Frommer's
Italy 2016

By Eleonora Baldwin,
Stephen Brewer,
Stephen Keeling,
Megan McCaffrey-Guerrera,
Michelle Schoenung
and Donald Strachan

Published by
Frommer Media LLC

Copyright © 2016 by Frommer Media LLC. All rights reserved. No part of this publication may be reproduced, stored in a retrieval system, or transmitted in any form or by any means, electronic, mechanical, photocopying, recording, scanning or otherwise, except as permitted under Sections 107 or 108 of the 1976 United States Copyright Act, without the prior written permission of the Publisher. Requests to the Publisher for permission should be addressed to Support@FrommerMedia.com.

Frommer's is a registered trademark of Arthur Frommer. Frommer Media LLC is not associated with any product or vendor mentioned in this book.

ISBN 978-1-62887-214-9 (paper), 978-1-62887-215-6 (e-book)
Editorial Director: Pauline Frommer
Editor: Holly Hughes
Production Editor: Lindsay Conner
Cartographer: Liz Puhl
Photo Editor: Dana Davis

For information on our other products or services, see www.frommers.com.
Frommer Media LLC also publishes its books in a variety of electronic formats. Some content that appears in print may not be available in electronic formats.

Manufactured in China

5 4 3 2 1

HOW TO CONTACT US

In researching this book, we discovered many wonderful places—hotels, restaurants, shops, and more. We're sure you'll find others. Please tell us about them, so we can share the information with your fellow travelers in upcoming editions. If you were disappointed with a recommendation, we'd love to know that, too. Please write to: Support@FrommerMedia.com

FROMMER'S STAR RATINGS SYSTEM

Every hotel, restaurant and attraction listed in this guide has been ranked for quality and value. Here's what the stars mean:

★ Recommended
★★ Highly Recommended
★★★ A must! Don't miss!

AN IMPORTANT NOTE

The world is a dynamic place. Hotels change ownership, restaurants hike their prices, museums alter their opening hours, and busses and trains change their routings. And all of this can occur in the several months after our authors have visited, inspected, and written about, these hotels, restaurants, museums and transportation services. Though we have made valiant efforts to keep all our information fresh and up-to-date, some few changes can inevitably occur in the periods before a revised edition of this guidebook is published. So please bear with us if a tiny number of the details in this book have changed. Please also note that we have no responsibility or liability for any inaccuracy or errors or omissions, or for inconvenience, loss, damage, or expenses suffered by anyone as a result of assertions in this guide.

CONTENTS

LIST OF MAPS

ABOUT THE AUTHORS

Eleonora Baldwin is a food and lifestyle writer, journalist, prolific blogger, and Italian culinary/travel show host who lives in Rome and provides insider knowledge on the Eternal City's dining scene, as well as small-group private culinary adventures in Italy. She is the author, editor, and photographer of popular blogs Aglio, Olio e Peperoncino (aglioolioepeperoncino.com), Rome City Guide for Kids (lolamamma.wordpress.com), and Roma Every Day (romatuttigg.blogspot.it). She has written, edited, and contributed to numerous travel and lifestyle publications, and her writing appears regularly in several online food columns.

Stephen Brewer has been savoring Italian pleasures ever since he sipped his first cappuccino while a student in Rome many, many years ago (togas had just gone out of fashion). He has written about Italy for many magazines and guidebooks and remains transported in equal measure by Bolognese cooking, Tuscan hillsides, the Bay of Naples, and the streets of Palermo.

Stephen Keeling has been traveling to Italy since 1985 and covering his favorite nation for Frommer's since 2007. He is co-author of the award-winning Frommer's family travel guide to Tuscany & Umbria, and has researched numerous travel books in Europe, Asia and the Americas. Stephen lives in New York City.

Megan McCaffrey-Guerrera's love affair with Italy began on her first visit at age 13. After a couple of decades and over a dozen trips to Italy, Megan made the move in 2003, making roots in the seaside village of Lerici on the Italian Riviera. She owns and operates, along with her Italian husband, Luigi, a boutique travel company specializing in customized trips all over Italy and the Mediterranean (www.bellavitaitalia.com). In addition to trip planning, Megan writes about Italy for several travel websites and travel guides, and in 2012 received her "Travel Associate" certification from the prestigious Travel Institute. Off-duty favorite activities include cooking up a storm to satisfy the household "black hole" (Luigi), learning to be a good "mamma" to baby Pietro, yoga, and Mediterranean swims.

Michelle Schoenung is an American journalist and translator in Milan who relocated to the Belpaese in 2000 for what was to be a yearlong adventure. Fifteen years on, she is pleased that Milan has evolved into a much more international and cosmopolitan city and has shed its image of merely being a foggy northern Italian business hub. Her writings and translations have appeared in magazines and books in the United States and Italy. In her free time, she likes to read, run, travel, cook and explore the city with her two rambunctious Italian-American sons.

Donald Strachan is a travel journalist who has written about Italy for publications worldwide, including "National Geographic Traveler," "The Guardian," "Sunday Telegraph," CNN.com, and many others. He has also written several Italy guidebooks for Frommer's, including "Frommer's EasyGuide to Rome, Florence, and Venice." For more, see www.donaldstrachan.com.

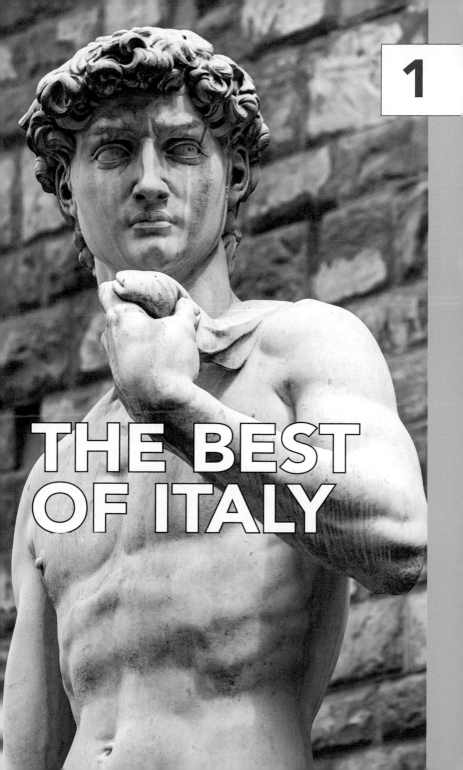

1

THE BEST OF ITALY

J ust hear the word "Italy" and you can already see it. The noble stones of ancient Rome and the Greek temples of Sicily. The wine hills of Piedmont and Tuscany, the ruins of Pompeii, and the secret canals and crumbling palaces of Venice. For centuries, visitors have come here looking for their own slice of the good life, and for the most part, they have found it.

Nowhere in the world is the impact of the Renaissance felt more fully than in its birthplace, **Florence,** the repository of artistic works left by Masaccio, Botticelli, Leonardo, Michelangelo, and many, many others. Much of the "known world" was once ruled from **Rome,** a city supposedly founded by twins Romulus and Remus in 753 B.C. There's no place with more artistic treasures—not even **Venice,** a seemingly impossible floating city that was shaped by its merchants and their centuries of trade with the Byzantine and Islamic worlds to the east.

Of course, there's more. Long before Italy was a country, it was a loose collection of city-states. Centuries of alliance and rivalry left a legacy of art and architecture in **Verona,** with its romance and an intact Roman Arena, and in **Mantua,** which blossomed during the Renaissance under the Gonzaga dynasty. **Padua** and its sublime Giotto frescoes are within easy reach of Venice, too. In **Siena,** ethereal art and Gothic palaces survive, barely altered since the city's heyday in the 1300s.

Earlier still, the eruption of Vesuvius in A.D. 79 preserved **Pompeii** and **Herculaneum** under volcanic ash for 2 millennia. It remains the best place to get close-up with everyday life in the time of the Roman Empire. The buildings of ancient Greece still stand at **Paestum,** in Campania, and at sites on **Sicily,** the Mediterranean's largest island.

The corrugated, vine-clad hills of the **Chianti** and the cypress-studded, emerald-green expanses of the **Val d'Orcia** serve up iconic images of **Tuscany.** Adventurous walkers of all ages can hike between the coastal villages of the **Cinque Terre,** where you can travel untroubled by the 21st century. Whether it's seafood along the Sicilian coast, pizza in **Naples,** pasta in **Bologna,** basil pesto in **Genoa,** or the red Barolo and Barbaresco wines of **Piedmont,** your taste buds are in for an adventure of their own. **Milan** and Florence are centers of world fashion. Welcome to *La Bella Italia!*

PREVIOUS PAGE: Michelangelo's statue of David, a copy outside the Palazzo Vecchio in Florence.

ITALY'S best AUTHENTIC EXPERIENCES

o **Dining Italian Style:** The most cherished pastime of most Italians is eating. There's no genuine "national" cuisine here: Each region and city has its own recipes handed down through generations. If the weather is fine and you're dining outdoors, perhaps with a view of a medieval church or piazza, you'll find the closest thing to food heaven. *Buon appetito!*

o **Exploring Rome's Mercato di Testaccio:** In 2012 the old Testaccio Market made way for a glass-paneled, modernist beauty, across the street from Rome's MACRO museum. Mingle with busy *signore* whose trolleys are chock-full of celery, carrots, and onions for the day's *ragù*, grab a slice of focaccia or some Roman street food, and pick up an authentic flavor of the Eternal City. See p. 152.

o **Cicchetti and a Spritz in Venice:** *Cicchetti*—tapaslike small servings, usually eaten while standing at a bar—are a Venetian tradition. Accompany the *cicchetti* with a spritz made with Aperol and sparkling Prosecco wine from the Veneto hills to make the experience complete. Your options are numerous, but some of the best spots to indulge arc on the San Polo side of the Rialto bridge. See p. 409.

o **Catching an Opera at Verona's Arena:** Summertime opera festivals in Verona are produced on a scale more human than those in such cities as Milan—and best of all, they are held under the stars. The setting is the ancient **Arena di Verona,** a site that's grand enough to accommodate as many elephants as might be needed for a performance of *Aïda*. See p. 425.

o **Slowing Down to Italy Pace:** Nothing happens quickly here: Linger over a glass of wine from the Tuscan hills, slurp a gelato made with seasonal fruit, enjoy the evening *passeggiata* (ritual walk) just like the locals. And they call it Slow Food for a reason.

ITALY'S best RESTAURANTS

o **Ora d'Aria** (Florence): Despite its historic location in an alleyway behind Piazza della Signoria, Florence's best dinner spot is unshakably modern. Head chef Marco Stabile gives traditional Tuscan ingredients a fresh (and lighter) makeover. Even if you can't stretch your budget to eat dinner here, take a walk down the medieval lane to watch kitchen staff at work through a picture window. See p. 213.

o **Ottava Nota** (Palermo): Palermo's old Arab quarter, the Kalsa, is buzzing once again, especially at this place that takes a creative angle on Sicilian cuisine. Ingredients come straight from the city's famous produce markets. See p. 626.

o **Trattoria dal Biassanot** (Bologna): Just about every restaurant in Bologna lays claim to the city's best *tagliatelle alla bolognese,* but many connoisseurs agree that this is the best spot in town. Under the wood beams of this gracious bistro, enjoy light-as-a-feather pastas. Even the bread is homemade. See p. 337.

o **Ai Artisti** (Venice): Venice's culinary rep is founded on the quality of the catch sold at its famous fish market. Both *primi* and *secondi* at Ai Artisti feature the freshest fish from the lagoon and farther afield. See p. 409.

ITALY'S best HOTELS

o **Santa Caterina** (Amalfi): What might be our favorite splurge on the peninsula is not outrageously posh, just magically transporting, set in citrus groves above the sea. Ceramic tiles, a smattering of antiques, and sea-view terraces grace the rooms, and a garden path and elevator descend to a private beach. Shoulder season rates and special offers help bring the cost out of the stratosphere. See p. 578.

o **La Dimora degli Angeli** (Florence): You walk a fine line when you try to bring a historic *palazzo* into the 21st century, and this place walks it expertly. Rooms are split over two floors, with contrasting characters—one romantic and modern-baroque in style; the second characterized by clean, contemporary lines and Scandinavian-influenced design. All are affordable and smack in the middle of Florence's shopping district. See p. 206.

o **BioCity** (Milan): For travelers on a tight budget, the BioCity is everything a hotel should be, and a little more. Built into a revamped 1920s villa, it's cozy, stylish, environmentally aware, equipped with all the gadgetry and connectivity you need, and the best value in what can be an expensive city. See p. 447.

o **Villa Spalletti Trivelli** (Rome): All-inclusive can be exclusive, especially when the experience of staying in an Italian noble mansion is part of the package. Opulence plus impeccable, understated service comes at a price, of course. When our lottery numbers come up, we will be booking a stay here—a long one. See p. 130.

ITALY'S best FOR FAMILIES

o **Climbing Pisa's Wonky Tower** (Tuscany): Are we walking up or down? Pleasantly disoriented kids are bound to ask as you spiral your way to the rooftop-viewing balcony atop one of the world's most famous pieces of botched engineering. Pisa is an easy day trip from Florence, and 8 is the minimum age for heading up its *Torre Pendente,* or Leaning Tower. See p. 286.

Gelato from artisan gelaterie, to be found all over Italy.

- **Acquario di Genova** (Liguria): After museums, churches, palaces, and more museums, Genoa's aquarium is a welcome change of direction, for everyone in the family. It may not be as large as some American super-aquariums, but it is beautifully designed (by architect Renzo Piano) and houses sharks, seals, and much weird and wonderful sea life, as well as a hummingbird sanctuary and great educational exhibits. See p. 509.

- **Exploring Underground Naples:** There is more to Naples than you can see at eye level. Head below its maze of streets to see remains of the ancient Greek and Roman cities that once stood here. As well as the Ágora and Forum, families can tour catacombs used for centuries to bury the Christian dead and tunnels that sheltered refugees from the cholera epidemic of 1884 and the bombs of World War II. See p. 548.

- **A Trip to an Artisan Gelateria:** Fluffy heaps of gelato, however pretty, are built with additives, stabilizers, and air pumped into the blend. Blue "Smurf" or bubble-gum-pink flavors are a pretty clear indication of chemical color enhancement, and ice crystals or grainy texture are telltale signs of engineered gelato—so steer clear. Authentic artisan *gelaterie* produce good stuff from scratch daily, with fresh seasonal ingredients and less bravado. See "Where to Eat" and "Gelato" sections in the individual chapters for our favorites: Rome (p. 146) and Florence (p. 218) have several of Italy's best joints.

ITALY'S most OVERRATED

- **Campo de' Fiori** (Rome): Yes, the piazza is stunning: This is the only square in Rome without a church, and its Renaissance light bounces off ocher and burnt sienna facades. But between 8am and 3pm, the piazza is a busy market where goods are geared (and priced) for tourists, not locals. Wait for the departure of the last boisterous pigeons and the vendors selling aprons embossed with the sculpted abs of Michelangelo's "David"; grab a slice of real Rome at sunset, when Campo de' Fiori reclaims its local, intimate, old Rome face. See p. 151.

- **Ponte Vecchio** (Florence): Sorry, lovers, but this isn't even the prettiest bridge in Florence, let alone one of the world's great spots for romantics. It's haphazard by design, packed at all hours, and hemmed in by shops that cater mostly to tourism. For a special moment with a loved one—perhaps even to "pop the question"—head downstream one bridge to the Ponte Santa Trínita. Built in the 1560s by Bartolomeo Ammanati, its triple-ellipse design is pure elegance in stone. At dusk, it is also one of Florence's best spots to take a photo of the Ponte Vecchio . . . if you must. See p. 186.

- **Capri** (Campania): We hate to say anything bad about such an enchanting beauty, but Capri falls victim to its justified popularity. Arrive in midsummer on a day excursion, corral through the gardens of Augustus, ride a boat through the Blue Grotto, shell out 5€ for a bottle of water . . . You will wish you could spend the night here, to enjoy the scenery and sparkling-white towns after the day-trippers leave, or to walk the scented flower paths in early spring. Any of which, of course, you can and should do. See p. 581.

ITALY'S best MUSEUMS

- **Vatican Museums** (Rome): The 100 galleries that constitute the Musei Vaticani are loaded with papal treasures accumulated over the centuries. Musts include the Sistine Chapel, such ancient Greek and Roman sculptures as "Laocoön" and "Belvedere Apollo," the frescoed "Stanze" executed by Raphael (among which is his "School of Athens"), and endless collections of pagan Greco-Roman antiquities and Renaissance art by European masters. See p. 77.

- **Galleria degli Uffizi** (Florence): This U-shaped High Renaissance building designed by Giorgio Vasari was the administrative headquarters, or *uffizi* (offices), for the dukes of Tuscany when the Medici called the shots round here. It's now the crown jewel of Europe's art museums, housing the world's greatest collection of Renaissance paintings, including icons by Botticelli, Leonardo da Vinci, and Michelangelo. See p. 177.

- **Accademia** (Venice): One of Europe's great museums, the Accademia houses an unequaled array of Venetian painting, exhibited chronologically from the 13th to the 18th century. Walls are hung with works by Bellini, Carpaccio, Giorgione, Titian, and Tintoretto. See p. 382.

- **Museo Archeologico Nazionale** (Naples): Come to see the mosaics and frescoes from Pompeii and Herculaneum—the original of the much reproduced "Attenti al Cane" ("Beware of the Dog") mosaic is here, as are the Villa of the Papyri frescoes. Much else awaits you, including the "Farnese Bull"—which once

The Vatican's famed spiral ramp.

decorated Rome's Terme di Caracalla—and some of the finest statuary to survive from ancient Europe. See p. 543.

- **Museo Egizio** (Turin): With a dazzling new refit unveiled in 2015, Turin's Egyptology museum has doubled in size and is now the finest collection of Egyptian artifacts anywhere outside Cairo. See p. 481.

- **Santa Maria della Scala** (Siena): The building is as much the star as the collections. This was a hospital from medieval times until the 1990s, when it was closed, and its frescoed wards, ancient chapels and sacristy, and labyrinthine basement floors were gradually opened up for public viewing. See p. 237.

ITALY'S best FREE THINGS TO DO

- **Get Rained on in Rome's Pantheon:** People often wonder whether the 9m (30-ft.) oculus in the middle of the Pantheon's dome has a glass covering. Visit this ancient temple in the middle of a downpour for your answer: The oculus is open to the elements, transforming the interior into a giant shower on wet days. In light rain, the building fills with mist, but during a full-fledged thunderstorm, the drops come down in a perfect 9m-wide shaft, splattering on the polychrome marble floor. Come on Pentecost to get rained on by a cloud of rose petals. See p. 98.

o **Surrender to the Madness of a Palermo Market:** In Sicily's capital—a crossroads between East and West for thousands of years—the chaotic, colorful street theater is a vignette of a culture that sometimes feels more Middle Eastern than European. The Vucciria isn't what it once was, however: Focus on the Capo and Ballarò markets. See p. 616.

o **Watch the Sun Rise Over the Roman Forum:** A short stroll from the Capitoline Hill down Via del Campidoglio to Via di Monte Tarpeo brings you to a perfect outlook: The terrace behind the Michelangelo-designed square provides a

Preserved fresco from Pompeii.

momentary photo op when the sun rises behind the Temple of Saturn, illuminating the archeological complex below in pink-orange light. Early risers can reward themselves with breakfast in the bakeries of the nearby Jewish Ghetto. See chapter 4.

o **Getting Hopelessly Lost in Venice:** You haven't experienced Venice until you have turned a corner convinced you're on the way somewhere, only to find yourself smack against a canal with no bridge, or in a little courtyard with no way out. All you can do is shrug, smile, and give the city's maze of narrow streets another try, because getting lost in Venice is a pleasure. See chapter 9.

o **Driving the Amalfi Coast:** The SS163, "the road of 1,000 bends," hugs vertical cliffsides and deep gorges, cutting through olive groves, lemon terraces, and whitewashed villages—against a background of the bluest ocean you can picture. One of the world's classic drives, it provokes fear, nausea, and wonder in equal doses; the secret is to make sure someone else is at the wheel. See p. 567.

ITALY'S best ARCHITECTURAL LANDMARKS

o **Brunelleschi's Dome** (Florence): It took the genius of Filippo Brunelleschi to work out how to raise a vast dome over the huge hole in Florence's cathedral roof. Though rejected for the commission to cast the bronze doors of the Baptistery, Filippo didn't sulk. He went away and became the city's greatest architect, and the creator of one of Italy's most recognizable landmarks. See p. 178.

o **The Gothic Center of Siena** (Tuscany): The shell-shaped Piazza del Campo stands at the heart of one of Europe's best-preserved medieval cities. Steep, canyonlike streets, icons of Gothic architecture like the Palazzo Pubblico, and ethereal Madonnas painted on gilded altarpieces transport you back to a time before the Renaissance. See p. 232.

o **Pompeii** (Campania): When Mt. Vesuvius blew its top in A.D. 79, it buried Pompeii under molten lava and ash, truncating the lives of perhaps 35,000 citizens and suspending the city in a time capsule. Today, still under the shadow of the menacing volcano, this poignant ghost town can be coaxed into life with very little imagination. See p. 562.

o **Valley of the Temples, Agrigento** (Sicily): The Greeks built these seven temples overlooking the sea to impress, and the honey-colored columns and pediments still do. Seeing these romantic ruins—some, like the Temple of Concordia, beautifully preserved, others, like the Temple of Juno, timeworn but still proud—is an experience of a lifetime. See p. 633.

Gazing over the Roman forum.

best UNDISCOVERED ITALY

- **The Aperitivo Spots and Craft Beer Bars of Rome:** Don't confuse *aperitivo* with happy hour: Predinner cocktails tickle appetites, induce conversation and flirting, and allow free access to all-you-can-eat buffets if you buy one drink. And Romans are increasingly turning to artisan-brewed beers for that one drink. See "Entertainment & Nightlife" in chapter 4.

- **Drinking Your Coffee al Banco:** Italians—especially city dwellers—don't often linger at a piazza table sipping their morning cappuccino. For them, a *caffè* is a pit stop: They order at the counter *(al banco)*, throw back the bitter elixir, and continue on their way, reinforced by a hit of caffeine. You will also save a chunk of change drinking Italian style. Your coffee should cost at least 50% less than the sit-down price, even in the handsome baroque surrounds of Turin's Piazza San Carlo. See p. 154.

- **Genoa's City Center:** Don't be fooled by a rough, industrial exterior: Genoa has Italy's largest *centro storico,* with beautiful architecture that rivals Venice. A restored old port, the Palazzo Reale, and the *palazzi* of Strada Nuova are just a few of the highlights in a trading city that got wealthy from the sea. See chapter 11.

- **The Art at Padua's Cappella degli Scrovegni:** Step aside, Sistine Chapel. Art lovers armed with binoculars behold this scene in awe—the cycle of frescoes by Giotto that revolutionized 14th-century painting. It is considered the most important work of art leading up to the Renaissance, and visiting is an unforgettable, intimate experience. See p. 421.

ITALY'S best ACTIVE ADVENTURES

- **Seeing Ferrara on Two Wheels:** Join the bike-mad *Ferraresi* as they zip along narrow, cycle-friendly lanes that snake through the city's old center, past the Castello Estense and the Renaissance elegance of the Palazzo Schifanoia. You can also take bikes on a circuit on top of the city's medieval walls. See p. 340.

- **Kayaking Around Venice:** At around 120€ per day, seeing Venice from a kayak is not cheap. But if you want to get a unique angle on the palaces and quiet canalside corners of Italy's fairytale floating city, there is nothing quite like it. See p. 393.

- **Riding on the New Monte Bianco Cable Cars, Valle d'Aosta:** In Italy's far northwestern corner, you can ride high on Europe's tallest mountain, departing from the hiking, biking, and skiing resort of Courmayeur. Standing 4,810m (15,780 ft.), Monte Bianco ("Mont Blanc" to the French) guards the border between France and Italy and is flanked by perilous glaciers and jagged granite peaks, all of which you can view from new cableways that opened in 2015. See p. 498.

o **Walking the Cinque Terre** (Liguria): The 3-mile path from Corniglia to Vernazza, and the 2-mile section from Vernazza to Monterosso, are the most rewarding in terms of sheer beauty. Find yourself rollercoastering along narrow paths surrounded by terraced vineyards, and olive and lemon groves that seem to hover over the sapphire Mediterranean Sea. This coastal path is best tackled in the early morning, before the crowds. Get lucky out of season and you might even have it to yourself. See p. 526.

ITALY'S best NEIGHBORHOODS

o **Testaccio, Rome:** The relaxed atmosphere of this working-class, all-Roman neighborhood is a perfect wind-down from the sightseeing hype and the crowds. Its appeal for travelers is growing, with museums, industrial design and architecture, lively nightlife, and especially culinary highlights, including the relocated Mercato di Testaccio. See chapter 4.

o **San Frediano, Florence:** Most Florentines have abandoned their *centro storico* to the visitors, but on the Arno's Left Bank in San Frediano, you'll find plenty of local action after dark. Dine at **iO** (p. 217), slurp a gelato by the river at **La Carraia** (p. 218), then drink until late at **Diorama** (p. 223) or catch an acoustic gig at **Volume** (p. 222).

Kayaking around Venice.

The streets of Oltrarno, Florence's "Left Bank."

- **Spaccanapoli, Naples:** It's often said Naples is Italy on overdrive, and the city goes up another gear in the narrow, crowded, laundry-strung lanes of its *centro storico*. Gird your loins, watch your wallet, and forget about a map—just plunge into the grid and enjoy the boisterous scene as you browse shops selling everything from *limoncello* and nativity scenes to fried snacks and the world's best pizza. It's a European *souk*. See chapter 12.

- **Cannaregio, Venice:** Cannaregio is a quiet residential neighborhood, with hidden churches graced by Tiepolo paintings, silent canals, and elegantly faded mansions. Here too is the old Ghetto Nuovo, a historic area of Jewish bakeries, restaurants, and old synagogues. It's all a great escape from the chaos around San Marco. See chapter 9.

ITALY IN CONTEXT

As with any destination, a little background reading can help you to understand more. Many Italy stereotypes are accurate—children are fussed over wherever they go, food and soccer are like religion, the north–south divide is alive and well, bureaucracy is a frustrating feature of daily life. Some are wide of the mark—not every Italian you meet will be open and effusive. Occasionally they do taciturn pretty well, too.

The most important thing to remember is that, for a land so steeped in history—3 millennia and counting—Italy has only a short history *as a country*. In 2011 it celebrated its 150th birthday. Prior to 1861, the map of the peninsula was in constant flux. War, alliance, invasion, and disputed successions caused that map to change color as often as a chameleon crossing a field of wildflowers. Republics, mini-monarchies, client states, Papal states, and city-states, as well as Islamic emirates, colonies, dukedoms, and Christian theocracies, roll onto and out of the pages of Italian history with regularity. In some regions, you'll hear languages and dialects other than Italian. It's part of an identity that is often more regional than it is national.

This confusing history explains why your Italian experience will differ wildly if you visit, say, Turin rather than Naples. (And why you should visit both, if you can.) The architecture is different; the food is different; the important historical figures are different, as are the local issues of the day. And the people are different: While the north–south schism is most often written about, cities as close together as Florence and Siena can feel very dissimilar. This chapter will help you understand why.

ITALY TODAY

The big Italian news for many travelers is the recent favorable movement in exchange rates. Last year's edition of this guide listed the US dollar/euro exchange rate at $1.37. At time of writing, it's $1.06. Everything in Italy just became 22% cheaper for visitors from across the Atlantic. (The Canadian dollar has moved less dramatically, but still in the right direction—from $1.51 to $1.33.) So, congratulations: You picked a good time to visit.

Many Italians have not been so lucky. One reason for the euro's plunge is a stubbornly slow European recovery from the global financial crisis—known here as the *Crisi*. It had a disastrous effect on Italy's

PREVIOUS PAGE: **Close-up of Swiss Guard at the Vatican.**

economy, causing the deepest recession since World War II. Public debt had grown to alarming levels—as high as 1,900 billion euros—and for more than a decade economic growth has been slow. As a result, 2011 and 2012 saw Italy pitched into the center of a European banking crisis, which almost brought about the collapse of the euro. By 2015, many Italians were beginning to see light at the end of their dark economic tunnel—a little, at least.

Populism has become a feature of national politics. A party led by comedian Beppe Grillo—the *MoVimento 5 Stelle* (Five Star Movement)—polled around a quarter of the vote in 2013 elections. By early 2014, in the postelectoral shakedown, former Florence mayor Matteo Renzi became Italy's youngest prime minister—at 39 years of age—heading a coalition of the center-left led by his Democratic Party (PD). Among his first significant acts was to name a governing cabinet made up of equal numbers of men and women, a ratio unprecedented in Italy. Opinion polling through mid-2015 showed Italians still favoring Renzi's reformism over rivals' policies.

Italy's population is aging, and a youth vacuum is being filled by immigrants, especially those from Eastern Europe, notably Romania (whose language is similar to Italian) and Albania, as well as from North Africa. Italy doesn't have the colonial experience of Britain and France, or the "melting pot" history of the New World; tensions were inevitable, and discrimination is a daily fact of life for many minorities. Change is coming—in 2013, Cécile Kyenge became Italy's first black government minister, and black footballer Mario Balotelli is one of the country's biggest sports stars. But it is coming too slowly for some.

A "brain drain" continues to push young Italians to seek opportunities abroad. The problem is especially bad in rural communities and on the islands, where the old maxim, "it's not what you know, it's who you know," applies more strongly than ever in these straitened times. By 2015, however, indicators suggested the worst of Italy's economic turmoil might be behind it. From top to toe, highlands to islands, fingers are firmly crossed that the good times are coming round again.

Vespas buzzing down the nighttime streets of Rome.

Italians know how to cook—just ask one. But be sure to leave plenty of time: Once an Italian starts talking food, it's a while before they pause for breath. Italy doesn't really have a unified national cuisine; it's more a loose grouping of regional cuisines that share a few staples, notably pasta, bread, tomatoes, and pig meat cured in many ways. On a **Rome** visit, you'll also encounter authentic local specialties such as *saltimbocca alla romana* (literally "jump-in-your-mouth"—thin slices of veal with sage, cured ham, and cheese) and *carciofi alla romana* (artichokes cooked with herbs, such as mint and garlic), and a dish that's become ubiquitous, *spaghetti alla carbonara*—pasta coated in a white sauce made with egg and *pecorino romano* (ewe's milk cheese), with added cured pork (*guanciale*, cheek, if it's authentic).

To the north, in **Florence and Tuscany,** you'll find seasonal ingredients served simply; it's almost the antithesis of "French" cooking, with its multiple processes. The main ingredient for almost any savory dish is the local olive oil, adored for its low acidity. The typical

Tuscan pasta is wide, flat *pappardelle*, generally tossed with a game sauce such as *lepre* (hare) or *cinghiale* (boar). Tuscans are fond of their own strong ewe's milk cheese, pecorino, made most famously around the Val d'Orcia town of Pienza. Meat is usually the centerpiece of any *secondo*: A *bistecca alla fiorentina* is the classic main dish, a T-bone-like wedge of meat. An authentic *fiorentina* should be cut only from the white Chianina breed of cattle. Sweet treats are also good here, particularly Siena's *panforte* (a dense, sticky cake); *biscotti di Prato* (hard, almond-flour biscuits for dipping in dessert wine, also known as *cantuccini*); and the *miele* (honey) of Montalcino.

Emilia-Romagna is the country's gastronomic center. Rich in produce, its school of cooking first created many pastas now common around Italy: tagliatelle, tortellini, and cappelletti (made in the shape of "little hats"). Pig also comes several ways, including in Bologna's mortadella (rolled, ground pork) and *prosciutto di Parma* (cured ham). Served in paper-thin slices, it's deliciously sweet. The distinctive cheese

THE MAKING OF ITALY
Prehistory to the Rise of Rome

Of all the early inhabitants of Italy, the most extensive legacy was left by the **Etruscans.** No one knows exactly where they came from, and the inscriptions that they left behind (often on graves in necropoli) are of little help—the Etruscan language has never been fully deciphered by scholars. Whatever their origins, within 2 centuries of appearing on the peninsula around 800 B.C., they had subjugated the lands now known as Tuscany (to which they left their name) and Campania, along with the **Villanovan** tribes that lived there.

From their base at **Rome,** the Latins remained free until they too were conquered by the Etruscans around 600 B.C. The new overlords introduced gold tableware and jewelry, bronze urns and terracotta statuary, and the art and culture of Greece and Asia Minor. They also made

Parmigiano-Reggiano is made by hundreds of small producers in the provinces of Parma and Reggio Emilia.

Probably the most famous dish of **Piedmont** and **Lombardy** is *cotoletta alla milanese* (veal dipped in egg and breadcrumbs and fried in olive oil)—the Germans call it Wienerschnitzel. *Osso buco* is another Lombard classic: shin of veal cooked in a ragout sauce. Turin's iconic dish is *bagna càuda*—literally "hot bath" in the Piedmontese language, a sauce made with olive oil, garlic, butter, and anchovies, into which you dip raw vegetables. Piedmont is also the spiritual home of *risotto*, particularly the town of Vercelli, which is surrounded by rice paddies.

Venice is rarely celebrated for its cuisine, but fresh seafood is usually excellent, and figures heavily in the Venetian diet. Grilled fish is often served with red radicchio, a bitter lettuce that grows best in nearby Treviso. Two classic nonfish dishes are *fegato alla veneziana* (liver and onions) and *risi e bisi* (rice and fresh peas).

Liguria also turns toward the sea for its inspiration, as reflected by its version of bouillabaisse, *burrida* flavored with spices. But its most famous food is pesto, a paste-sauce made with fresh basil, hard cheese, and crushed pine nuts, which is used to dress pasta, fish, and many other dishes.

The cookery of **Campania**—including spaghetti with clam sauce and pizza—is familiar to North Americans, because so many Neapolitans moved to the New World. Mozzarella is the local cheese, the best of it *mozzarella di bufala*, made with milk of buffalo, a species first introduced to Campania from Asia in the Middle Ages. Mixed fish fries (a *fritto misto*) are a staple of many a lunch table, and genuine Neapolitan pizza is in a class of its own.

Sicily has a distinctive cuisine, with strong flavors and aromatic sauces. One staple is *pasta con le sarde* (with pine nuts, wild fennel, spices, chopped sardines, and olive oil). In fact, fish is good and fresh pretty much everywhere (local swordfish is excellent). Desserts and homemade pastries include *cannoli*, cylindrical pastry cases stuffed with ricotta and candied fruit (or chocolate). Sicilian *gelato* is among the best in Italy.

Rome the governmental seat of Latium. "Roma" is an Etruscan name, and the ancient kings of Rome had Etruscan names: Numa, Ancus, and even Romulus.

The Etruscans ruled until the **Roman Revolt** around 510 B.C., and by 250 B.C. the Romans and their allies had vanquished or assimilated the Etruscans, wiping out their language and religion. However, many of the former rulers' manners and beliefs remained, and became integral to what we now understand as "Roman culture."

Meanwhile, the **Greeks**—who predated both the Etruscans and the Romans—had built powerful colonial outposts in the south, notably in Naples, founded as Greek "Neapolis." Remains of the *Àgora*, or market square, survive below **San Lorenzo Maggiore** (p. 550), in the old center of the city. The Greeks left behind crumbling stone monuments above ground too, including at the **Valley of the Temples,** Agrigento, Sicily (p. 633).

If you want to see the remains of Etruscan civilization, Rome's **Museo Nazionale Etrusco** (p. 108) and the Etruscan collection in Rome's **Vatican Museums** (p. 79) are a logical start-point. Florence's **Museo Archeologico** (p. 192) houses one of the greatest Etruscan bronzes yet unearthed, the "Arezzo Chimera." There are also fine Etruscan collections in **Volterra,** Tuscany (p. 267) and **Orvieto,** Umbria (p. 314).

The Roman Republic: ca. 510–27 B.C.

After the Roman Republic was established around 510 B.C., the Romans continued to increase their power by conquering neighboring communities in the highlands and forming alliances with other Latins in the lowlands. They gave to their allies, and then to conquered peoples, partial or complete Roman citizenship, with the obligation of military service. Citizen colonies were set up as settlements of Roman farmers or military veterans, including both **Florence** and **Siena.**

The stern Roman Republic was characterized by a belief in the gods, the necessity of learning from the past, the strength of the family, education through reading and performing public service, and most importantly, obedience. The all-powerful Senate presided as Rome defeated rival powers one after the other and came to rule the Mediterranean. The Punic Wars with **Carthage** (in modern-day Tunisia) in the 3rd century B.C. presented a temporary stumbling block, as Carthaginian general **Hannibal** (247–182 B.C.) conducted a devastating campaign across the Italian peninsula, crossing the Alps with his elephants and winning

Etruscan bronze of a she-wolf suckling twin brothers Romulus and Remus.

Ancient Roman ruins on the Capitoline Hill.

bloody battles by the shore of **Lago Trasimeno,** in Umbria, and at Cannae, in Puglia. In the end, however, Rome prevailed.

No figure was more towering during the late Republic, or more instrumental in its transformation into the Empire (see below), than **Julius Caesar,** the charismatic conqueror of Gaul—"the wife of every husband and the husband of every wife." After defeating the last resistance of the Pompeians in 45 B.C., he came to Rome and was made dictator and consul for 10 years. Conspirators, led by Marcus Junius Brutus, stabbed him to death at the Theater of Pompey on March 15, 44 B.C., the "Ides of March." The site (at Largo di Torre Argentina) is best known these days as the home to a feral cat colony.

The conspirators' motivation was to restore the power of the Republic and topple dictatorship. But they failed: **Mark Antony,** a Roman general, assumed control. He made peace with Caesar's willed successor, **Octavian,** and, after the Treaty of Brundisium which dissolved the Republic, found himself married to Octavian's sister, Octavia. This marriage, however, didn't prevent him from also marrying Cleopatra in 36 B.C. The furious Octavian gathered western legions and defeated Antony at the **Battle of Actium** on September 2, 31 B.C. Cleopatra fled to Egypt, followed by Antony, who committed suicide in disgrace a year later. Cleopatra, unable to seduce his successor and thus retain her rule of Egypt, followed suit with the help of an asp. The permanent end of the Republic was nigh.

Many of the standing buildings of ancient Rome date to periods after the Republic, but parts of the **Roman Forum** (p. 89) date from the Republic, including the **Temple of Saturn.** The adjacent **Capitoline Hill** and **Palatine Hill** have been sacred religious and civic places since the earliest days of Rome. Rome's best artifacts from the days of the Republic are housed inside the **Musei Capitolini** (p. 85). The greatest exponent of political oratory in the period was **Marcus Tullius Cicero** (106–43 B.C.), who wrote widely on philosophy and statesmanship, and was killed after expressing outspoken opposition to Mark Antony in his "Philippics."

The Roman Empire in Its Pomp: 27 B.C.–A.D. 395

Born Gaius Octavius in 63 B.C., and later known as Octavian, **Augustus** became the first Roman emperor in 27 B.C. and reigned until A.D. 14. His

EARLY ROMAN emperors

Caligula (r. A.D. 37–41): Young emperor whose reign of cruelty and terror ended when he was assassinated by his Praetorian guard

Nero (r. A.D. 54–68): The last emperor of the Julio-Claudian dynasty was another cruel megalomaniac who killed his own mother and may have started the Great Fire of Rome (A.D. 64)

Vespasian (r. A.D. 69–79): First emperor of the Flavian dynasty, who built the Colosseum (p. 88) and lived as husband-and-wife with a freed slave, Caenis

Domitian (r. A.D. 81–96): Increasingly paranoid authoritarian and populist who

became fixated on the idea that he would be assassinated—and was proven right

Trajan (r. A.D. 98–117): Virtuous soldier-ruler who presided over the moment Rome was at its geographically grandest scale, and also rebuilt much of the city

Hadrian (r. A.D.113–138): Humanist, general, and builder who redesigned the Pantheon (p. 98) and added the Temple of Venus and Roma to the Forum (p. 89)

Marcus Aurelius (r. A.D. 161–180): Philosopher-king, and the last of the so-called "Five Good Emperors," whose statue is exhibited in the Musei Capitolini (p. 85)

autocratic reign ushered in the *Pax Romana,* 2 centuries of peace. In Rome you can still see the remains of the **Forum of Augustus** (p. 89) and admire his statue in the **Vatican Museums** (p. 77).

By now, Rome ruled the entire Mediterranean world, either directly or indirectly, because all political, commercial, and cultural pathways led straight to Rome, the sprawling city set on seven hills: the Capitoline, Palatine, Aventine, Caelian, Esquiline, Quirinal, and Viminal. It was in this period that **Virgil** wrote his best-loved epic poem, "The Aeneid," which supplied a grandiose founding myth for the great city and empire. Also in this prosperous era, **Ovid** composed his erotic poetry and **Horace** wrote his "Odes."

The emperors brought Rome to new heights. But without the checks and balances formerly provided by the Senate and legislatures, success led to corruption. These centuries witnessed a steady decay in the ideals and traditions on which the Empire had been founded. The army became a fifth column of unruly mercenaries, and for every good emperor (Augustus, Claudius, Trajan, Vespasian, and Hadrian, to name a few) there were several cruel, debased, or incompetent tyrants (Caligula, Nero, Caracalla, and many others).

After Augustus died (by poison, perhaps), his widow, **Livia**—a shrewd operator who had divorced her first husband to marry Augustus—set up her son, **Tiberius,** as ruler through intrigues and poisonings. A series of murders and purges ensued, and Tiberius, who ruled during Pontius Pilate's trial and crucifixion of Christ, was eventually murdered in his late '70s. Murder was so common that a short time later, **Domitian** (ruled A.D. 81–96) became so obsessed with the possibility of assassination that he had the walls of his palace covered in mica so that he could see behind him at all times. (He was killed anyway.)

Excesses ruled the day—at least, if you believe surviving tracts written by contemporary chroniclers infused with all kinds of bias: **Caligula** supposedly committed incest with his sister, Drusilla, appointed his horse to the Senate, lavished money on egotistical projects, and proclaimed himself a god. Caligula's successor, his uncle **Claudius,** was poisoned by his final wife—his niece Agrippina—to secure the succession of **Nero,** her son by a previous marriage. Nero's thanks were to later murder not only his mother but also his wife (Claudius's daughter) and his rival, Claudius's son. The disgraceful Nero, an enthusiastic persecutor of Christians, committed suicide with the cry, "What an artist I destroy!"

By the 3rd century A.D., corruption had become so prevalent that there were 23 emperors in 73 years. Few, however, were as twisted as **Caracalla** who, to secure control, had his brother Geta slashed to pieces while Geta was in the arms of his mother, former empress Julia Domna.

Constantine the Great became emperor in A.D. 306, and in 330, he made Constantinople (or Byzantium) the new capital of the Empire, moving the administrative functions away from Rome altogether, partly because the menace of possible barbarian attacks in the west had increased. Constantine was the first Christian emperor, allegedly converting after he saw the "True Cross" in a dream, accompanied by the words *in this sign shall you conquer.* He defeated rival emperor Maxentius and his followers at the **Battle of the Milivan Bridge** (A.D. 312), a victory that's remembered by Rome's triumphal **Arco di Costantino** (p. 84). Constantine ended the persecution of Christians with the **Edict of Milan** (A.D. 313).

It was during the Imperial period that Rome flourished in architecture, advancing in size and majesty far beyond earlier cities built by the Greeks. **Classical orders** were simplified into types of column capitals: **Doric** (a plain capital), **Ionic** (a capital with a scroll), and **Corinthian** (a capital with flowering acanthus leaves). Much of this advance in building prowess was due to the discovery of a form of concrete and the fine-tuning of the arch, which was used with a logic, rhythm, and ease never before seen. Some of these monumental buildings still stand in Rome, notably **Trajan's Column** (p. 89), the **Colosseum** (p. 88), and Hadrian's **Pantheon** (p. 98), among many others. Elsewhere in Italy, Verona's **Arena** (p. 425) bears witness to the kinds of crowds that the brutal sport of gladiatorial combat could draw—Ridley Scott's 2000 Oscar-winning movie *Gladiator* isn't all fiction. Three **Roman cities** have been preserved, with street plans and, in some cases, even buildings remaining intact: doomed **Pompeii** (p. 562) and its neighbor **Herculaneum** (p. 560), both buried by Vesuvius's massive A.D. 79 eruption, and Rome's ancient seaport, **Ostia Antica** (p. 157). It was at Herculaneum that one of Rome's greatest writers perished, **Pliny the Elder** (A.D. 23–79). It's thanks to him, his nephew, **Pliny the Younger,** the

ALL ABOUT vino

Italy is the largest **wine**-producing country in the world; as far back as 800 B.C. the Etruscans were vintners. However, it wasn't until 1965 that laws were enacted to guarantee consistency in winemaking. Quality wines are labeled **"DOC"** (Denominazione di Origine Controllata). If you see **"DOCG"** on a label (the "G" means *garantita*), that denotes an even better quality wine region. **"IGT"** (Indicazione Geografica Tipica) indicates a more general wine zone—for example, "Umbria"—but still with some quality control.

Tuscany: Tuscan red wines rank with some of the finest in the world. **Sangiovese** is the prince of grapes here, and **chianti** from the hills south of Florence is the most widely known sangiovese wine. The best zone is **Chianti Classico,** where a lively ruby-red wine partners with a bouquet of violets. The Tuscan south houses two even finer DOCGs: mighty, robust **Brunello di Montalcino,** a garnet-red ideal for roasts and game; and almost purple **Vino Nobile di Montepulciano,** which has a rich, velvet body. End a meal with the Tuscan dessert wine called **vin santo,** which is usually accompanied by *biscotti* that you dunk into your glass.

Veneto and Lombardy: Reds around Venice and the Lakes vary from light and lunchtime-friendly **Bardolino** to **Valpolicella,** which can be particularly intense if the grapes are partly dried

before fermentation to make an **Amarone.** White, Garganega-based **Soave** has a pale amber color and a velvety flavor. **Prosecco** is the classic Italian sparkling white, and the base for both a Bellini and a Spritz—joints that use Champagne are doing it wrong.

Piedmont: The finest reds in Italy probably hail from the vineclad slopes of Piedmont, particularly those made from the late-ripening **Nebbiolo** grape in the Langhe hills south of Alba. The big names—with big flavors and big price tags—are **Barbaresco** (brilliant ruby red with a delicate flavor) and **Barolo** (also brilliant ruby red, and gaining finesse when it mellows into a velvety old age).

The South and Sicily: From the volcanic soil of Vesuvius, the wines of **Campania** have been extolled for 2,000 years. Homer praised **Falerno,** straw yellow in color. The key DOCG wines from Campania these days are **Greco di Tufo** (a mouth-filling, full white) and **Fiano di Avellino** (subtler and more floral). The wines of **Sicily**—once called a "paradise of the grape"—were extolled by the ancient poets, and table wines here are improving after a drop in quality (though not quantity). Sicily is also home to **Marsala,** a fortified wine first popularized by British port traders and now served with desserts; it also makes a great sauce for veal.

---

historians **Tacitus, Suetonius, Cassius Dio,** and **Livy,** and satirist **Juvenal,** that much of our knowledge of ancient Roman life and history was not lost.

The surviving Roman **art** had a major influence on the painters and sculptors of the Renaissance (see below). In Rome itself, look for the marble bas-reliefs (sculptures that project slightly from a flat surface) on the **Arco di Costantino** (p. 84), the sculpture and mosaic collections at the **Palazzo Massimo alle Terme** (p. 111), and the gilded equestrian statue of Marcus Aurelius at the **Musei Capitolini** (p. 85). The

Florentine Medici rulers were avid collectors of Roman statuary, much now at the **Uffizi** (p. 177). Naples's **Museo Archeologico Nazionale** (p. 543) houses the world's most extraordinary collection of Roman art, preserved for centuries under the lava at Pompeii.

The Fall of the Empire Through the "Dark Ages"

The Eastern and Western sections of the Roman Empire split in A.D. 395, leaving the Italian peninsula without the support it had once received from east of the Adriatic. When the **Goths** moved toward Rome in the early 5th century, citizens in the provinces, who had grown to hate the bureaucracy set up by **Emperor Diocletian,** welcomed the invaders. And then the pillage began.

Rome was first sacked by **Alaric I,** king of the Visigoths, in 410. The populace made no attempt to defend the city, other than trying vainly to buy him off (a tactic that had worked 3 years earlier); most people fled into the hills. The feeble Western emperor **Honorius** hid out in **Ravenna** the entire time, which from 402 he had made the new capital of the Western Roman Empire.

More than 40 troubled years passed. Then **Attila the Hun** invaded Italy to besiege Rome. Attila was dissuaded from attacking, thanks largely to a peace mission headed by Pope Leo I in 452. Yet relief was short-lived: In 455, **Gaiseric,** king of the **Vandals,** carried out a 2-week sack that was unparalleled in its savagery. The empire of the West lasted for only another 20 years; finally, in 476, the sacks and chaos ended the once-mighty city, and Rome itself was left to the popes, though it was ruled nominally from Ravenna by an Exarch from Byzantium (aka Constantinople).

Although little of the detailed history of Italy in the post-Roman period is known—and few buildings survive—it's certain that the spread of **Christianity** was gradually creating a new society. The religion was probably founded in Rome about a decade after the death of Jesus, and gradually gained strength despite early (and enthusiastic) persecution by the Romans. The best way today to relive the early Christian era is to visit Rome's Appian Way and its Catacombs, along the **Via Appia Antica** (p. 117). According to Christian tradition, it was here that an escaping Peter encountered his vision of Christ. The **Catacombs** (p. 118) were the

A Growing Taste for Beer

Italy will always be known, and adored, for its wine. But one gastronomic trend to watch out for as you travel is the growth in popularity of artisanal beer, especially among the young. Although supermarket shelves are still stacked with mainstream brands Peroni and Moretti, smaller stores and bars increasingly offer craft microbrews (known as *birre artigianali*). Italy had fewer than 50 breweries in 2000. That figure was well over 400 by 2015, and rising fast. You'll even find quality beers on the hallowed shelves of the occasional wine vendor.

first cemeteries of the Christian community of Rome, housing the remains of early popes and martyrs.

We have Christianity, along with the influence of Byzantium, to thank for the appearance of Italy's next great artistic style: the **Byzantine.** Painting and mosaic work in this era was very stylized and static, but also ornate and ethereal. The most accomplished examples of Byzantine art are found in the churches of **Ravenna** (p. 347). Later buildings in the Byzantine style include Venice's **Basilica di San Marco** (p. 372).

The Middle Ages: 9th Century to the 14th Century

A ravaged Rome entered the Middle Ages, its once-proud people scattered in rustic exile. A modest population lived in the swamps of the **Campus Martius.** The seven hills—now without water because the aqueducts were cut—stood abandoned and crumbling.

The Pope turned toward Europe, where he found a powerful ally in **Charlemagne,** king of the Franks. In 800, Pope Leo III crowned him emperor. Although Charlemagne pledged allegiance to the church and looked to Rome and its pope as the final arbiter in most religious and cultural affairs, he launched northwestern Europe on a course toward bitter opposition to the meddling of the papacy in temporal affairs.

The successor to Charlemagne's empire was a political entity known as the **Holy Roman Empire** (962–1806). The new Empire defined the end of the Dark Ages but ushered in a long period of bloody warfare. Magyars from Hungary invaded northeastern Lombardy and, in turn, were defeated by an increasingly powerful **Venice.** This was the great era of Venetian preeminence in the eastern Mediterranean; it defeated naval rival **Genoa** in the 1380 Battle of Chioggia; great buildings like the **Doge's Palace** (p. 377) were built; its merchants reigned over most of the eastern Mediterranean, and presided over a republic that lasted for a millennium. The Lion of St. Mark—symbol of the city's dominion—can be seen as far afield as **Bergamo** (p. 451), close to Milan.

Rome during the Middle Ages was a quaint backwater. Narrow lanes with overhanging buildings filled many areas that had once been showcases of imperial power. The forums, mercantile exchanges, temples, and theaters of the Imperial era slowly disintegrated. As the seat of the Roman Catholic Church, the state was almost completely controlled by priests, and began an aggressive expansion of church influence and acquisitions. The result was an endless series of power struggles. Between 1378 and 1417, competing popes—one in Rome, another **"antipope"** in Avignon—made simultaneous claims to the legacy of St. Peter.

Normans gained military control of Sicily from the Arabs in the 11th century, divided it from the rest of Italy, and altered forever the island's racial and ethnic makeup. The reign of **Roger II of Sicily** (r. 1130–54) is remembered for its religious tolerance and the multiethnic nature of the court, as well as its architecture. The **Palazzo dei Normanni** (p. 620), in Palermo, and nearby **Monreale** (p. 626), are just two among many great projects the Normans left behind.

In the mid–14th century, the **Black Death** ravaged Europe, killing perhaps a third of Italy's population; the unique preservation of Tuscan settlements like **San Gimignano** (p. 262) and **Siena** (p. 226) owes much to the fact that they never fully recovered after the devastation dished out by the 1348 plague. Despite such setbacks, Italian **city-states** grew wealthy from Crusade booty, trade, and banking.

The medieval period marks the beginning of building in stone on a mass scale. Flourishing from A.D. 800 to 1300, **Romanesque** architecture took its inspiration and rounded arches from ancient Rome. Architects built large churches with wide aisles to accommodate the masses. Pisa's **Campo dei Miracoli** (1153–1360s; p. 284) is typical of the Pisan-Romanesque style, with stacked arcades of mismatched columns in the cathedral's facade (and wrapping around the **Leaning Tower of Pisa**), and blind arcading set with diamond-shaped lozenges. The influence of Arab architecture is obvious—Pisa was a city of seafaring merchants.

Romanesque **sculpture** was fluid but still far from naturalistic. Often wonderfully childlike in its narrative simplicity, the work frequently mixes biblical scenes with the myths and motifs of local pagan traditions that were being incorporated into medieval Christianity. The 48 relief panels of the bronze doors of the **Basilica di San Zeno Maggiore** in

Siena's Palazzo Publico.

Verona (p. 425) rank among Italy's greatest surviving examples of Romanesque sculpture. The exterior of Parma's **Baptistery** (p. 354) sports a series of Romanesque friezes by Benedetto Antelami (1150–1230).

As the appeal of Romanesque and the Byzantine faded, the **Gothic** style flourished from the 13th to the 15th centuries. In architecture, the Gothic was characterized by flying buttresses, pointed arches, and delicate stained-glass windows. These engineering developments freed architecture from the heavy, thick walls of the Romanesque and allowed ceilings to soar, walls to thin, and windows to proliferate.

Although the Gothic age continued to be religious, many secular buildings also arose, including palaces designed to show off the prestige of various ruling families. Siena's civic **Palazzo Pubblico** (p. 234) and many of the great buildings of **Venice** (see chapter 9) date from this period. **San Gimignano** (p. 262), in Tuscany, has a preserved Gothic center. Milan's **Duomo** (p. 434) is one of Europe's great Gothic cathedrals.

Painters such as **Cimabue** (1251–1302) and **Giotto** (1266–1337), in Florence, **Pietro Cavallini** (1259–ca. 1330) in Rome, and **Duccio di Buoninsegna** (ca. 1255–1319) in Siena, began to lift art from Byzantine rigidity and set it on the road to realism. Giotto's finest work is his fresco cycle at Padua's **Cappella degli Scrovegni** (p. 421); he was the true harbinger of the oncoming Renaissance, which would forever change art and architecture. Duccio's 1311 "Maestà," now in Siena's

Milan's Duomo, a classic Gothic cathedral.

Museo dell'Opera Metropolitana (p. 235), influenced Sienese painters for centuries. Ambrogio Lorenzetti painted the greatest civic frescoes of the Middle Ages—his "Allegories of Good and Bad Government" in Siena's **Palazzo Pubblico** (p. 234)—before he succumbed to the Black Death, along with almost every great Sienese artist of his generation.

The medieval period also saw the birth of literature in the Italian language—which itself was a written version of the **Tuscan dialect,** primarily because the great writers of the age were Tuscans. Florentine **Dante Alighieri** wrote his *Divine Comedy* in the 1310s. Boccaccio's *Decameron*—kind of a Florentine *Canterbury Tales*—appeared in the 1350s.

The A-List of Italian Novels Available in English

- Alessandro Manzoni, *The Betrothed* (1827)
- Alberto Moravia, *The Conformist* (1951)
- Giuseppe Tomasi di Lampedusa, *The Leopard* (1958)
- Elsa Morante, *History: A Novel* (1974)
- Italo Calvino, *If on a Winter's Night a Traveler* (1979)
- Umberto Eco, *Foucault's Pendulum* (1988)
- Niccolo Ammaniti, *I'm Not Scared* (2001)

Renaissance & Baroque Italy

The story of Italy from the dawn of the Renaissance in the early 15th century to the "Age of Enlightenment" in the 17th and 18th centuries is as fascinating and complicated as that of the rise and fall of the Roman Empire.

During this period, **Rome** underwent major physical changes. The old centers of culture reverted to pastures and fields, and great churches and palaces were built with the stones of ancient Rome. Cows grazed on the crumbling Roman Forum. The city's construction boom did more damage to the ancient temples than any barbarian sack had done. Rare marbles were stripped from Imperial-era baths and used as altarpieces or sent to lime kilns. So enthusiastic was the papal destruction of Imperial Rome that it's a miracle anything is left.

Milan was a glorious Renaissance capital, particularly under the Sforza dynasty and Ludovico "Il Moro" (1452–1508), patron of Leonardo da Vinci. Smaller but still significant centers of power included the Gonzaga family's **Mantua** (p. 456) and the Este clan's **Ferrara** (p.339).

This era is best remembered because of its art, and around 1400 the most significant power in Italy was the city where the Renaissance began: **Florence** (see chapter 5). Slowly but surely, the **Medici** family rose to become the most powerful of the city's ruling oligarchy, gradually usurping the powers of the guilds and the republicans. They reformed law and commerce, expanded the city's power by taking control of neighbors such as **Pisa,** and also sparked a "renaissance," a rebirth, in painting, sculpture, and architecture. Christopher Hibbert's *The Rise and Fall of*

the House of Medici (2001) is the most readable account of the era.

Under the patronage of the Medici (as well as other powerful Florentine families), innovative young painters and sculptors went in pursuit of a greater degree of expressiveness and naturalism. **Donatello** (1386–1466) cast the first freestanding nude since antiquity (a bronze now in Florence's **Museo Nazionale del Bargello,** p. 181). **Lorenzo Ghiberti** (1378–1455) labored for 50 years on two sets of doors for Florence's **Baptistery** (p. 174), the most famous of which were dubbed the "Gates of Paradise." **Masaccio** (1401–28) produced the first

Ghiberti's Baptistery Doors, a Renaissance masterpiece in Florence.

painting that realistically portrayed linear perspective, on the nave wall of **Santa Maria Novella** (p. 190).

Next followed the brief period that's become known as the **High Renaissance:** The epitome of the Renaissance man, Florentine **Leonardo da Vinci** (1452–1519), painted his "Last Supper," now in Milan's **Santa Maria delle Grazie** (p. 441), and an "Annunciation" (1481), now hanging in Florence's **Uffizi** (p. 177) alongside countless Renaissance masterpieces from such great painters as Paolo Uccello, Sandro Botticelli, Piero della Francesca, and others. **Raphael** (1483–1520) produced a sublime body of work in 37 short years.

Skilled in sculpture, painting, and architecture, **Michelangelo** (1475–1564) and his career marked the apogee of the Renaissance. His giant "David" at the **Galleria dell'Accademia** (p. 191) in Florence is the world's most famous statue, and the **Sistine Chapel** frescoes have lured millions to the **Vatican Museums** (p. 77) in Rome.

Meanwhile in Venice, the father of the Venetian High Renaissance was **Titian** (1485–1576); known for his mastery of color and tonality, he was the true heir to great Venetian painters **Gentile Bellini** (1429–1507), **Giorgione** (1477–1510), and **Vittore Carpaccio** (1465–1525). Many of their masterpieces can be seen around **Venice** (see chapter 8).

As in painting, Renaissance **architecture** stressed proportion, order, classical inspiration, and mathematical precision. **Filippo Brunelleschi** (1377–1446), in the early 1400s, grasped the concept of "perspective" and provided artists with ground rules for creating the illusion of three dimensions on a flat surface. Ross King's *Brunelleschi's Dome* (2000) tells the story of his greatest achievement, the crowning of Florence's cathedral with that iconic ochre dome. Even **Michelangelo** took up architecture late in life, designing the Laurentian Library (1524) and New Sacristy (1524–34) at Florence's **San Lorenzo** (p. 189). He moved south (just as art's center of gravity did) to complete his crowning glory, the soaring dome of Rome's **St. Peter's Basilica** (p. 75).

The third great Renaissance architect—the most influential of them all—was **Andrea Palladio** (1508–80), who worked in a classical mode of columns, porticoes, pediments, and other ancient temple–inspired features. His masterpieces include fine churches in Venice.

In time, the High Renaissance stagnated, paving the way for the **baroque.** Stuccoes, sculptures, and paintings were carefully designed to complement each other—and the space itself—to create a unified whole. The baroque movement's spiritual home was Rome, and its towering figure was **Gian Lorenzo Bernini** (1598–1680), the greatest baroque sculptor, a fantastic architect, and a more-than-decent painter as well. Among many fine sculptures, you'll find his best in Rome's **Galleria Borghese** (p. 107) and **Santa Maria della Vittoria** (p. 111). Baroque architecture is especially prominent in the South: in the churches and devotional architecture of **Naples** (p. 535) and in **Siracusa** (p. 600), Sicily. **Turin** (p. 476) under the Savoys was remodeled by the baroque architecture of Guarino Guarini (1624–83) and **Filippo Juvarra** (1678–1736).

In music, most famous of the baroque composers is Venetian **Antonio Vivaldi** (1678–1741), whose "Four Seasons" is among the most regularly performed classical compositions of all time.

In painting, the baroque mixed a kind of super-realism based on using everyday people as models and an exaggerated use of light and dark—a technique called *chiaroscuro*—with compositional complexity and explosions of dynamic fury, movement, and color. The period produced many fine artists, notably **Caravaggio** (1571–1610). Among his masterpieces are the "St. Matthew" (1599) cycle in Rome's **San Luigi dei Francesi** (p. 98) and "The Acts of Mercy" in **Pio Monte della Misericordia** (p. 546), Naples. The baroque also had an outstanding female painter in **Artemisia Gentileschi** (1593–1652): Her brutal "Judith Slaying Holofernes" (1620) hangs in Florence's **Uffizi** (p. 177).

Frothy, ornate, and chaotic, **rococo** art was the baroque gone awry— and had few serious proponents in Italy. **Giambattista Tiepolo** (1696–1770) was arguably the best of the rococo painters, and specialized in ceiling frescoes and canvases with cloud-filled heavens of light. He worked extensively in Venice and the northeast. For rococo building— more a decorative than an architectural movement—look no further than Rome's **Spanish Steps** (p. 104) or the **Trevi Fountain** (p. 106).

At Last, a United Italy: The 1800s

By the 1800s, the glories of the Renaissance were a fading memory. From Turin to Naples, chunks of Italy had changed hands many, many times— between the Austrians, the Spanish, and the French, among autocratic thugs and enlightened princes, between the noble and the merchant classes. The 19th century witnessed the final collapse of many of the Renaissance city-states. The last of the Medici, Gian Gastone, had died in 1737, leaving Tuscany in the hands of Lorraine and Habsburg princes.

French emperor **Napoleon** brought an end to a millennium of Republic in **Venice** in 1797, and installed puppet or client rulers across the Italian peninsula. During the **Congress of Vienna** (1814–15), which followed Napoleon's defeat by an alliance of the British, Prussians, and Dutch, Italy was once again divided.

Political unrest became a fact of Italian life, some of it spurred by the industrialization of the north and some by the encouragement of insurrectionaries like **Giuseppe Mazzini** (1805–72). Europe's year of revolutions, **1848,** rocked Italy, too, with violent risings in Lombardy and Sicily. After decades of political machinations and intrigue, and thanks to the efforts of statesman **Camillo Cavour** (1810–61) and rebel general **Giuseppe Garibaldi** (1807–82), the Kingdom of Italy was proclaimed in 1861 and **Victor Emmanuel (Vittorio Emanuele) II** of Savoy became its first monarch. The kingdom's first capital was **Turin** (1861–65), seat of the victorious Piedmontese, followed by **Florence** (1865–71).

The establishment of the kingdom, however, didn't signal a complete unification of Italy because Latium (including Rome) was still under papal control and Venetia was held by Austria. This was partially resolved in 1866, when Venetia joined the rest of Italy after the **Seven Weeks' War** between Austria and Prussia. In 1871, Rome became the capital of the newly formed country, after the city was retaken on September 20, 1870. Present-day **Via XX Settembre** is the very street up which patriots advanced after breaching the city gates. The **Risorgimento**—the "resurgence," Italian unification—was complete.

Political heights in Italy seemed to correspond to historic depths in art and architecture. Among the few notable practitioners of this era, the most well known is probably Venetian **Antonio Canova** (1757–1822), Italy's major neoclassical sculptor, who became notorious for painting both Napoleon and his sister Pauline as nudes. His best work is in Rome's **Galleria Borghese** (p. 107). Tuscany also bred a late–19th-century precursor to French Impressionism, the **Macchiaioli** movement; see their works in the "modern art" galleries at Florence's **Palazzo Pitti** (p. 195).

If art was hitting an all-time low, **music** was experiencing its Italian golden age. It's bel canto **opera** for which the 19th century is largely remembered. **Gioachino Rossini** (1792–1868) was born in Pesaro, in the Marches, and found fame in 1816 with *The Barber of Seville*. The fame of **Gaetano Donizetti** (1797–1848), a prolific native of Bergamo, was assured when his *Anna Bolena* premiered in 1830. Both were perhaps overshadowed by **Giuseppe Verdi** (1813–1901), whose works such as *Rigoletto* and *La Traviata* have become some of the most whistled on the planet.

The 20th Century: Two World Wars & One Duce

In 1915, Italy entered **World War I** on the side of the Allies. Italy joined Britain, Russia, and France to help defeat Germany and the traditional enemy to the north, now the Austro-Hungarian Empire, and so to "reclaim" Trentino and Trieste. (Mark Thompson's *The White War* tells the story of Italy's catastrophic campaign.) In the aftermath of war and carnage, Italians further suffered with rising unemployment and horrendous inflation. As in Germany, this deep political crisis led to the emergence of a dictator.

On October 28, 1922, **Benito Mussolini,** who had started his Fascist Party in 1919, knew the country was ripe for change. He gathered 30,000 Black Shirts for his **March on Rome.** Inflation was soaring and workers had just called a general strike, so rather than recognizing a state under siege, **King Victor Emmanuel III** (1900–46) proclaimed Mussolini as the new government leader. In 1929, Il Duce—a moniker Mussolini began using from 1925—defined the divisions between the Italian government and the Pope by signing the Lateran Treaty, which granted political, territorial, and fiscal autonomy to the microstate of **Vatican City.** During the Spanish Civil War (1936–39), Mussolini's support of Franco's Fascists, who had staged a coup against the elected government of Spain, helped seal the Axis alliance between Italy and Nazi Germany. Italy was inexorably and disastrously sucked into **World War II.**

Deeply unpleasant though their politics were, the Fascist regime did sponsor some remarkable **architecture.** It's at its best in Rome's planned satellite community **EUR** (p. 117). In a city famed for Renaissance

Inside Milan's La Scala opera house.

works, Florence's **Santa Maria Novella station** (1934) is also a masterpiece—of modernism. Today the station has a plaque commemorating the Jews who were sent from the terminus to their deaths in Nazi Germany.

The era's towering figure in music was **Giacomo Puccini** (1858–1924); his operas *Tosca* (1900) and *Madame Butterfly* (1904) still pack houses worldwide.

After defeat in World War II, Italy's people voted for the establishment of the First Republic—overwhelmingly so in northern and central Italy, which counterbalanced a southern majority in favor of keeping the monarchy. Italy quickly succeeded in rebuilding its economy, in part because of U.S. aid under the **Marshall Plan** (1948–52). By the 1960s, as a member of the European Economic Community (founded by the **Treaty of Rome** in 1957), Italy had become one of the world's leading industrialized nations, and prominent in the manufacture of automobiles and office equipment. Fiat (from Turin), Ferrari (from Emilia-Romagna), and Olivetti (from northern Piedmont) were known around the world.

The country was plagued, however, by economic inequality between the industrially prosperous north and the depressed south, and during the late 1970s and early 1980s, it was rocked by domestic terrorism: These were the so-called **Anni di Piombo (Years of Lead),** during which extremists of the left and right bombed and assassinated with impunity. Conspiracy theories became the Italian staple diet; everyone from the state to shady Masonic lodges to the CIA was accused of involvement in what became in effect an undeclared civil war. The most notorious incidents were the kidnap and murder of Prime Minister **Aldo Moro** in 1978 and the **Bologna station bombing,** which killed 85 in 1980. You'll find a succinct account of these murky years in Tobias Jones's *The Dark Heart of Italy* (2003).

The postwar Italian **film industry** became respected for its innovative directors. **Federico Fellini** (1920–93) burst onto the scene with his highly individual style, beginning with *La Strada* (1954) and going on to such classics as *The City of Women* (1980). His *La Dolce Vita* (1961) defined an era in Rome.

In the early 1990s, many of the country's leading politicians were accused of corruption. These scandals uncovered as a result of the judiciary's **Mani Pulite (Clean Hands)** investigations—often dubbed **Tangentopoli** ("Bribesville")—provoked a constitutional crisis, ushering in the **Second Republic** in 1992.

Other resonant events in recent Italian history have centered on its religion. As much of the world watched and prayed, **Pope John Paul II** died in April 2005, at the age of 84, ending a reign of 26 years. A Vatican doctrinal hard-liner next took the papal throne as **Pope Benedict XVI.** He was succeeded by the surprisingly liberal **Pope Francis** in 2013, after Benedict became the first pope to resign since the 1400s.

WHEN TO GO

The best months for traveling in Italy are from **April to June** and **mid-September to October**—temperatures are usually comfortable, rural colors are richer, and the crowds aren't too intense (except around Easter). From **July through early September** the country's holiday spots teem with visitors. **Easter, May,** and **June** usually see the highest hotel prices in Rome and Florence.

August is the worst month in most places: Not only does it get uncomfortably hot, muggy, and crowded, but seemingly the entire country goes on vacation, at least from August 15 onward—and many Italians take off the entire month. Many family-run hotels, restaurants, and shops are closed (except at the spas, beaches, and islands, where most Italians head). Paradoxically, you will have many urban places almost to yourself if you visit in August. Turin and Milan, in particular, can seem virtual ghost towns, and hotels there (and often in Florence and Rome) are heavily discounted. Just be aware that many fashionable restaurants and nightspots are closed for the whole month.

From **late October to Easter,** many attractions operate on shorter (sometimes *much* shorter) winter hours, and some hotels are closed for renovation or redecoration, though that is less likely if you are visiting the cities. Many family-run restaurants take a week or two off sometime between **November and February;** spa and beach destinations become padlocked ghost towns.

Revelers at Carnivale, in Venice.

Weather

It's warm all over Italy in summer; it can be very hot in the south, and almost anywhere inland—landlocked cities on the plains of Veneto and Emilia-Romagna, and in Tuscany, can feel stifling during a July or August hot spell. The higher temperatures (measured in Italy in degrees Celsius) usually begin everywhere in May, often lasting until sometime in October. Winters in the north of Italy are cold, with rain and snow. A biting wind whistles over the mountains into Milan, Turin, and Venice. In Rome and the south the weather is warm (or at least, warm-ish) almost all year, averaging 10°C (50°F) in winter.

The rainiest months pretty much everywhere are usually October and November.

Italy's Average Daily High Temperature & Monthly Rainfall

ROME

	JAN	FEB	MAR	APR	MAY	JUNE	JULY	AUG	SEPT	OCT	NOV	DEC
TEMP. (°F)	55	56	59	63	71	77	83	83	79	71	62	57
TEMP. (°C)	12	13	15	17	21	25	28	28	26	21	16	13
RAINFALL (IN.)	3.2	2.8	2.7	2.6	2	1.3	.6	1	2.7	4.5	4.4	3.8

FLORENCE

	JAN	FEB	MAR	APR	MAY	JUNE	JULY	AUG	SEPT	OCT	NOV	DEC
TEMP. (°F)	49	53	60	68	75	84	89	88	81	69	58	50
TEMP. (°C)	9	11	15	20	23	28	31	31	27	20	14	10
RAINFALL (IN.)	1.9	2.1	2.7	2.9	3	2.7	1.5	1.9	3.3	4	3.9	2.8

VENICE

	JAN	FEB	MAR	APR	MAY	JUNE	JULY	AUG	SEPT	OCT	NOV	DEC
TEMP. (°F)	42	47	54	61	70	77	81	81	75	65	53	44
TEMP. (°C)	6	8	12	16	21	25	27	27	24	18	11	7
RAINFALL (IN.)	2.3	2.1	2.2	2.5	2.7	3	2.5	3.3	2.6	2.7	3.4	2.1

Public Holidays

Offices, government buildings (though not usually tourist offices), and shops in Italy are generally closed on: January 1 (*Capodanno,* or New Year); January 6 (*La Befana,* or Epiphany); Easter Sunday (*Pasqua*); Easter Monday (*Pasquetta*); April 25 (Liberation Day); May 1 (*Festa del Lavoro,* or Labor Day); June 2 (*Festa della Repubblica,* or Republic Day); August 15 (*Ferragosto,* or the Assumption of the Virgin); November 1 (All Saints' Day); December 8 (*L'Immacolata,* or the Immaculate Conception); December 25 (*Natale,* Christmas Day); December 26 (*Santo Stefano,* or St. Stephen's Day). You'll also often find businesses closed for the annual daylong celebration dedicated to the local saint (for example, on January 31 in San Gimignano, Tuscany).

Italy Calendar of Events

JANUARY

Festa di Sant'Agnese, Sant'Agnese Fuori le Mura, Rome. In this ancient ceremony, two lambs are blessed and shorn; their wool is used later for *palliums* (Roman Catholic vestments). January 21.

FEBRUARY

Carnevale, Venice. At this riotous time, theatrical presentations and masked balls take place throughout Venice and on the islands in the lagoon. The balls are by invitation only (except the Doge's Ball), but the street events and fireworks are open to everyone. www.carnevale. venezia.it. The week before Ash Wednesday, the beginning of Lent.

Festival della Canzone Italiana (Festival of Italian Popular Song), San Remo, Liguria. At this 6-day competition, major artists perform previously unreleased Italian songs. www.sanremo.rai.it. Late February.

MARCH

Festa di San Giuseppe, the Trionfale Quarter (north of the Vatican), Rome. The heavily decorated statue of the saint is brought out at a fair with food stalls, concerts, and sporting events. Usually March 19.

APRIL

Holy Week, nationwide. Processions and age-old ceremonies—some from pagan days, some from the Middle Ages—are staged. The most notable procession is led by the Pope, passing the Colosseum and the Roman Forum; a torchlit parade caps the observance. Beginning 4 days before Easter Sunday; sometimes late March but often April.

Easter Sunday (Pasqua), Piazza San Pietro, Rome. In an event broadcast around the world, the Pope gives his blessing from the balcony of St. Peter's.

Scoppio del Carro (Explosion of the Cart), Florence. At this ancient observance, a cart laden with flowers and fireworks is drawn by three white oxen to the Duomo, where at the noon Mass a mechanical dove detonates it from the altar. Easter Sunday.

MAY

Maggio Musicale Fiorentino (Florentine Musical May), Florence. Italy's oldest and most prestigious music festival emphasizes music from the 14th to the 20th centuries, but also presents ballet and opera. www.maggiofiorentino.it. Late April to end of June.

Mille Miglia, Brescia, Lombardy. Vintage and classic cars depart Brescia and spend 4 days parading around the towns and cities of northern and central Italy as part of the annual "1000 Miles." www.1000miglia.eu. Mid-May.

Concorso Ippico Internazionale (International Horse Show), Piazza di Siena, Rome. Top-flight international horse show held in the Villa Borghese. www. piazzadisiena.com. Late May.

JUNE

Festa di San Ranieri, Pisa, Tuscany. The city honors its patron saint with candlelit parades, followed the next day by eight-rower teams competing in 16th-century costumes. June 16 and 17.

Calcio Storico (Historic Football), Florence. A revival of a raucous 15th-century form of football, pitting four teams in medieval costumes against one another. The matches usually culminate on June 24, the feast day of St. John the Baptist. Late June.

Gioco del Ponte, Pisa, Tuscany. Teams in Renaissance costume take part in a long-contested "push-of-war" on the Ponte di Mezzo, which spans the River Arno. Last Sunday in June.

Arena di Verona Opera Festival, Verona, Veneto. The 20,000-seat remains of Verona's Roman-era amphitheater is the venue for Italy's most famous outdoor opera season, now over 100 years old. www.arena.it. Late June to early September.

La Biennale di Venezia (International Exposition of Contemporary Art), Venice. One of the most famous regular art events in the world takes place every 2 years (in odd-numbered years). www.labiennale.org. June to November.

JULY

Il Palio, Piazza del Campo, Siena, Tuscany. Palio fever grips this Tuscan hill town for a wild and exciting horse race dating from the Middle Ages. Pageantry, costumes, and the celebrations of the victorious *contrada* (sort of a neighborhood social club) mark the spectacle. It's a "no rules" event: Even a horse without a rider can win the race. July 2.

Umbria Jazz, Perugia, Umbria. One of Europe's top jazz festivals always attracts top-class artists. www.umbriajazz.com. Mid-July.

Festa del Redentore (Feast of the Redeemer), Venice. This festival marks the lifting of the plague in 1576, with fireworks, pilgrimages, and boating. www.redentorevenezia.it. Third Saturday and Sunday of July.

AUGUST

Il Palio, Piazza del Campo, Siena, Tuscany. See July for event description. The second annual staging is dedicated to the Assumption of the Virgin Mary. August 16.

Venice International Film Festival, Venice. Ranking after Cannes, this festival brings together stars, directors, producers, and filmmakers from all over the world to the Palazzo del Cinema on the Lido. Although many seats are reserved for jury members, the public can attend, too. www.labiennale.org/en/cinema. Late August to early September.

SEPTEMBER

Regata Storica, Grand Canal, Venice. A maritime spectacular: Many gondolas participate in the canal procession, although gondolas don't race in the regatta itself. www.regatastoricavenezia.it. First Sunday in September.

Vintage cars race around Lombardy in the annual Mille Miglia in May.

Festa di San Gennaro, Naples, Campania. The cathedral is the focal point for this celebration in honor of the city's patron saint. Twice a year a solemn procession is followed by the miraculous "liquefaction" of the holy blood. September 19, December 16, and 1st Sunday in May.

Palio di Asti, Asti, Piedmont. Riders race for Italy's "second" Palio around the central square of a provincial Piedmont town. Expect medieval pageantry and daring horsemanship in an event with 800 years of history. www.palio.asti.it. Third Sunday in September.

DECEMBER

La Scala Opera Season Opening, Teatro alla Scala, Milan. At the most famous house of them all, the season begins each December 7, the feast day of Milan's patron, St. Ambrose. It runs into the following July, then September to mid-November. Even though opening-night tickets are close to impossible to find, it is worth a try. www.teatroallascala.org.

Christmas Blessing of the Pope, Piazza di San Pietro, Rome. Delivered at noon from the balcony of St. Peter's Basilica, the Pope's words are broadcast to the faithful around the globe. December 25.

SUGGESTED ITALY ITINERARIES

taly is so vast and treasure-filled that it's hard to resist the temptation to pack in too much in too short a time. It's a dauntingly diverse and complex destination, and you can't even skim the surface in 1 or 2 weeks—so relax, don't try. If you're a first-time visitor with little touring time on your hands, we suggest you go just for the classic nuggets: Rome, Florence, and Venice could be packed into 1 very busy week, better yet in 2.

How can you accomplish that? Well, Italy ranks with Germany and France in offering mainland Europe's best-maintained highways (called *autostrade*). You'll pay a toll to drive on them (p. 638), but it's much quicker to use them than to trust your limited time to the array of minor roads, which can be *much* slower going.

The country also boasts one of the most efficient high-speed rail networks in the Western world. Rome, Bologna, and Milan are the key hubs of this 21st-century transportation empire—for example, from Rome's Termini station, Florence can be reached in only 95 minutes. In fact, if you're city-hopping between Rome, Florence, and Venice, you need never rent a car. Upgrades to the rail network mean that key routes are served by comfortable, fast trains. You'll only require a rental car if you plan rural detours.

The itineraries that follow introduce some of our favorite places. The pace may occasionally be a bit breathless for some visitors, so consider skipping a stop to have some chill-out time—after all, you're on vacation. Of course, you can also use any of our itineraries as a jumping-off point to develop your own custom-made adventure. *Buon viaggio!*

THE REGIONS IN BRIEF

Although bordered on the northwest by France, on the north by Switzerland and Austria, and on the east by Slovenia, Italy is a land largely surrounded by the sea. It isn't enormous, but the peninsula's boot shape gives you the impression of a much larger area. Here's a brief rundown of the cities and regions covered in this guide. See this guide's inside front cover for a map of Italy by region.

ROME & LATIUM   The region of **Latium** ("Lazio" in Italian) is dominated by **Rome,** capital of both an ancient empire and modern Italy. Much of the "civilized world" was once ruled from here, starting from the days when Romulus and Remus are said to have founded Rome, in 753 B.C. There's no place with more artistic monuments, or a bigger buzz—not even Venice or Florence.

PREVIOUS PAGE: **Country road lined with cypress trees.**

The baroque Trevi Fountain, a tourist gathering spot in Rome.

FLORENCE, TUSCANY & UMBRIA

Tuscany is one of Italy's most culturally and politically influential provinces—the development of Italy without Tuscany is simply unthinkable (in fact, today's Italian language is merely a standardized version of the medieval Florentine dialect). Nowhere in the world is the impact of the Renaissance still felt more fully than in its birthplace, **Florence,** the repository of artistic works left by Masaccio, Leonardo, Michelangelo, and others. The main Tuscan destinations beyond Florence are the smaller cities of **Lucca, Pisa,** and especially **Siena,** Florence's great historical rival, as well as the **Chianti** winelands. Neighboring **Umbria** is a land of rolling green hills, where olive groves thrive and the pace of life is sedate. It has outstanding art sights in **Perugia** and Etruscan **Orvieto.**

BOLOGNA & EMILIA-ROMAGNA

Italians don't agree on much, but one national consensus is that the food in **Emilia-Romagna** is probably the best in Italy. The capital, **Bologna,** also has museums, churches, and a fine university with roots in the Middle Ages. Among the region's other art cities, none is nobler than Byzantine **Ravenna,** with its mosaics dating to the time when it was capital of a declining Roman Empire.

VENICE & THE VENETO

Northeastern Italy is one of Europe's treasure troves, encompassing **Venice** (certainly the world's most unusual city) and the surrounding **Veneto** region. Aging, decaying, and sinking into the sea, Venice is so alluring we almost want to say, visit it even if you have to skip Rome and Florence. Also recommended are the art cities of the "Venetian Arc": **Verona,** with its Shakespearean romance and intact Roman Arena; and **Padua,** with its Giotto frescoes.

LOMBARDY, PIEDMONT & THE LAKES

Flat, fertile, and prosperous, **Lombardy** is dominated by **Milan.** However, despite Leonardo's "Last Supper," the La Scala opera house, shopping, and some major museums, Milan doesn't have the sights of Rome, Florence, or Venice—though Expo 2015 left a legacy of improved tourist services. You'll find charm (and a more manageable area to cover) in the neighboring cities of **Bergamo** and **Mantua.** Also competing for your time should be the photogenic lakes of **Como** and **Garda.**

Piedmont's largest city, **Turin,** is the home of the Fiat empire (and vermouth). Turin's best-known sight is the Sacra Sindone (Holy Shroud), which some Catholics believe is the cloth in which Christ's crucified body was wrapped.

LIGURIA   Comprising most of the **Italian Riviera,** the region of **Liguria** incorporates the major historical seaport of **Genoa,** charming, upscale harbors such as the one at **Portofino,** and Italy's best coastal hiking, among the traditional communities of the **Cinque Terre.**

CAMPANIA   Campania encompasses both the fascinating anarchy of **Naples** and the elegant beauty of **Capri** and the **Amalfi Coast.** The region also contains sites identified in ancient mythology (lakes defined as the entrance to the Kingdom of the Dead, for example) and some of the world's most renowned ruins, including **Pompeii** and **Herculaneum.**

SICILY   The largest island in the Mediterranean Sea, **Sicily** has a unique mix of bloodlines and architecture from medieval Normandy, Aragónese Spain, Moorish North Africa, ancient Greece, Phœnicia, and Rome. Cars and fashionable people clog the lanes of its capital, **Palermo.** Areas of ravishing beauty and eerie historical interest include **Syracuse** (Siracusa in Italian) and **Taormina,** and the ruins at **Agrigento** and **Selinunte.** Sicily's ruins are rivaled only by Rome itself.

THE BEST OF ITALY IN 1 WEEK: ROME, FLORENCE & VENICE

Let's be realistic: It's impossible to see these storied cities properly in a week. However, a fast, efficient rail network along the Rome–Florence–Venice axis makes it surprisingly easy to see a handful of the best that these graceful, art-stuffed cities have to offer. This weeklong itinerary treads the familiar highlights, but there's a reason why they are the country's most visited sights: They're sure to provide memories that will last a lifetime.

DAYS 1, 2 & 3: Rome ★★★

You could spend forever in the Eternal City, but 3 days is enough to get a flavor of it. There are two essential areas to focus on in a short visit. The first is the legacy of Imperial Rome, such as the **Forum, Campidoglio,** and **Colosseum** (p. 88). Bookend **DAY 1** with the Forum and Colosseum (one first, the other last) to avoid the busiest crowds; the same ticket is good for both. On **DAY 2,** tackle **St. Peter's Basilica** and the **Vatican Museums** (p. 77), with a collection unlike any other in the world that, of course, includes Michelangelo's **Sistine Chapel.** On **DAY 3,** it's a toss-up: Choose between

Italy in One Week

0 — 100 mi
0 — 100 km

1-3 Rome
4 & **5** Florence
6 & **7** Venice

the underground catacombs of the **Via Appia Antica** (p. 117); treading the cobbled streets of an ancient port at **Ostia Antica** (p. 158); or visiting some of the capital's quieter museum collections, including the **Palazzo Massimo alle Terme** (p. 111). Spend your evenings in the bars of **Campo de' Fiori** or **Monti** (p. 151) and the restaurants of **Trastevere** (p. 133) or **Testaccio** (p. 147). Toward the end of your third day, catch the late train to Florence. Make sure you have booked in advance: Walk-up fares are much more expensive than advanced tickets on the high-speed network.

DAYS 4 & 5: Florence: Cradle of the Renaissance ★★★

You have 2 whole days to explore the city of Giotto, Leonardo, Botticelli, and Michelangelo. Start with their masterpieces at the **Uffizi** (p. 177; you should definitely have booked admission tickets ahead), followed by the **Duomo** complex (p. 176): Scale Brunelleschi's ochre dome, and follow up with a visit to the nearby **San Giovanni Battista** (p. 480), **Museo Storico dell'Opera del Duomo** (p. 177), and **Campanile di Giotto** (p. 175). Start **DAY 5** with "David" at the **Accademia** (p. 191). For the rest of your time, spend it getting to know the art at the **Palazzo Pitti** (p. 195), the intimate wall paintings of **San Marco** (p. 192), and Masaccio's revolutionary frescoes in the **Cappella Brancacci** (p. 199). In the evenings, head south of the Arno for lively wine bars and better restaurants (p. 217). Leave on an early train on the morning of **DAY 6.**

DAYS 6 & 7: Venice: The City that Defies the Sea ★★★

You'll ride into the heart of Venice on a *vaporetto* (water bus), taking in the **Grand Canal,** the world's greatest thoroughfare. Begin your sightseeing at **Piazza San Marco** (p. 361). The **Basilica di San Marco** is right there, and after exploring it, visit the nearby **Palazzo Ducale (Doge's Palace;** p. 377) and its haunting **Bridge of Sighs.** Begin your evening with the classic Venetian *aperitivo,* an Aperol spritz (Aperol with sparkling Prosecco wine and soda) followed by *cicchetti* (Venetian tapas) before a late dinner. Make **DAY 7** all about the city's unique art: the **Gallerie dell'Accademia** (p. 382), the modern **Peggy Guggenheim Collection** (p. 383), and **San Rocco** (p. 386). Catch the latest train you can back to Rome. Or add another night—you can never stay too long in Venice.

Cafes line the Piazza San Marco in Venice.

The Best of Italy in 1 Week

SUGGESTED ITALY ITINERARIES

THE BEST OF ITALY IN 2 WEEKS

It's obviously difficult to see the top sights of Italy—and to see them properly—in just 2 weeks. But in this itinerary, we show you some of the best of them. We'll go beyond the well-trodden (and spectacular) Rome–Florence–Venice trail to include the southern region of Campania, specifically Pompeii, which has Italy's most precious Roman ruins. Additional stops in the center and north are Pisa (for the Leaning Tower and more) and Verona (the city of lovers since "Romeo and Juliet").

DAYS 1, 2 & 3: Rome ★★★

Follow the itinerary suggested in "The Best of Italy in 1 Week," above. Because an extra week allows you to add a trip to Pompeii, you can probably skip Ostia Antica. Choose your third day from between the catacombs of the **Via Appia Antica** (p. 117) and Rome's less visited museums.

DAY 4: Naples ★★

Leave Rome as early as you can so that you can take in the major attractions of Naples, the historic "capital" of southern Italy. There is an unparalleled collection of ancient artifacts at the **Museo Archeologico Nazionale** (p. 543), plus Titians and Caravaggios at the **Museo e Gallerie Nazionale di Capodimonte** (p. 544). After dark, wander **Spaccanapoli**—the old center's main east–west thoroughfare—then make a date with a **pizzeria**: Neapolitans stake a reasonable claim that pizza was invented here. After dinner, stroll the **Mergellina** boardwalk to enjoy the breezes and views of the Bay of Naples. Stay overnight in Naples, the first of 3 nights based here.

DAY 5: Pompeii ★★

On **DAY 5,** take the Circumvesuviana train 24km (15 miles) south of Naples to spend a day wandering Europe's best-preserved Roman ruins at **Pompeii** (p. 562). Be sure to pack water and lunch, because onsite services aren't great. The city was buried for almost 2,000 years, having suffered sudden devastation when nearby Vesuvius erupted in A.D. 79. Some of the great archaeological treasures of Italy—including the patrician villa **Casa dei Vettii** and the frescoed **Villa dei Misteri**—are here. Return to Naples for the night.

DAY 6: The Amalfi Coast ★★

On the morning of **DAY 6,** rent a car and drive 49km (30 miles) south of Naples along A3 until you see the turnoff for **Sorrento.** At Sorrento, head east along the curvy Amalfi Drive, of which Andre Gide said: "[There is] nothing more beautiful on this earth." The drive winds around the twisting, steep coastline, to the southern resorts of **Positano** and **Amalfi,** either of which would make an idyllic stopover to extend your stay. Allow at least 3 hours for this drive because it is slow moving. Alternatively, do the death-defying Amalfi Coast drive as part of an organized tour from Naples.

DAYS 7 & 8: Florence ★★★

Jump on the early high-speed train from Naples to Florence, then follow the itinerary suggested in "If You Have Only 1 Week," above. You'll be staying in Florence for the next 4 nights.

DAY 9: Gothic Siena ★★★

It's just over an hour to Siena on the *rapida* bus from Florence's bus station (p. 164). Leave early and set out immediately on arrival for **Piazza del Campo,** the shell-shaped main square, including its art-filled **Museo Civico** (inside the **Palazzo Pubblico**; p. 234). This is a flying visit, but you still have time to squeeze in a look at the **Duomo** (p. 176) and **Museo dell'Opera Metropolitana,** where you'll find Sienese master Duccio's giant "Maestà." Stop on the Campo for an early evening drink and then head to a restaurant in Siena's atmospheric back streets. Reserve an early table: The last bus back to Florence departs around 8:45pm.

DAY 10: Pisa & its Leaning Tower ★★

Most trains between Florence and Pisa take around an hour. On arrival, hop aboard the LAM Rossa bus outside Pisa Centrale Station, heading to the **Campo dei Miracoli** ("Field of Miracles"). The set-piece piazza here is one of the most photographed slices of real estate on the planet—and is home to the **Leaning Tower** (p. 286), of course. You can visit the **Duomo,** with its Arab-influenced Pisan-Romanesque facade, the **Battistero** with its carved pulpit and crazy acoustics, and the rest of the piazza's monuments and museums on the same combination ticket. You should book a slot ahead of time if you want to climb the Leaning Tower, however. For dining *alla pisana,* head away from the touristy piazza. The "real Pisa" lies in the warren of streets around the market square, **Piazza delle Vettovaglie.** Finish your visit with a stroll along the handsome promenade beside the **River Arno.** The last train back to Florence usually leaves at 10:30pm (though the 9:30pm train is quicker).

DAYS 11 & 12: Venice ★★★

Set your alarm clock for an early start: It takes around 2 hours to reach Venice from Florence aboard the Frecciargento high-speed train. Follow the itinerary suggested in "The Best of Italy in 1 Week," above.

DAY 13: Verona: City of Lovers & Gladiators ★★★

Although he likely never set foot in the place, Shakespeare placed the world's most famous love story, "Romeo and Juliet," here. Wander **Piazza dei Signori** and take in another square, **Piazza delle**

0   100 mi
0   100 km

L. Maggiore
L. Como
L. Garda
Aosta
Como
Trento
Udine
Milan **14**
Trieste
Turin
Piaoonza
Verona **13**
Venice **11 12**
Gulf of Venice
Parma
Modena
Bologna
Pula
Genoa
La Spezia
Rimini
FRANCE
MONACO
Ligurian Sea
Pisa **10**
Livorno
Florence **7 8**
SAN MARINO
Ancona
BOSNIA & HERZEGOVINA
CROATIA
Split
Mostar
Siena **9**
Perugia
Capraia
Elba
Bastia
Grosseto
Giglio
Viterbo
Ascoli Piceno
Pescara
Dubrovnik
Adriatic Sea
CORSICA (FRANCE)
Montecristo
VATICAN CITY
Rome **1-3**
L'Aquila
Ajaccio
Latina
Campobasso
Foggia
Barletta
Bari
Ponza
Olbia
Naples **4**
Pompeii **5 6**
Amalfi Coast
Brindisi
Taranto
Sassari
SARDINIA
Tyrrhenian Sea
Cosenza
Gulf of Taranto
Oristano
Ustica
AEOLIAN ISLANDS
Stromboli
Lipari
Catanzaro
Trapani
Palermo
Messina
Reggio di Calabria
EGADI ISLANDS
Mt. Etna
SICILY
Catania
Ionian Sea
Agrigento
Gela
Siracusa
TUNISIA
Ragusa
Strait of Sicily

1-3 Rome
4 Naples
5 Pompeii
6 The Amalfi Coast
7 & **8** Florence
9 Gothic Siena
10 Pisa
11 & **12** Venice
13 Verona
14 Milan

Erbe, before descending on the **Arena di Verona** (p. 425): Evoking Rome's Colosseum, it's the world's best-preserved gladiatorial arena, still used for monumental opera performances in summer months. Head back to Venice for the night. It is well worth booking your round-trip tickets ahead of time for the high-speed Frecciabianca train between Venice and Verona—the journey is just 1 hour, 10 minutes, compared with over 2 hours for a local train service.

DAY 14: Milan ★★

You should also prebook your Frecciabianca train connection between Venice and Milan, a journey of around 2½ hours. The most bustling city in Italy isn't only about industry and commerce. Milan possesses one of Europe's great Gothic cathedrals, the **Duomo** (p. 434). Its **Biblioteca-Pinacoteca Ambrosiana,** with cartoons by Raphael, houses one of Italy's great art collections. The city of St. Ambrose also hosts the **Pinacoteca di Brera** (p. 440), a treasure-trove of painting, laden with masterpieces from the likes of Mantegna and Piero della Francesca. Book ahead, too, to view Leonardo's fading but still magnificent "**Last Supper**" (p. 441). Stay overnight here if you are flying home or onward: It is one of the major transportation hubs of Europe.

ITALY FOR FAMILIES

Italy is probably the friendliest family vacation destination in all Europe. Practically, it presents few challenges. But if you're traveling by rental car with young children, be sure to request safety car seats ahead of time. Let the rental company know the age of your child and they will arrange for a seat that complies with EU regulations. Rail travelers should remember that reduced-price family fares are available on much of the high-speed network; ask when you buy your tickets or use a booking agent.

As you tour, don't go hunting for "child-friendly" restaurants or special kids' menus. There's always plenty available for little ones—even dishes that aren't offered to grown-up patrons. Never be afraid to ask if you have a fussy eater in the family. Pretty much any request is met with a smile.

Perhaps the main issue for travelers with children is spacing your museum visits so that you get a chance to see the masterpieces without having young kids suffer a meltdown after too many paintings of saints.

Remember to punctuate every day with a **gelato** stop—Italy makes the world's best ice cream. You will even find creative soy flavors for anyone with lactose intolerance. We also suggest planning fewer long, tiring daytrips out of town, especially by public transportation. And end your trip in Venice, which can seem to kids every bit as magical as a Disney theme park.

DAY 1: Rome's Ancient Ruins ★★★

History is on your side here: The wonders of **Ancient Rome** (p. 66) should appeal as much to kids (of almost any age) as to adults. There are plenty of gory tales to tell at the **Colosseum** (p. 88), where the bookshop has a good selection of city guides aimed at kids. After that, they can let off steam wandering the **Roman Forum** and the **Palatine Hill.** (The ruins of the **Imperial Forums** can be viewed at any time.) Cap the afternoon by exploring the **Villa Borghese** (p. 106), a monumental park in the heart of Rome where you can

Italy for Families

0 —— 100 mi
0 —— 100 km

1 Rome's Ancient Ruins
2 Rome: Living History
3 Rome: Underground
4 & 5 Florence
6 Pisa
7 & 8 Genoa & the Riviera di Levante
9 & 10 Lake Garda
11-13 Venice

rent bikes; there's a small zoo on the grounds. For dinner, head for some crispy crusts at an authentic Roman **pizzeria.**

DAY 2: Rome: Living History ★★★

Head early to **St. Peter's Basilica** (p. 75). They'll find it spooky wandering the Vatican grottoes, and few kids can resist climbing up to Michelangelo's dome at 114m (375 ft.). After time out for lunch, begin your assault on the **Vatican Museums** and the **Sistine Chapel.** Even if your kids don't like art museums, they will probably gawk at the grandeur. Later in the day head for the **Spanish Steps** (a good spot for some upscale souvenir shopping; see p. 104) before wandering over to the **Trevi Fountain.** Let them toss coins into the fountain, which is said to ensure a return to Rome—perhaps when they are older and can better appreciate the city's many more artistic attractions.

DAY 3: Rome: Underground ★★★

There are, literally, layers of history below the city streets, and kids will love to explore the catacombs of the **Via Appia Antica** (p. 117), the first cemetery of Rome's Christian community, and where the devout practiced their faith in secret during periods of persecution. **Context Travel** (p. 121) runs an excellent tour of the city's subterranean layers, which takes in **San Clemente** (p. 93) and Santi Giovanni e Paolo. It costs 285€ per party. Eat more **pizza** before you leave; Rome's pizzerias are matched only by those in Naples, to the south, and our next recommended stops all lie to the north. Leave on a late afternoon train to Florence.

DAYS 4 & 5: Florence ★★★

Florence is usually thought of as more of an adult city, but there's enough here to fill 2 family days, plus daytrips. With multiple nights here, you should take an apartment rather than a hotel room, to give you more space to spread out. Check out the websites **GoWithOh. com** or **HomeAway.com** for a good range of quality places. Close to the Duomo, **Residence Hilda** (p. 209) is a family-friendly hotel that rents large, apartment-style rooms with kitchenettes from 1 night.

Begin with the city's monumental main square, **Piazza della Signoria,** now an open-air museum of statues. The **Palazzo Vecchio** (p. 184) dominates one side; you can all tour it with special family-friendly guides, including a docent dressed as Cosimo de' Medici. You won't want to miss the **Uffizi.** With young children, you could turn your visit into a treasure trail of the museum's collection by first visiting the shop to select some postcards of the key artworks. On the second morning, kids will delight in climbing to the top of Brunelleschi's dome on the **Duomo** for a classic panorama. Get there early—queues lengthen through the day. You'll still have time to climb the 414 steps up to the **Campanile di Giotto,** run around in the **Giardino di Boboli,** and stroll the **Ponte Vecchio** at dusk. With older, fit children, you could add another day here, to allow time to see the Chianti hills on two wheels (see p. 169 for bike-rental info).

DAY 6: Pisa & its Leaning Tower ★★

If your kids are 7 or under, you should consider skipping **Pisa** (p. 286): 8 is the minimum age for the disorienting ascent up the bell tower of Pisa's cathedral, which more commonly goes by the

Genoa's Aquarium, a top attraction for families.

name the **Leaning Tower.** Elsewhere in the city, kids will love the hyperrealist monuments of the **Campo dei Miracoli** and learning about the city's Galileo links: He was born here, and supposedly discovered his law of pendulum motion while watching a swinging lamp inside the **Duomo.** Take them to taste a local specialty, *cecina*—a pizzalike garbanzo-bean flatbread served warm. Your day-long tour complete, whiz up the coast on the Frecciabianca fast train to Genoa. There is a luggage storage facility (*deposito bagagli*) at Pisa Centrale station.

DAYS 7 & 8: Genoa & the Riviera di Levante ★★

The industrial city-seaport of Genoa isn't an obvious choice for children, but it's here you'll find one of Italy's most enticing family attractions: The **Acquario di Genova** (p. 509), Europe's largest aquarium, where you can all enjoy a trip around the world's oceans. It requires a half-day to see properly, so get in early, and then head out to the **Riviera di Levante,** a coastline of pretty ports and rocky coves east of the city. Our favorite base around here is laid-back, romantic **Portofino,** where you can easily kill your second day in Liguria beside the azure sea.

DAYS 9 & 10: Lake Garda ★★★

Slow down for a couple of days by Italy's biggest inland lake, basing yourself perhaps around photogenic **Sirmione** (p. 472). Take a boat trip, hire a pedal boat or kayak, and generally enjoy lakeside life. In Sirmione you can scramble up high on the ramparts of the **Castello Scaligero** then ride the little train out to the Roman ruins at the

Grotte di Catullo, supposedly once a villa inhabited by poet Catullus (ca. 84 B.C.–ca. 54 B.C.). Look for lake fish on local menus. For active families with more time to spend, **Riva del Garda** (p. 473), close to the lake's northernmost point, is one of Europe's major windsurfing centers.

DAYS 11, 12 & 13: Venice: City on the Lagoon ★★★

In Venice, the fun begins the moment you arrive and take a *vaporetto* ride along the **Grand Canal.** Head straight for **Piazza San Marco** (p. 361), where children delight in feeding the pigeons and riding the elevator up the great **Campanile.** Catch the mosaics inside the **Basilica di San Marco,** which dominates the square. At the **Palazzo Ducale,** your kids can walk over the infamous **Bridge of Sighs.** As in Florence, make time for some art: Visit the **Gallerie dell'Accademia** (p. 382) and **San Rocco,** where kids view the episodic Tintoretto paintings like a picture book. If it's summer, save time for the beach at **Lido** (p. 392) and perhaps for getting a different angle on Venice's canals, from the seat of a **gondola** (p. 369).

A WHISTLESTOP WEEK-OR-SO FOR FOOD & WINE LOVERS

Italy has one of Europe's great cuisines—or rather, make that **several** of Europe's great cuisines. The nation's history as a collection of independent city-states and noble fiefdoms has left a richly diverse legacy in food. Each regional cuisine is committed to its own local produce and artisanal specialties, with treasured recipes that have been handed down through generations.

Italy is also the world's biggest wine producer. Although much of the output is undistinguished (if perfectly drinkable) table wine, some of the icons of world wine also hail from the peninsula. Our itinerary takes in just three of the great Italian red wine zones: **Montepulciano,** whose noble wine was known to the Etruscans; the **Chianti,** probably the first codified wine zone in the world; and **Piedmont,** whose robust reds Barolo and Barbaresco command top prices at restaurants across the globe.

DAYS 1 & 2: Rome ★★★

Italy's capital is packed with restaurants offering cuisine from across the peninsula—the **Trastevere, Monti,** and **Testaccio** neighborhoods are great for dining and drinks after dark. While here, look out for traditional Roman dishes like pasta with *cacio e pepe* (sheep's milk cheese and black pepper) or *saltimbocca alla Romana*—literally, "jump in the mouth," a veal cutlet with prosciutto and sage. **Gelato** is either Florentine or Sicilian in origin, depending on whom you speak to, but

Italy for Food & Wine Lovers

| L. Maggiore | L. Como | Trento | Udine |

Aosta · Como · Milan · Placenza · Verona · Venice · Trieste · L. Garda

Turin **89** · Parma · Modena · Bologna **67** · Genoa · La Spezia · Florence **45** · Pisa · Livorno · Siena · Montepulciano **3** · Perugia · Rome **12**

Legend:
- **1** & **2** Rome
- **3** Montepulciano
- **4** & **5** The Chianti
- **6** & **7** Bologna
- **8** & **9** Turin

it's in Rome you'll find some of the country's best (see p. 146). The city also has some of Italy's best craft beer bars (see p. 155). You'll need a rental car for your next leg. Collect it on your second afternoon and head north to Tuscany, to leave yourself a full day at your next stop.

DAY 3: Montepulciano ★★

Begin with a walk up the handsome, steep Corso from the town gate to **Piazza Grande,** monumental heart of the *comune.* Here you'll find the **Palazzo Comunale** (climb it for a panorama over the surrounding winelands) and **Cattedrale.** Oenophiles should make a beeline for the **Consorzio del Vino Nobile di Montepulciano** office, where you can taste vintages from small producers and seek advice for nearby wineries to visit. Our favorite cellar in the center is **Gattavecchi.** End the evening at **Acquacheta** (p. 249), where the menu's all about beef—"*bistecca numero uno,*" is how Contucci winemaker Adamo described it. Other local delicacies include sheep's milk cheese, *pecorino di Pienza.*

A vineyard in Chianti.

DAYS 4 & 5: the Chianti ★★★

Pick a base close to **Greve in Chianti** (p. 244) to lodge right at the heart of Tuscany's largest quality wine region. Sangiovese-based Chianti is a diverse wine: Chianti Classico denotes grapes from the original (and best) growing zone, and tasting opportunities abound at cellars such as **Villa Vignamaggio** and **Castello di Volpaia**—book ahead if you require a tour. The Chianti is also famed for its butchers, selling everything from cuts of fresh beef (ideal if you're staying in a villa) to salami made from a local breed of pig, the *Cinta Senese*. **Falorni,** in Greve, is outshone perhaps only by **Dario Cecchini,** in nearby Panzano. Also look out for Tuscan extra virgin olive oil—the local elixir is famed for its low acidity, and is among Italy's best.

DAYS 6 & 7: Bologna ★★

You've arrived in Italy's gastronomic capital; leave the rental car here—it's easy to continue onward by train. The agricultural plains of Emilia-Romagna are Italy's breadbasket. So much of the produce we think of as typical "Italian food" originally hails from here: cured prosciutto and Parmigiano-Reggiano cheese from Parma and Reggio nell'Emilia; the finest balsamic vinegar from Modena; mortadella and tortellini (filled pasta) from Bologna itself. Foodies should browse Bologna's markets, the **Mercato delle Erbe** and the **Quadrilatero,** a warren of lanes filled with enticing food shops. Make an evening reservation at a restaurant that specializes in classic Bolognese cooking; see p. 335 for some of our favorites.

DAYS 8 & 9: Turin ★

Lofty peaks dot the horizon north and west of the Piedmontese capital, and the cooking in Italy's northwest reflects the heartier and hardier mountain folk that live on the doorstep. Nearby Vercelli is Italy's rice capital—the town is surrounded by paddy fields—and *risotto* is at its best here. There's also a noticeable Ligurian current in Torinese food: The basil-based pesto is superb and the favorite slice-on-the-go isn't pizza but *farinata*, garbanzo bean flour flatbread dusted with rosemary or pepper. **Eataly** (p. 491), in the Lingotto neighborhood, stocks delicacies from across Italy. Sweet vermouth was also invented here; the classic local label is *Punt e Mes* ("point and a half" in Piedmontese dialect).

Fresh seafood stars on the menu in Italy's coastal cities.

HISTORIC CITIES OF THE NORTH

Often overshadowed by blockbusters like Rome and Florence, the cities of northern Italy make an excellent itinerary for second-time visitors to the country. Each city on our tour has a center with refined architecture, and a history of independence—as well as struggle with and eventual subjection to, the great regional powers, such as Venice. The logical start-point is Milan, gateway to Italy for flights from across the globe. Spend a day there, collect your rental car or rail tickets—all the train connections on this tour are easy—and set off early. The endpoint is Venice, where we recommend you extend your stay by as many days as you can; see chapter ## for full coverage of the city.

DAYS 1 & 2: Milan ★★ & Turin ★★

See Milan under "The Best of Italy in 2 Weeks," above. Spend **DAY 2** taking a daytrip by train to **Turin** (p. 476). The city of Fiat and football (meaning soccer) has a handsome baroque center, the finest Egyptian collection outside of Cairo at the **Museo Egizio** (p. 481), and views of the Alps surrounding the city from the top of the **Mole Antonelliana** tower (p. 480). It also has a food culture every bit as refined as Bologna's; Turin is the city of vermouth and on the doorstep of the Piedmont wine-growing region, so you need not go thirsty either. You can complete the rail journey between the cities in as little as 45 minutes: There's no need to relocate your base from Milan, if you prefer to minimize changes of lodging.

DAY 3: Bergamo ★★

Whether you arrive by train or car, alight in the **Lower Town** (Città Bassa) and ascend to the **Upper Town** (Città Alta) in style, on the town's century-old funicular railway. **Piazza Vecchia** (p. 454) is the architectural heart of the Upper Town. Beyond the arcades you'll find the Romanesque **Basilica di Santa Maria Maggiore** and the Renaissance **Cappella Colleoni,** with its frescoed ceiling by Venetian painter Tiepolo. You should also make time for the **Accademia Carrara** (p. 452), with its exceptional collection of northern Italian painting. Bergamo was the birthplace of composer Donizetti and has a lively cultural (largely operatic) program. You needn't relocate from your Milanese base: Bergamo is an easy daytrip from Milan.

DAY 4: Verona ★★★

A visit to northern Italy's most renowned small city (see p. 423) is less about ticking off sights than about soaking up the elegance of a place eternally (and fictionally) associated with Shakespeare's doomed lovers, Romeo and Juliet. If you're here in summer, make straight for the box office at the **Arena di Verona;** Italy's most intact Roman amphitheater still hosts monumental outdoor operatic productions, which you shouldn't miss. Your roaming should also take you to the **Basilica di San Zeno Maggiore,** one of Italy's most important Romanesque churches. Use Verona as a base for 2 nights and see Mantua as a day visit.

DAY 5: Mantua ★★

Landlocked it may be, but the Renaissance city of Mantua (p. 456) is almost completely, romantically surrounded by water—lakes fed

Juliet's balcony in Verona.

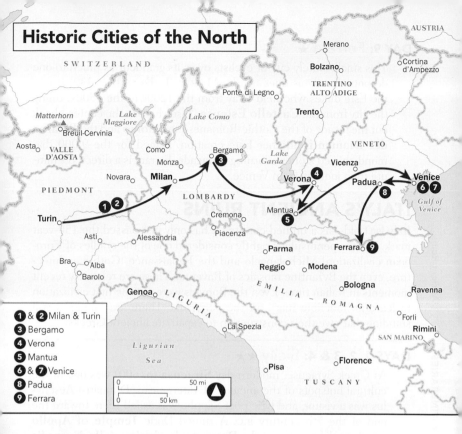

Historic Cities of the North

1 & **2** Milan & Turin
3 Bergamo
4 Verona
5 Mantua
6 & **7** Venice
8 Padua
9 Ferrara

by the River Mincio. It owes its grandeur almost entirely to one family, the Gonzaga dynasty, who built piazzas and palaces, and filled them with art by the greatest masters of the period, such as Mantegna. One day is just enough to see architect L. B. Alberti's **Basilica di Sant Andrea,** the frescoed **Palazzo Ducale,** and the Room of Giants inside the **Palazzo Te.**

DAYS 6 & 7: Venice ★★★

Follow the itinerary suggested in "The Best of Italy in 1 Week," p. 40. Use Venice as a base for your last 4 nights.

DAY 8: Padua ★

The most important painting stop in northern Italy is Giotto's frescoed **Cappella degli Scrovegni** (p. 421), but before you head there, stop in at the tourist office to buy a Padova Card—a discount ticket that buys you entrance to almost everything in town plus free public transportation or parking. The city is also the final resting place of St. Anthony of Padua, the second-most eminent Franciscan saint after St. Francis himself. Inside the **Basilica di Sant'Antonio** you'll find his tomb and some Donatello bronzes.

55

DAY 9: Ferrara ★

This small, stately city of cyclists owes its grandeur as much to one despotic family as does nearby Mantua. In Ferrara (p. 339) it was the Este dukes who held sway from the 1200s to the 1500s, ruling the city from the **Castello Estense.** Elsewhere in the center, check out the facade of the Gothic-Romanesque **Duomo** and the **Palazzo dei Diamanti,** another Este creation, named for the 9,000 diamond-shaped stones adorning its facade. Ferrara is a direct, 85-minute train journey from Venice.

ITALY'S ANCIENT RUINS

Italy isn't old—as a unified country, it has only just passed the 150-year mark. But the peninsula is rightly considered one of the cradles of European civilization. Michelangelo and the Renaissance, Gothic architecture, even the Byzantine mosaics of Ravenna: These are relatively recent moments in Italian time. Even the Romans were not the first civilization to leave an indelible mark on the peninsula. There are buildings still standing that owe their construction to expatriate ancient Greeks.

DAYS 1, 2, 3 & 4: Sicily ★★

As Greek Syracuse, modern-day **Siracusa** (p. 600) was one of the cultural hotspots of the ancient Mediterranean: Dramatist Aeschylus was a visitor, and lyric poet Sappho was exiled there toward the end of the 7th century B.C. A ruined Doric **Temple of Apollo** stands in the town, and the **Parco Archeologico della Neapolis** (p. 604) has a Greek theater still used to host dramas each summer. The southwest of the island has another cluster of ruins. If the main reason for your visit is to see Greek remains, you should probably make your base over there for at least half your time on Sicily. Allow a couple of days to tour coastal **Selinunte** (p. 631), **Segesta** (p. 630), and the Valley of the Temples at **Agrigento** (p. 633). The mosaics of the **Villa Romana del Casale** (p. 611) lie almost midway between the two—a worthy stop on your way past. You should rent a car for your time on Sicily. Catania, 67km (41 miles) north of Siracusa, is well connected by air with Rome (1 hr., 15 min. flight).

DAYS 5, 6 & 7: Rome ★★★

Rome is to ancient ruins as Coke is to fizzy brown liquids: This is the brand that counts when it comes to archaeology. Rome was the epicenter of a Republic and Empire that for centuries ruled most of Europe, and much of North Africa and the Middle East. Spend **DAY 5** walking ancient Rome's civic and spiritual heart, the **Foro Romano** (p. 90). The same ticket gets you into the **Colosseum** (p. 88). Between visits to those two, it makes sense to view the **Imperial Forums, Trajan's Markets,** and the city's best artifact

1-4 Sicily	
5-7 Rome	
8-10 Naples	
11 & 12 Florence	
13 Verona	

collection, at the **Musei Capitolini** (p. 85), whose new wing houses the equestrian bronze of philosopher-emperor Marcus Aurelius (r. A.D. 161–180). As well as the key archaeological sites, museums display an array of relics dug up here over the centuries: Add the ancient collections of the **Vatican Museums** (p. 77) and the busts and Roman art at the **Palazzo Massimo alle Terme** (p. 111) to your to-do list. The ruins of Rome's former seaport, **Ostia Antica** (p. 158), stand a short train journey from the city—it's a comfortable half-day roundtrip. On the way back into town, jump out at the Circo Massimo Metro stop to visit the **Terme di Caracalla** (p. 85) baths complex, and to admire for one last time the view of the **Palatine Hill** from the Circus Maximus. You could probably spend a month here just looking at the remnants of Ancient Rome.

DAYS 8, 9 & 10: Naples & Campania ★★

Ancient Naples—established as the fishing port of Parthenope, then re-founded as Neapolis in the 6th century B.C.—was a key settlement in Magna Graecia, or "Greater Greece." Dating to a later period, the Roman towns of **Pompeii** and **Herculaneum** (p.562

and p. 560) were preserved for centuries under the ash and lava after Vesuvius's cataclysmic eruption in A.D. 79. Remnants of the ancient world remain even in Naples's chaotic 21st-century *centro storico*: In the excavations below **San Lorenzo Maggiore** (p. 550) you can walk around the remains of the Roman Forum and Greek *Ágora* (market square). Naples's **Museo Archeologico Nazionale** (p. 543) preserves wall art from Pompeii and Roman statuary, including the "Farnese Bull." West of Naples, the amphitheater at **Pozzuoli** (p. 557) was once the third largest in the Roman world. Leave Naples on the high-speed Frecciarossa or Italo service late on day 10: It is just under 3 hours to Florence by rail. If you have a little more time on your hands, the **Amalfi Coast** (p. 564) makes an even more scenic base for exploring the ruins of Campania.

DAYS 11 & 12: Florence ★★★

Florence made its name and its fortune during the Renaissance period, in the 1400s and 1500s, and much of the center's art and architecture dates from that period. However, the city's **Museo Archeologico** (p. 192) houses relics from a civilization that predated even the Romans around here: the Etruscans. So many visitors to Florence zero in on Michelangelo & Co. that you may have the "Arezzo Chimera" and the museum's other precious relics to yourself. High on the hill north of Florence is a settlement that first rose under the Etruscans: **Fiesole** (p. 200) is an easy 20-minute bus journey from Florence. Now little more than an overgrown village, it has a preserved Roman theater and archaeological area where visitors can roam among the stones. In late 2014, parts of a Roman theater uncovered below the **Palazzo Vecchio** (p. 184) were opened to the public, too.

DAY 13: Verona ★★

It seems a little harsh to label the **Arena di Verona** (p. 425) "a ruin." This city's enormous amphitheater is the best preserved in Italy. Come in summer—and book ahead—to experience one of Europe's most atmospheric outdoor opera festivals.

ROME

4

Once it ruled the Western World, and even the partial, scattered ruins of that awesome empire, of which Rome was capital, are today among the most powerful sights on earth. To walk the Roman Forum, to view the Colosseum, the Pantheon, and the Appian Way—these are among the most memorable, instructive, and humbling experiences in all of travel. Equally thrilling are the sights of Christian Rome, which speak to the long and complex domination by this city of one of the world's major religions. Yet it's important to remember, too, that Rome is not just a place of the past, but one that lives and breathes and buzzes with Vespas in the here and now.

As a visitor to Rome, you will be constantly reminded of this city's extraordinary history. Take the time to get away from the tourist hordes to explore the intimate piazzas and lesser basilicas in the backstreets of Trastevere and the *centro storico*. Indulge in eno-gastronomic pursuits and stuff your days with cappuccinos, trattorias, wine bars, street food, and gelato. Have a picnic in Villa Borghese, take a vigorous walk along the Gianicolo, or nap in the grass against a fallen granite column at the Baths of Caracalla. Rome is so compact that without even planning too much you'll end up enjoying both its monuments and its simpler pleasures.

Walk the streets of Rome, and the city will be yours.

ESSENTIALS
Getting There

BY PLANE   Most flights arrive at Rome's **Leonardo da Vinci International Airport** (www.adr.it; ✆ **06-65951**), popularly known as **Fiumicino,** 30km (19 miles) from the city center. (If you're arriving from other European cities, you might land at Ciampino Airport, discussed below.) A tourist information office is at the airport's Terminal B, International arrivals; it's open daily from 9am to 6pm.

A *cambio* (money exchange) operates daily from 7am to 11pm, offering good rates, and there are ATMs in the airport.

There's a **train station** in the airport. To get into the city, follow the signs marked treni for the 31-minute shuttle ride to Rome's main station,

PREVIOUS PAGE: **Light streams through the oculus of the Pantheon.**

Stazione Termini. The shuttle (the Leonardo Express) runs from 5:52am to 11:36pm, every 30 minutes, for 14€ one-way. On the way, you'll pass a machine dispensing tickets, or you can buy them at the ticket booth near the tracks if you do not have change or small bills on you. *Tip:* When you arrive at Termini, get out of the train quickly and grab a baggage cart: It's a long schlep from the track to the exit or to other train connections, and baggage carts can be scarce.

A **taxi** from da Vinci airport to the city costs a flat-rate 48€ for the 1-hour trip, depending on traffic (hotels tend to charge 50€–60€ for pick-up service). The expense might be worth it if you have a lot of luggage. Note that the flat rate is applicable from the airport to central Rome and vice versa, but only if your central Rome location is inside the Aurelian Walls (most hotels are). Otherwise, standard metered rates apply, which can bump the fare to 75€ or higher.

If you arrive at **Ciampino Airport** (www.adr.it/ciampino; ℭ **06-65951**), you can take a Terravision bus (www.terravision.eu; ℭ **06-4880086**) to Stazione Termini. This takes about 45 minutes and costs 4€. A **taxi** from here costs a flat rate of 30€, provided you're going to a destination within the old Aurelian Walls. Otherwise, you'll pay the metered fare, but the trip is shorter (about 40 min.).

BY TRAIN OR BUS   Trains and buses (including trains from the airport) arrive in the center of old Rome at **Stazione Termini,** Piazza dei Cinquecento. This is the train, bus, and subway transportation hub for all of Rome, and it is surrounded by many hotels, especially budget ones.

If you're taking the **Metropolitana** (subway), follow the illuminated red-and-white M signs. To catch a bus, go straight through the outer hall and enter the sprawling bus lot of **Piazza dei Cinquecento.** You will also find a line of **taxis** parked out front.

The station is filled with services. There is an exchange window close to the end of platform 14 where you can change money, and an ATM at the end of platform 24. **Informazioni Ferroviarie** (in the outer hall) dispenses information on rail travel to other parts of Italy. There are also a **tourist information booth,** baggage services, newsstands, clean public toilets, and snack bars.

BY CAR   From the north, the main access route is the **Autostrada A1.** This highway links Milan with Naples via Bologna, Florence, and Rome. At 754km (469 miles), it is the longest Italian autostrada and is the "spinal cord" of Italy's road network. All the autostrade join with the **Grande Raccordo Anulare,** a ring road encircling Rome, channeling traffic into the congested city. *Tip:* Long before you reach this road, you should study a map carefully to see what part of Rome you plan to enter and mark your route accordingly. Route markings along the ring road tend to be confusing.

Warning: Return your rental car immediately on arrival, or at least get yourself to your hotel, park your car, and leave it there until you leave

Rome Top Attractions

PRATI

Vatican City & Prati

VATICAN CITY

Vatican Museums

St. Peter's

Castel Sant'Angelo

PIAZZA DEL POPOLO

Mausoleum of Augustus

PIAZZA NAVONA

CAMPO D. FIORI

Palazzo Farnese

Palazzo Spada

JEWISH GHETTO

Pantheon

Centro Storico

TRASTEVERE

TESTACCIO

Trastevere & Testaccio

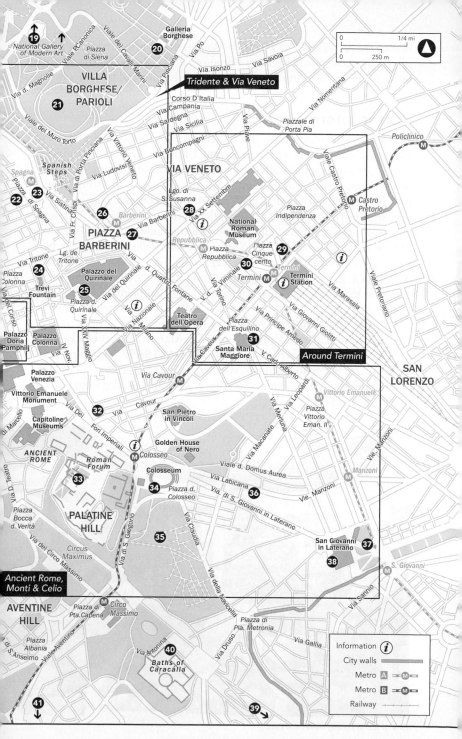

Rome. Think twice before driving in Rome—the traffic can be nightmarish. In any case, most of central Rome is a **ZTL (Zona Traffico Limitato),** off limits to nonresidents, and rigorously enforced by cameras. You will almost certainly be fined.

Visitor Information

Information, Internet, maps, and the Roma Pass (p. 66) are available at Tourist Information Points run by **Roma Capitale** (www.turismoroma.it) around the city. They're staffed daily from 9:30am to 7:15pm, except the one at Termini (daily 8am–7:45pm), which is located in "Centro Diagnostico" hall (Building F) next to platform 24; there's often a long line at this one, so if you're staying near other offices listed here, skip it. Additional offices are at Via della Conciliazione 4, near the Auditorium; Via Nazionale 183, near the Palazzo delle Esposizioni; on Piazza delle Cinque Lune, near Piazza Navona; on Via dei Fori Imperiali (for the Forum); at Via Santa Maria del Pianto 1, in the old Jewish Quarter; and on Via Marco Minghetti, at the corner of Via del Corso. There are also information points at both Fiumicino and Ciampino airports. All phone calls for Roma Capitale go to a central number: ✆ **06-060608** (www.060608.it).

Local travel agency **Enjoy Rome,** Via Marghera 8a, 3 blocks north of Termini (www.enjoyrome.com; ✆ **06-4451843;** Mon–Fri 9am–5:30pm and Sat 8:30–2pm), is also helpful at dispensing information and finding hotel rooms with no service charge (in anything from a hostel to a three-star hotel).

One of Rome's many street markets.

4

ROME | Essentials

City Layout

The bulk of what you'll want to visit—ancient, Renaissance, and baroque Rome (as well as the train station)—lies on the east side of the **Tiber River (Fiume Tevere),** which meanders through town. However, several important landmarks are on the other side: **St. Peter's Basilica** and the **Vatican,** the **Castel Sant'Angelo,** and the colorful **Trastevere** neighborhood. With the exception of those last sights, I think it's fair to say that Rome has the most compact and walkable city center in Europe.

That doesn't mean you won't get lost from time to time (most newcomers do). Arm yourself with a detailed street map of Rome (or a smartphone with a hefty data plan). Most hotels hand out a pretty good version of a city map.

The Neighborhoods in Brief

Much of the historic core of Rome does not fall under easy or distinct neighborhood classifications. Instead, when describing a location within the centro, most people's frame of reference is the name of the nearest large monument or square, like St. Peter's or Piazza di Spagna. Note that street addresses in Rome can be frustrating. Numbers usually run consecutively, with odd numbers on one side of the street, evens on the other. However, in the old districts the numbers sometimes run up one side and then run back in the opposite direction on the other side (so #50 could be potentially opposite #308).

VATICAN CITY & THE PRATI Vatican City is technically a sovereign state, although in practice it is just another part of Rome. The **Vatican Museums, St. Peter's,** and the **Vatican Gardens** take up most of the land area, and the popes have lived here for 6 centuries. The neighborhood north of the Vatican—called "Borgo Pio"—contains some good hotels (and several bad ones), but it is removed from the more happening scene of ancient and Renaissance Rome, and getting to and from those areas can be time-consuming. Borgo Pio is also rather dull at night and contains few, if any, of Rome's finest restaurants. The white collar **Prati** district, a middle-class suburb just east of the Vatican, is possibly a better choice, thanks to its smattering of affordable hotels, its shopping streets, and the fact that it boasts some excellent places to eat.

CENTRO STORICO & THE PANTHEON One of the most desirable (and busiest) areas of Rome, the **Centro Storico** ("Historic Center") is a maze of narrow streets and cobbled alleys dating from the Middle Ages and filled with churches and palaces built during the Renaissance and baroque eras. The only way to explore it is by foot. Its heart is **Piazza Navona,** built over Emperor Domitian's stadium and bustling with sidewalk cafes, *palazzi,* street artists, musicians, and pickpockets.

Rivaling Piazza Navona—in general activity, the cafe scene, and the nightlife—is the nearby area around the **Pantheon,** which remains from ancient Roman times and is surrounded by a district built much later.

roma **PASSES**

If you plan to do serious sightseeing in Rome (and why else would you be here?), the **Roma Pass** (www.romapass.it) is worth considering. For 36€ per card, valid for 3 days, you get free entry to the first 2 museums or archaeological sites you visit; express entry to the Colosseum; free admission to Museo della Repubblica Romana, Museo Carlo Bilotti, Museo Canonica, Museo delle Mura, Museo Napoleonico, and Villa di Massenzio; discounted entry to all other museums and sites; free use of the city's public transport network (bus, Metro, and railway lines; airport transfers not included); a free map; and free access to a special smartphone app. Note that the Vatican Museums are not part of the pass plan.

If your stay in Rome is shorter, you may want to opt for the **Roma Pass 48** Hours (28€) which offers the same benefits at the same museums and archaeological sites, except that only the first museum you visit is free and the ticket is only valid for 48 hours.

You can buy either of the Roma passes online (www.romapass.it) and pick them up at one of the city's Tourist Information Points; you can also order in advance by phone, with a credit card, at ✆ **06-060608.** Both kinds of Roma Passes are also sold directly at Tourist Information Point offices (see p. 64). The standard Roma Pass (but not the 48 Hours pass) can also be bought at participating museums and ATAC subway ticket offices.

A good alternative to consider is the **Archaeologia Card,** which for 27.50€ (buy at the first site you visit) grants admission to the following 9 sites for up to 7 days: the Colosseum, Palatine Museum and Roman Forum, Palazzo Massimo alle Terme, Palazzo Altemps, Crypta Balbi, the Baths of Diocletian, Cecilia Metella, Villa dei Quintili, and the Baths of Caracalla. With this pass, however, transport is not included, so if you plan to do a lot of sightseeing, the Roma Pass is a much better value.

South of Corso Vittorio Emanuele and centered on **Piazza Farnese** and the square of **Campo de' Fiori,** many buildings in this area were constructed in Renaissance times as private homes. West of Via Arenula lies one of the city's most intriguing districts, the old Jewish **Ghetto,** where the increasingly fashionable dining options far outnumber the hotels.

ANCIENT ROME, MONTI & CELIO   Although no longer the heart of the city, this is where Rome began, with the **Colosseum, Palatine Hill, Roman Forum, Imperial Forums,** and **Circus Maximus.** This area offers only a few hotels—most of them inexpensive to moderate in price—and not a lot of great restaurants. Many restaurant owners here have their eyes on the cash register and the tour-bus crowd, whose passengers are often herded in and out of these restaurants so fast that they don't know whether the food is any good. Just beyond the Circus Maximus is the **Aventine Hill,** south of the Palatine and close to the Tiber, now a leafy and rather posh residential quarter—with great city views. You will get much more of a neighborhood feel if you stay in **Monti** (Rome's oldest *rione*, or quarter) or **Celio,** respectively located north and south of the Colosseum. Both also have good dining, aimed at locals as well as visitors, and Monti especially has plenty of life from *aperitivo* o'clock and into the wee hours.

TRIDENTE & THE SPANISH STEPS   The northern part of Rome's center is sometimes known as the Tridente, so-called for the trident shape of the roads leading down from the apex of **Piazza del Popolo**—Via di Ripetta, Via del Corso, and Via del Babuino. The star here is unquestionably **Piazza di Spagna,** which attracts Romans and tourists alike to idly sit on its celebrated **Spanish Steps.** Some of Rome's most upscale shopping streets fan out from here, including **Via Condotti.** In fact, this is the most upscale part of Rome, full of expensive hotels, designer boutiques, and chic restaurants.

VIA VENETO & PIAZZA BARBERINI   In the 1950s and early 1960s, **Via Veneto** was the swinging place to be, as celebrities of la Dolce Vita paraded along the tree-lined boulevard to the delight of the paparazzi. The street is still the site of luxury hotels, cafes, and restaurants, although it's no longer such a happening spot, and the restaurants are mostly overpriced tourist traps.

To the south, Via Veneto comes to an end at **Piazza Barberini** and the magnificent **Palazzo Barberini,** begun in 1623 by Carlo Maderno and later completed by Bernini and Borromini.

VILLA BORGHESE & PARIOLI   We would call **Parioli** an area for connoisseurs, attracting those who shun the Spanish Steps and the overly commercialized Via Veneto. It is, in short, Rome's most elegant residential section, a setting for some of the city's finest restaurants, hotels, museums, and public parks. Geographically, Parioli is in fact framed by the green spaces of the **Villa Borghese** to the south and the **Villa Glori** and **Villa Ada** to the north. It lies adjacent to Prati but across the Tiber to the east; it's considered one of the safest districts in the city. All that being said, Parioli is not exactly central, so it can be a hassle as a base if you're dependent on public transportation.

AROUND STAZIONE TERMINI   The main train station adjoins **Piazza della Repubblica,** and is for many visitors their first introduction to Rome. Much of the area is seedy and filled with gas fumes from all the buses and cars, plus a fair share of weirdos. If you stay here, you might not score the typical Rome charm, but you'll have a lot of affordable options and a convenient location, near the city's transportation hub and not far from ancient Rome. There is a fair amount to see here, including the **Basilica di Santa Maria Maggiore,** the artifacts at **Palazzo Massimo alle Terme,** and the **Baths of Diocletian.**

The neighborhoods on either side of Termini (Esquilino and Tiburtino) have been slowly cleaning up, and some streets are now attractive. Most budget hotels on the Via Marsala side occupy a floor or several floors of a *palazzo* (palace); many of their entryways are drab, although upstairs they are often charming or at least clean and livable. In the area to the left of the station as you exit, the streets are wider, the traffic is heavier, and the noise level is higher. The area requires you to take just a little caution late at night.

TRASTEVERE In a Roman shift of the Latin *Trans Tiber*, Trastevere means "across the Tiber." This once medieval working-class district has been gentrified and is now overrun with visitors from all over the world. It started to transform in the 1970s when expats and other bohemians discovered its rough charm. Since then Trastevere has been filling up with tour buses, dance clubs, offbeat shops, sidewalk vendors, pubs, and little *trattorie* with English menus. There are even places to stay—mostly rather quaint rentals and airbnb's—but so far it hasn't burgeoned into a major hotel district. There are excellent restaurants and bars here, too.

The area centers on the ancient churches of **Santa Cecilia** and **Santa Maria in Trastevere,** and remains one of Rome's most colorful quarters, even if a bit overrun.

TESTACCIO & SOUTHERN ROME In A.D. 55, Emperor Nero ordered that Rome's thousands of broken amphorae and terracotta roof tiles be stacked in a pile to the east of the Tiber, just west of today's Ostiense Railway Station. Over the centuries, the mound grew to a height of around 61m (200 ft.) and then was compacted to form the centerpiece for one of the city's most unusual working-class neighborhoods, **Testaccio.** Houses were built on the perimeter of the amphorae mound and caves were dug into its mass to store wine and foodstuffs. Once home to slaughterhouses and Rome's former port on the Tiber, Testaccio is now known for its authentic Roman restaurants. It's also one of Rome's liveliest areas after dark.

Further south and east, the **Via Appia Antica** is a 2,300-year-old road that has witnessed much of the history of the ancient world. By 190 B.C., it extended from Rome to Brindisi on the southeast coast. Its most famous sights are the **Catacombs,** the graveyards of early Christians and patrician families (despite what it says in *Quo Vadis*, they weren't used as a place for Christians to hide while fleeing persecution). This is one of the most historically rich areas of Rome, great for a daytrip but not a convenient place to stay.

Getting Around

Central Rome is perfect for exploring on foot, with sites of interest often clustered together. Much of the inner core is traffic-free, so you will need to walk whether you like it or not. However, in many parts of the city walking may be uncomfortable because of the crowds, uneven cobblestones, heavy traffic, and narrow (if any) sidewalks. The hectic crush of urban Rome is considerably less during August, when many Romans leave town for vacation (but many restaurants and businesses close).

BY SUBWAY The **Metropolitana** (or **Metro;** www.romametropoli tane.it; ✆ **06-454640100**), is the fastest way to get around, operating 5:30am to 11:30pm Sunday to Thursday, and until 1:30am on Friday and Saturday. A big red **m** indicates the entrance to the subway. If your destination is close to a Metro stop, hop on, as your journey will be much faster than by taking surface transportation. There are currently three lines: Line A (orange) runs southeast to northwest via Termini, Barberini, Spagna and several stations in Prati near the Vatican; Line B (blue), runs north to south via Termini and stops in Ancient Rome; and a third, Line C (green), which is currently under construction and should be completed by 2020, runs from Monte Compatri in the southeast to San Giovanni (on Line A). The portion from Monte Compatri in the eastern outskirts of the city is currently connected as far as Centocelle, and should be extended to Piazza Lodi by the end of 2015.

Tickets are 1.50€ and are available from *tabacchi* (tobacco shops), many newsstands, and vending machines at all stations. Booklets of tickets are available at newsstands, *tabacchi* and in some terminals. You can also buy a **pass** on either a daily or a weekly basis (see "By Bus & Tram," below). To open the subway barrier, insert your ticket. If you have a Roma Pass (p. 66), touch it against the yellow dot and the gates will open. See the Metro map on the tear-out map in this guide.

BY BUS & TRAM Roman buses and trams are operated by **ATAC** (Agenzia del Trasporto Autoferrotranviario del Comune di Roma; www.atac. roma.it; ✆ **06-57003**). For 1.50€ you can ride to most parts of Rome on buses or trams, although it can be slow going in all that traffic, and the buses are often very crowded. A ticket is valid for 100 minutes, and you can get on many buses and trams (plus one journey on the Metro) during that time by using the same ticket. Tickets are sold in *tabacchi*, at newsstands and at bus stops, but there are seldom ticket-issuing machines on the vehicles themselves.

At Stazione Termini, you can buy **special timed passes:** a **BIG** (*biglietto giornaliero* or 1-day ticket) costs 6€, and a **CIS** (*carta settimanale*) is 24€ for 1 week. The **BTI** (*biglietto turistico,* or "tourist ticket") is 16.50€ for 3 days. If you plan to ride public transportation a lot—and if

---

Rome's Key Bus Routes

Although routes may change, a few reliable bus routes have remained valid for years in Rome:

o **40 (Express):** Stazione Termini to the Vatican via Via Nazionale, Piazza Venezia and Piazza Pia, by the Castel Sant'Angelo

o **64:** The "tourist route" from Termini, along Via Nazionale and through Piazza Venezia and along Via Argentina to Piazza San Pietro in the Vatican (**Head's up:** It's also known as the Pickpocket Express.)

o **75:** Stazione Termini to the Colosseum

o **H:** Stazione Termini via Piazza Venezia and the Ghetto to Trastevere via Ponte Garibaldi

Two Bus Warnings

Any map of the Roman bus system will likely be outdated before it's printed. Many buses listed on the "latest" map no longer exist; others are enjoying a much-needed rest, and new buses suddenly appear without warning. There's always talk of renumbering the whole system, so be aware that the route numbers we've listed might have changed by the time you travel.

Take extreme caution when riding Rome's overcrowded buses—pickpockets abound! This is particularly true on bus no. 64, a favorite of visitors because of its route through the historic districts and thus also a favorite of Rome's pickpocketing community. This bus has earned various nicknames, including the "Pickpocket Express" and "Wallet Eater."

Buses and trams stop at areas marked *fermata*. At most of these, a yellow or white sign will display the numbers of the buses that stop there and a list of all the stops along each bus's route, making it easier to scope out your destination. Generally, they run daily from 5am to midnight. From midnight until dawn, you can ride on special night buses (they have an "n" in front of their bus number), which run only on main routes. It's best to take a taxi in the wee hours—if you can find one. In a pinch call for one (see "By Taxi," below). **Bus information booths** at Piazza dei Cinquecento, in front of Stazione Termini, offer advice on routes.

you are skipping between the *centro storico*, Roman ruins, and Vatican, you likely will—these passes save time and hassle over buying a new ticket every time you ride. Purchase the appropriate pass for your length of stay in Rome. All the passes allow you to ride on the ATAC network, and are also valid on the Metro (subway). On the first bus you board, place your ticket in a small machine, which prints the day and hour you boarded, and then withdraw it. Do the same on the last bus you take during the valid period of the ticket. One-day and weekly tickets are also available at *tabacchi,* many newsstands, and at vending machines at all stations. If you plan to do a lot of sightseeing, however, the Roma Pass (p. 66) is a smarter choice.

Wi-Fi is gradually being rolled out across the public transport network. Look for the "Atac WiFi" sticker on the tram/subway doors. To access the service, connect to the "AtacWiFi" network and select "free navigation"; you can then register for free on the RomaWireless website. You only get 1 hour of surfing, but access to transport help websites like **www.muoversiaroma.it** is unlimited.

BY TAXI Don't count on hailing a taxi on the street or even getting one at a minor stand. If you're going out, have your hotel call one. At a restaurant, ask the waiter or cashier to dial for you. If you want to phone for yourself, try the city taxi service at ℂ **06-0609** (which will redirect to the nearest taxi rank, but you have to state the name of your location, and since you'll be speaking to a robot, correct pronunciation is key), or one of these radio taxi numbers: ℂ **06-6645,** 06-3570, or 06-4994. Taxis on call incur a surcharge of 3.50€.

The meter begins at 3€ (Mon–Fri 6am–10pm) for the first 3km (1¾ miles) and then rises 1.10€ per kilometer. The first suitcase is free. Every additional piece of luggage costs 1€. On Saturday and Sunday between 6am and 10pm the meter starts at 4.50€; from 10pm to 6am every day the meter starts at 6.50€. Trips from Termini incur a 2€ surcharge. Avoid paying your fare with large bills; invariably, taxi drivers claim that they don't have change, hoping for a bigger tip. In reality, a small tip is fine, but not necessary: Italians don't tip taxi drivers like Americans and, at most, will simply round up to the nearest euro. If the driver is really help-ful, a tip of 1€ to 2€ is sufficient. Many taxis accept credit cards, but it's best to check first, before getting on.

BY CAR   All roads might lead to Rome, but you don't want to drive once you get here. Because the reception desks of most Roman hotels have at least one English-speaking person, call ahead to find out the best route into Rome from wherever you are starting out. You will want to get rid of your rental car as soon as possible, or park in a garage.

If you want to rent a car to explore the countryside around Rome or drive to another city, you will save the most money if you reserve before leaving home (see chapter 13). If you decide to book a car here, **Hertz** is at Via Giovanni Giolitti 34 (www.hertz.com; *✆* **06-4740389;** Metro: Termini), and **Avis** is at Stazione Termini (www.avis.com; *✆* **06-4814373;** Metro: Termini). **Maggiore,** an Italian company, has an office at Stazione Termini (www.maggiore.it; *✆* **06-4880049;** Metro: Termini). Major agencies also have offices at the airport.

St. Peter's Basilica and the Vatican, viewed across the Tiber.

BY BIKE   Other than walking, the best way to get through the medieval alleys and small piazzas of Rome is perched on the seat of a bicycle. Despite being hilly, the heart of ancient Rome is threaded with bicycle lanes to get you through the murderous traffic. The most convenient place to rent a bike is **Bici & Baci,** Via del Viminale 5 (www.bicibaci. com; *℃* **06-4828443**), 2 blocks west of Stazione Termini. Prices start at 4€ per hour or 11€ per day.

[FastFACTS] ROME

Banks   In general, banks are open Monday to Friday 8:30am to 1:30pm and 3 to 4pm, but some banks keep afternoon hours from 2:45 to 3:45pm.

Dentists **American Dental Arts Rome,** Via del Governo Vecchio 73 (www. adadentistsrome.com; *℃* **06-6832613;** Bus: 41, 44, or 46B), uses the latest technology, including laser dental techniques.

Doctors   Call the U.S. Embassy at *℃* **06-46741** for a list of English-speaking doctors. All big hospitals have a 24-hour first-aid service (go to the emergency room, *pronto soccorso*). You'll find English-speaking doctors at the privately run **Salvator Mundi International Hospital,** Viale delle Mura Gianicolensi 67 (www.salvatormundi.it; *℃* **06-588961;** Bus: 75). For medical assistance, the **International Medical Center** is on 24-hour duty at Via Firenze 47 (www.imc84.com; *℃* **06-4882371;** Metro: Repubblica). You could also contact the **Rome American Hospital,** Via Emilio Longoni 69 (www.hcitalia.it/romeamericanhospital; *℃* **06-22551**), with English-speaking doctors on duty 24 hours. A more personalized service is provided 24 hours a day by **Medi-Call Italia,** Via Cremera 8 (www. medi-call.it; *℃* **06-8840113;** Bus: 86), which can arrange for a qualified doctor to make a house call at your hotel or anywhere in Rome. In most cases, the doctor will be a general practitioner who can refer you to a specialist if needed. Fees begin at around 100€ per visit and can go higher if a specialist or specialized treatments are necessary.

Embassies & Consulates   See chapter 13.

Emergencies   To call the police, dial *℃* **113;** for an ambulance *℃* **118;** for a fire *℃* **115.**

Internet Access
Wi-Fi is standard in nearly all Rome hotels, and is available for free in many cafes and information points. If you need a terminal try **Internet Train,** Via dei Marrucini 12 (www.internetcafe. it; *℃* **06-4454953;** Bus: 3, 71, or 492; Mon–Fri 9:30am–1am, Sat 3pm–1am, Sun 2pm–midnight); you'll get 30 minutes for 1.50€.

Mail   You can buy special stamps at the **Vatican City Post Office,** adjacent to the information office in St. Peter's Square (Mon–Fri 8:30am–7pm, Sat until 6pm). Convenient post offices in the old city include Via Monterone 1 (near the Pantheon); Via Cavour 277; Via Marsala 29 (on the north side of Termini); and Via Molise 2, near Piazza Barberini. Most are open Monday to Friday 8:30am to 3:30pm, with the Termini branch open Monday to Friday 8:20am to 7:05pm and Saturday 8:20am to 12:35pm.

Newspapers & Magazines   You can buy major publications including the *International New York Times* and the *London Times* at most newsstands. The English-language expat magazine *Wanted in Rome* (www. wantedinrome.com) comes out every 2 weeks and lists current events and shows. If

you want to try your hand at reading Italian, *Time Out* has a Rome edition.

Pharmacies A reliable pharmacy is **Farmacia Internazionale,** Piazza Barberini 49 (www.farmint.it; © **06-4825456;** Metro: Barberini), open 24 hours. Most pharmacies are open from 8:30am to 1pm and 4 to 7:30pm. In general, pharmacies follow a rotation system, so several are always open on Sunday.

Police Dial © **113.**

Safety Pickpocketing is the most common problem. Men should keep their wallets in their front pocket or inside jacket pocket. Purse snatching also happens on occasion, by young men speeding by on Vespas. To avoid trouble, stay away from the curb and keep your purse on the wall side of your body and place the strap across your chest. Don't lay anything valuable on al fresco tables or chairs, where it can be grabbed up. Groups of child pickpockets have long been a particular menace, although the problem isn't as severe as in years past. They might approach you with pieces of cardboard hiding their stealing hands. Just keep repeating a firm "*No!*"

EXPLORING ROME

Rome's ancient monuments, whether time-blackened or gleaming in the wake of a recent restoration, are a constant reminder that Rome was one of the greatest centers of Western civilization. In the heyday of the Empire, all roads led to Rome, with good reason. It was one of the first cosmopolitan cities, importing slaves, gladiators, great art, and even citizens from the far corners of the world. Despite its brutality and corruption, Rome left a legacy of law, a heritage of art, architecture, and engineering, and a canny lesson in how to conquer enemies by absorbing their cultures.

But ancient Rome is only part of the spectacle. The Vatican has had a tremendous influence on making the city a tourism center. Although Vatican architects stripped down much of the city's ancient glory during the Renaissance, looting ancient ruins (the Forum especially) for their precious marble, they created more treasures and even occasionally incorporated the old into the new—as Michelangelo did when turning the Diocletian's Baths complex into a church. And in the years that followed, Bernini adorned the city with the wonders of the baroque, especially his glorious fountains.

Bypassing the Lines

The endless lines outside Italian museums and attractions are a fact of life. But reservation services can help you avoid the wait, at least for some of the major museums. Buying a **Roma Pass** (p. 66) is a good start—holders can use a special entrance at the Colosseum, and for your first two (free) museums, you can skip the line (so be sure to choose busy ones).

For the **Vatican Museums,** buy an advance ticket at **http://biglieteriamusei.vatican.va**; you pay an extra 4€ but will be able to skip the line at the main entrance (which can be very, very long). Note that St. Peter's is not included in the perk: There is no way to jump the line there.

Coopculture (www.coopculture.it) operates an online ticket office, which allows you to skip the line at several sites, including the Colosseum and the Forum, with a reservation fee of 1.50€ and 2€ to print tickets in advance.

Select Italy also allows you to reserve your tickets for the Colosseum, the Roman Forum, Palatine Hill, the Galleria Borghese, plus many other museums in Florence and Venice. The cost varies depending on the museum—there's an agency fee on top of ticket prices—with several combination passes available. ✆ **800/877-1755** in the U.S., or buy your tickets online at **www.selectitaly.com**.

St. Peter's & the Vatican
VATICAN CITY

The world's smallest sovereign state, **Vatican City** is a truly tiny territory, comprising little more than St. Peter's Basilica and the walled headquarters of the Roman Catholic Church. There are no border controls, of course, though the city-state's 800 inhabitants (essentially clergymen and Swiss Guards) have their own radio station, daily newspaper, tax-free international pharmacy and petrol pumps, postal service, and head of state—the Pope. The Pope had always exercised a high degree of political independence from the rest of Italy in the form of the medieval Papal States, and this independence was formalized by the 1929 Lateran Treaty between Pope Pius XI and the Italian government to create the Vatican. The city is still protected by the flamboyantly uniformed (designed by Michelangelo) Swiss Guards, a tradition dating from the days when the Swiss, known as brave soldiers, were often hired out as mercenaries for foreign armies. Today the Vatican remains at the center of the Roman Catholic world, the home of the Pope—and the resting place of St. Peter. **St. Peter's Basilica** is obviously one of the highlights, but the only part of the Apostolic Palace itself that you can visit independently is the **Vatican Museums:** With its over 100 galleries, it's the biggest and richest museum complex in the world.

On the left side of Piazza San Pietro, the **Vatican Tourist Office** (www.vatican.va; ✆ **06-69882019;** Mon–Sat 8:30am–7:30pm) sells maps and guides that will help you make more sense of the riches you will be seeing in the museums; it also accepts reservations for tours of the Vatican Gardens.

The only entrance to St. Peter's for tourists is through one of the glories of the Western world: Bernini's 17th-century **St. Peter's Square (Piazza San Pietro).** As you stand in the huge piazza, you are in the arms of an ellipse partly enclosed by a majestic **Doric-pillared colonnade.** Stand in the marked marble discs embedded in the pavement near the fountains to see all the columns lined up in a striking optical/geometrical play. Straight ahead is the facade of St. Peter's itself, and to the right, above the colonnade, are the dark brown buildings of the **papal**

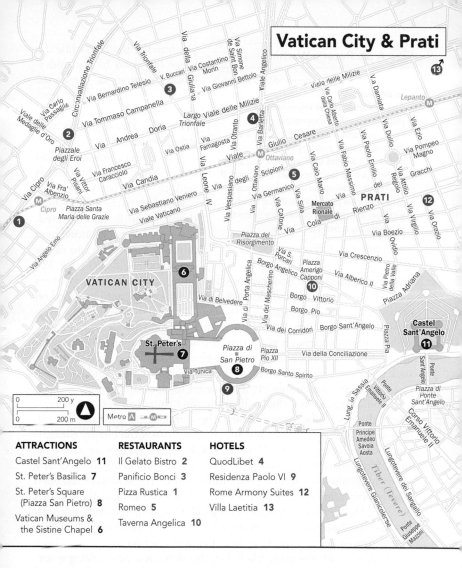

Vatican City & Prati

Lepanto

PRATI

Castel Sant'Angelo

VATICAN CITY

St. Peter's

Piazza di San Pietro

Piazza Pio XII

Tiber (Tevere)

| 0 | 200 y |
| 0 | 200 m |

Metro Ⓐ ═══Ⓜ═══

ATTRACTIONS	RESTAURANTS	HOTELS
Castel Sant'Angelo **11**	Il Gelato Bistro **2**	QuodLibet **4**
St. Peter's Basilica **7**	Panificio Bonci **3**	Residenza Paolo VI **9**
St. Peter's Square	Pizza Rustica **1**	Rome Armony Suites **12**
(Piazza San Pietro) **8**	Romeo **5**	Villa Laetitia **13**
Vatican Museums &	Taverna Angelica **10**	
the Sistine Chapel **6**		

apartments and the Vatican Museums. In the center of the square stands a 4,000-year-old **Egyptian obelisk,** created in the ancient city of Heliopolis on the Nile delta and appropriated by the Romans under Emperor Augustus. Flanking the obelisk are two 17th-century **fountains.** The one on the right (facing the basilica), by Carlo Maderno, who designed the facade of St. Peter's, was placed here by Bernini himself; the other is by Carlo Fontana.

St. Peter's Basilica ★★★ CHURCH   The Basilica di San Pietro, or simply **St. Peter's,** is the holiest shrine of the Catholic Church, built on the site of St. Peter's tomb by the greatest Italian artists of the 16th and 17th centuries. One of the lines on the right side of the piazza funnels you into the basilica, while the other two lead to the underground grottoes or the dome. Whichever you opt for first, you must be **properly dressed**—a rule that is very strictly enforced.

In Roman times, the Circus of Nero, where St. Peter is said to have been crucified, was slightly to the left of where the basilica is now located. Peter was allegedly buried here in A.D. 64 near the site of his execution, and in A.D. 324 Emperor Constantine commissioned a church to be built over Peter's tomb. That structure stood for more than 1,000 years, until it verged on collapse. The present basilica, mostly completed in the 1500s and 1600s, is predominantly High Renaissance and baroque. Inside, the massive scale is almost too much to absorb, showcasing some of Italy's greatest artists: Bramante, Raphael, Michelangelo, and Maderno. In a church of such grandeur—overwhelming in its detail of gilt, marble, and mosaic— you can't expect much subtlety. It is meant to be overpowering.

Going straight into the basilica, the first thing you see on the right side of the nave—the longest nave in the world, as clearly marked in the floor along with other cathedral measurements—is the chapel containing Michelangelo's graceful **"Pietà"** ★★★, one of Rome's greatest treasures. Created in the 1490s when the master was still in his 20s, it clearly shows his genius for capturing the human form. (The sculpture has been kept behind reinforced glass since an act of vandalism in the 1970s.) Note the lifelike folds of Mary's robes and her youthful features; although she would've been middle-aged at the time of the Crucifixion, Michelangelo portrayed her as a young woman to convey her purity.

Further inside the nave, Michelangelo's dome is a mesmerizing space, rising high above the supposed site of St. Peter's tomb. With a diameter of 41.5m (136 ft.), the dome is Rome's largest, supported by four bulky piers decorated with reliefs depicting the basilica's key holy relics: St. Veronica's handkerchief (used to wipe the face of Christ); the lance of St. Longinus, which pierced Christ's side; and a piece of the True Cross.

Under the dome is the twisty-columned **baldacchino** ★★, by Bernini, sheltering the papal altar. The 29m-high (96-ft.) ornate canopy was created in part, so it is said, from bronze stripped from the Pantheon. Bernini sculpted the face of a woman on the bases of each of the pillars; starting with the face on the left pillar (with your back to the entrance), circle the entire altar to see the progress of expressions from the agony of childbirth through to the fourth pillar, where the woman's face is replaced with that of her newborn baby.

Just before you reach the dome, on the right, the devout stop to kiss the foot of the 13th-century **bronze of St. Peter ★**, attributed to Arnolfo di Cambio. Elsewhere the church is decorated by more of Bernini's lavish sculptures, including his monument to Pope Alexander VII in the south transept, its winged skeleton writhing under the heavy marble drapes.

An entrance off the nave leads to the Sacristy and beyond to the **Historical Museum (Museo Storico)** or **treasury ★**, which is chock-full of richly jeweled chalices, reliquaries, and copes, as well as the late 15th-century bronze tomb of Pope Sixtus IV by Pollaiuolo.

You can also head downstairs to the **Vatican grottoes ★★**, with their tombs of the popes, both ancient and modern (Pope John XXIII got the most adulation until the interment of **Pope John Paul II** in 2005). Behind a wall of glass is what is assumed to be the tomb of St. Peter.

Visits to the **Necropolis Vaticana ★★** and St. Peter's tomb itself are restricted to 250 persons per day on guided tours (90 min.) You must send a fax or e-mail 3 weeks beforehand, or apply in advance in person at the Ufficio Scavi (©/fax **06-69873017;** e-mail: scavi@fsp.va; Mon–Fri 9am–6pm, Sat 9am–5pm), which is located through the arch to the left of the stairs up from the basilica. You specify your name, the number in your party, your language, and the dates you'd like to visit. When you apply at the Ufficio Scavi by fax or e-mail, you also need to specify how you would like to be contacted (by e-mail, fax, or postal address). For details, check **www.vatican.va**. Children 14 and under are not admitted to the Necropolis.

After you leave the grottoes, you find yourself in a courtyard and ticket line for the grandest sight in the basilica: the climb to **Michelangelo's dome ★★★**, about 114m (375 ft.) high. You can walk all the way up or take the elevator as far as it goes. The elevator saves you 171 steps, and you *still* have 320 to go after getting off. After you've made it to the top, you'll have a scintillating view over the rooftops of Rome and even the Vatican Gardens and papal apartments.

Piazza San Pietro. www.vatican.va. © **06-69881662.** Basilica (including grottoes) free admission. Necropolis Vaticana (St. Peter's tomb) 13€. Stairs to the dome 5€; elevator to the dome 7€; sacristy (with Historical Museum) free. Basilica (including the grottoes and treasury) Oct–Mar daily 7am–6:30pm, Apr–Sep daily 7am–7pm. Dome Oct–Mar daily 8am–5pm, Apr–Sept daily 8am–6pm. Metro: Cipro, Ottaviano/San Pietro.

Vatican Museums & the Sistine Chapel ★★★ MUSEUM   Nothing else in Rome quite lives up to the awe-inspiring collections of the **Vatican Museums,** a 15-minute walk from St. Peter's out of the north side of Piazza San Pietro. It's a vast treasure store of art from antiquity and the Renaissance gathered by the Roman Catholic Church throughout the centuries, filling a series of ornate Papal palaces, apartments, and galleries leading to one of the world's most beautiful buildings, the justly celebrated **Sistine Chapel** (considered part of the museums for admission purposes).

Note that the Vatican dress code also applies to the museums (no sleeveless blouses, no miniskirts, no shorts, no hats allowed), though it tends to be less rigorously enforced than at St. Peter's. Visitors can, however, take photos (no flash) and, even more dubiously, use mobile phones inside (with the exception of the Sistine Chapel). **Guided tours** are a good way to get the best out of a visit, and are the only way to visit the **Vatican Gardens.**

Obviously, one trip will not be enough to see everything here. Below are previews of the main highlights, showstoppers, and masterpieces on display (in alphabetical order).

APPARTAMENTO BORGIA (BORGIA APARTMENTS) ★ Created for Pope Alexander VI (the infamous Borgia pope) between 1492 and 1494, these rooms were frescoed with biblical and allegorical scenes by Umbrian painter Pinturicchio and his assistants. The rooms tend to be dimly lit, but look for what is thought to be the earliest European depiction of Native Americans, painted little more than a year after Columbus returned from the New World and Alexander had "divided" the globe between Spain and Portugal.

COLLEZIONE D'ARTE CONTEMPORANEA (COLLECTION OF MODERN RELIGIOUS ART) Opened in 1973 and spanning 55 rooms of almost 800 works, these galleries contain the Vatican's concession to modern art. Although there are some big names here and the quality is high, themes usually have a spiritual and religious component: Van Gogh's "Pietà, after Delacroix" is an obvious example, along with Francis Bacon's eerie "Study for a Pope II." You will also see works by Paul Klee ("City with Gothic Cathedral"), Siqueiros ("Mutilated Christ No. 467"), Otto Dix ("Road to Calvary"), Gauguin ("Religious Panel"), Chagall ("Red Pietà"), and a whole room dedicated to Georges Rouault.

MUSEI DI ANTICHITÀ CLASSICHE (CLASSICAL ANTIQUITIES MUSEUMS) The Vatican maintains four classical antiquities museums, the most important being the **Museo Pio Clementino ★★★**, crammed with Greek and Roman sculptures in the small Belvedere Palace of Innocent VIII. At the heart of the complex lies the Octagonal Court, where highlights include the sculpture of Trojan priest **"Laocoön" ★★★** and his two sons locked in a struggle with sea serpents, dating from around 40 B.C., and the exceptional **"Belvedere Apollo" ★★★** (a 2nd-c. Roman reproduction of an authentic Greek work from the 4th c. B.C.), the symbol of classic male beauty and a possible inspiration for Michelangelo's "David." Look out also for the impressive gilded bronze statue of **"Hercules"** in the Rotonda, from the late 2nd century A.D., and the **Hall of the Chariot,** containing a magnificent sculpture of a chariot combining

The Vatican Museums' antiquities include the famous sculpture of Laocoön.

Roman originals and 18th-century work by Antonio Franzoni.

The **Museo Chiaramonti ★** occupies the long loggia that links the Belvedere Palace to the main Vatican palaces, jam-packed on both sides with more than 800 Greco-Roman works, including statues, reliefs, and sarcophagi. In the **Braccio Nuovo ★** ("New Wing"), a handsome Neoclassical extension of the Chiaramonti sumptuously lined with colored marble, lies the colossal statue of the **"Nile" ★**, the ancient river portrayed as an old man with his 16 children, most likely a repro-duction of a long-lost Alexandrian Greek original.

The **Museo Gregoriano Profano ★**, built in 1970 (and therefore positively modern in Vatican terms), houses more Greek sculptures looted by the Romans (some from the Parthenon), mostly funerary steles and votive reliefs, as well as some choice Roman pieces, notably the restored mosaics from the floors of the public libraries in the **Baths of Caracalla** (p. 85).

MUSEO ETNOLOGICO (ETHNOLOGICAL MUSEUM) ★ Founded in 1926, this is an astounding assemblage of artifacts and artwork from cultures throughout the world, from ancient Chinese coins and notes, to plaster sculptures of Native Americans and ceremonial art from Papua New Guinea.

MUSEO GREGORIANO EGIZIO ★ Nine rooms are packed with plun-der from Ancient Egypt, including sarcophagi, mummies, pharaonic stat-uary, votive bronzes, jewelry, cuneiform tablets from Mesopotamia, inscriptions from Assyrian palaces, and Egyptian hieroglyphics.

MUSEO GREGORIANO ETRUSCO ★ The core of this collection is a cache of rare Etruscan art treasures dug up in the 19th century, dating from between the 9th and the 1st century B.C. The Romans learned a lot from the Etruscans, as the highly crafted ceramics, bronzes, silver, and gold on display attest. Don't miss the **Regolini-Galassi tomb** (7th c. B.C.), unearthed at Cerveteri. The museum is housed within the *palazzettos* of Innocent VIII (reigned 1484–92) and Pius IV (reigned 1559–65), the latter adorned with frescoes by Federico Barocci and Federico Zuccari.

PINACOTECA (ART GALLERY) ★★★ The great painting collections of the Popes are displayed within the Pinacoteca, including work from all the big names in Italian art, from Giotto and Fra' Angelico, to Perugino,

Raphael, Veronese, and Crespi. Early medieval work occupies Room 1, with the most intriguing piece a keyhole-shaped wood panel of the "Last Judgment" by Nicolò e Giovanni, dated to the late 12th century. **Giotto** takes center stage in Room 2, with the "Stefaneschi Triptych" (six panels) painted for the old St. Peter's basilica between 1315 and 1320. "Madonna del Magnificat," Bernardo Daddi's masterpiece of early Italian Renaissance art, is also here. **Fra' Angelico** dominates Room 3, his "Stories of St. Nicholas of Bari" and "Virgin with Child" justly praised (check out the Virgin's microscopic eyes in the latter piece). Carlo Crivelli features in Room 6, while decent work by Perugino and Pinturicchio graces Room 7, though most visitors press on to the **Raphael salon** ★★★ (Room 8), where you can view five paintings by the Renaissance master: The best are the "Coronation of the Virgin," the "Madonna of Foligno," and the vast "Transfiguration" (completed shortly before his death). Room 9 boasts Leonardo da Vinci's **"St. Jerome with the Lion" ★★**, as well as Giovanni Bellini's "Pietà." Room 10 is dedicated to Renaissance Venice, with Titian's "Madonna of St. Nicholas of the Frari" and Veronese's "Vision of St. Helen" being paramount. Don't skip the remaining galleries: Room 11 contains Barocci's "Annunciation," while Room 12 is really all about one of the masterpieces of the baroque, Caravaggio's **"Deposition from the Cross" ★★**. Crespi is featured in Room 15, Room 17 is full of Bernini sculpture, and the collection ends with an odd ensemble of Russian and Greek Orthodox icons in Room 18.

STANZE DI RAFFAELLO (RAPHAEL ROOMS) ★★ In the early 16th century, Pope Julius II hired the young Raphael and his workshop to decorate his personal apartments, a series of rooms on the second floor of the Pontifical Palace. Completed between 1508 and 1524, the **Raphael Rooms** now represent one of the great artistic spectacles inside the Vatican.

The **Stanza dell'Incendio** served as the Pope's high court room and later, under Leo X, a dining room. Most of its lavish fresco work has been attributed to Raphael's pupils. Leo X himself commissioned much of the artwork here, which explains the themes (past Popes with the name Leo). Note the intricate ceiling, painted by Umbrian maestro and Raphael's first teacher, Perugino.

Vatican Museums—Buy the Book

In the Vatican Museums, you'll find many overpacked galleries and few descriptive labels. To help you make sense of the incredible riches, pick up the **detailed guide** sold at the Vatican Tourist Office (14€), on the left side of the Piazza San Pietro.

Raphael is the main focus in the **Stanza della Segnatura,** originally used as a Papal library and private office and home to the awe-inspiring **"School of Athens" ★★★** fresco, depicting primarily Greek classical philosophers such as Aristotle, Plato, and Socrates. Many of the figures

papal AUDIENCES

When the pope is in Rome, he gives a public audience every Wednesday beginning at 10:30am (sometimes at 10am in summer). If you want to get a good seat near the front, arrive early, as security begins to let people in between 8 and 8:30am. Audiences take place in the Paul VI Hall of Audiences, although sometimes St. Peter's Basilica and St. Peter's Square are used to accommodate a large attendance in the summer. With the ascension of Pope Francis to the Throne of Peter in 2013, this tradition continues. You can check on the Pope's appearances and the ceremonies he presides over, including celebrations of Mass, on the Vatican website (www.vatican.va). Anyone is welcome, but you must first obtain a **free ticket;** without a reservation you can try the Swiss Guards by the Bronze Doors located just after security at St. Peter's (8am–8pm in summer and 8am–7pm in winter). You can pick up tickets here up to 3 days in advance, subject to availability.

If you would prefer to reserve a place in advance, download a request form at www.vaticantour.com/images/Vatican_Ticket_request.pdf or www.vatican.va and fax it to the **Prefecture of the Papal Household** at ☎ **06-69885863.** Tickets can be picked up at the office located just inside the Bronze Doors from 3 to 7:30pm on the preceding day or on the morning of the audience from 8 to 10:30am.

At noon on Sundays, the Pope speaks briefly from his study window and gives his blessing to the visitors and pilgrims gathered in St. Peter's Square (no tickets are required for this). From about mid-July to mid-September, the Angelus and blessing usually take place at the summer residence at Castelgandolfo, some 26km (16 miles) out of Rome and accessible by Metro and bus, though it is unclear whether Francis will continue to spend his summers there every year.

are thought to be based on portraits of Renaissance artists, including Bramante (on the right as Euclid, drawing on a chalkboard), Leonardo da Vinci (as Plato, the bearded man in the center), and even Raphael himself (in the lower-right corner with a black hat). On the wall opposite stands the equally magnificent "Disputa del Sacramento," where Raphael used a similar technique; Dante Alighieri stands behind the pontiff on the right, and Fra' Angelico poses as a monk (which in fact, he was) on the far left.

The **Stanza d'Eliodoro** was used for the private audiences of the Pope and was painted by Raphael immediately after he did the Segnatura. His aim here was to flatter his papal patron, Julius II: The depiction of the pope driving Attila from Rome was meant to symbolize the contemporary mission of Julius II to drive the French out of Italy. Finally, the **Sala di Costantino,** used for Papal receptions and official ceremonies, was completed by Raphael's students after the master's death, but based on his designs and drawings. It's a jaw-dropping space, commemorating four major episodes in the life of Emperor Constantine.

SISTINE CHAPEL ★★★   Michelangelo labored for 4 years (1508–12) to paint the ceiling of the Sistine Chapel; it is said he spent the entire time on his feet, paint dripping into his eyes. But what a result! Thanks to a massive restoration effort in the 1990s, the world's most famous fresco is today as vibrantly colorful and filled with roiling life as it was in 1512. And the chapel is still of central importance to the Catholic Church: This is where the Papal Conclave meets to elect new popes.

The "Creation of Adam," at the center of the ceiling, is one of the best known and most reproduced images in history, the outstretched hands of God and Adam—not quite touching—an iconic symbol of not just the Renaissance but the Enlightenment that followed. Nevertheless, it is somewhat ironic that this is Michelangelo's best-known work: The artist always regarded himself as a sculptor first and foremost.

The endless waiting in order to get into the chapel inevitably makes the sense of expectation all the greater, but despite the tour groups and the crowds, seeing the frescoes in person is a truly magical experience.

The ceiling **frescoes** are obviously the main showstoppers, though staring at them tends to take a heavy toll on the neck. Commissioned by Pope Julius II in 1508 and completed in 1512, they primarily depict nine scenes from the Book of Genesis (including the famed "Creation of Adam"), from the "Separation of Light and Darkness" at the altar end to the "Great Flood" and "Drunkenness of Noah." Surrounding these main frescoes are paintings of twelve people who prophesied the coming of

The ceiling of the Sistine Chapel, painted by Michelangelo.

Christ, from Jonah and Isaiah to the Delphic Sibyl. Once you have admired the ceiling, turn your attention to the altar wall. At the age of 60, Michelangelo was summoned to finish the chapel decor 23 years after he finished the ceiling work. Apparently saddened by leaving Florence, and depressed by the morally bankrupt state of Rome at that time, he painted these dark moods in his "Last Judgment," where he included his own self-portrait on a sagging human hide held by St. Bartholomew (who was martyred by being flayed alive).

Seeing the Vatican at Night

Vatican Museum visitors now can have the extraordinary opportunity of strolling through the galleries after sunset, at least on Friday nights from 7pm to 11pm (last entrance at 9:30) during the high tourist season, from the last Friday in April through July and the first Friday in September through the end of October. These twilight visits will allow access to important collections, including the Pio-Clementine Museum, the Egyptian Museum, the Upper Galleries (candelabra, tapestries and maps), the Raphael Rooms, the Borgia Apartments, the Collection of Modern Religious Art, and the Sistine Chapel. Booking online is mandatory; visit www.biglietteriamusei.vatican.va.

Yet the Sistine Chapel isn't all Michelangelo. The southern wall is covered by a series of astonishing paintings completed in the 1480s: "Moses Leaving to Egypt" by Perugino, the "Trials of Moses" by Botticelli, "The Crossing of the Red Sea" by Cosimo Rosselli (or Domenico Ghirlandaio), "Descent from Mount Sinai" by Cosimo Rosselli (or Piero di Cosimo), Botticelli's "Punishment of the Rebels," and Signorelli's "Testament and Death of Moses."

On the right-hand, northern wall are Perugino's "The Baptism of Christ," Botticelli's "The Temptations of Christ," Ghirlandaio's "Vocation of the Apostles," Perugino's "Delivery of the Keys," Cosimo Rosselli's "The Sermon on the Mount" and "Last Supper." On the eastern wall, originals by Ghirlandaio and Signorelli were painted over by Hendrik van den Broeck's "The Resurrection" and Matteo da Lecce's "Disputation over Moses" in the 1570s.

Vatican City, Viale Vaticano (a long walk around the Vatican walls from St. Peter's Sq.). www.museivaticani.va. ✆ **06-69884676.** Admission 16€ adults, 8€ children 6–13, free for children 5 and under; 2-hr tours of Vatican Gardens 32€ (no tours Wed or Sun). Mon–Sat 9am–6pm (ticket office closes at 4pm). Also open Fri 7–11pm (late Apr–July, Sept–Oct) per online booking. Also open last Sun of every month 9am–2pm (free admission). Closed Jan 1 and 6, Feb 11, Mar 19, Easter, May 1, June 29, Aug 14–15, Nov 1, and Dec 25–26. Reservations for advance tickets (reservation fee 4€) and guided tours (32€ per person) through www.biglietteriamusei.vatican.va. Metro: Ottaviano or Cipro–Musei Vaticani; bus 49 stops in front of the entrance.

NEAR VATICAN CITY

Castel Sant'Angelo ★★ CASTLE/PALACE This bulky cylindrical fortress on the Vatican side of the Tiber has a storied, complex history, beginning life as the mausoleum tomb of Emperor Hadrian in A.D. 138, and later serving as a castle (Pope Clement VII escaped the looting troops of Charles V here in 1527), papal residence in the 14th century, and military prison from the 17th century (Puccini used the prison as the setting for the third act of "Tosca"). Consider renting an audioguide at the entrance to help fully appreciate its various manifestations. The ashes and urns of Hadrian and his family have long since been looted and destroyed, and most of what you see today relates to the conversion of the structure into fortress and residence by the popes from the 14th century.

From the entrance a stone ramp *(rampa elicoidale)* winds its way to the upper terraces, from which you can see amazing views of the city and enjoy a coffee at the outdoor cafe. The sixth floor features the **Terrazza dell'Angelo,** crowned by a florid statue of the Archangel Michael cast in 1752 by the Flemish artist Peter Anton von Verschaffelt (location of the tragic denouement in "Tosca").

From here you can walk back down through five floors, including the Renaissance apartments (levels 3–5) used by some of Rome's most infamous Popes: Alexander VI (the Borgia pope) hid away in the castle after the murder of his son Giovanni in 1497, overwhelmed by grief (although his vows of moral reform were short lived). The art collection displayed throughout—ceramics, paintings, and sculpture—is fairly mediocre by Rome standards, although there are a few works by Carlo Crivelli and Luca Signorelli, notably a "Madonna and Child with Saints" from the latter.

Below the apartments are the grisly dungeons (**"Le Prigioni"**) used as torture chambers in the medieval period, and utilized especially enthusiastically by Cesare Borgia. The castle is connected to St. Peter's Basilica by **Il Passetto di Borgo,** a walled 800m (2,635-ft.) passage erected in 1277 by Pope Nicholas III, used by popes who needed to make a quick escape to the fortress in times of danger, which was fairly often. Fans of Dan Brown will recognize it from his novel *Angels and Demons*. Note that the dungeons, Il Passetto, and the apartments of Clement VII are only usually open on summer evenings (July–Aug Tues–Sun 8:30pm–1am; free 50-min. tours with admission, English tour at 10:30pm). Classical music and jazz concerts are also held in and around the castle in summer (Wed, Fri–Sun 9:30pm).

Lungotevere Castello 50. www.castelsantangelo.com. © **06-6819111.** Admission 11€. Tues–Sun 9am–7.30pm. Bus: 23, 40, 62, 271, 982, 280 (to Piazza Pia).

The Colosseum, Forum & Ancient Rome
THE MAJOR SIGHTS OF ANCIENT ROME

It will help enhance sightseeing experience if you know a little about the history and rulers of Ancient Rome: See p. 20 for a brief rundown.

Arco di Costantino (Arch of Constantine) ★★ MONUMENT
The photogenic triumphal arch next to the Colosseum was erected by the Senate in A.D. 315 to honor Constantine's defeat of the pagan Maxentius at the Battle of the Milvian Bridge (A.D. 312). Many of the reliefs

have nothing whatsoever to do with Constantine or his works, but they tell of the victories of earlier Antonine rulers (lifted from other, long-forgotten memorials).

Historically, the arch marks a period of great change in the history of Rome. Converted to Christianity by a vision on the eve of battle, Constantine ended the centuries-long persecution of the Christians, during which many followers of the new religion had been put to death in a gruesome manner. Although Constantine didn't ban paganism (which survived officially until the closing of the temples more than half a century later), he espoused Christianity himself and began the inevitable development that culminated in the conquest of Rome by the Christian religion. Btw. Colosseum and Palatine Hill. Metro: Colosseo.

Terme di Caracalla (Baths of Caracalla) ★ RUINS Named for the emperor Caracalla, a particularly unpleasant individual, the baths were completed in A.D. 217 after Caracalla's death. The richness of decoration has faded, and the lavishness can be judged only from the shell of brick ruins that remain. In their heyday, the baths sprawled across 11 ha (27 acres) and could handle 1,600 bathers at a time. Partially opened to the public in 2012, the tunnels below the complex give an idea of the scale of the hydraulic and heating systems that must have been needed to serve 8,000 or so Romans per day. The *palestra* (gym) is used for outdoor operatic performances in Rome (p. 154).
Via delle Terme di Caracalla 52. www.archeoroma.beniculturali.it. ✆ **06-39967700.** Admission 6€ (combined ticket with the Tomb of Cecelia Metella, p. 119). Oct Mon 8:30am–2pm, Tues–Sun 9am–6:30pm; Nov–Feb 15 Mon 8:30am–2pm, Tues–Sun 9am–4:30pm; Feb 16–Mar 15 Mon 8:30am–2pm, Tues–Sun 9am–5pm; Mar 16–Sept Mon 8:30am–2pm, Tues–Sun 9am–7pm. Last admission 1 hr. before closing. Bus: 118 or 628.

Musei Capitolini (Capitoline Museums) ★★ MUSEUM The masterpieces here are considered Rome's most valuable (recall that the Vatican Museums are *not* technically in Rome). They certainly were collected early: This is the oldest public museum *in the world.* So try and schedule adequate time, as there's much to see.

First stop is the courtyard of the **Palazzo dei Conservatori** (the building on the right of the piazza designed by Michelangelo, if you enter via the ramp from Piazza Venezia). It's scattered with gargantuan stone body parts—the remnants of a massive 12m (39-ft.) statue of the emperor Constantine, including his colossal head, hand, and foot. It's nearly impossible to resist snapping a selfie next to the giant foot.

On the *palazzo*'s ground floor, the unmissable works are in the first series of rooms. These include "Lo Spinario" **(Room III),** a lifelike bronze of a young boy digging a splinter out of his foot that was widely copied during the Renaissance; and the "Lupa Capitolina" **(Room IV),** a bronze statue from 500 B.C. of the famous she-wolf that suckled Romulus and Remus, the mythical founders of Rome. The twins were not on the original Etruscan statue, but added in the 15th century. **Room V** has

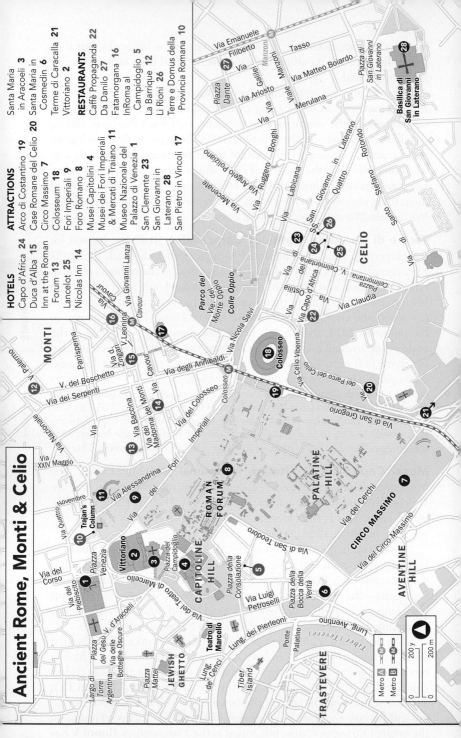

Ancient Rome, Monti & Celio

HOTELS

Capo d'Africa **24**
Duca d'Alba **15**
Inn at the Roman
Forum **13**
Lancelot **25**
Nicolas Inn **14**

ATTRACTIONS

Arco di Costantino **19**
Case Romane del Celio **20**
Circo Massimo **7**
Colosseum **18**
Fori Imperiali **9**
Foro Romano **8**
Musei Capitolini **4**
Musei dei Fori Imperiali
& Mercati di Traiano **11**
Museo Nazionale del
Palazzo di Venezia **1**
San Clemente **23**
San Giovanni in
Laterano **28**
San Pietro in Vincoli **17**

Santa Maria
in Aracoeli **3**
Santa Maria in
Cosmedin **6**
Terme di Caracalla **21**
Vittoriano **2**

RESTAURANTS

Caffè Propaganda **22**
Da Danilo **27**
Fatamorgana **16**
InRoma al
Campidoglio **5**
La Barrique **12**
Li Rioni **26**
Terre e Domus della
Provincia Romana **10**

Bernini's famously pained portrait of "Medusa," even more compelling when you see its writhing serpent hairdo in person.

Before heading upstairs, go toward the new wing at the rear, bathed in natural light thanks to a modern skylight ceiling, which houses the original equestrian **statue of Marcus Aurelius ★★★**, dating to around A.D. 180—the piazza outside, where it stood from 1538, now has a copy. There's a giant bronze head from a statue of Constantine (ca. A.D. 337) and the foundations of the original Temple of Jupiter that stood on the Capitoline Hill since its inauguration in 509 B.C.

The second-floor is known for its **picture gallery ★**, strong on baroque oil paintings, with masterpieces including Caravaggio's "John the Baptist" and "The Fortune Teller" (1595) and Guido Reni's "St. Sebastian" (1615).

An underground tunnel takes you under the piazza to the other part of the Capitoline Museums, the **Palazzo Nuovo,** via the **Tabularium ★**. This was built in 78 B.C. to house ancient Rome's city records, and was later used as a salt mine and then as a prison. The atmospheric stone gallery was opened to the public in the late 1990s to exhibit inscriptions, and also to provide access to one of the best balcony **views ★★★** in Rome: along the length of the Forum toward the Palatine Hill.

Much of the Palazzo Nuovo is dedicated to statues that were excavated from the forums below and brought in from outlying areas like Hadrian's Villa in Tivoli (p. 159). If you're running short on time at this point, head straight for the 1st-century **"Capitoline Venus" ★★**, in Room III—a modest girl covering up after a bath—and in Room IV, a chronologically arranged row of busts of Roman emperors and their families. Another favorite is the beyond handsome **"Dying Gaul" ★★**, a Roman copy of a lost ancient Greek work. Lord Byron considered the statue so lifelike and moving, he included mention of it in his poem "Childe Harold's Pilgrimage."

Piazza del Campidoglio 1. www.museicapitolini.org. ⓒ **060608.** Admission 13€. Tues–Sun 9am–8pm. Last admission 1 hr. before closing. Bus: C3, H, 40, 44, 60, 80B, 190, 780, or 781.

Circo Massimo (Circus Maximus) ★ HISTORIC SITE Today an almost formless ruin, the once-grand circus was pilfered repeatedly by medieval and Renaissance builders in search of marble and stone. But if you squint, and take in its elongated oval proportions and ruined tiers of benches, visions of *Ben-Hur* may dance before your eyes. At one time, 250,000 Romans could assemble on the marble seats while the emperor observed the games from his box high on the Palatine Hill. What the Romans called a "circus" was a large arena enclosed by tiers of seats on three or four sides, used especially for sports or spectacles.

The circus lies in a valley between the Palatine and Aventine hills. Next to the Colosseum, it was the most impressive structure in ancient Rome, in one of the most exclusive neighborhoods. For centuries, chariot races filled it with the cheers of thousands.

When the dark days of the 5th and 6th centuries fell, the Circus Maximus seemed a symbol of the ruination of Rome. The last games were held in A.D. 549 on the orders of Totilla the Goth, who had seized Rome twice. He lived in the still-glittering ruins on the Palatine and apparently thought the chariot races in the Circus Maximus would lend his rule credibility. After 549, the Circus Maximus was never used again, and the demand for building materials reduced it, like so much of Rome, to a great dusty field.

Btw. Via dei Cerchi and Via del Circo Massimo. Metro: Circo Massimo.

Colosseum (Colosseo) ★★★ ICON   No matter how many pictures you've seen, the first impression you'll have of the Colosseum is amazement at its sheer enormity. Its massive bulk looks as if it has been plopped down among the surrounding buildings, and not the other way around.

Your first view of the Flavian Amphitheater (the Colosseum's original name) should be from the outside, and it's important to walk completely around its 500m (1,640-ft.) circumference. It doesn't matter where you start, but do the circle and look at the various stages of ruin before delving in. Note the different column styles on each level. Black soot from passing cars has left its mark on the columns, but a full-on conservation makeover (running through 2016) will work to eliminate much of it.

Once inside, walk onto the partially reconstructed wooden floor, which once covered the hypogeum, the place where gladiators and beasts waited their turn in the arena. Vespasian ordered the construction of the elliptical bowl, called the Amphitheatrum Flavium, in A.D. 72; it was inaugurated by Titus in A.D. 80. The stadium could hold as many as 87,000 spectators, by some counts, and seats were sectioned on three levels, dividing the people by social rank and gender. There were 80 entrances, allowing the massive crowds to be seated within a few minutes, historians say. Most events were free, but all spectators had to obtain a terracotta disc, called a tessera, to enter.

The Colosseum was built as a venue for gladiator contests and wild animal fights, but when the Roman Empire fell, it was abandoned and eventually overgrown with vegetation. You'll notice on the top of the "good side," as locals call it, that there are a few remaining supports that once held the canvas awning that covered the stadium during rain or for the summer heat. Much of the ancient travertine that once sheathed its outside was used for palaces like the nearby Palazzo Venezia and Palazzo Cancelleria near the Campo de' Fiori.

Note: The same ticket that you buy for the Colosseum includes admission to the Forum and Palatine Hill, and is valid for 2 days.

Piazzale del Colosseo. www.archeoroma.beniculturali.it. ✆ **06-39967700.** Admission 12€ (includes Roman Forum & Palatine Hill). Nov–Feb 15 daily 8:30am–4:30pm; Feb 16–Mar 15 daily 8:30am–5pm; Mar 16–27 daily 8:30am–5:30pm; Mar 28–Aug daily 8:30am–7:15pm; Sept daily 8:30am–7pm; Oct daily 8:30am–6:30pm. Last admission 1 hr. before closing. Guided tours (45 min.) in English daily at 10:15, 10:45, 11:15, and 11:45am, 12:30, 1:45, and 3pm. Tours 5€. Metro: Colosseo.

Fori Imperiali (Imperial Forums) ★ RUINS   Begun by Julius Caesar as an answer to the overcrowding of Rome's older forums, the Imperial Forums were, at the time of their construction, flashier, bolder, and more impressive than the buildings in the Roman Forum. This site conveyed the unquestioned authority of the emperors at the height of their absolute power.

Alas, Mussolini felt his regime was more important than the ancient one, and issued the controversial orders to cut through centuries of debris and buildings to carve out Via dei Fori Imperiali, thereby linking the Colosseum to the grand 19th-century monuments of Piazza Venezia. Excavations under his Fascist regime began at once, and many archaeological treasures were revealed (and then—*argh!*—destroyed).

The best view of the Forums is from the railings on the north side of Via dei Fori Imperiali; begin where Via Cavour joins the boulevard. (Visitors are not permitted down into the ruins.) Closest to the junction are the remains of the **Forum of Nerva,** built by the emperor whose 2-year reign (A.D. 96–98) followed the assassination of the paranoid Domitian. You'll be struck by how much the ground level has risen in 19 centuries. The only really recognizable remnant is a wall of the Temple of Minerva with two fine Corinthian columns. This forum was once flanked by that of Vespasian, which is now gone.

The next along is the **Forum of Augustus ★★**, built before the birth of Christ to commemorate the Emperor Augustus's victory over Julius Caesar's assassins, Cassius and Brutus, in the Battle of Philippi (42 B.C.).

Continuing along the railing, you'll see the vast semicircle of **Trajan's Markets ★★**, whose teeming arcades were once stocked with merchandise from the far corners of the Roman world. They collapsed long ago, leaving only a few cats to watch after things. The shops once covered a multitude of levels; you can visit the part that has been transformed into the **Museo dei Fori Imperiali** (see p. 93).

In front of the Markets, the **Forum of Trajan ★★** is the newest and most beautiful of the Imperial Forums, built between A.D. 107 and 113, and designed by Greek architect Apollodorus of Damascus (who also laid out the adjoining market building). There are many statue fragments and pedestals bearing still-legible inscriptions, but more interesting is the great Basilica Ulpia, whose gray marble columns rise roofless into the sky. This forum was once regarded as one of the architectural wonders of the world. Beyond the Basilica Ulpia is **Trajan's Column ★★★**, in magnificent condition, with an intricate bas-relief sculpture depicting Trajan's victorious campaign (although, from your vantage point, you'll be able to see only the earliest stages).

The **Forum of Julius Caesar ★★**, the first of the Imperial Forums to be built, lies on the opposite side of Via dei Fori Imperiali, adjacent to the Roman Forum. This was the site of the stock exchange, as well as the Temple of Venus.

Along Via dei Fori Imperiali. Metro: Colosseo.

Foro Romano (Roman Forum) & Palatino (Palatine Hill) ★★★

RUINS   When it came to cremating Caesar, sacrificing a naked victim, or just discussing the day's events, the Roman Forum was the place to be. Traversed by the **Via Sacra (Sacred Way)** ★, the main thoroughfare of ancient Rome, the Forum flourished as the center of Roman life in the days of the Republic, before it gradually lost prestige (but never spiritual draw) to the Imperial Forums (see above).

You'll see only ruins and fragments, an arch or two, and lots of over-turned boulders, but with some imagination you can feel the rush of history here. That any semblance of the Forum remains today is miraculous because it was used for years as a quarry (as was the Colosseum). Eventually it reverted to a *campo vaccino* (cow pasture). But excavations in the 19th century and later in the 1930s began to bring to light one of the world's most historic spots. (Not without controversy: *Some* of what you see here has no definitive ancient heritage—it was rebuilt as later generations imagined it.)

By day, the columns of now-vanished temples and the stones from which long-forgotten orators spoke are mere shells. Bits of grass and weeds grow where a triumphant Caesar was once lionized. But at night, when the Forum is silent in the moonlight, it isn't difficult to imagine Vestal Virgins still guarding the sacred temple fire.

You can spend at least a morning wandering through the ruins of the Forum. We'd suggest you enter via the gate on Via dei Fori Imperiali. Turn right at the bottom of the entrance slope to walk west along the old Via Sacra toward the arch. Just before it on your right is the large brick **Curia** ★★, the main seat of the Roman Senate, built by Julius Caesar, rebuilt by Diocletian, and consecrated as a church in A.D. 630.

The triumphal **Arch of Septimius Severus** ★★ (A.D. 203), will be your next important sight, displaying time-bitten reliefs of the emperor's victories in what are today Iran and Iraq. During the Middle Ages, Rome became a provincial backwater, and frequent flooding of the nearby river helped bury (and thus preserve) most of the Forum. Some bits did still stick out aboveground, including the top half of this arch, which was used to shelter a barbershop!

Just to the left of the arch, you can make out the remains of a cylindrical lump of rock with some marble steps curving off it. That round stone was the **Umbilicus Urbus,** considered the center of Rome and of the entire Roman Empire; the curving steps are those of the **Imperial Rostra** ★, where great orators and legislators stood to speak and the people gathered to listen. Nearby, a much-photographed trio of fluted columns with Corinthian capitals supports a bit of architrave from the corner of the **Temple of Vespasian and Titus** ★★ (emperors were routinely turned into gods upon dying).

Start heading to your left toward the eight Ionic columns marking the front of the **Temple of Saturn** ★★ (rebuilt in 42 B.C.), which

THREE free views TO REMEMBER FOR A LIFETIME

The Forum from the Campidoglio Standing on Piazza del Campidoglio, outside the Musei Capitolini (p. 85), walk around the right side of the Palazzo Senatorio to a terrace overlooking the best panorama of the Roman Forum, with the Palatine Hill and Colosseum as a backdrop. At night, the Forum is dramatically floodlit and its ruins look even more haunting.

The Whole City from the Janiculum Hill From many vantage points in the Eternal City, the views are panoramic. But one of the best spots for a memorable vista is the Janiculum Hill (Gianicolo), above Trastevere. Laid out before you are Rome's rooftops, peppered with domes ancient and modern. From up here, you will understand why Romans complain about the materials used to build the Vittoriano (p. 96)—it's a white shock in a sea of rose- and honey-colored stone. Walk 50 yards north of the famous balcony (favored by tour buses) for a slightly better angle, from the Belvedere 9 Febbraio 1849.

The Aventine Hill & the Priori dei Cavalieri di Malta The mythical site of Remus' original settlement, the Aventine (Aventino) is now a leafy, upscale residential neighborhood—but also blessed with some magical views. From Via del Circo Massimo walk through the gardens along Via di Valle Murcia, and keep walking in a straight line. Along your right side, gardens offer views over the dome of St. Peter's. When you reach Piazza dei Cavalieri di Malta, look through the keyhole of the Priory gate (on the right) for a "secret" view of the Vatican.

housed the first treasury of republican Rome. It was also the site of one of the Roman year's biggest annual blowout festivals, the December 17 feast of Saturnalia, which, after a bit of tweaking, Christians now celebrate as Christmas. Turn left to start heading back east, past the worn steps and stumps of brick pillars outlining the enormous **Basilica Julia ★★**, built by Julius Caesar. Further along, on the right, are the three Corinthian columns of the **Temple of the Dioscuri ★★★**, dedicated to the Gemini twins, Castor and Pollux. Forming one of the most photogenic sights of the Roman Forum, a trio of columns supports an architrave fragment. The founding of this temple dates from the 5th century B.C.

Beyond the bit of curving wall that marks the site of the little round **Temple of Vesta** (rebuilt several times after fires started by the sacred flame within), you'll find the reconstructed **House of the Vestal Virgins** (A.D. 3rd–4th c.). The temple was the home of the consecrated young women who tended the sacred flame in the Temple of Vesta. Vestals were girls chosen from patrician families to serve a 30-year-long priesthood. During their tenure, they were among Rome's most venerated citizens, with unique powers such as the ability to pardon condemned criminals. The cult was quite serious about the "virgin" part of the job description—if one of Vesta's earthly servants was found to have "misplaced" her virginity, the miscreant Vestal was buried alive, because it was forbidden to shed a Vestal's blood. (Her amorous accomplice was merely flogged to death.) The overgrown rectangle of their gardens is lined with broken, heavily worn statues of senior Vestals on pedestals.

The path dovetails back to Via Sacra. Turn right, walk past the so-called "Temple of Romulus," and then left to enter the massive brick remains and coffered ceilings of the 4th-century **Basilica of Constantine and Maxentius ★★** (Basilica di Massenzio). These were Rome's public law courts, and their architectural style was adopted by early Christians for their houses of worship (the reason so many ancient churches are called "basilicas").

Return to the path and continue toward the Colosseum. Veer right to the Forum's second great triumphal arch, the extensively rebuilt **Arch of Titus ★★** (A.D. 81), on which one relief depicts the carrying off of treasures from Jerusalem's temple. Look closely and you'll see a menorah among the booty. The war that this arch glorifies ended with the expulsion of Jews from the colonized Judea, signaling the beginning of the Jewish Diaspora throughout Europe. You can exit behind the Arch—and there's another exit, accessing the Campidoglio from the opposite end of the Forum.

From here you can climb the **Palatine Hill ★** (Palatino), on the same ticket. The Palatine, tradition tells us, was the spot on which the first settlers built their huts under the direction of Romulus. In later years, the hill became a patrician residential district that attracted such citizens as Cicero. In time, however, the area was gobbled up by imperial palaces and drew a

Ruins of the Temple of the Dioscuri in the Roman Forum.

famous and infamous roster of tenants, such as Livia (some of the frescoes in the House of Livia are in miraculous condition), Tiberius, Caligula (murdered here by members of his Praetorian Guard), Nero, and Domitian

Only the ruins of its former grandeur remain today, but it's worth the climb for the panoramic views of both the Roman and the Imperial Forums, as well as the Capitoline Hill and the Colosseum. You can also enter from here, and do the entire tour in reverse.

Via della Salara Vecchia 5/6. ⓒ **06-39967700.** Admission 12€ (includes Colosseum). Oct 30–Dec and Jan 2–Feb 15 daily 8:30am–4:30pm; Feb 16–Mar 15 daily 8:30am–5pm; Mar 16–24 daily 8:30am–5:30pm; Mar 25–Aug daily 8:30am–7:15pm; Sept daily 8:30am–7pm; Oct 1–29 daily 8:30am–6:30pm. Last admission 1 hr. before closing. Guided tours are given daily at 11am, lasting 1 hr., costing 4€. Metro: Colosseo.

Museo dei Fori Imperiali & Mercati di Traiano (Museum of the Imperial Forums & Trajan's Markets) ★ RUINS/MUSEUM   The
museum occupies the ruins of boutiques, food stores, and workshops that formed Emperor Trajan's Market (call it the World's First Shopping Mall). All in all, it's home to 172 marble fragments from the Fori Imperiali; here are also original remnants from the Forum of Augustus and Forum of Nerva.

Created in A.D. 100–110, but having fallen into total ruin, this once-bustling market was rebuilt in the Middle Ages and then extensively excavated under Mussolini. The Imperial Forums, many of which are still being excavated, are hard for ordinary visitors to comprehend, so the museum uses replicas to help visitors orient themselves, and many galleries house models and recreations of the various forums and temples. It also houses a giant head of Constantine, found in 2005 in an old sewer. It's expensive (11€), so recommended only for those with a deeper historical interest in Ancient Rome.

Via IV Novembre 94. www.mercatiditraiano.it. ⓒ **060608.** Admission 11€. Tues–Sun 9am–7pm. Last admission 1 hr. before closing. Bus: 53, 80, 85, 87, 175, 186, 271, 571, or 810.

OTHER ATTRACTIONS NEAR ANCIENT ROME
Basilica di San Clemente ★★ CHURCH   This isn't just another Roman church—far from it. In this church-upon-a-church, centuries of history peel away. In A.D. 4th century, a church was built over a secular house from the 1st century, beside which stood a pagan temple dedicated to Mithras (god of the sun). Down in the eerie grottoes (which you explore on your own), you'll discover well-preserved frescoes from the 9th to the 11th centuries. The Normans destroyed this lower church, and a new one was built in the 12th century. Its chief attraction is the mosaic from that period adorning the apse, as well as a chapel honoring St. Catherine of Alexandria with 1428 frescoes by Masolino.

Via San Giovanni in Laterano (at Piazza San Clemente). www.basilicasanclemente.com. ⓒ **06-7740021.** Basilica free admission; excavations 5€. Mon–Sat 9am–12:30pm and 3–6pm; Sun noon–6pm. Last admission 20 min. before closing. Bus: 53, 85, or 117.

Basilica di San Giovanni in Laterano ★ CHURCH   This church (not St. Peter's) is the cathedral of the diocese of Rome, where the pope comes to celebrate Mass on certain holidays. Built in A.D. 314 by Constantine, it has suffered the vicissitudes of Roman history, forcing many overhauls. Only parts of the baptistery remain from the original.

The present building is characterized by an 18th-century facade by Alessandro Galilei (statues of Christ and the Apostles ring the top). Note that a 1993 terrorist bomb caused severe damage to the facade. Borromini gets the credit for the interior, built for Pope Innocent X. In a purportedly misguided attempt to redecorate, frescoes by Giotto were destroyed; remains attributed to Giotto were discovered in 1952 and are now on display against the first inner column on the right.

Across the street is the **Santuario della Scala Santa (Palace of the Holy Steps),** Piazza San Giovanni in Laterano 14 (✆ 06-7726641). Allegedly, the 28 marble steps here (now covered with wood for preservation) were originally at Pontius Pilate's villa in Jerusalem, and Christ climbed them the day he was brought before Pilate. According to medieval tradition, the steps were brought from Jerusalem to Rome by Constantine's mother, Helen, and they've been in this location since 1589. Today pilgrims from all over the world come here to climb the steps on their knees. This is one of the holiest sites in Christendom, although some historians say the stairs might date only from the 4th century.
Piazza San Giovanni in Laterano 4. ✆ **06-69886433.** Free admission. Daily 7am–6:30pm. Metro: San Giovanni.

Case Romane del Celio ★ RUINS   The 5th-century Basilica of SS. Giovanni e Paolo stands over a residential complex consisting of several Roman houses of different periods. A visit here will provide you with a unique picture of how generations of Romans lived. Preserved at the labyrinthine site is a residence from the 2nd century A.D., a single home of a wealthy family, and a 3rd-century A.D. apartment building for artisans.

According to tradition, this was the dwelling of two Roman officers, John and Paul (not the Apostles), who were beheaded during the reign of Julian the Apostate (361–63), when they refused to serve in a military campaign. They were later made saints, and their bones were said to have been buried at this site. A religious sect, the Passionists, excavated the site in 1887, discovering naked genii figures painted on the walls. Scandalized at such a realistic depiction of male genitalia, they blurred some of the most obvious anatomical details. The two-story construction, with some 20 rooms, also contains a small museum room with finds from the site and fragmentary 12th-century frescoes.
Piazza Santi Giovanni e Paolo 13 (entrance on Clivo di Scauro). www.caseromane.it. ✆ **06-70454544.** Admission 6€ adults, 4€ ages 12–18. Thurs–Mon 10am–1pm and 3–6pm. Metro: Colosseo or Circo Massimo.

Museo Nazionale del Palazzo di Venezia ★ MUSEUM   Best remembered today as Mussolini's Fascist headquarters in Rome, the palace was built in the 1450s as the Rome outpost of the Republic of Venice—hence the name. It later became the Austrian Embassy, after Venice's republican government was dissolved by Napoleon. Today, a few of its rooms are given over to a modest collection of exhibits; highlights include Giorgione's enigmatic "Double Portrait" and some early Tuscan altarpieces. Car noise is a constant companion as you tour—the palace's formerly tranquil gardens are now one of Rome's busiest intersections, Piazza Venezia.

Via del Plebiscito 118. www.museopalazzovenezia.beniculturali.it. © **06-6780131.** Admission 5€. Tues–Sun 8:30am–7:30pm. Bus: 30, 40, 46, 62, 70, 87, or 916.

San Pietro in Vincoli (St. Peter in Chains) ★ CHURCH   This church, which has undergone recent renovations, was founded in the 5th century to house the supposed chains that bound St. Peter in Palestine (they're preserved under glass below the main altar). But the drawing card is the tomb of Pope Julius II, which features one of the world's most famous sculptures: **Michelangelo's "Moses"** ★★. Michelangelo was to have carved 44 magnificent figures for the tomb. That didn't happen, of course, but the Pope was given a great consolation prize—a figure intended to be "minor" that's now numbered among Michelangelo's masterpieces. Don't leave without a quick look at the unusual "skeleton tombs," in the left aisle.

Piazza San Pietro in Vincoli 4A. © **06-97844952.** Free admission. Spring–summer daily 8:30am–12:30pm and 3:30–6:30pm (fall–winter to 5:30pm). Metro: Colosseo or Cavour.

Santa Maria in Aracoeli ★ CHURCH   On the Capitoline Hill, this landmark church was built for the Franciscans in the 13th century. According to legend, Augustus once ordered a temple erected on this spot, where a prophetic sibyl forecast the coming of Christ. Interior highlights include a coffered Renaissance ceiling and the tombstone of Giovanni Crivelli (1432) carved by the great Florentine Renaissance sculptor, Donatello. The church is also known for the **Cappella Bufalini** ★ (first chapel on the right), frescoed by Pinturicchio with scenes illustrating the life and death of St. Bernardino of Siena.

You have to climb a long flight of steep steps to reach the church, unless you're already on neighboring Piazza del Campidoglio, in which case you can cross the piazza and climb the steps on the far side of the Musei Capitolini (p. 85).

Scala dell'Arcicapitolina 12. © **06-69763838.** Free admission. Daily 9am–12:30pm and 2:30–5:30pm. Bus: C3, H, 40, 44, 60, 80B, 190, 780, or 781.

Santa Maria in Cosmedin ★ CHURCH   People come to this little church not for great art treasures, but to see the **"Mouth of Truth,"** a large disk under the portico. As Gregory Peck demonstrated to Audrey Hepburn in the film *Roman Holiday*, the mouth is supposed to chomp down on the hands of liars. (According to local legend, a former priest used to keep a scorpion in back to bite the fingers of anyone he felt was lying.) The purpose of this disk—which is not of particular artistic interest—is unclear. One hypothesis says that it was one of Rome's many "talking statues." If you wanted to rat someone out, all you'd have to do was drop an anonymous note into the open mouth. The church itself was erected in the 6th century but was subsequently rebuilt. A Romanesque bell tower was added at the end of the 11th century.

Piazza della Bocca della Verità 18. ℭ **06-6787759.** Free admission. Summer daily 9:30am–5:50pm; winter daily 9:30am–5pm. Bus: 23, 81, 160, 280, or 628.

Vittoriano ★ MONUMENT   It's impossible to miss the white Brescian marble Vittorio Emanuele monument that dominates the corner where Via dei Fori Imperiali meets Piazza Venezia. The city's most flamboyant and frankly, disliked, landmark was built in the late 1800s to honor the first king of a united Italy. It has been compared to everything from a wedding cake to a Victorian typewriter, and has been ridiculed because of its harsh white color in a city of honey-gold tones. An eternal flame burns at the Tomb of the Unknown Soldier. For a panoramic view over the city, a glass elevator whisks you to the **Terrazza delle Quadrighe (Terrace of the Chariots) ★**.

Piazza Venezia. ℭ **06-6780664.** Admission to elevator 7€. Mon–Thurs 9:30am–5:45pm, Fri–Sun 9:30am–6:45pm. Bus: 53, 80, 85, 87, 175, 186, 271, 571, or 810.

Centro Storico & the Pantheon

CENTRO STORICO

Just across the Tiber from the Vatican and Castel Sant'Angelo lies the true heart of Rome, the **Centro Storico** or "historic center," roughly the triangular wedge of land that bulges into a bend of the river. Although the area lay outside the Roman city, it came into its own during the Renaissance, and today its streets and alleys are crammed with piazzas, elegant churches, and lavish fountains, all buzzing with scooters and people.

PIAZZA NAVONA & NEARBY ATTRACTIONS

Rome's most famous square, **Piazza Navona ★★★**, is a gorgeous baroque gem, lined with cafes and restaurants and often crammed with tourists, street artists, and pigeons by day and night. Its long, thin shape follows the contours of the old Roman Stadium of Domitian, where chariot races once took place, still a ruin until a mid–17th-century makeover by Pope Innocent X. The twin-towered facade of 17th-century **Sant'Agnese in Agone** lies on the piazza's western side, while the **Fontana dei Quattro Fiumi (Fountain of the Four Rivers) ★★★** opposite is one of three great fountains in the square, this one a typically exuberant creation of Bernini, topped with an Egyptian obelisk. The four stone personifications below symbolize the world's greatest rivers: the Ganges, Danube, River Plate, and Nile. It's fun to try to figure out which is which. (**Hint:** The figure with the shroud on its head is the Nile, so represented because the river's source was unknown at the time.) At the south end is the **Fontana del Moro (Fountain of the Moor),** also by

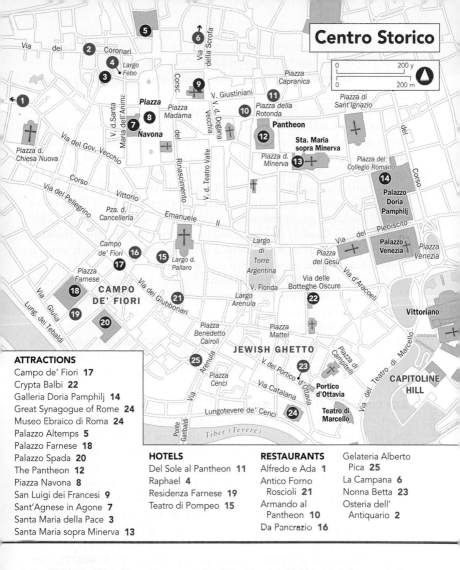

Centro Storico

Bernini; the **Fontana di Nettuno (Fountain of Neptune)** is a 19th-century addition.

　　Art lovers should make the short walk from the piazza to **Santa Maria della Pace** ★★ on Arco della Pace, a 15th-century church given the usual baroque makeover by Pietro da Cortona in the 1660s. The real gems are inside, beginning with Raphael's **"Four Sibyls"** ★★ fresco, above the arch of the Capella Chigi, and the **Chiostro del Bramante (Bramante cloister)** ★, built between 1500 and 1504 and the first work of the Renaissance master in the city. The church is normally open on Monday, Wednesday, and Saturday from 9am to noon, while the cloister opens Tuesday to

Sunday from 10am to 8pm. The church is free, but admission to the cloister, which hosts temporary art exhibitions, costs 10€.

Palazzo Altemps ★★ MUSEUM   Inside this 15th-century *palazzo*, today a branch of the National Museum of Rome, is one of Rome's most charming museums. It's rarely crowded yet houses some of Rome's most famous private and public art collections. The collection is small, but the works are individually superb; much of it was once part of the famed **Boncompagni Ludovisi Collection,** created by Cardinal Ludovico Ludovisi (1595–1632) and sold at auction in 1901.

Among the highlights is the **"Ludovisi Ares"** ★★, a handsome 2nd-century copy of a late 4th-century B.C. Greek statue of Mars (Ares to the Greeks). Equally renowned is the **"Ludovisi Gaul"** ★, a marble depiction of a Gaulish warrior plunging a sword into his chest, looking backwards defiantly as he supports a dying woman with his left arm—a 2nd-century Roman copy of a 3rd-century B.C. Hellenistic original. Also worth a look is the **"Ludovisi Throne,"** a sculpted block of white marble, thought to date from the 5th century B.C., depicting Aphrodite rising from the sea. Elsewhere the "Juno Ludovisi" is a massive, 1st-century marble head of the goddess Juno.

Piazza di Sant'Apollinare 46, near Piazza Navona. ℂ **06-39967700.** Admission 7€ (also valid at Palazzo Massimo alle Terme, Terme di Diocleziano, and Crypta Balbi for 3 days). Tues–Sun 9am–7:45pm. Last admission 1 hr. before closing. Bus: 30, 70, 81, 87, 130, 492, or 628.

San Luigi dei Francesi ★★ CHURCH   For a painter of such stratospheric standards as Caravaggio, it is impossible to be definitive in naming his "masterpiece." However, the **"Calling of St. Matthew"** ★★, in the far-left chapel of Rome's French church, must be a candidate. The panel dramatizes the moment Jesus and Peter "called" the customs officer to join them, in Caravaggio's distinct *chiaroscuro* (extreme light and shade) style. Around the same time (1599–1602) Caravaggio also painted the other two St. Matthew panels in the Capella Contarelli—including one depicting the saint's martyrdom. Other highlights inside include Domenichino's masterful "Histories of Saint Cecilia" fresco cycle.

Via di Santa Giovanna d'Arco 5. www.saintlouis-rome.net. ℂ **06-688271.** Free admission. Mon–Wed and Fri–Sat 10am–12:30pm and 3–7pm; Thurs 10am–12:30pm; Sun 3–7pm. Bus: C3, 30, 70, 81, 87, 116, 186, 492, or 628.

THE PANTHEON & NEARBY ATTRACTIONS

The Pantheon stands on **Piazza della Rotonda,** a lively square with cafes, vendors, and great people-watching.

The Pantheon ★★★ HISTORIC SITE   Of all ancient Rome's great buildings, only the Pantheon ("Temple to All the Gods") remains intact. It was originally built in 27 B.C. by Marcus Agrippa but was entirely reconstructed by Hadrian in the early 2nd century A.D. This remarkable building, 43m (142 ft.) wide and 43m (142 ft.) high (a perfect sphere resting in a cylinder) is among the architectural wonders of the world, even today. Hadrian himself is credited with the basic plan, an architectural design that was unique for the time. There are no visible arches or vaults holding up the dome; instead they're sunk into the concrete of the building's walls. The ribbed dome outside is a series of almost weightless cantilevered bricks.

Animals were once sacrificed and burned in the center, with the smoke escaping through the only means of light, the oculus, an opening at the top 5.5m (18 ft.) in diameter. The interior would have been richly decorated, with white marble statues of Roman gods ringing the central space in its niches. Nowadays, apart from the jaw-dropping size of the space, the main things of interest are the tombs of two Italian kings (Vittorio Emanuele II and his successor, Umberto I), and the resting place of **Raphael** (fans still bring him flowers), between the second and third chapel on the left. The Pantheon has been used as a Catholic church since the 7th century, the **Santa Maria ad Martyres,** but informally known as "Santa Maria della Rotonda."

Piazza della Rotonda. ℂ **06-68300230.** Free admission. Mon–Sat 8:30am–7:30pm; Sun 9am–6pm. Mass Sat 5pm, Sun 10:30am (only Mass attendees allowed to enter at these times). Bus: 30, 40, 62, 64, 81, or 492 to Largo di Torre Argentina.

Santa Maria sopra Minerva ★ CHURCH   Just 1 block behind the Pantheon, Santa Maria sopra Minerva is Rome's most significant Dominican church and the only significant Gothic church downtown. True, the facade is in the Renaissance style (the church was begun in 1280 but worked on until 1725), but inside, the arched vaulting is pure Gothic. The main art treasures here are the "Statua del Redentore" (1521), a statue of Christ by **Michelangelo** (just to the left of the altar), and a wonderful fresco cycle in the **Cappella Carafa** (on the right before the altar), created by Filippino Lippi between 1488 and 1493 to honor St. Thomas Aquinas. Devout Catholics flock to the venerated tomb of **Saint Catherine of Siena** under the high altar—the room where she died in 1380 was reconstructed behind the Sacristy by Antonio Barberini in 1637 (far left corner of the church). **Fra' Angelico,** the Dominican friar and painter, also rests here, in the **Cappella Frangipane e Maddaleni-Capiferro** (to the left of the altar).

Piazza della Minerva 42. www.basilicaminerva.it. ℂ **06-69920384.** Free admission. Daily 8am–7pm. Bus: 116.

Crypta Balbi ★ MUSEUM/RUINS   The newest and perhaps most intriguing of all the branches of the National Museum of Rome, the Crypta Balbi houses the archeological remains of the vast portico belonging to the 1st-century B.C. **Theatre of Lucius Cornelius Balbus,** discovered here in 1981. The ground floor's exhibits chronicle the history of the site through to the medieval period and the construction of the Conservatorio di Santa Caterina della Rosa. The second floor ("Rome from Antiquity to the Middle Ages") explores the transformation of the city between the 5th and 9th centuries, using thousands of ceramic objects, coins, lead seals, bone and ivory implements, precious stones, and tools found on the site.

Via delle Botteghe Oscure 31. www.archeoroma.beniculturali.it. ✆ **06-39967700.** Admission 7€ adults (also valid for Palazzo Massimo alle Terme, Palazzo Altemps, and Terme di Diocleziano for 3 days). Tues–Sun 9am–7:45pm. Bus: 30, 40, 64, 70, 87, 190, 271, 492, 571, 810, or 916.

Galleria Doria Pamphilj ★★ ART MUSEUM   One of the city's finest rococo palaces, the Palazzo Doria Pamphilj is still privately owned by the aristocratic Doria Pamphilj family, but their stupendous art collection is open to the public. Make sure you grab a free audio tour at the entrance.

The *galleria* extends through the old apartments, the paintings displayed floor-to-ceiling among antique furniture, drapes, and richly decorated walls. The Dutch and Flemish collection is especially strong, with highlights including a rare Italian work by Pieter Brueghel the Elder, "Battle in the Port of Naples," and his son Jan Brueghel the Elder's "Earthly Paradise with Original Sin." Among the best Italian works are two paintings by Caravaggio, the moving "Repentant Magdalene" and his wonderful "Rest on the Flight into Egypt," hanging near "Salome with the Head of St. John," by Titian. There's also Raphael's "Double Portrait," an "Annunciation" by Filippo Lippi, and a "Deposition from the Cross" by Vasari. The gallery's real treasures, however, occupy a special room: Bernini's bust of the Pamphilj **"Pope Innocent X"** ★, and **Velázquez's celebrated, enigmatic painting** ★★ of the same man.

Via del Corso 305 (just north of Piazza Venezia). www.dopart.it. ✆ **06-6797323.** Admission 11€ adults, 7.50€ students. Daily 9am–7pm, last admission 6pm. Bus: 64 to Piazza Venezia.

CAMPO DE' FIORI

The southern section of the Centro Storico, **Campo de' Fiori** is another neighborhood of narrow streets, small piazzas, and ancient churches. Its main focus remains the piazza of **Campo de' Fiori** ★ itself, whose workaday fruit and veg stalls are a real contrast to the cafes and street entertainers of Piazza Navona. An excessively expensive (and often low-quality) open-air food market runs Monday through Saturday from early in the morning until around 2pm, or whenever the food runs out. From the center of the piazza rises a statue of the severe-looking monk **Giordano Bruno,** whose presence is a reminder that heretics were occasionally burned at the stake here: Bruno was executed by the Inquisition in 1600. Curiously this is the only *piazza* in Rome that doesn't have a church in its perimeter.

Built from 1514 to 1589, the **Palazzo Farnese** ★, on Piazza Farnese just to the south of the Campo, was designed by Sangallo and Michelangelo, among others, and was an astronomically expensive project for the time. Its famous residents have included a 16th-century member of the Farnese family, plus Pope Paul III, Cardinal Richelieu, and the former Queen Christina of Sweden, who moved to Rome after abdicating. During the 1630s, when the heirs couldn't afford to maintain the *palazzo*, it

Market stalls on the lively main square Campo de' Fiori.

was inherited by the Bourbon kings of Naples and was purchased by the French government in 1874; the French Embassy is still located here, so the building is closed to the general public. For the best view of it, cut west from Via Giulia along any of the narrow streets—we recommend Via Mascherone or Via dei Farnesi.

Palazzo Spada ★ MUSEUM Built around 1540 for Cardinal Gerolamo Capo di Ferro, Palazzo Spada was purchased by the eponymous Cardinal Spada in 1632, who then hired Borromini to restore it—most of what you see today dates from that period. Its richly ornate facade, covered in high-relief stucco decorations in the Mannerist style, is the finest of any building from 16th-century Rome. The State Rooms are closed (the Italian Council of State still meets here), but the richly decorated courtyard and corridor, Borromini's masterful illusion of perspective *(la prospettiva di Borromini),* and the four rooms of the **Galleria Spada** are open to the public. Inside you will find some absorbing paintings, such as the "Portrait of Cardinale Bernardino Spada" by Guido Reni, and Titian's "Portrait of a Violinist," plus minor works from Caravaggio, Parmigianino, Pietro Testa, and Giambattista Gaulli.

Piazza Capo di Ferro 13. © **06-6874893.** Admission 5€. Tues–Sun 8:30am–7:30pm. Bus 46, 56, 62, 64, 70, 87, or 492.

THE JEWISH GHETTO

The southern part of Campo de' Fiori merges into the old **Jewish Ghetto,** established near the River Tiber by a Papal Bull in 1555, which required all the Jews in Rome to live in one area. Walled in, overcrowded, prone to floods and epidemics, and on some of the worst land in the city, it was an extremely grim place to live. After the Ghetto was abolished in

101

1882, its walls were finally torn down and the area largely reconstructed. Today the **Via Portico d'Ottavia** lies at the heart of a flourishing Jewish Quarter, with Romans flocking here to soak up the festive atmosphere and sample the Roman-Jewish and Middle Eastern food.

The **Great Synagogue of Rome** (Tempio Maggiore di Roma; www.romaebraica.it; © **06-6840061**) was built from 1901 to 1904 in an eclectic style evoking Babylonian and Persian temples. The synagogue was attacked by terrorists in 1982 and since then has been heavily guarded by *carabinieri,* a division of the Italian police armed with machine guns.

Museo Ebraico di Roma (Jewish Museum of Rome) ★ MUSEUM
On the premises of the Great Synagogue of Rome, this museum chronicles the history of not only Roman Jews but Jews from all over Italy. There are displays of works of 17th- and 18th-century Roman silversmiths, precious textiles from all over Europe, and a number of parchments and marble carvings that were saved when the Ghetto's original synagogues were demolished. Admission includes a guided English-language tour of the synagogue.

Via Catalana. www.museoebraico.roma.it. © **06-6840061.** Admission 11€ adults, 4€ for students, free for children 10 and under. Mid-June to mid-Sept Sun–Thurs 10am–7pm and Fri 10am–4pm; rest of year Sun–Thurs 10am–5pm and Fri 9am–2pm.

The Tridente & the Spanish Steps

The northern half of central Rome is known as the **Tridente** thanks to the trident shape formed by three roads—Via di Ripetta, Via del Corso, and Via del Babuino—leading down from **Piazza del Popolo.** The area around **Piazza di Spagna** and the **Spanish Steps** was once the artistic quarter of the city, attracting English poets Keats and Shelley, German author Goethe, and Italian film director Federico Fellini (who lived on Via Margutta). Institutions such as Caffè Greco and Babington's Tea Rooms are still here (see p. 141), though you will be lucky to see any artists today through the throngs of tourists and shoppers.

PIAZZA DEL POPOLO

Elegant **Piazza del Popolo** ★★ is haunted with memories. According to legend, the ashes of Nero were enshrined here, until 11th-century residents began complaining to the pope about his imperial ghost. The **Egyptian obelisk** dates from the 13th century B.C.; it was removed from Heliopolis to Rome during Augustus's reign (it once stood at the Circus Maximus).

The current piazza was designed in the early 19th century by Valadier, Napoleon's architect. Standing astride the three roads that form the "trident" are almost-twin baroque churches, **Santa Maria dei Miracoli** (1681) and **Santa Maria di Montesanto** (1679). The stand-out church, however, is across from them, at the piazza's northern curve: the 15th-century **Santa Maria del Popolo** ★★, with its splendid baroque

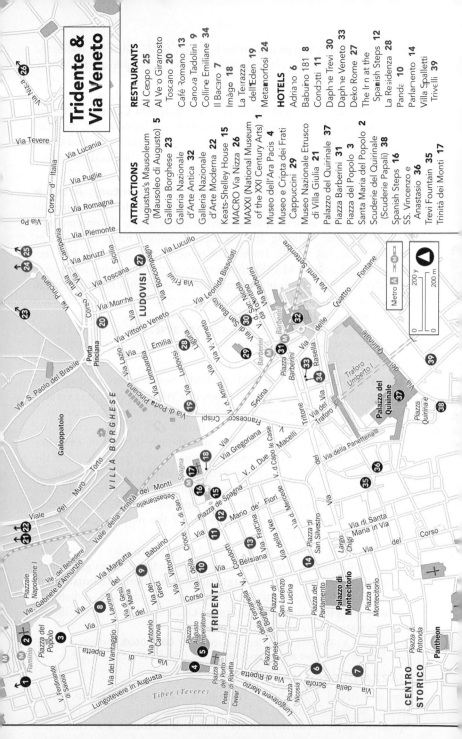

Tridente & Via Veneto

ATTRACTIONS

Augustus's Mausoleum (Mausoleo di Augusto) **5**
Galleria Borghese **23**
Galleria Nazionale d'Arte Antica **32**
Galleria Nazionale d'Arte Moderna **22**
Keats-Shelley House **15**
MACRO Via Nizza **26**
MAXXI (National Museum of the XXI Century Arts) **1**
Museo dell'Ara Pacis **4**
Museo e Cripta dei Frati Cappuccini **29**
Museo Nazionale Etrusco di Villa Giulia **21**
Palazzo del Quirinale **31**
Piazza Barberini **31**
Piazza del Popolo **3**
Santa Maria del Popolo **2**
Scuderie del Quirinale (Scuderie Papali) **38**
Spanish Steps **16**
SS. Vincenzo e Anastasio **36**
Trevi Fountain **35**
Trinità dei Monti **17**

RESTAURANTS

Al Ceppo **25**
Al Ve o Girarrosto Toscano **20**
Café Romano **13**
Canova Tadolini **9**
Colline Emiliane **34**
Il Bacaro **7**
Imàgo **18**
La Terrazza dell'Eden **19**
Metamorfosi **24**

HOTELS

Adria no **6**
Babuino 181 **8**
Condotti **11**
Daphne Trevi **30**
Daphne Veneto **33**
Deko Rome **27**
The Inn at the Spanish Steps **12**
La Residenza **28**
Panda **10**
Parlamento **14**
Villa Spalletti **Trivelli 39**

Metro A [] M []

200 y
200 m

103

facade modified by the great Bernini between 1655 and 1660. Inside the church, look for Raphael's mosaic series the "Creation of the World" adorning the interior dome of the **Capella Chigi** (the second chapel on the left). **Pinturicchio** decorated the main choir vault with frescoes such as the "Coronation of the Virgin." The **Capella Cerasi** (to the left of the high altar) contains gorgeous examples of baroque art: an altarpiece painting of "The Assumption of Mary" by Carracci, and on either side two great works by Caravaggio, "Conversion on the Road to Damascus" and "The Crucifixion of Saint Peter."

MAXXI (National Museum of the XXI Century Arts) ★

MUSEUM   Ten minutes north of Piazza del Popolo by tram, you leave the Renaissance far behind at MAXXI, a masterpiece of contemporary architecture with bending and overlapping oblong tubes designed by Anglo-Iraqi architect Zaha Hadid. The museum is divided into two sections, MAXXI art and MAXXI architecture, primarily serving as a venue for temporary exhibitions of contemporary work in both fields (although it does have a small and growing permanent collection). The building is worth a visit in its own right.

Via Guido Reni 4a. www.fondazionemaxxi.it. ✆ **06-39967350.** Admission 11€, free children 13 and under. Tues–Fri and Sun 11am–7pm; Sat 11am–10pm. Metro: Flaminio, then tram 2.

Museo dell'Ara Pacis ★★ MUSEUM

Set in a very modern glass building, which you can explore for free, the "Altar of Peace" was created in 9 B.C. to honor the achievements of (soon-to-be-Emperor) Augustus in subduing tribes north of the Alps. The marble Altar of Peace temple-like monument was later lost to memory, and though signs of its existence were discovered in the 16th century, it wasn't until the 1930s that the ancient monument was fully excavated. After World War II it lay virtually abandoned until the 1970s, but true restoration began in the 1980s. The current museum building containing it, finished in 2006 to a design by American architect Richard Meier, is one of the most poignant showcases of Imperial Rome.

The exhibit complex housing the *Ara Pacis* provides context, with interactive displays in English and Italian. Note that you get great views of the huge, overgrown ruin of **Augustus's Mausoleum (Mausoleo di Augusto)** from here, but the 1st-century B.C. tomb itself—where the ashes of emperors Augustus, Caligula, Claudius, Nerva, and Tiberius were once stored—is closed to the public.

Lungotevere in Augusta. http://en.arapacis.it. ✆ **06-060608.** Admission 8.50€. Tues–Sun 9am–7pm (last admission 6pm). Bus: C3, 70, 81, 87, 186, 492, 628, or 913.

PIAZZA DI SPAGNA

The undoubted highlight of Tridente is **Piazza di Spagna,** which attracts hordes of Romans and tourists alike to lounge on its celebrated **Spanish Steps (Scalinata della Trinità dei Monti) ★★**, the largest

Tourists gather on the Spanish steps.

stairway in Europe, and enjoy the view onto Bernini's "Fontana della Barcaccia," a fountain shaped like an old boat. The Steps are especially enchanting in early spring, when they become framed by thousands of blooming azaleas, but they are heaving with flower dealers, trinket sellers, and photographers year-round.

In an odd twist, the monumental stairway of 135 steps and the square take their names from the Spanish Embassy (it used to be headquartered here), but were actually funded, almost entirely, by the French. That's because the Trinità dei Monti church at the top was under the patronage of the Bourbon kings of France at the time. They were built from 1723 to 1725.

Trinità dei Monti itself is a 16th-century church with a stately baroque facade perched photogenically at the top of the Steps, behind yet another Roman obelisk, the "Obelisco Sallustiano." It's worth climbing up just for the views. Inside, the artistic highlights include works by Daniele da Volterra, a pupil of Michelangelo, notably a fresco of the "Assumption" in the third chapel on the right; the last figure on the right is said to be a portrait of the maestro himself. In the second chapel on the left is Volterra's critically acclaimed "Deposition" in monochrome, which imitates a sculpture by clever use of *trompe l'oeil*.

Keats-Shelley House ★ MUSEUM   At the foot of the Spanish Steps is the 18th-century house where the Romantic English poet John Keats died of consumption on February 23, 1821 at age 25. Since 1909, when it was bought by well-intentioned English and American literary types, it has been a working library established in honor of Keats and fellow Romantic Percy Bysshe Shelley, who drowned off the coast of Viareggio with a copy of Keats' works in his pocket. Mementos range from kitsch to extremely moving. The apartment where Keats spent his last months, tended by his close friend Joseph Severn, shelters a death mask of Keats as well as the "deadly sweat" drawing by Severn. Both Keats and Shelley are buried in their beloved Rome, at the Protestant cemetery near the Pyramid of Cestius, in Testaccio (p. 147).
Piazza di Spagna 26. www.keats-shelley-house.org. ✆ **06-6784235.** Admission 5€. Mon–Sat 10am–1pm and 2–6pm. Metro: Spagna.

Palazzo del Quirinale ★★ HISTORIC SITE   Until the end of World War II, this palace was home of the king of Italy; before the crown resided here, it was the summer residence of the pope. Since 1946 the palace has been the official residence of the President of Italy, but parts of it are open to the public on Sunday mornings.

Although it can't compare to Rome's major artistic showstoppers (there's little art or furniture in the rooms), the palace's baroque and neo-classical walls and ceilings are quite a spectacle. Few rooms anywhere are as impressive as the richly decorated 17th-century **Salone dei Corazzieri,** the **Sala d'Ercole** (once the apartments of Umberto I but completely rebuilt in 1940), and the tapestry-covered 17th-century **Sala dello Zodiaco.** Despite its Renaissance origins (nearly every important architect in Italy worked on some aspect of its sprawling premises), this *palazzo* is rich in associations with ancient emperors and deities. The colossal statues of the "Dioscuri," Castor and Pollux, which now form part of the fountain in the piazza, were found in the nearby Baths of Constantine; in 1793 Pius VI had an ancient Egyptian obelisk moved here from the Mausoleum of Augustus. The sweeping view of the city from the piazza, which crowns the highest of the seven ancient hills of Rome, is itself worth the trip.

Piazza del Quirinale. www.quirinale.it. © **06-46991.** Admission 5€, free ages 17 and under and 65 and over. Sun 8:30am–noon. Closed late June to early Sept. Metro: Barberini.

Trevi Fountain (Fontana di Trevi) ★★ MONUMENT   As you elbow your way through the summertime crowds around the **Trevi Fountain,** you'll find it hard to believe that this little piazza was nearly always deserted before 1950, when it began "starring" in films. The first was *Three Coins in the Fountain,* and later it was the setting for an iconic scene in Federico Fellini's 1960 masterpiece *La Dolce Vita.* It was also also where Audrey Hepburn's character in *Roman Holiday* gets her signature haircut. To this day, thousands of euros worth of coins are tossed into the fountain every day.

Supplied with water from the Acqua Vergine aqueduct and a triumph of the baroque style, the fountain was based on the design of Nicola Salvi and was completed in 1762. The design centers on the triumphant figure of Neptune, standing on a shell chariot drawn by winged steeds and led by a pair of tritons. Two allegorical figures in the side niches represent good health and fertility. The fountain is currently undergoing restoration, with completion scheduled for Autumn 2015.

On the southwestern corner of the piazza is an unimpressive church, **SS. Vincenzo e Anastasio,** with a strange claim to fame. Within it survive the relics (hearts and intestines) of several popes.

Piazza di Trevi. Metro: Barberini.

Villa Borghese & Parioli

Villa Borghese ★★, in the heart of Rome, is not actually a villa but one of Europe's most elegant parks, 6km (3¾ miles) in circumference. It provides access to the Galleria Borghese in the former Villa Borghese Pinciana (which really is a villa). Cardinal Scipione Borghese created the park in the 1600s. Umberto I, king of Italy, acquired it in 1902 and presented it to the city of Rome. With landscaped vistas, the heart-shaped greenbelt is crisscrossed by roads, but you can escape from the traffic and seek a shaded area under a tree to enjoy a picnic or relax. On a sunny weekend, it's a pleasure to stroll here and see Romans at play, relaxing or inline skating. There are a few casual cafes and some food vendors. You can also rent bikes or segways here. In the northeast area of the park is a conservation zoo; the park is also home to a few outstanding museums.

Galleria Borghese ★★★ ART MUSEUM   On the far northeastern edge of the Villa Borghese, the Galleria Borghese occupies the former Villa Borghese Pinciana, built between 1609 and 1613 for Cardinal Scipione Borghese, an early patron of Bernini and an astute collector of work by Caravaggio. Today the gallery displays much of his collection and a lot more besides, making this one of Rome's great art treasures. It's also one of Rome's most pleasant sights to tour, thanks to the curators' mandate that only a limited number of people be allowed in at any one time (see the last paragraph of this section for more on that).

The ground floor is a **sculpture gallery** par extraordinaire, housing Canova's famously risqué statue of Paolina Borghese, sister of Napoleon and wife of the reigning Prince Camillo Borghese (when asked if she was uncomfortable posing nude, she reportedly replied, "No, the studio was heated."). The genius of Bernini reigns supreme in the following rooms, with his "David" (the face of which is thought to be a self-portrait), and his **"Apollo and Daphne" ★★** seminal works of baroque sculpture. Look out also for Bernini's Mannerist sculpture next door, "The Rape of Persephone." Caravaggio is represented by the "Madonna of the Grooms," his shadowy "St. Jerome," and his frightening **"David Holding the Head of Goliath" ★★**.

Upstairs lies a rich collection of paintings, including Raphael's ultra-graceful "Deposition" and his sinuous "Lady with a Unicorn." There's also a series of self-portraits by Bernini, and his lifelike busts of Cardinal Scipione and Pope Paul V. One of Titian's best, **"Sacred and Profane Love" ★**, lies in one of the final rooms. Guided tours of the galleries in English (5€) run 9:10am to 11:10am, but failing that opt for the

audioguides, as English labeling in the museum is minimal. No photographs are allowed inside the museum.

Important information: No more than 360 visitors at a time are allowed on the ground floor, and no more than 90 are allowed on the upper floor, during set 2-hour windows. **Reservations are essential,** so call ✆ **06-32810** (Mon–Fri 9am–6pm; Sat 9am–1pm). You can also make reservations by visiting **www.tosc.it**, or by stopping by in person on your first day to reserve tickets for a later date. If you are having problems making a reservation in advance, ask your hotel to help out.

Piazzale del Museo Borghese 5 (off Via Pinciana). www.galleriaborghese.it. ✆ **06-8413979.** Admission 11€ plus 2€ mandatory "service charge." Audioguides 5€. Tues–Sun 8:30am–7:30pm. Bus: 5, 19, 52, 116, 204, 490, or 910.

MACRO Via Nizza ★★ MUSEUM   Rome's contemporary art museum was recently expanded to occupy an entire block of early-1900s industrial buildings, formerly the Peroni beer factory, located near the Porta Pia gate of the Aurelian walls. Designed by French architect Odile Decq, the museum hosts contemporary art exhibits with edgy installations, visuals, events, and multimedia screenings. Another branch of the museum is housed in a converted slaughterhouse in Testaccio (p. 147).

Via Nizza 138. www.museomacro.org. ✆ **06-671070400.** Admission 14.50€ (combined ticket with MACRO Testaccio). Tues–Sun 10:30am–7:30pm. Last admission 30 min. before closing. Bus: 38, 89. Tram: 3, 19.

Museo Carlo Bilotti ★ ART MUSEUM   Fans of Greek-born Italian artist **Giorgio de Chirico** should make a pilgrimage to this small modern art gallery, created thanks to the generosity of Carlo Bilotti, an Italian-American collector who donated 23 artworks to Rome in 2006. Though long overshadowed by the more famous Surrealists, De Chirico was a major influence on the Surrealist movement in the early 20th century—the themes of loneliness and isolation explored in his "metaphysical" paintings can be compared to American artist Edward Hopper.

Housed in a 16th-century palace in the Villa Borghese, the museum consists of two small rooms, and though the work is good, we recommend it for art aficionados only. Works to look out for include the elegant "Portrait of Tina and Lisa Bilotti" by Andy Warhol, a rare restrained piece by the Pop Art master, and Larry Rivers' depiction of Carlo Bilotti himself. De Chirico dominates Room 2, with 17 paintings representing all his memorable themes from the second half of the 1920s through to the 1970s. Here also is the beguiling "Summer," an abstract work by Tuscan Gino Severini.

Villa Borghese, at Viale Fiorello La Guardia. www.museocarlobilotti.it. ✆ **06-0608.** Admission free. June–Sept Tues–Fri 1–7pm; Oct–May Tues–Fri 10am–4pm. Metro: Flaminio.

Museo Nazionale Etrusco di Villa Giulia (National Etruscan Museum) ★★★ MUSEUM   The great Etruscan civilization was one of Italy's most advanced, although it remains relatively mysterious, in part because of its centuries-long rivalry with Rome. Once Rome had absorbed the Etruscans in the 3rd century B.C., the Romans set about eradicating all evidence of the Etruscans' achievements, as they did with most of the peoples they conquered

Today this museum, housed in the handsome Renaissance Villa Giulia, built by Pope Julius III between 1550 and 1555, is the best place in Italy to learn about the Etruscans, thanks to a cache of precious artifacts, sculptures, vases, monuments, tools, weapons, and jewels. Fans of ancient history could spend several hours here, but for those with less time, here's a quick list of the unmissable sights: The most striking attraction is the stunning **Sarcofago degli Sposi (Sarcophagus of the Spouses)** ★★, a late 6th-century B.C. terracotta funerary monument featuring a life-sized bride and groom, supposedly lounging at a banquet in the afterlife (there's a similar monument in Paris's Louvre). Equally fascinating are the **Pyrgi Tablets,** gold-leaf inscriptions in both Etruscan and Phoenician from the 5th century B.C., and the **Apollo of Veii,** a huge painted terracotta statue of Apollo dating to the 6th century B.C. The **Euphronios Krater** is also housed here, a renowned and perfectly maintained red-figured Greek vase from the 6th century B.C., which returned home from the New York Met after a long legal battle won by Italy in 2006.

Piazzale di Villa Giulia 9. www.villagiulia.beniculturali.it. ✆ **06-3226571.** Admission 8€. Tues–Sun 8:30am–7:30pm. Bus: 926. Tram: 3, 19.

Galleria Nazionale d'Arte Moderna (National Gallery of Modern Art) ★ ART MUSEUM   Housed in the monumental Bazzani Building, constructed for the exhibition celebrating the 50th anniversary of "United Italy" in 1911, this "modern" art collection ranges from unfashionable neoclassical and Romantic paintings and sculpture to better 20th-century works. Quality varies, but fans should seek out van Gogh's "Gardener" and "Portrait of Madame Ginoux" in Room 15, the handful of Impressionists in Room 14 (Cézanne, Degas, Monet, and Rodin), and Klimt's harrowing "Three Ages" in Room 16. Surrealist and Expressionist works by Miró, Kandinsky, and Mondrian appear in Room 22, and Pollock's "Undulating Paths" and Calder's "Mobile" hold court in Room 27. One of Warhol's "Hammer and Sickle" series is tucked away in Room 30.

Frankly, the museum is primarily a showcase for **modern Italian painters,** a group inevitably laboring under the mighty shadow of their Renaissance and baroque forebears, but talented nonetheless. Be sure to check out especially the rooms dedicated to Giacomo Balla (no. 34), Giacomo Manzù (no. 35), Renato Guttuso (no. 37), and Pino Pascali (no. 40).

Viale delle Belle Arti 131. www.gnam.beniculturali.it. ✆ **06-322981.** Admission 8€, free children 17 and under. Tues–Sun 8:30am–7:30pm. Bus: 88, 95, 490, or 495.

Via Veneto & Piazza Barberini

Piazza Barberini lies at the foot of several Roman streets, among them Via Barberini, Via Sistina, and Via Vittorio Veneto. It would be a far more pleasant spot were it not for the heavy traffic swarming around its principal feature, Bernini's **Fountain of the Triton (Fontana del Tritone)** ★. For more than 3 centuries, the strange figure sitting in a vast open clam has been blowing water from his triton. Off to one side of the piazza is the aristocratic side facade of the **Palazzo Barberini,** named for one of Rome's powerful families; inside is the **Galleria Nazionale d'Arte Antica** (see below). The Renaissance Barberini reached their peak when a son was elected pope as Urban VIII; he encouraged Bernini and gave him patronage.

As you walk up **Via Vittorio Veneto,** look for the small fountain on the right corner of Piazza Barberini—it's another Bernini, the **Fountain of the Bees (Fontana delle Api).** At first they look more like flies, but they're the bees of the Barberini, the crest of that powerful family complete with the crossed keys of St. Peter above them. (Keys were always added to a family crest when a son was elected pope.)

Museo e Cripta dei Frati Cappuccini (Museum and Crypt of the Capuchin Friars) ★★ RELIGIOUS SITE/MUSEUM

One of the most mesmerizingly macabre sights in all Christendom, this otherwise modest museum dedicated to the Capuchin order ends with a series of six chapels in the crypt, adorned with thousands of skulls and bones woven into mosaic "works of art." To make this allegorical dance of death, the bones of more than 3,700 Capuchin brothers were used. Some of the skeletons are intact, draped with Franciscan habits. The creator of this chamber of horrors? The tradition of the friars is that it was the work of a French Capuchin. Their literature suggests that you should consider the historical context of its origins, a period when Christians had a rich and creative cult of the dead and great spiritual masters meditated and preached with a skull in hand. But whatever you believe, the experience is undeniably spooky (you can take photographs). The entrance is halfway up the first staircase on the right of the church of the Convento dei Frati Cappuccini, completed in 1630 and rebuilt in the early 1930s.

Beside the Convento dei Frati Cappuccini, Via Vittorio Veneto 27. www.cappuccini viaveneto.it. © **06-88803695.** Admission 6€, 4€ ages 17 and under. Daily 9am–7pm, last admission 6:30pm. Metro: Barberini.

Galleria Nazionale d'Arte Antica (National Gallery of Ancient Art) ★★ ART MUSEUM

On the southern side of **Piazza Barberini,** the grand **Palazzo Barberini** houses the Galleria Nazionale d'Arte Antica, a trove of Italian art from primarily the early Renaissance to late baroque periods. Some of the art on display is wonderful, but the building itself is the main attraction, a baroque masterpiece begun by Carlo Maderno in 1627 and completed in 1633 by Bernini, with additional work by Borromini (notably a whimsical spiral staircase). The **Salone di Pietro da Cortona** in the center is the most captivating space, with a *trompe l'oeil* ceiling frescoed by Pietro da Cortona, a depiction of "The Triumph of Divine Providence."

The initial galleries on the lower two floors cover the early Renaissance, with some modest crowd-pleasers such as Piero di Cosimo's "St. Mary Magdalene" (Room 10). But most of the devotional work will appeal strictly to aficionados. Beyond these first galleries lies the core of the museum, covering the High Renaissance and baroque periods, which has more intriguing works, including Raphael's "La Fornarina," a baker's daughter thought to have been the artist's mistress (look for Raphael's name on the woman's bracelet); paintings by Tintoretto and Titian (Room 15); a portrait of English King Henry VIII by Holbein (Room 16); and a couple of typically unsettling El Grecos in Room 17, "The Baptism of Christ" and "Adoration of the Shepherds." Caravaggio dominates room 20 with the justly celebrated "Judith and Holofernes" and **"Narcissus" ★★**.

The newer galleries on the top floor cover the less fashionable late baroque era, featuring the work of painters such as Luca Giordano (Room 25) and other Neapolitans. Bernini's "Portrait of Urban VIII" certainly stands out in Room 26. If you run out of time, you can skip the final galleries (they cover the even less appealing late 17th and 18th c.), although the classic Venetian scenes by Canaletto (Room 30) are always a pleasure.

Via delle Quattro Fontane 13. www.galleriabarberini.beniculturali.it. © **06-4814591.** Admission 7€; combined with Palazzo Corsini 9€. Tues–Sun 8:30am–7pm; last admission 6pm. Metro: Barberini.

Around Stazione Termini

Palazzo Massimo alle Terme ★★ MUSEUM   A third of Rome's assortment of ancient art can be found at this branch of the Museo Nazionale Romano; among its treasures are a major coin collection, extensive maps of trade routes (with audio and visual exhibits on the network of traders over the centuries), and a vast sculpture collection that includes portrait busts of emperors and their families, as well as mythical figures like the Minotaur and Athena. But the real draw is on the second floor, where you can see some of the oldest of Rome's **frescoes ★★**; they depict an entire garden, complete with plants and birds, from the Villa di Livia a Prima Porta. (Livia was the wife of Emperor Augustus and was deified after her death in A.D. 29.)

Largo di Villa Peretti. www.archeoroma.beniculturali.it. © **06-39967700.** Admission 7€; ticket valid for Terme di Diocleziano (see below), Palazzo Altemps (p. 98) and Crypta Balbi (p. 99). Tues–Sun 9am–7:45pm. Last admission 1 hr. before closing. Metro: Termini or Repubblica.

Santa Maria della Vittoria ★ CHURCH   This pretty little baroque church has the classic Roman travertine facade and an ornate interior. But a visit here is all about one artwork: Gian Lorenzo Bernini's **"Ecstasy of St. Teresa" ★★★**. Crafted from marble between 1644 and 1647, it shows the Spanish saint at the moment of her ecstatic encounter with an angel (the so-called "Transverberation"). To say Bernini's depiction is a

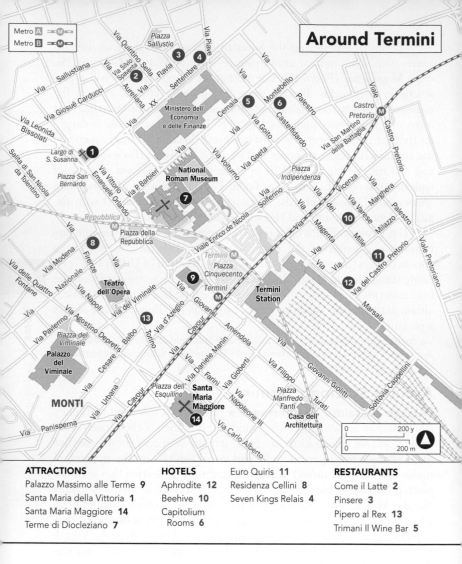

Metro B

Around Termini

little on the erotic side would be an understatement. The Cornaro family, who sponsored the chapel's construction, is depicted as witnesses to the moment from a "balcony" on the right.

Via XX Settembre 17 (at Largo S. Susanna). www.chiesasantamariavittoriaroma.it. ✆ **06-42740571.** Free admission. Mon–Sat 8:30am–noon and 3:30–6pm, Sun 3:30–6pm. Metro: Repubblica.

Santa Maria Maggiore (St. Mary Major) ★ CHURCH   This majestic church, one of Rome's four papal basilicas, was founded by Pope Liberius in A.D. 358 and rebuilt on the orders of Pope Sixtus III from 432 to 440. Its 14th-century **campanile** is the city's loftiest. Much doctored in the 18th century, the church's facade isn't an accurate reflection of the treasures inside. The basilica is noted for the 5th-century Roman mosaics in its nave, and for its coffered ceiling, said to have been gilded with gold brought from the New World. The church also contains the **tomb of Bernini,** Italy's most important baroque sculptor–architect. Ironically, the man who changed the face of Rome with his elaborate fountains is buried in a tomb so simple that it takes a sleuth to track it down (to the right, near the altar).

Piazza di Santa Maria Maggiore. ✆ **06-69886800.** Free admission. Daily 9am–7pm. Bus: C3, 16, 70, 71, 75, 360, 590, 649, 714, or 717.

Terme di Diocleziano (Baths of Diocletian) ★ MUSEUM/

RUINS   Roman recycling at its finest. Originally this spot held the largest of Rome's hedonistic baths (dating back to A.D. 298 and the reign of Emperor Diocletian) but during the Renaissance a church, a vast cloister, and a convent were built around and into the ruins—much of it designed by Michelangelo, no less. Today the entire hodgepodge is part of the Museo Nazionale Romano, and this juxtaposition of Christianity, ancient ruins, and exhibit space makes for a compelling museum stop that's usually quieter than the city's blockbusters. There's a large collection of inscriptions and other stone carvings from the Roman and pre-Roman periods, alongside statuary. Only Aula 10 remains of the vast baths, which accommodated 3,000 at a time when they opened in the early 4th century. The baths were abandoned in the 6th century, when invading Goth armies destroyed the city's aqueducts. *Note:* The museum is undergoing restoration and only sections may be open.

Viale E. di Nicola 78. www.archeoroma.beniculturali.it. ✆ **06-39967700.** Admission 7€; ticket valid for Palazzo Massimo alle Terme (see above), Palazzo Altemps (p. 98) and Crypta Balbi (p. 99). Tues–Sun 9am–7:45pm. Last admission 1 hr. before closing. Metro: Termini or Repubblica.

Trastevere

Galleria Nazionale d'Arte Antica in Palazzo Corsini ★ PALACE/

ART MUSEUM   Palazzo Corsini first found fame (or more accurately, notoriety) as the home of Queen Christina of Sweden. Christina moved to Rome when she abdicated the Swedish throne after converting to Catholicism, but her most famous epithet is "Queen without a realm, Christian without a faith, and a woman without shame," which stemmed from her open bisexuality, which in the 17th century was frowned upon—at least publicly. Several other big names stayed in this beautiful palace, including Michelangelo as well as Napoleon's mother, Letizia. Today one wing houses a moderately interesting museum with mostly the runoff from Italy's national art collection. Worth a look is Caravaggio's "St. John the Baptist" (1606), and panels by Luca Giordano, Fra' Angelico, and Poussin; otherwise the palace history and legend are more interesting than the museum itself.

Via della Lungara 10. www.galleriacorsini.beniculturali.it. ✆ **06-68802323.** Admission 5€, free for children 17 and under. Tues–Sun 8:30am–7:30pm. Bus: 125.

San Francesco d'Assisi a Ripa ★ CHURCH   This church was built on the site of a convent where St. Francis stayed when he came to Rome to see the pope in 1219. His simple cell is preserved inside. It is also yet another small Roman church with a Bernini treasure: The "Tomb of Beata Ludovica Albertoni" (1675) is unmistakably by the hand of the Roman baroque master, with its delicate folds of marble and the ecstatic expression on the face of its subject. Ludovica was a noblewoman who died in 1533 having dedicated her life to the city's poor. The sculpture is in the last chapel on the left.

Piazza di San Francesco d'Assisi 88. ℭ **06-5819020.** Free admission. Mon–Sat 10am–1pm and 2–6:30pm, Sun 2–6:30pm. Bus: 23, 44, 75, or 280.

Santa Cecilia in Trastevere ★ CHURCH   A still-functioning convent with a peaceful courtyard garden, Santa Cecilia contains the partial remains of a "Last Judgment," by Pietro Cavallini (ca. 1293), a masterpiece of Roman medieval painting. (Enter to the left of the main doors; a *suora* will accompany you upstairs to see it.) Inside the airy church is a late 13th-century baldacchino by Arnolfo di Cambio, over the altar. The church is built on the reputed site of Cecilia's long-ago palace, and for a small fee you can descend under the church to inspect the ruins of Roman houses, as well as peer through a gate at the stucco grotto beneath the altar.

Piazza Santa Cecilia 22. www.benedettinesantacecilia.it. ℭ **06-45492739.** Church free admission; Cavallini frescoes 2.50€; excavations 2.50€. Main church and excavations daily 9:30am–12:30pm and 4–6pm. Frescoes Mon–Sat 10am–12:30pm. Bus: H, 44, or 125/Tram 8.

Santa Maria in Trastevere ★ CHURCH   This ornate Romanesque church at the colorful heart of Trastevere was founded around A.D. 350 and is one of the oldest in Rome. The body was added around 1100, and the portico was added in the early 1700s. The restored mosaics on the apse date from around 1140, and below them are the 1293 mosaic scenes depicting the "Life of the Virgin Mary" by Pietro Cavallini. The faded mosaics on the facade are from the 12th or 13th century, and the octagonal fountain in the piazza is an ancient Roman original that was restored and added to in the 17th century by Carlo Fontana.

Piazza Santa Maria in Trastevere. ℭ **06-5814802.** Free admission. Daily 9:30am–12:30pm and 3–5:30pm. Bus: H or 125/Tram: 8.

Villa Farnesina ★ HISTORIC HOME   This place should never have been called the Villa Farnesina at all: It was originally built for Sienese banker Agostino Chigi in 1511, but it was acquired (and renamed) by the Farnese family in 1579. With two such wealthy Renaissance patrons, it's hardly surprising that the interior decor is top drawer. The villa's architect Baldassare Peruzzi began the decoration, with frescoes and motifs rich in myth and symbolism. He was later assisted by Sebastiano del Piombo, Sodoma, and, most notably, Raphael. Raphael's **"Loggia of Cupid and Psyche"** ★★ was frescoed to mark Chigi's marriage to

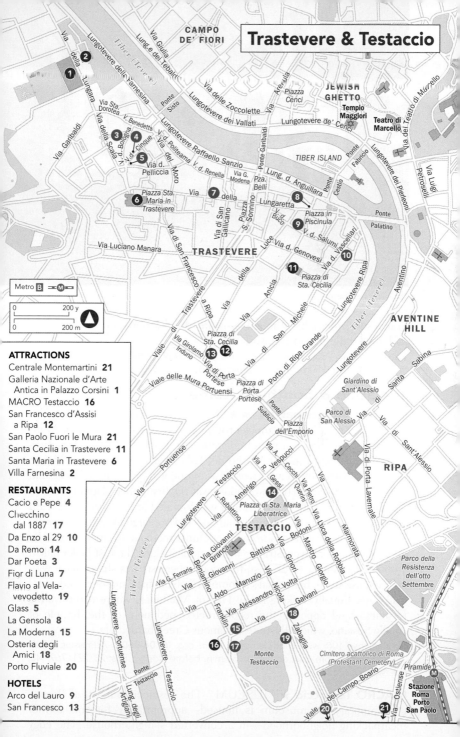

Trastevere & Testaccio

The streets of Trastevere.

Francesca Ordeaschi—though assistants Giulio Romano and Giovanna da Udine did much of the work.

Via della Lungara 230. www.villafarnesina.it. ✆ **06-68077268.** Admission 6€. Mon–Sat 9am–2pm; 2nd Sun of month 9am–5pm. Bus: 23, 125, 271, or 280.

Testaccio & Southern Rome

Centrale Montemartini ★★ MUSEUM The renovated boiler rooms of Rome's first thermoelectric plant, named after Giovanni Montemartini, now house a grand collection of Roman and Greek statues originally displayed in the Museo del Palazzo dei Conservatori, Museo Nuovo and Braccio Nuovo, creating a unique juxtaposition of classic and industrial archeology. The powerhouse was the first public plant to produce electricity for the city of Rome, and was founded at the turn of the 19th century on Via Ostiense, where it still occupies a large block between the ex-wholesale market, the Gazometro (defunct methane gas meter), and the bank of the Tiber River. Striking installations include the vast boiler hall, a 1,000-square-meter (10,764-sq.-ft.) room where statues share space with an immense steam boiler that's a complex web of pipes, masonry, and metal walkways. Equally striking is the Hall of Machines, where two towering turbines stand opposite the reconstructed pediment of the Temple of Apollo Sosiano, which illustrates a famous Greek battle.

Via Ostiense 106. www.centralemontemartini.org. ✆ **06-0608.** Admission 7.50€. Tues–Sun 9am–7pm. Last admission 30 min. before closing. Bus: 23, 271, 769, N2, N3. Metro: Garbatella.

MACRO Testaccio ★ MUSEUM The Testaccio outpost of Rome's contemporary art museum is housed—appropriately for this former meatpacking neighborhood—in a converted slaughterhouse. The edgy programs and exhibits are a mix of installations, visuals, events, and special viewings. Opening times are made for night owls: Make a late visit before going on to Testaccio's bars and restaurants.

Piazza Orazio Giustiniani 4. www.museomacro.org. (℅ **06-671070400.** Admission 14.50€ (combined ticket with MACRO Via Nizza). Tues–Sun 4–10pm. Last admission 30 min. before closing. Bus: 63, 630, or 719.

San Paolo Fuori le Mura (St. Paul Outside the Walls) ★

CHURCH   The giant Basilica of St. Paul, whose origins date from the time of Constantine, is Rome's fourth great patriarchal church. It was erected over the tomb of St. Paul and is the second-largest church in Rome after St. Peter's. The basilica fell victim to fire in 1823 and was subsequently rebuilt—hence the relatively modern look. From the inside, its windows may appear to be stained glass, but they're actually translucent alabaster that illuminates a forest of single-file columns and mosaic medallions (portraits of the various popes). Its most important treasure is a 12th-century marble Easter candelabrum by Vassalletto, who's also responsible for the remarkable cloisters containing twisted pairs of columns enclosing a rose garden. Miraculously, the baldacchino by Arnolfo di Cambio (1285) wasn't damaged in the fire; it now shelters the tomb of St. Paul the Apostle.

Via Ostiense 190 (at Piazzale San Paolo). www.basilicasanpaolo.org. ℅ **06-69880800.** Basilica free admission; cloisters 4€. Basilica daily 7am–6:30pm. Cloisters daily 8am–6:15pm. Metro: Basilica di San Paolo.

The Via Appia (Appian Way) & the Catacombs

Of all the roads that led to Rome, **Via Appia Antica** (begun in 312 B.C.) was the most famous. It eventually stretched all the way from Rome to the seaport of Brindisi, through which trade with Greece and the East was funneled. (According to Christian tradition, it was along the Appian Way that an escaping Peter encountered the vision of Christ, causing him to go back into the city to face martyrdom.) The road's initial stretch in Rome is lined with the monuments and ancient tombs of patrician Roman families—burials were forbidden within the city walls as early as

---

Mussolini's City of the Future

South of the city center, the outlying **EUR suburb** ★ (the acronym stands for *Esposizione Universale Romana*) was designed and purpose-built by Mussolini in the Fascist era to stage the planned World Fair of 1942—canceled due to World War II. Though never completed, EUR's mix of rationalist and classical-inspired elements will enthuse anyone with a serious interest in architecture.

Perfect symmetry and sleek marble-lined avenues house a number of museums, corporate headquarters and office agglomerates, connected to the *centro* by the modern thoroughfare Via Cristoforo Colomb. The residential area that later grew around the EUR business district is not particularly exciting, but it is verdant and quiet—a nice getaway from bustling central Rome.

the 5th century B.C.—and, below ground, miles of tunnels hewn out of the soft *tufa* stone.

These tunnels, or catacombs, were where early Christians buried their dead and, during the worst times of persecution, held clandestine church services. A few of them are open to the public, so you can wander through musty-smelling tunnels whose walls are gouged out with tens of thousands of burial niches, including small niches made for children. Early Christians referred to each chamber as a *dormitorio*—they believed the bodies were only sleeping, awaiting resurrection (which is why they could not countenance the traditional Roman practice of cremation). In some you can still discover the remains of early Christian art. The obligatory guided tours feature occasionally biased history, plus a dash of sermonizing, but the guides are very knowledgeable.

The Appia Antica park is a popular Sunday lunch picnic site for Roman families, following the half-forgotten pagan tradition of dining in the presence of one's ancestors on holy days. The Via Appia Antica is closed to cars on Sundays, left for the picnickers, bicyclists, and inline skaters. See **www.parcoappiaantica.it** for more on the park, including downloadable maps.

To reach the catacombs area, take bus no. 218 from the San Giovanni Metro stop; to find the bus stand, walk through the gates from the Metro and wait at the halt on the opposite side of the road to the Basilica. Around 2 or 3 buses run every hour during daylight hours. This bus bumps along the basalt cobbles of the Appia Antica for a bit and then veers right on Via Ardeatina at Domine Quo Vadis church. After a long block, it stops at the square Largo Ardeatina, near the gate to the San Callisto catacombs. From here, you can walk right on Via delle Sette Chiese to the Domitilla catacombs or fork left on Via delle Sette Chiese to San Sebastiano. *Tip:* This bus service can be unreliable. If you are in a hurry to accommodate your visit to the catacombs, take a cab (p. 70).

Catacombe di San Callisto (Catacombs of St. Callixtus) ★★
RELIGIOUS SITE/TOUR   "The most venerable and most renowned of Rome," said Pope John XXIII of these funerary tunnels. These catacombs are often packed with tour-bus groups, and they have perhaps the cheesiest tour, but the tunnels are phenomenal. They're the first cemetery of the Christian community of Rome, burial place of 16 popes in the 3rd century. They bear the name of St. Callixtus, the deacon whom Pope St. Zephyrinus put in charge of them and who was later elected pope (A.D. 217–22) himself. The complex is a network of galleries structured in four levels and reaching a depth of about 20m (65 ft.), the deepest in the area. There are many sepulchral chambers and almost half a million tombs of early Christians.

Entering the catacombs, you see the most important crypt, that of nine popes. Some of the original marble tablets of their tombs are

A Noble Survivor

Of all the monuments on the Appian Way itself, the most impressive is the **Tomb of Cecilia Metella** ★, within walking distance of the catacombs. The cylindrical tomb, clad in travertine and topped with a marble frieze, honors the wife of one of Julius Caesar's military commanders from the republican era. Why such an elaborate tomb for a figure of relatively minor historical importance? Other mausoleums may have been even more elaborate, but Cecilia Metella's earned enduring fame simply because her tomb has remained while the others have decayed. Part of the reason is its symbiotic relationship with the early 14th-century **Castle Caetani** attached to the rear. For centuries, the tomb survived being plundered for building materials because of the castle, which was built to guard the road and collect tolls; in later eras, the castle was spared because it was attached to the romantic ruin of the tomb. Admission to the tomb, on a combined ticket with the Baths of Caracalla (p. 85), is 6€, free for children 17 and under.

preserved. Also commemorated is St. Cecilia, patron of sacred music (her relics were moved to her church in Trastevere during the 9th c.; see p. 114). This early Christian martyr received three ax strokes on her neck, the maximum allowed by Roman law, which unfortunately for her, failed to kill her outright. Farther on are the Cubicles of the Sacraments, with 3rd-century frescoes.

Via Appia Antica 110–26. www.catacombe.roma.it. 𝄞 **06-5130151**. Admission 8€ adults, 5€ children ages 7–15. Thurs–Tues 9am–noon and 2–5pm. Closed late Jan to late Feb. Bus: 218.

Catacombe di Domitilla ★★★ RELIGIOUS SITE/TOUR The oldest of the catacombs is the hands-down winner for most enjoyable experience. Groups are relatively small, and guides are entertaining and personable. The catacombs—Rome's longest at 18km (11 miles)—were built below land donated by Domitilla, a noblewoman of the Flavian dynasty who was exiled from Rome for practicing Christianity. They were rediscovered in 1593, after a church abandoned in the 9th century collapsed. The visit begins in the sunken church founded in A.D. 380, the year Christianity became Rome's state religion.

There are fewer "sights" here than in the other catacombs, but this is the only catacomb where you'll still see bones; the rest have emptied their tombs to rebury the remains in ossuaries on the inaccessible lower levels. Elsewhere in the tunnels, 4th-century frescoes contain some of the earliest representations of Saints Peter and Paul. Notice the absence of crosses: It was only later that Christians replaced the traditional fish symbol with the cross. During this period, Christ's crucifixion was a source of shame to the community. He had been killed like a common criminal.

Via delle Sette Chiese 282. www.domitilla.info. 𝄞 **06-5110342**. Admission 8€ adults, 5€ children ages 6–14. Wed–Mon 9am–noon and 2–5pm. Closed mid-Dec to mid-Jan. Bus: 714 (to Piazza Navigatori).

Catacombe di San Sebastiano (Catacombs of St. Sebastian) ★

RELIGIOUS SITE/TOUR   Today the tomb and relics of St. Sebastian are in the ground-level basilica, but his original resting place was in the catacombs underneath it. Sebastian was a senior Milanese soldier in the Roman army who converted to Christianity and was martyred during Emperor Diocletian's persecutions, which were especially brutal in the first decade of the 4th century. From the reign of Valerian to that of Constantine, the bodies of Sts. Peter and Paul were also hidden in the catacombs, which were dug from *tufa,* a soft volcanic rock that hardens on exposure to the air. The church was built in the 4th century and remodeled in the 17th century.

The tunnels here, if stretched out, would reach a length of 11km (6¾ miles). In the tunnels and mausoleums are mosaics and graffiti, along with many other pagan and Christian objects, as well as four Roman tombs with their frescoes and stucco fairly intact, found in 1922 after being buried for almost 2,000 years.

Via Appia Antica 136. www.catacombe.org. ⓒ **06-7850350.** Admission 8€ adults, 5€ children 6–15. Mon–Sat 10am–4:30pm. Closed Nov 26–Dec 26. Bus: 118

Especially for Kids

There's a real "Jekyll and Hyde" quality to exploring Rome with kids. On the one hand, it's a capital city, big, busy, and hot, and with public transportation that doesn't always work too well. On the other, the very best parts of the city for kids—Roman ruins, subterranean worlds, and *gelato*—are aspects you'd want to explore anyway. Seeing Rome with kids doesn't demand an itinerary redesign—at least, if you're willing to skip some of the marquee museums. And despite what you have heard about its famous seven hills, much of the center is mercifully flat, and pedestrian. The election of a center-left mayor in 2013 means the city is likely to become even more pedestrian-friendly in future. His immediate banning of private cars from the roads around the Forum and Colosseum is likely the first of several measures aimed at creating a Rome that is friendlier for little visitors, and making its precious ruins even more enjoyable places to visit.

Food is pretty easy too: Roman **pizzas** are some of the best in the world—see "Where to Eat," p. 134, for our favorites. Ditto the ice cream, or *gelato* (p. 146). Restaurants in pretty much any price category will be happy to serve up a simple *pasta al pomodoro* (pasta with tomato sauce) to a fussy eater.

The city is shorter on green spaces than European cities like London, but the landscaped gardens of the **Villa Borghese** have plenty of space for them to let off steam. Pack a picnic or rent some bikes (p. 72). The **Parco Appia Antica** (www.parcoappiaantica.it) is another family favorite, especially on a Sunday or national holiday when the old cobbled road is closed to traffic. The park's **Catacombs** (p. 117) are eerie enough to satisfy grisly young minds, but also fascinating Christian and historical sites in their own right.

ORGANIZED tours

Forget the flag-waving guides leading a herd of dazed travelers around monuments. There's a better class of professionally guided tours, which deliver top-notch insider expertise, focused themes, and personalized attention, plus perks such as skipping long admission lines and having bespoke after-hours experiences.

One of the leading tour operators in Rome, **Context Travel** ★ (www.context-travel.com; ℭ **800/691-6036** in the U.S., or 06-96727371) uses local scholars—historians, art historians, preservationists—to lead their small-group walking tours through Rome's monuments, museums, and historic piazzas, as well as culinary walks and excellent family programs. Custom-designed tours are also available. Prices of the regular tours are high, beginning at 60€ for 2 hours, but most participants consider them a highlight of their trips.

Walks of Italy (www.walksofitaly. com; ℭ **06-95583331**) also runs excellent guided walking tours of Rome; their 2½-hour introductory tour costs 29€, and more in-depth explorations of the Colosseum, Vatican Museums, and Forum go for 59€ to 99€.

Enjoy Rome, Via Marghera 8a (www. enjoyrome.com; ℭ **06-4451843**), offers a number of "greatest hits" walking tours, plus an early evening tour of the Jewish Ghetto and Trastevere, and a bus excursion to the Catacombs and the Appian Way that visits a ruined ancient aqueduct that most Romans, let alone tourists, never see. Tours cost 30€ to 50€ per person, but entrance fees are not included.

The self-styled "storytellers of the new millennium" at **Through Eternity** (www. througheternity.com; ℭ **06-7009336**) are a group of art historians and architects; what sets them apart is their theatrical delivery, helped along by the dramatic scripts that many of the guides seem to follow. It can be a lot of fun, but it's not for everyone. Through Eternity also offers twilight tours, food tours, and after-hours tours of the Vatican, allowing you to see its treasures without fighting the crowds (it's a tremendous experience). A 5-hour tour of the Vatican is 67€; other tours range from 39€ to 109€.

Museums, of course, are trickier. You can probably get kids fired up more easily for the really ancient stuff. The bookshop at the **Colosseum** (p. 88) has a good selection of guides to the city aimed at under-12s, themed on gladiators and featuring funny or cartoonish material. Make that an early stop. We have taken a 6-year-old to the **Musei Capitolini** (p. 85), and she loved hunting down the collection's treasures highlighted on the free museum leaflet. It was like a themed treasure hunt, and bought us a couple of hours to admire the exhibits—and the chance to see them from a new and unexpected angle, too. The multiple ground levels below **San Clemente** (p. 93) and the **Case Romane del Celio** (p. 94) are another obvious draw for small visitors.

Aspiring young gladiators may even want to spend 2 hours at the **Scuola Gladiatori Roma (Rome Gladiator School),** where they can prepare for a duel in a reasonably authentic way. You can book through **Viator.com**, or find out more about the program at **www.gsr-roma.com**.

The gardens of the Villa Borghese, popular with families.

Away from the museums, kids will also likely enjoy some of the cheesier city sights—at the very least these will make some good family photos to share on Facebook or Instagram. Build in some time to place your hands in the Bocca della Verità, at **Santa Maria in Cosmedin** (p. 95), to throw a coin in the **Trevi Fountain** (p. 106), and to enjoy watching the feral cats relaxing amid the ruins of **Largo di Torre Argentina.** There is a cat sanctuary here that gives basic healthcare to Rome's many strays.

If you want to delve deeper into the city as a family, check out the tours on **Context Travel**'s family program (see Organized Tours, p. 121), such as walks and workshops about mythology, underground Rome, or "How Rome Works," which covers some of the Romans' fiendishly clever engineering. The 2- to 3-hour tours are pricey (255€–355€ per family) but first rate, and you will have the docent all to yourselves.

WHERE TO STAY

Rome's standard hotels are notoriously overpriced. So, when you stay here, unusual solutions—rental apartments, B&Bs, even convents and monasteries—have two great virtues: They're cheaper than standard facilities and, often, more memorable.

Breakfast in all but the highest echelon of hotels is often a buffet with coffee, fruit, rolls, and cheese. It's not always included in the rate, so check the listing carefully. If you are budgeting and breakfast is a payable extra, skip it and go to a nearby cafe-bar. It will likely be much cheaper.

Nearly all hotels are heated in the cooler months, but not all are air-conditioned in summer, which can be vitally important during a stifling July or August. The deluxe and first-class properties usually are, but after that, it's a tossup. Be sure to check before you book if it's important to you.

SELF-CATERING APARTMENTS

Anyone looking to get into the local swing of things should stay in a short-term rental apartment. A centrally located, "economical" double room in a Rome hotel goes for about 120€ per night, and it may be cramped and dark, with few amenities. For the same price or less, you could have your own spacious one-bedroom apartment with a terrace, washing machine, A/C, and a fridge to keep your wine in. Properties of all sizes and styles, in every price range, are available for stays of 3 nights to several weeks.

Nearly every rental apartment in Rome is owned and maintained by a third party (that is, not the rental agency). That means that the decor and flavor of the apartments, even in the same price range and neighborhood, can vary widely. Every reputable agency, however, puts multiple photos of each property they handle on its website, so that you'll have a sense of what you're getting into. The photos should be accompanied by a list of amenities, so if A/C and a washing machine are important to you, but you can live without Wi-Fi, be sure to check for those features. Note also that **www.airbnb.com**, the platform that allows individuals to rent their own apartments to guests, covers Rome.

It's standard practice for local rental agencies to collect 30% of the total rental amount upfront to secure a booking. When you get to Rome and check in, the balance of your rental fee is often payable in cash only. Upon booking, the agency should provide you with detailed "check-in" procedures. Sometimes, you're expected to call a cell or office phone when you arrive, and then the keyholder will meet you at the front door of the property at the agreed-upon time. *Tip:* Before the keyholder disappears, make sure you have a few numbers to call in case of an emergency. Otherwise, most apartments come with information sheets that list neighborhood shops and services. Beyond that, you're on your own, which is what makes an apartment stay such a great way to do as the Romans do.

RECOMMENDED AGENCIES **Cross Pollinate** (www.cross-pollinate. com; © **06-99369799**), a multi-destination agency with a decent roster of apartments and B&Bs in Rome, was created by the American owners of the Beehive Hotel in Rome. Each property is inspected before it gets listed. **GowithOh** (www.gowithoh.com; © **800/567-2927** in the U.S.) is a hip rental agency that covers 12 European cities, Rome among them. The website is fun to navigate and has sections on how to save money as well as over 400 apartments for rent in the city. **Eats & Sheets** (www.eatsandsheets. com; © **06-83515971**) is a small boutique collective comprising two B&Bs (near the Vatican and Colosseum), and 11 beautiful apartments for rent, most in the *centro storico*. **Roman Reference** (www.romanreference.

com; ℂ **06-48903612**) offers no-surprises property descriptions (with helpful and diplomatic tags like "better for young people") and even includes the "eco-footprint" for each apartment. You can expect transparency and responsiveness from the plain-dealing staff. **Rental in Rome** (www.rent-alinrome.com; ℂ **06-69905533**) has an alluring website—with videoclips of the apartments—and the widest selection of midrange and luxury apartments in the prime *centro storico* zone (there are less expensive ones, too). **Bed & Breakfast Association of Rome** (www.b-b.rm.it) handles both self-catering apartments and rooms for rent within private apartments, some of which charge as little as 30€.

MONASTERIES & CONVENTS

Staying in a convent or a monastery can be a great bargain. But remember, these are religious houses, which means the decor is most often stark and the rules extensive. Cohabitating is almost always frowned upon—though marriage licenses are rarely required—and unruly behavior is not tolerated (so, no staggering in after too much *limoncello* at dinner). Plus, there's usually a curfew. Most rooms in convents and monasteries do not have private bathrooms, but ask when making your reservation in case some are available. However, if you're planning a mellow, "contemplative" trip to Rome, and you can live with these parameters, convents and monasteries are an affordable and fascinating option. The place to start is **www.monasterystays.com**, which lays out all your monastic options for the Eternal City and can make all the bookings for you.

Around Vatican City & Prati

For most visitors, this is a rather dull area to be based in. It's well removed from the ancient sites, and not a great restaurant neighborhood. But if the main purpose of your visit centers on the Vatican, you'll be fine here, and you will be joined by thousands of other pilgrims, nuns, and priests (see map p. 75).

EXPENSIVE

Residenza Paolo VI ★★   The only hotel actually within the Vatican state, Residenza Paolo is plugged into the walls of the venerated Augustinian Order headquarters, where it's been based since 1886. As a result, there's no city sales tax. Taking breakfast on the rooftop terrace is a special treat, as this narrow strip overlooks St. Peter's Square—if the timing's right, you'll see the Pope himself blessing crowds (usually on Sun). As for the rooms they are all done with simple elegance, featuring terracotta or hardwood floors, heavy drapes and oriental rugs, and quality beds. The downside? Just like their in-Rome-proper rival hotels, square footage is at a premium in many of the guestrooms. There's a 15% discount on bookings 3 nights and over.

Via Paolo VI 29. www.residenzapaolovi.com. ℂ **06-684870.** 35 units. 135€–599€ double. Rates include breakfast. Parking nearby from 20€. Metro: Ottaviano. **Amenities:** Bar; babysitting; room service; Wi-Fi (15€ per day).

Villa Laetitia ★★★   This elegant hotel overlooking the River Tiber is the work of Anna Fendi, member of the Roman fashion dynasty and a nifty designer in her own right. Thanks to Anna, the rooms are anything but traditional, despite the 1911 villa setting surrounded by tranquil gardens. The decor features accents like bold patterns on the beds and floors and modern art on the walls. The Stendhal Room is our favorite, with black and white floor tiles with matching bedspread, cool clear acrylic furniture, a small kitchenette painted fire-engine red, and a secluded balcony that flirts with the morning sun.

Lungotevere delle Armi 22–23. www.villalaetitia.com. © **06-3226776.** 14 units. 200€–280€ double. Parking nearby 20€. Metro: Lepanto. **Amenities:** Restaurant; bar; airport transfer (55€); babysitting; fitness room; room service; spa; Wi-Fi (free).

MODERATE

QuodLibet ★★★   The name is Latin for "what pleases" and we'll be frank: Everything is pleasing here. This upscale B&B boasts spacious rooms, gorgeous artwork and furnishings, and generous breakfasts (the breads come from the bakery just next door, as does the aroma wafting in). All the rooms are set on the 4th floor of an elegant building (with elevator and A/C), so it's quieter than many places. It's located just a 10-minute walk from the Vatican Museums, and a block from the Metro (which allows you to reach other parts of the city easily). Saving the best for last is host Gianluca, a man with charm and a deep knowledge of both Rome and what will interest visitors. A top pick!

Via Barletta 29. www.quodlibetroma.com. © **06-1222642.** 4 units. 70€–180€ double. Rates include breakfast. Metro: Ottaviano. **Amenities:** Wi-Fi (free).

Rome Armony Suites ★★   A warning: Rome Armony Suites is almost always booked up months in advance, so if you're interested in it, be sure to book early! Why so popular? The answer starts with service; owner Luca and his son Andrea are charming, sensitive hosts, who are especially good with first-time visitors to Rome. As for the rooms, they're big, plush, clean, and modern, with minimalist decor, tea and coffee facilities, and a fridge in each unit. For breakfast, you get a voucher to use in Brown & Co., a cafe around the corner. Final perk: an excellent location.

Via Orazio 3. www.romearmonysuites.com. © **348-3305419.** 6 units. 120€–260€ double. Rates include breakfast. Metro: Ottaviano. **Amenities:** A/C; Wi-Fi (free).

Ancient Rome, Monti & Celio

There aren't many hotel rooms on Earth with a view of a 2,000-year-old amphitheater, so there's a definite "only in Rome" feeling to lodging on the edge of the ancient city (see map p. 86). The negative side to residing in this area—and it's a big minus—is that the streets adjacent to those ancient monuments have little life outside tourism. There's a lot more going on in **Monti,** Rome's oldest "suburb" (only 5 min. from the Forum) which is especially lively after dark (so expect noisy streets until late).

Celio has even more of a neighborhood vibe, and a local, gentrified life quite separate from tourism.

If you're after a little more room, **Residenza Leonina ★**, Piazza degli Zingari 4 (www.residenzaleonina.com; ℭ **06-48906885**), offers a few modern, spacious apartments in the heart of Monti for about 100€ to 195€ per night. You can get better deals if you book direct and, best of all, one of central Rome's best gelato vendors is literally at the doorstep (see "Getting Your Fill of Gelato," p. 146).

EXPENSIVE

Capo d'Africa ★★ This exquisite boutique hotel, located in the heart of Imperial Rome and set in an early 20th-century *palazzo*, offers a truly unique lodging experience. With sweeping vistas from the manicured roof terrace (the hotel's top perk: you eat breakfast up here), elegant design, and an all-around upscale vibe, guests are welcomed as they would be in any relaxed and unpretentious Roman home. The rooms, too, are magnificent: light-filled, spacious, sharp and modern, with cherrywood furniture, touches of glass and chrome, incredibly comfy beds, marble bathrooms, and plenty of cupboard space, so you need never see your bags after you arrive.

Via Capo d'Africa 54. www.hotelcapodafrica.com. ℭ **06-772801.** 65 units. 380€–430€ double. Rates include breakfast. Parking 45€. Bus: 53, 85, or 117. **Amenities:** Restaurant; bar; exercise room; room service; Wi-Fi (free)

The Inn at the Roman Forum ★★★ This small hotel is tucked down a medieval lane, on the edge of Monti, with the forums of several Roman emperors as neighbors. Its midsized rooms are sumptuously decorated, with designs that fuse the contemporary and baroque traditions of the city. The two rooms on the top floor have private gardens, which offer total tranquility, plus there's a shared roof terrace where sunset *aperitivo* is served each evening with unforgettable views of the Vittoriano and the Palatine Hill. The ground floor even has its own archaeological dig. The Inn isn't cheap, but the views alone more than make up for it.

Via degli Ibernesi 30. www.theinnattheromanforum.com. ℭ **06-69190970.** 12 units. 390€–990€ double. Rates include breakfast. Parking 30€. Metro: Cavour. **Amenities:** Bar; concierge; room service; Wi-Fi (10€ per day).

MODERATE

Duca d'Alba ★★ Hip and chic Monti doesn't have many full-service hotels—at least, not yet. The Duca d'Alba is located on one of the main drags, with all the nightlife and authentic dining you'll need. Rooms in the main building are cozy (read: small) and contemporary, with modern furniture and gadgetry, but even smaller bathrooms. If you want to spring for more than moderate rates, the annex rooms next door have a *palazzo* character, with terracotta-tiled floors, oak and cherrywood furniture, more space, and street-facing rooms that are soundproofed. Those on the second floor are the brightest. *Tip:* If you offer to pay in cash, you'll receive a 12% discount.

Via Leonina 14. www.hotelducadalba.com. ✆ **06-484471.** 33 units. 120€–412€ double. Rates include breakfast. Metro. Cavour. **Amenities:** Bar; babysitting (prebooking essential); Wi-Fi (free).

Lancelot ★   Expect warmth and hospitality from the minute you walk in the door. The English-speaking staff, who all have been here for years, are the heart and soul of Lancelot, and the reason why the hotel has so many repeat guests. The room decor is simple, and most of the units are spacious, immaculately kept, and light-filled, thanks to large windows. Ask for the 6th-floor rooms that have private terraces overlooking Ancient Rome—they're well worth the 20€ extra you pay. What makes this place truly remarkable are the genteel, chandelier-lit common areas for meeting other travelers, *Room With A View*-style. Unusual for Rome, there's also private parking, for which you'll need to book ahead.

Via Capo d'Africa 47. www.lancelothotel.com. ✆ **06-70450615.** 61 units. 130€–196€ double. Rates include breakfast. Parking 10€ (prebooking essential). Bus: 53, 85, or 117. **Amenities:** Restaurant (set dinner 25€ incl. wine); bar; babysitting; Wi-Fi (free).

Nicolas Inn ★★   This tiny B&B, run by a welcoming American–Lebanese couple, makes the perfect base for those who want to concentrate on Rome's ancient sights—the Colosseum is 1 block in one direction, the Forum 3 blocks in the other. Rooms are a good size and decorated with wrought-iron beds, cool tiled floors, and heavy wooden furniture. Best of all, light floods in through large windows. Guests take breakfast at a local café—with unlimited espresso. Downers: no children under 5, and no credit cards accepted.

Via Cavour 295. www.nicolasinn.com. ✆ **06-97618483.** 4 units. 100€–180€ double. Rates include breakfast (at nearby cafe). Metro: Cavour or Colosseo. **Amenities:** Airport transfer (60€); concierge; Wi-Fi (free).

The Centro Storico & Pantheon

Travelers who want to immerse themselves in the atmosphere of Rome's lively Renaissance heart will prefer staying in this area rather than the more commercial Tridente district, or quieter Vatican. You'll be looking at a lot of walking, but that's a reason many visitors come here in the first place—to wander and discover the glory that was and is Rome. Many restaurants and cafes are within an easy walk of all the hotels located here (see map p. 97).

EXPENSIVE

Del Sole al Pantheon ★   This place oozes history, dating back, incredibly, to 1467. Famous guests have included Jean-Paul Sartre and Simone de Beauvoir, as well as Italian 15th-century poet Ludovico Ariosto and 19th-century composer Pietro Mascagni, among others. Rooms are decorated with lavish period decor, lots of brocade drapery, fine fabrics, and classic furniture. Each room comes equipped with air conditioning and satellite TV, and some feature unbeatable views of the Pantheon.

Piazza della Rotonda 63. www.hotelsolealpantheon.com. ✆ **06-6780441.** 32 units. 240€–422€ double. Rates include breakfast. Parking nearby 45€. Bus: 64. **Amenities:** Airport transfer (60€); bar; babysitting; room service; Wi-Fi (5€ per day; not available in annex building).

Raphael ★★ Planning on proposing? This ivy-covered palace, just off Piazza Navona, is just the kind of special-occasion place to pick, with luxurious rooms, enthusiastic staff, and a roof terrace with spectacular views across Rome. It's a gorgeous hotel, highlighted by 20th-century artwork inside, including Picasso ceramics in the lobby, and paintings by Mirò, Morandi, and De Chirico scattered across the property. The standard rooms are all decorated in elegant Victorian style, with antique furnishings and hardwood floors. Some may prefer staying in the quirky Richard Meier–designed executive suites that blend contemporary with Asian design and feature oak paneling, contemporary art, and Carrara marble.

Largo Febo 2, Piazza Navona. www.raphaelhotel.com. ✆ **06-682831.** 50 units. 280€–730€ double. Rates include breakfast. Valet parking 50€. Bus: 64. **Amenities:** Restaurant; bar; babysitting; concierge; exercise room; room service; sauna; Wi-Fi (free).

MODERATE

Residenza Farnese ★★ This little gem is tucked away in a stunning 15th-century mansion, within stumbling distance of the Campo de' Fiori. Most rooms are spacious and artsy, with colorful comforters and wallpaper, tiled floors and a vaguely Renaissance theme. Standard rooms are a little smaller. If you book via the website with 21 days advance, a 10% discount is applied on every day of your stay. Another perk: the downright generous spread of fresh fruit, cheese, ham, sausage, egg, and yogurt for breakfast, plus a free minibar in each room.

Via del Mascherone 59. www.residenzafarneseroma.it. ✆ **06-68210980.** 31 units. 92€–310€ double. Rates include breakfast. Parking 15€ (reservations required). Bus: 64, 70, 81, or 87. **Amenities:** Airport transfer (free with min. 4-night stay); bar; concierge; room service; Wi-Fi (free).

Teatro di Pompeo ★★ History buffs will appreciate this small B&B, literally built on top of the ruins of the 1st-century Theatre of Pompey, where on the Ides of March Julius Caesar was stabbed to death (p. 139). The lovely breakfast area beneath the lobby is actually part of the arcades of the old theater, with the original Roman stone walls. The large rooms themselves are not Roman in style, but feel plush, with exposed wood-beam ceilings, cherrywood furniture, and terracotta-tiled floors. Some rooms feature a view of the internal courtyard, while others overlook the small square, and all are quiet despite the Campo de' Fiori crowds right behind the hotel. Staff members are extremely helpful, and they all speak English. *Tip:* Avoid the Trattoria Der Pallaro restaurant next door; it's a tourist trap.

Largo del Pallaro 8. www.hotelteatrodipompeo.it. ✆ **06-68300170.** 13 units. 165€–220€ double. Rates include breakfast. Bus: 46, 62, or 64. **Amenities:** Bar; babysitting; room service; Wi-Fi (free).

Tridente, Via Veneto & Parioli

The heart of the city is a great place to stay if you're a serious shopper or enjoy the romantic, somewhat nostalgic locales of the Spanish Steps and Trevi Fountain. But expect to part with a lot of extra Euro for the privilege. This is one of the most elegant areas in Rome (see map p. 103).

EXPENSIVE

Babuino 181 ★★   Leave Renaissance and baroque Italy far behind at this sleek, contemporary hotel, with relatively spacious rooms featuring Frette linens, iPod docks, and even a Nespresso machine for cappuccino and espresso lovers. The bathrooms are heavy on the marble and mosaics, and shuttered windows with hefty curtains provide a perfectly blacked-out and quiet environment for light sleepers. Breakfast buffet is an additional 18€.

Via del Babuino 181. www.romeluxurysuites.com/babuino. ℰ **06-32295295.** 24 units. 250€–680€ double. Metro: Flaminio. **Amenities:** Bar; airport transfer (65€); babysitting; concierge; room service; Wi-Fi (free).

Deko Rome ★★★   Honeymooners love Deko Rome, but then, so does everyone who stays here. It is, quite simply, an exceptionally warm and welcoming place, a true boutique hotel (just nine rooms) occupying the second floor of an elegant early 20th-century *palazzo*. The interior blends antiques, vintage 60s pieces, and contemporary design for rooms that are chic in a way that's happily retro and quite comfortable; as a bonus, each room comes with an iPad and flatscreen TV. Add in the friendly, fun owners (Marco and Serena) and excellent location, close to Via Veneto, and Deko is understandably hugely popular. It fills up quickly—reservations many months in advance are essential. Save 20€ if you pay in cash.

Via Toscana 1. www.dekorome.com. ℰ **06-42020032.** 9 units. 210€–250€. Rates include breakfast. Parking (nearby) 25€. Bus: 910 (from Termini). **Amenities:** Airport transfer (50€); bar; babysitting; Wi-Fi (free).

The Inn at the Spanish Steps ★★★   Set in one of Rome's most desiderable locations on the famed Via dei Condotti shopping magnet, this lavish guesthouse is the epitome of luxe. Rooms are fantasias of design and comfort, some with parquet floors and cherubim frescoes on the ceiling, others decked out with wispy fabrics draping plush, canopied beds. Swank amenities include flatscreen TVs, iPod docks, a computer-lending program, Jacuzzi tubs, double marble sinks, curling irons, pet amenities, and so forth. Note that some rooms are located in the annex building, and these tend to be larger than the ones in the main building. The perfectly manicured rooftop garden provides beautiful views, to be enjoyed at breakfast—where there's a generous buffet spread—or at sunset, frosted glass of *vino* in hand.

Via dei Condotti 85. www.atspanishsteps.com. ℰ **06-69925657.** 24 units. 370€–750€ double. Rates include breakfast. Metro: Spagna. **Amenities:** Bar; babysitting; airport transfer (55€); concierge; room service; Wi-Fi (free).

Villa Spalletti Trivelli ★★★ This really is an experience rather than a hotel, an early 20th-century neoclassical villa remodeled into an exclusive 12-room guesthouse, where lodgers mingle in the gardens or the magnificent great hall, as if invited by an Italian noble for the weekend. There is no key for the entrance door; ring a bell and a staff member will open it for you, often offering you a glass of complimentary prosecco as a welcome. Onsite is a Turkish bath, a sizeable and modern oasis for those who want extra pampering, while rooms feature elegant antiques and Fiandra damask linen sheets, with sitting area or separate lounge, REN toiletries, and satellite LCD TV. And the minibar? All free, all day. Via Piacenza 4. www.villaspalletti.it. ✆ **06-48907934.** 12 units. 450€–710€ double. Rates include breakfast. Free parking. Metro: Barberini. **Amenities:** Restaurant; bar; concierge; exercise room; room service; spa; sauna; Wi-Fi (free).

MODERATE

Daphne Trevi & Daphne Veneto ★ These jointly managed B&B properties, minutes from the Trevi fountain, are a relatively good value, even in the summer. Daphne Trevi occupies an 18th-century building with a range of rooms, and Daphne Veneto is a 19th-century structure with single rooms and larger doubles (rooms on the third and fourth floors have rooftop views). In both locations the staff is super helpful. The rooms are also similar in both: cozy and clean (but no TVs), with small showers and desktop or laptop computers for guests' use (but note that Wi-Fi isn't great in most rooms; the first floor is best). The main difference between the two is location; Trevi lies on an older, quieter cobblestone street, and Veneto is on a wider, busier thoroughfare. Via di San Basilio 55. www.daphne-rome.com. ✆ **06-87450086.** 8 units. 130€–230€ double. Rates include breakfast. Nearby parking 30€. Metro: Barberini. **Amenities:** Airport transfers (55€); Wi-Fi (free).

Hotel Adriano ★★★ Secluded in a maze of small alleyways, but just 5 minutes from the Pantheon, the Adriano occupies an elegant 17th-century *palazzo*. The rooms boast an incredibly stylish and trendy modern design, with blond-wood built-ins and designer furniture carefully chosen for each room. The hotel drips with atmosphere. Note that if you opt for an "annex" room this is quite a different experience, more akin to a self-catering apartment. Via di Pallacorda 2. www.hoteladriano.com. ✆ **06-68802451.** 77 units. 90€–220€ double. Rates include breakfast. Parking nearby 40€. Bus: 175 or 492. **Amenities:** Bar; babysitting; bikes; concierge; gym; Wi-Fi (free).

Hotel Condotti ★ This cozy guesthouse can be a tremendously good deal depending on when you stay and when you book (hint: Those who book well in advance and through a discounter get the best rates). For your money you'll get a clean, unpretentious room, though the common areas aspire higher with marble floors, antiques, tapestries, and a Venetian-glass chandelier. Overall it's worth considering for its proximity to the Spanish Steps, great deals online (especially during off-season), and free Internet (with accees to terminals in the lobby).

Via Mario de' Fiori 37. www.hotelcondotti.com. © **06-6794661.** 16 units. 150€ and way, way up. Rates include breakfast. Metro: Spagna. **Amenities:** Airport transfer (65€); bar; babysitting; bikes; room service; Wi-Fi (free).

La Residenza ★ Considering its location just off Via Veneto, this hotel is a smart deal, with renovated, modern rooms, all relatively spacious with a couple of easy chairs or a small couch in addition to a desk. Families with children are especially catered to, with quad rooms and junior suites on the top floor featuring a separate kids' alcove with two sofa beds, and an outdoor terrace with patio furniture. In addition to free Wi-Fi in the rooms, there are terminals in the lobby where you can check the Internet. The breakfast buffet is excellent and includes quality charcuterie and cheeses, homemade breads and pastries. Two more perks: free Friday cocktails, and a welcome fruit basket on arrival.

Via Emilia 22–24. www.hotel-la-residenza.com. © **06-4880789.** 29 units. 120€–250€ double. Rates include buffet breakfast. Parking (limited) 20€. Metro: Barberini. **Amenities:** Bar; babysitting; room service; Wi-Fi (free).

INEXPENSIVE

Panda ★ Panda has long been popular among budget travelers, and its rooms get booked up quickly. Rooms are spare, but not without a bit of old-fashioned charm, like characteristic Roman *cotto* (terracotta) floor tiles and exposed beams. The cheaper singles and doubles do not have a private bathroom; the triples are with full private bath only. The en-suite bathrooms tend to be cramped, however. Right outside your doorstep, there are several great cafes and wine bars where you can start the day with espresso beverages, or end your night with alcoholic ones.

Via della Croce 35. www.hotelpanda.it. © **06-6780179.** 28 units (8 with bathroom). 68€–78€ double without bathroom; 90€–130€ double with bathroom. Metro: Spagna. **Amenities:** Wi-Fi (free).

Parlamento ★ Set on the top floors of a 17th-century *palazzo*, this is the best budget deal in the area, as all of its rooms have private bathrooms and are equipped with flatscreen satellite TVs, desks, exposed beams, and parquet or terracotta floors. Breakfast is served on the rooftop terrace—you can also chill up there with a glass of wine in the evening. Note that air-conditioning usually costs a little extra. The Trevi Fountain, Spanish Steps, and Pantheon are all within a 5- to 10-minute walk.

Via delle Convertite 5 (at Via del Corso). www.hotelparlamento.it. © **06-69921000.** 23 units. 124€–210€ double. Rates include breakfast. Parking nearby 30€. Metro: Spagna. **Amenities:** Airport transfer 55€; bar; concierge; room service; Wi-Fi (free).

Around Termini

Known for its concentration of cheap hotels, the Termini area (see map p. 112) is about the only part of the center where you can score a high-season double for under 100€. The streets around **Termini** station are not the most picturesque, and parts of the neighborhood are downright seedy, but it's very convenient for transportation and access to most of Rome's top sights. Termini is the only spot where Rome's main Metro lines intersect, and buses and trams leave from the concourse outside to every part of the city.

There are some upscale hotels around here, but if you have the dollars to spend on a truly luxe hotel, choose a prettier neighborhood.

MODERATE

Aphrodite ★   It's all about value and location at this oasis of tranquility right across the street from the chaos of Termini station—though there *is* a high convenience/poor character tradeoff. Still, these modern rooms are spotless, with wood floors and pretty bathrooms boasting sinks with polished travertine counters. The California-style rooftop terrace and friendly service are a further bonus. Need more convincing? The Terravision airport bus stops right outside. *One warning:* If you are a light sleeper, request a room at the back, or bring powerful earplugs.

Via Marsala 90. it.hotelaphrodite.com. ℂ **06-95227496.** 60 units. 110€–205€ double. Rates include breakfast. Metro: Termini. **Amenities:** Bar; babysitting (prebooking essential); concierge; Wi-Fi (free).

Residenza Cellini ★★   And for every rule, there's an exception. In this case, the lovely Cellini is the exception to the "don't spend top dollar to stay near Termini" rule. The feeling of refinement begins the second you walk through the door to find a vase of fresh lilies in the elegant, high-ceilinged hall. Antique-styled rooms are proudly traditional, with thick walls (so no noise from your neighbors), solid Selva furniture, and handsome parquet floors. It's not all about the past, however: Beds have orthopedic mattresses topped with memory foam, everything is made from anti-allergenic, natural materials, and there are satellite TV, splendid bathrooms with Jacuzzi bathtub or hydro-jet showers, and air conditioning to keep rooms cool all summer. Service is top notch and wonderfully personal.

Via Modena 5. www.residenzacellini.it. ℂ **06-47825204.** 11 units. 95€–250€ double. Rates include breakfast. Parking 35€. Metro: Repubblica. **Amenities:** Babysitting (prebooking essential); Wi-Fi (free).

Seven Kings Relais ★★   There's a hipster retro feel to the decor of this striking hotel, kitted out with dark wooden furniture, chocolate-brown bedspreads, and modern tiled floors. Rooms are also unusually large—especially nos. 104, 201, and 205. Despite its location right on one of Rome's busiest thoroughfares, there's no noise: An external courtyard and modern soundproofing see to that. Breakfast is a 24-hour self-service bar with tea, coffee, and biscuits, and the reception staff works around the clock.

Via XX Settembre 58A. www.7kings.eu. ℂ **06-42917784.** 11 units. 90€–220€ double. Metro: Repubblica. **Amenities:** Babysitting (prebooking essential); Wi-Fi (free).

INEXPENSIVE

Beehive ★★   Conceived as part hostel and part hotel, the Beehive is a unique Rome lodging experience. The eco-minded American owners offer rooms for a variety of budgets. Some have private bathrooms, others have shared facilities or are actual six-bed dorms—but all are decorated with flair, adorned with artworks or flea-market treasures. The garden with trees and secluded reading/relaxing spaces is the biggest plus. There's also a walk-in American breakfast, open to all comers, where you can get fruit, oatmeal, or eggs any way you like, as well as weekend brunches and value vegan buffets some evenings (8€ including a glass of wine).

Via Marghera 8. www.the-beehive.com. © **06-44704553.** 12 units. 70€–80€ double; dorm beds 25€–35€. Metro: Termini or Castro Pretorio. **Amenities:** Restaurant; Wi-Fi (free).

Capitolium Rooms ★   This intimate B&B occupies the second-floor wing of a handsome townhouse. The rooms are well lit, with antique-style white furniture, and beds with soft mattresses. Sure, the decor is a little old-fashioned, but so is the warmth of the welcome. Pricing, especially out of high season (Apr–June), is negotiable—email them directly and strike a deal, but insist on one of the five rooms with a view over the leafy colonial square. A couple of units are also large enough for families.

Via Montebello 104. www.capitoliumrooms.com. © **06-4464917.** 7 units. 50€–210€ double. Rates include breakfast. Parking 15€–22€. Metro: Termini or Castro Pretorio. **Amenities:** Wi-Fi (free).

Euro Quiris ★   There's not a frill in sight at this government-rated one star a couple of blocks north of the station. Rooms are on the 5th floor and simply decorated with functional furniture, but they are spotless, and mattresses are a lot more comfortable than you have a right to expect in this price bracket. Bathrooms are a good size, too. The friendly reception staff dispenses sound local knowledge, including tips on where to have breakfast in cafes nearby, and the Beehive's American breakfast is just round the corner (see above). No credit cards accepted.

Via dei Mille 64. www.euroquirishotel.com. © **06-491279.** 9 units. 40€–160€ double. Metro: Termini. **Amenities:** Wi-Fi (free).

Trastevere

This was once an "undiscovered" neighborhood—but no longer. Being based here does give some degree of escape from the busy (and pricey) *centro storico,* however. And there are bars, shops, and restaurants galore among its narrow cobblestone lanes (see map p. 115). The panorama from the **Gianicolo** (p. 91) is also walkable from pretty much everywhere in Trastevere.

INEXPENSIVE

Arco del Lauro ★★   Hidden in Trastevere's snaking alleyways, this serene little B&B is split between two adjacent sites on the ground floor of a shuttered pink *palazzo*. Rooms have parquet floors and simple decor, with a mix of modern and period furnishings, but modern, plush beds. Rooms can't be defined as large, but they all feel spacious thanks to original, lofty wood ceilings. Breakfast is taken at a nearby cafe; there's also coffee and snacks laid out around the clock. Credit cards are not accepted. Via Arco de' Tolomei 29. www.arcodellauro.it. ✆ **06-97840350.** 6 units. 85€–145€ double. Rates include breakfast (at nearby cafe). Bus: 125/Tram: 8. **Amenities:** Babysitting (2 weeks' prebooking essential); Wi-Fi (free).

San Francesco ★   There's a local feel to staying here that has disappeared from much of Trastevere, perhaps because it's at the very edge of the neighborhood, close to the Porta Portese gate in an area that hasn't been gentrified or over-exploited. All rooms are bright, with color-washed walls and modern tiling. Doubles are fairly small, but the bathrooms are palatial. The grand piano in the lobby adds a touch of old-time charm; a top-floor garden with bar overlooks terracotta rooftops and pealing church bell towers. Via Jacopo de Settesoli 7. www.hotelsanfrancesco.net. ✆ **06-48300051.** 24 units. 80€–184€ double. Price includes breakfast. Parking 20€–25€. Bus: 44 or 125. Amenities: Bar; babysitting (prebooking essential); Wi-Fi (free).

WHERE TO EAT

Rome remains a top destination for food lovers, and offers more dining diversity today than ever. Many of its *trattorie* haven't changed their menus in a quarter of a century, but there's an increasing number of creative places with chefs willing to experiment and revisit tradition.

Restaurants generally serve lunch between 1 and 2:30pm, and dinner between about 8 and 10:30pm. At all other times, most restaurants are closed—though a new generation is moving toward all-day dining, with a limited service at the "in-between" time of mid-afternoon.

If you have your heart set on any of these establishments below, we seriously recommend *reserving ahead of arrival.* Hot tables go quickly, especially on high-season weekends—often twice: once for the early dining tourists, and then again by locals, who dine later, typically around 9pm.

Pick up a Gina "PicNic"

The best place for a picnic in Rome is the Borghese Gardens, now made super-easy thanks to **Gina PicNic,** Via San Sebastianello 7a (www.ginaroma.com; ✆ **06-6780251;** daily 11am–8pm), just 1 block downhill from the park. It's not cheap, but it's certainly elegant. Gina's deli will provide you with a picnic basket complete with a thermos of Italian coffee, glasses, and fine linens for a meal to be enjoyed in the fabled gardens. For 40€, two people can enjoy quiches, salads, huge *panini* stuffed with a variety of meats, tomato, eggplant, and mozzarella, along with a fresh fruit salad, chocolate dessert, biscotti, water, and even wine (20€ extra). Order 1 day before and pick up around noon; return the basket when you're done.

A *servizio* (tip or service charge) is almost always added to your bill, or included in the price. Sometimes it is marked on the menu as *coperto e servizio* (bread, cover charge, and service). You can of course leave extra if you wish — a couple of euros as a token. Don't go overboard on the tipping front, and watch out for unsavory practices. More than once we have overheard waitstaff telling foreign tourists that service *wasn't* included, when the menu clearly stated (in Italian) that it was.

Vatican City & Prati

For restaurant locations, see map p. 75. If you just want a quick, yet very tasty sandwich to munch on before or after the Vatican safari, **Duecentogradi,** is a top-notch panino joint with lots of tasty choices, located right across from the Vatican walls at Piazza Risorgimento 3 (www. duecentogradi.it; ℭ **06-39754239;** Mon–Sat 11–2am; Sun 7pm–2am).

EXPENSIVE

Taverna Angelica ★★ MODERN ITALIAN/SEAFOOD   Considering how close this restaurant is to St. Peter's, it offers surprisingly good value for the money. Specialties include spaghetti with crunchy bacon and leeks, *fettuccine* with king prawns and eggplant, turbot with crushed almonds, and a delectable black-bread encrusted lamb with potato flan. The seafood is always fresh and simply cooked, from octopus carpaccio to sea bream with rosemary. Service is excellent, and the wine list carefully selected. Save room for the addictive chocolate dessert. Reservations are required.

Piazza A. Capponi 6. www.tavernaangelica.it. ℭ **06-6874514.** Main courses 18€– 24€; pastas 10€–14€. Daily 7pm–midnight; Sun noon–2:30pm. Closed 10 days in Aug. Metro: Ottaviano.

MODERATE

Pizza Rustica ★★★ PIZZA   Known for good reason as the "Michelangelo of pizza," celebrity chef Gabriele Bonci has always had a cult following in the Eternal City. And since he's been featured on TV shows overseas as well as written up by influential bloggers, you can expect long lines at his recently expanded pizzeria once known as Pizzarium. No matter—it's worth waiting for some of the best pizza you'll ever taste, sold by the slice or by weight. His ingredients are fresh and organic, the crust is perfect, and the toppings often experimental (try the mortadella and crumbled pistachio, or the beguiling roasted potatoes and mozzarella). Hang around, as toppings change in quick rotation. There's also a good choice of Italian craft IPAs and wheat beers, and wines by the glass. Note that there are only a handful of benches outside for seating, and reservations aren't taken.

Via della Meloria 43. ℭ **06-39745416.** Pizza 12€–14€ for large tray. Daily 11am– 10pm. Metro: Cipro.

Romeo ★★ MODERN ITALIAN The collaboration between a famous bakery dynasty, and Michelin-star chef Cristina Bowerman of **Glass** (p. 145), offers a refreshing, contemporary detour from traditional Roman cooking, with American-inspired sandwiches, a wide range of salumi, and creative pasta dishes served in sleek, modern premises. Musts include the signature foie gras sandwich served with sweet mango mayonnaise, and ravioli stuffed with asparagus and Castelmagno cheese. The restaurant proper is in the back but you can opt for a more casual lunch of pizza, quiches, or sandwiches from the counters up front.

Via Silla 26/a. www.romeo.roma.it. © **06-32110120.** Main courses 13€–25€. Mon–Sat 9am–midnight, Sun 10am–midnight. Metro: Ottaviano.

INEXPENSIVE

Il Gelato Bistrò ★★★ GELATO Claudio Torcè's artisanal ice cream shop is credited with starting a natural, gluten-free gelato movement in Rome, but what makes this place really enticing (and why it doesn't really fit on our recommended "classic" gelato list; p. 146) are its savory flavors (out of a total 150). These are especially good during the happy hour *aperitivo* (dubbed *aperigelato*), when wine and cocktails are served. Prepare for gelato made from sweet bell peppers, chili, green tea, and even oyster and smoked salmon, paired with crudités, cold cuts, and even sushi. Purists can still get an incredible chocolate and pistachio, too, plus free Wi-Fi.

Circonvallazione Trionfale 11/13. © **06-39725949.** Cup from 2.50€. Tues–Thurs 8am–11pm, Fri 8am–midnight, Sat 9am–1am, Sun 9am–midnight. Metro: Cipro.

Panificio Bonci ★★ BAKERY The newest addition to the Gabriele Bonci empire is not another pizzeria but a traditional bakery, with naturally leavened bread (including seasonal delights, such as pumpkin bread), cakes, cookies, croissants, and puffy *pizzette* with tomato sauce, sold by weight. During holiday season Bonci bakes some of the best panettone in town, characterized by innovative twists on the classic recipe.

Via Trionfale 36. © **06-39734457.** Cakes, pizza 3€–5€. Mon–Sat 7:30–10pm; Sun 9:30am–3pm (July–Aug Mon–Sat 9:30am–3pm and 5–9pm). Closed 1 week in mid-Aug. Metro: Ottaviano.

Ancient Rome, Monti & Celio

For restaurant locations, see map p. 86. If all you need is a snack, there's no beating **Gaudeo,** Via del Boschetto 112 (www.gaudeo.it; ©**06-98183689**), where a freshly baked roll loaded with the finest prosciutto, mozzarella, salami, and a whole lot more costs between 4€ and 10€.

EXPENSIVE

InRoma al Campidoglio ★ ITALIAN Once a social club for Rome's film industry, InRoma sits on a cobbled lane opposite the Palatine Hill. The food is consistently good thanks to careful sourcing of premier ingredients from around Italy. Meals might start with *caprese di bufala affumicata* (salad of tomatoes and smoked buffalo mozzarella) followed by *tagliata* (griddled

A Roman deli.

beef strip steak) with a red wine reduction. You can eat inside in an under-stated romantic setting, but we recommend you reserve on the terrace for a table to remember. A 12€ light lunch is based on classic Roman pastas like *all'amatriciana* (cured pork, tomato, and pecorino cheese).

Via dei Fienili 56. www.inroma.eu. 📞 **06-69191024.** Main courses 18€–30€. Daily noon–4pm and 6:30–11:30pm. Bus: C3, 80D, 81, 160, or 628.

MODERATE

Caffè Propaganda ★ MODERN ITALIAN   This all-day eatery—part lively Parisian bistro, part cocktail bar—is a safe bet for scoring a good meal within eyeshot of the Colosseum. Diners lounge on caramel-colored leather banquettes and choose from a diverse menu that mixes Roman classics such as *carbonara* (pasta with cured pork, egg, and cheese), with familiar international dishes like Caesar salad (or an 18€ hamburger). When the chef gets whimsical, he offers treats like deep-fried *alici* (whole anchovy) served in a paper bag. Service is relaxed by North American standards, so only eat here if you have time to linger. The mixology department, led by star bartender Patrick Pistolesi, skill-fully assembles Propaganda's signature cocktails.

Via Claudia 15. www.caffepropaganda.it. 📞 **06-94534255.** Main courses 15€–22€. Tues–Sun 12:30pm–12:30am. Metro: Colosseo/Tram: 3.

Da Danilo ★★ ROMAN   The general rule is: Don't dine near the sta-tion, but there are a few exceptions. Rightly popular with Roman busi-ness lunchers and *cucina romana* aficionados, this intimate eatery offers authentic Rome and Lazio fare, prepared with quality local ingredients. Don't let the informal setting—homey wood paneling and soccer celeb-rity photos on the walls—trick you: This trattoria's fine food and atten-tion to detail ranks it as some of Rome's best local cuisine. Classics include one of the city's best *cacio e pepe* pasta dish (sheep's milk Pecorino cheese and black pepper), served out of a massive, scooped out

Pecorino cheese round; the house *carbonara*, creamy and egg-forward; and homemade gnocchi served, as traditions dictates, exclusively on Thursday. The beef tartare, grilled lambchops, and lardo-laced ribeyes are menu strong points, as are all the daily meat specials. The wine list features a good choice of elegant Lazio labels, and there are always interesting tastings and events hosted in the small private room.

Via Petrarca 13. www.trattoriadadanilo.it. ✆ **06-77200111.** Main courses 12€–17€. Tues–Sat 12:30–3pm and 7:30–midnight. Closed 2 weeks in Aug. Metro: Vittorio Emanuele and Manzoni.

La Barrique ★★ MODERN ROMAN   This cozy, contemporary *enoteca* (a wine bar with food) has a kitchen that knocks out farm-to-table fresh fare that complements the well-chosen wine list. The atmosphere is lively and informal, with rustic place settings and friendly service—as any proper *enoteca* should be. Dishes come in hearty portions on a daily-changing menu. Expect the likes of *bocconcini di baccalà* (salt-cod morsels), crispy on the outside and served with a rich tomato dipping sauce; or *crostone* (a giant crostino) topped with grilled burrata cheese, chicory, and cherry tomatoes. Wines are available by the glass, quarter-liter, or half-liter.

Via del Boschetto 41B. ✆ **06-47825953.** Main courses 10€–18€. Mon–Fri 12:30–2:30pm; Mon–Sat 6:30–11:30pm. Metro: Cavour.

L'Asino d'Oro ★★ CONTEMPORARY UMBRIAN/ROMAN   This isn't your typical Roman eatery. Helmed by Lucio Sforza, a renowned chef from Orvieto, L'Asino d'Oro offers a seriously refined take on the flavors of central Italy without a checked tablecloth in sight; instead, the setting is contemporary with a Scandinavian feel thanks to the light-wood interior. As for the food, it's marked by creativity and flair, in both flavor and presentation. Expect bizarre pairings and flavor combos—like *lumache in umido piccante al finocchietto selvatico* (snail stew with wild fennel) or fettuccine in duck liver and vin santo sauce—but they work!

Via del Boschetto 73. www.facebook.com/asinodoro. ✆ **06-48913832.** Main courses 13€–17€. Tues–Sat 12:30–2:30pm; Mon–Sat 7:30–10:30pm. Closed last 2 weeks in Aug. Metro: Cavour.

Terre e Domus della Provincia Romana ★★ CONTEMPORARY ROMAN   Located in the stunning Palazzo Valentini, opposite the Trajan Column, with sleek, modern décor and floor-to-ceiling windows that overlook the Vittoriano and Trajan Markets, the newly managed "enoteca" belonging to the county of Rome, strictly showcases only the best in local wines and products, plus produce grown at the Rebibbia prison in Rome. The menu lists traditional Roman classics, and an abundance of seasonal, vegetable-driven dishes: we loved the gnocchi *cacio e pepe* and classic amatriciana. Don't miss the local artichokes, which are in their prime between February and May.

Foro di Traiano 82–84. www.palazzovalentini.it. ✆ **06-69940273.** Main courses 10€–15€. Daily 7:30am–midnight. Metro: Cavour. Bus: 80, 85, 87, or 175.

INEXPENSIVE

Li Rioni ★★ PIZZA   This fab neighborhood pizzeria is close enough to the Colosseum to be convenient, but just distant enough to avoid the dreaded "touristy" label that applies to so much dining in this part of town. Roman-style pizzas baked in the wood-stoked oven are among the best in town, with perfect crisp crusts. There's also a bruschetta list (from around 4€) and a range of salads. Outside tables can be cramped, but there's plenty of room inside. If you want to eat late, booking is essential or you'll be fighting for a table with hungry locals.

Via SS. Quattro 24. www.lirioni.it. ✆ **06-70450605.** Pizzas 5.50€–9€. Wed–Mon 7:30–11:30pm. Bus: 53, 85, or 117.

Centro Storico & the Pantheon

For restaurant locations, see map p. 97. Vegetarians looking for massive salads (or anyone who just wants a break from all those heavy meats and starches) can find great food at the neighborhood branch of **L'Insalata Ricca,** Largo dei Chiavari 85 (www.linsalataricca.it; ✆ **06-68803656;** daily noon–midnight). It also offers free Wi-Fi.

EXPENSIVE

Da Pancrazio ★ ROMAN   At this traditional Roman restaurant, the premises *almost* outshine the food. The restaurant's built over the ruins of the 1st-century B.C. Theatre of Pompey (where Julius Caesar was infamously murdered), and its various dining rooms and spaces are decked out with charming historical decor, from Roman-style benches and carved capitals to Belle Epoque paintings and furnishings (the restaurant opened in 1922). As for the menu, go for the classic Roman fare the kitchen does best, such as *abbacchio al forno con patate* (baked lamb with potatoes) or the *spaghetti alla carbonara.*

Piazza del Biscione 92. www.dapancrazio.it. ✆ **06-6861246.** Main courses 15€–27€. Thurs–Tues 12:30–3pm and 7:30pm–11pm. Closed 3 weeks in Aug. Bus: 46, 64, 84, or 916 to Largo di Torre Argentina.

Osteria dell'Antiquario ★ MODERN ITALIAN/ROMAN   Here's a romantic restaurant, where tables are lit by candlelight in the evenings and in the summer you can sit on the terrace overlooking the Palazzo Lancillotti. The menu is mostly Roman, but there are inventive detours such as lobster soup, linguine with grouper sauce, gnocchi with clams and wild mushrooms, or a special cannelloni. Fresh fish here is especially good, with tuna, turbot, prawns, and swordfish brought in daily.

Piazzetta di S. Simeone 26–27, Via dei Coronari. www.osteriadellantiquario.it. ✆ **06-6879694.** Main courses 15€–30€. Daily 7–11pm; Sept–June also daily noon–2:30pm. Closed 15 days in mid-Aug, Christmas, and Jan 6–30. Bus: 70, 81, or 90.

MODERATE

Alfredo e Ada ★ ROMAN   No menus here, just the waiter—and it's usually owner Sergio explaining, in Italian, what the kitchen is preparing that day. You'll typically be offered Roman trattoria classics like eggplant parmigiana, artichoke lasagna, excellent carbonara, or tripe. The whole place oozes character, with shared tables, scribbled walls festooned with drawings and paintings, and the house wine poured into carafes from a tap in the wall. With only five tables, try to make a reservation or get here early. This sort of place is becoming rare in Rome—enjoy it while you can.

Via dei Banchi Nuovi 14. ✆ **06-6878842.** Main courses 10€–18€. Tues–Sat 12:30pm–midnight. Closed Aug. Bus: 46B, 98, 870, or 881.

Armando al Pantheon ★ ROMAN/VEGETARIAN   Despite being just a few steps from the Pantheon, this typical Roman trattoria remains an authentic, family-owned business serving as many locals as tourists. Chef Armando Gargioli took over the place in 1961 and his sons now run the business. Roman favorites to look out for include the *pasta e ceci* (pasta and chickpeas; Fri only), the Jewish-influenced *aliciotti all'indivia* (endive and roasted anchovies; Tues only), and the fabulous *abbacchio* (roast lamb). Another bonus: Vegetarians get their own, fairly extensive, menu. Good wine list with local labels.

Salita dei Crescenzi 31. www.armandoalpantheon.it. ✆ **06-68803034.** Main courses 10€–24€. Mon–Fri noon–3pm and 7–11pm; Sat noon–3pm. Closed Aug. Bus: 30, 40, 62, 64, 81, or 492.

La Campana ★★ ROMAN/TRADITIONAL ITALIAN   Rome's oldest and most traditional restaurant is located in a small alley a stone's throw from Piazza Navona and the Pantheon. Family atmosphere and a classic Roman elegance permeate the spacious, well-lit rooms. The atmosphere is convivial yet refined, with a lovely mixture of regulars and locals. There's a broad selection of *antipasti* displayed on a long table at the entrance, and the menu (which changes daily) features authentic *cucina romana* classics like pasta with oxtail ragout, tripe, gnocchi, *cacio e pepe*, and myriad vegetarian choices. The wine list includes interesting local labels, and the staff and service are impeccable.

Vicolo della Campana 18. www.ristorantelacampana.com. ✆ **06-6875273.** Main courses 12€–18€. Tues–Sun noon–3pm and 7:30–11pm. Bus: 30, 70, 81, 87, 186, 492, or 628.

Nonna Betta ★★ ROMAN/JEWISH   Though not strictly kosher, this is the only restaurant in Rome's old Jewish quarter historically owned and managed by Roman Jews. Traditional "nonna" dishes include delicious *carciofi alla giudia,* deep-fried artichokes, served with small pieces of fried food, like battered cod filet, stuffed and fried zucchini flowers, carrot sticks, and whatever vegetable is in season. Don't forego the *baccalà* with onions and tomato or the tagliolini with chicory and mullet roe. There are Middle Eastern specialties such as falafel and couscous on the menu as well, and all desserts are homemade, including a stellar pistachio cake.

Via del Portico d'Ottavia 16. www.nonnabetta.it. ✆ **06-68806263**. Main courses 10€. Sun–Fri noon–3pm and 7–11pm. Bus: 23, 63, 280, 630, or 780. Tram 8.

INEXPENSIVE

Antico Forno Roscioli ★★ BAKERY   The Rosciolis have been running this celebrated bakery for three generations since the 1970s, though the premises has been knocking out bread since at least 1824. Today it's the home of the finest crusty sourdough in Rome, assorted cakes, and addictive pastries and biscotti, as well as exceptional Roman-style *pizza bianca* and *pizza rossa* sold by weight. Note that this is a take-out joint, with very limited seating inside and only a few stand-up tables out front—and the wider range of pizza toppings is only available from noon to 2:30pm. But you could always take your food to nearby Piazza Farnese. The unmissable Roscioli restaurant and *salumeria* deli is around the corner, at Via dei Giubbonari 21.

Via dei Chiavari 34. www.anticofornoroscioli.it. *€* **06-6864045.** Pizza from 4.50€ (sold by weight). Mon–Sat 7am–7:30pm. Tram: 8.

Tridente, the Spanish Steps & Via Veneto

For restaurant locations, see map p. 103. The historic cafes near the Spanish Steps are saturated with history but, sadly, tend to be overpriced tourist traps, where mediocre cakes or even a cup of coffee or tea will cost 5€. Nevertheless, you may want to pop inside the two most celebrated institutions: **Babington's Tea Rooms** (www.babingtons.com; *€* **06-6786027;** daily 10am–9:30pm), which was established in 1893 at the foot of the Spanish Steps by a couple of English *signore,* and **Caffè Greco,** Via dei Condotti 86 (www.anticocaffegreco.eu; *€* **06-6791700;** daily 9am–8pm), Rome's oldest bar, opened in 1760, which has hosted Keats, Ibsen, Goethe, and many other historical *cognoscenti.*

EXPENSIVE

Al Ceppo ★★ MARCHIGIANA/ROMAN   The setting of this Parioli dining institution is that of an elegant 19th-century parlor, with chandeliers, flower arrangements, family portraits on the walls, and an open kitchen featuring a wood-stoked hearth, where various meats are roasted before your eyes. Service is performed with the grace proper of the two sisters running it. Cristina and Marisa are originally from the Le Marche region northeast of Rome, and regional hallmark dishes are represented here: *marchigiana*-style rabbit, fish stews, fresh seafood, and porchetta. You'll also find veal, pork, and a variety of pastas. If the braised beef cheek is on the menu, don't forego that mystical experience.

Via Panama 2 (near Piazza Ungheria). www.ristorantealceppo.it. *€* **06-8419696.** Main courses 18€–32€. Tues–Sun 12:30–3pm and 8–11pm. Closed last 2 weeks in Aug. Bus: 52 or 910.

Café Romano ★ CONTEMPORARY ROMAN   The official restaurant of the posh Hotel d'Inghilterra lies on one of Rome's "fashion streets," a suitably upscale location for this temple to fine dining. Chef Antonio Vitale is the current maestro, his seasonal, contemporary menus utilizing fresh produce and riffing on traditional Roman dishes. Starters such as zucchini flowers stuffed with buffalo mozzarella, burrata cheese and salmon roe are classic. The pasta with seafood and grated mozzarella adds some of his Neapolitan hometown flavor. For the main course, there's duck leg served with potato pie, and the roasted veal shank with asparagus, which are both refined, tantalizing versions of Roman favorites.

In Hotel d'Inghilterra, Via Borgognona 4. www.niquesahotels.com. ☏ **06-69981500.** Main courses 23€–3€. Daily 7–10:30am and noon–10:30pm. Metro: Spagna.

Imàgo ★★★ INTERNATIONAL   The views of Rome from this 6th-floor hotel restaurant are jaw-dropping, a gorgeous panorama of the old city laid out before you, glowing pink as the sun goes down. The food is equally special, with chef Francesco Apreda's reinterpretation of Italian cuisine, which borrows heavily from Indian and Japanese culinary schools. The Michelin star–awarded menus change seasonally, but might include duck breast tandoori-style, sake-glazed black cod with purple baby vegetables, or even a lavender-flavored casserole of quail and sea scallops. Reservations are essential; jackets required for the gentlemen.

In Hotel Hassler, Piazza della Trinità dei Monti 6. www.imagorestaurant.com. ☏ **06-69934726.** Main courses 39€–46€; 9-course tasting menu 140€; 6-course vegetarian menu 120€. Daily 7:30–10:30pm. Metro: Spagna.

La Terrazza dell'Eden ★★★ MODERN ITALIAN/INTERNATIONAL   This restaurant on the top floor of the Hotel Eden offers superb cuisine and breathtaking views that sweep from Villa Borghese below, all the way to St. Peter's. Exciting young chef Fabio Ciervo offers an interesting angle on continental classics; starters may include smoked lobster with wild black rice, and will set the stage for fragrant risotto with cherries, Champagne rosé, and *pigeon de Bresse* and more tempting choices of pastas. Menus change seasonally, but expect a range of fresh fish like sea bass, mullet, and turbot dishes, and some twists on Roman-style meat courses, from lamb in a crust of mixed herbs with mushrooms and lemon thyme sauce, to roast saddle of venison and suckling pig sausage with Bronte pistachio, jazzed up with a piquant quince and liquorice sauce. Forget showing up without an advance reservation.

In Hotel Eden, Via Ludovisi 49. www.dorchestercollection.com. ☏ **06-47812752.** Main courses 35€–55€; 6-course fixed-price gourmet menu, excluding wine 120€. Daily 12:30–2:30pm and 7:30–10:30pm. Metro: Barberini.

Metamorfosi ★★★ MODERN ITALIAN   The prestigious Michelin star–awarded restaurant is a feast for both the eyes and the taste buds. The minimalistic decor—soft tones of chocolate and beige dotted with subtle floral accents—balances the cuisine's flair for astonishing creations. Chef Roy Caceres, a native of Colombia, likes to trigger emotions in his guests, spanning beyond smell and taste, and telling a story with each beautifully crafted dish. With a penchant for squab dishes, Caceres shines in risotto and pasta preparations, along with elegant meat and fish interpretations. Be prepared for creamy cheese ravioli mixed with salmon, hazelnut, and smoked pepper; risotto wrapped in a thin saffron film; winsomely presented glazed eel with farro and sweet onion sorbet; and crispy lamb with almonds, eggplant, and gin-juniper ice cream. The menu also offers two creative tasting menus, each featuring the restaurant's showpieces, and diners can benefit from the helpful guidance of a very talented sommelier.

Via Giovanni Antonelli 30/32. www.metamorfosiroma.it. © **06-8076839.** Main courses 25€–30€. Mon–Fri 12:30–3pm and 8–11:30pm; Sat 7:30–midnight. Bus: 168, 223, 910, and 926.

MODERATE

Al Vero Girarrosto Toscano ★★ TUSCAN   This Dolce Vita stalwart has been popular with celebrities and gourmands since its opening in the 1960s. Since then, the restaurant's praised traditional Roman cuisine has been slowly replaced by universally acclaimed Tuscan recipes, for which it now draws the same VIP crowds and carnivores south of the Arno. The decor is as classic as the menu, with warm wood paneling, elegant finishings, and a cozy fireplace that doubles as open-hearth grill. Don't miss classic Tuscan hors d'oeuvres like liver crostini and assorted bruschettas, but do focus your attention on equally classic hearty soups like pasta and beans and droolsome *ribollita* (minestrone enhanced with kale, cannellini beans, and bread). Grilled meats play a starring role here with *girarrosto* (Tuscan barbecue) classics like the Fiorentina (a 2-lb. T-bone steak), succulent tenderloin, filet, or a platter of mixed grilled ribs, chops, and sausage. There's a good wine list, with a clear slant toward regional labels.

Via Campania 29. www.alverogirarrostotoscano.it. © **06-42013045.** Main courses 18€–35€. Daily 12:30–3pm and 7:30pm–midnight. Bus: 52, 53, 217, 360 or 910.

Canova Tadolini ★★ ROMAN   Few restaurants are so steeped in history as this place. Antonio Canova's sculpture studio was kept as a workshop by the descendants of his pupil Adamo Tadolini until 1967, explaining why even today it is littered with tools and sculptures in bronze, plaster, and marble. The whole thing really does seem like a museum, with tables squeezed between models, casts, drapes, and bas-reliefs. The Sala Giulio is dominated by a giant copy of a statue of Pope Leo XIII (the original stands on the Pope's tomb) by Giulio Tadolini (grandson of Adamo), while the whimsical (and slightly creepy) Sala Anatomia is decorated with odd bits of marble arms, legs, and thighs once attached to complete sculptures. The pasta menu features tasty versions of *spaghetti alle vongole* and *alla carbonara,* while entrees offer more interest, from the veal chop grilled and served with rustic potatoes and rosemary, to the sliced skirt steak salad with arugula, cherry tomatoes, and Parmesan.

Via del Babuino 150A–B. www.canovatadolini.com. © **06-32110702.** Main courses 11€–25€. Mon–Sat 8am–8:30pm. Metro: Spagna.

Colline Emiliane ★★ EMILIANA-ROMAGNOLA   This family-owned restaurant tucked in an alley beside the the Trevi Fountain has been serving traditional dishes from Emilia-Romagna since 1931. Service is excellent and so is the food: Classics include *tortelli di zucca* (stuffed pasta pockets flavored with crushed Amaretto biscuits) and magnificent *tagliatelle alla Bolognese*. Save room for the chocolate tart or lemon meringue pie for dessert. Reservations are essential.

Via degli Avignonesi 22 (off Piazza Barberini). ✆ **06-4817538.** Main courses 14€– 25€. Tues–Sun 12:30–2:45pm; Tues–Sat 7:30–10:45pm. Closed Sun in July and all of Aug. Metro: Barberini.

Il Bacaro ★ MODERN ITALIAN Although it's housed in a 17th-century *palazzo,* this is a modern Roman bistro with contemporary takes on traditional trattoria dishes. Expect pasta with swordfish or tuna, or a braised skewer of prawns wrapped in precious melting strips of lardo, served on vegetable velouté, and Argentine beef steaks dotted with flecks of pâté, or, when available, shaved white truffles from Piedmont. Desserts revolve around a sensational selection of mousses paired with Bavarian chocolate, hazelnuts, caramel, and pistachio. The wine list features more than 600 labels, many well-priced varietals from all over Italy, and with just as much attention paid to French wines.

Via degli Spagnoli 27 (near Piazza delle Coppelle). www.ilbacaroroma.com. ✆ **06-6872554.** Main courses 14€–24€. Daily 10am–1am. Metro: Spagna.

Around Termini

For restaurant locations, see map p. 112.

EXPENSIVE

Pipero al Rex ★★★ CONTEMPORARY ROMAN Who said Termini can't be romantic? Located on the ground floor of the Rex Hotel, this tastefully decorated dining room serves 6 to 7 tables for a total of 16 covers, lined with white tablecloths and flooded in warm lighting. Sommelier and consummate host Alessandro Pipero works the front of the Michelin-star dining room; while Chef Luciano Monosilio runs the kitchen. Service is impeccable and never intrusive, and the menu features an interesting selection of classic spaghetti carbonara (portion size and relative price chosen starting at a plate of 50 grams for only 10€), or more modern chocolate-filled tortellini in bone broth. Main courses shine in the duck breast tartare, or the anglerfish served with licorice and Jerusalem artichoke.

Via Torino 149. www.hotelrex.net. ✆ **06-4815702.** Main courses 30€–25€; 9-course tasting menu 80€. Mon–Sat 12:30–2:30pm and 7:30–10:30pm. Metro: Termini.

MODERATE

Trimani Il Wine Bar ★ MODERN ITALIAN This small bistro and impressively stocked wine bar attracts white collars and wine lovers in a modern and relaxed ambience, accompanied by smooth jazz. Dishes are made to suit the wines: Seasonal pasta *primi* might include a salad of octopus, fava beans, and potato spiked with olives and almonds. Refined entrees might include rabbit stuffed with asparagus, and Luganega sausage served with a zucchini puree. There's a well-chosen wines-by-the-glass list that changes daily. If you just want a snack to accompany your vino, cheese and salami platters range from 9€ to 13€.

Via Cernaia 37B. www.trimani.com. ℂ **06-4469630.** Main courses 10€–18€. Mon–Sat 11:30am–3pm and 5:30pm–midnight. Closed Sat mid-Jun to mid-Sept. Closed 2 weeks in mid-Aug. Metro: Repubblica or Castro Pretorio.

INEXPENSIVE

Pinsere ★★ PIZZA *Pinsa* is not your average pizza, rather an ancient Roman preparation: an oval focaccia made with a blend of four organic flours and olive oil that's left to rise for 2-3 days. The result is a fragrant, feather-light single-portion snack. The small Pinsere bakery bakes pinsa on request, tops each with a variety of ingredients, and sells them over a tiny counter for an even smaller price. Favorites are Campionessa with pureed pumpkin, smoked cheese and pancetta; classic tomato, basil and *bufala,* or the summer plain pinsa stuffed with silken slices of prosciutto and fresh figs. Toppings and fillings are seasonal and change in quick rotation. There's also a good choice of salads and soups, plus bottled beers and soft drinks. Note that there is no seating, and reservations aren't taken.

Via Flavia 98. ℂ **06-42020924.** Pinsa 1€–4,50€ according to topping. Mon–Fri 9am–4pm. Bus: 60, 60L, 61,62,82, 492, 910.

Trastevere

For restaurant locations, see map p. 115. Popular craft-beer bar **Bir and Fud** (p. 156) also serves pizzas and traditional snacks like *supplì* (fried rice croquettes filled with mozzarella and tomato sauce) to hungry drinkers. It serves food in the evening daily, and at lunchtime from Thursday through Sunday.

EXPENSIVE

Glass ★★★ CONTEMPORARY ROMAN Sleek modernism rules here, in design and cuisine alike. Walls are stark white and floors are polished, and the menu is a mix of innovation and cosmopolitan flair. Listings change monthly, but expect the likes of tagliatelle with wild asparagus, black garlic, and lemon followed by sumac-scented lamb with purple potato chips. Thanks to the skills of Michelin-starred chef Cristina Bowerman, this is one of Rome's hottest tables—reservations are essential.

Vicolo del Cinque 58. www.glass-restaurant.it. ℂ **06-58335903.** Main courses 29€–50€; fixed-price menus 75€–100€. Tues–Sun 7:30–11:30pm. Closed 2 weeks in Jan, 2 weeks in July. Bus: 125.

La Gensola ★★★ SEAFOOD/ROMAN This family-run restaurant is considered one of the best seafood destinations in Rome. The ambience is warm and welcoming, like a true Trastevere home; decor is cozy and intimate, with soft lighting and a life-sized wood-carved tree in the middle of the main dining room. Fish-lovers flock here for the trademark spaghetti with sea urchin, the fish-forward *amatriciana,* and general traditional Roman cuisine with a marine twist. The incredibly fresh fish is sourced daily in Lazio's best coastal sea auctions. Besides melt-in-your-mouth calamari, shrimp and tuna, ceviche, carpaccios and tartare, the

GETTING YOUR FILL OF gelato

Don't leave town without trying one of Rome's outstanding **ice-cream parlors.** However, choose your Italian ice carefully: Don't buy close to the tourist-packed piazzas, and avoid places with vats full of brightly colored, air-pumped gelato. The best gelato is made only from natural ingredients, which impart a natural color (if the pistachio gelato is bright green, for example, rather than grayish-green, move on). Take your cone (*cono*) or small cup (*coppetta*) and walk as you eat—sitting down on the premises or ordering at outside tables is usually more expensive. The recommended spots below are generally open mid-morning to late, sometimes after midnight on summer weekends. Cones and small cups rarely go beyond 2.50€.

One of Rome's oldest artisan gelato makers, **Gelateria Alberto Pica** ★★★ (Via della Seggiola 12; ℂ **06-6868405;** Bus: H, 63, 780, or 810; Tram 8) produces top-quality gelato churned with ingredients sourced locally, including their own wild strawberries grown in the family's countryside estate. Just a few of our *many* faves include rice with cinnamon; Sicilian pistachio; honey & orange and Amalfi lemon.

At the fabulous (and gluten-free) **Fatamorgana** ★★★ (Piazza degli Zingari 5, Monti; www.gelateriafatamorgana.it;

ℂ **06-86391589;** Metro: Cavour), creative flavors are the hallmark, and there's a firm commitment to seasonal and organic ingredients. Try *crema di zenzero* (cream of ginger), *cioccolato Lapsang Souchong* (chocolate with smoked black tea), or a surprising basil-walnut-honey combo.

In the Termini area, tiny but sleek **Come il Latte** (Via Silvio Spaventa 24; www.comeillatte.it; ℂ **06-42903882;** Metro: Repubblica or Castro Pretorio) turns out artisan gelatos in flavors ranging from salted caramel, to mascarpone and crumbled cookies, to espresso coffee, to rice with cinnamon; fruit flavors change according to the season and market availability. Committed to short-supply-chain sustainability, the charming gelateria adds props like an American drinking fountain and old-school vat containers.

Trastevere's best artisan gelato, **Fior di Luna** ★★★ (Via della Lungaretta 96; www.fiordiluna.com; ℂ **06-64561314;** Bus: H or 780/Tram: 8), is made with natural and fair-trade produce. The stars of the small but mighty menu are the intense and incredibly rich chocolate flavors, spiked with fig or orange or made with single *cru* cocoa, and the perfect pistachio.

grill churns out succulent beefsteaks and other non fish-based dishes. Reservations, which are mandatory on the weekend, can also be made online, via the restaurant's website, which is in Italian only.
Piazza della Gensola 15. www.osterialagensola.it. ℂ **06-58332758.** Main courses 15€. Daily 12:30–3pm and 7:30–11:30pm. Bus: 125.

MODERATE

Cacio e Pepe ★ ROMAN   This ultra-traditional trattoria, complete with paper tablecloths, a TV in the background showing the game, the owner chatting up the ladies, and a bustling crowd of patrons waiting to be seated, is a Trastevere neighborhood stalwart. On the menu, besides name-sake pasta *cacio e pepe* you won't go wrong with other classic Roman pasta dishes, such as *amatriciana* (tomato and *guanciale*, cured pork jowel) and a very good rendition of *carbonara* (egg, pecorino, and crispy guanciale)—be ready for hearty portions. For *secondo*—if you have room left—keep it simple; consider *polpette* (stewed meatballs), *saltimbocca alla romana* (veal cutlets with sage and ham), and simple grilled meats, all sold at sensible prices. Vicolo del Cinque 15. www.osteriacacioepepe.it. *©* **06-89572853.** Main courses 9€–18€. Daily 7pm–midnight; Sun also 12:30–3pm. Bus: 125.

Da Enzo al 29 ★★ ROMAN   This classic and untouristy Trastevere family-run trattoria serves traditional Roman cuisine in a friendly and relaxed atmosphere, with a few outdoor tables looking out on some of Trastevere's quaintest cobbled alleys. *Cucina romana* including classic carbonara, *amatriciana,* and *cacio e pepe* win the gold, but do consider the ravioli stuffed with ricotta and spinach, and the house meatballs braised in tomato sauce. Local wines can be ordered by the jug or glass, and desserts (among them, a good mascarpone with wild strawberries) come served in either full or half portions, which is good, considering Enzo's hefty servings.
Via dei Vascellari 29. www.daenzoal29.com. *©* **06 5812260.** Main courses 8€–15€. Mon–Sat 12:30–3pm and 7:30–11:00pm. Bus: 125.

INEXPENSIVE

Dar Poeta ★ PIZZA   Many consider this the best pizza in Rome. I wouldn't go that far, but "the poet" does serve up a passable pie with good toppings, creatively combined. The lines are long to eat in, but you can also order a pie for takeout from the host. Popular signature pizzas are the *patataccia* (potatoes, creamed zucchini, and *speck* [a smoked prosciutto]) and the decadent dessert calzone, filled with fresh ricotta and Nutella.
Vicolo del Bologna 45. www.darpoeta.com. *©* **06-5880516.** Pizzas 5€–9€. Daily noon–11pm. Bus: 125.

Testaccio

Rome's old meatpacking district is a major dining zone (see map p. 117). The old slaughterhouses have been transformed into art venues, markets, and museum **MACRO** (p. 108), but restaurants here still specialize in meats from the *quinto quarto* (the "fifth quarter")—the leftover parts of an animal after the slaughter, typically offal like sweetbreads, tripe, tails, and other goodies you won't find on most American menus. This is an area to eat *cucina romana*—either in the restaurants recommended below, or from any street-food stall in the **Nuovo Mercato di Testaccio** (p. 152). If you book a food-themed tour of Rome, you will almost certainly end up down here.

EXPENSIVE

Checchino dal 1887 ★★ ROMAN   For haute *quinto quarto* fare, this is your best bet. Testaccio has been changing rapidly, but not Checchino. It's a pricier choice than most of the other restaurants in this area, but Romans from all over the city keep coming back when they want authentic *tonnarelli al sugo di coda* (pasta with a stewed oxtail sauce for which Checchino holds a secret recipe) and *pajata* (veal intestines) cooked any number of ways—with *rigatoni* pasta, roasted, or in a stew. Via di Monte Testaccio 30. www.checchino-dal-1887.com. ℂ **06-5743816.** Main courses 12€–27€; fixed-price menu 40€–65€. Tues–Sat 12:30–2:45pm and 8–11:45pm. Closed Aug and last week in Dec. Bus: 83, 673, or 719.

MODERATE

Flavio al Velavevodetto ★★ ROMAN   Flavio's plain dining room is burrowed out of the side of Rome's most unusual "hill"—a large mound made from amphorae discarded during the Roman era (see p. 68). But this is one of the best places in the city to try well-prepped classic Roman pastas like *cacio e pepe,* and *quinto quarto* entrees at fair prices. The *misto umido* is an ideal sampler for first-timers, with portions of *polpette* (meatballs), *coda alla vaccinara* (oxtail), and *involtini* (stuffed rolled veal), enough for three to share. Homemade desserts are tasty, but the *tiramisù* wins the gold.
Via di Monte Testaccio 97–99. www.ristorantevelavevodetto.it. ℂ **06-5744194.** Main courses 9€–30€. Daily 12:30–3pm and 7:45–11pm. Bus: 83, 673, or 719.

Osteria degli Amici ★★ MODERN ROMAN   This intimate and friendly *osteria,* on the corner of nightclub central and the hill of broken amphorae, serves everything from traditional Roman cuisine to creative interpretations. Charming friends Claudio and Alessandro base their menu on fresh produce sourced at the nearby market, as well as their combined experience gathered by working in famous kitchens around the world. Signature musts include golden-crusted fried mozzarella *in carrozza,* and the wide selection of pastas, ranging from classic *carbonara* to large *paccheri* tubes with mussels, clams, and cherry tomatoes. My favorite remains *gricia coi carciofi,* a tomatoless *amatriciana* with slivers of braised artichoke. Let the honest vino flow and leave room for the apple tartlet with cinnamon gelato.
Via Nicola Zabaglia 25. ℂ **06-5781466.** Main courses 14€–18€. Wed–Mon 12:30–3pm and 7:30pm–midnight. Bus: 83, 673, or 719.

Porto Fluviale ★ MODERN ITALIAN   This multi-functional restaurant—part trattoria, part street-food stall, part pizzeria—can accommodate pretty much whatever you fancy, whenever you fancy it. The decor is modern and vaguely industrial, with a daytime clientele made up of families and white collars—the vibe gets younger after dark. From the various menus, best bets are the 30 or so *cicchetti,* small plates that allow you to test and taste the kitchen's range. You can share a few platters of *carpaccio di baccalà* (thin sliced of salt-cod), *maialino* (roasted suckling pig with pureed apple and rosemary), and *burrata e pomodori* (Apulian mozzarella pouch filled with a creamy milky filling, served with tomatoes). Most items on the regular menu (*primi* and *secondi*) also come in half portions, and there are burgers under 10€. But skip the pizzas; they're fairly nondescript.

Via del Porto Fluviale 22. www.portofluviale.com. © **06-5743199.** Main courses 8€–19€; set lunch 12€–20€. Daily 10:30am–2am. Metro: Piramide.

INEXPENSIVE

Da Remo ★★ PIZZA   Mentioning "Testaccio" and "pizza" in the same sentence elicits one typical response from locals: Da Remo, which is a Roman institution. In the summer, reservations at least 2 days in advance are wise. Every crisp-crusted pizza is made for all to see behind the open counters. The most basic ones (Margherita and Marinara) start at around 6€. If it's too crowded on a summer evening, order your pizza for takeout and eat it in the quaint park across the street. No credit cards.

Piazza Santa Maria Liberatrice 44. © **06-5746270.** Pizzas 7€–15€. Mon–Sat 7pm–1am. Bus: 83, 673, or 719.

La Moderna ★★ PIZZA/MODERN ITALIAN   For lovers of Neapolitan-style pizza (thicker rim), consider this pizzeria and cocktail bar with an unabashed passion for motion pictures: In addition to the movie memorabilia, there's even a functioning silver screen in one of the main dining rooms. The decor flirts with Paris bistros and New York delis, with lots of vintage posters and furnishings, a warm and cozy atmosphere. Besides an impressive mixology department and signature pizzas, the menu is graced with spaghetti *aglio, olio e peperoncino,* a classic home-style preparation made with properly assembled garlic, olive oil, and chili pepper flakes. The cuisine also includes offal—why not? You're in Testaccio. So be prepared for braised tongue and grilled sweetbreads. La Moderna also offers up street food with a wide selection of frankfurters, burgers, and delicious all-Roman *trapizzini* (triangular pizza pockets filled with local classics, like tripe or meatballs). An impressive choice of Italian and foreign craft beers and excellent music complete the warm setting.

Via Galvani 89. www.lamoderna-testaccio.com. © **06-5750123.** Pizzas 7€; Main courses 9€–15€. Daily 7:30am–2am. Bus: 83, 673, or 719.

SHOPPING

Rome offers temptations of every kind. In our limited space below we've summarized streets and areas known for their shops. The monthly rent on the famous streets is very high, and those costs are passed on to you. Nonetheless, a stroll down some of these streets presents a cross section of the most desirable wares in Rome.

Note that **sales** usually run twice a year, in January and July.

The Top Shopping Streets & Areas

AROUND PIAZZA DI SPAGNA   Most of Rome's haute couture and seriously upscale shopping fans out from the bottom of the Spanish Steps.

Upscale shopping around Piazza di Spagna.

Via Condotti is probably Rome's poshest shopping street, where you'll find Prada, Gucci, Bulgari, and the like. A few more down-to-earth stores have opened, but it's still largely a playground for the superrich. Neighboring **Via Borgognona** is another street where both the rents and the merchandise are chic and ultraexpensive, but thanks to its pedestrian-only access and handsome baroque and neoclassical facades, it offers a nicer window-browsing experience. Shops are more densely concentrated on **Via Frattina,** the third member of this trio of upscale streets. Chic boutiques for adults and kids rub shoulders with ready-to-wear fashions, high-end chains, and a few tourist tat vendors. It's usually thronged with shoppers who appreciate the lack of motor traffic.

VIA COLA DI RIENZO The commercial heart of the Prati neighborhood bordering the Vatican, this long, straight street runs from the Tiber to Piazza Risorgimento. Via Cola di Rienzo is known for stores selling a wide variety of merchandise at reasonable prices—from jewelry to fashionable clothing, bags, and shoes. Among the most prestigious is the historic Roman perfume store, **Bertozzini Profumeria dal 1913,** at no. 192 (✆ **06-6874662**). You will also find the department store **Coin** at no. 173 (with a large supermarket in the basement), the largest branch of venerable gourmet food store **Castroni** at no. 196 (www.castroni.it), and the smaller, more selective gourmet grocery **Franchi** at no. 200 (www. franchi.it), a good source for parmigiano cheese.

VIA DEL CORSO With less of a glamour quotient (and less stratospheric prices) than Via Condotti or Via Borgognona, Via del Corso boasts affordable styles aimed at younger consumers. Occasional gems are scattered amid the international shops selling jeans and sporting equipment. In general, the most interesting stores are toward the Piazza del Popolo end of the street (**Via del Babuino** here has a similar profile), plus there's a branch of department store **La Rinascente** (www.larinascente.it; ✆ **06-6784209**) at Piazzale Colonna 357. Sidewalks are narrow, so it's not a convenient street to window-shop with a stroller or young children.

VIA DEI CORONARI An antique-lover's souk. If you're shopping, or just window-shopping for antiques or vintage-style souvenir prints, then spend an hour walking the length of this pretty, pedestrian-only street.

VIA MARGUTTA This beautiful, tranquil street is home to numerous art stalls and artists' studios—Federico Fellini used to live here—though all the stores tend to offer the same

A Pause Before Purchasing

Although Rome has many wonderful boutiques, the shopping is generally better in **Florence**. If you're continuing on to there, you may want to hold off a bit, as you're likely to find a better selection and better prices.

sort of antiques and mediocre paintings these days. You have to shop hard to find real quality. Highlights include **Bottega del Marmoraro** at no. 53b, the studio of master stonecarver Sandro Fiorentini, and **Valentina Moncada**'s hugely popular contemporary art gallery at no. 54 (www.valentinamoncada.com; ✆ **06-3207956**).

MONTI Rome's most fashion-conscious central neighborhood has a pleasing mix of indie artisan retailers, hip boutiques, and honest, everyday stores frequented by locals, where there's not a brand name in sight. Roam the length of **Via del Boschetto** for one-off fashions, designer ateliers, and unique, gift-sized homewares. In fact, you can roam in every direction from the spot where Via del Boschetto meets **Via Panisperna.** Turn off on nearby **Via Urbana** or **Via Leonina,** where boutiques jostle for shopfront space with cafes that are ideal for a break or light lunch. Via Urbana also hosts the weekly **Mercatomonti** (see "Rome's Best Markets," below).

Rome's Best Markets

Campo de' Fiori ★ Central Rome's food market has been running since at least the 1800s. It's no longer the place to find a produce bargain, but is still a genuine slice of Roman life in one of its most attractive squares. The market runs Monday through Saturday from 7am to around 1 or 2pm. Campo de' Fiori. No phone. Bus: H, 23, 63, 116, 271, 280, 780, or 810/Tram: 8.

Eataly ★★ Not strictly a market, but a four-floor homage to Italian ingredients and cooking. Thirty different breads, 25 shelving bays of pasta, two aisles of olive oil . . . and that's just scratching the surface of what's under this one roof. Browse the cookbooks, chocolate, local wines and beer and cheese, or stop for a meal in one of the ingredient-themed restaurants and food bars (although prices are a little steep). This foodie heaven is open daily from 10am to midnight. Piazzale XII Ottobre 1492. www. roma.eataly.it. ✆ **06-90279201.** Metro: Piramide. Follow signs from Metro exit gates to "Air Terminal," then "Piazza XII Ottobre;" take the escalator up and then walk around to the right.

Mercatomonti ★★ Everything from contemporary glass jewelry to vintage cameras, handmade clothes for kids and adults, and one-off designs to wear or admire is sold here in the heart of trendy Monti, in a commandeered parking garage (where else?). The market runs Sundays from 10am to 6pm. Via Leonina 46. www.mercatomonti.com. No phone. Metro: Cavour.

Nuovo Mercato di Testaccio (New Testaccio Market) ★★

In 2012, the old Testaccio market building was replaced by this modern, daringly modernist, sustainably powered market building. It's the best place to go produce shopping with the Romans. There's everything you could want to pack a picnic—cheese, cured meats, seasonal fruit—as well as meat, fish, and fresh vegetables (ideal if you are self-catering in the city). There are also clothes and kitchenware stalls, but the food is the star. For instant gratification, sample the street food at **Mordi e Vai** ★★, Box 15 (www.mordievai.it; ✆ **339-1343344**). The likes of a *panino* filled with warm Roman recipes like veal and artichokes in a piquant gravy costs 4€. The market runs Monday through Saturday from 6am to 2:30pm. Btw. Via Luigi Galvani and Via Aldo Manuzio (at Via Benjamin Franklin). No phone. Bus: 83, 673, or 719.

Nuovo Mercato Trionfale (New Trionfale Market) ★★★

Replacing the old and rickety Via Andrea Doria market, this modern, working class (and rather unattractive) structure houses over 250 stalls, which more than make up for its exterior looks. Vendors sell top choice, local (and value) produce, meat, fish, cheese, eggs, baked goods and spices, as well as household wares. Keep an eye out for terrific butchers, exquisite fishmongers, and awesome local produce. A handful of stalls specializing in international ingredients sell everything from okra and pomelo to habanero chilis and hopia. If you plan to shop, bring cash; only a few fishmongers and butchers here accept credit cards. The market runs Monday through Saturday from 7am to 2pm; on Tuesdays and Fridays it stays open until 5pm. Via Andrea Doria 3. ✆ **06-39743501.** Tram: 19. Metro: Cipro

Fresh tomatoes at a market stall in Rome.

Porta Portese ★   Trastevere's vast weekly flea market stretches all the way from the Porta Portese gate along Via di Porta Portese to Viale di Trastevere. Expect to find everything. It runs Sundays from dawn until mid-afternoon. Via di Porta Portese. No phone. Tram: 8.

ENTERTAINMENT & NIGHTLIFE

Even if you don't speak Italian, you can generally follow the listings of special events and evening entertainment featured in *La Repubblica,* a leading national newspaper published in Rome. See also the "TrovaRoma" section of its city website, **www.roma.repubblica.it**. *Wanted in Rome* (www.wantedinrome.com) has listings of opera, rock, English-language cinema showings, and such and gives an insider look at expat Rome. **Un Ospite a Roma** (www.unospitearoma.it), available both online and in print, free at concierge desks and tourist information centers, is full of details on what's happening around the city. Free magazine and website *Romeing* (www.romeing.it) is worth consulting for events and lifestyle updates on the contemporary scene. Also check **InRome-Now.com** for monthly updates of cultural events.

Unless you're dead set on making the Roman nightclub circuit, try what might be a far livelier and less expensive option—sitting late at night on **Via Veneto, Piazza della Rotonda, Piazza del Popolo,** or one of Rome's other piazzas, all for the (admittedly inflated) cost of an espresso, a cappuccino, or a Campari and soda. For clubbers, it is almost impossible to predict where the next hot venue will appear, but if you like it loud and late—and have an adventurous streak—jump in a cab to **Monte Testaccio** or **Via del Pigneto** and bar-hop wherever takes your fancy. In Trastevere, there's always a bit of life along **Via Politeana** around the spot where it meets **Piazza Trilussa.**

Performing Arts & Live Music

While Rome's music scene in Rome doesn't have the same vibrancy as Florence's, nor the high-quality opera of Milan's La Scala or **La Fenice** in Venice (p. 418), classical music fans are still well catered to. In addition to the major venues featured below, be on the lookout for concerts and one-off events in churches and salons around the city. Check **www.operainroma.com** for a calendar of opera and ballet staged by the Opera in Roma association at the **Chiesa Evangelica Valdese,** Via IV Novembre 107. The **Pontificio Instituto di Musica Sacra,** Piazza Sant'Agostino 20A (www.musicasacra.va; **✆ 06-6638792**) and **All Saints' Anglican Church,** Via del Babuino 153 (www.accademiaoperaitaliana.it; **✆ 06-7842702**) both regularly run classical music and operatic evenings.

Alexanderplatz ★   An established stalwart of Rome, Alexanderplatz has been the home of Rome's jazz scene since the early 1980s. If there's a good act in the city, you will find it here. Via Ostia 9. www.alexander platzjazzclub.com. ✆ 06-39742171. Cover 10€. Metro: Ottaviano.

Auditorium–Parco della Musica ★★ Multiple stages showcase a broad range of music—from James Taylor to tango festivals and world music, to the classical chamber and symphonic music of the Accademia Nazionale di Santa Cecilia. The massive, purpose-built complex itself is a postmodern work of art, designed by architect Renzo Piano. Viale Pietro de Coubertin 30. www.auditorium.com. ✆ **02-60060900.** Bus: M, 53, or 910/Tram: 2D.

Teatro dell'Opera di Roma ★★ This is where you will find the marquee operas such as *La Traviata, Carmen,* and *Tosca.* There's also a full program of classical concerts with top-rank orchestras and ballet. In summer the action moves outdoors for a short season of unforgettable open-air operatic performances at the ruined **Baths of Caracalla** (p. 85). Piazza Beniamino Gigli 7. www.operaroma.it. ✆ **06-48160255.** Tickets 17€–150€. Metro: Repubblica.

The Teatro dell'Opera.

Cafes

Remember: In Rome and everywhere else in Italy, if you just want to drink a quick coffee and bolt, walk up to *il banco* (the bar), order *"un caffè, per favore"* or *"un cappuccino,"* and don't move. They will make it for you to drink on the spot. It will cost more (at least double) to sit down to drink it, and outdoor table service is the most expensive way to go. Even in the heart of the city center, a short coffee *al banco* should cost no more than 1€; add around .20€ for a *cappuccino.* Expect to pay up to five times that price if you sit outdoors on a marquee piazza. Most cafes in the city serve a decent cup of coffee, but here's a small selection of places worth hunting down. (For our top picks on *gelaterie,* see page 146.)

With its shabby-chic interior and namesake fig tree backdrop to charming outdoor seating where locals play chess at tables with mismatched chairs, **Bar del Fico ★** (Piazza del Fico 26; www.bardelfico.com; ✆ **06 6880 8413**) is one of Rome's most beloved aperitivo spots and coveted see-and-be-seen nightlife destinations. **Sant'Eustachio il Caffè** ★★ (Piazza Sant'Eustachio 82; www.santeustachioilcaffe.it; © **06-68802048**) roasts its own Fairtrade Arabica beans over wood. The unique taste and bitter kick to its brews ensures there's usually a friendly crowd a few deep at the bar. (Unless you ask, the coffee comes with sugar.) Debate still rages among Romans as to whether the city's best cup of coffee is served at Sant'Eustachio or at **Tazza d'Oro** ★, near the Pantheon (Via degli Orfani 84; www.tazzadorocoffeeshop.com; © **06-6789792**). Jacketed baristas work at 100mph at **Spinelli** ★ (Via dei Mille 60; no phone; weekdays only), a no-nonsense locals' cafe. Join the throng at the bar for a morning *cappuccino* and *un cornetto* (a croissant) filled with jam, *crema* (pastry cream), Nutella, or white chocolate. There's a cold-food buffet at lunch.

Wine Bars, Cocktail Bars & Craft Beer Bars

For Rome's most creative modern cocktails in a casual environment, visit **Caffè Propaganda** (p. 137).

APERITIVO CULTURE

The mass social phenomenon of the *aperitivo* (happy hour—and so much more) can be a great way to meet, or at least observe the particular ways of, real Romans. It started in hard-working northern cities like Milan, where you'd go to a bar after leaving the office and, for the price of one drink (usually under 10€), get access to an unlimited buffet of high-quality food—like chunks of *parmigiano*, cured meats, fresh green salad, or other pasta salads. Luckily for Rome (a decidedly less industrious city), the custom trickled down here, and now the city is filled with casual little places to drop in for a drink (from 6 or 7pm onward) and eat to your heart's content of all these tasty finger foods. All the places listed here are fine for families, too—Italian kids love aperitivo (minus the alcohol)!

Rome, Illuminated

When the sun goes down, Rome's palaces, ruins, fountains, and monuments are bathed in a theatrical white light. During your stay in Rome, be sure to make time for a memorable evening stroll past the solemn pillars of old temples or the cascading torrents of Renaissance fountains glowing under the blue-black sky.

The **Fountain of the Naiads** ("Fontana delle Naiadi") on Piazza della Repubblica, the **Fountain of the Tortoises** ("Fontana della Tartarughe") on Piazza Mattei, the **Fountain of Acqua Paola** ("Fontanone") at the top of the Janiculum Hill, and the **Trevi Fountain** (p. 106) are particularly

beautiful at night. The **Capitoline Hill** (or Campidoglio) is magnificently lit after dark, with its measured Renaissance facades glowing like jewel boxes. The view of the Roman Forum seen from the rear of Piazza del Campidoglio is perhaps the grandest in Rome (see "Three Free Views to Remember for a Lifetime" box, p. 91). If you're across the Tiber, the Vatican's **Piazza San Pietro** (p. 74) is impressive at night without the crowds. And a combination of illuminated architecture, baroque fountains, and sidewalk shows makes **Piazza Navona** (p. 96) even more delightful at night.

Look for signs in the window and follow your nose. The **Monti** neighborhood is a good place to begin. The **Terre Domus Enoteca Provincia di Roma** (see below) also does good *aperitivo*.

Ai Tre Scalini ★ This little *bottiglieria* (wine bar) is the soul of Monti. There's a traditional menu, as well as a long wine list with bottles sourced from across Italy. Arrive early or call to reserve a table: This place is usually jammed. Via Panisperna 251. ✆ **06-48907495.** Metro: Cavour.

Bir and Fud ★ Around 15 beers on tap (most of them Italian craft brews, and some brewed as strong as 9%) as well as carb-heavy snacks like pizza and *supplì* (fried rice balls). It's 5€ for a small beer. Via Benedetta 23. www.birandfud.it. ✆ **06-5894016.** Bus: 23, 125, 271, or 280.

Cavour 313 ★★ A wine bar that's as traditional and genuine as you will find, this close to the ruins. There are over 30 wines by the glass (from 3.50€) as well as cold cuts, cheese, and vegetable platters, or excellent carpaccio to partner the wines. Closed Sunday in summer. Via Cavour 313. www.cavour313.it. ✆ **06-6785496.** Metro: Colosseo and Cavour.

La Bottega del Caffè ★ Beers, wine, cocktails, *aperitivo*—there's a little of everything at one of Monti's busiest neighborhood bars. Piazza Madonna dei Monti 5. ✆ 06-64741578. Metro: Cavour.

Litro ★★ A wonderful addition to Rome's dining and drinking scene: a wine bar located in Monteverde Vecchio (residential area above Trastevere) that serves natural wines, cocktails and snacks sourced from Lazio-based purveyors of traditional cured meats and cheeses, plus bruschette, stellar alcoholic sorbets. Via Fratelli Bonnet 5. ✆ **06-45447639.** Bus: 75, 982.

NO.AU ★ Tricked out a little like a Barcelona cava bar, and located right in the old center, this place has craft beers from local brewer Birra del Borgo on tap plus a selection of wines (red, white, and sparkling) from around 5€ a glass. NO.AU (pronounced "knowhow," almost) is set back in a narrow alley to provide a little escape from the chaos. Closed Monday. Piazza di Montevecchio 16. ✆ **06-45652770.** Bus: 30, 46, 62, 64, 70, 81, 87, 116, or 571.

Open Baladin ★★ If anyone ever tells you that "Italians don't do good beer," send them to this bar near the Ghetto. A 40-long row of taps lines the bar, with beers from their own Piedmont brewery and across Italy (including many local to the Lazio region). Via degli Specchi 5–6. www.openbaladin.com. ✆ **06-6838989.** Tram: 8.

Stravinskij Bar ★ An evening at this award-winning cocktail bar inside one of Rome's most famous grand hotels is always a regal, exclusive affair. Mixology, ingredients, and canapés are all top-notch. Inside Hotel de Russie, Via del Babuino 9. ✆ **06-32888874.** Metro: Spagna.

SIDE TRIPS FROM ROME
Ostia Antica ★★

24km (15 miles) SW of Rome

The ruins of Rome's ancient port are a must-see for anyone who can't make it to Pompeii. It's a more comfortable daytrip than Pompeii, on a similar theme: the chance to wander around the preserved ruins of an ancient Roman settlement that has been barely touched since its abandonment.

Ostia, at the mouth of the Tiber, was the port of Rome, serving as the gateway for riches from the far corners of the Empire. Founded in the 4th century B.C., it became a major port and naval base under two later emperors, Claudius and Trajan. A prosperous city developed, full of temples, baths, theaters, and patrician homes.

Ostia flourished between the 1st and 3rd centuries, and survived until around the 9th century before it was abandoned. Gradually it became little more than a malaria bed, a buried ghost city that faded into history. A papal-sponsored commission launched a series of digs in the 19th century; however, the major work of unearthing was carried out under Mussolini's orders from 1938 to 1942 (the work had to stop because of the war). The city is only partially dug out today, but it's believed that all the chief monuments have been uncovered. There are quite a few impressive ruins—this is no dusty field like the Circus Maximus.

A word to the wise: There is no need for hiking boots, but the Roman streets underfoot are all clad in giant basalt cobblestones. Bear that in mind when choosing footwear for the day.

ESSENTIALS

GETTING THERE   Take the Metro to Piramide, changing lines there for the Lido train to Ostia Antica. (From the platform, take the exit for "Air Terminal" and turn right at the top of the steps, where the station name changes to Porta San Paolo.) Departures to Ostia are about every half-hour; the trip takes 25 minutes and is included in the price of a Metro single-journey ticket or Roma Pass (p. 66). It's just a 5-minute walk to the excavations from the Metro stop: Exit the station, walk ahead and over the footbridge, and then continue straight ahead until you reach the car park. The ticket booth is to the left.

VISITOR INFORMATION   The site opens daily at 8:30am. Closing times vary with the season, ranging from 7:15pm in high season (April through August) to 4:30pm off-season (November to February 15), so check times beforehand at **www.ostiaantica.beniculturali.it** or call ✆ **06-56350215.** Note that the ticket office closes 1 hour before the ruins close. Admission costs 8€ (10€ if there's an additional exhibition), free for ages 17 and under and 65 and over. The 2€ map on sale at the ticket booth is a wise investment.

PARKING   The car park, on Viale dei Romagnoli, costs 2.50€ for an unlimited period. Arrive early if you're driving: It is fairly small.

EXPLORING OSTIA ANTICA

The principal monuments are all labeled. On arrival, visitors first pass the *Necropoli* (burial grounds, always outside the city gates in Roman towns and cities). The main route follows the giant cobblestones of the **Decumanus ★** (the main street) into the heart of Ostia. The **Piazzale delle Corporazioni ★★** is like an early version of Wall Street: This square contained nearly 75 corporations, the nature of their businesses identified by the patterns of preserved mosaics. Near by, Greek dramas were performed at the **Teatro,** built in the early days of the Empire. The theater as it looks today is the result of much rebuilding. Every town the size of Ostia had a **Forum ★**, and the layout is still intact: A well-preserved **Capitolium** (once the largest tremple in Ostia) faces the remains of the 1st-century A.D. **Temple of Roma and Augustus**.

Elsewhere in the grid of streets are the ruins of the **Thermopolium,** which was a bar; its name means "sale of hot drinks." Of an *insula*, a Roman block of apartments, **Casa Diana** remains, with its rooms arranged around an inner courtyard. The **Terme di Nettuno ★** was a vast baths complex; climb the building at its entrance for an aerial view of its well-preserved mosaics. In addition in the enclave is a **museum** displaying Roman statuary along with fragmentary frescoes.

WHERE TO EAT

There is no real need to eat by the ruins—a half-day here should suffice, and Ostia is within easy reach of the abundant restaurants of Rome's city center. The obvious alternative is a picnic; the well-stocked foodie magnet **Eataly** (see p. 151) is only a couple of minutes from the Lido platform at Piramide Metro station, making it easy to grab provisions when you make the Metro interchange. There are perfect picnic spots beside fallen columns or old temple walls. If you really crave a sit-down meal, **Allo Sbarco di Enea**, Viale dei Romagnoli 675 (✆ **06-5650034**) has a menu of trattoria staples, a shaded garden, and two-course tourist menus starting at 12€, excluding drinks. There's also a snack and coffee bar outside Ostia's Metro station.

Tivoli & the Villas ★★

32km (20 miles) E of Rome

Perched high on a hill east of Rome, Tivoli is an ancient town that has always been something of a retreat from the city. In Roman times it was known as Tibur, a retirement town for the wealthy; later during the Renaissance, it again became the playground of the rich, who built their country villas out here. To do justice to the gardens and villas that remain—especially if the Villa Adriana is on your list, as indeed it should be—you'll need time, so it's worth setting out early.

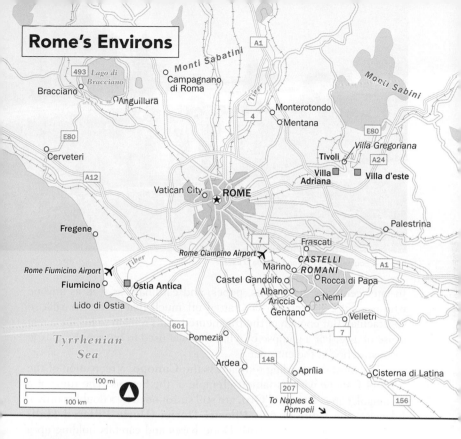

Rome's Environs

Lago di Bracciano · 493

Monti Sabatini

Monti Sabini

Bracciano

Anguillara

Campagnano di Roma

Tiber

A1

Monterotondo

Mentana

4

E80

E80

Villa Gregoriana

Cerveteri

Tivoli

A24

Villa d'este

Villa Adriana

A12

Vatican City

ROME

Palestrina

Fregene

7

Frascati

CASTELLI ROMANI

A1

Tiber

Rome Ciampino Airport

Marino

Rome Fiumicino Airport

Ostia Antica

Castel Gandolfo

Rocca di Papa

Fiumicino

Albano

Nemi

Lido di Ostia

Ariccia

Genzano

Velletri

Tyrrhenian Sea

601

Pomezia

7

Ardea

148

Aprília

Cisterna di Latina

0   100 mi
0   100 km

207

To Naples & Pompeii ↘

156

ESSENTIALS

GETTING THERE   Tivoli is 32km (20 miles) east of Rome on Via Tiburtina, about an hour's drive with traffic (the Rome–L'Aquila *autostrada*, A24, is usually faster). If you don't have a car, take Metro Line B to Ponte Mammolo. After exiting the station, transfer to a Cotral bus for Tivoli (www.cotralspa.it). Cotral buses depart every 15 to 30 minutes during the day (2.20€ one-way). Villa d'Este is in Tivoli itself, close to the bus stop; to get to Villa Adriana you need to catch another bus (the orange no.4; buy tickets at a *tabacchi* in the center of Tivoli).

EXPLORING TIVOLI & THE VILLAS

Villa Adriana (Hadrian's Villa) ★★★ HISTORIC SITE/RUINS

The globe-trotting Emperor Hadrian spent the last 3 years of his life in the grandest style. Less than 6km (3¾ miles) from Tivoli, between 118 and 138 A.D. he built one of the greatest estates ever conceived, and he filled acre after acre with some of the architectural wonders he'd seen on his many travels. Hadrian erected theaters, baths, temples, fountains, gardens, and canals bordered with statuary, filling the palaces and temples with sculpture, some of which now rest in the museums of Rome.

Neptune Fountain and fishpond at Villa d'Este.

In later centuries, barbarians, popes, and cardinals, as well as anyone who needed a slab of marble, carted off much that made the villa so spectacular. But enough of the fragmented ruins remain to inspire a real sense of awe. For a glimpse of what the villa used to be, see the plastic reconstruction at the entrance.

The most outstanding remnant is the **Canopo,** a recreation of the town of Canope with its famous Temple of the Serapis. The ruins of a rectangular area, **Piazza d'Oro,** are still surrounded by a double portico. Likewise, the **Edificio con Pilastri Dorici (Doric Pillared Hall)** remains, with its pilasters with Doric bases and capitals holding up a Doric architrave. The apse and the ruins of some magnificent vaulting are found at the **Grandi Terme (Great Baths),** while only the north wall remains of the **Pecile,** otherwise known as the *Stoà Poikile di Atene* or "Painted Porch," which Hadrian discovered in Athens and had reproduced here. The best is saved for last—the **Teatro Marittimo,** a circular maritime theater in ruins with its central building enveloped by a canal spanned by small swing bridges.

For a closer look at some of the items excavated, you can visit the museum on the premises and a visitor center near the villa parking area. Largo Marguerite Yourcenar 1, Tivoli. www.villaadriana.beniculturali.it. © **0774-530203.** Admission 11€. Daily 9am–sunset (about 7:30pm in May–Aug, 5pm Nov–Jan, 6pm Feb, 6.30pm Mar and Oct, and 7pm Apr and Oct). Bus: 4 from Tivoli.

Villa d'Este ★★ PARK/GARDEN Like Hadrian centuries before, Cardinal Ippolito d'Este of Ferrara ordered this villa built on a Tivoli hillside in the mid–16th century. The dank Renaissance structure, with its second-rate paintings, is not that interesting; the big draw for visitors is the **spectacular gardens** below (designed by Pirro Ligorio).

As you descend the cypress-studded garden slope you're rewarded with everything from lilies to gargoyles spouting water, torrential streams, and waterfalls. The loveliest fountain is the **Fontana dell Ovato,** by Ligorio. But nearby is the most spectacular engineering achievement: the **Fontana dell'Organo Idraulico (Fountain of the Hydraulic Organ),** dazzling with its music and water jets in front of a baroque chapel, with four maidens who look tipsy (the fountain "plays" every 2 hours from 10:30am).

The moss-covered **Fontana dei Draghi (Fountain of the Dragons),** also by Ligorio, and the so-called **Fontana di Vetro (Fountain of Glass),** by Bernini, are also worth seeking out, as is the main promenade, lined with 100 spraying fountains. The garden is worth hours of exploration, but it involves a lot of walking, with some steep climbs.

Piazza Trento 5, Tivoli. www.villadestetivoli.info. ✆ **0774-332920.** Admission 11€ (8€ Nov–Apr). Tues–Sun 8:30am to 1 hr. before sunset. Bus: Cotral service from Ponte Mammolo (Roma–Tivoli); the bus stops near the entrance.

Villa Gregoriana ★ PARK/GARDEN   Villa d'Este dazzles with artificial glamour, but the Villa Gregoriana relies more on nature. Originally laid out by Pope Gregory XVI in the 1830s, the gardens were reopened in 2005 after a $5.5-million restoration. The main highlight is the panoramic waterfall of Aniene, with the trek to the bottom on the banks of the Anio studded with grottoes and balconies that open onto the chasm. The only problem is that if you do make the full descent, you might need a helicopter to pull you up again (the climb back up is fierce). From one of the belvederes, there's a view of the **Temple of Vesta** on the hill. A former school has been converted into a visitor center designed by architect Gae Aulenti.

Largo Sant'Angelo, Tivoli. www.villagregoriana.it. ✆ **06-39967701.** Admission 6€. Apr–Oct Tues–Sun 10am–6:30pm; Mar, Nov, and Dec Tues–Sun 10am–4pm. Bus: Cotral service from Ponte Mammolo (Roma–Tivoli); the bus stops near the entrance.

WHERE TO EAT

Tivoli's gardens make for a pleasant picnic place (see **Eataly,** p. 151), but if you crave a sit-down meal, **Antica Trattoria del Falcone,** Via del Trevio 34 (www.ristoranteilfalcone.it; ✆ **0774-312358**) is a dependable option in Tivoli itself. Just off Largo Garibaldi, it's been open since 1918 and specializes in excellent pizza (ask for the pizza menu), Roman pastas, and roast meats. It is open daily 11:30am to 4pm and 6:30 to 11:30pm.

FLORENCE

5

otticelli, Michelangelo, and Leonardo da Vinci all left their mark on Florence, the cradle of the Renaissance. With Brunelleschi's dome as a backdrop, follow the River Arno to the Uffizi Gallery (Florence's foremost museum) and soak in centuries of great painting. Wander across the Ponte Vecchio (Florence's iconic bridge), taking in the tangle of Oltrarno's medieval streets. Then sample seasonal Tuscan cooking in a Left Bank trattoria. You've discovered the art of fine living in this masterpiece of a city.

Michelangelo's "David" stands tall (literally) behind the doors of the **Accademia,** and nearby are the delicate paintings of Fra'Angelico in the convent of **San Marco.** Works by Donatello, Masaccio, and Ghiberti fill the city's churches and museums. Once home to the Medici, the **Palazzo Pitti** is stuffed with Raphaels and Titians, and backed by the fountains of the regal **Boboli Garden.**

But it's not just about the art. Florentines love to shop, too, and Italy's leather capital offers a bounty of handmade gloves, belts, bags, and shoes sold from workshops, family-run boutiques, and high-toned stores, as well as at tourist-oriented **San Lorenzo Market.** Splurge on designer wear from fashion houses along **Via de' Tornabuoni**—this city is the home of Gucci, Pucci, and Ferragamo.

As for Florentine cuisine, it's increasingly cosmopolitan, but flavors are often still Tuscan at heart. Even in fine restaurants, meals might kick off with *ribollita* (seasonal vegetable stew) before moving onto the chargrilled delights of a *bistecca alla fiorentina* (Florentine beefsteak on the bone)—all washed down with a **Chianti Classico.** At lunchtime order a plate of cold cuts and pecorino cheese, or if you're feeling adventurous, *lampredotto alla fiorentina* (a sandwich of cow's stomach stewed in tomatoes and garlic).

When you've dined to your fill, retire to a wine bar in the **Oltrarno,** or to one of the edgier joints of **Santo Spirito** and **San Frediano.** If you're keen on opera, classical, theater, or jazz, you'll find those here, too.

ESSENTIALS
Getting There

BY PLANE Several European airlines serve Florence's **Amerigo Vespucci Airport** (www.aeroporto.firenze.it; ✆ **055-306-15** switchboard, 055-306-1300 for flight info), also called **Peretola,** just 5km (3 miles)

FACING PAGE: **Dome of the Duomo.**

northwest of town. There are no direct flights to or from the United States, but you can make connections through London, Paris, Amsterdam, Frankfurt, and other major European cities. The half-hourly **SITA-ATAF Vola in bus** to and from downtown's bus station at Via Santa Caterina da Siena 17 (☎ **800-424-500**), beside the train station, takes 20 minutes and costs 6€ one-way or 10€ round-trip. Metered **taxis** line up outside the airport's arrival terminal and charge a flat rate of 20€ to the city center (22€ on holidays, 24€ after 10pm; additional 1€ per bag).

The closest major international airport with seasonal direct flights to North America is Pisa's **Galileo Galilei Airport** (www.pisa-airport.com; ☎ **050-849-300**), 97km (60 miles) west of Florence. Until the **PisaMover** airport transit service opens (at press time scheduled for a Dec 2015 debut), train connections to Florence involve a short bus journey (1.30€) or taxi ride (10€) from Pisa airport to Pisa Centrale, where you can catch a state rail service to Florence (60–80 min.; 8€). Alternatively, 18 daily buses operated by **Terravision** (www.terravision.eu) connect downtown Florence directly with Pisa Airport in just over 1 hour. One-way tickets are 5€ adults, 4€ children ages 5 to 12; round-trip fares are 10€ and 8€.

BY TRAIN Florence is Tuscany's rail hub, with regular connections to all of Italy's major cities. To get here from Rome, take the high-speed **Frecciarossa** or **Frecciargento** trains (1½ hr.; www.trenitalia.com) or rival high-speed trains operated by **Italo** (www.italotreno.it; p. 641). High-speed trains run to Venice (2 hr.) via Bologna and Padua.

Most Florence-bound trains roll into **Stazione Santa Maria Novella,** Piazza della Stazione, which you'll see abbreviated as **S.M.N.** The station is an architectural masterpiece, albeit one dating to Italy's Fascist period, rather than the Renaissance; it lies on the northwestern edge of the city's compact historic center, a 10-minute walk from the Duomo and a brisk 15-minute walk from Piazza della Signoria and the Uffizi.

BY CAR The **A1 autostrada** runs north from Rome past Arezzo to Florence and continues to Bologna, and **unnumbered superhighways** run to and from Siena (the *SI-FI raccordo*) and Pisa (the so-called *FI-PI-LI*). To reach Florence from Venice, take the A13 southbound then switch to the A1 at Bologna.

Driving to Florence is easy; the problems begin once you arrive. Almost all cars are banned from the historic center—only residents or merchants with special permits are allowed into this camera-patrolled *zona a trafico limitato* (the "ZTL"), which was further extended in early 2015. Have the name and address of your hotel ready and the traffic police will wave you through. You can drop off baggage there (the hotel will organize a temporary ZTL permit); then you must relocate to a parking lot (special rates are available through most hotels).

Your best bet for overnight or longer-term parking is one of the city-run garages. The best deal—better than many hotels' garage rates—is at the **Parterre parking lot** under Piazza Libertà at Via Madonna delle Tosse 9 (✆ **055-5030-2209**). It's open round the clock, costs 2€ per hour, or 10€ for the first 24 hours, 15€ for the second, then 20€ per day; it's 70€ for up to a week's parking. More info on parking at **www.firenzeparcheggi.it**.

Don't park your car overnight on the streets in Florence without local knowledge; if you're towed and ticketed, it will set you back substantially, and the headaches to retrieve your car are beyond description. If this happens to you, start by calling the vehicle removal department (the *Recupero Veicoli Rimossi*) at ✆ **055-422-4142**.

Visitor Information

TOURIST OFFICES   The most convenient tourist office is at Via Cavour 1R (www.firenzeturismo.it; ✆ **055-290-832**), 2 blocks north of the Duomo. The office is open Monday through Friday from 9am to 6pm, Saturday 9am to 2pm. Its free map is quite adequate for navigation purposes—no need to upgrade to a paid version.

The train station's nearest tourist office (✆ **055-212-245**) is opposite the terminus at Piazza della Stazione 5. With your back to the tracks, take the left exit, cross onto the concrete median, and bear right; it's across the busy road junction ahead. The office is usually open Monday through Saturday from 9am to 7pm (sometimes only to 2pm in winter) and Sunday 9am to 2pm. This office gets crowded; unless you're really lost, press on to the Via Cavour office.

Another helpful office is under the Loggia del Bigallo on the corner of Piazza San Giovanni and Via dei Calzaiuoli (✆ **055-288-496**); it's open Monday through Saturday from 9am to 7pm (often 5pm mid-Nov to Feb) and Sunday 9am to 2pm.

WEBSITES   The official Florence information website, **www.firenzeturismo.it**, contains a wealth of reasonably up-to-date information. The site also has a downloadable PDF with the latest opening hours for all the major city sights. The best-informed city blogs are written in Italian by locals: **Io Amo Firenze** (www.ioamofirenze.it) is handy for reviews of the latest eating, drinking, and events in town. For one-off exhibitions and culture, **Art Trav** (www.arttrav.com) is an essential bookmark. For more updated Florence info, go to **www.frommers.com/destinations/florence**.

City Layout

Florence is a smallish city, sitting on the Arno River and petering out to olive-planted hills rather quickly to the north and south, but extending farther west and east along the Arno valley with suburbs and light

The address system in Florence has a split personality. Private homes, some offices, and hotels are numbered in black (or blue), but businesses, shops, and restaurants are numbered independently in red. (That's the theory anyway; in reality, the division between black and red numbers isn't so clear-cut.) The result is that 1, 2, 3 (black) addresses march up the block numerically oblivious to their 1R, 2R, 3R (red) neighbors. You might find the doorways on one side of a street numbered 1R, 2R, 3R, 1, 4R, 2, 3, 5R.

The color codes occur only in the *centro storico* and other old sections of town; outlying districts didn't bother with this confusing system.

industry. It has a compact center that is best negotiated on foot. No two major sights are more than a 25-minute walk apart, and most of the hotels and restaurants in this chapter are in the relatively small *centro storico* (historic center), a compact tangle of medieval streets and *piazze* (squares) where visitors spend most of their time. The bulk of Florence, including most of the tourist sights, lies north of the river, with the **Oltrarno,** an old working artisans' neighborhood, hemmed in between the Arno and the hills on the south side.

The Neighborhoods in Brief

THE DUOMO The area surrounding Florence's gargantuan cathedral is as central as you can get. The Duomo itself is halfway between the two monastic churches of Santa Maria Novella and Santa Croce, as well as at the midpoint between the Uffizi Gallery and the Ponte Vecchio to the south and San Marco and the Accademia (home of Michelangelo's "David") to the north. The streets south of the Duomo make up a medieval tangle of alleys and tiny squares heading toward Piazza della Signoria.

This is one of the oldest parts of town, and the streets still vaguely follow a grid laid down when the city was a Roman colony. The site of the Roman city's forum is today's **Piazza della Repubblica.**

The Duomo neighborhood is, understandably, one of the most hotel-heavy parts of town, offering a range from luxury inns to student dives and everything in between. However, several places around here rest on the laurels of their sublime location; you need to be choosy. The same goes for dining in the area.

PIAZZA DELLA SIGNORIA This is the city's civic heart and perhaps the best base for museum hounds—the Uffizi Gallery, Bargello sculpture collection, and **Ponte Vecchio** are all nearby. It's a well-polished part of the tourist zone but still retains the narrow medieval streets where Dante grew up. The few blocks just north of the Ponte Vecchio have reasonable shopping, but unappealing modern buildings were planted here to replace those destroyed during World War II. The entire neighborhood can be stiflingly crowded in peak season—Via Por Santa Maria is one to avoid—but in those moments when you catch it empty of tour groups, it remains the romantic heart of pre-Renaissance Florence. As with the Duomo neighborhood, you need to be *very* choosy when picking a restaurant or even an ice cream around here.

SAN LORENZO & THE MERCATO CENTRALE   This wedge of streets between the train station and the Duomo, centered on the Medici's old family church of **San Lorenzo** and its Michelangelo-designed tombs, is market territory. The vast indoor **Mercato Centrale** (food market) is here, and many of the streets are filled daily with stalls hawking leather and other souvenirs at **San Lorenzo Market.** It's a colorful neighborhood, blessed with many budget hotels and a growing choice of good, affordable dining spots, but it's not the quietest part of town.

PIAZZA SANTA TRÍNITA   This piazza sits just north of the river at the south end of Florence's shopping mecca, **Via de' Tornabuoni,** home to Gucci, Armani, and more. It's a pleasant, well-to-do (but still medieval) neighborhood in which to stay, even if you don't care about haute couture. If you're an upscale shopping fiend, there's no better place to be.

SANTA MARIA NOVELLA   This neighborhood, bounding the western edge of the *centro storico,* has two characters: an unattractive zone around the train station, and a nicer area south of it between the church of Santa Maria Novella and the river. In general, the train-station area is the least appealing part of town in which to base yourself. The streets are mostly heavily trafficked and noisy, and you're a little removed from the medieval atmosphere. This area does, however, have more good budget

In June, teams in Renaissance costumes play a 15th-century form of football.

options than any other quarter, especially along **Via Faenza** and its tributaries. Try to avoid staying on busy **Via Nazionale.**

The situation improves dramatically as you move east into the San Lorenzo area (see above), or pass Santa Maria Novella church and head south toward the river. **Piazza Santa Maria Novella** and its tributary streets have seen a few stylish boutique hotels open in the last decade.

SAN MARCO & SANTISSIMA ANNUNZIATA   On the northern edge of the *centro storico,* these two churches are fronted by *piazze*—**Piazza San Marco,** a busy transport hub, and **Piazza Santissima Annunziata,** the most architecturally unified square in the city. The neighborhood is home to Florence's university, the **Accademia,** the San Marco paintings of Fra' Angelico, and quiet streets with some hotel gems. The walk back from the heart of the action isn't as far as it looks on a map, and you'll likely welcome the escape from tourist crowds. But it's not (yet) a great dining or nightlife neighborhood.

SANTA CROCE   The art-filled church at the eastern edge of the *centro storico* is the focal point of one of the most genuine neighborhoods left in the center. Few tourists roam too far east of **Piazza Santa Croce,** so if you want to feel like a local, stay here. The streets around the Mercato di Sant'Ambrogio and Piazza de' Ciompi have an especially appealing, local feel, and they get lively after dark. The Santa Croce neighborhood boasts some of the best restaurants and bars in the city—*aperitivo* time is vibrant along **Via de' Benci,** and there is always something going on along **Via Panisperna** and the northern end of **Via de' Macci.**

THE OLTRARNO, SAN NICCOLÒ & SAN FREDIANO   "Across the Arno" is the artisans' neighborhood, still dotted with workshops. It began as a working-class neighborhood to catch the overflow from the expanding medieval city on the opposite bank, but became a chic area for aristocrats to build palaces on the edge of the countryside. The largest of these, the **Pitti Palace,** later became the home of the grand dukes and today houses a set of paintings second only to the Uffizi in scope.

The Oltrarno's lively tree-shaded center, **Piazza Santo Spirito,** is lined with bars and close to some great restaurants (and lively nightlife, too). West of here, the neighborhood of **San Frediano** is becoming ever more fashionable, and **San Niccolò** at the foot of Florence's southern hills is a buzzing nightlife spot. You may not choose to stay around here— the hotel range isn't great—but when evening draws nigh, cross one of the bridges to eat and drink better, at better prices, than you will generally find in the *centro storico.*

Getting Around

Florence is a **walking** city. You can stroll between the two top sights, Piazza del Duomo and the Uffizi, in 5 minutes or so. The hike from the most northerly major sights, San Marco and the Accademia, to the most southerly, the Pitti Palace across the Arno, should take no more than 30 minutes. From Santa Maria Novella eastward across town to Santa Croce is a flat 20- to 30-minute walk. But beware: **Flagstones,** some of them uneven, are everywhere—wear sensible shoes with some padding and foot support.

BY BUS   You'll rarely need to use Florence's efficient **ATAF bus system** (www.ataf.net; ✆ **800-424-500** in Italy) since the city is so compact. Bus tickets cost 1.20€ and are good for 90 minutes, irrespective of how many changes you make. A 24-hour pass costs 5€, a 3-day pass 12€, and a 7-day pass 18€. Tickets are sold at *tabacchi* (tobacconists), some bars, and most newsstands. If you cannot find a machine or vendor near your stop, pay 2€ to buy a ticket onboard, or if you have an Italian cellphone number (p. 647), text the word "ATAF" to ✆ **488-0105** to buy a validated ticket for 1.50€ using your prepaid phone credit. *Note:* Once on board, validate your ticket in the box near the rear door to avoid a steep fine. Since traffic is limited in most of the historic center, buses make runs on principal streets only, except for four tiny electric buses (*bussini* services C1, C2, C3, and D) that trundle about the *centro storico*. The most useful lines to outlying areas are no. 7 (for Fiesole) and nos. 12 and 13 (for Piazzale Michelangiolo). Buses run from 7am until 8:30 or 9pm daily, with a limited night service on a few key routes (mostly local-focused).

BY TAXI   Taxis aren't cheap, and with the city so small and the one-way system forcing drivers to take convoluted routes, they aren't an economical way to get about. They're most useful to get you and your bags between the train station and your hotel. The standard rate is .91€ per kilometer, with a whopping 3.30€ to start the meter (that rises to 5.30€ on Sun; 6.60€ 10pm–6am), plus 1€ per bag. There's a taxi stand outside the train station; otherwise, call **Radio Taxi** at ✆ **055-4242.** For the latest taxi information, see **www.4242.it**.

BY BICYCLE & SCOOTER   Many of the bike-rental shops in town are located between San Lorenzo and San Marco. They include **Alinari,** Via San Zanobi 38R (www.alinarirental.com; ✆ **055-280-500**), which rents bikes (2.50€ per hour; 12€ per day) and mountain bikes (3€ per hour; 18€ per day). It also hires out 100cc scooters (15€ per hour; 55€ per day). Another renter with similar prices is **Florence by Bike,** Via San Zanobi 54R (www.florencebybike.it; ✆ **055-488-992**).

BY CAR   Trying to drive in the *centro storico* is a frustrating, useless exercise, and moreover, unauthorized traffic is not allowed past signs marked **ztl.** On top of that, 2013 saw the introduction of a city charge even for residents to drive into the center to park, and rules became even tighter in April 2015. You need a permit to do anything beyond dropping off and picking up bags at your hotel. Park your vehicle in one of the underground lots on the center's periphery and pound the pavement. (See "By Car" under "Getting There," p. 164.)

[FastFACTS] FLORENCE

Business Hours

Hours mainly follow the Italian norm (see p. 645). In Florence, however, many of the larger and more central shops stay open through the midday *riposo* or nap (note the sign *orario nonstop*).

Doctors

Tourist-oriented **Medical Service Firenze** is at Via Roma 4, in the city center (www.medicalservice.firenze.it; ℓ **055-475-411**). It's open for walk-ins Monday to Friday 11am to noon, 1 to 3pm, and 5 to 6pm; Saturday 11am to noon and 1 to 3pm only. **Dr. Stephen Kerr** has an office at Piazza Mercato Nuovo 1 (www.dr-kerr.com; ℓ **335-836-1682** or 055-288-055), with office hours Monday through Friday from 3 to 5pm without an appointment (appointments are available 9am–3pm). The consultation fee is 50€, slightly less if you show a student ID card.

Hospitals

The most central hospital is **Santa Maria Nuova,** a block northeast of the Duomo on Piazza Santa Maria Nuova (ℓ **055-69-381**), with an emergency room (*pronto soccorso*) open 24 hours. There is a comprehensive guide to medical services, including specialist care, on the official Florence city website: See **www.firenze-turismo.it**.

Internet Access

Every hotel we recommend now offers wireless Internet, usually for free but occasionally for a small fee. If you have your own laptop or smartphone, several bars and cafes offer free Wi-Fi to anyone buying a drink or snack. There's free Wi-Fi at the **Mercato Centrale** (p. 215), too.

Mail & Postage

Florence's **main post office** (ℓ **055-273-6428**), at Via Pellicceria 3, off the southwest corner of Piazza della Repubblica, is open Monday through Friday from 8:20am to 7:05pm, Saturday 8:20am to 12:35pm.

Newspapers & Magazines

Florence's national daily paper, *La Nazione*, is on sale everywhere. *The Florentine* (www.theflorentine.net) is the city's English-language publication, widely available at bars, cafes, and hotels. Overseas English-language newspapers are also available: The newsstands at the station are a safe bet, as is a booth under the arcade on the western side of Piazza della Repubblica. You will find the *Financial Times, Wall Street Journal,* and London *Guardian,* alongside the usual *International New York Times*.

Pharmacies

There is a 24-hour pharmacy (also open Sun and state holidays) in **Stazione Santa Maria Novella** (ℓ **055-216-761;** ring the bell opposite taxi rank btw. 11pm and 7am). On holidays and at night, look for the sign in any pharmacy window telling you which ones are open locally.

Police

To report lost property or passport problems, call the *questura* (police headquarters) at ℓ **055-49-771. Note:** It is illegal to knowingly buy fake goods anywhere in the city (and yes, a "Louis Vuitton" bag at 10€ counts as *knowingly*). You may be served a hefty on-the-spot fine if caught.

Safety

As in any city, plenty of pickpockets are out to ruin your vacation, and in Florence you'll find light-fingered youngsters (especially around the train station), but otherwise you're safe. Do steer clear of the Cascine Park after dark, when you may run the risk of being mugged; likewise the area around Piazza Santo Spirito and in the backstreets behind Santa Croce after all the nightlife has gone off to bed. And you probably won't want to hang out with the late-night heroin addicts shooting up on the Arno mud flats below the Lungarno embankments on the edges of town. See chapter 14 for more safety tips.

DISCOUNT tickets FOR THE CITY

Visitors to Florence in mid-2013 got a shock when they went to purchase the discount **Firenze Card** (www.firenzecard.it). Launched in 2011 at 50€ per person, the card was suddenly priced at 72€, still today's price. So is it a good buy? If you are planning a busy, culture-packed break here, the Firenze Card works out to good value. If you only expect to see a few museums, skip it.

For the culture vultures out there, the "new" card (still valid for 72 hr.) now allows one entrance to each of 60 sites; the list includes a handful that are free anyway, but also the Uffizi, Accademia, Cappella Brancacci, Palazzo Pitti, Brunelleschi's dome, San Marco, and many more. In fact, *everything* we recommend in this chapter is included in the price of the card, even sites in Fiesole (p. 200). It also gets you into shorter lines, taking ticket prebooking hassles out of the equation—another saving of 3€ to 4€ for busy museums, above all the Uffizi and Accademia. It also includes 3 days' free bus travel (which you likely won't use) and free public Wi-Fi (which you might).

Amici degli Uffizi membership (www.amicidegliuffizi.it) is the ticket to choose if you want to delve deeper into a smaller range of Florence museums, especially if you want to make multiple visits to the vast collections at the Uffizi and Palazzo Pitti, or if you plan on visiting Florence more than once in a given year. It costs 60€ for adults, 40€ ages 18 to 26, 100€ for a family, and is valid for a calendar year (Jan 1–Dec 31). It grants admission (without queuing) into 15 or so state museums, including the Uffizi, Accademia, San Marco, Bargello, Cappelle Medicee, and everything at the Palazzo Pitti. Children 17 and under enter free with a paying adult, and membership permits multiple visits. Join Tuesday to Saturday inside Uffizi entrance no. 2. Take photo ID, plus a little patience: The desk is not always staffed.

The Opera del Duomo has also dispensed with single entry tickets to its sites in favor of a value *biglietto cumulativo*, the **Grande Museo del Duomo** ticket. It covers Brunelleschi's dome, the Baptistery, Campanile di Giotto, Museo Storico dell'Opera, and crypt excavations of Santa Reparata (inside the cathedral) for 10€, free for accompanied children up to age 14. It also gets you into the Duomo without queuing (in theory). Buy it at the ticket office almost opposite the Baptistery, on the north side of Piazza San Giovanni. It includes enough to fill a busy half-day, at least. See **www.ilgrandemuseodelduomo.it** for more details.

EXPLORING FLORENCE

Most museums accept cash only at the door. **Precise opening times can change** without notice, especially at city churches (for example, the Baptistery sometimes remains open until 11pm in summer). The tourist office maintains an up-to-date list of hours. Note, too, that the **last admission** to the museums and monuments listed is usually between 30 and 45 minutes before the final closing time.

Piazza del Duomo

The cathedral square is always crowded—filled with tourists and caricature artists during the day, strolling crowds in the early evening, and knots of students strumming guitars on the Duomo's steps at night. The

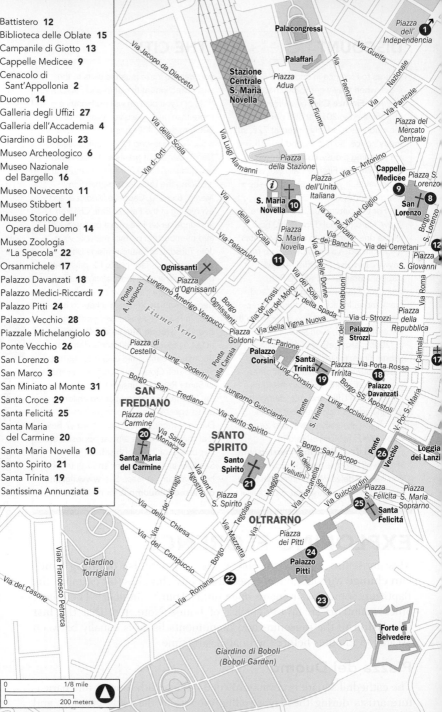

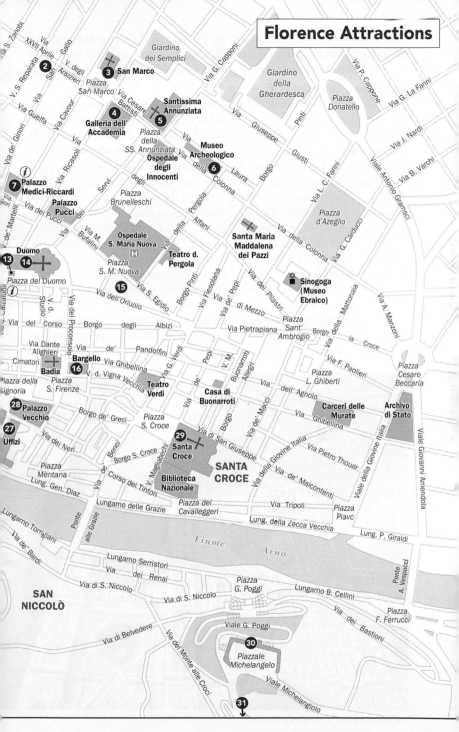

Florence Attractions

San Marco

Santissima Annunziata

Galleria dell' Accademia

Museo Archeologico

Palazzo Medici-Riccardi

Palazzo Pucci

Ospedale degli Innocenti

Ospedale S. Maria Nuova

Teatro d. Pergola

Santa Maria Maddalena dei Pazzi

Duomo

Sinogoga (Museo Ebraico)

Bargello

Teatro Verdi

Casa di Buonarroti

Carceri delle Murate

Archivio di Stato

Palazzo Vecchio

Uffizi

Badia

Santa Croce

Biblioteca Nazionale

SANTA CROCE

SAN NICCOLÒ

Piazzale Michelangelo

Fiume Arno

piazza's vivacity amidst the glittering facades of the cathedral and the Baptistery doors keep it an eternal Florentine sight—and now that it has been closed to traffic since 2009, it's a more welcoming space than ever.

Battistero (Baptistery) ★★★ RELIGIOUS SITE In choosing a date to mark the beginning of the Renaissance, art historians often seize on 1401, the year Florence's powerful wool merchants' guild held a contest to decide who would receive the commission to design the **North Doors** ★★ of the Baptistery to match the Gothic **South Doors,** cast 65 years earlier by Andrea Pisano. The era's foremost Tuscan sculptors each cast a bas-relief bronze panel depicting their own vision of the "Sacrifice of Isaac." Twenty-two-year-old Lorenzo Ghiberti, competing against Donatello, Jacopo della Quercia, and Filippo Brunelleschi, won. He spent the next 21 years casting 28 bronze panels and building his doors.

The result so impressed the merchants' guild—not to mention the public and Ghiberti's fellow artists—that they asked him in 1425 to do the **East Doors** ★★★, facing the Duomo, this time giving him the artistic freedom to realize his Renaissance ambitions. Twenty-seven years later, just before his death, Ghiberti finished 10 dramatic lifelike Old Testament scenes in gilded bronze, each a masterpiece of Renaissance sculpture and some of the finest examples of low-relief perspective in Italian art. Each illustrates episodes in the stories of Noah (second down

The ornate façade of Florence's Duomo.

on left), Moses (second up on left), Solomon and the Queen of Sheba (bottom right), and others. The panels mounted here are excellent copies; the originals are in the **Museo Storico dell'Opera del Duomo** (see p. 177). Years later, Michelangelo was standing before these doors and someone asked his opinion. His response sums up Ghiberti's accomplishment as no art historian could: "They are so beautiful that they would grace the entrance to Paradise." They've been nicknamed the Gates of Paradise ever since.

The Baptistery, with its glittering bronze doors by Lorenzo Ghiberti.

The building itself is ancient. It is first mentioned in city records in the 9th century and was probably already 300 years old by then. Its interior is ringed with columns pilfered from ancient Roman buildings and is a spectacle of mosaics above and below. The floor was inlaid in 1209, and the ceiling was covered between 1225 and the early 1300s with glittering **mosaics ★★**. Most were crafted by Venetian or Byzantine-style workshops, which worked off designs drawn by the era's best artists. Coppo di Marcovaldo drew sketches for the over 7.8m-high (26-ft.) "Christ in Judgment" and the "Last Judgment" that fills over a third of the ceiling. Bring binoculars (and a good neck masseuse) if you want a closer look.

Piazza San Giovanni. www.ilgrandemuseodelduomo.it. ℂ **055-230-2885**. Admission included with 10€ Grande Museo del Duomo ticket. Mon–Wed and Fri–Sat 8:15–10:15am and 11:15am–6:30pm; Thurs 8:15am–6:30pm; Sun 8:15am–1:30pm. Bus: C2.

Campanile di Giotto (Giotto's Bell Tower) ★★ HISTORIC SITE

In 1334, Giotto started the cathedral bell tower but completed only the first two levels before his death in 1337. He was out of his league with the engineering aspects of architecture, and the tower was saved from falling by Andrea Pisano, who doubled the thickness of the walls. Andrea, a master sculptor of the Pisan Gothic school, also changed the design to add statue niches—he even carved a few of the statues himself—before quitting the project in 1348. Francesco Talenti finished the job between 1350 and 1359. The **reliefs** and **statues** in the lower levels—by Andrea Pisano, Donatello, Luca della Robbia, and others—are all copies; the weatherworn originals are housed in the Museo Storico dell'Opera del Duomo (see p. 177). We recommend climbing the 414

A MAN & HIS dome

Filippo Brunelleschi, a diminutive man whose ego was as big as his talent, managed in his arrogant, quixotic, and brilliant way to invent Renaissance architecture. Having been beaten by Lorenzo Ghiberti in the contest to cast the **Baptistery** doors (see p. 174), Brunelleschi resolved that he would rather be the top architect than the second-best sculptor and took off for Rome to study the buildings of the ancients. On returning to Florence, he combined subdued gray *pietra serena* stone with smooth white plaster to create airy arches, vaults, and arcades of perfect classical proportions in his own variant on the ancient Roman orders of architecture. He designed **Santo Spirito,** the elegant **Ospedale degli Innocenti,** and a new sacristy for **San Lorenzo,** but his greatest achievement was erecting the dome over Florence's cathedral.

The Duomo—at that time the world's largest church—had already been built, but nobody had been able to figure out how to cover the daunting space over its center without spending a fortune. No one was even sure whether they could create a dome that would hold up under

its own weight. Brunelleschi insisted he knew how, and once granted the commission, revealed his ingenious plan—which may have been inspired by close study of Rome's **Pantheon** (p. 98).

He built the dome in two shells, the inner one thicker than the outer, both shells thinning as they neared the top, thus leaving the center hollow and removing a good deal of the weight. He also planned to construct the dome of giant vaults with ribs crossing them, and dovetailed the stones making up the actual fabric of the dome. In this way, the walls of the dome would support themselves as they were erected. In the process of building, Brunelleschi found himself as much an engineer as architect, constantly designing winches and hoists to carry the materials (plus food and drink) faster and more efficiently up to the level of the workmen.

His finished work speaks for itself, 45m (148 ft.) wide at the base and 90m (295 ft.) high from drum to lantern. For his achievement, Brunelleschi was accorded a singular honor: He is the only person ever buried in Florence's cathedral.

steps to the top; the **view** ★★ is memorable as you ascend, and offers the best close-up shot in the entire city of Brunelleschi's dome.

Piazza del Duomo. www.ilgrandemuseodelduomo.it. © **055-230-2885.** Admission included with 10€ Grande Museo del Duomo ticket. Daily 8:15am–6:50pm. Bus: C2, 14, or 23.

Duomo (Cattedrale di Santa Maria del Fiore) ★★ CATHE-DRAL   By the late 13th century, Florence was feeling peevish: Its archrivals Siena and Pisa sported flamboyant new cathedrals while it was saddled with the tiny 5th- or 6th-century cathedral of Santa Reparata. So in 1296, the city hired Arnolfo di Cambio to design a new Duomo, and he raised the facade and the first few bays before his death (around 1310). Work continued under the auspices of the Wool Guild and architects Giotto di Bondone (who concentrated on the bell tower) and Francesco Talenti (who expanded the planned size and finished up to the drum of the dome). The facade we see today is a neo-Gothic composite designed by Emilio de Fabris and built from 1871 to 1887.

The Duomo's most distinctive feature, however, is its enormous **dome** ★★★ (or *cupola*), which dominates the skyline and is a symbol of Florence itself. The raising of this dome, the largest in the world in its time, was no mean architectural feat, tackled by Filippo Brunelleschi between 1420 and 1436 (see "A Man & His Dome," p. 176). You can climb up between its two shells for one of the classic panoramas across the city— something that is not recommended for claustrophobes or anyone with no head for heights. **Get there early:** Queues can be extremely long.

The cathedral is rather Spartan inside, though check out the optical illusion equestrian "statue" of English mercenary soldier Sir John Hawkwood on the north wall, painted in 1436 by Paolo Uccello.

Piazza del Duomo. www.ilgrandemuseodelduomo.it. ✆ **055-230-2885.** Admission to church free; Santa Reparata and cupola included with 10€ Grande Museo del Duomo ticket. Church Mon–Wed and Fri 10am–5pm; Thurs 10am–4:30pm (July–Sept until 5pm, May until 4pm); Sat 10am–4:45pm; Sun 1:30–4:45pm. Cupola Mon–Fri 8:30am–6:20pm; Sat 8:30am–5pm; Sun 1–4pm. Bus: C1 or C2.

Museo Storico dell'Opera del Duomo (Cathedral Works Museum) ★★ ART MUSEUM Florence's Cathedral Museum reopened in late 2015 with double the space to show off what is Italy's second-largest collection of devotional art after Rome's Vatican Museums (p. 77). The site itself is significant: It once housed the workshop where Michelangelo sculpted his statue of "David." The museum's prize exhibit is the centerpiece: After a restoration completed in 2012, the original **Gates of Paradise** ★★★ cast by Lorenzo Ghiberti in the early 1400s (see "Baptistery," p. 174) look better than ever. You can see them in a re-creation of their original space on the piazza, and read from interpretation panels that explain the Old Testament scenes.

Also here is a Michelangelo **"Pietà"** ★★ that nearly wasn't. Early on in the process he had told students that he wanted this "Pietà" to stand at his tomb, but when he found an imperfection in the marble, he began attacking it with a hammer (look at Christ's left arm). The master never returned to the work, but his students later repaired the damage. The figure of Nicodemus was untouched, legend has it, because this was a self-portrait of the artist—a Michelangelo legend that, for once, is probably true. Elsewhere are works by Donatello, Verrocchio, and others.

Piazza del Duomo 9 (behind cathedral). www.ilgrandemuseodelduomo.it. ✆ **055-230-2885.** Admission included with 10€ Grande Museo del Duomo ticket. Mon–Sat 9am–7:30pm; Sun 9am–1:45pm. Bus: C1.

Around Piazza della Signoria & Santa Trínita

Galleria degli Uffizi (Uffizi Gallery) ★★★ ART MUSEUM There is no collection of Renaissance art on the planet that can match the Uffizi. Period. For all its crowds and other inconveniences, the Uffizi

Interior courtyard of the Uffizi Gallery.

remains a must-see. And what will you see? Some 60-plus rooms and marble corridors—built in the 16th century as the Medici's private office complex, or *uffici*—all jam-packed with famous paintings, among them Giotto's "Ognissanti Madonna," Botticelli's "Birth of Venus," Leonardo da Vinci's "Annunciation," Michelangelo's "Holy Family," and many, many more.

Start with **Room 2** for a look at the pre-Renaissance, Gothic style of painting. Compare teacher and student as you examine Cimabue's "Santa Trínita Maestà," painted around 1280, and Giotto's **"Ognissanti Madonna"** ★★★ done in 1310. The similar subject and setting for both paintings allows the viewer to see how Giotto transformed Cimabue's iconlike Byzantine style into something real and human. Giotto's Madonna actually looks like she's sitting on a throne, her clothes emphasizing the curves of her body, whereas Cimabue's Madonna and angels float in space, looking like portraits on coins, with stiff positioning. Also worth a look-see: Duccio's **"Rucellai Madonna"** ★ (1285), a founding work of the ethereal Sienese School of painting.

Room 3 showcases the Sienese School at its peak, with Simone Martini's dazzling **"Annunciation"** ★★ (1333) and Ambrogio Lorenzetti's "Presentation at the Temple" (1342). The Black Death of 1348 wiped out this entire generation of Sienese painters, and most of that city's population along with them. **Room 6** shows Florentine painting at its most decorative, in the style known as "International Gothic." The iconic work is Gentile da Fabriano's **"Procession of the Magi"** ★★★ (1423). The line to see the newborn Jesus is full of decorative and comic elements, and is even longer than the one outside the Uffizi.

Room 8 contains the unflattering profiles of the Duke Federico da Montefeltro of Urbino and his duchess, done by **Piero della Francesca** around 1465. The subjects are portrayed in an unflinchingly realistic way. The duke, in particular, exposes his warts and his crooked nose, broken in a tournament. This focus on earthly, rather than Christian, elements harkens back to the teachings of classical Greek and Roman times, and is made all the more vivid by depiction (on the back) of the couple riding chariots driven by the humanistic virtues of faith, charity, hope, and modesty (for her) and prudence, temperance, fortitude, and justice (for him).

Also here are works by **Filippo Lippi** from the mid–15th century. His most celebrated panel, **"Madonna and Child with Two Angels" ★★**, dates from around 1465. The background, with distant mountains on one side and water on the other, framing the portrait of a woman's face, was shamelessly stolen by Leonardo da Vinci 40 years later for his "Mona Lisa." Lippi's work was also a celebrity scandal. The woman who modeled for Mary was said to be Filippo's lover—a would-be nun called Lucrezia Buti whom he had spirited away from her convent before she could take vows—and the child looking toward the viewer the product of their union. That son, Filippino Lippi, became a painter in his own right, and some of his works hang in the same room. However, it was Filippo's student (who would, in turn, become Filippino's teacher) who would go on to become one of the most famous artists of the 15th century. His name was Botticelli.

Rooms 10 to 14—still collectively numbered as such, even though the partition walls were knocked down in 1978—are devoted to the works of Sandro Filipepi, better known by his nickname "Little Barrels," or Botticelli. Botticelli's 1485 **"Birth of Venus" ★★** hangs like a highway billboard you have seen a thousand times. Venus's pose is taken from classical statues, while the winds Zephyr and Aura blowing her to shore, and the muse welcoming her, are from Ovid's "Metamorphosis." Botticelli's 1478 **"Primavera" ★★★**, its dark, bold colors a stark contrast to filmy, pastel "Venus," defies definitive interpretation (many have tried). But again it features Venus (center), alongside Mercury, with the winged boots, the Three Graces, and the goddess Flora. Next to it Botticelli's "Adoration of the Magi" contains a self-portrait of the artist—he's the one in yellow on the far right.

Leonardo da Vinci's **"Annunciation" ★★★** anchors **Room 15.** In this painting, though completed in the early 1470s while Leonardo was still a student in Verrocchio's workshop, da Vinci's ability to orchestrate the viewer's focus is already masterful: The line down the middle of the brick corner of the house draws your glance to Mary's delicate fingers, which themselves point along the top of a stone wall to the angel's two raised fingers. Those, in turn, draw attention to the mountain in the center of the two parallel trees dividing Mary from the angel, representing the gulf between the worldly and the spiritual. Its unusual perspective was painted to be viewed from the lower right.

Reopened in 2012 after restoration, the **Tribuna** ★ is an octagonal room added to the Uffizi by Francesco I in the 1580s. Although visitors can no longer walk through it, you can view the mother-of-pearl ceiling and the **"Medici Venus"** ★★, a Roman statue dating from the 1st century B.C. Note the similarities to Botticelli's painted Venus.

As soon as you cross to the Uffizi's west wing—past picture windows with views of the Arno River to one side and the perfect, Renaissance perspective of the Uffizi piazza to the other—you're walloped with another line of masterpieces. However, it is hard to be certain of the precise layout you'll encounter, as the museum is undergoing a major facelift, to create the "New Uffizi." Among the highlights of this "second half" is Michelangelo's 1505–08 **"Holy Family"** ★. The twisting shapes of Mary, Joseph, and Jesus recall those in the Sistine Chapel in Rome for their sculpted nature and the bright colors. The torsion and tensions of the painting (and other Michelangelo works) inspired the next generation of Florentine painters, known as the **Mannerists.** Andrea Del Sarto, Rosso Fiorentino, and Pontormo are all represented in the revamped **Sale Rosse (Red Rooms)** downstairs. Here too, the Uffizi has a number of Raphaels, including his recently restored and often-copied **"Madonna of the Goldfinch"** ★★ (Room 66), with a background landscape lifted from Leonardo and Botticelli.

Titian's reclining nude **"Venus of Urbino"** ★★ (Room 83) is another highlight of the later works. It's no coincidence that the edge of the curtain, the angle of her hand and leg, and the line splitting floor and bed all intersect at the forbidden part of her body. Opened in 2013, the **Sale Gialle (Yellow Rooms)** features a trio of paintings by Caravaggio, notably an enigmatic **"Bacchus"** ★, and many by the 17th- to 18th-century *caravaggieschi* artists who aped his *chiaroscuro* (bright light and dark shadows) style of painting. Greatest among them was Artemisia

Gentileschi, a rare female baroque painter. Her **"Judith Slaying Holofernes"** ★ (ca. 1612), is one of the more bloody paintings in the gallery, and shares Room 90 with Caravaggio.

Rooms 46 to 55 also opened in 2012 to showcase the works of foreign painters in the Uffizi—the museum owns a vast and varied collection, much of which lay in storage until the opening of these new galleries. The best among the so-called **Sale Blu (Blue Rooms)** is the Spanish gallery, with works by Goya, El Greco's "Sts. John the Evangelist and Francis" (1600), and Velázquez's **"Self-Portrait"** ★. **Room 49** displays two of Rembrandt's most familiar self-portraits.

If you find yourself flagging at any point (it happens to us all), there is a **coffee shop** at the far end of the west wing. Prices are in line with the piazza below, plus you get a great close-up of the Palazzo Vecchio's facade from the terrace. Fully refreshed, you can return to discover works by the many great artists we didn't have space to cover here: Cranach and Dürer; Giorgione, Bellini, and Mantegna; and Uccello, Masaccio, Bronzino, and Veronese. The collection goes on and on (there are countless Roman statues and friezes, too). There is nowhere like it in Italy, or the world.

Piazzale degli Uffizi 6 (off Piazza della Signoria). www.uffizi.firenze.it. © **055-238-8651.** (Reserve tickets at www.firenzemusei.it or © 055-294-883.) Admission 8€ (12.50€ when there's a temporary exhibition). Tues–Sun 8:15am–6:50pm. Bus: C1 or C2.

Museo Nazionale del Bargello (Bargello Museum) ★★

MUSEUM   This is the most important museum anywhere for Renaissance **sculpture**—and often inexplicably quieter than other museums in the city. In a far cry from its original use as the city's prison, torture chamber, and execution site, the Bargello now stands as a three-story art museum containing some of the best works of Michelangelo, Donatello, and Ghiberti, as well as of their most successful Mannerist successor, Giambologna.

In the ground-level Michelangelo room, you'll witness the variety of his craft, from a whimsical 1497 **"Bacchus"** ★★ to a severe, unfinished "Brutus" of 1539. "Bacchus," created when Michelangelo was just 22, really looks like he's drunk, leaning back a little too far, his head off kilter, with a cupid about to bump him over. Nearby is Giambologna's twisting **"Mercury"** ★, who looks like he's about to take off from the ground, propelled by the breath of Zephyr.

Upstairs an enormous vaulted hall is filled with some of Donatello's most accomplished sculptures, including his original "Marzocco" (from outside the Palazzo Vecchio; p. 184), and **"St. George"** ★ from a niche on the outside of Orsanmichele. Notable among them is his bronze **"David"** ★★ (which some think might correctly be named "Mercury"), done in 1440, the first freestanding nude sculpture since Roman times. The classical detail of these sculptures, as well as their naturalistic poses and reflective mood, is the essence of the Renaissance style.

PIAZZA DELLA Signoria

When the medieval Guelph party finally came out on top after their political struggle with the Ghibellines, they razed part of the old city center to build a new palace for civic government. It's said the Guelphs ordered architect Arnolfo di Cambio to build what we now call the **Palazzo Vecchio** (see p. 184) in the corner of this space, but to be careful that not 1 inch of the building sat on the cursed former Ghibelline land. This odd legend was probably fabricated to explain Arnolfo's quirky off-center architecture.

The space around the *palazzo* became the new civic center of town, L-shaped **Piazza della Signoria** ★★, named after the oligarchic ruling body of the medieval city (the "Signoria"). Today, it's an outdoor sculpture gallery, teeming with tourists, postcard stands, horses and buggies, and expensive outdoor cafes. If you want to catch the square at its serene best, come around 8am.

The statuary on the piazza is particularly beautiful, starting on the far left (as you're facing the Palazzo Vecchio) with Giambologna's equestrian statue of "Grand Duke Cosimo I" (1594). To its right is one of Florence's favorite sculptures to hate, the **"Fontana del Nettuno"** ("Neptune Fountain"; 1560–75), created by Bartolomeo Ammannati as a tribute to Cosimo I's naval ambitions but nicknamed by the Florentines "Il Biancone," or "Big Whitey." The **porphyry plaque** set in the ground in front of the fountain marks the site where puritanical monk Savonarola held the Bonfire of the Vanities: With his fiery apocalyptic preaching, he whipped the Florentines into a reformist frenzy, and hundreds filed into this piazza, arms loaded with paintings, clothing, and other effects that represented their "decadence." They threw it all onto the flames.

To the right of Neptune is a long, raised platform fronting the Palazzo Vecchio known as the *arringheria*, from which soapbox speakers would lecture to crowds before them (we get our word "harangue" from this). On its far left corner is a copy (original in the Bargello; see p. 181) of Donatello's **"Marzocco,"** symbol of the city, with a Florentine lion resting his raised paw on a shield emblazoned with the city's emblem, the *giglio* (lily). To its right is another Donatello replica, **"Judith Beheading Holofernes."** Farther down is a man who needs little introduction, Michelangelo's **"David,"** a 19th-century copy of the original now in the Accademia. Near enough to David to look truly ugly in comparison is Baccio Bandinelli's **"Hercules and Cacus"** (1534). Poor Bandinelli was trying to copy Michelangelo's muscular male form but ended up making his Heracles merely lumpy.

At the piazza's south end is one of the square's earliest and prettiest embellishments, the **Loggia dei Lanzi** ★★ (1376–82), named after the Swiss guard of lancers *(lanzi)* whom Cosimo de' Medici stationed here. The airy loggia was probably built on a design by Andrea Orcagna—spawning another of its many names, the Loggia di Orcagna (yet another is the Loggia della Signoria). At the front left stands Benvenuto Cellini's masterpiece in bronze, **"Perseus"** ★★★ (1545), holding out the severed head of Medusa. On the far right is Giambologna's **"Rape of the Sabines"** ★★, one of the most successful Mannerist sculptures in existence, and a piece you must walk all the way around to appreciate, catching the action and artistry of its spiral design from different angles. Talk about moving it indoors, safe from the elements, continues . . . but for now, it's still here.

Exploring Florence

FLORENCE

Side by side on the back wall are the contest entries submitted by Ghiberti and Brunelleschi for the commission to do the Baptistery doors in 1401. Both had the "Sacrifice of Isaac" as their biblical theme, and both displayed innovative use of perspective. Ghiberti won the contest, perhaps because his scene is more thematically unified. Brunelleschi could have ended up a footnote in the art history books, but instead he gave up the chisel and turned his attentions to architecture instead, which turned out to be a wise move (see "A Man & His Dome," p. 176). Via del Proconsolo 4. www.polomuseale.firenze.it. **℃ 055-238-8606.** Admission 4€ (7€ when there's a temporary exhibition). Daily 8:15am–1:50pm (until 5pm during exhibition). Closed 1st, 3rd, and 5th Sun, and 2nd and 4th Mon of each month. Bus: C1 or C2.

Orsanmichele ★★ RELIGIOUS SITE/ARCHITECTURE   This bulky structure halfway down Via dei Calzaiuoli looks more like a Gothic warehouse than a church—which is exactly what it was, built as a granary and grain market in 1337. After a miraculous image of the Madonna appeared on a column inside, however, the lower level was turned into a shrine and chapel. The city's merchant guilds each undertook the task of decorating one of the outside Gothic tabernacles around the lower level with a statue of their guild's patron saint. Masters such as Ghiberti, Donatello, Verrocchio, and Giambologna all cast or carved masterpieces to set here (those remaining are mostly copies, including Donatello's "St. George").

In the dark interior, the elaborate Gothic **Tabernacle ★** (1349–59) by Andrea Orcagna protects a luminous 1348 "Madonna and Child" painted by Giotto's student Bernardo Daddi, to which miracles were ascribed during the Black Death of 1348–50.

Every Monday (9am–5pm) you can access the upper floors, which house many of the original sculptures that once adorned Orsanmichele's exterior niches. Among the treasures of the so-called **Museo di Orsanmichele ★** are a trio of bronzes: Ghiberti's "St. John the Baptist" (1412–16), the first life-size bronze of the Renaissance; Verrocchio's "Incredulity of St. Thomas" (1483); and Giambologna's "St. Luke" (1602). Climb up one floor further, to the top, for an unforgettable 360° **panorama ★★** of the city. The Museo is staffed by volunteers, so donate if you are able. Via Arte della Lana 1. ℃ **055-210-305.** Free admission. Daily 10am–5pm. Bus: C2.

Palazzo Davanzati ★★ PALACE/MUSEUM   One of the best preserved 14th-century palaces in the city offers a fascinating glimpse into domestic life in the medieval and Renaissance period. It was originally built for the Davizzi family in the mid-1300s, then bought by the Davanzati clan; check out the latter's family tree, dating back to the 1100s, on the wall of the ground-floor courtyard. The palace's painted wooden ceilings and murals have aged well (even surviving World War II damage), but the emphasis remains not on the décor, but on providing visitors with insights into medieval life for a noble Florentine family: feasts and festivities in the Sala Madornale; a private, internal well to secure water supply when things got sticky; and magnificent bedchamber frescoes from the 1350s, which recount, comic-strip style, "The Chatelaine of Vergy," a 13th-century morality tale. An interesting footnote: In 1916, a New York auction of furnishings from this very same palace launched a "Florentine style" trend in U.S. interior design circles.

Via Porta Rossa 13. www.polomuseale.firenze.it. *©* **055-238-8610.** Admission 2€. Daily 8:15am–1:50pm. Closed 2nd and 4th Sun, and 1st, 3rd, and 5th Mon of each month. Bus: C2.

Palazzo Vecchio ★★ PALACE   The core of Florence's fortresslike town hall was built from 1299 to 1302 to the designs of Arnolfo di Cambio, Gothic master builder. The palace was home to the various Florentine governments (and is today to the city government). When Duke Cosimo I and his Medici family moved to the *palazzo* in 1540, they redecorated: Michelozzo's 1453 **courtyard** ★ was left architecturally intact but frescoed by Vasari with scenes of Austrian cities, to celebrate the 1565 marriage of Francesco de' Medici and Joanna of Austria.

A grand staircase leads up to the **Sala dei Cinquecento,** named for the 500-man assembly that met here in the pre-Medici days of the Florentine Republic. It's also the site of the greatest fresco cycle that ever wasn't. Leonardo da Vinci was commissioned in 1503–05 to paint one long wall with a battle scene celebrating Florence's victory at the 1440 Battle of Anghiari. Always trying new methods and materials, he decided to mix wax into his pigments. Leonardo had finished painting part of the wall, but it wasn't drying fast enough, so he brought in braziers stoked with hot coals to try to hurry the process. As others watched in horror, the wax in the fresco melted under the intense heat and the colors ran down the walls to puddle on the floor. The search for whatever remains of his work continues; some hope was provided in 2012 with the discovery of pigments used by Leonardo in a cavity behind the current wall. Michelangelo was supposed to paint a fresco on the opposite wall, but he never got past the preparatory drawings before Pope Julius II called him to Rome to paint the Sistine Chapel. Eventually, the bare walls were covered by Vasari and assistants from 1563 to 1565, with subservient frescoes exalting Cosimo I and the military victories of his regime, against Pisa (on the near wall) and Siena (far wall). Opposite the door you enter is Michelangelo's statue of **"Victory"** ★, carved from 1533 to 1534 for Pope Julius II's tomb but later donated to the Medici.

The first series of rooms on the upper floor is the **Quartiere degli Elementi,** frescoed with allegories and mythological characters again by Vasari. Crossing the balcony overlooking the Sala dei Cinquecento, you enter the **Apartments of Eleonora di Toledo ★,** decorated for Cosimo's Spanish wife. Her small **private chapel ★★★** is a masterpiece of mid-16th-century fresco painting by Bronzino. Farther on, under the coffered ceiling of the **Sala dei Gigli,** you'll see Domenico Ghirlandaio's fresco of "St. Zenobius Enthroned," with figures from Republican and Imperial Rome, and Donatello's original **"Judith and Holofernes"** ★ bronze (1455), one of his last works. In late 2014, the palace's basement was opened up for visitors to view the **Scavi del Teatro Romano** ★, the remnants of Roman Florentia's theater, upon which the Palazzo was built. Remains of the walls and an intact paved street have been uncovered.

Visitors can also climb the **Torre di Arnolfo ★★,** the palace's crenellated tower. If you can bear the small spaces and 418 steps, the views

The Piazza della Signoria and the Palazzo Vecchio.

from the top of this medieval skyscraper are sublime. The 95m (312-ft.) Torre is closed during bad weather; the minimum age to climb it is 6, and children ages 17 and under must be accompanied by an adult.

Piazza della Signoria. www.museicivicifiorentini.comune.fi.it. ℂ **055-276-8325.** Admission to Palazzo or Torre 10€; admission to both, or to Palazzo plus Scavi 14€; admission to everything 18€. Palazzo/Scavi: Fri–Wed 9am–7pm (Apr–Sept until 11pm); Thurs 9am–2pm. Torre: Fri–Wed 10am–5pm (Apr–Sept 9am–9pm); Thurs 10am–2pm. Bus: C1 or C2.

Ponte Vecchio ★ ARCHITECTURE   The oldest and most famous bridge across the Arno, the Ponte Vecchio was built in 1345 by Taddeo Gaddi to replace an earlier version. The overhanging shops have lined the bridge since at least the 12th century. In the 16th century, it was home to butchers until Ferdinand I moved into the Palazzo Pitti across the river. He couldn't stand the stench, so he evicted the meat cutters and moved in classier gold- and silversmiths, and jewelers, who occupy it to this day.

The Ponte Vecchio's fame saved it in 1944 from the Nazis, who had orders to blow up all the bridges before retreating out of Florence as Allied forces advanced. They couldn't bring themselves to reduce this span to rubble—so they blew up the ancient buildings on either end instead to block it off. The **Great Arno Flood** of 1966 wasn't so discriminating, however, and severely damaged the shops. A private night watchman saw the waters rising alarmingly and called many of the goldsmiths at home, who rushed to remove their valuable stock before it was washed away.

Via Por Santa Maria/Via Guicciardini. Bus: C3 or D.

The Ponte Vecchio spans the River Arno.

Vasari's Corridor

The enclosed passageway that runs along the top of the Ponte Vecchio is part of the **Corridoio Vasariano (Vasari Corridor) ★**, a private elevated link between the Palazzo Vecchio and Palazzo Pitti, and now hung with the world's best collection of artists' self-portraits. Duke Cosimo I, distressed by the idea of mixing with the hoi polloi on his way to work, commissioned Vasari to design his V.I.P. route in 1565. It's often possible to walk the corridor, although closures for restoration work are common. Inquire at the tourist office. **Context Travel** (p. 121) operates a 2-hour guided walk through the corridor, costing 190€ per person (pricey, but worth it), plus the admission price of the Uffizi. **CAF Tours** (p. 202) runs a shorter walk along the corridor for 65€. Booking in advance for any corridor tour is essential.

Santa Trínita ★★ CHURCH Beyond Bernardo Buontalenti's late-16th-century **facade** lies a dark church, rebuilt in the 14th century but founded by the Vallombrosans before 1177. The third chapel on the right has what remains of the detached frescoes by Spinello Aretino, which were found under Lorenzo Monaco's 1424 "Scenes from the Life of the Virgin" frescoes covering the next chapel along. In the right transept, Domenico Ghirlandaio frescoed the **Cappella Sassetti ★** in 1483 with a cycle on the "Life of St. Francis," but true to form he set all the scenes against Florentine backdrops and peopled them with portraits of contemporary notables. His "Francis Receiving the Order from Pope Honorius" (in the lunette) takes place under an arcade on the north side of Piazza della Signoria—you'll recognize the Loggia dei Lanzi in the middle, and on the left, the Palazzo Vecchio. (The Uffizi between them hadn't been built yet.)

The south end of the piazza leads to the **Ponte Santa Trínita ★★**, Florence's most graceful bridge. In 1567, Ammannati built a span here that was set with four 16th-century statues of the seasons in honor of the marriage of Cosimo II. After the Nazis blew up the bridge in 1944, it was rebuilt, and all was set into place —save the head on the statue of Spring, which remained lost until a team dredging the river in 1961 found it by accident. If you want to photograph the Ponte Vecchio, head here at dusk. Piazza Santa Trínita. ℂ **055-216-912.** Free admission. Mon–Sat 8am–noon and 4–6pm; Sun 8–10:45am and 4–6pm. Bus: C3, D, 6, or 11.

Around San Lorenzo & the Mercato Centrale

Until a controversial—and *perhaps* temporary—move in 2014, the church of San Lorenzo was lost behind the leather stalls and souvenir carts of Florence's vast **San Lorenzo street market** (see "Shopping," later in this chapter). In fact, the bustle of commerce characterizes the whole neighborhood, centered on both the tourist market and the nearby **Mercato Centrale** food hall, whose upper floor became a major informal dining destination when it opened in 2014 (see p. 219).

The Medici Chapels.

Cappelle Medicee (Medici Chapels) ★ MONUMENT/MEMORIAL
When Michelangelo built the New Sacristy between 1520 and 1533
(finished by Vasari in 1556), it was to be a tasteful monument to Lorenzo
the Magnificent and his generation of relatively pleasant Medici. When
work got underway on the adjacent **Cappella dei Principi (Chapel of
the Princes)** in 1604, it was to become one of Italy's most god-awful
and arrogant memorials, dedicated to the grand dukes, some of Florence's most decrepit tyrants. The Cappella dei Principi is an exercise in
bad taste, a mountain of cut marbles and semiprecious stones—jasper,
alabaster, mother-of-pearl, agate, and the like—slathered onto the walls
and ceiling with no regard for composition and still less for chromatic
unity. The pouring of ducal funds into this monstrosity began in 1604
and lasted until the rarely conscious Gian Gastone de' Medici drank
himself to death in 1737, without an heir—but teams kept doggedly at
the thing, and they were still finishing the floor in 1962.

Michelangelo's **Sagrestia Nuova (New Sacristy)** ★★, built to
jibe with Brunelleschi's Old Sacristy in San Lorenzo proper (see below),
is much calmer. (An architectural tidbit: The windows in the dome taper
as they get near the top to fool you into thinking the dome is higher.)
Michelangelo was supposed to produce three tombs here (perhaps four)
but ironically got only the two less important ones done. So Lorenzo de'
Medici ("the Magnificent")—wise ruler of his city, poet of note, grand
patron of the arts, and moneybags behind much of the Renaissance—
ended up with a mere inscription of his name next to his brother Giuliano's on a plain marble slab against the entrance wall. Admittedly, they did
get one genuine Michelangelo sculpture to decorate their slab, a not
quite finished **"Madonna and Child"** ★.

On the left wall of the sacristy is Michelangelo's **"Tomb of
Lorenzo"** ★, duke of Urbino (and Lorenzo the Magnificent's grandson),
whose seated statue symbolizes the contemplative life. Below him on the

elongated curves of the tomb stretch "Dawn" (female) and "Dusk" (male), a pair of Michelangelo's most famous sculptures. This pair mirrors the similarly fashioned "Day" (male) and "Night" (female) across the way. One additional point "Dawn" and "Night" brings out is that Michelangelo perhaps hadn't seen too many naked women.

Piazza Madonna degli Aldobrandini (behind San Lorenzo, where Via Faenza and Via del Giglio meet). (C) **055-238-8602.** Admission 6€ (8€ when there's a temporary exhibition). Daily 8:15am–4:50pm. Closed 1st, 3rd, and 5th Mon, and 2nd and 4th Sun of each month. Bus: C1, C2, or 22.

Palazzo Medici-Riccardi ★ PALACE   Built by Michelozzo in 1444 for Medici "godfather" Cosimo il Vecchio, this is the prototype Florentine *palazzo*, on which the more overbearing Strozzi and Pitti palaces were later modeled. It remained the Medici private home until Cosimo I officially declared his power as duke by moving to the city's traditional civic brain center, the Palazzo Vecchio. A door off the courtyard leads up a staircase to the **Cappella dei Magi,** the oldest chapel to survive from a private Florentine palace; its walls are covered with dense and colorful Benozzo Gozzoli **frescoes** ★★ (1459–63) in the International Gothic style. Rich as tapestries, the walls depict an extended "Journey of the Magi" to see the Christ child, who's being adored by Mary in the altarpiece.

Via Cavour 3. www.palazzo-medici.it. (C) **055-276-0340.** Admission 7€ adults, 4€ ages 6–12. Thurs–Tues 9am–7pm. Bus: C1, 14, or 23.

San Lorenzo ★ CHURCH   A rough brick anti-facade hides what is most likely the oldest church in Florence, founded in A.D. 393. It was later the Medici family's parish church, and Cosimo il Vecchio, whose wise behind-the-scenes rule made him popular with the Florentines, is buried in front of the high altar. The plaque marking the spot is inscribed pater patriae—"Father of the Homeland." Off the left transept, the **Sagrestia Vecchia (Old Sacristy)** ★ is one of Brunelleschi's purest pieces of early Renaissance architecture. The focal sarcophagus contains Cosimo il Vecchio's parents, Giovanni di Bicci de' Medici and his wife, Piccarda Bueri. A side chapel is decorated with an early star map showing the night sky above the city in the 1440s—a scene that also features in Brunelleschi's Pazzi Chapel, in Santa Croce; see p. 195. On the wall of the left aisle is Bronzino's huge fresco of the **"Martyrdom of San Lorenzo"** ★. The poor soul was roasted on a grill in Rome.

Piazza San Lorenzo. (C) **055-214-042.** Admission to church 4.50€; admission to library 3€; combined admission 7€. Church: Mon–Sat 10am–5:30pm; Mar–Oct also Sun 1:30–5:30pm. Laurentian Library: Mon–Sat 9:30am–1:30pm. Bus: C1.

Near Piazza Santa Maria Novella

The two squat obelisks in **Piazza Santa Maria Novella** ★, resting on Giambologna tortoises, once served as turning posts for "chariot" races held here from the 16th to the mid–19th century. Once a down-at-heel part of the center, the area now has some of Florence's priciest hotels.

Museo Novecento ★ MUSEUM Inaugurated in 2014, this museum covers 20th-century Italian art in a multitude of media. Crowds are often sparse—let's face it, you're in Florence for the 1400s, not the 1900s—but that's no reflection on the quality of the collection, which spans 100 years of visual arts in reverse chronological order. Exhibits include works by major names such as De Chirico and Futurist Gino Severini, and closer examinations of Florence's role in fashion and Italy's relationship with European avant-garde art. Our favorite spot, though, is the top-floor **screening room** ★★ where a 20-minute movie clip montage plays on a loop. It shows Florence as represented by a century of movie-makers from Arnaldo Ginna's 1916 *Vita Futurista* to recent films such as *Room with a View* and *Tea with Mussolini*.

Piazza Santa Maria Novella 10. www.museonovecento.it. ℭ **055-286-132.** Admission 8€. Apr–Sept daily 9am–7pm (closes at 2pm on Thurs and 11pm on Fri); Oct–Mar daily 9am–6pm (closes 2pm on Thurs). Bus: 6 or 11.

Santa Maria Novella ★★ CHURCH Of all Florence's major churches, the home of the Dominicans is the only one with an original **facade** ★★ that matches its era of greatest importance. The lower Romanesque half was started in the 14th century by architect Fra' Jacopo Talenti, who had just finished building the church itself (begun in 1246). Renaissance architect and theorist Leon Battista Alberti finished the facade, adding a classically inspired Renaissance top that not only went

Santa Maria Novella.

seamlessly with the lower half but also created a Cartesian plane of perfect geometry. Inside, on the left wall, **Masaccio's "Trinità"** ★★★ (ca. 1425) is the first painting ever to use perfect linear mathematical perspective. Florentine citizens and artists flooded in to see the fresco when it was unveiled, many remarking in awe that it seemed to punch a hole back into space, creating a chapel out of a flat wall. The **transept** is filled with frescoed chapels by Filippino Lippi and others. The **Sanctuary** ★ behind the main altar was frescoed after 1485 by Domenico Ghirlandaio with the help of his assistants and apprentices, probably including a young Michelangelo. The left wall is covered with a cycle on the "Life of the Virgin" and the right wall with a "Life of

St. John the Baptist." (Read from the bottom upward; there are boards that explain the scenes.) The works are not just biblical stories but also snapshots of the era's fashions and personages, full of portraits of the Tornabuoni family who commissioned them.

For many years the church's frescoed cloisters were treated as a separate site; they have been reunited at last, all now accessible on one admission ticket. (Although, confusingly, there are two separate entrances, through the church's garden and via the tourist office at the rear, on Piazza della Stazione.) The **Chiostro Verde (Green Cloister)** ★★ was partly frescoed between 1431 and 1446 by Paolo Uccello, a Florentine painter who became increasingly obsessed with the mathematics behind perspective. His Old Testament scenes include a "Universal Deluge," which ironically was badly damaged by the Great Arno Flood of 1966. Off the cloister, the **Spanish Chapel** ★ is a complex piece of Dominican propaganda, frescoed in the 1360s by Andrea di Bonaiuto. The **Chiostro dei Morti (Cloister of the Dead)** ★ is one of the oldest parts of the convent, and was another area badly damaged in 1966. Its low-slung vaults were decorated by Andrea Orcagna and others.

Piazza Santa Maria Novella/Piazza della Stazione 4. www.chiesasantamarianovella.it. ✆ **055-219-257.** Admission 5€. Mon–Thurs 9am–5:30pm; Fri 11am–5:30pm; Sat 9am–5pm; Sun 1–5pm (July–Sept noon–5pm). Bus: C2, 6, 11, or 22.

Near San Marco & Santissima Annunziata

Cenacolo di Sant'Apollonia ★ ART MUSEUM   Painter Andrea del Castagno (1421–57) learned his trade painting the portraits of condemned men in the city's prisons, and it's easy to see the influence of his apprenticeship on the faces of the Disciples in his version of **"The Last Supper,"** the first painted in Florence during the Renaissance. The giant fresco, completed around 1447, covers an entire wall at one end of this former convent refectory. It is easy to spot Judas, banished to the other side of the communal table and painted as a satyr with a faux-marble panel in turmoil above his head. Above Castagno's "Last Supper," his "Crucifixion," "Deposition," and "Entombment" complete the sequence of the final days of the Christian story.

Via XXVII Aprile 1. ✆ **055-238-8607.** Free admission. Daily 8:15am–1:50pm. Closed 1st, 3rd, and 5th Sun and 2nd and 4th Mon of each month. Bus: 1, 6, 11, 14, 17, or 23.

Galleria dell'Accademia ★★ ART MUSEUM   **"David"** ★★★—"Il Gigante"—is much larger than most people imagine, looming 4.8m (16 ft.) on top of a 1.8m (6-ft.) pedestal. He hasn't faded with time, either; a 2004 cleaning still makes the marble gleam as if it were the original unveiling day in 1504. Viewing the statue is a pleasure in the bright and spacious room custom-designed for him after the icon was moved to the Accademia in 1873, following 300 years of pigeons perching on his head in Piazza della Signoria. Replicas now take the abuse there, and at

Piazzale Michelangiolo. The spot high on one flank of the Duomo, for which he was originally commissioned, stands empty.

But the Accademia is not only about "David"; you will be delighted to discover he is surrounded by an entire museum

Seeing 'David' Without a Reservation

The wait to get in to see "David" can be an hour or more if you didn't reserve ahead or buy a Firenze Card (p. 171). Try getting there before the museum opens in the morning or an hour or two before closing time.

stuffed with other notable Renaissance works. Michelangelo's unfinished **"Prisoners"** ★★ statues are a contrast to "David," with the rough forms struggling to free themselves from the raw stone. They also provide a unique glimpse into how Michelangelo worked a piece of stone; he famously said that he tried to free the sculpture within from the block, and you can see this quite clearly here. Rooms showcase paintings by Perugino, Filippino Lippi, Giotto, Giovanna da Milano, Andrea Orcagna, and others. Via Ricasoli 60. www.polomuseale.firenze.it. © **055-238-8609.** (Reserve tickets at www.firenzemusei.it or © 055-294-883.) Admission 8€ (12.50€ when there's a temporary exhibition). Tues–Sun 8:15am–6:50pm. Bus: C1, 1, 6, 14, 19, 23, 31, or 32.

Museo Archeologico (Archaeological Museum) ★ MUSEUM   If you can force yourselves away from the Renaissance, rewind a millennium or two at one of the most important archaeological collections in central Italy, which has a particular emphasis on the **Etruscan** period. You will need a little patience, however: The collection is not easy to navigate, and displays are somewhat user-unfriendly. Exhibits also have a habit of moving around, but you will easily find the **"Arezzo Chimera"** ★★, a bronze figure of a mythical lion–goat–serpent dating to the 4th century B.C. It is perhaps the most important bronze sculpture to survive from the Etruscan era, and at time of writing, it was displayed alongside the "Arringatore," a life-size bronze of an orator dating to the 1st century, just as Etruscan culture was being subsumed by Ancient Rome. On the top floor is the **"Idolino"** ★, an exquisite and slightly mysterious, lithe bronze. The collection is also strong on Etruscan-era *bucchero* pottery and funerary urns, and Egyptian relics that include several sarcophagi displayed in a series of eerie galleries. One bonus: With other visitors so focused on medieval and Renaissance sights in the city, you may have the place almost to yourself. Piazza Santissma Annunziata 9b. © **055-23-575.** Admission 4€. Tues–Fri 8:30am–7pm; Sat–Mon 8:30am–2pm (Aug closed Sun). Bus: 6, 19, 31, or 32.

San Marco ★★★ ART MUSEUM   We have never understood why this place is not mobbed; perhaps because it showcases, almost exclusively, the work of Fra' Angelico, Dominican monk and Florentine painter in the style known as "International Gothic." This is the most important collection in the world of his altarpieces and painted panels, residing in the former 13th-century convent the artist-monk once called home. Seeing it all in one place allows you to truly appreciate how his decorative impulses and the sinuous lines of his figures mark his work as standing right on the cusp of the Renaissance. The most moving and unusual work is his **"Annunciation"** ★★★, but a close second is the intimate frescoes of the life of Jesus—painted not on one giant wall, but scene by scene on the individual walls of small monks' cells that honeycomb the upper floor. The idea was that these scenes, painted by Fra' Angelico and his assistants, would aid in the monks' prayer and contemplation. The final cell on the left corridor belonged to the fundamentalist firebrand preacher Savonarola, who briefly incited the populace of the most art-filled city in the world to burn their "decadent" paintings, illuminated manuscripts, and anything else he felt was a worldly betrayal of Jesus' ideals. (Ultimately, he ran afoul of the pope.) You'll see his notebooks, rosary, and what's left of the clothes he wore that day in his cell, as well as an anonymous panel painted to show the day in 1498 when he was burned at the stake in Piazza della Signoria. There is much more Fra' Angelico secreted around the cloisters, including a **"Crucifixion"** ★ in the Chapter House. The former Hospice is now a gallery dedicated to Fra' Angelico and his contemporaries; look out especially for his **"Tabernacolo dei Linaioli"** ★★, still glowing after a 2011 restoration, and a seemingly weightless **"Deposition"** ★★.

Piazza San Marco 1. www.polomuseale.firenze.it. ✆ **055-238-8608.** Admission 4€. Mon–Fri 8:15am–1:50pm; Sat–Sun 8:15am–4:50pm. Closed 1st, 3rd, and 5th Sun and 2nd and 4th Mon of each month. Bus: C1, 1, 6, 7, 10, 11, 14, 17, 19, 20, 23, 25, 31, or 32.

Santissima Annunziata ★ CHURCH   In 1233, seven Florentine nobles had a spiritual crisis, gave away all their possessions, and retired to the forests to contemplate divinity. In 1250, they returned to what were then fields outside the city walls and founded a small oratory, proclaiming they were Servants of Mary, or the Servite Order. The oratory was enlarged by Michelozzo (1444–81) and later redesigned in the baroque style. The main art interest is in the **Chiostro dei Voti (Votive Cloister),** designed by Michelozzo with Corinthian-capitaled columns and decorated with some of the city's finest **Mannerist frescoes** ★★ (1465–1515). Rosso Fiorentino provided an "Assumption" (1513) and Pontormo a "Visitation" (1515) just to the right of the door. Their master, Andrea del Sarto, contributed a "Birth of the Virgin" (1513), in the far right corner, one of his finest works. To the right of the door into the church is a damaged but still fascinating "Coming of the Magi" (1514) by del Sarto, who included a self-portrait at the far right, looking out at us from under his blue hat. In the excessively baroque **interior,** just to the left as you enter is a huge tabernacle hidden under a mountain of *ex votos* (votive offerings). It was designed by Michelozzo to house a small painting of the "Annunciation." Legend holds that this painting was started by a friar who, vexed that he couldn't paint the Madonna's face as beautifully as it should be, gave up and took a nap. When he awoke, he found an angel had filled in the face for him.

On **Piazza Santissima Annunziata** ★★ outside, flanked by elegant Brunelleschi porticos, is an equestrian statue of "Grand Duke

Ferdinando I" by Giambologna. It was his last work, cast in 1608 after his death by his student Pietro Tacca, who also did the two fountains of fantastic mermonkey-monsters. You can stay right on this spectacular piazza, at one of our favorite Florence hotels, the Loggiato dei Serviti (p. 209).

Piazza Santissima Annunziata. ✆ **055-266-181.** Free admission. Cloister: daily 7:30am–12:30pm and 4–6:30pm. Church: daily 4–5:15pm. Bus: 6, 19, 31, or 32.

Around Piazza Santa Croce

Piazza Santa Croce is pretty much like any grand Florentine square— an open space ringed with souvenir and leather shops and thronged with tourists. Once a year (during late June) it's covered with dirt and violent, Renaissance-style soccer is played on it in the tournament known as **Calcio Storico Fiorentino.**

Santa Croce ★★ CHURCH   The center of Florence's Franciscan universe was begun in 1294 by Gothic master Arnolfo di Cambio in order to rival the church of Santa Maria Novella being raised by the Dominicans across the city. The church wasn't consecrated until 1442, and even then it remained faceless until the neo-Gothic **facade** was added in 1857. This art-stuffed complex demands 2 hours of your time to see properly. The Gothic **interior** is vast, and populated with the tombs of famous Florentines. Starting from the main door, immediately on the right is the tomb containing the bones of the most venerated Renaissance master, **Michelangelo Buonarroti,** who died in Rome in 1564 at the ripe age of 89. The pope wanted him buried in the Eternal City, but Florentines managed to sneak his body back to Florence. Two berths along from Michelangelo's monument is a pompous 19th-century cenotaph to **Dante Alighieri,** one of history's great poets, whose *Divine Comedy* codified the Italian language. (Exiled from Florence, Dante is buried in Ravenna—see p. 351.) Elsewhere, seek out monuments to philosopher **Niccolò Machiavelli, Gioacchino Rossini** (1792–1868), composer of *The Barber of Seville,* sculptor **Lorenzo Ghiberti,** and scientist **Galileo Galilei** (1564–1642).

The right transept is richly decorated with **frescoes.** The **Cappella Castellani** was frescoed with stories of saints' lives by Agnolo Gaddi, with a tabernacle by Mino da Fiesole and a "Crucifix" by Niccolò Gerini. Agnolo's father, Taddeo Gaddi—one of Giotto's closest followers— painted the **Cappella Baroncelli** ★ (1328–38) at the transept's end. The frescoes depict scenes from the "Life of the Virgin," and include an "Annunciation to the Shepherds," the first night scene in Italian fresco. Giotto himself frescoed the two chapels to the right of the high altar. (Whitewashed over in the 17th century, they were uncovered from 1841 to 1852 and inexpertly restored.) The **Cappella Peruzzi** ★, on the right, is a late work with many references to antiquity, reflecting Giotto's trip to Rome's ruins. The more famous **Cappella Bardi** ★★ even appeared in the movie *A Room with a View;* key panels, featuring episodes in the life

Michelangelo's tomb in the church of Santa Croce.

of St. Francis, include the "Trial by Fire Before the Sultan of Egypt" on the right wall (notice the subtle expressions and poses of the figures); and, one of Giotto's best-known works, the "Death of St. Francis," in which monks weep and wail with convincing pathos.

Outside in the cloister is the **Cappella Pazzi** ★, one of Filippo Brunelleschi's architectural masterpieces (faithfully finished after his death in 1446). Giuliano da Maiano probably designed the porch that now precedes the chapel, set with glazed terracottas by Luca della Robbia. (It was restored in 2015 thanks to an international Kickstarter project run by the church.) The rectangular chapel is one of Brunelleschi's signature pieces, decorated with his trademark *pietra serena* gray stone. It is the defining example of (and model for) early Renaissance architecture. Curiously, the ceiling of the smaller dome depicts the night sky at the same moment as the Old Sacristy in San Lorenzo (p. 189). From the cloister you can enter the **Museo dell'Opera** to see the Cimabue **"Crucifix"** ★ that was almost destroyed by the Arno Flood of 1966, which became an international symbol of the ruination wreaked by the river that November day.

Piazza Santa Croce. www.santacroceopera.it. ℂ **055-246-6105.** Admission 6€ adults, 4€ ages 11–17. Mon–Sat 9:30am–5:30pm; Sun 2–5:30pm. Bus: C1, C2, or C3.

The Oltrarno, San Niccolò & San Frediano

Museo Zoologia "La Specola" ★ MUSEUM The wax anatomical models are one reason this museum may be the only one in Florence where kids eagerly pull their parents from room to room. Creepy collections of threadbare stuffed-animal specimens transition into rooms filled with lifelike human bodies suffering from dismemberments, flayings, and eviscerations—all in the name of science. These wax models served as anatomical illustrations for medical students studying at this scientific institute from the 1770s. The grisly wax plague dioramas in the final room were created in the early 1700s to satisfy the lurid tastes of Cosimo III.

Via Romana 17. www.msn.unifi.it. ℂ **055-275-6444.** Admission 6€ adults, 3€ children 6–14 and seniors 65 and over. June–Sept daily 10:30am–5:30pm; Oct–May Tues–Sun 9:30am–4:30pm. Bus: 11, 36, or 37.

Palazzo Pitti (Pitti Palace) ★★ MUSEUM/PALACE Although built by and named after a rival of the Medici—merchant Luca Pitti—in the 1450s, this gigantic *palazzo* soon fell into Medici hands. It was the Medici family's principal home from the 1540s, and continued to house Florence's rulers until 1919. The Pitti contains five museums, including one of the world's best collections of canvases by Raphael. Out back are elegant Renaissance gardens, the **Boboli** (see below).

In the art-crammed rooms of the Pitti's **Galleria Palatina ★★,** paintings are displayed like cars in a parking garage, stacked on walls above each other in the "Enlightenment" method of exhibition. Rooms are alternately dimly lit, or garishly bright; this is how many of the world's great art treasures were seen and enjoyed by their original commissioners. You will find important historical treasures amid the Palatina's vast and haphazard collection; some of the best efforts of Titian, Raphael, and Rubens line the walls. Botticelli and Filippo Lippi's **"Madonna and Child" ★** (1452) provide the key works in the **Sala di Prometeo (Prometheus Room).** Two giant versions of the "Assumption of the Virgin," both by Mannerist painter Andrea del Sarto, dominate the **Sala dell'Iliade (Iliad Room).** Here you will also find another Biblical woman painted by Artemisia Gentileschi, "Judith." The **Sala di Saturno (Saturn Room) ★** is stuffed with Raphaels; next door in the **Sala di Giove (Jupiter Room)** you'll find his sublime, naturalistic portrait of **"La Velata" ★★,** as well as **"The Ages of Man" ★.** The current attribution of the painting is awarded to Venetian Giorgione, though that has been disputed.

At the **Appartamenti Reali (Royal Apartments)** you get an excellent feeling for the conspicuous consumption of the Medici Grand Dukes and their Austrian and Belgian Lorraine successors—and see some notable paintings in their original, ostentatious setting. The rooms earned their "Royal" label because Italy's first king lived here for several years during Italy's 19th-century unification process—when Florence was Italy's second capital, after Turin—until Rome was finally conquered and the court moved there. Much of the stucco, fabrics, furnishings, and general decoration is in thunderously poor taste, but you should look out for Caravaggio's subtle canvas **"Knight of Malta" ★.**

The opulence of the Galleria Palatina at the Pitti Palace.

The Pitti's "modern" gallery, the **Galleria d'Arte Moderna ★**, has a fairly good collection, this time of 19th-century Italian paintings with a focus on Romanticism, Neoclassical works, and the **Macchiaioli** a school of Italian painters who worked in an "impressionistic style" before the French Impressionists. If you have limited time, make right for the major works of the latter, in Sala 18 through 20, which displays the Maremma landscapes of **Giovanni Fattori ★** (1825–1908).

The Pitti's pair of lesser museums—the **Galleria del Costume** (Costume Gallery) and **Museo degli Argenti** (Museum of Silverware)—combine to show that wealth and taste do not always go hand in hand. One thing you will notice in the Costume Gallery is how much smaller the locals were just a few centuries ago.

Piazza de' Pitti. Galleria Palatina, Apartamenti Reali, and Galleria d'Arte Moderna: ✆ **055-238-8614;** reserve tickets at www.firenzemusei.it or ✆ 055-294-883. Admission 8.50€ (13€ when there's a temporary exhibition). Tues–Sun 8:15am–6:50pm. Museo degli Argenti and Galleria del Costume: ✆**055-238-8709.** Admission (includes Giardino di Boboli and Giardino Bardini) 7€ (10€ when there's a temporary exhibition). Same hours as Giardino di Boboli; see below. Cumulative ticket for everything, including Giardino di Boboli (see below), valid 3 days, 11.50€ (not available during temporary exhibition). Bus: C3, D, 11, 36, or 37.

Giardino di Boboli (Boboli Garden) ★★ PARK/GARDEN

The statue-filled park behind the Pitti Palace is one of the earliest and finest Renaissance gardens, laid out mostly between 1549 and 1656 with box hedges in geometric patterns, groves of ilex (holm oak), dozens of statues, and rows of cypress. Just above the entrance through the courtyard of the Palazzo Pitti is an oblong **amphitheater** modeled on Roman circuses, with a **granite basin** from Rome's Baths of Caracalla and an **Egyptian obelisk** of Ramses II. In 1589 this was the setting for the wedding reception of Ferdinando de' Medici's marriage to Christine of Lorraine. For the occasion, the Medici commissioned entertainment from Jacopo Peri and Ottavio Rinuccini, who decided to set a classical story entirely to music and called it "Dafne"—the world's first opera. (Later, they wrote a follow-up hit "Eurdice," performed here in 1600; it's the first opera whose score has survived.) At the south end of the park, the **Isolotto ★** is a dreamy island marooned in a pond full of huge goldfish, with Giambologna's "L'Oceano" sculptural composition at its center. At the north end, down around the end of the Pitti Palace, are some fake caverns filled with statuary, attempting to invoke a classical sacred grotto. The most famous, the **Grotta Grande,** was designed by Giorgio Vasari, Bartolomeo Ammannati, and Bernardo Buontalenti between 1557 and 1593; dripping with phony stalactites, it's set with replicas of Michelangelo's unfinished "Prisoners" statues. You can usually get inside on the hour (but not every hour) for 15 minutes.

Entrance via Palazzo Pitti. www.polomuseale.firenze.it. ✆ **055-238-8791.** Admission (includes Giardino Bardini, Museo degli Argenti, and Museo del Costume) 7€ (10€ during compulsory temporary exhibition). Nov–Feb daily 8:15am–4:30pm; Mar daily

8:15am–5:30pm; Apr–May and Sept–Oct daily 8:15am–6:30pm; June–Aug daily 8:15am–7:30pm. Closed 1st and last Mon of month. Cumulative ticket for everything in Palazzo Pitti and Giardino di Boboli, valid 3 days, 11.50€ (not available during temporary exhibition). Bus: C3, D, 11, 36, or 37.

Piazzale Michelangiolo (Michelangelo) ★ SQUARE   This panoramic piazza is a required stop for every tour bus. The balustraded terrace was laid out in 1869 to give a sweeping **vista** ★★ of the entire city, spread out in the valley below and backed by the green hills of Fiesole beyond. The bronze replica of "David" here points right at his original home, outside the Palazzo Vecchio.
Viale Michelangelo. Bus: 12 or 13.

San Miniato al Monte ★★ CHURCH   High atop a hill, its gleaming white-and-green facade visible from the city below, San Miniato is one of the few ancient churches of Florence to survive the centuries virtually intact. The current building began to take shape in 1013, under the auspices of the powerful Arte di Calimala guild, whose symbol, a bronze eagle clutching a bale of wool, perches on the **facade** ★★. This Romanesque facade is a particularly gorgeous bit of white Carrara and green Prato marble inlay. Above the central window is a 13th-century mosaic of "Christ Between the Madonna and St. Miniato" (a theme repeated in the apse). The **interior** has a few Renaissance additions, but they blend in well with the overall medieval aspect—an airy, stony space with a raised choir at one end, painted wooden trusses on the ceiling, and tombs interspersed with inlaid marble symbols of the zodiac paving the floor. Below the choir is an 11th-century **crypt** with remains of frescoes by Taddeo Gaddi. Off to the right of the raised choir is the **sacristy,** which Spinello Aretino covered in 1387 with cartoonish yet elaborate frescoes depicting the **"Life of St. Benedict"** ★. Off the left aisle of the nave is the 15th-century **Cappella del Cardinale del Portogallo** ★★, a collaborative effort by Renaissance artists built to honor young Portuguese humanist Cardinal Jacopo di Lusitania, who was sent to study in Perugia but died an untimely death at age 25 in Florence. Note: It's worth timing your visit to come here when the Benedictine monks are celebrating mass in Gregorian chant at 5:30pm.

Around the back of the church is San Miniato's **monumental cemetery** ★, one enormous "city of the dead," whose streets are lined with tombs and mausoleums built in elaborate pastiches of every generation of Florentine architecture (with a marked preference for the Gothic and the Romanesque). It's a peaceful spot, soundtracked only by birdsong and the occasional tolling of the church bells.
Via Monte alle Croci/Viale Galileo Galilei (behind Piazzale Michelangiolo). © **055-234-2731.** Free admission. Daily 9:30am–1pm and 3–7pm (closed some Sun afternoons and often open through *riposo* in summer). Bus: 12 or 13.

Santa Felicità ★ CHURCH   The 2nd-century Greek sailors who lived in this neighborhood brought Christianity to Florence with them, and this little church was probably the second to be established in the city, the first edition of it rising in the late 4th century. The current version was built in the 1730s. The star works are in the first chapel on the right, the Brunelleschi-designed **Cappella Barbadori-Capponi**, with paintings by Mannerist master Pontormo (1525–27). His **"Deposition"** ★★ and frescoed "Annunciation" are rife with his garish color palette of oranges, pinks, golds, lime greens, and sky blues, and exhibit his trademark surreal sense of figure.

Piazza Santa Felicità (2nd left off Via Guicciardini across the Ponte Vecchio). © **055-213-018**. Free admission (1€ to operate chapel lights). Mon–Sat 9:30am–12:30pm and 3:30–5:30pm. Bus: C3 or D.

Santa Maria del Carmine ★★★ CHURCH   Following a 1771 fire that destroyed everything but the transept chapels and sacristy, this Carmelite church was almost entirely reconstructed in high baroque style. To see the **Cappella Brancacci** ★★★ in the right transept, you have to enter through the cloisters (doorway to the right of the church facade) and pay admission. The frescoes here were commissioned by an enemy of the Medici, Felice Brancacci, who in 1424 hired Masolino and his student Masaccio to decorate it with a cycle on the "Life of St. Peter." Masolino probably worked out the cycle's scheme and painted a few scenes along with his pupil before taking off for 3 years to serve as court painter in Budapest, Hungary, while Masaccio kept painting, quietly creating the early Renaissance's greatest frescoes. Masaccio eventually left for Rome in 1428, where he died at age 27; the cycle was completed between 1480 and 1485 by Filippino Lippi. Masolino was responsible for the "St. Peter Preaching," the upper panel to the left of the altar, and the two top scenes on the right wall, which shows his fastidious, decorative style in a long panel of "St. Peter Healing the Cripple" and "Raising Tabitha," and his "Adam and Eve." Contrast this first man and woman, about to take the bait offered by the snake, with the **"Expulsion from the Garden"** ★★, opposite it, painted by Masaccio. Masolino's figures are highly posed, expressionless models. Masaccio's Adam and Eve, on the other hand, burst with intense emotion. The top scene on the left wall, the **"Tribute Money"** ★★, is also by Masaccio, and it showcases another of his innovations, linear perspective. The two scenes to the right of the altar are Masaccio's as well—the **"Baptism of the Neophytes"** ★★ is among his masterpieces.

Piazza del Carmine. www.museicivicifiorentini.comune.fi.it. © **055-276-8224**. Free admission to church; Cappella Brancacci 6€. Mon and Wed–Sat 10am–5pm; Sun 1–5pm. Bus: D.

Santo Spirito ★ CHURCH   One of Filippo Brunelleschi's masterpieces of architecture, this 15th-century church doesn't look like much from the outside (no true facade was ever built). But the **interior** ★ is a marvelous High Renaissance space—an expansive landscape of proportion and mathematics worked out in classic Brunelleschi style, with coffered ceiling, lean columns topped by Corinthian capitals, and the stacked perspective of arched arcading. Good late-Renaissance and baroque paintings are scattered throughout, but the best stuff lies in the transepts, especially the **Cappella Nerli ★**, with a panel by Filippino Lippi (right transept). The church's extravagant **baroque altar** has a ciborium inlaid in *pietre dure* around 1607—and frankly, looks a bit silly against the restrained elegance of Brunelleschi's architecture. The sacristy displays a wooden "Crucifix" that has, controversially, been attributed to Michelangelo. See (and judge) for yourself.

Piazza Santo Spirito ★ outside is one of the focal points of the Oltrarno, shaded by trees and lined with trendy cafes that see some bar action in the evenings. There are often a few farmers selling their fruit and vegetables on the piazza.

Piazza Santo Spirito. ✆ **055-210-030.** Free admission. Mon–Tues and Thurs–Sat 10am–12:30pm and 4–5:30pm; Sun 4–5:30pm. Bus: C3, D, 11, 36, or 37.

Side Trip to Fiesole

Although it's only a short city bus ride away from Florence, **Fiesole ★** is very proud of its status as an independent municipality. In fact, this hilltop village high the greenery above Florence predates that city in the valley by centuries.

Etruscans from Arezzo probably founded a town here in the 6th century B.C., on the site of a Bronze Age settlement. *Faesulae* became the most important Etruscan center in the region, and although it eventually became a Roman town—conquered in 90 B.C., it built a theater and adopted Roman customs—it always retained a bit of Etruscan otherness. Following the barbarian invasions, it became part of Florence's administrative district in the 9th century yet continued to struggle for self-government. Medieval Florence settled things in 1125 by attacking and razing the entire settlement, save the cathedral and bishop's palace.

Fiesole Essentials

To get to Fiesole, take bus no. 7 from Florence. It departs from Via La Pira, down the right flank of San Marco. A scenic 25-minute ride through the greenery above Florence takes you to Fiesole's main square, Piazza Mino. The **tourist office** is at Via Portigiani 3 (www.fiesole-foryou.it; ✆ **055-596-1311**). From March through October it's open daily (Apr–Sept 10am–6:30pm, Mar and Oct 10am–5:30pm); from November through February, it's open Wednesday to Monday from 10am to 1:30pm.

Fiesole's sights all use a single admission ticket, costing 12€ adults, 8€ students age 7 to 25 and seniors 65 and over; a family ticket costs 24€. Prices are 2€ per person lower from Monday to Thursday, when the missable Museo Bandini is closed. All sites are open the same hours as the tourist office, which doubles as the ticket office. For more information, visit **www.museidifiesole.it** or call ✆ **055-596-1293.**

An oasis of cultivated greenery still separates Florence from Fiesole. Even with the big city so close by, Fiesole endures as a Tuscan small town, mostly removed from Florence at its feet, and hence a perfect escape from summertime crowds. It stays relatively cool all summer long, and while you sit at a cafe on Piazza Mino, sipping an iced cappuccino, the lines at the Uffizi and pedestrian traffic around the Duomo seem very distant indeed.

San Francesco ★ MONASTERY/MUSEUM The ancient highpoint of the Etruscan and Roman town is now occupied by a tiny church and monastery. The 14th-century church has been largely overhauled, but at the end of a small nave hung with devotional works—Piero di Cosimo and Cenni di Francesco are both represented—is a fine "Crucifixion and Saints" altarpiece by Neri di Bicci. Off the cloisters is a quirky little **Ethnographic Museum,** stuffed with objects picked up by Franciscan missionaries, including an Egyptian mummy and Chinese jade and ceramics. Entrance to the church's painted, vaulted **crypt** is through the museum. To reach San Francesco, you will climb a sharp hill—pause close to the top, where a little balcony provides perhaps the best **view** ★★★ of Florence, and the wine hills of the Chianti beyond.

Via San Francesco (off Piazza Mino). ✆ **055-59-175.** Free admission. Daily 9am–noon and 3–5pm (7pm in summer). Bus: 7.

Teatro Romano (Roman Theater) ★ RUINS Fiesole's archaeological area is romantically overgrown with grasses, amid which sit sections of column, broken friezes, and other remnants of the ancient world. It is also dramatically sited, terraced into a hill with views over the olive groves and forests north of Florence. Beyond the **Roman Theater** ★ (which seated 1,500 in its day), three rebuilt arches anchor the remains of the 1st-century A.D. **baths.** In Roman times, the baths were a place where all social classes mixed, but the sexes were kept strictly apart. Near the arches, a cement balcony over the far edge of the archaeological park gives you a good look at the best remaining stretch of the 4th century B.C. **Etruscan town walls.** At the other end of the park from the baths, the floor and steps of a 1st-century B.C. **Roman Temple** were built on top of a 4th-century B.C. Etruscan one dedicated to Minerva. To the left are oblong **Lombard tombs** from the 7th century A.D., when this part of Fiesole was a necropolis.

Via Portigiani 1. ✆ **055-596-1293.** For admission and hours, see "Fiesole Essentials," above. Bus: 7.

Organized Tours

To really get under the surface of the city, book an insightful culture tour with **Context Travel** ★★ (www.contexttravel.com; ✆ **800/691-6036** in the U.S. or 06-96727371 in Italy). Led by academics and other experts in their field on a variety of themes, from the gastronomic to the archaeological and artistic, these tours are limited to six people and cost around

70€ per person. Context also conducts a guided walk through the Vasari Corridor (subject to availability; see p. 187). The quality of Context's walks are unmatched, and well worth the above-average cost.

Offerings from **CAF Tours** (www.caftours.com; ✆ **055-283-200**) include the chance to walk on the cathedral's roof terraces (1½ hr.; 50€), as well as several walks and cooking classes costing from 25€ to over 100€. **ArtViva** (www.italy.artviva.com; ✆ **055-264-5033**) has a huge array of walking tours and museum guides starting at 29€, including the distinctly dark "Sex, Drugs, and the Renaissance" walking tour (2¼ hr.; 39€). **I Just Drive** (www.ijustdrive.us; ✆ **055-093-5928**) offers fully equipped cars (Wi-Fi, complimentary bottle of Prosecco) plus English-speaking driver for various themed visits; for example, you can ride in a Bentley limousine up to San Miniato al Monte on a dusk "Gregorian Chant Tour" (1½ hr.), to hear monks' evening prayers. Websites such as **Viator.com** and **GetYourGuide.com** also have a range of locally organized tours and activities, reviewed by travelers.

Especially for Kids

You have to put in a bit of work to reach some of Florence's best views—and the climbs, up claustrophobic, medieval staircases, are a favorite with many kids. The Cupola of **Santa Maria del Fiore** (p. 176), the **Palazzo Vecchio's** (p. 184) Torre di Arnolfo, and the **Campanile di Giotto** (p. 175) are perfect for any youngster with a head for heights.

The best activities with an educational component are run by the **Museo dei Ragazzi** ★★ (www.musefirenze.it; ✆ **055-276-8224**), not a standalone museum but a program that offers child's-eye tours in English around the Palazzo Vecchio, led by guides in period costumes. Lively activities focus on life at the ducal court—pitched at children ages 5–10 or 10-plus ("At Court with Donna Isabella")—or take kids into the workshop to learn fresco or tempera painting. Book online, email to inquire on **info@muse.comune.fi.it**, or stop by the desk next to the Palazzo Vecchio ticket booth.

You'll need a bus (no. 4) or a taxi to get to the site, but budding medievalists and Harry Potter fans will thank you for a visit to **Museo Stibbert** ★, Via Stibbert 26 (www.museostibbert.it; ✆ **055-475-520**). It's essentially the giant toy box of an eccentric Anglo-Italian arms-and-armor collector, which was made into a private museum in 1906. Among the mayhem, with every variety of historic weapon, armor, and shield from Europe and the Islamic world, the museum boasts the biggest collection of Japanese armor outside of Tokyo. The museum is open Monday to Wednesday 10am to 2pm, Friday to Sunday 10am to 6pm. Admission costs 8€, 6€ for children ages 4 to 12.

When your youngsters simply need a crowd-free timeout space, head for the **Biblioteca delle Oblate,** Via dell'Oriuolo 26 (www.bibliotecadelleoblate.comune.fi.it; ✆ **055-261-6526**), where you'll find a library with books for little ones (including in English), as well as space to spread out, color, or draw. It's free and open 9am to 6:45pm, except for Monday morning and all day Sunday (closed 2 weeks mid-Aug). The Oblate's **cafe** (p. 222) is an excellent place to kick back.

There's only one game in town when it comes to spectator sports: *calcio.* To Italians, soccer/football is something akin to a second religion, and an afternoon at the stadium can offer you more insight into local culture than a lifetime in the Uffizi. The Florence team, **Fiorentina ★** (nicknamed *i viola,* "the purples") is often among the best in Italy's top league, *Serie A.* You can usually catch them alternate Sundays from September through May at the **Stadio Comunale Artemio Franchi**, Via Manfredo Fanti 4 (www.violachannel.tv). Book tickets online or head for an official ticket office on arrival (take photo ID): There is a sales desk on the Mercato Centrale's upper floor (p. 215) and at Via dei Sette Santi 28R (at Via Giovanni Dupré), open from 9:30am on matchdays. With kids, get seats in a Tribuna (stand) rather than the Curva, where the fanatical fans sit. To reach the stadium from the center, take bus no. 10 or 20 from San Marco (10–15 min.). You can get kitted out in home colors at **Alè Viola,** Via del Corso 58R (✆ **055-295-306**).

You can skip the subtitles at an original 1920s cinema right in the center that shows daily movies in their original language: **Odeon Firenze ★**, Piazza Strozzi (www.odeonfirenze.com; ✆ **055-214-068**). The labyrinthine and well-stocked traditional toy store **Dreoni** is at Via Cavour 31R (www.dreonigiocattoli.eu; ✆ **055-216-611**).

Cycling is a pleasure in the riverside Parco delle Cascine: See p. 169 for bike rental advice. And remember: You are in the **gelato** capital of the world. At least one multiscoop gelato per day is the minimum recommended dose; see p. 218.

WHERE TO STAY

In the past few years, thanks to a rapidly growing number of beds and national economic crises, the forces of supply and demand have brought hotel prices in Florence down . . . a little. Few hoteliers expect major changes to their rates in coming years. Add to that recent welcome movements in the euro–dollar and euro–pound exchange rates and you have a hotel market that's as favorable to visitors as it's ever been. That said, it is still difficult to find a high-season double you'd want to stay in for much less than 100€.

Some of those price drops have been added back in taxes: Since 2012, Florence's city government has levied an extra 1€ to 1.50€ per person per night per government-rated hotel star, for the first 5 nights of any stay. The tax rose slightly again in 2015. It is payable on arrival, and is not usually included in quoted rates.

Peak hotel season is Easter through early July, September through early November, and December 23 through January 6. May, June, and

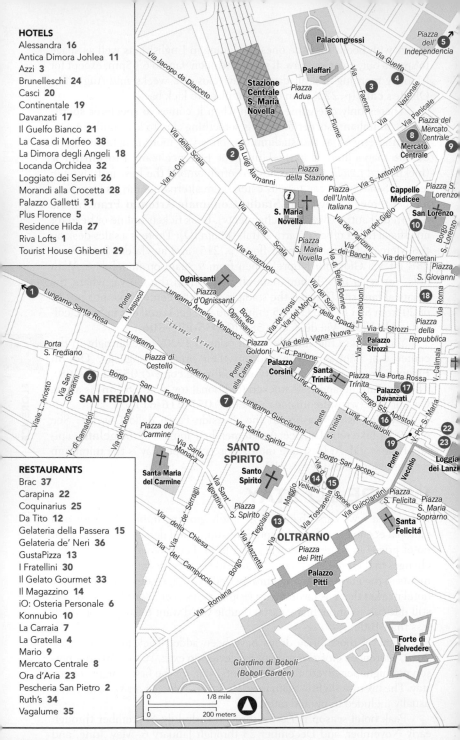

HOTELS
Alessandra **16**
Antica Dimora Johlea **11**
Azzi **3**
Brunelleschi **24**
Casci **20**
Continentale **19**
Davanzati **17**
Il Guelfo Bianco **21**
La Casa di Morfeo **38**
La Dimora degli Angeli **18**
Locanda Orchidea **32**
Loggiato dei Servizi **26**
Morandi alla Crocetta **28**
Palazzo Galletti **31**
Plus Florence **5**
Residence Hilda **27**
Riva Lofts **1**
Tourist House Ghiberti **29**

RESTAURANTS
Brac **37**
Carapina **22**
Coquinarius **25**
Da Tito **12**
Gelateria della Passera **15**
Gelateria de' Neri **36**
GustaPizza **13**
I Fratellini **30**
Il Gelato Gourmet **33**
Il Magazzino **14**
iO: Osteria Personale **6**
Konnubio **10**
La Carraia **7**
La Gratella **4**
Mario **9**
Mercato Centrale **8**
Ora d'Aria **23**
Pescheria San Pietro **2**
Ruth's **34**
Vagalume **35**

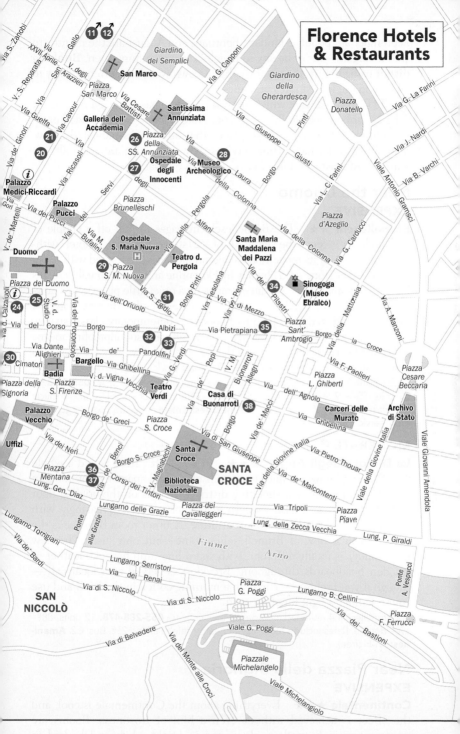

Florence Hotels & Restaurants

September are popular; January, February, and August are the months to grab a bargain—never be shy to haggle if you're coming then. **Booking direct** using phone, email, or the hotel's own website is often the key to unlocking the lowest rates or complimentary extras.

To help you decide which area you'd like to base yourself in, consult "The Neighborhoods in Brief," p. 166. Note that we have included parking information only for those places that offer it. As indicated below, many hotels offer babysitting services; however, these are generally "on request." At least a couple of days' notice is advisable.

Near the Duomo

EXPENSIVE

Brunelleschi ★★   The Brunelleschi manages to pull off a couple of neat tricks. It exceeds the standards of a 21st-century "design hotel" without losing track of its roots: Rooms and public areas are framed with *pietra serena*, the gray stone used liberally by Florentine architect Brunelleschi. It's big but feels small, thanks to an entrance on a quiet little piazza and a labyrinthine layout, arranged around the oldest standing building in Florence. Rooms are midsized, with parquet floors and contemporary-classic styling. Although many look onto Via Calzaiuoli, impressive soundproofing means you won't hear the noise. Apparently the hotel is a favorite of author Dan Brown, since it appears in both *The Da Vinci Code* and *Inferno*.

Piazza Santa Elisabetta 3 (just off Corso). www.hotelbrunelleschi.it. © **055-27-370.** 96 units. 234€–919€ standard double; 287€–929€ superior double. Rates include breakfast. Parking 35€–39€. Bus: C2. **Amenities:** 2 restaurants; bar; concierge; gym; room service; Wi-Fi (free).

MODERATE

La Dimora degli Angeli ★★★   In 2012, this B&B added a whole new floor, and now occupies two levels of a grand apartment building in one of the city's busiest shopping districts. Rooms on the original floor are for romantics; bright, modern wallpaper contrasts pleasingly with iron-framed beds and traditional furniture. (Corner room Beatrice is the largest, with a view of Brunelleschi's dome—but only just.) The new floor, below, is totally different, with sharp lines and bespoke leather or wooden headboards throughout. Breakfast is served at a local cafe—though if you prefer, you can grab a morning coffee in the B&B and use your token for a light lunch instead.

Via Brunelleschi 4. www.ladimoradegliangeli.com. © **055-288-478.** 12 units. 88€–190€ double. Rates include breakfast (at nearby cafe). Parking 26€. Bus: C2. **Amenities:** Wi-Fi (free).

Near Piazza della Signoria

EXPENSIVE

Continentale ★★★   Everything about the Continentale is cool, and the effect is achieved without even a hint of frostiness. Rooms are uncompromisingly modern, decorated in bright white and bathed in natural light. Deluxe units are built into a medieval riverside tower, which have mighty walls and medieval-sized windows (that is, small). Standard rooms are large (for Florence), and there's a retro-1950s feel to the overall styling. Communal areas are a major hit, too: A relaxation room has a glass wall with a front-row view of the Ponte Vecchio. Top-floor **La Terrazza** (p. 223) serves Florence's best rooftop cocktails.

Vicolo dell'Oro 6R. www.lungarnocollection.com. $\mathcal{C}$ **055-27-262.** 43 units. 180€–730€ double. Parking 35€–37€. Bus: C3 or D. **Amenities:** Bar; concierge; gym; spa; Wi-Fi (free).

Between San Lorenzo & San Marco

MODERATE

Il Guelfo Bianco ★★ Decor in this former noble Florentine family home retains its authentic *palazzo* feel, though carpets have been added for comfort and warmth. No two rooms are the same—stone walls this thick cannot just be knocked through—and several have antiques integrated into their individual schemes. Grand rooms at the front (especially 101, 118, and 228) have spectacular Renaissance coffered ceilings and masses of space. Bathrooms are plainer by comparison. Sleep at the back and you'll wake to an unusual sound in Florence: birdsong. Under the same ownership, the small adjacent restaurant **Bistrot Il Desco** (www.ildescofirenze.it; $\mathcal{C}$ **055-288-330**) serves seasonal Mediterranean dishes made with organic ingredients (many from their own farm), and is open to guests and nonguests alike. Reservations are recommended.

Via Cavour 29 (near corner of Via Guelfa). www.ilguelfobianco.it. $\mathcal{C}$ **055-288-330.** 40 units. 99€–300€ double. Rates include breakfast. Valet parking 27€–33€. Bus: C1, 14, or 23. **Amenities:** Restaurant; bar; babysitting (prebooking essential); concierge; room service; Wi-Fi (free).

INEXPENSIVE

Casci ★ The front part of the palace now occupied by the Casci was once composer Gioachino Rossini's Florence digs. This affordable, central hotel has long been a Frommer's favorite, and the partial pedestrianization of Via Cavour makes it an even more attractive city base. Rooms follow a labyrinthine layout, split between Rossini's old *piano nobile* and a now-joined former convent to the rear, where the bigger rooms are located, including a couple of spacious family units. Rooms are simply decorated and some can get a little dark, though a rolling program of modernization is installing new, light-toned furniture to counteract that—now in 16 rooms and counting. The welcome from some of Florence's friendliest family hoteliers is an unchanging feature.

Via Cavour 13 (btw. Via dei Ginori and Via Guelfa). www.hotelcasci.com. $\mathcal{C}$ **055-211-686.** 25 units. 80€–150€ double; 100€–190€ triple; 120€–230€ quad. Rates include breakfast. Valet parking 21€–25€. Bus: C1, 14, or 23. Closed 2 weeks in Dec. **Amenities:** Bar; babysitting (10€/hr.); concierge; Wi-Fi (free).

Near Piazza Santa Trínita
MODERATE

Alessandra ★ This typical Florentine *pensione* immediately transports you back to the age of the gentleman and lady traveler. Decor has grown organically since the place opened as a hotel in 1950—Alessandra is a place for evolution, not revolution. A pleasing mix of styles is the end result: Some rooms with hefty armoires, carved headboards, gilt frames, and gold damask around the place; others with eclectic postwar furniture, like something from a period movie set. A couple rooms have views of the Arno, while front-side rooms overlook Borgo SS. Apostoli, one of the center's most atmospheric streets.

Borgo SS. Apostoli 17. www.hotelalessandra.com. ✆ **055-283-438.** 27 units. 150€–180€ double. Rates include breakfast. Garage parking 25€. Bus: C3, D, 6, 11, 36, or 37. Closed a few days around Christmas. **Amenities:** Wi-Fi (free).

Davanzati ★★ Although installed inside a historic building, the Davanzati never rests on its medieval laurels: There is still a laptop in every room for guest use, HD movies are streamed to your TV, and lobby newspapers come on an iPad. Rooms are simply decorated in the Tuscan style, with color-washed walls; half-canopies over the beds add a little flourish. Room 100 is probably the best family hotel room in Florence, full of nooks, crannies, and split-levels that give the adults and the kids a sense of private space. A complimentary evening drink for all guests remains part of the Davanzati's family welcome.

Via Porta Rossa 5 (on Piazza Davanzati). www.hoteldavanzati.it. ✆ **055-286-666.** 27 units. 122€–211€ double; 152€–243€ superior (sleeps up to 4). Rates include breakfast. Valet parking 26€. Bus: C2. **Amenities:** Bar; babysitting; concierge; Wi-Fi (free).

Between Santa Maria Novella & San Lorenzo
INEXPENSIVE

Azzi ★ This quirky, bohemian joint is also known as the Locanda degli Artisti. Each of its original 16 rooms is brightly decorated, and most feature an antique piece or colorfully painted wall to add ambience. Floorboards are artfully distressed (both by time and by design), and pictures or wall mirrors have wistfully weathered frames. In short, each is exactly the kind of room you could imagine for a struggling artist to lay his or her head at night. Refitted in 2013, 8 new rooms have a different feel, with laminate flooring, white furniture, and shiny travertine bathrooms. Frommer's readers booking direct (mention this book) get 10% to 15% off published room rates and 3€ off overnight parking.

Via Faenza 88R. www.hotelazzi.com. ✆ **055-213-806.** 24 units. 54€–130€ double; 95€–140€ triple. Rates include breakfast. Garage parking 18€. Bus: 2, 12, 13, 22, 28, 36, 37, or 57. **Amenities:** Bar; Wi-Fi (free).

Plus Florence ★★ There's simply nowhere in Florence with as many services for your buck—including seasonal indoor and outdoor swimming pools—all in a price bracket where you are usually fortunate to get an en suite bathroom (and Plus has those, too). The best rooms in this large, well-equipped hostel are in the new wing, added in 2013 and housing private rooms only. Units here are dressed in taupe and brown, with subtle uplighting and space (in some) for up to four beds. The only minuses: an un-picturesque building; and the location, between two busy roads (light sleepers should request a room facing the internal courtyard).

Via Santa Caterina d'Alessandria 15. www.plusflorence.com. © 055-462-8934. 187 units. 40€–100€ double; 50€–130€ triple. Bus: 20. **Amenities:** Restaurant; bar; concierge; gym; 2 swimming pools; sauna; Wi-Fi (free).

Near San Marco & Santissima Annunziata
EXPENSIVE

Residence Hilda ★★   There's not a hint of the Renaissance here: These luxurious mini-apartments are all bright-white decor and designer soft furnishings, with stripped-wood flooring and modern gadgetry to keep everything running. Each is spacious, cool in summer, and totally soundproofed against Florence's permanent background noise. Every apartment also has a mini-kitchen, equipped just fine for preparing a simple meal—ideal if you have kids in tow. In 2015, deluxe units also added Nespresso machines, yoga mats, and an exercise bike. Unusually for apartments, they are all bookable by the single night and upward.

Via dei Servi 40 (2 blocks north of the Duomo). www.residencehilda.it. © 055-288-021. 12 units. 150€–450€ per night for apartments sleeping 2–4. Valet parking 31€. Bus: C1. **Amenities:** Airport transfer; babysitting; concierge; room service; Wi-Fi (free).

MODERATE

Antica Dimora Johlea ★★   There is a real neighborhood feel to the streets around this *dimora* (traditional Florentine home) guesthouse, which means evenings are lively and Sundays are dead (although it's under a 10-min. walk to San Lorenzo). Standard-sized rooms are snug; upgrade to a deluxe if you need more space, but there is no difference in the standard of decor, a mix of Florentine and earthy boho styling. Help yourself to coffee, a soft drink, or a glass of wine from the honesty bar and head up to a roof terrace for knockout views over the terracotta rooftops to the center and hills beyond. It is pure magic at dusk. No credit cards.

Via San Gallo 80. www.johanna.it. © 055-463-3292. 6 units. 90€–180€ double. Rates include breakfast. Valet parking 20€. Bus: C1, 1, 6, 11, 14, 17, or 23. **Amenities:** Bar; Wi-Fi (free).

Loggiato dei Serviti ★★   Stay here to experience Florence as the gentleman and lady visitors of the Grand Tour did. For starters, the building is a genuine Renaissance landmark, built by Sangallo the Elder in the 1520s. There is a sense of faded grandeur and unconventional luxury throughout—no gadgetry or chromotherapy showers here, but you will find rooms with writing desks and vintage ambience. No unit is small, but standard rooms lack a view of either Brunelleschi's dome or the perfect piazza outside. Air conditioning is pretty much the only concession to the 21st century—and you will love it that way.

Piazza Santissima Annunziata 3. www.loggiatodeiservitihotel.it. © **055-289-592.** 37 units. 120€–330€ double. Rates include breakfast. Valet parking 21€. Bus: C1, 6, 14, 19, 23, 31, or 32. **Amenities:** Babysitting (prebooking essential); concierge; Wi-Fi (free).

Morandi alla Crocetta ★★ Like many in Florence, this hotel is built into the shell of a former convent. Morandi alla Crocetta has retained the original convent layout, meaning some rooms are snug—though that does not apply to two rooms added in 2014, ranged around the old cloister downstairs. Anyway, what you lose in size, you more than gain in character: Every single one oozes *tipico fiorentino*. Rooms have parquet flooring thrown with rugs and dressed with antique wooden furniture. Original Zocchi prints of Florence, made in 1744, are scattered around the place. It's definitely worth upgrading to a superior room if you can: These have more space and either a private courtyard terrace or, in one, original frescoes decorating the entrance to the former convent chapel, though the chapel is now permanently sealed off. The hotel is located on a quiet street.

Via Laura 50 (1 block east of Piazza Santissima Annunziata). www.hotelmorandi.it. © **055-234-4747.** 12 units. 100€–167€ double. Rates include breakfast. Garage parking 24€. Bus: 6, 19, 31, or 32. **Amenities:** Bar; babysitting (prebooking essential); concierge; Wi-Fi (free).

Tourist House Ghiberti ★ A pleasing mix of the traditional and the modern prevails at this backstreet guesthouse named after a famous former resident—the creator of the Baptistery's "Gates of Paradise" had workshops on the top floor of the *palazzo*. Rooms have plenty of space, with high ceilings, herringbone terracotta floors, whitewashed walls, and painted wood ceilings in a vaguely Renaissance style. There is a sauna and Jacuzzi for communal use, so you can soak away the aches and pains of a day's sightseeing; memory-foam mattresses added in 2014 should help with that, too. Email direct if you want to bag the best room rate.

Via M. Bufalini 1. www.touristhouseghiberti.com. © **055-284-858.** 6 units. 64€–179€ double. Rates include breakfast. Garage parking 20€–25€. Bus: C1, 14, or 23. **Amenities:** Jacuzzi; sauna; Wi-Fi (free).

Near Santa Croce
MODERATE

La Casa di Morfeo ★ For a cheery, affordable room in the increasingly lively eastern part of the center, look no further than this small hotel that opened in 2012 on the second floor of a grand, shuttered palace. There is no huge difference in quality among the guest rooms. Each is midsized, with modern gadgetry, and painted in bright contemporary colors, each individual scheme corresponding to the flower after which the room is named. Our favorite is Mimosa, painted in light mustard, with a ceiling fresco and a frontside view over Via Ghibellina. Colored lighting brings a bit of fun to every unit, too.

Via Ghibellina 51. www.lacasadimorfeo.it. ⒸⒸ **055-241-193.** 9 units. 75€–240€ double. Rates include breakfast. Bus: C2 or C3. **Amenities:** Wi-Fi (free).

Palazzo Galletti ★★   Not many hotels within a sensible budget give you the chance to live like a Florentine noble. Rooms here were all refreshed in 2015, and have towering ceilings and an uncluttered arrangement of carefully chosen antiques. Most have frescoed or painted wood showpiece ceilings. Bathrooms, in contrast, have sharp, contemporary lines, and are decked out in travertine and marble. Aside from two street-facing suites, every room has a small balcony, ideal for a pre-dinner glass of wine. If you're here for a once-in-a-lifetime trip, spring for the "Giove" or (especially) "Cerere"; both are large suites, and the latter has walls covered in original frescoes from the 1800s. In-room Wi-Fi is free if you book direct and mention this Frommer's guide.

Via Sant'Egidio 12. www.palazzogalletti.it. ⒸⒸ **055-390-5750.** 11 units. 100€–170€ double; 170€–240€ suite. Rates include breakfast. Garage parking 30€. Bus: C1, C2, 14, or 23. **Amenities:** Wi-Fi (5€/day).

INEXPENSIVE

Locanda Orchidea ★   Over several visits to Florence, this has been a go-to inn for stays on a tight budget. Rooms range over two floors of a historic *palazzo*—the best of them facing a quiet, leafy rear courtyard where wisteria flowers each spring. Furniture is a fun mix of mismatched flea-market finds and secondhand pieces; tiled floors and bold print wallpaper and fabrics keep up the charmingly outdated feel. Note that bathrooms are shared (they have good water pressure), and there is no A/C or onsite breakfast. But for value, character, and welcome, this place is hard to beat in this price bracket.

Borgo degli Albizi 11 (close to Piazza San Pier Maggiore). www.hotelorchidea florence.it. ⒸⒸ **055-248-0346.** 7 units. 42€–80€ double. Garage parking 18€–22€. Bus: C1 or C2. **Amenities:** Wi-Fi (free).

West of the Center

MODERATE

Riva Lofts ★★   The traditional Florentine alarm call—a morning mix of traffic and tourism—is replaced by birdsong when you awake in one of the stylish rooms here, on the banks of the River Arno. A former stone-built artisan workshop, Riva has had a refit to match its "loft" label: There's a taupe-and-white scheme with laminate flooring, floating staircases, marble bathrooms with rainfall showers, and clever integration of natural materials in such features as original wooden workshop ceilings. Breakfast is served until 11:45am and noon checkouts are standard—a seriously traveler-friendly touch. The center is a 30-minute walk, or jump on one of Riva's vintage-style bikes and cycle to the Uffizi along the Arno banks. Yet another standout feature in this price bracket: a shaded garden with outdoor plunge pool.

Via Baccio Bandinelli 98. www.rivalofts.com. ☏ **055-713-0272.** 9 units. 165€–255€ double. Rates include breakfast. Garage parking 20€ (or park out front for free). Bus: 6/Tram: T1 (3 stops from central station). **Amenities:** Bar; bike rental (free); outdoor pool; Wi-Fi (free).

Apartment Rentals & Alternative Accommodations

It's the way of the modern world: Global players in apartment rental have finally overtaken most of the local specialists in Florence. Online agency **Cross Pollinate** ★ (www.cross-pollinate.com; ☏ **06-99369799**) still has a Florence apartment portfolio worth checking. **GoWithOh.com** ★ has a user-friendly website that incorporates verified guest feedback into its wide portfolio of high-quality city apartments. **HomeAway.com,** TripAdvisor-owned **HolidayLettings.co.uk,** and **Airbnb.com** are also well stocked with central and suburban apartments.

An alternative budget option is to stay in a **religious house.** A few monasteries and convents in the center receive guests for a modest fee, including the **Suore di Santa Elisabetta,** Viale Michelangiolo 46 (near Piazza Ferrucci; www.csse-roma.eu; ☏ **055-681-1884**), in a colonial villa just south of the Ponte San Niccolò. The **Istituto Oblate dell'Assunzione,** Borgo Pinti 15 (☏ **055-2480-582**), has simple, peaceful rooms in a Medici-era building ranged around a courtyard garden east of the center. The easiest way to build a monastery and convent itinerary in Florence and beyond is via agent **MonasteryStays.com** ★. Remember that most religious houses have a curfew, generally 11pm or midnight.

Tip: For basic grocery shopping in the center, try **Conad City,** Via dei Servi 56R (☏ **055-280-110**), or any central branch of **Supermercato il Centro**.

WHERE TO EAT

Florence is well-supplied with restaurants, though in the most touristy areas (around the Duomo, Piazza della Signoria, Piazza della Repubblica, and Ponte Vecchio), you must choose carefully—many eateries are of low quality or charge high prices, and sometimes both. The highest concentrations of excellent *ristoranti* and *trattorie* are around **Santa Croce** and across the river in the **Oltrarno** and **San Frediano.** There's also an increasing buzz around **San Lorenzo,** particularly since the top floor of the Mercato Centrale (see below) opened in 2014. The area's rep for catering to the lowest common denominator when it comes to visitors may soon be a thing of the past. Bear in mind that menus at restaurants in Tuscany can change weekly or even (at some of the very best places) daily. The city has also got much more **gluten-savvy.** If you're a celiac or have any sort of food intolerance, don't be afraid to ask.

Reservations are strongly recommended if you have your heart set on eating anywhere in particular, especially at dinner on weekends.

Near the Duomo
MODERATE
Coquinarius ★ TUSCAN   There is a regular menu here—pasta; mains such as wild boar medallions or stuffed pigeon; traditional desserts. But the real pleasure is tucking into a couple of sharing plates and quaffing from the excellent wine list. Go for something from an extensive carpaccio list (beef, boar, octopus, swordfish, and more) or pair a *misto di salumi e formaggi* (mixed Tuscan salami and cheeses) with a full-bodied red wine, to cut through the strong flavors of the deliciously fatty and salty pork and Tuscan sheep's milk cheese, pecorino.

Via delle Oche 11R. www.coquinarius.com. ℂ **055-230-2153.** Main courses 8€–18€. Daily 12:30–3:30pm and 6:30–10:30pm. Bus: C1 or C2.

INEXPENSIVE
I Fratellini ★ LIGHT FARE   This hole-in-the-wall has been serving food to go since 1875. The drill is simple: Choose a filling, pick a drink, then eat your fast-filled roll on the curb opposite or find a nearby piazza perch. There are around 30 fillings to choose from, including the usual Tuscan meats and cheeses—salami, pecorino, cured ham—and more flamboyant combos such as goat cheese and Calabrian spicy salami or *bresaola* (air-dried beef) and wild arugula. A glass of wine to wash it down costs from 1.80€. No credit cards. Lunchtime lines can be long.

Via dei Cimatori 38R (at corner of Via Calzaiuoli). www.iduefratellini.it. ℂ **055-239-6096.** Sandwiches 3€. Daily 9:30am–7pm (July–Aug often closed Sun). Bus: C2.

Near Piazza della Signoria
EXPENSIVE
Ora d'Aria ★★ CONTEMPORARY TUSCAN   If you want to see what the latest generation of Tuscan chefs can do in a kitchen, this place should top your list. The mood is modern and elegant, yet never stuffy. Dishes are subtle and creative, and combine traditional Tuscan ingredients in an original way. The menu changes daily, but expect the likes of spaghetti with extract of peppers, capers, and smoked ricotta, or piglet with spiced pear. If you can't stretch the budget for a dinner here, book a table at lunch to taste simpler, cheaper (14€–18€) dishes such as cold salad of salt cod with Pratese vermouth and sweet potato, served in full-size or half-price "tapas" portions. Reservations essential.

Via dei Georgofili 11–13R (off Via Lambertesca). www.oradariaristorante.com. ℂ **055-200-1699.** Main courses 32€–45€ (at dinner); tasting menu 70€–75€. Tues–Sat 12:30–2:30pm; Mon–Sat 7:30–10pm. Closed 3 weeks in Aug. Bus: C3 or D.

Near San Lorenzo & the Mercato Centrale

MODERATE

Konnubio ★★★ CREATIVE TUSCAN/VEGAN   There's a warm glow (candles and low-watt lighting) about this place that opened in 2014—it makes you instantly happy, and the cooking keeps you there. Ingredients are largely Tuscan, but combined creatively, such as in warm octopus salad with cherry tomatoes and olives, or ravioli stuffed with guinea hen and served with truffle cream sauce. There's an extensive vegan menu, too, including pumpkin with baked tofu, capers, and confit tomato. Under brick vaults and a covered courtyard, it could work for a romantic dinner; but you won't be out of place in a family group either (there's a kids' menu). It feels like refined dining, but in a price category that gets you a so-so bowl of pasta in much of the center.
Via dei Conti 8R. www.konnubio.it. ℂ **055-238-1189.** Main courses 12€–27€. Daily noon–3pm and 7–11pm. Bus: C1.

La Gratella ★★ FLORENTINE/GRILL   It doesn't look much—a workers' canteen on a nondescript side street—but looks don't matter much when you can source and cook meat like they do here. Star of the show is the *bistecca alla fiorentina*, a large T-bone-like cut grilled on the bone and brought to the table over coals. It is sold by weight and made for sharing; expect to pay about 50€. Pair this or any market-fresh meat on the menu with simple Tuscan sides like *fagioli all'uccelletto* (stewed beans and tomatoes). They cater to celiacs, too.
Via Guelfa 81R. www.trattorialagratella.com. ℂ **055-211-292.** Main courses 12€–18€. Daily noon–3pm and 7–11pm. Bus: 1, 6, 11, 14, 17, or 23.

INEXPENSIVE

Mario ★ TRADITIONAL FLORENTINE   There is no doubt that this traditional market workers' trattoria is now firmly on the tourist trail. But Mario's clings to the traditions and ethos it adopted when it first fired up the burners in its kitchen 60 years ago. Food is simple, hearty, and served at communal tables—"check in" on arrival and you will be offered seats together wherever they come free. Think *zuppa di fagioli* (bean

---

It's All Tripe

New York has the hot dog. London has pie and mash. Florence has . . . cow's intestine in a sandwich. The city's traditional street food, *lampredotto* (the cow's fourth stomach) stewed with tomatoes, has made a big comeback over the last decade, including on the menus of some fine-dining establishments. The best places to sample it are still the city's *trippai*, tripe vendors who sell it from vans around the center, alongside "regular" sandwiches. The most convenient vendors are in **Piazza de' Cimatori** and on **Via de' Macci** at Piazza Sant'Ambrogio. A hearty, nutritious lunch should come to around 4€. Most are open Monday through Saturday, but close in August, when Florentines flee the city.

soup) followed by traditional Tuscan piquant beef stew, *peposo,* or *vitello arrosto* (roast veal). No credit cards.

Via Rosina 2R (north corner of Piazza Mercato Centrale). www.trattoriamario.com. ☎ **055-218-550.** Main courses 6.50€–14€. Mon–Sat noon–3:30pm. Closed Aug. Bus: C1.

Mercato Centrale ★★★ MODERN ITALIAN   In 2014 the upper floor of Florence's produce market reopened as a bustling shrine to the best modern Italian street food. There are counters selling dishes from all over the country, including **Sud,** one of the city's best pizzerias. Don't fancy pizza? There are counters selling filled pasta, vegetarian and vegan dishes, cold cuts and cheeses, fresh fish dishes, Chianina burgers and meatballs, and lots more. It works perfectly for families who can't agree on a dinner choice. Or just stop by for a drink and soak up the buzz: There's a beer bar (disappointing) and enoteca (superb).

Piazza Mercato Centrale. www.mercatocentrale.it. ☎ **055-239-9798.** Dishes 5€–13€. Daily 10am–midnight. Bus: C1.

Near Santa Maria Novella

MODERATE

Pescheria San Pietro ★★ SEAFOOD   It takes a big serving of confidence to open a seafood restaurant—on two floors—in one of Florence's less-fashionable quarters. This place, opened in 2014, has the chops (and the chefs) to pull it off. The fishy focus hardly wavers: A route through the menu might take in tuna carpaccio, followed by *tagliatelle* with baby sardines, then a *gran fritto* (mixed fry) of seafood and vegetables in tempura batter—though you'd do well to manage that, because portions are generous. With open kitchens, clanking cutlery, brisk service, and a great value "business lunch" (14.50€ all-in, including a glass of wine), San Pietro is classic seafood bistro all over. There's also a 6-item vegetarian menu (dishes 11€–12€).

Via Alamanni 7R. www.pescheriasanpietro.it. ☎ **055-238-2749.** Main courses 16€–24€. Daily 11:30am–11pm. Bus: C2, D, 29, 30, or 35/Tram: T1.

Near San Marco & Santissima Annunziata

San Marco is the place to head for *schiacciata alla fiorentina,* olive-oil flatbread loaded with savory toppings. You will find some of the best at **Pugi,** Piazza San Marco 9B (www.focacceria-pugi.it; ☎ **055-280-981**), open 7:45am (Sat 8:30am) to 8pm Monday to Saturday, but closed most of August.

MODERATE

Da Tito ★★ TUSCAN/FLORENTINE   Every night feels like party night at one of central Florence's rare genuine neighborhood trattorias. (And for that reason, it's usually packed—book ahead.) The welcome and the dishes are authentically Florentine, with a few modern Italian curveballs: Start, perhaps, with the *risotto con piselli e guanciale* (rice with fresh peas and cured pork cheek) before going on to a traditional grill such as *lombatina di vitella* (veal chop steak). The neighborhood location, a 10-minute walk north of San Lorenzo, and mixed clientele keep the quality consistent.

Via San Gallo 112R. www.trattoriadatito.it. ✆ **055-472-475.** Main courses 10€–18€. Mon–Sat 12:30–2pm and 7:30–10:30pm. Bus: C1, 1, 7, 20, or 25.

Near Santa Croce
MODERATE

Brac ★★ VEGETARIAN   An artsy cafe-bookshop for most of the day, at lunch and dinner this place turns into one of Florence's best spots for vegetarian and vegan food. There are plenty of seasonal salads and creative pasta dishes, but a *piatto unico* works out best for hungry diners: one combo plate loaded with three dishes from the menu, perhaps pear carpaccio with pecorino cheese and walnuts; potato and broccoli lasagne with ginger and parsley sauce; plus an eggplant and mozzarella *pane carasau* (Sardinian flatbread). The atmosphere, with tables ranged around an internal courtyard, is intimate and romantic—yet singletons won't feel out of place eating at the counter out front. Booking at dinner is a must in high season and on weekends.

Via dei Vagellai 18R. www.libreriabrac.net. ✆ **055-094-4877.** Main courses 10€–14€. Daily noon–midnight. Bus: C1, C3, or 23.

Ruth's ★ KOSHER/VEGETARIAN   Ruth's bills itself as a "kosher vegetarian" joint, but you will also find fish on the menu. It's small (around 12 tables), so book ahead if you want to be certain of a table. The interior is cafe-like and informal, the menu likewise. Skip the Italian *primi* and go right for Eastern Mediterranean *secondi* such as vegetarian couscous with harissa or fish moussaka, a layered bake of eggplant, tomato, salmon, and spiced rice served with salad and *caponata* (a cold vegetable preserve). A rabbi from the adjacent synagogue oversees the kosher credentials.

Via Farini 2a. www.kosheruth.com. ✆ **055-248-0888.** Main courses 10€–18€. Sun–Fri noon–3pm; Sat–Thurs 7:30–10:30pm. Bus: 6, 19, 31, or 32.

Dining in Florence.

Vagalume ★★ MODERN ITALIAN   The style is *"tapas fiorentine"*—there are no "courses" and no pasta, and you compile a dinner from a range of good-sized dishes in any order you please. Dishes change daily, but could include the likes of a soufflé of Gorgonzola, hazelnuts, and zucchini; rabbit stewed in Vernaccia wine with olives; a "tarte tatin" of beetroot and burrata cheese; or a marinated mackerel salad with fennel and orange. To go with the modern menu, there's stripped-back decor, jazz-funk played in the background on an old vinyl record player, and an emphasis on beers—three on tap, plus a bottle list that is strong on European styles. The wine list is short, but expertly chosen.

Via Pietrapiana 40R. www.facebook.com/vagalume.firenze. © **055-246-6740.** Dishes 7€–14€. Daily 6pm–2am. Closed 2 weeks in Feb. Bus: C2 or C3.

In the Oltrarno & San Frediano

EXPENSIVE

iO: Osteria Personale ★★ CONTEMPORARY TUSCAN   There's a definite hipster atmosphere, with the stripped brick walls and young staff, but the food ethos here is ingrained, too. Ingredients are usually familiar Tuscan flavors, but combined in a way you may not have seen before. The menu always has a good range of seafood, meat, and vegetarian dishes: Perhaps tempura artichoke flowers stuffed with taleggio cheese and marjoram, followed by guinea-hen ravioli, then roasted octopus with garbanzo-bean cream and cumin. Reservations are always advisable.

Borgo San Frediano 167R. www.io-osteriapersonale.it. © **055-933-1341.** Main courses 17€–20€; tasting menus 40€ 4 dishes, 55€ 6 dishes. Mon–Sat 7:30–10pm. Closed 10 days in Jan and all of Aug. Bus: D or 6.

MODERATE

Il Magazzino ★ FLORENTINE   A traditional *osteria* that specializes in the flavors of old Florence, it looks the part, too, with its terracotta tiled floor and barrel vault, chunky wooden furniture, and hanging lamps. If you dare, this is a place to try tripe or *lampredotto* (intestines), the traditional food of working Florentines, prepared expertly here in ravioli, boiled, or *alla fiorentina* (stewed with tomatoes and garlic). The rest of the menu is carnivore-friendly too: Follow *tagliatelle al ragù bianco* (pasta ribbons with a "white" meat sauce made with a little milk instead of tomatoes) with *guancia di vitello in agrodolce* (veal tongue stewed with baby onions in a sticky-sweet sauce).

Piazza della Passera 3. © **055-215-969.** Main courses 9€–18€. Daily noon–3pm and 7:30–11pm. Bus: C3 or D.

INEXPENSIVE

GustaPizza ★★ PIZZA   Florentines aren't known for their pizza-making skills, so I guess it's just as well that this place is run by Calabrians. Pizzas are in the Naples style, with fluffy crusts, doughy bases, and just the classic toppings on a menu that you could write on the back of a napkin: Margherita (cheese, tomato, basil) and Napoli (cheese, tomatoes, anchovies, oregano, capers) are joined by a couple of simple specials, such as mozzarella and basil pesto. It is self-service, but there are a few

tables if you want to eat with a knife and fork (no reservations). On warm days, eat takeout round the corner on the steps of Santo Spirito.
Via Maggio 46R. **℗ 055-285-068.** Pizzas 4.50€–8€. Tues–Sun 11:30am–3pm and 7–11pm. Closed 3 weeks in Aug. Bus: C3, D, 11, 36, or 37.

Gelato

Florence has a fair claim to being the birthplace of gelato, and has some of the world's best *gelaterie*—but many, many poor imitations too. Steer clear of spots around major attractions with air-fluffed mountains of ice cream and flavors so full of artificial colors they glow in the dark. If you can see the Ponte Vecchio or Piazza della Signoria from the front door of the gelateria, you may want to move on. You might only have to walk a block, or duck down a side street, to find a genuine artisan in the gelato kitchen. Opening hours tend to be discretionary: When it's warm, many open until 11pm or beyond.

Carapina ★★ Militant seasonality ensures the fruit gelato here is the best in the center. *Note:* This branch usually closes at 7pm.
Via Lambertesca 18R. www.carapina.it. **℗ 055-291-128.** Cone from 2.50€. Bus: C3 or D. Also at: Piazza Oberdan 2R (**℗ 055-676-930**).

Gelateria della Passera ★★ Milk-free water ices here are among the most intensely flavored in the city, and relatively low in sugary sweetness. Try the likes of pink grapefruit or jasmine tea gelato.
Via Toscanella 15R (at Piazza della Passera). www.gelaterialapassera.wordpress.com. **℗ 055-291-882.** Cone from 2€. Bus: C3 or D.

Gelateria de' Neri ★ There's a large range of fruit, white, and chocolate flavors here, but nothing overelaborate. If the ricotta and fig flavor is offered, you are in luck.
Via dei Neri 9R. **℗ 055-210-034.** Cone from 1.80€. Bus: C1, C3, or 23.

La Carraia ★★ Packed with locals late into the evening on summer weekends—for a good reason. The range is vast, quality high.
Piazza N. Sauro 25R. www.lacarraiagroup.info. **℗ 055-280-695.** Cone from 1.50€. Bus: C3, D, 6, 11, 36, or 37. Also at: Via de' Benci 24R (**℗ 329-363-0069**).

Il Gelato Gourmet di Marco Ottaviano ★★ It's all about the seasonal, produce-led flavors at this place that opened in 2014. Choice can include Sicilian pistachio or Pastiera, based on a Neapolitan cake.
Via Palmieri 34R (at Piazza San Pier Maggiore). **℗ 055-234-1036.** Cone from 2€. Bus: C1 or C2.

SHOPPING

After Milan, Florence is **Italy's top shopping city**—beating even the capital, Rome. Here's what to buy: leather, fashion, shoes, marbleized paper, hand-embroidered linens, artisan and craft items including ceramics, Tuscan wines, handmade jewelry, *pietre dure* (known also as "Florentine mosaic," inlaid semiprecious stones), and antiques.

General Florentine **shopping hours** are Monday through Saturday from 9:30am to noon or 1pm and 3 or 3:30 to 7:30pm, although increasingly, many shops are staying open on Sunday and through that midafternoon *riposo* or nap (especially the larger stores and those around tourist sights). Some close Monday mornings instead.

The Top Shopping Streets & Areas

AROUND SANTA TRÍNITA   The cream of the crop of Florentine shopping lines both sides of elegant **Via de' Tornabuoni,** with an extension along **Via della Vigna Nuova** and other surrounding streets. Here you'll find the big Florentine fashion names like **Gucci ★** (at no. 73R; www. gucci.com; ✆ 055-264-011), **Pucci ★** (at no. 22R; www.emiliopucci. com; ✆ **055-265-8082**), and **Ferragamo ★** (at no. 5R; www.fer ragamo.com; ✆ **055-292-123**), ensconced in old palaces or minimalist boutiques. Stricter traffic controls have made shopping Via de' Tornabuoni a more sedate experience, though somewhat at the expense of surrounding streets.

AROUND VIA ROMA & VIA DEI CALZAIUOLI   These are some of Florence's busiest streets, packed with storefronts offering mainstream shopping. It is here you will find the city's major department stores, **Coin,** Via dei Calzaiuoli 56R (www.coin.it; ✆ **055-280-531**), and **La Rina- scente,** Piazza della Repubblica (www.rinascente.it; ✆ **055-219-113**), alongside quality clothing chains such as Geox and Zara. **La Feltrinelli RED,** Piazza delle Repubblica 26 (www.lafeltrinelli.it; ✆ **199-151- 173**), is the center's best bookstore. A three-floor branch of upscale food-market minichain **Eataly,** Via de' Martelli 22 (www.eataly.net; ✆ **055-015-3601**), lies just north of the Baptistery.

AROUND SANTA CROCE   The eastern part of the center has seen a flourishing of one-of-a-kind stores, with an emphasis on young, independent fashions. **Borgo degli Albizi** and its tributary streets are worth roaming. This is also where you will find the **Mercato delle Pulci** (see below).

Florence's Best Markets

Mercato Centrale ★★   The center's main market stocks the usual fresh produce, but you can also browse for (and taste) cheeses, salamis and cured hams, Tuscan wines, takeout food, and more. It is picnic-packing heaven. It runs Monday to Saturday until 2pm (until 5pm Sat for most of the year). Upstairs is street-food nirvana, all day, every day; see p. 215. Btw. Piazza del Mercato Centrale and Via dell'Ariento. No phone. Bus: C1.

Mercato delle Pulci ★★   The little piazza behind the Loggia del Pesce—originally built under Cosimo I for the city's fishmongers—hosts a daily flea market. Rifle through the little shanty-style shops in search of costume jewelry, Tiffany lamps, secondhand dolls and books, vintage postcards, weird objects, and other ephemera. The market runs daily, although not every unit is open every day. Piazza de' Ciompi. No phone. Bus: C2 or C3.

Mercato di San Lorenzo ★

The city's tourist street market is a fun place to pick up T-shirts, marbleized paper, or a city souvenir. Leather wallets, purses, bags, and jackets are another popular purchase—be sure to assess the workmanship, and haggle shamelessly. The market runs daily; watch out for pickpockets. In 2014 it was controversially ejected from part of its traditional home, in Piazza San Lorenzo, and now spreads around Piazza del Mercato Centrale; whether it will ever move back is as yet undecided. Via dell'Ariento and Via Rosina. No phone. Bus: C1.

Food stall in the Mercato Centrale.

Crafts & Artisans

Florence has a longstanding reputation for its craftsmanship. Although the storefront display windows along heavily touristed streets are often stuffed with cheap imports and mass-produced goods, if you search around you can still find genuine handmade, top-quality items.

To get a better understanding of Florence's artisans, including a visit to a workshop, **Context Travel** (p. 121) runs a guided walk around the Oltrarno, Florence's traditional craft area. The "Made in Florence" walk costs 80€ and lasts 3 hours.

Madova ★ For almost a century, this has been the best city retailer for handmade leather gloves, lined with silk, cashmere, or lambs' wool. Expect to pay between 40€ and 60€ for a pair. You may not expect it this close to the Ponte Vecchio, but Madova is the real deal. Closed Sundays. Via Guicciardini 1R. www.madova.com. ✆ **055-239-6526.** Bus: C3 or D.

Masks of Agostino Dessi ★ This little shop is stuffed floor to ceiling with handmade Carnevale and *commedia dell'arte* masks, made from papier-mâché, leather, and ceramics, and then hand-finished expertly. Via Faenza 72R. ✆ **055-287-370.** Bus: C1.

Officina Profumo-Farmaceutica di Santa Maria Novella ★★★

A shrine to scents and skincare, this is also Florence's most historic herbal pharmacy, with roots in the 17th century, when it was founded by Dominicans based in the adjacent convent of Santa Maria Novella. Nothing is cheap, but the perfumes, cosmetics, moisturizers, and other products are made from the finest natural ingredients and packaged exquisitely. Via della Scala 16. www.smnovella.it. ✆ **055-216-276.** Bus: C2.

Parione ★ This traditional Florentine stationer stocks notebooks, marbleized paper, fine pens, and handmade wooden music boxes. Via dello Studio 11R. www.parione.it ✆ **055-215-030.** Bus: C1 or C2.

Scuola del Cuoio ★★ Florence's leading leather school is also open house for visitors. You can watch trainee artisans at work (Mon–Fri) then visit the small shop to buy the best soft leather. Portable items like wallets and bags are a good buy. Closed Sundays in off-season. Via San Giuseppe 5R (or enter through Santa Croce, via right transept). www.scuoladelcuoio.com. ✆ **055-244-534.** Bus: C3.

ENTERTAINMENT & NIGHTLIFE

Florence has excellent, mostly free listings publications. At the tourist offices, pick up the free monthly *Informacittà* (www.informacitta.net), which is strong on theater, concerts, and other arts events, as well as markets. Younger and hipper *Zero* (http://firenze.zero.eu) is hot on the latest eating, drinking, and nightlife. It is available free from trendy cafe-bars, shops, and sometimes the tourist office. *Firenze Spettacolo,* a 2€ Italian-language monthly sold at newsstands, is the most detailed and up-to-date listing of nightlife, arts, and entertainment. English-language magazine *The Florentine* publishes downloadable weekly events and listings at **www.theflr.net/weekly**.

If you just want to wander and see what grabs you, you will find plenty of tourist-oriented action in bars around the city's main squares. For something a little livelier—with a more local focus—check out **Borgo San Frediano, Piazza Santo Spirito,** or the northern end of **Via de' Macci,** close to where it meets Via Pietrapiana. **Via de' Benci** is usually buzzing around *aperitivo* time, and is popular with an expat crowd. **Via de' Renai** and the bars of San Niccolò around the **Porta San Miniato** are often lively too, with a mixed crowd of tourists and locals.

Performing Arts & Live Music

Florence does not have the musical cachet of Milan, Venice, Naples, or Rome, but there are two symphony orchestras and a fine music school in Fiesole, as well as great expectations for its new opera house (see below). The city's theaters are respectable, and most major touring companies stop in town. Get tickets to all cultural events online—they will send an e-mail with collection instructions—or buy in person at **Box Office,** Via delle Carceri 1 (www.boxofficetoscana.it; ✆ **055-210-804**).

Many performances staged in concert halls and other spaces are sponsored by the **Amici della Musica** (www.amicimusica.fi.it; ✆ **055-607-440**), so check their website to see what is on while you are here.

Opera di Firenze ★★ This vast new concert hall and arts complex seats up to 1,800 in daring modernist surrounds. Much delayed, the venue hosted its first Maggio Musicale Fiorentino in 2014. Piazzale Vittorio Gui. www.operadifirenze.it. ✆ **055-277-9350.** Tickets 10€–100€. Tram: T1.

St. Mark's ★   Operatic duets and full-scale operas in costume are the lure here. The program sticks to crowd pleasers like *Carmen, La Traviata,* and *La Bohème,* and runs most nights of the week all year. Via Maggio 18. www.concertoclassico.info. ✆ **340-811-9192.** Tickets 20€–35€. Bus: D, 11, 36, or 37.

Teatro Verdi ★   Touring shows, "serious" popular music, one-off revues, classical music and dance, and the Orchestra della Toscana, occupy the stage at Florence's leading theater. Via Ghibellina 97. www.teatrover dionline.it. ✆ **055-212-320.** Closed 2nd half of July and all Aug. Bus: C1, C2, C3, or 23.

Volume ★   By day, it's a laid-back cafe and art space selling coffee, books, and crepes. By night, a buzzing bar with regular acoustic sets. Piazza Santo Spirito 5R. www.volumefirenze.com. ✆ **055-238-1460.** Bus: C3, D, 11, 36, or 37.

Cafes

Florence no longer has a glitterati or intellectuals' cafe scene, and when it did—from the late-19th-century Italian Risorgimento era through *la dolce vita* of the 1950s—it was basically copying the idea from Paris. Although they're often overpriced tourist spots today—especially around **Piazza della Repubblica**—Florence's high-toned cafes are fine if you want pastries served to you while you sit and people-watch.

Caffetteria delle Oblate ★   A relaxing terrace popular with local families and students, and well away from the tourist crush (and prices) on the streets below. As a bonus, it has unique view of Brunelleschi's dome. Also serves light lunch and *aperitivo.* Top floor of Biblioteca dell'Oblate, Via del Oriuolo 26. www.lospaziochesperavi.it. ✆ **055-263-9685.** Bus: C1 or C2.

Le Terrazze ★   The prices, like the perch, are a little elevated (3€–5€ for a coffee). But you get to enjoy your drink on a hidden terrace in the sky, with just the rooftops, towers, and Brunelleschi's dome for company. Top floor of La Rinascente, Piazza della Repubblica. www.larinascente.it. ✆ **055-219-113.** Bus: C2.

Rivoire ★   If you are going to choose one overpriced pavement cafe in Florence, make it this one. The steep prices (6€ a cappuccino, 4.50€ for a small mineral water) help pay for the rent of one of the prettiest slices of real estate on the planet. Piazza della Signoria (at Via Vacchereccia). www.rivoire.it. ✆ **055-214-412.** Bus: C2.

Wine Bars, Cocktail Bars & Craft Beer Bars

If you want to keep it going into the small hours, you will likely find Italian **nightclubs** to be rather cliquey—people usually go in groups to hang out and dance only with one another. There's plenty of flesh showing, but no meat market. Singles hoping to find random dance partners will often be disappointed. Out in the northwestern 'burbs, **Tenax,** Via Pratese 46 (www.tenax.org; ✆ **335-523-5922**), attracts big-name DJs on Friday and Saturday nights.

Giant wine casks at Cantinetta dei Verrazzano.

Beer House Club ★★ The best artisan beers from Tuscany, Italy, and further afield. Their own line, brewed for the bar in nearby Prato, includes IPA, Imperial Stout, and Saison styles. Between 5 and 8pm, house beers are 5€ a pint instead of 6€. Corso Tintori 34R. www.beerhouseclub.it. 𝄐 **055-247-6763.** Bus: C1, C3, or 23.

Caffè Sant'Ambrogio ★ This fine wine and cocktail bar is in a lively part of the center, northeast of Santa Croce. It is popular with locals without being too achingly hip. In summer, the action spills out onto the little piazza and church steps outside. Piazza Sant'Ambrogio 7R. www.caffesantambrogio.it. No phone. Bus: C2 or C3.

Cantinetta dei Verrazzano ★★ One of the coziest little wine and food bars in the center is decked out with antique wooden wine cabinets, in genuine *enoteca* style. The wines come from the first-rate Verrazzano estate, in Chianti (see p. 244). Via dei Tavolini 18R. www.verrazzano.com. 𝄐 **055-268-590.** Bus: C2.

Diorama ★★ Opened in 2014, this tiny bar has a small terrace, Formica tables, craft beers (5€–7€), hot dogs (3.50€), and a local vibe. Via Pisana 78R. www.dioramafirenze.com. 𝄐 **055-228-6682.** Bus: 6.

Golden View Open Bar ★ One of the city's most elegant *aperitivo* spots. Pay 10€ to 14€ for a cocktail or glass of sparkling wine and help yourself to the buffet between 7 and 9:30pm every night. There is also live jazz 3 nights a week from 9:15pm. Via dei Bardi 58R. www.goldenviewopenbar.com. 𝄐 **055-214-502.** Bus: C3 or D.

Il Santino ★★ This tiny wine bar stocks niche labels from across Italy, and serves exquisite "Florentine tapas" plates (5€–10€) to munch while you sip. Via Santo Spirito 60R. 𝄐 **055-230-2820.** Bus: D, 11, 36, or 37.

La Terrazza at the Continentale ★★ There are few surprises on the list here—a well-made Negroni, Moscow Mule, Bellini, and the like—and prices are a little steep at 15€ to 18€ a cocktail. But the setting, on a rooftop right by the Ponte Vecchio, makes them cheap at the price. The atmosphere is fashionable but casual (wear what you like) and staff is supremely welcoming. Arrive at sundown to see the city below start to twinkle. Inside Continentale Hotel, Vicolo dell'Oro 6R. 𝄐 **055-27-262.** Bus: C3 or D.

Mostodolce ★   Burgers, pizza, Wi-Fi, and sports on the screen—so far, so good. And Mostodolce also has its own artisan beer on tap, brewed just outside Florence at Prato (some are very strong). Happy hour is 3:30 to 7:30pm, when it is .50€ off a beer. Via Nazionale 114R. www.mostodolce.it/firenze. ℂ **055-230-2928.** Bus: 1, 6, 11, 14, 17, or 23.

Volpi e L'Uva ★   The wines by the glass list is 30-strong, the atmosphere is relaxed, and the terrace on a little piazza beside Santa Felicità is a delight. It's the kind of place you just sink into. Glasses from 4€. Closed Sundays. Piazza dei Rossi 1. www.levolpieluva.com. ℂ **055-239-8132.** Bus: C3 or D.

6

TUSCANY

R enaissance artists famously left behind some of the world's greatest art and architecture in Tuscany—the Leaning Tower of Pisa, Piero della Francesca's fresco cycle in Arezzo, Ambrogio Lorenzetti's civic "Allegories" in Siena's Museo Civico. Such masterpieces took root here because these were some of the great cities of medieval Europe, set amid beguiling landscapes carpeted with cypresses and vineyards.

Soaking up culture is certainly part of the allure of Tuscany, one of Italy's most popular tourist regions. Equally inviting, however, is the chance to partake of superb food and wine, served with genuine warmth. Even a simple meal can seem like a work of art in places as bountiful as the Val di Chiana or the Val d'Orcia. Somehow it only makes sense that full-bodied red wines should come from towns as appealing as Montepulciano and Montalcino, and character-filled whites from proud little San Gimignano. Art, scenery, food, wine—you may well come to believe that all the good things in life come together in Tuscany.

SIENA ★★★

70km (43 miles) S of Florence, 232km (144 miles) N of Rome

Florence's longtime rival, this medieval city of rose-colored brick seems to have come out on top in terms of grace and elegance. With steep, twisting stone alleys and proud churches, palaces, and crenellated public buildings draped across its gentle hillsides, Siena is for many admirers the most beautiful town in Italy. At its heart is a ravishing piazza, and from its heights rises a magnificent duomo of striped marble.

The city trumpets the she-wolf as its emblem, a holdover from its days as Saena Julia, the Roman colony founded by Augustus about 2,000 years ago (though the official Sienese myth has the town founded by the sons of Remus, younger brother of Rome's legendary forefather). Civic projects and artistic prowess reached their greatest heights in the 13th and 14th centuries, when artists invented a distinctive Sienese style while banking and a booming wool industry made Siena one of the richest Italian republics. Then, in 1348, the Black Death killed more than half of the population, decimating the social fabric and devastating the economy. Siena never recovered, and much of the city has barely changed since, inviting you to slip into the rhythms and atmosphere of the Middle Ages.

PREVIOUS PAGE: **Tuscan countryside at sunset**

Essentials

GETTING THERE

BY TRAIN   Some 19 trains daily connect Siena with **Florence** (usually 90 min.), via Empoli. Siena's **train station** is at Piazza Roselli, about 3km (1¾ miles) north of town. To get into town, take the no. 9 or 10 bus to Piazza Gramsci (buy your ticket at the newsstand in the station). Don't take the bus that stops in front of the station, but go into the big brick shopping center across the street and take the escalator down to the underground bus stop. Be sure to say "Gramsci" when you board, or you can end up in a far-flung outlying district. You can also take a series of escalators up to town from the shopping center—these too are poorly marked, but as long as you're going up you're moving in the right direction.

BY BUS   Buses are faster and let you off right in town: TRAIN SpA (www.trainspa.it) and SITA (www.sitabus.it) express buses (*corse rapide;* around 25 daily; 75 min.) and slower buses (*corse ordinarie;* 14 daily; 95 min.) operate between **Florence**'s main bus station and Siena's Piazza Gramsci. Siena is also connected with **San Gimignano** (at least hourly Mon–Sat, either direct or with a change in Poggibonsi; 65–80 min. not including layover), **Perugia** (two to four daily; 90 min.), and **Rome**'s Tiburtina station (five to nine daily; 3 hr.).

BY CAR   There's a fast road direct from **Florence** (it has no marked route number; follow the green signs toward Siena), or take the more scenic route, down the Chiantigiana SS222. From **Rome** get off the A1 north at the Val di Chiana exit and follow the SS326 west for 50km (31 miles). From **Pisa** take the highway toward Florence and exit onto the SS429 south just before Empoli (100km/62 miles total). The easiest way into the center is from the Siena Ovest highway exit. There's **parking** (www.sienaparcheggi. com; ✆ **0577/228711**) in well-signposted lots outside the city gates. An especially handy lot is Santa Caterina, from which escalators whisk you up to town. Most charge between .50€ and 1.60€ per hour. Many hotels have discount arrangements with lots; around 15€ per day is standard.

GETTING AROUND

You can get anywhere you want to go on foot, with a bit of climbing. **Minibuses,** called *pollicini* (www.sienamobilita.it; ✆ **0577/204246**), run quarter-hourly (every half-hour Sat afternoon and all day Sun) from the main gates into the city center from 6:30am to 8:30pm. You can also call for a radio **taxi** at ✆ **0577/49222** (7am–9pm only); there's a taxi queue at the train station and in town at Piazza Matteotti.

VISITOR INFORMATION

The **tourist office,** where you can get a fairly useless free map or pay .50€ for a detailed one, is at Piazza del Campo 56 (www.terresiena.it; ✆ **0577/280551**). It's open Monday to Saturday 9am to 7pm (10am–5pm Nov–Mar), Sunday 10am to 1pm.

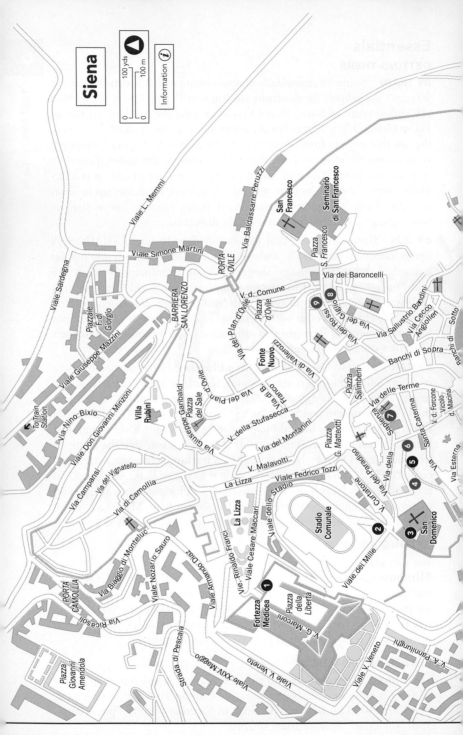

Siena

100 yds
100 m

Information ⓘ

To Train Station

Piazzale F. di Giorgio

Viale Sardegna

Viale L. Memmi

Viale Simone Martini

BARRIERA SAN LORENZO

PORTA OVILE

Via Baldassarre Peruzzi

San Francesco

Seminario di San Francesco

Piazza S. Francesco

Via dei Baroncelli

V. d. Comune

Piazza d'Ovile

Via dei Rossi

Via del Giglio

Via Sallustio Bandini

Via di Cecco Angiolieri

Banchi di Sopra

Banchi di Sotto

Viale Giuseppe Mazzini

Via Nino Bixio

Viale Don Giovanni Minzoni

Villa Rubini

Piazza Garibaldi

Piazza del Sale

Via di B. del Pian d'Ovile

Via del Plan d'Ovile

Fonte Nuovo

Via di Vallerozzi

V. della Stufasecca

Via Giuseppe Garibaldi

Via dei Montanini

Piazza Salimbeni

Via delle Terme

V. d. Forcone

Vicolo d. Macina

Piazza G. Matteotti

Via della Sapienza

Santa Caterina

Via Esterna

Via Campansi

Via del Vignatello

Via di Camollia

V. Malavolti

La Lizza

Viale Federico Tozzi

V. Curtatone

Via del Paradiso

San Domenico

Viale dello Stadio

Stadio Comunale

Viale dei Mille

Via di Camollia

PORTA CAMOLLIA

Via Ricasoli

Via Biaggio di Monteluc

Via Nozario Sauro

Viale Armando Diaz

Viale Cesare Maccari

Vie. Rinaldo Franci

La Lizza

Piazza della Libertà

Fortezza Medicea

V.G. Marconi

Piazza Giovanni Amendola

Strada di Pescaia

Viale XXIV Maggio

Viale V. Veneto

V.A. Pannilunghi

Viale V. Veneto

1
2
3
4
5
6
7
8
9

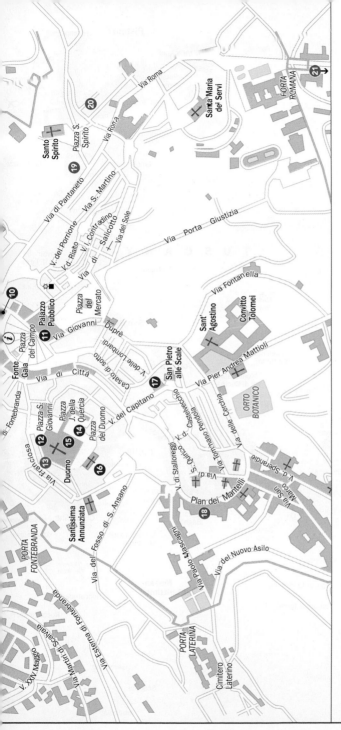

RESTAURANTS

Antica Osteria da Divo **13**
Kopakabana **8**
La Chiacchera **6**
La Sosta di Violante **19**
L'Osteria **9**

HOTELS

Antica Torre **20**
Campo Regio Relais **7**
Hotel Alma Domus **4**
Palazzo Ravizza **18**
Santa Caterina **21**

ATTRACTIONS

Archivio di Stato **10**
Baptistery **12**
Casa di Santa Caterina **5**
Duomo **15**
Enoteca Italiana **1**
Museo Civico/
   Palazzo Pubblico **11**
Museo dell'Opera
   Metropolitana **14**
Pinacoteca Nazionale **17**
San Domenico **3**
Santa Maria della Scala **16**
Siena Hotels Promotion **2**

Florence
Siena
TUSCANY
UMBRIA

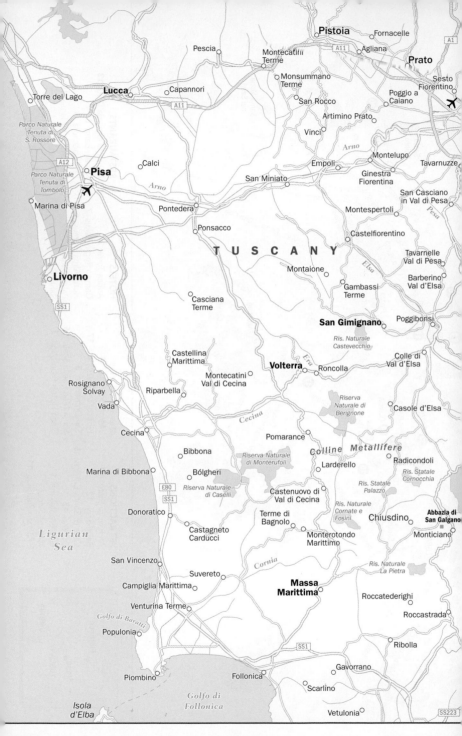

Tuscany

0 ——— 10 mi
0 ——— 10 km

Vaglia
Vicchio
Fiesole
Rufina
Stia
EMILIA-ROMAGNA
Florence
(Firenze)
Sieve
Pontassieve
Arno
Rignano
sull'Arno
Vallombrosa
Poppi
Chiusi della
Verna
Grassina
Bibbiena
Pieve Santo
Stefano
Impruneta
Sto. Stefano a Tizzano
Reggello
Rassina
Caprese
Michelangelo
San Polo in Chianti
Pian de Sco
Strada in Chianti
Figline
Valdarno
Castelfranco di Sopra
SS71
Sansepolcro
Vicchiomaggio
SS222
Area Naturale
Protetta di Int.
Locale Le Balze
Loro Ciuffenna
Castello di Verrazzano
Capolona
Anghiari
Greve in Chianti
San Giovanni
Valdarno
Castiglion
Fibocchi
Giovi-Ponte
alla Chiassa
Montefioralle
Villa Vignamaggio
Fontodi
**Panzano
in Chianti**
Montevarchi
Valdarno
Arno
A1
Ris. Naturale
Reg. Valle
dell'Inferno e
Bandella
Laterina
Monterchi
Castello di Volpaia
Levane
Ris. Naturale
Reg. Ponte a
Buriano e Penna
UMBRIA
Chianti
Radda in Chianti
Bucine
Pergine Valdarno
Arezzo
Castellina
in Chianti
Gaiole
in Chianti
Ambra
Battifolle-
Ruscello
Quercegrossa
A1
Rigutino
Monteriggioni
Castelnuovo
Berardenga
Monte
San Savino
Castiglion
Fiorentino
Siena
E78
SS73
Val di Chiana
Soviclle
Rapolano
Terme
Lucignano
Foiano
dei Chiana
Cortona
Isola d'Arbia
SS326
SS71
Asciano
Terontola
SS223
Monteroni
d'Arbia
Sinalunga
Lago
Trasimeno
Ombrone
Abbazia di Monte
Oliveto Maggiore
Ris. Naturale
to Merse
Vescovado
Torrita
di Siena
A1
Montepulciano
Stazione
Castiglione
del Lago
Merse
Buonconvento
Ris. Naturale
Basso Merse
Montepulciano
Ris. Naturale
Farma
San Quirico
d'Orcia
Pienza
UMBRIA
Montalcino
Chianciano Terme
Panicale
Bagno
Vignoni
Ris. Naturale
Lucciolabella
Ris. Naturale
Pietraporciana
Chiusi
Tavernelle
**Abbazia di
Sant'Antimo**
Castiglione
d'Orcia
Sarteano
Piegaro
Orcia
Cetona
Città
della Pieve
Paganico
Radicófani
San Casciano
dei Bagni
Campagnatico
Cinigiano
Arcidosso
Fabro
E78
Pianacastagnaio
SS2
Ficulle

231

Siena should offer a free bottle of wine to visitors who manage to figure out the bewildering range of reduced-price cumulative ticket combos on offer. The two you should care about and purchase (at participating sights) are the **Musei Comunali** pass (11€; valid for 2 days), for admission to Museo Civico and Santa Maria della Scala, both of which are must-sees, and the **OPA pass,** for entry to the Duomo, Museo dell'Opera Metropolitana, Baptistery, Cripta, and Oratorio di San Bernardino for 12€ Mar–Oct and 8€ Nov–Feb—the savings on entrance to the first three alone, not to be missed, make the pass a good investment.

Exploring Siena

At the heart of Siena is a serious contender for the most beautiful square in Italy—the sloping, scallop-shell-shaped Piazza del Campo (Il Campo). Laid out in the 1100s on the site of the Roman forum, the welcoming expanse is a testament to the city's civic achievements; it's anchored by a crenellated town hall, the Palazzo Pubblico (1297–1310), and the herringbone brick pavement is divided by white marble lines into nine sections representing the city's medieval ruling body, the Council of Nine. A poor 19th-century replica of Jacopo della Quercia's 14th-century fountain, the Fonte Gaia, is on one side of the square (some of the restored, but badly eroded, original panels are in Santa Maria della Scala (see p. 237). The dominant public monument is the slender 100m-tall (328-ft.) brick Torre del Mangia (1338–48), named for a slothful bell ringer nicknamed Mangiaguadagni, or "profit eater." (There's an armless statue of him in the courtyard.) From the platform atop the tower's 503 steps, the undulating Tuscan hills seem to rise and fall to the ends of the earth (admission to tower 8€, mid-Oct to Feb 10am–4pm, Mar to mid-Oct 10am–7pm).

Archivio di Stato ★ MUSEUM   Tucked into a 1469 Florentine Renaissance-style palazzo off the southeast corner of the Campo, this state archive displays such historic documents as Boccaccio's will and Jacopo della Quercia's contract for designing the Fonte Gaia fountain. Most riveting, however, is a remarkable set of wooden covers dating back to 1258 and made for the city's account books, the "Tavolette di Biccherna." They're painted with religious scenes, scenes of daily working life, and important events in Siena's history.
Via Banchi di Sotto 52. *②* **0577–241–745.** Free admission. Mon–Sat hourly viewings at 9:30, 10:30, and 11:30am

Duomo ★★★ CATHEDRAL   Much of the artistic greatness of Siena comes together in this black-and-white-marble cathedral, begun in the 12th century and completed in the 13th century, a magnificent example of Italian Gothic architecture. You're likely to come away from a visit with a great appreciation for the Pisanos, father and son. Nicola was the principal architect of the church, until he fell out of favor with the group

Siena's Piazza del Campo with the Palazzo Publico and the Torre del Mangia.

overseeing construction and left Siena; young Giovanni did much of the carving on the facade, where a vast army of prophets and apostles appears around the three portals (most of the originals are now in the Museo dell'Opera Metropolitana; see p. 235). They both worked on the pulpit, where the faithful could gaze upon sumptuously sculpted scenes of the life of Christ and the prophets and evangelists.

Beneath the pulpit spreads a flooring mosaic of 59 etched and inlaid marble panels (1372–1547), a showpiece for 40 of Siena's medieval and Renaissance artistic luminaries. Most prolific among them was Domenico Beccafumi, born into a local peasant family and adopted by his lord, who saw the boy's talent for drawing. Beccafumi studied in Rome but returned to Siena and spent much of his career designing 35 scenes for the flooring (from 1517–47); his richly patterned images are a repository of Old Testament figures. Matteo di Giovanni, another Sienese, did a gruesome Slaughter of the Innocents—a favorite theme of the artist, whose fresco of the same scene is in Santa Maria della Scala (see p. 237). Many of the panels are protected by cardboard overlays and uncovered only from mid–August to early October in honor of the Palio.

Umbrian Renaissance master Bernardino di Betto (better known as Pinturicchio, or Little Painter, because of his stature) is the star in the **Libreria Piccolomini,** entered off the left aisle. Cardinal Francesco Piccolomini built the library in 1487 to house the illuminated manuscripts of his famous uncle, a popular Sienese bishop who later became Pope Pius II. (Cardinal Piccolomini himself later became Pope Pius III— for a mere 18 days, before dying in office.) Pinturicchio's frescoes depict 10 scenes from the Pope Pius II's life, including an especially dramatic departure for the Council of Basel as a storm rages in the background.

In the **Baptistery** (not a separate building but beneath the choir), the great early Renaissance trio of Sienese and Florentine sculptors— Jacopo della Quercia, Lorenzo Ghiberti, and Donatello—crafted the gilded bronze panels of the baptismal font. Donatello wrought the dancing figure of Salome in the "Feast of Herod," and della Quercia did the statue of St. John that stands high above the marble basin.

Piazza del Duomo. www.operaduomo.siena.it. *©* **0577/283048.** Admission on cumulative ticket, or 4€, except when floor uncovered 7€. Mar–Oct Mon–Sat 10:30am–7pm, Sun 1:30–6pm; Nov–Feb Mon–Sat 10:30am–5:30pm, Sun 1:30–5:30pm. Baptistery: Piazza San Giovanni (down the stairs around the rear right flank of the Duomo). *©* **0577/283048.** Admission on cumulative ticket, or 4€. Mar–Oct Mon–Sat 10:30am–7pm, Sun 1:30–6pm; Nov–Feb Mon–Sat 10:30am–5:30pm, Sun 1:30–5:30pm.

Museo Civico/Palazzo Pubblico ★★★ MUSEUM   Presiding over the Piazza del Campo, this great Gothic-style town hall houses some the city's finest artistic treasures. Siena's medieval governors, the Council of Nine, met in the **Sala della Pace**, and to help ensure they bore their duties responsibly, in 1338 Ambrogio Lorenzetti frescoed the walls with what has become the most important piece of secular art to survive from medieval Europe. His "Allegory of Good and Bad Government and Their Effects on the Town and Countryside" provides not only a moral lesson but also a remarkable visual record of the Siena and the surrounding countryside as it appeared in the 14th century. Probably not by accident, the good government frescoes are nicely illuminated by natural light, while scenes of bad government are cast in shadow and have also deteriorated over the years. In an uplifting panorama on the good side of the room, the towers, domes, and rooftops of Siena appear much as they do today, with horsemen, workers, and townsfolk going about their daily affairs; in the countryside, genteel lords on horseback overlook bountiful fields. On the bad government side, streets are full of rubble, houses are collapsing, and soldiers are killing and pillaging; in the countryside, fields are barren and villages are ablaze.

Among other frescoes in these rooms is Sienese painter Simone Martini's greatest work, and his first, a "Maestà" (or Majesty), finished in

Something New Under the Duomo

Siena's "newest" work of art is a cycle of frescoes painted between 1270 and 1275, discovered during excavation work in 1999. The colorful works are on view in a subterranean room called the **Cripta**, though it was never used as a burial crypt. Most likely the room was a lower porch for the duomo (staircases lead to the nave), but it became a storeroom when the choir area above was expanded. What remains are fascinating fragments of scenes from the New Testament, full of emotion and painted in vibrant colors. Scholars are still trying to determine who painted what in the room. Entry is included on the OPA pass (see p. 232), which includes the Duomo upstairs and other sights, or otherwise is 6€.

The Duomo of Siena.

1315 (he went over it again in 1321), in the **Sala del Mappamondo**. He shows the Virgin Mary as a medieval queen beneath a royal canopy, surrounded by a retinue of saints, apostles, and angels. The work introduces not only a secular element to a holy scene but also a sense of three-dimensional depth and perspective that later came to the fore in Renaissance painting. Mary's presence here in the halls of civil power reinforces the idea of good government, with the Virgin presiding as a protector of the city. Just opposite is another great Martini work (though the attribution has been called into question), the "Equestrian Portrait of Guidoriccio da Fogliano." The depiction of a proud mercenary riding past a castle he has just conquered was part of a long lost "castelli," or "castles," fresco cycle that showed off Sienese conquests.

Palazzo Pubblico, Piazza del Campo. © **0577/292226.** Admission on cumulative ticket with Torre del Mangia 13€; or 7.50€ adults with reservation, 8€ adults without reservation; 4€ students and seniors 65 and over with reservation, 3.50€ students and seniors without reservation; free for ages 11 and under. Nov–Mar 15 daily 10am–6pm; Mar 16–Oct daily 10am–7pm. Bus: A (pink), B.

Museo dell'Opera Metropolitana ★★ MUSEUM In 1339, Siena decided to show off its political, artistic, and spiritual prominence by expanding the Duomo. Work had just begun when the Black Death killed more than half the city's inhabitants in 1348, and the project ground to a halt, never to be resumed—partly because it was later discovered that the foundations could not support the massive structure. The aborted nave of the so-called "New Duomo" has now been repurposed to house many of the church's treasures. Here you can see the glorious-if-worse-for-wear statues by Giovanni Pisano that once adorned the façade, as well as a 30-sq-m (323-sq-ft) stained-glass window made for the apse in the late 1280s, with nine colorful panels—beautifully illuminated to full effect in these new surroundings—depicting the Virgin Mary, Siena's four patron saints, and the four Biblical Evangelists.

Upstairs is the "Maestà" by Duccio di Buoninsenga, an altarpiece which was declared a masterpiece from the day it was unveiled in 1311, carried in a solemn procession from the painter's workshop on Via Stalloreggi to the Duomo's altar. As a contemporary wrote, "all honorable citizens of Siena surrounded said panel with candles held in their hands, and women and children followed humbly behind." The front depicts the Madonna and Child surrounded by saints and angels while the back once displayed 46 scenes from the lives of Mary and Christ. In 1711 the altarpiece was dismantled and pieces are now in collections around the world, though what remains here shows the genius of Duccio, who slowly broke away from a one-dimensional Byzantine style to imbue his characters with nuance, roundness, and emotion.

The **Facciatone,** a walkway atop the would-be facade of the "New Duomo," is the city's second most popular viewpoint, with a stunning perspective of the cathedral across the piazza and sweeping views over the city's rooftops to Siena's favorite height, the Torre del Mangia towering over the Campo.

Piazza del Duomo 8. www.operaduomo.siena.it. © **0577/283048.** Admission on cumulative ticket, or 6€. Mar–Oct Mon–Sat 10:30am–7pm, Sun 1:30–6pm; Nov–Feb Mon–Sat 10:30am–5:30pm, Sun 1:30–5:30pm.

Pinacoteca Nazionale ★ ART MUSEUM The greatest works of Sienese art have long since been dispersed to museums around the world, but here you can still get an overview of the works of the city's major artists, especially those working in the 12th through the 16th centuries, nicely displayed in the Brigidi and Buonsignori palaces. What you'll soon notice is that while the Renaissance was flourishing in Florence, Siena held to its old ways—these works are rich in Byzantine gold and an almost Eastern influence in the styling. The collection tends to shift around a bit, but a walk through the second floor galleries will show you what you want to see.

Among the works by Duccio (of the famous "Maestà" in the Museo dell'Opera, p. 235) is an enchanting "Madonna and Child with Saints," in which a placid, otherworldly looking Mary holds a very wise-looking Jesus. Simone Martini (painter of Siena's other great "Maestà," in the Museo Civico, p. 264) did the wonderful "Agostino Novello" altarpiece, in which St. Augustine is shown performing all sorts of heroic deeds, such as flying over boulders to save a monk trapped in a ravine; in many of the panels you'll notice Sienese street scenes. Works by the Lorenzetti brothers include some charming landscapes by Ambrogio (artist of the "Allegory of Good and Bad Government" in the Palazzo Pubblico, p. 234);

SIENA'S saintly SCHOLAR

Catherine Benincasa (1347–1380), one of 25 children of a wealthy Sienese cloth dyer, had her first vision of Christ when she was 5 or 6 and vowed to devote her entire life to God. She took a nun's veil but not the vows when a teenager, was wed "mystically" to Christ when she was 21, and became known for helping the poor and infirm. She and her followers traveled throughout central Italy promoting "the total love for God" and a stronger church. Not only did she found a woman's monastery outside Siena, she served as Siena's ambassador to Pope Gregory XI in Avignon. Encouraging his return to Rome, she continued to write him and other Italian leaders and to travel extensively, begging for peace and the reform of the clergy and the papal

states. She fasted almost continually, which eventually took such a toll on her health, she died at age 33. She was canonized as St. Catherine of Siena in 1461 by Pope Pius II—himself a native of Siena (see the Libreria Piccolomini, p. 233).

The cavernous, stark church of **San Domenico** in Piazza San Domenico (free admission; 9am–6:30pm daily) houses Catherine's venerated head, preserved in a gold reliquary, and her thumb. Her family home, **The Casa di Santa Caterina,** Costa di Sant'Antonio (℃ **0577/44177;** free admission; 9am–6pm daily), has been preserved as a religious sanctuary; the former kitchen is now an oratory with a spectacular 16th-century majolica-tiled floor.

his "Castle on the Lake" is almost surrealistic, an architectural fantasy reminiscent of the 20th-century works of Giorgio di Chirico. Pietro's "Madonna of the Carmelites," an altarpiece the artist executed for the Carmelite church in Siena, shows the Virgin and Child in a distinctly medieval setting, surrounded by members of the order in 14th-century garb, along with a typically Sienese landscape, complete with horsemen and planted hillsides. Domenico Beccafumi's cartoons, or sketches, for his floor panels in the Duomo are on the first floor.

Via San Pietro 29. ℃ **0577/286143.** Admission 4€. Sun–Mon 9am–1pm; Tues–Sat 8:15am–7:15pm.

Santa Maria della Scala ★★ MUSEUM   One of Europe's first hospitals, probably founded around 1090, Santa Maria della Scala raised abandoned children, took care of the infirm, fed the poor, and lodged pilgrims who stopped in Siena on their way to and from Rome. These activities are recorded in scenes in the **Sala del Pellegrinaio** (Pilgrims' Hall), where colorful depictions of patients and healers from the Middle Ages looked down upon rows of hospital beds as recently as the 1990s. These are some of the finest secular works of the Middle Ages, color-rich 15th-century frescoes by Domenico di Bartolo and others, showing such scenes as surgeons dressing a leg wound or holding a flask of urine to the light, or caregivers offering fresh clothing to an indigent young man. One of Bartolo's panels encapsulates an orphan's lifetime experience at the hospital, as he pictures infants being weaned, youngsters being instructed

A DAY AT THE races

Siena lets its guard down every year, on July 2 and again on August 16, when the **Palio delle Contrade** transforms the Piazza del Campo into a racetrack, with hordes of spectators squeezing through the city's narrow alleyways to watch. This aggressive bareback horserace around the Campo involves 10 of Siena's 17 *contrade* (districts), chosen by lot to participate, and is preceded by a showy flag-waving ceremony and parade. The race itself is over in just 2 minutes. Frenzied celebrations greet the winning rider, and the day is rounded off with communal feasts in each district.

To witness the event, you'll end up standing for hours in the sun and waging battle to get to a toilet. An easier way to enjoy the experience is to settle for the trial races, also held in the Campo (starting June 29 and Aug 13). There's a crowd, but it's smaller and tamer. While trial races are not as fast and furious as the real thing, they are just as photogenic and fun to watch. There are usually six in the mornings (9am) and late evenings (7:45pm June, 7:15pm Aug).

Another way to view the Palio in comfort is to reserve a spot in the temporary stands, on one of the surrounding terraces, or even at a window overlooking the campo. You should reserve a year in advance and expect to pay at least 350€ and as much as 700€ a person. Among the travel agents handling arrangements is **2Be Travel Designers** (www.paliotickets.com).

by a stern-looking mistress, and a young couple being wed (young women raised in the hospital were given dowries). As these activities transpire, a dog and cat scuffle, foundlings climb up ladders toward the Virgin Mary, and wealthy benefactors stand on Oriental carpets.

Elsewhere in the hospital complex you'll see other frescoes and altarpieces commissioned by the hospital as it acquired huge landholdings and considerable wealth over the centuries. One gallery houses some original panels from Jacopo della Quercia's 14th-century fountain in the Piazza del Campo, the Fonte Gaia. In the cellars is the dark and eerie **Oratorio di Santa Caterina della Notte**, where St. Catherine (see p. 237) allegedly passed her nights in prayer.

Piazza del Duomo 2. www.santamariadellascala.com. ☎ **0577/534571.** Admission on cumulative ticket, or 9€, free for ages 11 and under. Mar 17–Oct 15 Mon–Wed 10:30am–4:30pm, Thurs–Sun 10:30am–6:30pm; Oct 16–Mar 16 daily 10:30am–4:30pm.

Where to Stay

It's best to come to this popular town with a reservation. If you don't have one, stop by the **Siena Hotels Promotion** booth on Piazza San Domenico (www.hotelsiena.com; ☎ **0577/288084**), where for 1.50€ to 4€, depending on the category of hotel, they'll find you a room and reserve it—but remember, this is a private agency that works on commission with hotels, so their selection is limited to hotels with which they have a deal. The booth is open Monday through Saturday from 9am to 7pm (until 8pm in summer). The city tourist office also books accommodations for a fee.

Antica Torre ★   A 16th-century tower house dishes up no end of medieval atmosphere, with eight smallish rooms tucked onto four floors. If you don't mind the climb, the two on the top floor come with the advantage of views across the tile rooftops, and just treading on the old stones on the staircase is a pleasure. All rooms have marble floors, brick and timbered ceilings, handsome iron bedsteads, and plenty of other character, which for some guests may compensate for the fairly cramped quarters, small bathrooms, and lack of many hotel services. Continental breakfast (extra) can get the day off to a rocky start, literally, as it's served downstairs in a rough-hewn stone vault.
Via di Fiera Vecchia 7. www.anticatorresiena.it. ℂ **0577/222255.** 8 units. 70€–99€ double. **Amenities:** Wi-Fi (free).

Campo Regio Relais ★★   A *Room with a View* ambiance pervades this stylish old house a ten-minute walk from the Campo. Two of the rooms do have spectacular views up a hillside crowned with the Duomo, and all guests enjoy the same stunning vista from the breakfast room/lounge and terrace. The old-fashioned *pensione* ambiance is enhanced with a sophisticated take on modern updates that includes rich fabrics and traditionally elegant furnishings, chic rather than staid. Amenities include an honesty bar, a library, attentive service, and excellent breakfast.
Via della Sapienza 25. www.camporegio.com. ℂ **0577/222073.** 6 units. Doubles 150€–450€ w/buffet breakfast. Usually closed Jan to mid-Mar. **Amenities:** Wi-Fi (free).

Hotel Alma Domus ★   This modern re-do of the former drying rooms of a medieval wool works is run by the nuns of St. Catherine, who provide crisply homey and spotless lodgings with a slightly contemporary flair. Terraced into the hillside below San Domenico church, near the Fontebranda (the oldest and most picturesque of the city's fountains), the place has a quiet, retreatlike air—even a meditative, monastic calm, if you choose to see it that way—along with a great perk: city-view balconies in the more expensive rooms. Less expensive rooms do not have views or air conditioning. Breakfast is included, but it's a bit basic; you may prefer to walk up the hill and enjoy a cappuccino in the Campo.
Via Camporegio 37. www.hotelalmadomus.it. ℂ **0577/44177.** 28 units. 85€–120€ double. Rates include breakfast. Bus: A (red). **Amenities:** Smoke-free rooms, Wi-Fi (free).

Palazzo Ravizza ★★★   Generations of travelers have fallen under the spell of this 17th-century Renaissance *palazzo*, where high ceilings, oil paintings, highly polished antiques, and the gentle patina of age all suggest an era of grand travel. High-ceilinged salons are set up for lounging, with deep couches and card tables, even a grand piano, and a large garden in the rear stretches towards green hills. All the rooms are different, though most have wood beams and a surfeit of period detail, including some frescoes and coffered ceilings; furnishings throughout are comfortable and traditionally stylish. While this wonderful old place has the aura of a country hideaway, it's right in the city center, just a few streets below the Piazza del Campo.

Pian dei Mantellini 34 (near Piazza San Marco). www.palazzoravizza.it. ✆ **0577/280462.** 35 units. 130€–180€ double. Rates include breakfast. Free parking. Closed early Jan to early Feb. Bus: A (green, yellow). **Amenities:** Bar; babysitting; concierge; room service; smoke-free rooms; Wi-Fi (free).

Santa Caterina ★★ You'll forgo a city center location to stay here, but being just outside the walls—literally so, as this is the first house after Porta Roma, about a 10-minute walk from Piazza del Campo—has the advantage of making you feel like you are in the countryside. A large, shady garden enhances the feeling, and you can breakfast and enjoy a drink under the trees in good weather; for indoor lounging, there's a snug little bar, a well-upholstered, book-lined lounge, and a glass-enclosed breakfast room. Most of the cozy and atmospheric rooms, with wood-beamed ceilings, simple wood furnishings, and nice old prints on the walls, face the back, where wide-sweeping views of the green Val d'Orcia seem to go on forever. One choice room has a little balcony overlooking this scene, and a few others are bi-level, with bedrooms tucked beneath the eaves. Just make sure to get a rear-facing room, because facing the street out front would mean missing the wonderful view.

Via Enea Silvio Piccolomini 7. www.hscsiena.it. ✆ **0577/221105.** 22 units. 130€–150€ double. Rates include buffet breakfast. Bus: A (pink) or 2. **Amenities:** Babysitting; bikes; concierge; parking (fee); smoke-free rooms; Wi-Fi (free).

Where to Eat

The **Enoteca Italiana** in the 16th-century Fortezza Medicea di Santa Barbara is the only state-sponsored wine bar in Italy, in vaults that were built for Cosimo de' Medici in 1560 (www.enoteca-italiana.it; ✆ **0577/228843;** Mon noon–8pm; Tues–Sat noon–1am). You can sample a choice selection of Italian wines by the glass and accompany your choices with small plates of meats and cheeses. Every Italian city has a favorite *gelateria,* and Siena's is **Kopakabana,** at Via de' Rossi 52–54 (www.gelateriakopakabana.it; ✆ **0577/223744;** mid-Feb to mid-Nov noon–8pm, later in warm weather), with flavors that include *panpepato,* based on the peppery Sienese cake.

Antica Osteria da Divo ★★ CONTEMPORARY SIENESE It's hard to know what cuisine would best suit this almost-eerie setting of brick vaulting, exposed timbers, walls of bare rock, and even some Etruscan tombs—either some sort of medieval gruel or else something innovatively refined, which luckily is where this menu goes. Many of the offerings are uniquely Sienese, as in *pici alla lepre* (thick spaghetti in hare sauce), *sella di cinghiale* (saddle of wild boar braised in Chianti), or a breast of guinea fowl (*faraona*) roasted with balsamic vinegar. Such meals are well paired with vegetables, often caramelized onions or crisp roasted potatoes with herbs. Service is outstanding, and as befits one of

If the Disney empire were to set up shop in Tuscany, it would have some ready made stage sets near Siena. **Monteriggioni,** 14km (8 1/2 miles) northwest of Siena along the SS2, is one of the most perfectly preserved fortified villages in all of Italy. The town was once a Sienese outpost, begun in 1213, where soldiers patrolled the walls and kept an eye out for Florentine troops from the towers— an image that Dante once likened to the circle of Titans guarding the lowest level of Hell. All 14 of these vantage points have survived, and you can climb up for a view (admission 3.50€, open Apr–Sept, daily 9:30am–1:30pm and 2–7:30pm). A walk from one end of Monteriggioni to the other takes about 5 minutes—as you pass, note the stone houses and garden plots tucked against the walls, which once kept townsfolk nourished during times of siege. The **tourist office** is at Piazza Roma 23, 53035 Monteriggioni (www.monteriggioniturismo.it; © **0577/304810**). Siena city buses 130A and 130R run out to Monteriggioni every hour.

The enchanting **Abbey of San Galgano,** in a grassy meadow on the banks of the River Merse, has a great *Sword in the Stone*-like back story. Galgano, born in Siena in 1148, was pursuing his career as a knight when he had a vision of the archangel Michael, who led him up a steep path to a circular temple outside the village of Montesiepi, where he met the 12 apostles. Moved by the vision, Galgano went off to Montesiepi, drove his sword into a stone to renounce his knighthood, and built a round stone hermitage. After his death in 1182, his simple dwelling was expanded into a spectacular rotunda, with a dome built of 24 alternating rows of brick and stone. This became the center of a community of Cistercian monks who were also great church builders (they designed the cathedral in Siena). The brothers later built a Gothic abbey down the hill, which after the Black Death decimated their community, crumbled into an evocative ruin— you can prowl around it, admiring its high arches, carved capitals, and stone settings for long-vanished stained-glass windows. The saint's tomb is up the hill in the Hermitage; though his body long ago went missing, his sword remains in the stone, with only its handle protruding. The **abbey** (www.prolocochiusdino.it; © **055/756700**) is outside the village of Chiusdino about 40km (25 miles) southwest of Siena via S73. It is open daily, June–August 9am–8pm, March–May and September–October 9am–7pm, and November–February 10am–5pm. Admission is 2€.

the most romantic meals in town, the intimate spaces are beautifully candlelit at night.

Via Franciosa 25–29 (2 streets down from the left flank of the Duomo). www.osteria dadivo.it. © **0577/284381.** Main courses 20€–24€. Wed–Mon noon–2:30pm and 7–10:30pm. Closed 2 weeks Jan–Feb. Bus: A (green, yellow).

La Chiacchera ★★ SIENESE   A hole in the wall is an apt description for this tiny, rustically decorated room tucked halfway along a steep alleyway. The climb can help work up an appetite or work off the large portions of *ribollita* (hearty bread and vegetable soup), *salsicce e fagioli* (sausage and white beans); or *tegamata di maiale* (a Sienese pork casserole). Good weather provides a unique dining experience on the street out in front, where the legs of the tables and chairs have been cut to accommodate the steep slope.

Costa di Sant'Antonio 4 (near San Domenico). www.osterialachiacchera.it. © **0577/ 280631.** Main courses 7€–8€. Daily noon–3pm and 7pm–midnight. Bus: A (red).

La Sosta di Violante ★★ SIENESE   This warm, friendly, rose-hued room is only a 5-minute walk from Piazza del Campo but just far enough off the beaten track to seem like a getaway (*sosta* means rest or break, as in "take a break"). The surroundings and menu attract a mostly neighborhood crowd that has come to count on the kitchen for excellent preparations of *parpadelle, pici,* and other classic Tuscan pastas in rich sauces. Grilled Florentine steaks are another specialty, but so are many unusual vegetarian menu choices, including delicious *fritelle di pecorino* (pecorino cheese fritters) and a cauliflower (*cavolfiore*) soufflé. Any civic-minded Sienese would get this reference to Violante, the Bavarian-born 18th-century duchess who, after the death of her Medici husband from syphilis, became a beneficent governor of Siena and divided the city into its famous present-day *contrade* (districts).

Via di Pantaneta 115. www.lasostadiviolante.it. © **0577/43774.** Main courses 7€–15€. Mon–Sat 12:30–2:30pm and 7:30–10:30pm. Bus: A (pink).

L'Osteria ★★ TUSCAN/GRILL   One of Siena's great culinary treasures is this simple tile-floored, wood-beamed room where straightforward local cuisine is expertly prepared and served at extremely reasonable prices. Truffles occasionally appear in some special preparations, but for most of the year the short menu sticks to the classics—*pici al cinghale* (pasta with wild boar sauce), tripe (*trippa*) stew, and thick steaks, accompanied by *fagioli bianchi* (white beans) and *patate fritte* (fried potatoes). Service can be brusque, but that's just because nightly crowds keep the waiters hopping.

Via de' Rossi 79–81. © **0577/287592.** Main courses 8€–21€. Mon–Sat 12:30–2:30pm and 7:30–10:30pm. Bus: A (red).

Shopping

Siena is famous for its *panforte,* a sweet, dense cake created by city bakers in the Middle Ages and still sold in shops all over town. Made from candied fruit and nuts glued together with honey, it resembles a gloopy fruit cake. Each shop has its own recipe, with the most popular varieties being sweet Panforte Margherita and bitter Panforte Nero. Try a slice at **Drogheria Manganelli,** Via di Città 71–73 (© **0577/280002**), which has made its own *panforte* and soft *ricciarelli* almond cookies since the 19th century.

Authentic Sienese ceramics feature only three colors: black, white, and the reddish-brown "burnt sienna," or *terra di Siena.* **Ceramiche Artistiche Santa Caterina,** with showrooms at Via di Città 74–76 (© **0577/283098**), sells high-quality pieces, courtesy of Maestro Marcello Neri, who trained at Siena's premier art and ceramics institutions, and his son, Fabio.

A Side Trip into the Chianti

For many visitors to Italy, heaven on earth is the 167 sq. km (64 sq. miles) of land between Florence and Siena, known as the Chianti. Tra versing the gentle hillsides on the SR222, the Chiantigiana, is a classic drive, especially the stretch between Castellina in Chianti and Greve. Landscapes are smothered in vineyards and olive groves, punctuated by woodland and peppered with *case coloniche*—stone farmsteads with trademark square dovecotes protruding from the roofs.

First stop for wine lovers is **Radda in Chianti,** 36km (22 miles) north of Siena; the turnoff is just north of Castellina. This important wine center retains its medieval street plan and a bit of its walls. The center of town is the 15th-century **Palazzo del Podestà,** studded with the mayoral coats of arms of past *podestà*. **Porciatti** will give you a taste of traditional salami and cheeses at their *alimentari* on Piazza IV Novembre 1 at the gate into town (www.casaporciatti.it; ✆ **0577/738055**).

Seven kilometers (4⅓ miles) north of Radda on a secondary road is the **Castello di Volpaia ★★** (www.volpaia.com; ✆ **0577/738066**), a Florentine holding that was buffeted by Sienese attacks from the 10th to 16th centuries. The still-impressive central keep is all that remains, but it's surrounded by an evocative 13th-century *borgo* (village) containing the Renaissance La Commenda church. You can tour the winery daily; the tour includes a tasting of the wines and their fantastic olive oil. The central

Tuscan vineyards.

tower has an enoteca for drop-in tastings and sales, plus award-winning (and scrumptious) olive oils and farm-produced white and red vinegars.

Back on the Chiantigiana (SR222), the next town is **Panzano in Chianti,** 12km (7 miles) north of Radda, known for its embroidery and a butcher, **Antica Macelleria Cecchini,** Via XX Luglio 11 (www.dario cecchini.com; ✆ **055/852020**). Dario Cecchini is fast becoming one of the most famous butchers in the world, entertaining visitors with classical music and tastes of his products while perhaps reciting the entirety of Dante's *Inferno* from memory.

Just north of Panzano, the SR222 takes you past the turnoff for Lamole. Along that road you'll find **Villa Vignamaggio** ★★ (www.vignamaggio. com; ✆ **055/854661**), a russet-orange villa surrounded by cypress and elegant gardens where Lisa Gherardini, who grew up to pose for Leonardo da Vinci's "Mona Lisa," was born in 1479. In 1404 the estate's wine was the first red wine to be referred to as "chianti." Book ahead at least a week to tour the cellar and gardens, sample the wines, or even stay overnight in atmosphere-laden rooms (from 180€ for a double).

Greve in Chianti, 8km (5 miles) north of Panzano on the SR222, is the center of the wine trade and the unofficial capital of Chianti. The central **Piazza Matteotti** is a rough triangle surrounded by a mismatched patchwork arcade—each merchant had to build the stretch in front of his own shop. Greve is the host of Chianti's annual September wine fair, and there are, naturally, dozens of wine shops in town. The best is the **Enoteca del Chianti Classico,** Piazzetta Santa Croce 8 (✆ **055/853297**). At Piazza Matteotti 69–71 is another famous butcher, **Macelleria Falorni** (www.falorni.it; ✆ **055/854363**), established in 1700 and still containing a cornucopia of hanging *prosciutti* and dozens of other cured meats, along with a decent wine selection. It's open daily.

The **Castello di Verrazzano** (www.verrazzano.com; ✆ **055/854243** or 055/290684), 6km (4 miles) northwest of Greve, is a significant stop for Americans: the ancestral home of the Verrazzano family, birthplace in 1485 of Giovanni Verrazzano, who discovered New York. The estate has been making wine since at least 1170; free tastings are offered daily at the roadside shop. Their "jewel" is a 100% sangiovese called Sasello, while the Bottiglia Particolare (Particular [Special] Bottle) is a Super Tuscan wine, at 70% sangiovese and 30% cab. Tours of the gardens and cellars run Monday through Friday (book a week or more ahead in high season), and there's a rustic farmhouse inn, Foresteria Casanova, with rooms from 94€ double.

From here it's another 29km (17 miles) to Florence, or 50km (30 miles) back to Siena—allow a little over an hour without stops for the return trip.

MONTEPULCIANO ★★

67km (41 miles) SE of Siena, 124km (77 miles) SE of Florence, 186km (116 miles) N of Rome

Sipping a delicious ruby wine in a friendly hill town is a good reason to trek across the beautiful Tuscan countryside. There are few better places to aim for than Montepulciano, with its medieval alleyways, Renaissance palaces, and famous violet-scented, orange-speckled Vino Nobile di Montepulciano.

Montepulciano is also a good base for exploring other hill towns, especially nearby Pienza and Montalcino, and for making excursions into the Val d'Orcia, that enchanting region of rolling green hills and stream-watered valleys.

Essentials

GETTING THERE

Driving is the best method: From Siena, the most scenic route is south on the SS2 to San Quirico d'Orcia, where you get the SS146 eastbound through Pienza to Montepulciano.

Six TRA-IN **buses** (www.trainspa.it; ℭ **0577/204111**) run daily from Siena (1½ hr.). From Florence, **LFI** (ℭ **0578/31174**) buses run three times daily (none on Sun) to Bettolle, where you transfer for the bus to Montepulciano (2¼ hr. total).

GETTING AROUND

Montepulciano's Corso is very steep indeed. If you are unfit, or suffer from health problems, take the bus. Little orange *pollicini* connect the junction just below the Porta al Prato and Piazza Grande in about 8 minutes. The official point of origin is "the fifth tree on the right above the junction." Tickets cost 1€ each way (buy them on the bus) and run every 20 minutes.

VISITOR INFORMATION

Montepulciano's **tourist office** is in the parking lot just below Porta al Prato (www.prolocomontepulciano.it; ℭ **0578/757341**). It's open Monday–Saturday from 9:30am to 12:30pm and 3 to 6pm (until 8pm in summer); in August it stays open 9:30am to 8pm.

Exploring Montepulciano

It's all uphill from **Porta al Prato,** where the Medici balls above the gate hint at Montepulciano's long association with Florence. The steep climb up the Corso comes with a look at some impressive palaces. At no. 91 is the massive **Palazzo Avignonesi,** with grinning lions' heads, and across the street is the **Palazzo Tarugi** (no. 82). Both are by Vignola, the late Renaissance architect who designed Rome's Villa Giulia. The lower level of the facade of the **Palazzo Bucelli** (no. 73) is embedded with a patchwork of Etruscan reliefs and funerary urns, placed there by a former resident, 18th-century antiquarian scholar Pietro Bucelli, to show off his collection.

At the top of the street, the highest point in a very high town is **Piazza Grande.** You might recognize the 14th-century **Palazzo Comunale** from the 2009 vampire movie *Twilight: New Moon*—it was filmed here, though the story was supposedly set in Volterra. One side of the piazza is taken up by the rambling façade of the never-completed **Cattedrale di Santa Maria Assunta**.

A short and level walk north along Via Ricci brings you to **Piazza San Francesco**, where views extend south to Lago Trasimeno in Umbria and northeast across the golden folds of hills toward Siena.

Cattedrale di Santa Maria Assunta ★ CATHEDRAL   Montepulciano's bare-brick, homely cathedral was erected in 1680 on the site of a much earlier church (only a relatively new 15th-century bell tower was left in place). The plan was to build a landmark worthy of its noble neighbors on Piazza Grande, but the city ran out of funds, and the exterior was never sheathed in marble as planned. Inside is Montepulciano's great work of art, a 1401 gold-hued altarpiece by Taddeo di Bartolo (1363–1422) of "The Assumption of the Virgin with Saints." This is one of the greatest works by Bartolo, one of Siena's post-Black-Death generation of artists; he must have been pleased with it, as he included his self-portrait among the apostles gathered around the tomb of Mary. You can't get too

The steep, winding streets of Montepulciano.

close to the massive triptych soaring above the high altar, which is a shame, because the charm lies in the detail of the many various panels. The main sections show the death of the Virgin, with the apostles by her bedside; her ascension into Heaven, as the apostles survey her empty tomb; and the Virgin's coronation, an extremely popular theme among 14th- and 15th-century Italian artists in which Christ crowns his mother as queen of Heaven. Surrounding these scenes are various adoring saints and, along the bottom, episodes from the life of Christ. One particularly charming vignette shows a child shinnying up a tree to get a better view of Christ entering Jerusalem.

The cathedral's other masterpiece is the remnants of a marble

Montepulciano

Scale: 0 – 100 yds / 0 – 100 m

Map labels:

Sant'Agostino
Palazzo Avignonesi
Palazzo Tarugi
Santa Lucia
Logge del Grano
Via di Gracciano nel Corso
Pal. Cocconi
Palazzo Bucelli
San Francesco
Via d. Poggiolo
Palazzo Burati-Bellarmino
Porta delle Grassi
Palazzo Ricci
Palazzo Cervini
Palazzo Venturi
Porta Gozzano
Via Voltaia nel Corso
Palazzo d. Capitano
Via Ricci
Palazzo Comunale
Piazza Grande
Palazzo Grugni
Via di San Biagio
Via di Collazzi
Via d. Fortezza
Duomo
Gesù
Via della Circonvallazione
Teatro Poliziano
Via di Oriolo
Poliziano's House
Via dell'Opio nel Corso
Fortezza
Porta delle Farine
Via Poliziano
Santa Maria dei Servi

ATTRACTIONS
Cattedrale di Santa Maria 7
Contucci 8
Gattavecchi 12
Palazzo Comunale 5
Palazzo Tarugi 3
Tempio di San Biagio 9

HOTELS
Mueble il Riccio 4
Osteria del Borgo 6
Vicolo dell'Oste 1

RESTAURANTS
Acquacheta 11
Caffè Poliziano 2
Fattoria Pulcino 13
Osteria del Conte 10

sculptural group by the Florentine architect and sculptor Michelozzo (1396–1472), crafted between 1427 and 1436 for the tomb of papal secretary Bartolomeo Aragazzi. You'll see Michelozzo's light touch throughout Tuscany: he redesigned the Palazzo Vecchio and designed the Palazzo Medici in Florence; and sculpted the statue of St. John over the door of Florence's Duomo. Unfortunately you'll have to walk around the church to see his work here, as the tomb was disassembled in the 17th century (some pieces were stolen and eventually ended up in the Victoria and Albert Museum London). Look for a reclining, hooded statue of the deceased to the right of the central entrance door, and figures of fortitude and justice standing on either side of the high altar; leaning against a nearby pillar is the figure of St. Bartholomew, after whom Aragazzi was named.

Piazza Grande. No phone. Daily 9am–12:30pm and 3:15–7pm. Free admission.

Tempio di San Biagio ★ CHURCH This lovely church just outside the town walls, completed in 1534, is the masterwork of Antonio da Sangallo the Elder. Best known for fortresses and other military defenses, here Sangallo he broke out of the mold to create a beautiful travertine church on the plan of a Greek cross, with the four arms of equal length radiating from a central dome. Since the church is in open countryside with no other buildings nearby, it's easy to admire its classical unity. The interior is as refined as the exterior but, like many a great beauty, a bit dull at close inspection.

Via di San Biagio. No phone. Daily 9am–12:30pm and 3:30–7:30pm. Free admission.

Where to Stay

Meuble il Riccio ★★   This atmospheric 800-year-old palazzo near Piazza Grande, passed down through the innkeeper's family, really lays on the charm—in the arcaded, mosaic-tiled courtyard, the vast antiques-and-art-filled salon and breakfast room, the homey lounge, or the rooftop terrace overlooking the checkerboard landscapes of the Valdichiana far below the town. Some rooms do justice to the surroundings with palatial expanses and terraces of their own, while others are simpler and viewless but not without character. In all rooms look for the replicas of carved wooden *ricci,* hedgehogs, that once emblazoned the 13th-century façade. Ivana and Giorgio Caroti are on hand to dispense advice and make restaurant reservations, and they serve delicious homemade pastries at breakfast and drinks throughout the day.

Via di Tolosa 21. www.ilriccio.net. ☏ **0578/757713.** 10 units. 100€–110€ double. Rates include buffet breakfast. **Amenities:** Bar; Wi-Fi (free).

Osteria del Borgo ★   Wood beams and exposed brickwork supply these bright, good-sized rooms and apartments with plenty of rustic Tuscan charm, while the comfortably stylish furnishings and modern baths lend them a chic flair. The hilltop perch is just off one side of Piazza Grande, so views from some rooms and the shared courtyard are expansive. A homey restaurant downstairs serves Tuscan specialties and spills out to a nice terrace in good weather.

Via Ricci. www.osteriadelborgo.it. ☏ **0578/716799.** 5 units. 90€–120€ double. Rates include buffet breakfast. Free parking. **Amenities:** Restaurant; Wi-Fi (free).

Vicolo dell'Oste ★★   Tuscan chic prevails in this house on a narrow lane off the Corso, just below the top of the hill and Piazza Grande. Wood-beamed ceilings set off streamlined contemporary furnishings, while such deluxe touches as large Jacuzzis are tucked into the corners of some rooms. Practical amenities include streamlined kitchens in several rooms. While there are no communal spaces, breakfast is served in a nearby café, and innkeepers Giuseppe and Luisa seem to always be near at hand to take care of your needs.

Via delle Oste. www.vicolodelloste.it. ☏ **0578/758393.** 5 units. 95€–100€ double. Rates include breakfast. **Amenities:** Wi-Fi (free).

Where to Eat

With a local wine that pairs especially well with hearty sauces and red meat, it's no accident that food in Montepulciano is typically Tuscan,

Wine Tasting in Montepulciano

The **Gattavecchi** *cantine* (wineries), Via di Collazzi 74 (www.gattavecchi.it; ✆ 0578/757110), burrow under Santa Maria dei Servi. Its cellars have been in use since before 1200, originally by the friars of the adjacent church. Older still is the tiny room at the bottom chiseled from the rock; it was probably an Etruscan tomb. Gattavecchi's Vino Nobile is top-notch, as is the 100% Sangiovese Parceto. Tasting is free. **Contucci** (www.contucci.it; ✆ 0578/757006), in the 11th-century cellars of a historic palace in Piazza Grande, has a fine range of Vino Nobile wines grown on four soil types, all between the magical numbers of 200m (656 ft.) and 400m (1,312 ft.) altitude. According to winemaker Adamo Pallecchi, this is crucial. The cantina is open for free tasting every day of the year. Opposite the Duomo, the **Palazzo del Capitano del Popolo** is another stop for wine buffs. Turn right from the corridor for the **Consorzio del Vino Nobile di Montepulciano** (www.consorziovinonobile.it; ✆ 0578/757812; 11:30am–1:30pm and 2–6pm Mon–Fri, 2–6pm Sat from week after Easter–Oct), which offers a rotating menu of tastings for a small fee. Local wineries without a shop in town also sell by the bottle here, and if you're heading into the country for some wine touring, staff can provide maps and ideas. Across the corridor, the **Strada del Vino Nobile** office (www.stradavinonobile.it; ✆ 0578/717484) can help you arrange a local wine itinerary.

relying heavily on game, beef from the Valdichiana, and thick pastas like hand-rolled *pici* topped with rich sauces. Aside from the town's many tasting rooms, you can also quaff the local wines and taste local salamis and cheeses in an atmospheric old cafe, the late-19th-century **Poliziano,** on the Corso (number 27, ✆ 0578/758615).

Acquacheta ★★★ SOUTHERN TUSCAN/GRILL   If you're craving steak, you'll want to include a meal in this cellar eatery, where the emphasis is on local products. In a rustic dining room, long and narrow, seating is at shared tables, where meat is sold by weight and brought to your table by a cleaver-wielding chef for your approval before it goes onto the grill. A choice of pastas and sauces (mix and match as you please) are also available, as are hearty salads. Please don't ask for a separate wine glass—drinking water and wine from the same glass is an age-old tradition in simple eateries in these parts.

Via del Teatro 22 (down right side of Palazzo Contucci from Piazza Grande). www.acquacheta.eu. ✆ 0578/717086. Reservations essential. Main courses 7€–18€. Wed–Mon noon–3pm and 7:30–10:30pm. Closed mid-Jan to mid-Mar.

Fattoria Pulcino★ SOUTHERN TUSCAN/GRILL   Several of the larger wineries around Montepulciano have rustic dining rooms, and this is one of the most pleasant of them. There's a totally satisfying selection of grilled meats straight from the farm, prepared to order, as well as homemade pastas, all served up with mesmerizing views of the rolling countryside and Montepulciano crowning its hilltop. *Pici di Montepulciano,* the

local, thick, hand-rolled spaghetti, is topped with rich sauces, and anything you order is to be washed down with the estate's Vino Nobile.
Via SS146, 3km/2 miles SE of Montepulciano. ✆ **339/1403162.** www.pulcinoristo rante.com. Main courses 8€–16€. Daily noon–10pm. Shorter hours in winter.

Osteria del Conte★SOUTHERN TUSCAN   A trek to the top of town is well rewarded with a delicious meal in this simple room overseen by a mother-and-son team who are devoted to home cooking and warm hospitality. You can put yourself in their hands with a set menu, which includes several local specialties and wine, or choose from a nice a la carte selection—the *pici all'aglione* (handmade spaghetti with garlic sauce) is a memorable first course, and most of the meats are grilled to order.
Via di San Donato 19. www.osteriadelconte.it. ✆ **0578/756062.** Main courses 9€–14€. Thurs–Tues 12:30–2:30pm and 7:30–9:30pm.

Side Trips from Montepulciano

PIENZA ★★
14km (9 miles) west of Montepulciano, 55km (34 miles) southeast of Siena

A 20-minute drive west of Montepulciano on the SS146, this lovely Tuscan hilltown sits perched above the Val d'Orcia, with glorious landscapes of vineyards and wheat fields in every direction; its narrow side streets are lined with shops selling the town's famous pecorino (sheep's milk cheeses) and honey. But Pienza has a unique noble heritage, dating to the mid-15th century, when it was rebuilt by humanist Pope Pius II and architect Bernardo Rossellino to be the ideal Renaissance town. Piazzas and palaces, spaces and perspectives, were to be designed to reflect Renaissance ideals of rationality and humanism, and to instill the populace with notions of peace and harmony. Rossellino's budget was 10,000 florins and he spent 50,000, but Pius was so pleased with the transformation of his birthplace that he scrapped the old name of Corsignano and named the town after himself. Sadly, Pius died soon thereafter, and most of his plans for palaces, churches, piazzas and a grid of well-ordered streets were never realized.

Park outside the town walls and follow the main street, **Corso Rossellino,** to the center of town: the splendid **Piazza Pio II**, the focal point of Pius's town-planning dream and a Renaissance stage set of architectural perfection. Here you'll find the two main buildings of Pius' ambitious dream: A church (the **Duomo)** and the pope's own residence (**Palazzo Piccolomini**). Pienza's **tourist office** is also here, inside the Palazzo Vescovile on Piazza Pio II, Corso Rossellino 30, 53026 Pienza (www.pienza.info; ✆ **0578/749905;** open Wed–Mon 10am–1pm and 3–6pm from Mid-March to Oct, weekends only the rest of the year).

Duomo ★ CATHEDRAL   The light-drenched domus vitrea (literally "a house of glass") fulfilled Pius' notion that the structure should symbolize enlightenment. The exterior represents Renaissance ideals of unity

Cheese in Pienza.

with a façade of three blind arches, atop which the pope rather immodestly placed his coat of arms. The light-drenched interior was in part inspired by the pope's travels in Germany, where he admired the local style of church architecture, hall churches lit by tall windows. For all of its perfection, the structure showed signs of a serious flaw almost as soon as it was completed—the hillside on which it is built is unstable, and the foundations are slowly shifting (as you walk toward the rear, you'll notice the floor slightly slopes).

Piazza Pio II. No phone. Free admission. Daily 7am–1pm and 2:30–7pm.

Palazzo Piccolomini ★ HISTORIC SITE   Pope Pius, of course, had to have a residence worthy of his lofty status, and his dining room, bedroom, library, and other chambers are appropriately regal, and rather stuffy. The pope's descendants lived here until 1968, and nothing in the cavernous salons is very exciting (the dry-as-dust audio guide doesn't help, either). The bright spot is the palazzo's hanging garden and triple-decked loggia, reached through the painted courtyard; you can linger a while to take in the incredible views south over the Val d'Orcia. With a setting like this it's easy to see why Pius II, born Silvio Piccolomini into an impoverished branch of a noble Sienese family, wanted to return to this humble town of his birth after an event-filled life as a humanist scholar, itinerant diplomat, and pope from 1458 to 1464.

Piazza Pio II. © **0578/74392.** www.palazzopiccolominipienza.it. Admission 7€ adults, 5€ students and children 6–17, free for children under 5. Mid-Mar to mid-Oct Tues–Sun 10am–6:30pm; mid-Oct to mid Mar Tues–Sun 10am–4:30pm.

Where to Eat

Trattoria Latte di Luna ★   Just about everyone who's in Pienza at mealtimes seems to squeeze through the narrow door of this family-run trattoria, where home-cooked meals are prepared by mom in the kitchen and served by dad and daughter in the yellow stucco dining room. *Pici all'aglione* (with spicy tomato-and-garlic sauce) or *zuppa di pane* (a local variant on *ribollita*, with more cabbage) are stellar starters, followed by wild boar or suckling pig in season or grilled steaks any time. The dessert of choice is the house-made *semifreddi* flavored with walnuts and seasonal fruits and berries.

Corso Rossellino, next to Porta al Ciglio. ℰ **0578/748606.** Main courses 7–16€. Wed–Mon 12:15–2:15pm and 7:15–9:15pm.

MONTALCINO ★★

23km (14 miles) west of Pienza; 28km (17 miles) west of Montepulicano; 40km (25 miles) south of Siena

Montalcino presents a warm welcome on the approach from the Ombrone River valley below, its medieval houses clinging higglety-pigglety to precipitous alleys beneath prickly towers. Of course, if you know wine, you're aware that scenery is not the town's real calling card—that's Brunello di Montalcino, one of the world's most acclaimed reds, of which the town produces more than 3.5 million bottles a year, along with 3 million of its lighter-weight cousin Rosso di Montalcino.

For many centuries, however, Montalcino wasn't concerned with wine at all, but with its shifting allegiances to the ever-battling rival powers of Florence and Siena. The little town was once known as the "Republic of Siena at Montalcino" for housing Sienese refugees after Florence conquered Siena in 1555 (see **La Fortezza**, below). Montalcino soon fell to Florence, however, and more or less languished until the 1960s, when the world began waking up to the fact that the local sangiovese grosso grapes—known as "Brunello" to the locals—yielded a wine to be reckoned with. Today Montalcino is flourishing, mostly because of the wine trade. As an added bonus, two fine medieval abbeys can be visited in the countryside nearby.

The **tourist office** is at Costa del Municipio, www.prolocomontalcino.it; ℰ **0577/849331;** 10am–1pm and 2–5:40pm daily, closed Mon Nov–Mar.

La Fortezza ★ HISTORIC SITE   Built in 1361, this castle's moment arrived when the Sienese holed up here for 4 years after their city's final defeat by Florence in 1555 (ironically, the fortress had only recently been expanded and strengthened by Florence's Medici dukes). You can wander round the pentagonal walls and scale a ladder to the highest turret for a view across hills and dales all the way to Siena—but do so before you sample wine in the on-premise enoteca, perhaps the only tasting room in the world with ramparts.

Piazzale Fortezza. www.enotecalafortezza.it. ℰ **0577 849211.** Admission on cumulative ticket with Museo di Montalcino, or 4€, 2€ children 6–17. Nov–Mar daily 10am–6pm, Apr–Oct daily 9am–8pm.

Museo di Montalcino ★ ART MUSEUM   Coming upon this small collection is a bit of a treat, as the cloisters of the church of Sant'Agostino house a trove of masterpieces that you wouldn't expect to find in such a small town. The painting galleries are devoted largely to Sienese artists, whose cold, Byzantine influences are not always immediately appealing. However, many of these artists were bold innovators of their times, in the years after the plague of 1348 killed more than half the population of Europe. The Virgin Mary, the favorite subject of early Renaissance painters, shows up in works of Bartolo di Fredi and Luca Tomme; Fredi's multi-panel painting of "The Coronation of Mary" is considered to be his masterpiece. The "Madonna dell'Unita (Madonna of Humility)," by Sano di Pietro (1406–1481), was quite radical in its time, showing Mary kneeling on a cushion rather than seated on her traditional throne. Girolano di Benvenuto (1470–1524) depicts the apostle Thomas witnessing the Virgin's empty, flower-filled tomb as she ascends to Heaven and throws him her belt. Andrea della Robbia's terracotta statue of St. Sebastian, who looks rather boyish and calm considering he's about to be shot full of arrows, brings the collection into the full flowering of the Renaissance in the late 15th century. A corny life-size model of an Etruscan warrior is the crowd-pleaser in the archaeological collection, displaying relics of locals who have inhabited the region, as you'll learn, for more than 200,000 years.

Via Ricasoli 31. ✆ **0577/846014**. Admission on cumulative ticket with Fortezza, or 4.50€, children 3€. Tues–Sun 10am–1pm and 2–5:40pm.

Abbazia di Sant'Antimo ★★★ RELIGIOUS SITE

This exquisite Romanesque abbey of pale yellow stone nestles serenely in a valley amidst vines and silvery olive groves at the foot of the village of Castelnuovo dell'Abate, 9km (6 miles) south of Montalcino. Legend has it that the first stone here was laid on the order of Charlemagne in A.D. 781, after an angel cured his plague-stricken entourage on a journey from Rome. While that story is debatable, the monastery does date to the 8th century and may have once housed the relics of namesake Saint Anthimus, an early Christian priest. Near the entrance, on one side of the campanile, is a charming medieval relief of the Madonna and Child, and carvings of mythological animals and geometric designs surround the doors. Inside the columned interior, the elaborate

A monk at Abbazia di Sant'Antimo.

carving continues; look on the right side for an intricate depiction of Daniel in the lion's den. In the chapel, 15th-century frescoes by Giovanni di Asciano show scenes from the Life of St. Benedict, rich in earthy details (one scene features two blatantly amorous pigs). The French monks who have inhabited the abbey since 1992 fill Sant'Antimo with their haunting Gregorian chant during six daily prayer services, open to the public, usually at 7am, 9am, 11am, 12:45pm, 2:45pm, 7pm, and 8:30pm (9pm in the summer). A well-marked cross-country hiking trail to the monastery from Montalcino takes about 2 hours. For a quicker return, ask for a bus timetable at Montalcino's tourist office.

Via Della Badia di Sant'Antimo, Castelnuovo dell'Abate. www.antimo.it. © **0577–835659.** Free admission. Open Mon–Sat 10:30am–12:30pm and 3–6:30pm, Sun 9:15am–12:45pm and 3–6pm.

Monte Oliveto Maggiore ★★★ RELIGIOUS SITE The most famous of Tuscany's rural monasteries is set in the scarred hills of the Crete Senesi, 22km (13 miles) northeast of Montalcino. Founded in 1313 by a group of wealthy Sienese businessmen who wanted to devote themselves to the contemplative life, the Olivetan order built this red-brick monastic complex in the early 15th century. Lovely as it is, what draws most visitors today is one of the masterpieces of High Renaissance narrative painting: a 36-scene fresco cycle by Luca Signorelli and Sodoma illustrating the Life of St. Benedict. Signorelli started the job in 1497, finishing nine scenes before skipping town to work on Orvieto's Duomo, where he created his masterpiece, a Last Judgment (see page 263). Antonio Bazzi, who arrived in 1505 and finished the cycle by 1508, is better known as "Il Sodoma" (probably a reference to his predilection for young men, although he was married at least three times and may have some 30 children). Look for a self-portrait of Sodoma in scene 3—he's the richly dressed fellow with flowing black hair, accompanied by two pet badgers, a chicken, and a tamed raven. To follow the cycle's narrative, start in the back lefthand corner as you enter, with a scene of the young Benedict, astride a spirited white horse, leaving his parents' home to study in Rome. The scenes are especially appealing because of their precise details of medieval life: check out the construction crews in scene 11, or the harlots smuggled into the monastery in scene 19 (allegedly, the abbot made Sodoma add clothing to the nudes he'd first painted). Also inside the church are gorgeous choir stalls crafted in intarsia in 1505 by the monk Giovanni da Verona, showing city scenes with remarkably detailed perspective.

SP 451, Strada di Monte Oliveto. www.monteolivetomaggiore.it. © **0577–707611.** Free admission. Daily 9:15am–noon and 3:15–6pm daily (until 5pm in winter).

Where to Eat

Fiaschetteria Italiana ★★ Montalcino's most popular drinking spot, in the center of town on Piazza del Popolo, was founded in 1888 by Ferrucci Biondi Santi, a pioneer in the development of Brunello. He

Sampling the Vino

Brunello di Montalcino is one of Italy's mightiest reds, a brawny wine that can hold its own with the rarest *bistecca alla fiorentina*. It's also the perfect accompaniment to game, pungent mushroom sauces, and aged cheeses. Brunello exudes the smell of mossy, damp earth and musky berries; it tastes of dark, sweet fruits and dry vanilla, and as the deep ruby liquid mellows to garnet, the wine takes on its characteristic complex and slightly tannic aspect.

Although Montalcino has produced wine for centuries, its flagship Brunello is a recent development, born out of late 19th-century sangiovese experiments. Most Brunellos are drinkable after about 4 to 5 years in the bottle, while the complex ones are best after 10 years or so

(few last beyond 30 years). Montalcino's wine consortium, **Consorzio del Vino Brunello di Montalcino** (www.consorzio brunellodimontalcino.it; © **0577-848246**) is at Piazza Cavour 8, where staff members can provide information on the local wines and steer you to vineyards that are open to the public. For a full day of winery visits without worrying about driving, you can board the **Brunello Wine Bus** (www.lecameredi-bacco.com; © **0577/846021**), which operates from mid-June to November. The bus leaves Montalcino at 9am on Tuesday, Thursday, and Saturday for a trip to six or so renowned wineries, returning at 8pm. The cost is 25€ a person, plus additional tasting fees.

modeled his establishment on Caffe Florian in Venice, which is why locals refer to the Art Deco establishment with red velvet sofas and marble-top tables as "The Florian." The square out front may not be as grand as the Piazza San Marco but it's certainly picturesque in its own way. Prince Charles is among the famous patrons who have quaffed the excellent Brunellos and other wines offered here. Snacks and light meals are available, and the coffee, almost as treasured as the wines, is hands-down the best for miles around.

Piazza del Popolo 6. www.caffefiaschetteriaitaliana.com. © **0577/849-043.** Main courses 8€–12€. Daily 7:30am–11pm, closed Thurs Nov–Mar.

AREZZO

53km (32 miles) NE of Montepulicano

This lively little city on the eastern flanks of the Valdichiana is not nearly as well known or as often visited as its more famous Tuscan neighbors, but this doesn't mean that Arezzo doesn't have a lot to show off. Within a fairly unremarkable 20th-century perimeter (much of it built atop the rubble left by Allied bombings in World War II), you'll find an enticing medieval city of cobbled streets climbing to the charmingly lopsided Piazza Grande. An elegant loggia designed by native son Giorgio Vasari (author of the gossipy *Lives of the Artists*) anchors one side of the piazza, while the rest of the space seems to be rather casually draped across the slope, with slanting cobblestones and an irregular shape. The Duomo, seeming a bit forlorn, crowns the hilltop, while next it to the green expanse of the Parco del Prato, with airy views of the countryside, surrounds a ruined, 16th-century fortress.

Arezzo's rich cultural life has left it with a number of art-filled churches. Famous natives of Arezzo include not only Vasari but Piero della Francesca, from nearby Sansepolcro, the poet Petrarch (1304–74), and actor and director Roberto Benigni, who filmed parts of the 1999 Oscar-winning *La Vita è Bella* (*Life Is Beautiful*) here.

Arezzo is just off the A1 autostrada, putting it within fairly easy reach of Montepulciano by car; there's also bus service (**LFI,** www.lfi.it; ✆ **0578/324294**) from Montepulciano with a change in Sinalunga, or you can take the bus to Chiusa and then a train to Arezzo, as Arezzo is on a main north-south train line. There are several **tourist information offices** (www.arezzoturismo.it) in the center: At Piazza della Repubblica 28, ✆ **0575/377-678;** Palazzo Communale, Piazza Libertà 1, ✆ **0575/401-945;** San Sebastiano Church, Via Ricasoli, ✆ **0575/403-574;** and inside the Logge Vasari, Piazza Grande 13, ✆ **0575/182-4358.**

Basilica di San Francesco ★★★ CHURCH   The timed-entry admission only lets you spend about 25 minutes in front of Piero della Francesca's fresco of the "Legend of the True Cross," but that is reason enough to come to Arezzo. One of the greatest artists of the Renaissance painted one of the world's greatest fresco cycles, in a league with the Sistine Chapel, between 1452 and 1466. The 10 panels are remarkable for their grace, narrative detail, compositional precision, perfect perspective, depth of humanity, and dramatic light effects—"the most perfect morning light in all Renaissance painting," wrote art historian Kenneth Clark. The full religious significance of the story may escape you, but with stalwart knights and fair ladies, the scenes seem like a medieval romance. The beauty is in the details: heaving bosoms, pouty lips, and dreamy eyes, along with some wonderful ancient and medieval finery. The artist seems unable to render a human face without adding an aesthetic humanity that calls out to us from the plaster. You may have seen these frescoes in the film *The English Patient,* in a scene in which Kip hoists Hana past the frescoes by means of ropes and pulleys; we see her expressions of delight and

"Legend of the True Cross," by Piero della Francesca, in Arezzo.

wonder as she comes face to face with Piero's colorful ladies and gents. You'll feel the same, even when earthbound and jostling for a good look with your co-viewers.

Piazza San Francesco. www.pierodellafrancesca.it. © 0575/352727. Church: Mon–Sat 8:30am–noon and 2:30–6:30pm, Sun 9:45–10:45am and 1–5pm. Admission free. Piero cycle open Mon–Fri 9am–6:30pm, Sat 9am–5:30pm, Sun 1–5:30pm, admission only with timed-entry tickets (30 min), reservations required by phone, website, or in person. Piero tickets 8€, 5€ students and children under 17.

Casa di Vasari (House of Vasari) ★★ HISTORIC HOUSE

Giorgio Vasari was born in Arezzo in 1511, just as the Renaissance was flowering all around him. Though he never achieved the greatness of many of the other artists working around him, Vasari helped define the period—and may have even coined the term "Renaissance" for the creative flowering that led Europe out of the Dark Ages. An architect as well an artist—he designed the Palazzo degli Uffizi in Florence (see p. 177)—Vasari is best known for *Lives of the Most Excellent Painters, Sculptors and Architects,* a rather juicy account of the great masters, many of whom Vasari knew personally. He settled down here in his hometown in 1540 and set about frescoing the walls and ceilings of his gracious house with classical themes and portraits. Check out his playful fresco "Virtue, Envy, and Fortune" in which each of the three competing figures appears most prominent depending on where you're standing. In the Room of Celebrities, Vasari painted portraits of Michelangelo, Adrea del Sarto, and other notable contemporaries, surrounding himself with the cultural greats of his day. Vasari's copious correspondence, including 17 letters from Michelangelo, is also sometimes on view. While the original furnishings are no longer in place, part of the beautiful garden remains, and like the rest of the house provides a glimpse at a cultured Renaissance lifestyle.

Via XX Settembre 55. © **0575/409040**. Admission 4€, 2€ students and children under 17. Wed–Mon 9:15am–noon and 3:15–6pm daily (until 5pm in winter).

Cattedrale di Arezzo ★ CATHEDRAL

This big and austere Gothic barn, at the highest point in town, reveals some nice surprises once you step inside the coldly stark interior. First to catch your eye will be the stained-glass windows by Guillaume de Marcillat (1470–1529), a French master, summoned to Rome to work for the popes, who spent the last ten years of his life in Arezzo creating these seven magnificent windows. His colorful scenes include the Calling of St. Matthew, the Baptism of Christ, the Expulsion of Merchants from the Temple, the Adulteress, and the Raising of Lazarus along the right wall; and Saints Silvester and Lucy in the chapel to the left of the apse. (Lucy has a amazingly serene face, considering that she's about to have her eyes gouged out.) Another fine artwork is the robust Mary Magdalene portrayed in a fresco by Piero Della Francesco in an arch near the sacristy door. Take some time to inspect the stone-carved scenes on the tomb of Guido Tarlati, an Aretine bishop who died in 1327—though a this man of the cloth, he seems to have been constantly at war, clad in armor and besieging castles with glimpses of Arezzo in the background. (He was eventually excommunicated.) In the chapel on the left near the entrance, a series of bright and pretty terra-cottas by Andrea della Robbia show the Assumption, the Crucifixion, and a Madonna and Child.

Piazza del Duomo. 𝒞 **0575/23991.** Free admission. Daily 7am–12:30pm and 3–6:30pm.

Santa Maria della Pieve ★★ CHURCH   Most great churches are intended to draw the eye heavenward, but few achieve the effect quite as dramatically and almost playfully as this 12th-century arched façade. Three stacked arcades of beige stone subtly narrow as they rise above a five-arched lower floor and the narrow street below, and above it all rises a bell tower with five rows of windows. The effect is all the more powerful since the church is built on a slope, so the towering façade is often viewed from below.

Inside is an altarpiece by Pietro Lorenzetti, a Sienese artist who would eventually perish when the Black Death devastated the city in 1348. His work here is multi-tiered like the church's façade, with figures getting smaller on each successive layer. The paintings are unusually vivacious for the typically remote Sienese school. It is one of relatively few medieval altarpieces that remains in situ in the church for which it was intended. Some of the remains of the town's patron saint, Donato—a 4th-century bishop of Arezzo—are here, too, in a beautiful gold reliquary.

Corso Italia 7. 𝒞 **0575/22629**. Free admission. May–Sept daily 8am–7pm, Oct–Apr daily 8am–noon and 3–6pm.

Where to Eat

In all but the worst weather, Aretines turn out for the evening *passeggiata*. Two prime spots to sit on a terrace and enjoy a pre-dinner glass of wine or aperitif while watching the comings and goings are **Caffe dei Costanti** in Piazza San Francesco (𝒞 **0575/1824075**) and **Caffe Vasari** (𝒞 **0575/21945**) under the Loggia overlooking Piazza Grande, a good place to perch even in the rain.

Antica Osteria l'Agania ★ TUSCAN   On any given night half the town seems to be packing into these two floors of plain, brightly lit dining rooms, yet the waitstaff never seems daunted by the din or the crowds. All of the pastas are homemade from organic ingredients (five types are available, topped with a choice of five sauces), produce is market fresh, and the meats are from local farms. Daily specials usually include such local favorites as *trippa* (tripe) and *grifi e polenta* (chunks of veal stomach in polenta), but lighter fare is almost always available, too, and specials often include eggs topped with fresh asparagus or *tartufo* (dried truffles), especially tasty when accompanied with a Pinot Grigot. The house wine is excellent, and very inexpensive, and the house grappa puts the perfect finish on a meal.

Via Mazzini 10. www.agania.com. ✆ **0575/295381.** Main courses 7€–9€. Tues–Sun 12:30–2:30pm and 7:30–10:30pm.

CORTONA

34km (22 miles) S of Arezzo; 31km (19 miles) NE of Montepulciano

Draped across a green mountainside above terraced olive groves, austere-looking Cortona is a steep medieval city, where cut-stone staircases take the place of many streets. In recent years, the book and film *Under the Tuscan Sun* have brought waves of appreciative fans to town, but Cortona has survived the onslaught. The somber streets and stage-set piazzas are a bit more crowded in summer than they once were, but the town's appeal—including some significant art treasures, and romantic misty views over the wide Valdichiana—is as strong as ever.

Note that if you arrive by **train**, the Camucia/Cortona train station (✆ **0575/603018**), is 5km (3 miles) below town in the workaday town of Camucia, where many services are located as well. **LFI buses** run from here up to Cortona, but not as frequently as you'll wish—only once an hour at some periods during the day. You can buy your ticket on the bus, 1.60€. In historic Cortona, you'll find a **tourist office** at Piazza Signorelli 9, in the courtyard beyond the Museo dell'Accademia Etrusca ticket office (www.cortonaweb.net; ✆ **0575/637223**).

Via Nazionale, known as the **Rugapiana** ("flat street," since it's the only one in town that even comes close to fitting that description) runs east-west through the medieval town to **Piazza della Repubblica,** presided over by a stern city hall loaded with towers, a stone staircase, and wooden balconies. On the northern corner the square opens into **Piazza Signorelli**, a lovely expanse named for the town's famous Renaissance artist, Luca Signorelli (1445-1523). This piazza was once the headquarters of Cortona's Florentine governors, whose coats of arms adorn the **Casali Palace** (now home to the excellent Etruscan museum, see below). From here, streets lead down to the **Piazza del Duomo** and a treasure trove of art in the **Museo Diosceano** (see below). Other street climb steeply uphill from Piazza Signorelli to the **Basilica di**

Santa Margharita and, even higher, the hilltop **Medici Fortress**. You can, however, stay on level ground—as many strollers choose to do—and walk east along Via Nazionale to **Piazza Garibaldi**. This airy balcony at the edge of town extends into public gardens where views look south to Lago Trasimeno in Umbria and west across the Valdichiana to Montepulciano.

Basilica di Santa Margherita ★ CHURCH   High above the town, this somber 19th-cenutry church with a red-and-white striped interior would be quite forgettable if it were not for the intriguing story of its patron, Margaret of Cortona (1247–1297), a humble follower of St. Francis. In her late twenties, Margaret—the former mistress of the lord of a castle near Montepulciano—devoted her life to fasting and caring for the sick and poor, establishing a hospital and order of nursing sisters. The 13th-century crucifix through which she carried on a prayer dialogue with God hangs in the church, and her embalmed body—to which the intervening centuries have not been terribly kind—lies in full view in a lavish 14th-century Gothic tomb above the main altar.

Piazza Santa Margherita. ✆ **0575/603116**. Free admission. Apr–Oct daily 8–noon and 3–7; Nov–Mar 9–noon and 3–6.

Church of San Francesco ★ CHURCH   This rather simple Romanesque church with its wood-raftered ceiling is the second Franciscan church ever built (the first, in Assisi, was begun around 1228, while this one dates to 1245). This church contains the tomb of Brother Elias of Cortona, who administered the Franciscan Order after Francis' death in 1226. It also houses three precious relics of St. Francis himself—his tunic, his manuscript of the New Testament, and a cushion he often used. On the high altar is the Reliquary of the Holy Cross, an ornate 10th-century ivory tablet containing a fragment of Christ's cross, presented to Elias by the Byzantine Emperor in 1244. The artist Luca Signorelli, who died in Cortona in 1523, is believed to be buried in the crypt.

Via Berrettini. ✆ **0575/603205**. Free admission. Daily 9am–5:30pm.

Fortezza di Girifalco ★ HISTORIC SITE   It's all uphill to Cortona's rugged defenses, built in 1556 on the orders of Duke Cosimo di Medici (from the days when Cortona was a prosperous art city under Medici rule). The torturous stepped ascent is enlivened by 15 modern mosaics depicting the Stations of the Cross, by the Futurist artist Gino Severini (1883–1966), a Cortona native. By the second time Christ falls, you'll feel like doing the same, though you can pause for a restorative drink at the bar by the Basilica Santa Margherita (see above). The views from the four surviving bastions reward the climb, extending all the way across the Valdichiana to Montepulciano, south into Umbria toward Lago Trasimeno, and north toward Arezzo and the colossal Monte Amiata.

Viale Raimondo Bistacci. ✆ **0575/637235**. Admission 3€. Hours vary but usually Sat–Sun 10am–7pm.

Museo dell'Accademia Etrusca ★ MUSEUM   In pre-Roman Italy, Cortona was one of the 12 cities of the Etruscan confederation, and so many artifacts from that era were discovered nearby that an Etruscan Academy was founded in 1727. The collection is now housed in the Palazzo Casali, a 13th-century mansion built for the city's governors. The original upper floors evoke the medieval period, while lower galleries have received a smart contemporary overhaul. The lower galleries tackle the Etruscan and Roman history of Cortona, with lots of gold from excavated tombs and the enigmatic Cortona Tablet, a 200-word document inscribed in bronze. On the sprawling upper floors, the most intriguing object is a one-of-a-kind oil lamp from the late 4th century B.C., decorated with human heads, allegorical figures, and a few virile Pans playing their pipes, all surrounding a leering Gorgon's head on the bottom.

Piazza Signorelli 9. www.cortonamaec.org. ✆ **0575/637235**. Admission 10€, 7€ children under 17, 3€ students. Apr–Oct daily 10am–7pm (closed Mon Nov–Mar).

Museo Dioscoceano ★ MUSEUM   Displayed in the former church of the Gesu, almost every work in this small collection is a masterpiece. Pride of place, however, belongs to Fra' Angelico and Luca Signorelli. The Fra Angelico gem is an altarpiece from 1436 that offers a splendid "Annunciation," graced by his mastery of perspective and command of minute detail—notice the delicate feathers on Gabriel's wings, the angel's precious garment embroidered in gold, the Virgin's elaborate robes, and the carpet of wildflowers (the new Eden) on which her house sits. Luca Signorelli, who was born in Cortona around 1450, is represented by a vividly detailed "Deposition" originally painted for the cathedral in Cortona in 1502. The painter instilled his figure of Christ with so much realism and passion, a legend soon began to circulate that he modeled the figure on his son, who had died of the plague that year. Signorelli's "Communion of the Apostles" (1512) in the same room shows the artist's strong sense of perspective and architectural space; notice Judas in the foreground, hiding the host in his purse—ashamed of his imminent betrayal, he can't swallow it.

Piazza del Duomo. ✆ **0575-4027268**. Admission 5€. Daily 10am–7pm (closed Mon Nov–Mar. 5€.

Where to Eat
Ristorante la Loggetta ★★★ TUSCAN/GRILL   You would probably be happy eating canned spaghetti while savoring the view over the Piazza della Repubblica from this restaurant's namesake loggia—or for that matter, while eating under the enchanting stone-and-brick vaults inside. It's a moot point, however, as the food here is very well done, and nicely, if rather stiffly, served. The kitchen is acclaimed for its preparations of beef from the Valdichiana, often served with a rich, red-wine reduction.

Piazza di Pescharia. www.laloggetta.com. ✆ **0575/95395**. Main courses 9€–28€. Thurs–Tues 12:15–2:30pm and 7:15–9:30pm.

Trattoria Dardano ★ TUSCAN/GRILL   Cortonans come to this simple, single, brightly lit room for meat—roasted here over a charcoal fire, all from local butchers, with the emphasis on *bistecca alla fiorentina* from cattle raised in the valley below town (generally considered to be the best beef in Italy). *Pollo* (chicken), *anatra* (duck), *miale* (pork) and *faraona* (guinea hen) also go onto the flames. The heaping platters are usually preceded by *crostini neri* (little black toasts), with chicken liver, some local salamis, and often *ribollita*, the thick Tuscan soup, all accompanied by local wine.

Via Dardano 24. ✆ **0575/601944.** www.trattoriadardano.com. Main courses 8€–13€. Thurs–Tues noon–2:45pm and 6:40–10pm.

Trattoria la Grotta ★ TUSCAN   For many regulars, any meal in this medieval, brick-vaulted dining room or in the tiny courtyard just off Piazza della Reppubblica must include the house gnocchi, made with a perfect touch and light as a feather. All the pastas are house made, and topped with rich, sweet sauces, while fresh, locally grown zucchini and artichokes are a light antidote for the deftly grilled steaks. The house wine is delicious and very reasonably priced.

Piazza Baldelli 3. ✆ **0575/630271**. trattorialagrotta.it. Main course 8€–18€. Wed–Mon noon–2 and 7:30–11.

SAN GIMIGNANO ★★

42km (26 miles) NW of Siena, 52km (32 miles) SW of Florence

Let's just get the clichés out of the way, shall we?—"Manhattan of the Middle Ages" and "City of Beautiful Towers." There, it's said. As every brochure will tell you, in the 12th and 13th centuries more than 70 towers rose above the tile roofs of San Gimignano, built partly to defend against outside invaders but mostly as command centers and status symbols for San Gimignano's powerful families. A dozen towers remain, and from the distance, as you approach across the rolling countryside, they do indeed appear like skyscrapers and give the town the look of a fantasy kingdom. Once inside the gates, you'll also better understand the reference to Manhattan, because visitors throng the narrow lanes shoulder to shoulder, laying asunder the medieval aura you've come to savor. Almost everyone traveling the hill town circuit makes a stop here, while bus tours pour in from Siena and Florence, and Italians come on weekend outings. If you want to be swept back to the Middle Ages, you're best off visiting during the week in off season, or late on weekday afternoons after the buses have loaded up for the return journey.

Essentials

GETTING THERE   Approximately 30 daily **trains** run between **Siena** and **Poggibonsi** (one about every half hour, trip time: 25–40 min.), from where more than 30 buses make the 25-minute run to San Gimignano

San Gimignano.

Monday through Saturday; only six buses run on Sunday. Buses stop at Porta San Giovanni; you can easily walk into town from here, but shuttle buses are also available to take you up to Piazza della Cisterna (.75€, buy a ticket from a newsstand or on the bus).

SITA (www.sitabus.it; ✆ **055/47821**) and TRAIN SpA (www.train spa.it; ✆ **0577/204111**) codeshare **buses** run at least hourly (fewer on Sun) for most of the day from both **Florence** (50 min.) and **Siena** (45 min.) to Poggibonsi. Many of those buses make an immediate connection with buses to San Gimignano (a further 20–25 min.; see above). From **Siena** there are also 10 direct buses (a 1¼ hr. journey) Monday through Saturday.

Arriving by **car,** take the Poggibonsi Nord exit off the **Florence-Siena** highway or the SS2. San Gimignano is 12km (7½ miles) from Poggibonsi.

VISITOR INFORMATION The **tourist office** is at Piazza Duomo 1 (www.sangimignano.com; ✆ **0577/940008**). It's open daily March through October from 9am to 1pm and 3 to 7pm, and November through February from 9am to 1pm and 2 to 6pm.

Exploring San Gimignano

You'll see the town at its lively best if you come on a Thursday or Saturday morning, when the interlocking **Piazza della Cisterna** and **Piazza del Duomo** fill with market stalls.

Collegiata ★★ CHURCH   San Gimignano's main church is awash in frescoes, including one around the main door: a gruesome "Last Judgment" by Sienese artist Taddeo di Bartolo (1410) in which mean-looking little devils taunt tortured souls. Bartolo allegedly modeled some of the characters after townsfolk who rubbed him the wrong way. Much of the nave is also covered in the flat, two-dimensional frescoes of the Sienese school—in

Outdoor Art

Towers and medieval ambience aside, you'll also be delighted to discover that San Gimignano is awash in frescoes—in churches, public buildings, and even outdoors. In Piazza Pecori, reached through the archway to the left of the Collegiata's facade, is a fresco of the "Annunciation," possibly painted in 1482 by the Florentine Domenico Ghirlandaio.

The door to the right of the tourist office leads into a courtyard of the Palazzo del Commune, where Taddeo di Bartolo's 14th-century "Madonna and Child" is flanked by two works on the theme of justice by Sodoma, including his near-monochrome "St. Ivo"—an appropriate presence, given Ivo's role as patron saint of lawyers.

effect, a comic-strip-like Poor Man's Bible, illustrating familiar stories for the illiterate faithful in simple and straightforward fashion. The left wall is frescoed with 26 scenes from the Old Testament (look for an especially satisfying panel showing the Pharaoh and his army being swallowed by the Red Sea) and the right wall with 22 scenes from the New Testament (a very shifty looking Judas receives his 30 pieces of silver for betraying Christ).

The best frescoes in the church are the two in the tiny Cappella di Santa Fina off the right aisle, where Renaissance master Domenico Ghirlandaio decorated the walls with airy scenes of the life of Fina—a local girl who, though never officially canonized, is one of San Gimignano's patron saints. Little Fina was so devout, when she fell ill with paralysis she refused a bed and lay instead on a board, never complaining even when worms and rats fed off her decaying flesh. As you'll see in one of the panels, St. Gregory appeared and foretold the exact day (his feast day, March 12) on which Fina would die. She expired right on schedule and began working miracles immediately—all the bells in town rang spontaneously at the moment of her death. The second panel shows her funeral and another miracle, in which one of her nurses regained the use of her hand (paralyzed from long hours cradling the sick girl's head) when she laid it in Fina's lifeless hand.

Piazza del Duomo. ⏰ **0577/940316.** Admission 3.50€ adults, 1.50€ ages 6–18. Apr–Oct daily 9:30am–7pm, Nov–Mar Sat 11am–5:30pm

Museo Civico & Torre Grossa ★★ MUSEUM   The late 13th-century home of the city government, Palazzo del Commune, is topped with San Gimignano's tallest tower, the aptly named Torre Grossa (Big Tower), finished in 1311. Your reward for a climb to the top will be views of the cityscape and rolling countryside of the Val d'Elsa, but save your 5€ and enjoy the same outlook for free by making the 5-minute climb uphill from Piazza del Duomo to the ruined Rocca.

Inside the Camera del Podestà (Room of the Mayor) are San Gimignano's most famous frescoes, Memmo di Filippuccio's "Scenes of Married Life." In one scene, a couple takes a bath together, and in the other, the scantily-clad fellow climbs into bed beside his naked wife. The great treasure in the adjoining painting gallery is the "Coppo di Marcovaldo Crucifix," an astonishingly touching work in which a vulnerably human figure of Christ is surrounded by six intricate little scenes of the Crucifixion. The artist Coppo, a Florentine soldier, was captured by the Sienese, who soon realized what a treasure they had in him; his masterpieces show a transition away from flat Byzantine style to more varied texture and three-dimensionality.

St. Fina's head (for her biography, see the Collegiata, above) is in a room to the right, in the "Tabernacle of Santa Fina" (1402), painted with scenes of four of the teenager saint's miracles. Taddeo di Bartolo, who did the terrifying "Last Judgment" in the Collegiata, painted the "Life of St. Gimignano (or Geminianus)" for this room. The town's namesake saint, St. Gimignano was a 5th-century bishop of Modena who allegedly conjured up a dense fog to save his flock from an attack by Attila the Hun. Hearing the news, the little town then known as Silvia changed its name to San Gimignano to buy a bit of insurance. Gimignano cradles his namesake town in his lap, towers and all, figuratively offering it his protection.

Piazza del Duomo. (℃ **0577/990312.** Admission 6€ adults, 5€ ages 6–18 and 65 and over. Apr–Oct daily 9:30am–7pm; Nov–Feb daily 11am–5:30pm; Mar, 10am–5:30pm.

Sant'Agostino ★ CHURCH   An especially appropriate presence in this 13th-century church at the north end of town is St. Sebastian, the "saint who was martyred twice." In 1464, a plague swept through San Gimignano and, when it finally passed, the town hired the Florentine painter Benozzo Gozzoli to paint a thankful scene. (As a stop on trade and pilgrimage routes, the town would be decimated by the plague time and again, giving the townspeople a special affinity for St. Sebastian, who was also prone to repeated bad fortune.) The fresco shows St. Sebastian getting some divine help to fend off the arrows soldiers are shooting into his torso. In real life, the 3rd-century early Christian could not stay out of harm's way. When Sebastian proclaimed his faith, the emperor Diocletian ordered that he be taken to a field and shot full of arrows (for which he has rather cynically been named the patron saint of archers). Sebastian miraculously survived and was nursed back to health. Once back on his feet, he stood on a step and harangued Diocletian as he passed in royal procession, and the emperor had him bludgeoned to death on the spot. Gozzoli also frescoed the choir behind the main altar floor-to-ceiling with 17 scenes from the life of St. Augustine, a worldly well-traveled scholar who, upon having to make the decision to give up his concubine, famously prayed, "Grant me continence and chastity but not yet." The scenes are straightforward (without a great deal of religious symbolism) and rich in landscape and architectural detail.

Piazza Sant'Agostino. (℃ **0577/907012.** Free admission. Daily 7am–noon and 3–7pm (Nov–Apr closes at 6pm, and Jan to mid-Apr closed Mon mornings).

Where to Eat & Stay

San Gimignano's slightly peppery, dry white wine, **Vernaccia di San Gimignano,** is the only DOCG white wine in Tuscany, and it has quite a provenance, too: It's cited in Dante's *Divine Comedy.* A relaxing place to sip a glass or two is **diVinorum**, in former stables with a small terrace at Via degli Innocenti 5 (© 0577–907–192). At the famous **Gelateria di Piazza**, Piazza della Cisterna 4 (www.gelateriadipiazza.com; © 0577–942–244), master gelato maker Sergio offers creative combinations like refreshing Champeigmo, with sparkling wine and pink grapefruit, and *crema di Santa Fina,* made with saffron and pine nuts.

Chiribiri ★ ITALIAN   A tiny vaulted cellar almost next to the walls, Chiribiri seems more serious about what it sends out of the kitchen than many of the more expensive places closer to the center of town do. Ravioli with pumpkin, white beans and sage, beef in Chianti, wild boar stew, and other Tuscan classics are done well and served without fuss. Note: they don't take credit cards.

Piazzetta della Madonna 1. © **0577/941948.** Main courses 8€–12€. Daily 11am–11pm.

Dorandò ★★ TUSCAN   Three stone-walled rooms with brick-vaulted ceilings are the setting for San Gimignano's most elegant and best dining, though there's nothing fussy about the cooking. Ingredients are locally sourced and recipes are decidedly local—beef is done in a sauce of Chianti classic, local pork comes with an apple puree, and *cibrèo,* a rich ragout, comes with chicken livers and giblets scented with ginger and lemon. If you want to include a dinner here on an overnight in San Gimignano, you'll need a reservation.

Vicolo dell'Oro 2. www.ristorantedorando.it. © **0577/941862.** Main courses 20€–24€. Tues–Sun noon–2:30pm and 7–9:30pm (daily Easter–Sept). Closed Dec 10–Jan 31.

Hotel l'Antico Pozzo ★★★   When this 15th-century palazzo was a convent, the namesake "ancient well" served a grim purpose—young novices were dangled over the depths when they resisted *droit de seigneur,* the feudal rights of noblemen to have their way with young women living on their lands. That might not be the most inviting inducement to stay at a hotel, but the present incarnation just may be the best in town, and it's all about taste, elegance, and comfort. Reached by a broad stone staircase (or an elevator if you choose), some of the character-filled rooms are beamed and frescoed, others have nice views of the town and Rocca. All are good-sized and beautifully decorated, with classic furnishings that sometimes include canopied beds, along with fine prints and other appointments. A grassy garden in the rear is an especially welcome treat from the daytime crowds.

Via San Matteo 87. www.anticopozzo.com. © **0577/942014.** 18 units. 90€–170€ double. Rates include breakfast. **Amenities:** Bar; Wi-Fi (free).

La Cisterna ★   Behind the ivy-clad entrance right on the town square, here you'll find rooms that vary considerably in size and outlook—some of the smaller ones overlook a quaint but viewless courtyard, while larger rooms and suites may feature balconies and views that extend for miles. Furnishings throughout are simply and unobtrusively traditional Tuscan, with wrought-iron bedsteads and some flourishes like arches, tile floors, and stone walls to impart a bit of character, although the surroundings—and the service, too—can seem a bit impersonal. The restaurant and terrace out front, along with a view-filled, glassed-in dining room upstairs, serve Tuscan food that is a lot better than you'd expect, given the presence of large tour groups that often pile in for lunch.

Piazza della Cisterna 24. www.hotelcisterna.it. © **0577/940328.** 48 units. 85€–145€ double. Rates include breakfast. **Amenities:** Restaurant, bar, Wi-Fi (free).

VOLTERRA ★★

29km (18 miles) SW of San Gimignano, 50km (31 miles) W of Siena

In the words of the writer D. H. Lawrence, Volterra is "on a towering great bluff that gets all the winds and sees all the world." Volterra seems to rear higher than any other Tuscan town, rising a precipitous 540m (1,772 ft.) above the Valdera valley below. (You'll see the town long before you arrive.) Along its narrow ridge, a warren of medieval alleys fall steeply off the main piazza.

Lawrence came here to study the Etruscans, who took the 9th-century-B.C. town established by the Villanovan culture and, by the 4th century B.C., had turned it into Velathri, one of the largest centers in Etruria's 12-city confederation. Seeing their haunting bronzes and alabaster funerary urns is a compelling reason to venture here—that is, unless you're a fan of Stephanie Meyer's teen vampire trilogy, *Twilight,* in which case you're here to see the home town of the Volturi vampire coven.

Essentials

GETTING THERE   Driving is the easiest way to get here: Volterra is on the SS68 about 30km (19 miles) from the Colle di Val d'Elsa exit on the Florence-Siena highway. From San Gimignano, head southwest on the secondary road to Castel di San Gimignano, where you can pick up the SS68.

From **Siena,** there are 16 daily TRA-IN **buses** (www.trainspa.it) that make the 20- to 30-minute trip to **Colle di Val d'Elsa,** from which there are four daily buses to Volterra (50 min.). From **San Gimignano,** first take a bus to Poggibonsi (20 min.) then link up with those Colle di Val d'Elsa buses to Volterra. From **Florence,** take one of five daily buses (three on Sun) to Colle di Val d'Elsa and transfer there (2½–3 hr. total). Six to 10 **CPT** (www.cpt.pisa.it) buses run to Volterra Monday through Saturday from **Pisa** (change in Pontedera; 2–2½ hr. total).

VISITOR INFORMATION   Volterra's helpful **tourist office,** Piazza dei Priori 19–20, 56048 Volterra (www.volterratur.it; © **0588/87257**), offers both tourist information and free hotel reservations. It's open daily from 9:30am to 1pm and 2 to 6pm.

Exploring Volterra

The most evocative way to enter Volterra is through **Porta all'Arco,** the main 4th-century B.C. gateway to the Etruscan city. Via die Priori leads steeply uphill from there to Volterra's stony medieval heart, the **Piazza dei Priori,** where the Gothic **Palazzo dei Priori** (1208–57) is said to be the first city hall in Tuscany, and the model for Florence's Palazzo Vecchio and many other civic buildings in the region. The squat tower in the eastern corner is festooned with a little pig (*porcellino*), hence its name, **Torre del Porcellino.** Enjoy the view of the square with a coffee or glass of wine and a panino at one of the tables in front of Bar Priori. The modest-looking **Duomo**, behind the piazza, is worth checking out inside for a life-size wood group of the "Deposition from the Cross," carved around 1228 by anonymous Pisan masters and painted in bright colors. With their fluidity and emotional expressiveness the figures look surprisingly contemporary.

Church of San Francesco ★ CHURCH Volterra's 13th-century Franciscan church, just inside the Porta San Francesco, has one overwhelming reason to visit: Halfway up the right aisle is the **Cappella Croce del Giorno**, frescoed with the "Legend of the True Cross" in medieval Technicolor by Cenni di Francesco in 1410. While not nearly as beautifully executed as Piero della Francesca's telling of the same story in the church of San Francesco in Arezzo (see page 260), Cenni's version of this popular medieval tale is quite compelling, especially with his knack for reproducing the dress and architecture of his era. Though the artist worked for some of the most important families in Florence, this is his only remaining signed work and shows a unique style: golden backgrounds, flattened space, and elongated figures with elegant features.

Piazza San Francesco. No phone. Free admission. Daily 8:30am–6:30pm.

Museo Etrusco Guarnacci ★★ MUSEUM Volterra's remarkable collection of Etruscan artifacts is dusty, poorly lit, and devoid of a lot of English labeling. It is nonetheless a joyful celebration of the farmers, seafarers, and miners who flourished between the Tiber and Arno rivers from about 800 B.C. until their assimilation by Rome in the 1st century A.D. (the name "Tuscany" is derived from "Etruscan"). The bulk of the holdings are on the ground floor, with row after row of 600 **Etruscan funerary urns**, most from the 3rd century B.C., but some from as early as the 7th century B.C. Ashes were placed in these caskets, which were topped with elaborately carved lids that show snippets of life from more than 2 millennia ago—finely dressed characters lounging with wine cups to offer to the gods, or horse and carriage rides into the underworld. One of the finest, the **Urna degli Sposi,** is a striking portrait of a husband and wife, both very old, somewhat dour-faced and full of wrinkles, together in death as in life. The Etruscans also crafted bronze sculptures, and one of the finest is a lanky young man with a beguiling smile known as the "Ombra

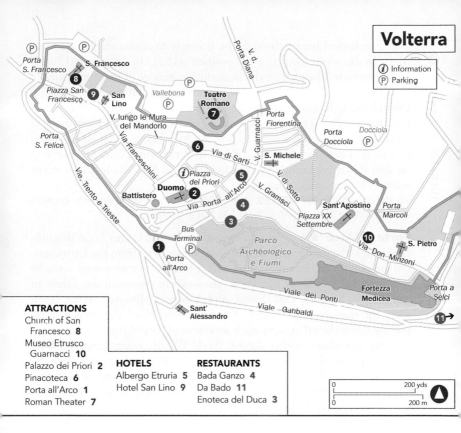

Volterra

(i) Information
(P) Parking

ATTRACTIONS
Church of San
  Francesco **8**
Museo Etrusco
  Guarnacci **10**
Palazzo dei Priori **2**
Pinacoteca **6**
Porta all'Arco **1**
Roman Theater **7**

HOTELS
Albergo Etruria **5**
Hotel San Lino **9**

RESTAURANTS
Bada Ganzo **4**
Da Bado **11**
Enoteca del Duca **3**

0 ————— 200 yds
0 ————— 200 m

della Sera (Shadow of the Evening)"—so called because the elongated shape looks so much like a shadow stretched in evening light.

Via Don Minzoni 15. *(C)* **0588/86347.** Admission by cumulative ticket with Pinacoteca 10€, or 8€. Summer daily 9am–7pm; winter daily 8:30am–1:45pm.

Pinacoteca ★ MUSEUM   While much of Volterra preserves the Etruscan, Roman, and medieval past, the town's worthy painting gallery transports you to the Renaissance with several standout paintings. Room 4 has a remarkably intact 1411 polyptych of the "Madonna with Saints" signed by Taddeo di Bartolo, who traveled throughout Tuscany and left works in Pisa, Montepulciano, and nearby San Gimignano (see p. 263). The fellow in the red cape and beard in the tiny left tondo is the original Santa Claus, St. Nicholas of Bari. In room 11 is "Christ in Glory with Saints" (1492), the last great work of Florentine Domenico Ghirlandaio, one of the Florentine masters of the Renaissance. The figures create a perfectly oval architectural frame for the Flemish-inspired landscape of the background. If you look hard, you can spot a giraffe being led along the road—an exotic animal that had only recently been acquired by the Medici for their menagerie. In Room 12 hangs a remarkably colored "Annunciation" (1491) by Luca Signorelli—note the great rush of feeling as the archangel bursts through the doorway to announce the news to Mary. In the same room is a "Deposition" (1521) by 26-year-old Rosso Fiorentino, a red-headed (and reportedly hot-headed) Florentine painter, who ended up going to France to work at the Chateau Fontainbleau. Considered to be his masterpiece, this altarpiece was originally done for the Duomo. Painted in his odd color palette of flat grays and reds, it unusually portrays this solemn scene of Christ being taken off the cross as a swirl of action, with sashes flapping in the wind, workers scurrying up and down precarious-looking ladders, and the whole tragic event seeming frantic and disorganized.

Via del Sarti 1. ℭ **0588/87580.** Admission by cumulative ticket with Etruscan Museum 10€, or 6€. Daily 9–6:45 (until 1:45 Nov–mid-Mar).

Porta all'Arco ★★ Volterra's greatest landmark, this huge magnificent gate is the only round arch to come down to us from the Etruscans. On the outside are mounted three basalt heads—features worn away by well over 2,000 years of wind and rain—said to represent the Etruscan gods Tinia (Jupiter), Uni (Juno), and Menrva (Minerva). What fascinated the Romans was the arch's keystone, from which they took inspiration for the arches that were such an essential part of their architecture. The gateway almost didn't survive World War II, when retreating German troops decided to blow it up to block the Allied advance through the city. Volterrans dug up the surrounding paving stones and temporarily plugged the opening, convincing the Germans not to destroy a gate that no one could pass through anyway.

Porta all'Arco. No phone. Free admission.

Roman Theater ★ ARCHEOLOGICAL SITE Walk along Via Lungo le Mure, a walkway atop the medieval ramparts, to overlook the impressive remains of Volterra's Roman theater and baths. These are some of the best-preserved Roman remains in Tuscany, dating back to the 1st century B.C., though parts of the theater were torn up for building materials during the construction of the medieval walls. The view from up here is the best way to see it all, but if you do want to wander among the stones, there's an entrance down on Viale Francesco Ferrucci.

Viale Francesco Ferrucci. ℭ **0588/86050.** Admission 3.50€. Summer daily 10:30am–5:30pm; winter Sat–Sun 10am–4pm.

Where to Stay

Staying within Volterra's city walls can be a charming experience, especially in the evening when residents regain their historic town. Choices are fairly limited, so book ahead if you're planning a visit in the busy period May through September.

Albergo Etruria ★★ The lounge and guest kitchen are homey touches, but the real attraction of this cozy lodging is the roof garden, a leafy retreat where the greenery is backed by the town's brick towers and

The hill town of Volterra.

tile rooftops. Parts of an Etruscan wall enhance the historic character of the old house, but rooms are charmingly up to date, filled with comfortable, attractive furniture handpicked by the friendly owners. The Piazza dei Priori is only a few steps away from this stylish retreat.

Via Matteotti 32. www.albergoetruria.it. *©* **0588/87377.** 21 units. 69–99€ double. Rates include buffet breakfast. **Amenities:** Wi-Fi (free).

Hotel San Lino ★ There's a slightly institutional ring to the hallways and some of the guest rooms here, probably because for many centuries the 13th-century palazzo served as a cloistered convent. The large enclosed gardens are still in place, and a little terrace at one end looks across miles of countryside; there's also a small pool, the only one within the city walls and reason enough to stay here in the heat of the summer. Some rooms seem rather functional, but others are nicely turned out with a mix of contemporary and traditional Tuscan furnishings; the best of them overlook the garden and the sweeping landscapes beyond.

Via San Lino 6 (near Porta San Francesco). www.hotelsanlino.com. *©* **0588/85250.** 44 units. 90€–110€ double. Rates include buffet breakfast. **Amenities:** Restaurant; bar; pool; Wi-Fi (free).

Where to Eat

Bada Ganzo ★ MODERN TUSCAN   The room is traditional, but the menu offers a contemporary take on Volterran cuisine: dishes such as ravioli with *pecorino Volterrano e noci* (local sheep's milk cheese and hazelnuts), *pollo arrosto al vino e uvetta* (chicken roasted with wine and raisins), and often some specials with truffles. The few tables out front are an especially atmospheric place to dine on a summer evening.

Via dei Marchesi 13. *©* **0588/80508.** Main courses 8€ and 12€. Daily noon–3pm and 7:30–10:30pm.

crafty **VOLTERRANS**

The Etruscans made good use of the easily mined local stone, a translucent calcium sulfate known as alabaster—witness the hundreds of **alabaster** sarcophagi in the Guarnacci museum (see p. 268). Alabaster became a major industry in Volerra again at the end of the 19th century, when the material was much in demand for lampshades, with the rise of electric lighting. Today local artisans work alabaster into a mind-boggling array of objects, from fine art pieces to some remarkable kitsch.

Plaques around town denote the workshops of some of the best traditional artisans, where you will find only hand-worked items. Via Porta all'Arco has several fine shops, including the showroom of internationally known **Paolo Sabatini**, at no. 45 (www.paolosabatini. com; *✆* 0588/87594), whose alabaster sculptural pieces often combine wood and stone. The large **Rossi Alabastri** (www.rossialabastri.com; *✆* 0588/86133) shop at Piazzetta della Pescheria, at one end of the Roman theater panoramic walk, shows off some especially distinctive lighting pieces, as well as alabaster bowls, fruits, and all sorts of other easily portable items. At **alab'Arte**, Via Orti S. Agostino 28 (www.alabarte.com;

✆ **0588/87-968)**, near the Guarnacci museum, Roberto Cini and Giorgio Finazzo create classical and contemporary sculptural pieces of museum quality—in fact, they are often called upon to help restore sculpture in churches and museums around Italy.

You'll find the work of many other local artisans at The **Società Cooperativa Artieri Alabastro**, Piazza dei Priori 4/5 (*✆* **0588/87590**), a showroom and sales outlet for smaller workshops. To learn more about the town's alabaster industry, visit the **Ecomuseo dell'Alabastro**, Piazzetta Minucci (*✆* **0588/87580**; admission 3.50€, open 9:30am–7:30pm daily in summer, 10:30am–4:30pm in winter).

Alabaster isn't the only craft in town. **Fabula Etrusca**, Via Lungo le Mura del Mandorlo 10 (www.fabulaetrusca.it; *✆* **0588–87401**) sells intricate handmade jewelry modeled after original Etruscan designs. For prints and lithographs created from hand-engraved zinc plates—another local artisan specialty—visit **L'Istrice**, Via Porta all'Arco 23 (*✆* **0588/85422**), and **Bubo Bubo**, Via Roma 24 (www.labositrice.it; *✆* **0588/80307**).

Da Bado ★★ TUSCAN   Owner Giacomo's mom, Lucia, is in the kitchen of this neighborhood favorite in the San Lazzero neighborhood, just outside the walls a short walk from the Etruscan museum. She prepares a few daily choices that often include *zuppa volterrana* (bread and vegetable soup) and *baccalà rifatto* (pan-fried salted codfish stewed with tomatoes), along with *pappardelle alla lepre* (wide fettuccine with rabbit sauce) and other hearty pastas well suited to the homey, stone arched surroundings. Lucia also makes the jams that fill her delicious home-made tortes (cakes). A café in front serves coffee and pastries all day, Da Bado. Borgo San Lazzero 9. *✆* **0588/80402**. Main courses 8€–13€. Thurs–Tues 12:30–2:30pm and 7:30–10:30pm.

Enoteca del Duca ★★ MODERN TUSCAN   You'll have a choice of surroundings at Voltera's best restaurant: the rather elegant high-ceilinged dining room, a bottle-lined enoteca, or a pretty patio out back. Wherever you choose to enjoy them, the offerings are innovative and refined takes on Tuscan classics: all the salamis and cheeses are from local producers, *lavagnette* (homemade egg pasta) comes with a sauce of celery and pecorino pesto, and local beef is grilled to perfection. Some of the wines come from the owners' vineyards.

Via di Castello 2. www.enoteca-delduca-ristorante.it. ✆ **0588/81510.** Main courses 15€–25€. Wed–Mon 12:30–3pm and 7:30–10pm (also Tues dinner in summer).

A Side Trip to Massa Marittima

The road south from Volterra leads 65km (40 miles) over stark mountains to Massa Marittima, a hill town perched high above the coastal plain. You'll pass through a desolate region known as the Maremma, a region that was once fertile farmland for the Etruscans but by the Middle Ages had become swampy and riddled with malaria; for centuries afterward, only *butteri* (cowboys) ventured across the empty landscapes. These hills surround you with a forlorn beauty that is a stark contrast to the green forests and vineyard-clad slopes usually associated with Tuscany.

GETTING THERE   The only easy way to reach Massa Marittima is by car, a twisty-turny trip of at least an hour and a half from Volterra on SR439. From Siena, head southwest on the SS73 then the SS441 for 67km (41 1/2 miles). The nearest train station is at Follonica (2½ hrs from Rome, 80 min. from Pisa) where buses go on to Massa. The **tourist office** is at Via Todini 3-5 (www.altamaremmaturismo.it; ✆ **0566/902756**), down the right side of the Palazzo del Podestà. It's open 9:30am to 1pm and 2 to 6:30pm, but it's closed on Mondays, when all the town museums are also closed.

Massa Marittima has been a mining town since Etruscan times, and in the 14th century drew up the first mining code in European history, one of the most important legislative documents of the Middle Ages. The town is divided between the lower Città Vecchia (Old Town) and the upper Città Nuova (New Town) established by the Sienese after they subdued Massa in 1335. The Città Vecchia clusters around triangular **Piazza Garibaldi**, where the **Duomo** sits rather off-kilter off to one side. Carved panels above the main door celebrate the life of St. Cerbonius, the town's 9th-century bishop and patron, who was born in North Africa and shipwrecked on the shores of Tuscany. (He was known for having a way with animals: When invading Visigoths locked him in a pen with a ferocious bear, the beast suddenly slinked down onto its haunches and licked the saint's feet.) The remains of Cerbonius are inside in the elaborately carved Arca di San Cerbone.

From the narrow end of Piazza Garibaldi, Via Moncini branches steeply up from Via della Libertà toward the **Porta alla Silici**, part of the fortifications the Sienese built when they revamped the Città Nuova in 1337. An arch connects the fortress to the 1228 **Torre del Candeliere** (www.museidimaremma.it; ✆ **0566/902289**), where you can climb to the top for views over the ramparts (admission 3€; open generally Tues–Fri 10am–1pm and 3–6pm, Sat–Sun 10:30am–6pm; closed Mondays).

The **Museo d'Arte Sacra** (Corso Diaz 36, www.museidimaremma.it; ℭ **0566/901954**), houses the town's great art treasure, a "Maestà" painted in the late 1330s by Ambrogio Lorenzetti, who did the "Allegory of Good and Bad Government" in Siena (see page 234). This painting is infused with humanity; notice how Mary gazes lovingly at her child Jesus as he clutches at her gown, a touching representation of the maternal bond. Faith, Hope, and Charity sit at her feet, and among the saints looking on is black-robed St. Cerbonius, a flock of miraculously tamed wild geese milling about his feet. During the baroque era, when Byzantine paintings were considered to be primitive, the painting was shoved aside and it wasn't rediscovered until 1867, by which point it had been divided into five pieces and nailed together to serve as an ash bin. The museum is open Tuesday through Sunday from 10am to 1pm and 3 to 6pm (11am–1pm and 3–5pm Nov–Mar). Admission is 5€ adults and 3€ children 13 and under and seniors 60 and over.

The nearby **Museo degli Organi Meccanici**, on the top floor of the 12th-century Chiesa e Convento di San Pietro all'Orto (Corso Diaz 28; www.museodegliorgani.it; ℭ **0566/940282**) is a sanctuary for church organs, rescued from churches across Italy (some date as far back as 1600) and restored to working order. The staff often performs impromptu concerts that are quite transporting, as light filters through the stained-glass windows. (Admission 4€, 3€ for children and seniors; open June–Sept 10am–1pm and 4–7pm; Mar–May 4–6pm, Oct to mid-Jan 10:30am–12:30pm and 3–6pm; closed mid-Jan to Feb).

Massa Maritima.

Exhibits at the Museo della Miniera on Via Corridoni (www.museidimaremma.it; © 0566/902289) explicate the town's mining history; the main reason to visit is to take a guided 45-minute tour down a reconstructed 1940s mineshaft (usually in Italian only). Tours run hourly, Tuesday to Sunday 10am to noon and 3 to 5:15pm (last tour 4:30pm Nov–Mar); admission is 5€ for adults; 3€ for children under 16.

LUCCA ★★

72km (45 miles) W of Florence

Lucca is often called the forgotten Tuscan town, because it's just far enough off the beaten track to be left out of package-tour itineraries. But travelers have been waxing poetic about the place for a long time. In the 19th century, novelist Henry James called Lucca "a charming mixture of antique character and modern inconsequence"—the "inconsequence" bit meaning that Lucca, beautifully preserved within its 16th- and 17th-century walls, is much more a remnant of ages past than a part of the modern world. The Etruscans were here as early as 700 B.C., and the Romans after them, and the city flourished as a silk center in the Middle Ages. No doubt such a long and colorful history inspired Lucca's native son Giacomo Puccini (1858–1924), composer of *Tosca, Madame Butterfly, Turandot*, and *La Bohème,* some of the most romantic operas of all time. Lucca can seem like a stage set, and it's easy to look at the icing-white, four-tiered facade of the church of San Michele (Victorian art critic John Ruskin said it would be difficult to invent anything more noble) and hear the strains of "O Mio Bambino Caro."

Essentials

GETTING THERE   Lucca is on the Florence-Viareggio **train** line, with about 30 trains daily (fewer on Sun) connecting with **Florence** (75–90 min.). A similar number of trains make the short hop to/from **Pisa** (30 min.). The **station** is a short walk south of Porta San Pietro.

By **car,** the A11 runs from Florence past Prato, Pistoia, and Montecatini before hitting Lucca. Inside the walls, you'll usually find a pay-parking space underground at **Mazzini** (enter from the east, through the Porta Elisa, and take an immediate right).

A **VaiBus** (www.vaibus.it) service runs hourly from Florence (70 min.) and from Pisa (50 min.) to Lucca's Piazzale Verdi.

GETTING AROUND   A set of *navette* (electric **minibuses**) whiz down the city's peripheral streets, but the flat center is easily traversed on foot. Or, to really get around like a Lucchese, **rent a bike**—see the box "Get in the Saddle," p. 278, for rental information.

Taxis line up at the train station (© 0583/494989), Piazzale Verdi (© 0583/581305), and Piazza Napoleone (© 0583/491646).

VISITOR INFORMATION   The main **tourist office** is inside the north side of the walls at Piazza Santa Maria 35 (www.luccaturismo.it;

① 0583/919931; daily 9am–7pm, sometimes later in summer). The *comune* also has a small **local info office** on Piazzale Verdi (① 0583/ 442944), which keeps similar hours.

For **events** and concert listings, pick up the English-language monthly *Grapevine* for 2€ at most newsstands.

Exploring Lucca

Lucca has many remarkable architectural landmarks, but the first you'll notice are its incredibly intact city walls—more than 4km (2½ miles) of them, with 11 bastions and six gates; some stretches are 18m (59 ft.) wide. Topping the walls, the tree-shaded **Passeggiata delle Mura** can be circumnavigated on foot or by bike (see "Get in the Saddle," p. 278), as you peer across Lucca's rooftops toward the hazy mountains.

The most curious feature of Lucca's street plan is **Piazza Anfiteatro,** near the north end of Via Fillungo, the main shopping street. This semicircle of handsome medieval houses stands atop what were once the grandstands of a 1st- or 2nd-century-A.D. Roman amphitheater. Near by, **Torre Guinigi** rises from the 14th-century palace of Lucca's iron-fisted rulers; notice that the tower is topped with a grove of ilex trees, one of many such gardens that once flourished atop the city's defensive towers. Climb the 230 steps for a spectacular view of Lucca's skyline, the snow-capped Apuan Alps and the rolling green valley of the River Serchio (3.50€ adults, 2.50€ children 6–12 and seniors 65 and over; open daily, Apr–May 9am–7:30pm, June–Sept 9am–6:30pm, Oct and Mar 9:30am– 5:30pm, Nov–Feb 9:30am–4:30pm).

Biking Lucca's city walls.

Lucca's narrow medieval lanes reward wanderers with many surprises. One is the facade of **San Frediano,** Piazza San Frediano (① 0583/493627), glittering with a two-story-tall 13th-century mosaic that depicts the Apostles watching Christ's ascent to heaven. And as you stroll, notice how many shopfronts display early 20th-century Art Nouveau signs etched in glass, adding an elegant grace note to the city's medieval atmosphere.

Cattedrale di San Martino ★★ CATHEDRAL Completed in 1070 to house one of the most renowned artifacts in Christendom, the Volto Santo (more on that below), Lucca's ornate Duomo does justice to its prized procession. On

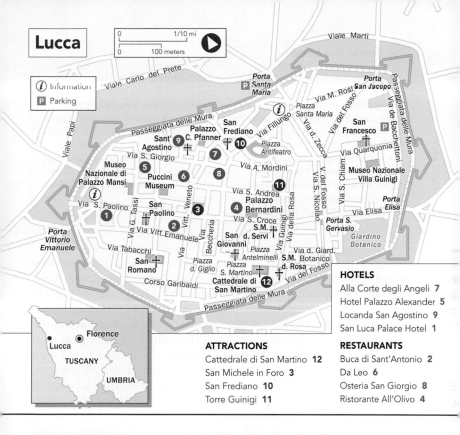

Lucca

HOTELS
- Alla Corte degli Angeli **7**
- Hotel Palazzo Alexander **5**
- Locanda San Agostino **9**
- San Luca Palace Hotel **1**

ATTRACTIONS
- Cattedrale di San Martino **12**
- San Michele in Foro **3**
- San Frediano **10**
- Torre Guinigi **11**

RESTAURANTS
- Buca di Sant'Antonio **2**
- Da Leo **6**
- Osteria San Giorgio **8**
- Ristorante All'Olivo **4**

the facade, three arches open to a deep portico sheathed in marble; above it rise three tiers of arcaded loggias supported by dozens of little columns, each different. Legend has it that the Lucchese commissioned many artists to carve the columns, with the promise of hiring the best to do them all; they used all the entries and never paid anyone. A pair of binoculars will help you pick out the elaborate carvings of figures, animals, vines, and geometric patterns in the loggias and on the portico. St. Martin, the former Roman soldier to whom the cathedral is dedicated, figures prominently—look for the statue of him ripping his cloak to give half to a scantily clad beggar. A labyrinth is carved into the wall of the right side of the portico, intended for the faithful to make a figurative pilgrimage to the center of the maze, as if to Jerusalem, before entering the church. A Latin inscription reads, "This is the labyrinth built by Daedalus of Crete; all who entered therein were lost, save Theseus, thanks to Ariadne's thread."

Inside, the handsome sweep of inlaid pavement and the high altar are the work of the 15th-century Lucca native Matteo Civitali, as is the **Tempietto,** an octagonal, freestanding chapel of white and red marble in the left nave: this is where you'll find the famous **Volto Santo.** As the

Get in the Saddle

The popular way to get around Lucca, you'll soon learn, is on a bike. Enjoy the medieval lanes and squares on foot, but equip yourself with two wheels for a ride on the Passeggiata della Mura, atop the medieval walls. You can do so in style on one of the neon-green or Barbie-pink models from **Antonio Poli,** near the tourist office at Piazza Santa Maria 42 (www.biciclettepoli.com; ✆ **0583/ 493787;** daily 8:30am–7:30pm, closed

Sun mid-Nov to Feb and Mon mornings year-round). On the same street, bikes are also available from **Cicli Bizzarri,** Piazza Santa Maria 32 (www.ciclibizzarri. net; ✆ **0583/496031;** Mon–Sat 8:30am– 1pm and 2:30–7:30pm, plus Sun same hours, Mar to mid-Sept). The going rates are 3€ an hour for a regular bike, 4€ to 4.50€ for a mountain bike, and 6.50€ for a tandem.

story goes, this crucifix was carved by Nicodemus, the biblical figure who helped remove Christ's body from the cross. Nicodemus, however, did not complete the face, fearing he could not do the holy visage justice. He fell into a deep sleep, and when he awoke he discovered a beautiful face miraculously carved on the crucifix (and that's just the beginning of the story; see "The Plot Thickens," below). The cathedral's other great treasure is the **Tomb of Ilaria Carretto Guinigi**, the young wife of Lucca ruler Paolo Guinigi, who died in 1405 at the age of 26; she lives on, accompanied by a little dog (a sign of her faithfulness) in a beautiful image carved by Jacopo della Quercia, the Sienese sculptor whose work so heavily influenced Michelangelo.

Piazza San Martino. ✆ **0583/957068.** Admission to church free; transepts and Ilaria tomb 2€ adults, 1.50€ children 6–14. Cumulative ticket for tomb, Museo, and San Giovanni 6€ adults, 4€ children 6–14. Mon–Fri 9:30am–5:45pm (closes 4:45pm Nov– Mar), Sat 9:30am–6:45pm, Sun 9:30–10:45am and noon–6pm.

San Michele in Foro ★ CHURCH   The magnificent facade of the Cattedrale di San Martino (see above) is matched, or even outdone for visual drama, by the delicately stacked arches and arcades of this 12th-century church that rises above the site of Lucca's Roman forum. The show begins just above the main portal, where St. Michael slays a dragon as mythical creatures look on. Above that two lions flank a rose window, then begin four soaring tiers of little columns; these are inlaid with intricate carvings and topped with human heads, flowers, and animals. Above each row is a frieze on which real and mythical animals jump and run. The two top tiers are narrow and freestanding, surmounted by a statue of a bronze-winged **St. Michael the Archangel** flanked by two trumpeting cohorts. The interior is rather dull by comparison, although it is enlivened with a fine painting of "Sts. Roch, Sebastian, Jerome, and Helen" by Filippino Lippi in the right transept. The offspring of a notorious relationship between the painter Fra Filippo Lippi and a young nun, Lucrezia Buti, Filippino became one of the most accomplished painters of the late 15th century; his work shows the influence of his father as well as his teacher, Sandro Botticelli. The great composer Giacomo Puccini, who was born in 1858 down the block at Via Poggio no. 30 (a plaque marks the site), once sang in the church choir here.

Piazza San Michele. (*) **0583/48459.** Free admission. Summer daily 7:40am–noon and 3–6pm; winter daily 9am–noon and 3–5pm.

Where to Stay

Lucca has many B&B–style inns. For a complete listing, ask the tourist board for the handy booklet "Extra Alberghiero."

Alla Corte degli Angeli ★★   Some of the most charming accommodations in Lucca flow across four floors of this beautifully restored and maintained pink *palazzo* just off Via Fillungo, the main shopping street. It's hard not to fall for the gimmicky decor, which provides just the right touch of playful ambience in the smallish but extremely tasteful rooms. In each, colorful murals incorporate a flower, and rich draperies and upholstered headboards pick up the theme; a scattering of antique pieces and excellent lighting enhance the air of stylish comfort. Some of the good-sized bathrooms have both showers and hydromassage tubs. Given the tightly packed medieval neighborhood, a room on an upper floor ensures an extra amount of sunlight—third-floor Paolina is an especially good choice because it has two exposures.

Via degli Angeli 23 (off Via Fillungo). www.allacortedegliangeli.com. (*) **0583/469204.** 10 units. 130€–210€ double. Rates include buffet breakfast. Garage parking 15€. Closed 2 weeks in Jan. **Amenities:** Bikes; concierge; Wi-Fi (free).

Hotel Palazzo Alexander ★   Stepping into this 12th-century palace tucked into medieval streets feels a bit like walking onto an operatic stage set, and the feeling certainly doesn't let up as you settle in amid gilded and polished wood, reproduction antiques, old prints, and plush fabrics. You might have *putti* (cherubs) grinning down on you from the frescoed ceiling, while at the same time marble baths, Jacuzzi tubs in

The Plot Thickens

According to medieval legend, St. Nicodemus stashed the Volto Santo crucifix in a cave for safekeeping, where an 8th-century Italian bishop discovered it while on pilgrimage to the Holy Land (the location came to him in a dream). The bishop put the crucifix adrift in a boat, which magically washed up on the shores of northern Italy. Once again, the relic was set loose, this time in a driverless wagon pulled by two oxen, and all by itself it arrived in Lucca. First placed in the church of San Frediano, it miraculously moved itself to the cathedral. Throughout the medieval era, the Volto Santo and the legends attached to it attracted pilgrims from throughout Europe. On May 3 and September 13 to 14, the Lucchese walk in a candlelit procession from San Frediano to the cathedral, where the famous statue awaits them, dressed in gold and wearing a gold crown.

some rooms, excellent beds and fine linens, and other amenities are thoroughly up to date. The good-sized rooms are named after Puccini operas, and some of the especially charming suites have vaulted and beamed ceilings reminiscent of Rodolfo's *La Bohème* garret—well, that is, if the young poet had lived very, very well. Luckily, this quirkily stylish little inn offers service as memorable as the surroundings.

Via Santa Giustina 28. www.hotelpalazzoalexander.it. © **0583/47615.** 9 units. From 80€ double. Rates include buffet breakfast. **Amenities:** Bar; Wi-Fi (free).

Locanda San Agostino ★★ Three large, stylish, and atmospheric guest rooms are tucked away in this moody old palace. Four-poster beds, polished antiques, old oil painitngs, and elegant wall coverings provide a homey and fairly luxurious ambience, as does the raised hearth in the attractive lounge/breakfast room and the wisteria-shaded terrace. The aptly named Teatro room comes with a big bonus—a private balcony with views over the ruins of a Roman theater.

Piazza San Agostino 3. www.locandasantagostino.it. © **0583/467-884.** 3 units. From 100€ double. Rates include buffet breakfast. Amenities: Wi-Fi (free).

San Luca Palace Hotel ★★ A sense of tasteful, old-world comfort begins in the downstairs hall and sitting room and continues into the large guest rooms, nicely done up with parquet floors, well-coordinated fabrics and draperies (green color schemes in some rooms, red in others). There are many nice flourishes, like inviting table-and-chair arrangements in all the rooms and small "reading" alcoves with day beds in many. This old palace just inside the walls also has plenty of practical conveniences, including an easy-to-reach location (parking is adjacent) just a short stroll from the sights and train station. There's no in-house restaurant, but an extremely pleasant bar off the lobby serves light snacks.

Via San Paolino 103 (off Piazza Napoleone). www.sanlucapalace.com. © **0583/317446.** 26 units. 85€ double. **Amenities:** Bar; Wi-Fi (free).

Where to Eat

Lucca's extra-virgin olive oil appears on every restaurant table. An atmospheric 19th-century pastry shop, **Taddeucci,** Piazza San Michele 34 (www.taddeucci.net; © **0583/494933**), is famous for *buccellato,* a Lucca specialty—a ring-shaped sweet bread flavored with raisins and fennel seeds. For a fortifying (and addictive) snack, stop by **Amedo Giusti,** Via Santa Lucia 18 (© **0583/496285**), where focaccia with many different toppings emerge piping hot from the oven. Sample Lucca's excellent DOC wines at **Enoteca Vanni,** Piazza San Salvatore 7 (www.enotecavanni.com; © **0583/491902**).

Buca di Sant'Antonio ★ LUCCHESE Almost three and half centuries old, Lucca's most venerable dining room coasts a bit on its reputation these days, but sitting in the handsome tile-floored surroundings amid copper pots and brass instruments is still a terribly pleasant experience—and usually requires a dinnertime reservation. We also like the nicely formal service, with waiters in bow ties, and the welcoming glass of prosecco that launches a meal of traditional Lucchese dishes. The menu changes regularly, but usually includes such house specialties as *farro alla garfagnana* (spelt, or barley, soup) and *coniglio in umido* (rabbit stew). A house dessert is *buccellato*, a ring-shaped confection like a coffee cake named for the bread that sustained Roman legionnaires.

Via della Cervia 3 (a side alley just west of Piazza San Michele). ✆ **0583/55881.** Main courses 15€. Tues–Sat 12:30–3pm and 7:30–10:30pm; Sun 12:30–3pm.

Da Leo ★★ LUCCHESE/TUSCAN   It's a good sign when you have to veer off the well-beaten path to find a place, even better when anyone you ask along the way knows how to get there. The pleasantly old-fashioned room with plastic-draped tablecloths has been serving local classics for 50 years, and the *minestra di farro arrosto di maialino con patate* (roast piglet and potatoes), *coniglio* (rabbit), and other authentic Lucchese fare remain as good as ever. This is the place to try the typically Luccan *zuppa di farro,* a soup made with spelt, a barleylike grain cooked al dente.

Via Tegrimi 1 (just north of Piazza San Salvatore). www.trattoriadaleo.it. ✆ **0583/ 492236.** Main courses 9€–16€. Daily noon–2:30pm and 7:30–10:30pm.

Osteria San Giorgio ★ LUCCHESE/TUSCAN   This local favorite has a courtyard out front and comfortably informal rooms decorated with old photos, all tucked away on a quiet street near the Piazza Anfiteatro. The menu is geared to neighbors looking for a home-cooked meal: several soups, including a hearty *farro alla luchesse* (beans and barley), *coniglio stufato con olive taggiasche e uva* (rabbit stew with olives and grapes), and a local seafood favorite, *baccalà alla griglia con ceci* (grilled cod with chickpeas). Servers seems to know just about everyone who comes in the door and extend a warm welcome to newcomers as well.

Via San Giorgio 26. www.osteriasangiorgiolucca.it. ✆ **0583/953233.** Main courses 8€–13€. Daily noon–3pm and 7–10:30pm.

Ristorante All'Olivo ★ LUCCHESE/SEAFOOD   This is where the Lucchese come when they're in the mood for fish. Taking a seat in one of its four comfortable and elegant little rooms—one with a fireplace, another like a covered garden—definitely elevates a meal to a special occasion. The fish and seafood is brought in daily from the nearby Tuscan port of Viareggio it and appears in a bounty of seafood pastas, grilled seafood platters, a nice choice of *antipasti di mare,* and a simply prepared catch of the day. Meat lovers will not be disappointed with the hearty roasts and grilled Tuscan steaks.

Piazza San Quirico 1. www.ristoranteolivo.it. ✆ **0583/496264.** Main courses 12€– 20€. Mon–Sat 12:30–2pm and 7:30–10pm.

Entertainment & Nightlife

Every evening at 7pm, the Chiesa di San Giovanni hosts an opera recital or orchestral concert dedicated to hometown composer Giacomo Puccini, in a series called **Puccini e la sua Lucca** (Puccini and His Lucca; www.puccinielasualucca.com). Tickets are 17€ (13€ for those 22 and under) and can be purchased all day inside San Giovanni. Just try listening to "Nessun Dorma" in this lovely church in the composer's hometown without chills running up and down your spine. The shore of nearby Lago di Massaciuccoli provides the backdrop for the summer **Puccini Festival** ★ (www.puccinifestival.it; © **0584/359322**), the biggest annual date in a local opera lover's calendar. There's a seasonal ticket office at Viale Puccini 257a, in Torre del Lago, or book tickets online (35€–125€).

PISA ★★

85km (53 miles) south of Lucca, 76km (47 miles) W of Florence

It's ironic that one of the most famous landmarks in a country that has given Western civilization many of if its greatest art and architecture is in fact an engineering failure. Built on sandy soil too unstable to support so much heavy marble, Pisa's famous tower began to lean even while it was still under construction. Eight centuries later, however, the Leaning Tower puts Pisa on the map. Seeing it, maybe climbing it, and touring other landmarks on the Campo dei Miracoli (Field of Miracles) is probably why you'll come to this city near the northwestern coast of Tuscany.

Pisa began as a seaside settlement around 1000 B.C. and was expanded into a naval trading port by the Romans in the 2nd century B.C. By the 11th century, the city had grown into one of the peninsula's most powerful maritime republics. In 1284, however, Pisa's battle fleet was destroyed by Genoa at Meloria (off Livorno), forcing Pisa's long slide into twilight. Florence took control in 1406 and, despite a few small rebellions, stayed in charge until Italian unification in the 1860s.

Today Pisa is lively and cosmopolitan, home to a university founded in 1343, one of Europe's oldest. Once away from the Campo dei Miracoli, however, there's not a whole lot to see, so you may want to join the ranks of day trippers who visit from Florence or nearby Lucca.

Essentials

GETTING THERE   There are around 25 train runs between Lucca and Pisa every day (25–35 min.); from **Florence,** 50 daily trains make the trip (60–90 min.). On the Lucca line, day-trippers should get off at **San Rossore station,** a few blocks west of Piazza del Duomo and the Leaning Tower. All other trains—and eventually the Lucca one—pull into **Pisa Centrale** station. From here, bus no. 4 or the **LAM Rossa** bus will take you close to Piazza del Duomo.

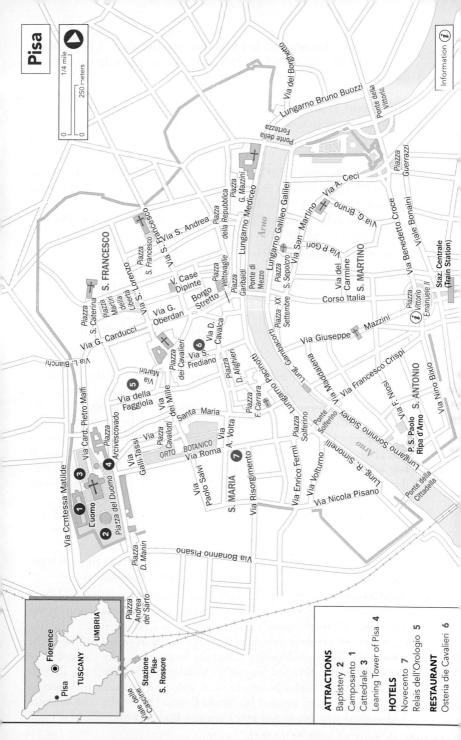

Pisa

0 1/4 mile
0 250 meters

Information ⓘ

TUSCANY
Florence
Pisa
UMBRIA

Stazione Pisa-S. Rossore

Via delle Cascine

Piazza Andrea del Sarto

Via Bonanno Pisano

Via Contessa Matilde

Piazza D. Manin

Via Card. Pietro Malfi

Piazza del Duomo

L'uomo

Piazza Arcivescovado

Via della Faggiola

Via L. Bianchi

Piazza S. Caterina

Via G. Carducci

S. FRANCESCO

Piazza Martiri della Libertà

Via S. Lorenzo

Piazza S. Francesco

Via S. Francesco

Via S. Andrea

Piazza G. Mazzini

Ponte della Fortezza

Via del Bastione

Lungarno Bruno Buozzi

Ponte della Vittoria

V. Case Dipinte

Via G. Oberdan

Borgo Stretto

Piazza Vettovaglie

Piazza della Repubblica

Lungarno Mediceo

Arno

Via S. Frediano

Piazza dei Cavalieri

Via D. Cavalca

Via D. Alighieri

Piazza XX Settembre

Ponte di Mezzo

Piazza Garibaldi

Lungarno Galileo Galilei

Via San Martino

Via A. Ceci

Via G. Bruno

Via P. Gori

Piazza S. Sepolcro

S. MARTINO

Via del Carmine

Corso Italia

Piazza Cairoli

Lung. Gambacorti

Via Mazzini

Via Giuseppe

Lungarno Pacinotti

Piazza F. Carrara

Piazza Solferino

Ponte Solferino

Santa Maria

Via Cavallotti

Piazza Cavallotti dei Mille

Via Galli-Tassi

Via del Borgo

Via S. Maria

BOTANICO ORTO

Via Roma

Via A. Volta

Via Paolo Salvi

S. MARIA

Via Risorgimento

Via Enrico Fermi

Via Volturno

Via Nicola Pisano

Lung. R. Simoneili

Lungarno Sonnino Sidney

Arno

Ponte della Cittadella

Via Madalena

Via Francesco Crispi

Via F. Niosi

S. ANTONIO

P. S. Paolo Ripa d'Arno

Via Nino Bixio

Piazza Vittorio Emanuele II

ⓘ

Viale Bonaini

Via Benedetto Croce

Piazza Guerrazzi

Staz. Centrale (Train Station)

ATTRACTIONS

Baptistery **2**
Camposanto **1**
Cattedrale **3**
Leaning Tower of Pisa **4**

HOTELS

Novecento **7**
Relais dell'Orologio **5**

RESTAURANT

Osteria die Cavalieri **6**

283

There's a Florence-Pisa fast **highway** (the so-called FI.PI.LI) along the Arno valley. Take the SS12 or SS12r from Lucca. For details on parking locations and charges, see **www.pisamo.it**.

Tuscany's main international airport, **Galileo Galilei** (www.pisa-airport.com), is just 3km (2 miles) south of the center. Trains zip you from the airport to Centrale station in 5 minutes; the LAM Rossa bus departs every 9 minutes for Centrale station and then the Campo. A metered taxi ride costs 10€ to 15€ (drivers accept credit cards).

GETTING AROUND CPT (www.cpt.pisa.it; ✆ **050/884284** or 800/012773 in Italy) runs the city's **buses.** Bus no. 4 and the LAM Rossa bus run to near the Campo dei Miracoli.

Taxis can be found on Piazza della Stazione and Piazza del Duomo. Call a radio taxi at ✆ **050/541600** or 055/555330.

VISITOR INFORMATION The main **tourist office** is at Piazza Vittorio Emanuele II 16 (www.pisaunicaterra.it; ✆ **050/42291;** Mon–Sat 9am–7pm, Sun 9am–4pm). There's also a desk inside the arrivals hall at the airport (✆ **055/502518;** daily 9:30am–11:30pm).

To find out what's going on in town, pick up a copy of the monthly *ToDo* (often in bars and cafes), or visit **www.todomagazine.it**.

Exploring Pisa

On a grassy lawn wedged into the northwest corner of the city walls, medieval Pisans created one of the most dramatic squares in the world. Dubbed the **Campo dei Miracoli (Field of Miracles),** Piazza del Duomo contains an array of elegant buildings that heralded the Pisan-Romanesque style. A subtle part of its appeal, aside from the beauty of the white marble-sheathed marble buildings, is its spatial geometry. If you were to look at an aerial photo of the square and draw connect-the-dot lines between the doors and other focal points, you'd come up with all sorts of perfect triangles and tangential lines.

Admission charges for the monuments and museums of the Campo are tied together in a complicated way. Admission to the cathedral is free with a ticket to any other sight. Any other single sight is 5€; any two sights cost 7€; and three cost 8€. Admission to the Leaning Tower is separate (see below). For more information, visit **www.opapisa.it**.

Baptistery ★★ CHURCH   Italy's largest baptistery (104m/341 ft. in circumference), begun in 1153 and capped with a Gothic dome in the 1300s, is built on the same unstable soil as the Leaning Tower. The first thing you will notice is a decided tilt—not nearly as severe as that of the tower, but this round ornate structure leans noticeably towards the cathedral. The unadorned interior is considered to be where the Renaissance, with its emphasis on classical style and humanism, began to flower, in the pulpit created by Nicola Pisano (1255–60). The sculptor had studied sarcophagi and other ancient Roman works that the Pisan navy brought back from Rome as booty, and the classic influence on his work is obvious—note the nude Roman god Hercules taking his place next to statues of St. Michael and St. John the Baptist. In scenes of the life of Christ, figures wear tunics and Mary wears the headdress of a Roman matron. If the baptistery is not too crowded, stand near the middle and say something loudly; the sound will reverberate for quite awhile, thanks to the structure's renowned acoustics.

Piazza del Duomo. www.opapisa.it. ✆ **050/835011.** For prices, see above. Open daily, Apr–Sept 8am–8pm; Oct 9am–7pm; Nov–Feb 10am–5pm; Mar 9am–6pm. Bus: E, 4, LAM Rossa.

Camposanto ★ CEMETERY   Pisa's monumental cemetery, where the city's aristocracy was buried until the 18th century, was begun in 1278, when Crusaders began shipping back loads of dirt from Golgotha (the mount where Christ was crucified). Giovanni di Simone (architect of the Leaning Tower) enclosed the field in a marble cloister, and the walls were eventually covered by magnificent 14th- and 15th-century frescoes, mostly destroyed by Allied bombings in World War II. One of the few remaining, a "Triumph of Death," inspired the 19th-century composer Franz Liszt to write his "Totentanz" ("Dance of Death"). Roman sarcophagi, used as funerary monuments, fared better (84 of these survive), as did the huge chains that medieval Pisans used to protect their harbor, which now hang on the cemetery walls.

Piazza del Duomo. www.opapisa.it. ✆ **050/835011.** For prices, see above. Same hours as the Baptistery; see above. Bus: E, 4, LAM Rossa.

Cattedrale ★★ CATHEDRAL   Pisa's magnificent white marble cathedral will forever be associated with Galileo Galilei (1564–1642), a native son and founder of modern physics. Bored during church services, he discovered the law of perpetual motion (a pendulum's swings always take the same amount of time) by watching the swing of a bronze chandelier now known as the "Lamp of Galileo." (It's also said, though the story is probably apocryphal, that Galileo climbed the adjacent Leaning Tower and dropped two wooden balls of differing sizes that hit the ground at the same time, thus proving that gravity exerts the same force on objects no matter what they weigh.) The exuberant cathedral, with its intricate tiers of arches and columns, is quite remarkable in its own right. Heavily influenced by Pisa's contact through trade with the Arab world, it has come to be the prime example of distinctive Pisan Romanesque architecture. Giovanni Pisano, whose father, Nicola, sculpted the pulpit in the Baptistery (see above) created the pulpit here (1302–11), covering it with detailed scenes from the New Testament. Now considered among the great masterpieces of Gothic sculpture, the relief panels were deemed too old-fashioned by the church's 16th-century restorers, who packed them away in crates until they were reassembled, rather clumsily, in 1926.

Piazza del Duomo. www.opapisa.it. ✆ **050/835011.** For prices, see above. Same hours as the Baptistery and Camposanto; see above. Bus: E, 4, LAM Rossa.

Leaning Tower of Pisa ★★★ Construction began on the bell tower of Pisa Cathedral in 1173. Three stories into the job, it became apparent the structure was leaning distinctly, whereupon architects Guglielmo and Bonnano Pisano called off the work. A century later, Giovanni di Simone resumed the job, having quite literally gone back to the drawing board—he tried to compensate for the tilt by making successive layers taller on one side than the other, thus giving the tower a slight banana-like curve. Over the centuries engineers have poured concrete into the foundations and tried other solutions, all in vain. By the late 20th century the tower was in such serious danger of collapse, it was closed and braced with cables. Crews removed more than 70 tons of earth from beneath the structure, allowing it to slightly right itself as it settled. With a lean of only 4m (13 ft.), compared to a precarious 4.6m (15 ft.) before the fix, the tower has been deemed stable for now and safe to climb once again. But before you do, take time to notice just how lovely the multi-color marble tower is, with eight arcaded stories that provide a mesmerizing sense of harmony as you look up its height.

The only way to climb the tower is to book a visit in the office on the north side of the piazza—or, for peak season, book online well in advance. Visits are limited to 30 minutes, and you must be punctual for your slot or you'll lose your chance to climb the 293 steps. Children under 8 are not permitted to climb the tower, and those aged 8 to 18 need to be accompanied by an adult (8–12s must hold an adult's hand at all times). Leave bags at the cloakroom next to the ticket office behind the cathedral. Piazza del Duomo. www.opapisa.it. ✆ **050/835011.** Admission 18€. Same hours as the Baptistery, Camposanto, and Cattedrale; see above. Bus: E, 4, LAM Rossa.

The Tower of Pisa.

Where to Eat & Stay

Most visitors comes to Pisa on a day trip, which helps keep hotel prices down but also limits quality options. The low season for most hotels in Pisa is August. For pizza or *cecina* (a garbanzo-bean flour flatbread served warm), stop in at **Il Montino,** Vicolo del Monte (✆ **050/598695**), a favorite slice stop for Pisans.

Osteria die Cavalleri ★ PISAN   The "Restaurant of the Knights" operates out of stone rooms that date to the 12th century; the cooking is traditionally Tuscan but founded on the contemporary Slow Food principles of fresh and local. Being Pisa, this means seafood, including *tagliolini* with razor clams and a classic *baccala,* dried cod lightly battered and fried; some hearty meat choices, such as *pappardelle* with rabbit sauce and grilled steaks; and robust vegetable soups. You can get away with a one-dish meal here—in fact, it's encouraged at lunchtime, when a crowd of local office workers packs in.

Via San Frediano 16. ✆ **050/580858.** Main courses 10€–14€. Mon–Fri 12:30–2pm and 7:45–10pm, Sat 7:45–10pm.

Novecento ★   These small and simple rooms set around a courtyard in an old villa are strictly contemporary, not an antique armoire in sight. Instead, Philippe Starck chairs and contemporary upholstered headboards are set against colored accent walls. A lush garden is filled with lounge chairs and quiet corners, and off to one side is the best room in the house, a self-contained, cottage-like unit. For guests desiring a bit more greenery, Pisa's Botanical Garden is just up the street. The Campo Santo is a straightforward 10-minute walk away.

Via Roma 37. www.hotelnovecento.pisa.it. ✆ **050/500323.** 14 units. 60€–150€ double. Rates include breakfast. Parking on street (10€ per day). **Amenities:** Wi-Fi (free).

Relais dell'Orologio ★★   Maria Luisa Bignardi provided Pisa with its only truly remarkable place to stay when she converted her family mansion into refined yet relaxing guest quarters. The large garden and cozy top floor "attic" lounge provide a relaxing refuge from the crowds in the Campo, just a 5-minute walk away. Guest rooms are filled with family heirlooms, some colorful architectural details, and lots of 21st-century conveniences, including excellent beds and marble bathrooms. Some of the rooms are quite small, though for a bit extra you can settle into a larger room or one overlooking the garden. Signora Bignardi also runs the 12-room **Relais dei Fiori,** Via Carducci 35 (www.relaisdeifiori. com; ✆ **050/556054**), where small but very attractive doubles start at 70€. At both, travelers 65 and older get a 20% discount in some periods.

Via della Faggiola Ugiccione 12–14. www.hotelrelaisorologio.com. ✆ **050/830361.** 21 units. 90€–180€ double. Rates include buffet breakfast. **Amenities:** Restaurant; bar; Wi-Fi (free).

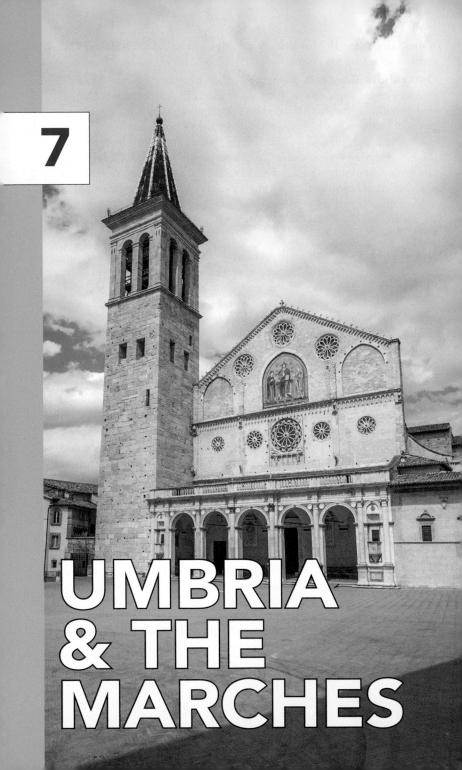

7

UMBRIA
& THE
MARCHES

It's easy to think of Umbria as second to Tuscany, its more-visited neighbor to the north, but that's a good thing—being slightly out of the limelitght is one of the region's great assets. Perugia, Spoleto, Gubbio, and dozens of other noble hill towns are a little quieter than their Tuscan neighbors—a bit easier to enjoy, yet still filled with rival-worthy art treasures, from Giotto's famous fresco cycle in Assisi to Signorelli's horrifying view of Judgment Day in Orvieto. Even less visited are the rugged valleys of the Marches to the east, where charming towns like Urbino get a fraction of the tourist traffic they deserve. Umbrian landscapes are a picturesque mix of vineyards and olive groves, golden checkerboard valleys, and unspoiled forests, edged by the western slopes of the Appenine mountains. These mellow, almost otherworldly landscapes are an apt setting for a region often called "la terra dei santi" (land of the saints), in homage to the beloved St. Francis of Assisi and his followers, reminders of whom are everywhere.

PERUGIA ★★

164km (102 miles) SE of Florence, 176km (109 miles) N of Rome

Perugia is Umbria's capital, but it's most appealing in its guise of medieval hill town. Ancient alleys drop precipitously off **Corso Vannucci,** the cosmopolitan shopping promenade, and Gothic palaces rise above stony piazzas. The city produced and trained some of Umbria's finest artists, whose works fill the excellent art gallery. Thousands of students from Perugia's two universities impart the old streets with youthful energy, and Perugia's most famous product, chocolate, adds a sweet note to the town's appeal.

Essentials

GETTING THERE **Ryanair** (www.ryanair.com; ✆ **0871/246-0000**) flights connect London Stansted with Perugia's **Aeroporto Internazionale dell'Umbria** (www.airport.umbria.it; ✆ **075/592141**), 10km (6 miles) east of the city at San Egidio. Flights are usually met by a minibus outside the terminal, taking you to Perugia train station and Piazza Italia (30–40 min.; 3.50€), but heading back there are just three buses per day, so check times in advance (just 1 bus Sat–Sun). Taxis to or from the airport cost around 25€.

Facing Page: **Spoleto Cathedral.**

Two **rail** lines serve Perugia. The state railway connects with **Rome** (2–3 hr.; most trains require a change at Foligno) and **Florence** (2¼ hr.; most trains require a change at Terontola) every couple of hours. There are also hourly trains to **Assisi** (20–30 min.) and **Spoleto** (1¼ hr.). The station is a few kilometers southwest of the center at Piazza Vittorio Veneto (© **147/888088**), but well connected with buses to/from Piazza Italia (1€). Perugia's seven-stop, 3km (2-mile) long "minimetro" also makes the run from the station up to stops in the town center (1.50€, buy tickets in machines). The station for the **Umbria Mobilità–operated regional railway** (© **800/512141**), Sant'Anna, is in Piazzale Bellucci (near the bus station). These tiny trains serve **Todi** every couple of hours.

SULGA lines (www.sulga.it; © **075/5009641**) has one **bus** (Mon and Fri) from Florence (6pm; 2 hr.), six or seven daily from Assisi (30 min.) and Todi (40 min.), and around six a day from Rome (2½ hr.). Morning buses usually stop at the airport; the station is in Piazza Partigiani and connected to Piazza Italia by escalator. **Umbria Mobilità** (www.umbriamobilita.it; © **800/512141**) buses connect Perugia with Assisi (six buses daily; 50 min.), Gubbio (six buses daily; 1 hr., 10 min.), and Todi (six buses daily; 1 hr., 15 min.).

Perugia is connected by three fast and free **roads.** The Raccordo Perugia-A1 runs east-west between the A1, Lago Trasimeno, and Perugia, bypassing the city to link with the E45 (aka SS3bis). The E45 runs south to Todi and Terni (for Rome). Heading southeast, the SS75bis connects the E45 at Perugia with Assisi and Spoleto. Parking in town is fairly abundant. The most convenient parking is at the underground pay lots at Piazza Partigiani, from which escalators take you up to Piazza Italia (with some amazing underground scenery along the route; see box p. 295). For information about parking in Perugia, visit **www.sipaonline.it**.

VISITOR INFORMATION   The **tourist office,** at Piazza Matteotti 18 (www.regioneumbria.eu; © **075/573-6458**), is open daily from 8:30am to 6:30pm. You can also pick up a copy of *Viva Perugia* (1€) at newsstands to find out what's going on around town.

Exploring Perugia

Piazza Italia is like a balcony hanging over the hillside at one end of town. From this airy square, sophisticated **Corso Vannucci** flows through the massive Palazzo dei Priori to **Piazza IV Novembre**, where the cathedral stands. The square's focal point is really the elaborate **Fontana Maggiore,** with its carved panels and figures crafted by Nicola Pisano and his son Giovanni 1278 and 1280. It's especially entertaining to stroll up the corso in the early evening, when it becomes the stage set for one of Italy's most lively and decorous evening *passeggiate*.

Cappella di San Severo ★ CHURCH   Don't be fooled by the 18th-century exterior of this modest chapel; the 14th-century chapel inside

contains a real treasure. Before young Raphael Sanzio made a name for himself in Florence and Rome, he settled briefly in Perugia, where in 1504 he painted the first of the many frescoes that would make him famous in his own lifetime (not to mention vaulting him into the triumvirate of great Renaissance masters, alongside Leonardo DaVinci and Michaelangelo). Unfortunately only the upper half of his "Holy Trinity" remains here, and that is damaged. The work seems touchingly modest compared to the complex "School of Athens" and other works he later did for the Vatican palaces and chapels. As energetic in life as he was in his work, Raphael ran a huge workshop, had dozens of wealthy patrons, was in line to be a cardinal, and died on his 37th birthday, allegedly after a lustful session with his mistress. After Raphael's death, his then-septuagenarian teacher, Perugino, painted the six saints along the bottom of the fresco.

Piazza Raffaello. ✆ **075/573-3864.** Admission 3€ adults, 2€ seniors 65 and over, 1€ children 7–14, free for children 6 and under; includes admission to Pozzo Etrusco, valid 1 week. Apr–Oct Tues-Sun 10am–1:30pm and 2:30–6pm (also open Mon in Apr and Aug); Nov–Mar Tues–Sun 11am–1:30pm and 2:30–5pm.

Galleria Nazionale ★★★ MUSEUM The world's largest repository of Umbrian art, this gallery covers seven or so centuries and showcases dozens of artists. Pride of place belongs to the altarpieces by Perugino, who was born nearby in Città della Pieve and spent much of his career working in Perugia (although he also studied alongside Leonardo da Vinci in Florence and executed frescoes in the Sistine Chapel in Rome). Among Perugino's works in Rooms 22–26 are delicate landscapes, sweet Madonnas, and grinning Christ childs that reveal his spare, precise style. Their transcendent beauty seems ironic, given that Perugino was openly anti-religion. They certainly reveal nothing of his fairly turbulent life—he was arrested in Florence for assault and battery and barely escaped exile; sued Michelangelo for defamation of character; and more than once was censored for reusing images and lacking originality. He persevered, however, and worked prodigiously until his death at age 73, leaving a considerable fortune.

The museum's other showpiece is by a Tuscan, Piero della Francesca, who completed his "Polyptych of Perugia" for the city's church of Sant'Antonio in 1470. The symmetry, precise placement of figures and objects, and realistic dimensions belie the artist's other occupation as a mathematician; at the same time, his figures are robustly human, real flesh and blood. Della Francesca works sheer magic at the top of the piece, in a scene of the Annunciation, when an angel appears to Mary to tell her she will be the mother of the son of God. She's standing in a brightly lit cloister, and the illusion of pillars leading off into the distance is regarded as one of the greatest examples of perspective in Renaissance art.

Palazzo dei Priori, Corso Vannucci 19. ✆ **075/574-1247.** Admission 6.50€ adults, 3.25€ ages 18–25 (E.U. citizens only), free for children 17 and under and seniors 65 and over (EU citizens only). Daily 8:30am–7:30pm (closed 1st Mon of every month).

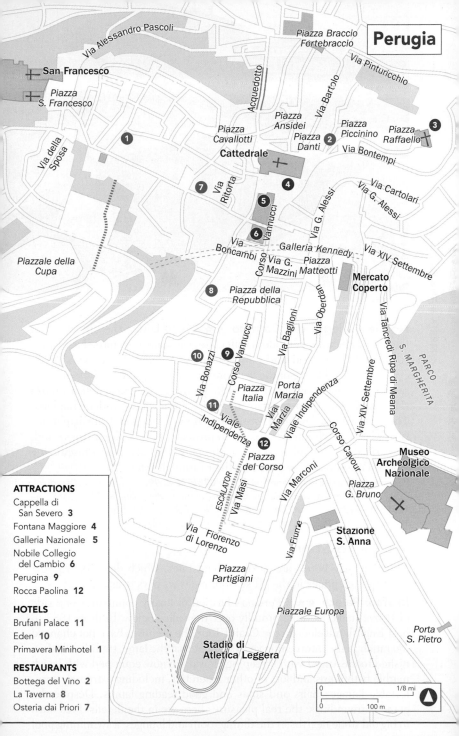

Perugia

ATTRACTIONS

Cappella di
San Severo **3**

Fontana Maggiore **4**

Galleria Nazionale **5**

Nobile Collegio
del Cambio **6**

Perugina **9**

Rocca Paolina **12**

HOTELS

Brufani Palace **11**

Eden **10**

Primavera Minihotel **1**

RESTAURANTS

Bottega del Vino **2**

La Taverna **8**

Osteria dai Priori **7**

City of Perugia.

Nobile Collegio del Cambio ★★ MUSEUM   The cubicles and fluorescent lighting of modern office life will seem even more banal after you visit the frescoed and paneled meeting rooms of Perugia's Moneychanger's Guild, one of the best-preserved "office suites" of the Renaissance. Perugino was hired in 1496 to fresco the Sala dell' Udienza (Hearing Room), perhaps with the help of his young student Raphael. The images merge religion (scenes of the Nativity and Transfiguration) with classical references (female representations of the virtues) and, most riveting of all, glimpses of 15th-century secular life, a fascinating look at Perugians of the time and their sartorial tastes.

Palazzo dei Priori, Corso Vannucci 25. ℂ **075/572-8599.** Admission 4.50€ adults, 2.50€ seniors 65 and over, free for children 12 and under. Mar–Oct Mon–Sat 9am–12:30pm and 2:30–5:30pm, Sun 9am–1pm; Nov–Feb Tues–Sat 8am–2pm, Sun 9am–12:30pm, except Dec 20–Jan 6 when summer hours apply.

Where to Stay

Most Perugian hotels are flexible about rates, which dive 40% to 50% below posted prices in the off season; it always pays to ask.

Brufani Palace ★★   Perugia's bastion of luxury commands one side of Piazza Italia, looming proudly over the valley below. Built in 1883 to host English travelers on the Grand Tour, the premises have not changed too much in the intervening years, except that the large, traditionally furnished rooms (most with sweeping views) are now equipped with lavish marble bathrooms and lots of other amenities, including extremely comfortable lounge chairs and sofas and good reading lamps. Despite the grand surroundings, the real pleasures here are in the details: fires burn in big old stone hearths in the dining room and lounges; a swimming pool has been carved out of subterranean brick vaults, with see-through panels exposing Etruscan ruins beneath; and a large rooftop terrace is a perfect spot for a glass of wine at sunset.

Piazza Italia 12. www.brufanipalace.com. © **075/573-2541.** 94 units. From 150€ double. Rates include buffet breakfast. **Amenities:** Restaurant/bar (tables on the piazza in summer); babysitting; concierge; small exercise room; indoor pool; room service; Wi-Fi (free with most rates).

Eden ★ This comfortable little inn occupies the top floor of a 13th-century building in the city center (an elevator takes you up), and the airy accommodations seem a world removed from the medieval city below. Furnishings are contemporary, with colorful accent walls and modern art; the compact, bathrooms are up to date; and a pleasant breakfast room that doubles as a lounge is sleek and functional. Outside the tall windows are an enticing jumble of rooftops, towers, and narrow stone lanes. When you're ready to go down and explore the sights, the friendly management supplies an insightful, self-guided itinerary of their own design.

Via Cesare Caporali 9. www.hoteleden.perugia.it. © **075/572-8102.** 12 units. 65€–95€ double. Rates include breakfast. Garage parking 25€ per day. **Amenities:** Wi-Fi (free).

Primavera Minihotel ★★ It's well worth the climb up the three flights of stairs to reach this aerie-like retreat atop a house just down some twisty streets from Piazza della Repubblica. The rooftop locale means all the tall windows frame views of rooftops and the green valleys spread out below the town. Best are from a room one additional flight up, with its own large terrace, though there's not a bad room in the house. All are different, some with Art Nouveau pieces, some with traditionally rustic furnishing and Deruta pottery, others quite contemporary. All have hardwood floors and lots of timber, stone, and other architectural details, and all surround a welcoming lounge/breakfast room (though you'll have to pay extra for breakfast).

Via Vincioli 8. www.primaveraminihotel.it. © **075/572-1657.** 8 units. 65€–90€ double. Garage parking 15€ per day. **Amenities:** Wi-Fi (free).

Perugia's Medieval Pompeii

Beneath Piazza Italia is some remarkable underground scenery. Around 1530 the Perugians rebelled against Pope Paul III over a tax on salt (to this day, Perugian bread is salt-free). In retribution, the Pope demolished more than one-quarter of the city, and built his **Rocca Paolina** atop the ruins. After Italian unification in 1860, locals ripped the castle to pieces and built Piazza Italia on top. Today, however, the vaults of the Pope's fort and the even older remains of medieval dwellings and streets are in full view beneath the piazza. You can clamber through doorless entrances, climb the remains of stairways, walk through empty rooms, and wander at will through the brick maze. Enter the underground city daily (no admission fee) from the escalators that connect the lower-town's Piazza Partigiani, with its car park and bus station, and Piazza Italia (daily 6:15am–1:45am).

The City of *Cioccolato* and Jazz

Perugia is a chocoholic's paradise. **Perugina** has been making candy here since 1907 and now pumps out 120 tons of the brown stuff a day, including 1½ million Baci (kisses), its gianduja-and-hazelnut bestseller. You can buy them and other products at the Perugina shop at Corso Vannucci 101 (© **075/573-4760**). Perugia hosts a weeklong **Eurochocolate**

Festival (www.eurochocolate.com) every year from mid- to late October. The highlight is the chocolate-carving contest, when the scraps of 1,000kg (455-lb.) blocks are handed out for sampling. **Umbria Jazz** (www.umbriajazz.com), one of Europe's top jazz festivals, draws top international names to town for 2 weeks in mid-July.

Where to Eat

Plenty of cheap *pizzerie* feed the student population. The best is **Il Segreto di Pulcinella,** Via Larga 8, off Via Bonazzi and a short walk from Piazza della Repubblica (© **075/573-6284**). Pizzas cost 4€ to 7€, and it's open Tuesday through Sunday (noon–2:30pm and 8:30pm–midnight).

Bottega del Vino ★ UMBRIAN   A snug, vintage-photo-lined room right off Piazza IV Novembre dispenses wines by the glass and accompanies them with a nice assortment of Umbrian hams and cheeses—perfect for an evening *aperitivo* at one of the tables out front as all of Perugia promenades by. Small lunch and dinner menus include salads and a couple of pastas, as well as a dish or two of the day, which might be a steak or roasted leg of lamb. Live jazz often continues into the small hours, making this a popular after-dinner spot, too.

Via del Sole 1. © **075/571-6181.** Main courses 13€. Tues–Sun noon–3pm and 7pm–midnight. Closed Jan.

La Taverna ★★ UMBRIAN   For many Perugians, a tiny courtyard down a flight of steps from Corso Vannucci is the epicenter of good dining. In warm weather, tables fill the courtyard; inside, barrel-vaulted ceilings shimmer with candlelight in evening, and the service and the cooking are similarly warm and down to earth. Everything, from bread to pasta to desserts, is made in house and typically Umbrian: Papardelle is sauced with a hearty Umbrian ragù, *caramelle rosse al gorgonzola* (beet ravioli with Gorgonzola) is made with beets from a local farm, and the grilled and roasted meats are seasoned with fresh herbs from the surroundings hillsides. Chef Claudio will make his way to your table at some point to ensure that everything is *tutto bene.*

Via delle Streghe 8 (near Corso Vannucci's Piazza Repubblica). © **075/572-4128.** Main courses 9€–16€. Tues–Sun 12:30–2:30pm and 7:30–11pm.

Osteria dai Priori ★ UMBRIAN   You'll pass through a wine shop downstairs and climb a flight of stairs to reach this welcoming brick-vaulted room with contemporary blond furnishings, where the emphasis is on local ingredients and age-old Umbrian recipes. A portion of slowly cooked small beans (*fagiolina*) is paired with eggs and onions and bread salad; *gnoccconi* (large potato dumplings) are stuffed with fresh ricotta; slow-roasted pork shank (*stinco di mialale*) is served with crisp potatoes. The staff will eagerly walk you through the ever-changing menu and pair wines with each course.

Via dei Priori 39. ℭ **075/572-7098.** Main courses 9€–12€. Wed–Mon noon–3pm and 7:30–10:30.

A Side Trip to Gubbio

Gubbio, 39 km (24 miles) northeast of Perugia, is hands-down the most medieval-looking town in Umbria, with a crenelated skyline backed by a tree-covered mountain. At its stony heart is Piazza Grande, where the harsh expanse is softened from the south side by views of misty hills and the wide valley that spreads beneath them.

GETTING THERE   By **car,** the SS298 branches north from Perugia, off the E45, through rugged scenery. Gubbio is not served by train, but there are eight or nine daily **Umbria Mobilità buses** (www.umbriamobilita. it; ℭ **800/512141**) from **Perugia** to Piazza 40 Martiri (70 min.), named for citizens killed by the Nazis for aiding partisans during World War II

EXPLORING GUBBIO

If you want to avoid the climb up to Piazza Grande, take the free elevator at the junction of Via Repubblica and Via Baldassini (daily 7:45am–7pm). The tourist office is nearby at Via della Repubblica 15 (www.comune.gub bio.pg.it; ℭ **075/922-0693** or 075/922-0790). It's open Monday through Friday from 8:30am to 1:45pm and 3:30 to 6:30pm, Saturday from 9am to 1pm and 3:30 to 6:30pm, and Sunday from 9:30am to 1pm and 3 to 6pm; October through March, all afternoon hours are 3 to 6pm.

Monte Igino ★ PARK/GARDEN   An open-air funicular whisks you to the top of this 908m (2,980-ft.) summit in about 5 minutes for yet more stupendous Umbrian views. On the ascent you can be glad you are not taking part in the May 15 Corso dei Ceri, when teams race up the mountainside carrying 15-foot-long wooden battering ram–like objects called ceri, or "candles." The race is part of festivities honoring St. Ubaldo, the bishop who allegedly smooth-talked Frederick Barbarossa out of sacking the town in the 1150s and was sainted for his efforts. The saint's corpse is up here, too, languishing in a glass casket at the Basilica di Sant'Ubaldo, a 5-minute walk from the top station of the funicular. The **Funivia Colle Eletto** (www.funiviagubbio.it; ℭ **075-927-3881**) runs Monday to Friday 10am to 1:15pm and 2:30 to 6:30pm, Saturday to Sunday 9:30am to 1:15pm and 2:30 to 7pm (hours can vary month to month). Round-trip tickets are 5€ adults, 4€ children 4 to 13; one-way tickets are 4€ adults, 3€ children.

Museo del Palazzo dei Consoli ★★ MUSEUM   The former home of the town government is a solidly Gothic-looking palace, almost improbably so, with crenellations, a tower, and an imposing stone staircase that

Go Jump in the Lake

Lago Trasimeno, Italy's fourth-largest lake, washes up against the Tuscany–Umbria border between Cortona and Perugia. The shallow waters aren't quite a match for the romance and beauty of Como and the other lakes in the north, but Trasimeno is nonetheless a refreshing splash of blue amid olive groves and sunflower fields. The lakeshore was the site of a big moment in history, too—in 271 b.c., Hannibal, having just breached the Alps, lured 16,000 Roman soldiers into an ambush somewhere on the northern shore (just where is a matter of debate) and massacred them.

A well-equipped spot from which to enjoy the lake is **Castiglione del Lago,** 50km (30 miles) west of Perugia, where you can swim from a pebbly beach or do a bit of biking on shoreline paths; you

can rent bikes for about 10€ a day at **Cicli Valentini**, Via Firenze 68/B (℃ **333/9678327**; ciclivalentini.it); it's open Sat–Sun 9am–1pm and 3:30–8pm.

Hourly ferry trips of about half an hour cross the lake to the picturesque island of **Isola Maggiore**, an especially nice place to take a dip in the relatively uncrowded waters, or to buy lace from the few local women who carry on a long-standing island craft tradition. Just stepping ashore on Isola Maggiore, you'll be following in the footsteps of St. Francis, who spent Lent of 1213 here. Allegedly, the saint even charmed the local fish—when Francis threw a pike given to him by a fisherman back into the lake, the grateful creature swam alongside his savior until the saint gave him a special blessing.

seems to demand you climb up from Piazza Grande. The main hall, where the medieval commune met, houses the sleep-inducing town museum, where one prize stands out amid the old coins and bits of pottery: the seven **Eugubine Tables**, inscribed on bronze from 200 to 70 b.c., which provide the only existing record of the Umbri language transposed in Etruscan and Latin letters—in other words, ancient Umbria's Rosetta Stone. The tablets mainly detail the finer points of animal sacrifice and divination through watching the flight patterns of birds. A local farmer turned up the tablets while he was plowing his fields in 1444, and city officials convinced him to sell them for 2 years' worth of grazing rights. In your explorations be sure to find the secret corridor that leads from the back of the ceramics room to the Pinacoteca upstairs, via the medieval toilets.

Piazza Grande. ℃ **075/927-4298.** Admission 5€ adults, 2.50€ children 7–25, free for children 7 and under and seniors. Apr–Sept daily 10am–1pm and 3–6pm; Oct–Mar daily 10am–1pm and 2–5pm.

WHERE TO EAT

Grotta dell'Angelo ★ ITALIAN/UMBRIAN   A long barrel-vaulted dining room where locals have been gathering for the past 700 years or so is the place to sit in winter, while warm-weather dining is on a vine-shaded terrace. Wherever you eat, enjoy homemade gnocchi and other pastas, followed by flame-grilled sausages and other meats roasted over the open fire—the whole roast chicken stuffed with fennel is especially delicious.

Via Gioia 47. www.grottadellangelo.it. ℃ **075/927-3438.** Main courses 9€–14€. Wed–Mon 12:30–2:30pm and 7:30–11pm. Closed Jan 7–Feb 7.

A Side Trip to Urbino

One of the steepest hill towns in Italy, the time-capsule Renaissance city of Urbino carpets adjoining ridges with a lovely compilation of towers, domes, and red-tile roofs. Though the glory days of this remote and hard-to-reach town wound down about 500 years ago, it's still prosperous and lively, and you'll be sharing the streets and squares with students at Urbino's famous university. The only easy way to get here from Perugia is by car, 113km (68 miles) northeast through mountainous terrain on the SP3. The trip takes a slow hour and 45 minutes, but you won't mind, as the landscape puts on quite a show, its rippling hills carpeted with a patchwork of fields and forests and topped with occasional walled village. Stash your car in the large parking lot at Borgo del Mercatale (1.20€ per hour), and then attack the steep cobblestone streets on foot.

Lovely as it is, Urbino's main draws are definitely art-related: It's the home town of Raphael, the Renaissance painter of glorious frescos, and the outstanding art collection of Duke Frederico da Montefeltro, housed in his magnificent palace.

Palazzo Ducale/Galleria Nazionale delle Marche ★★ MUSEUM

Wise and worldly Duke Frederico da Montefeltro (1422–82) paced the halls of this palace and contemplated his vast holdings from the study window, all the while dreaming up some of the most enlightened ideals of the Renaissance. (One of the palace's most enchanting rooms is that study, beautifully paneled with intarsia depicting classical and humanistic writers as well as great religious thinkers.) The duke famously came up with the concept of *sprezzatura*, the ideal of maintaining grace under

The hill town of Urbino, in the Marches.

pressure. Duke Frederico and his son, Guidobaldo, oversaw a court that was so enlightened that Baldassare Castiglione set his 1507 bestseller, *Book of the Courtier,* in the palace's Hall of Vigils. Father and son were also patrons of some of the great artists of their day, whose works are now among those hanging in the salons and staterooms. Quite in keeping with the duke's enlightened notions is "Ideal City," attributed to Piero della Francesca; the artist's "Flagellation," commissioned by the duke and still among the palace's treasures, is one of the Renaissance's finest accomplishments in perspective. Less lofty, subjectwise, is Paolo Uccello's similarly masterful work of perspective, "The Profanation of the Host," a piece of 15th-century anti-Semitic propaganda depicting a popular tale in which a pawnbroker attempts to cook the sacred communion wafer (believed to be transformed into the body of Christ during the eucharist), as blood seeps under his door and attracts bailiffs.

Piazza Duca Frederico. www.galleriaborghese.it © **0722/2760.** Admission 5€. Mon 8:30am–2pm, Tues–Sun 8:30am–7:15pm.

Raphael's Birthplace ★ MUSEUM   One of the great artists of the High Renaissance (you may have seen his work at Cappella di San Severo in Perugia, p. 290, and his best efforts at the Vatican, p. 80) was born here in 1483. In fact, you can even see here his earliest known work, a modest boyhood fresco on one of the rough walls, "Madonna and Child." Compare it to his "Portrait of a Young Woman," in the nearby Palazzo Ducale, which shows the genius of his mature style. Near that painting in the museum, look also for works by Raphael's lesser-known father, Giovanni Santi, who was a court painter to the duke.

Via Rafaello 57. Admission 3€. Mar–Oct Mon–Sat 9am–1pm and 3–7pm, Sun 10am–1pm; Nov–Feb Mon–Sat 9am–2pm, Sun 10am–1pm.

WHERE TO EAT

Taverna degli Artisti ★ ITALIAN   These vaulted underground rooms, one with colorful frescoes, are the place to try *Strozzapretti con salmone, asparagi, funghi,* thick elongated pasta (the name means "priest choker") with a creamy sauce of salmon, asparagus, and mushrooms. It's an Urbino favorite that even locals claim is expertly done here. Their other pastas and pizzas are excellent, too.

Via Bramante 52. © **0722/2676**. Main courses 10€–15€. Daily 12:30–2:30pm and 7:30–10pm.

ASSISI ★★★

27km (17 miles) E of Perugia

St. Francis is still working miracles: His birthplace remains a lovely Umbrian hilltown, despite a steady onslaught of visitors. Many pilgrims come to pay homage to Francis at the Basilica di San Francisco, and almost as many are drawn by the frescoes celebrating his life with which

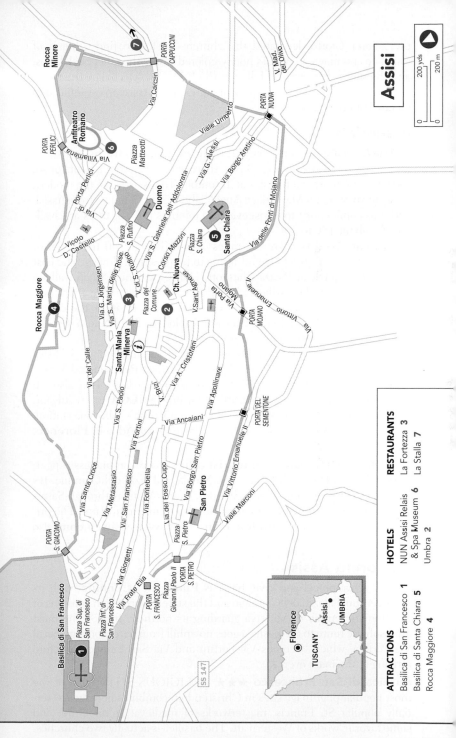

Assisi

0   200 yds
0   200 m

SS 147

TUSCANY

Florence

UMBRIA

Assisi

Basilica di San Francesco
Piazza Sup. di San Francesco
Piazza Inf. di San Francesco

PORTA S. GIACOMO

Via Santa Croce

Via del Calle

Rocca Maggiore

PORTA PERLICI

Porta Perlici

Via di

Vicolo D. Castello

Anfiteatro Romano

Via Villamena

PORTA CAPPUCCINI

Via Carceri

Rocca Minore

Piazza Matteotti

Duomo

Piazza S. Rufino

Via S. Rufino

V. di S. Rufino

Via S. Maria delle Rose

Via G. Jørgensen

Via S. Paolo

Via Metastasio

Vie San Francesco

Via Fontini

Via Fontebella

Via del Fosso Cupo

Via Frate Elia

Via Giorgetti

PORTA S. FRANCESCO

Piazza Giovanni Paolo II

PORTA S. PIETRO

Piazza S. Pietro

San Pietro

Via Borgo San Pietro

Via Ancaiani

Via Apollinare

Via A. Cristofani

V. Brizi

Santa Maria Minerva

Piazza del Comune

Ch. Nuova

Corso Mazzini

Via S. Gabriele dell'Addolorata

Via del Addolorata

Piazza S. Chiara

Santa Chiara

Via S. Chiara

V. Sant'Agnese

Via Porta Mojano

PORTA MOJANO

Il Mojano

Via delle Fonti di Mojano

Via Borgo Aretino

Via G. Alessi

Viale Umberto

PORTA NUOVA

V. Mad. del Olivo

Via Vittorio Emanuele II

Viale Marconi

PORTA DEL SEMENTONE

PORTA DEL SEMENTONE

the painter Giotto decorated the church. You'll also find a blend of romance and magic in Assisi's honey-colored stone, the quiet back lanes, and the mists that rise and fall over the Val di Spoleto below the town. With its saintly presence and pleasant ambience, Assisi an essential stop on any Umbrian tour.

Essentials

GETTING THERE   From **Perugia,** there are about 20 **trains** daily (25–30 min.). From **Florence** (2–3 hr.), there are trains every 2 hours or so, though some require a transfer at Terontola. Trains arrive in the modern valley town of Santa Maria degli Angeli, about 5km (3 miles) from Assisi, with bus connections to Assisi every 20 minutes (1€), or **taxis** are available for about 15€ to 20€.

By **car,** Assisi is 18km (11 miles) east of Perugia, off the SS75bis. The center's steep streets are off limits to non-resident drivers. The best strategy is to **park** in Piazza Matteotti (1.15€ per hour), keep walking west, and finish at the basilica; it's all downhill. A dependable alternative is the Mojano multi-story garage (1.05€ first 2 hrs.; 1.45€/hr. thereafter) halfway up the hill from Piazza Giovanni Paolo II to Porta Nuova. Escalators whisk you into the center of town.

Eight Umbria Mobilità **buses** (www.umbriamobilita.it; 🕿 **800/512141**) run seven times daily (Mon–Fri) between **Perugia** and Assisi's Piazza Matteotti (50 min.; 3.20€; 4€ if you pay on the bus). They also run about five buses a day from **Gubbio** (1¾ hr.). **SULGA** (www.sulga.it; 🕿 **075/500-9641**) runs two buses daily from **Rome**'s Tiburtina station, taking about 3 hours, and one daily trip from Piazza Adua in **Florence,** which takes about 2½ hours.

VISITOR INFORMATION   The **tourist office** (www.comune.assisi.pg.it; 🕿 **075/812534**) is in the Palazzo S. Nicola on Piazza del Comune. It's open summer daily from 8am to 6:30pm, winter Monday through Saturday from 8am to 2pm and 3 to 6pm, Sunday from 9am to 1pm. The private websites **www.assisionline.com** and **www.assisiweb.com** also have good info.

Exploring Assisi

Assisi's geographical and civic heart is **Piazza del Comune**, with its 13th-century Palazzo del Capitano and the stately Corinthian columns of the Roman Tempio di Minerva guarding its northern fringe. The most atmospheric route to the basilica goes downhill from here along medieval Via Portica, which becomes Via Fortini and Via San Francesco before arriving at the main event.

Basilica di San Francesco ★★★ RELIGIOUS SITE   One of the most popular pilgrimage sites in Christendom combines homage to eternally popular St. Francis, masterworks of medieval architecture, and some favorite works of Western art. The basilica is actually two churches,

The World's Favorite Saint

For Christian pilgrims the magic of Assisi is all about St. Francis, one of the patron saints of Italy (along with Catherine of Siena). Founder of one of the world's largest monastic orders, he is generally considered to be just about the holiest person to walk the earth since Jesus. Born to a wealthy merchant, Francis was a spoiled young man of his time, until he did an about-turn in his early 20s and dedicated himself to a life of poverty. His meekness, love of animals, and invention of the Christmastime crèche scenes have all helped ensure his popularity. Though Francis traveled as far as Egypt (in an unsuccessful attempt to convert the sultan and put an end to the Crusades), he is most associated with the gentle countryside around Assisi, where he spent months praying and fasting in lonely hermitages.

lower and upper; the lower church is dark and somber, a place of contemplation, while the upper church soars into light-filled Gothic vaults, instilling a sense of celebration. This assemblage was begun soon after the saint's death in 1226, under the guidance of Francis's savvy and worldly colleague, Brother Elias. The lower church was completed in 1230, and the upper church in 1280. The steeply sloping site just outside the city walls was previously used for executions and known as the Hill of Hell. The presence of the patron saint of Italy, in spirit as well as in body, now makes this one of Italy's most uplifting sights. His kindness, summed up in his saying, "For it is in giving that we receive," seems to permeate the soft gray stones, and the frescoed spaces move the devout to tears and art lovers to fits of near-religious ecstasy.

The Lower Church Entered off Piazza Inferiore di San Francesco (the lower of the two squares abutting the church), the basilica's bottom half is a cryptlike church that is indeed, first and foremost, a crypt, housing the stone **sarcophagus of St. Francis**, surrounded by four of his disciples. An almost steady stream of the faithful files past the monument, many on their knees. Inside is the saint's remarkably intact skeleton. Most saints of the Middle Ages fell victim to the purveyors of relics, who made enormous profit dispensing bones, a finger here, a toe there. It's said that Brother Elias, Francis' savvy colleague, had the foresight to seal the coffin in stone, and it remained undetected until 1818. The dimly lit atmosphere is greatly enlivened with the presence of many rich frescoes, including Simone Martini's action-packed depictions of the "Life of St. Martin" in the **Cappella di San Martino** (1322–1326). Martini displays his flair for boldly patterned fabrics and his familiarity with detailed manuscript illumination (many such manuscripts would have passed through his native Siena, on the pilgrimage route from northern Europe to Rome). Martini was also, like St. Martin, a knight, which may have influenced his depictions of the saint—who was a Roman soldier—being investitured, ripping his cloak to share it with a beggar, and renouncing chivalry and weaponry in favor of doing good deeds. The imagery is not out of keeping with Francis, who as a youth dreamed of being a soldier.

Giotto and his assistants frescoed the **Cappella della Santa Maria Maddalena**, with the "Life of St. Mary Magdalene" (1303–1309). An incredibly moving cycle of "Christ's Passion" (1316–1319) by Pietro Lorenzetti includes a hauntingly humane "Deposition," in which the young Sienese artist depicts a gaunt Christ and sorrowful Mary, displaying a naturalism and emotion not before seen in painting.

The Upper Church   Entering the light-filled Gothic interior of the Upper Church, you'll first encounter **scenes of the New Testament** by Cimabue, the last great painter of the Byzantine style; some critics say only the "Crucifixion" (1277) is his, and the rest of the scenes are by his assistants. In any case, it's rather ironic he's here at all. The artist was infamous for his stubbornness and difficult personality (in the *Divine Comedy*, Dante places him in Purgatory among the proud, adding the comment, "Cimabue thought to hold the field of painting, and now Giotto hath the cry.") It's Giotto who famously holds court in this church, with his 28-part fresco cycle on **"The Life of St. Francis,"** completed in the 1290s. Even nonreligious viewers love these scenes of the saint removing his clothing to renounce material processions, marrying poverty (symbolized by a woman in rags), and preaching to the birds (the perennial favorite scene, and the subject of ubiquitous postcards for sale around town).

Piazza Superiore di San Francesco. www.sanfrancescoassisi.org. ✆ **075/819001.** Free admission. Lower Church daily 6am–7pm; Upper Church daily 8:30am–7pm.

Basilica di Santa Chiara ★ CHURCH   One of the first followers of St. Francis was a young woman, Chiara (Clare, in English), daughter of a count and countess, who was so swept away by the teachings of the young zealot that she allowed him to cut her hair and dress her in sackcloth. She founded the order of the Poor Dames (now known as Poor Clares), whose members continue to renounce material possessions, and her remains lie in this vast, stark church on full view, with her face covered in wax. Also in this church, the **Oratorio del Crocifisso** preserves the venerated 12th-century crucifix from which the figure of Christ allegedly spoke to St. Francis and asked him to rebuild his church (the reference was to the organization, which had by then become mired in politics, corruption, and warfare). As Clare lay ill on Christmas Eve 1252, she allegedly voiced regrets that she would not be able to attend services in the then-new Basilica di San Francisco. Suddenly, in a vision, she saw and heard the

---

Dress Appropriately

San Francesco and Santa Chiara have a strict dress code. Entrance is *forbidden* to those wearing shorts or miniskirts or showing bare shoulders. You also must remain silent and cannot take photographs in the Upper Church of San Francesco.

mass clear as a bell and in Technicolor, a miracle for which she was named the patron saint of television in 1958.

Piazza Santa Chiara. © **075/812282.** Free admission. Daily 6:30am–noon and 2–7pm (6pm in winter).

Rocca Maggiore ★★ CASTLE   This civic show of might is built of bleached yellow stone atop a steep hillside very high above the city. Some claim that a sharp-eyed observer can see all the way to the Mediterranean on a clear day, but that's probably an oxygen-deprivation vision induced by the climb through narrow medieval lanes and up the pine-scented hillside. Hyberbole aside, views across the Umbrian plain below are wonderful—quite a bit more exhilarating than the dull displays of costumes and weapons in the restored keep and soldiers quarters. Save the admission fee for a glass of wine when you get back down.

Piazzale delle Libertà Comunali, at the top of town, at the ends of Via della Rocca, Via del Colle, and the stepped Vicolo San Lorenzo off Via Porta Perlici. © **075/815292.** Admission 5€ adults; 3.50€ students, children 8–18, and seniors 65 and over; free for children 7 and under; joint ticket with Foro Romano and Pinacoteca Comunale 8€ and 5€. June–Aug daily 9am–8pm; Apr–May and Sept–Oct daily 10am–6:30pm; Nov–Feb daily 10am–4:30pm; Mar 10am–5:30pm.

Where to Stay

Never show up in Assisi, especially from Easter to fall, without a hotel reservation. Don't even think of showing up without a reservation on pilgrim-thronged **church holidays** or the **Calendimaggio,** a spring celebration the first weekend (starting Thurs) after May 1, when the town divides itself into "upper" and "lower" factions that date to the 1300s; it's a celebration full of processions, medieval contests of strength and skill, and late-night partying—all in 14th-century costume, of course. At these times you may wind up stuck overnight in one of the bus-pilgrimage facilities 4km (2½ miles) away in Santa Maria degli Angeli. The official central booking office is **Consorzio Albergatori ed Operatori Turistici di Assisi,** Via A. Cristofani 22a (www.visitassisi.com; © **075/816-566**).

NUN Assisi Relais & Spa Museum ★★   A dramatic change of pace from Assisi's heavily medieval aura is in full force at this contemporary redo of a centuries-old convent. Handsome guest quarters have all-white surfaces and bursts of bright colors, accented with stone walls and arches, and boldly turned out with Eames chairs, laminate tables, and high-tech lighting. A two-level suite with a hanging sleeping loft is focused on a massive 13th-century fresco of saints in the wilderness, bound to instill nighttime visions. A lavish breakfast buffet and other meals are served in a stark, white-vaulted, modern version of the refectory, and downstairs are hedonistic pleasures the former tenants could never have dreamed of—two pools, a series of saunas and steam rooms, and a state-of-the-art spa.

Eremo delle Carceri 1A. www.nunassisi.com. © **075/815-5150.** 18 units. From 260€ double. Rates include breakfast. **Amenities:** Restaurant; bar; concierge; indoor pools; room service; sauna; steam room; spa; Wi-Fi (free).

Umbra ★★   Assisi lodgings just don't get any homier than the Laudenzi family's welcoming little inn, down a tiny alley from Piazza del Comune. A gate opens into a shady patio and beyond are welcoming, if a bit outdated, guest rooms with vaulted ceilings, fresco fragments, and other historic remnants here and there, all nicely furnished with old-fashioned armoires and dressers. Views over rooftops to the valley below unfold through the tall windows, from the private terraces off the choicest rooms, and the rooftop terrace for all guests to enjoy. The dining room is one of the most pleasant places to eat in town and extends into a lovely garden.

Via Delgli Archi 6 (off the west end of Piazza del Comune). www.hotelumbra.it. ✆ 075/812240. 24 units. 85€–130€ double. Rates include breakfast. Garage parking 10€ per day. Closed mid-Jan to Easter. **Amenities:** Restaurant; bar; babysitting; bikes; concierge; room service; Wi-Fi (free).

Villa Zuccari ★★   If you have a car, you can easily visit Assisi from any number of smaller nearby towns. The little wine village of Montefalco, about 20 minutes south, is especially appealing, given the presence of dozens of wineries and this old family estate, where you will feel like a guest in a gracious Italian home. You will also be within easy reach of Spello, Trevi, Spoleto, Todi, and other hill towns that spill down the Umbrian hillsides. But you might be tempted to stay put on your own large terrace or in the palm-shaded garden surrounding a pool. Inside, the airy, light-filled bedrooms are especially large and comfortably equipped with soft armchairs, king-sized beds, and some nice antiques; the big bathrooms are sheathed in marble. Welcoming lounges are filled with books and pottery, and dinners are served in a vaulted room that glistens with terracotta tiles.

Locanda San Luca (just east of Montefalco). www.villazuccari.com. ✆ 0742/399402. 34 units. From 135€ double. **Amenities:** Restaurant; bar; pool; Wi-Fi (free).

Where to Eat

Several of Assisi's restaurants and bars serve a local flatbread called *torta al testa,* usually split and stuffed with cheeses, sausages, and vegetables (spinach is popular). It's a meal in itself and a fast and cheap lunch.

La Fortezza ★★ UMBRIAN   You don't have to veer far off the beaten track to find the Chiocchetti family's plain, stone-walled dining room, where the focus is on authentic Umbrian home cooking. Both body and soul benefit from their specialties, such as *cannelloni all'Assisiana* (fresh pasta sheets wrapped around a veal *ragù,* all baked under parmigiano) and *coniglio in salsa di mele* (rabbit roasted in a sauce of wine and apples).

Vicolo della Fortezza/Piazza del Comune (up the stairs near the Via San Rufino end). www.lafortezzahotel.com. ✆ 075/812993. Main courses 10€–13€. Fri–Wed 12:30–2:30pm and 7:30–9:30pm. Closed Feb and 1 week in July.

La Stalla ★★ GRILL/UMBRIAN   It's not often that the term "old barn" is associated with good dining, but a meal in these rustic and rather raucous converted livestock stalls, with stone walls and low ceilings, can be the highlight of a trip to Assisi (even the servers seem to be having a good time). The pleasant, 15-minute walk out here will work up an appetite, so begin with the *assaggini di torta al testo*, small samplers of Assisian flatbread stuffed with cheese, meat, and vegetables, then move through the hearty selection of pastas to the simple servings of steak, pork and sausage skewers, chicken, and even potatoes that come off the grill. Decent house wines compliment the meals, which you can enjoy on a terrace in good weather.

Santuario della Carceri 24 1½ km (less than 1 mile) from center, direction Eremo. ℂ **075/812317.** Main courses 8€–13€. Tues–Sun noon–2:30 and 7–10:30pm.

SPOLETO ★

63km (39 miles) SE of Perugia

Spoletto can seem to be the center of the cultured world in June, when the **Festival dei Due Mondi** (aka Spoleto Festival) brings performers and audiences from all over the world to town. For most of the year, though, Spoleto is just another lovely Umbrian hill town, sweeping up a steep hillside. The pleasant warren of steep streets and airy piazzas are lined with artifacts from the Roman past and prosperous Middle Ages, and include one of Italy's most beautifully situated cathedrals.

Essentials

GETTING THERE Spoleto is a main **rail** station on the Rome-Ancona line, and 16 daily trains from **Rome** stop here (about 1½ hr.). From **Perugia,** take one of the 20 daily trains to Foligno (25 min.) to transfer to this line for the final 20-minute leg. From outside the station, take bus A, B, or C to Piazza Carducci on the edge of the old town.

By **car,** the town sits on the old Roman Via Flaminia, now the SS3. There's usually plenty of parking, but the easiest option is to make for the Spoletosfera parking garage, signposted from the SS3's Spoleto Sud exit (1€ per hour). Escalators from the lot run up the hillside to the top of town, allowing you to get off at well-signposted levels (for Piazza della Libertà, the Duomo, and so on).

VISITOR INFORMATION The **information center** at Piazza della Libertà 7 (www.visitspoleto.it; ℂ **0743/220773**) hands out heaps of info and an excellent map. It's open daily (Mon–Fri 9am–1:30pm and 2–7pm, Sat 9am–1pm, and Sun 10am–1pm and 3:30–6:30pm).

Exploring Spoleto

You won't spend much time in the Lower Town, but a highlight is the 11th-century Romanesque **San Gregorio di Maggiore,** Piazza della Vittoria (ℂ **0743/44140**), which replaced an earlier oratory here in a cemetery of Christian martyrs. The church's namesake saint was killed in a spectacle at the nearby amphitheater in A.D. 304, as were a supposed 10,000 lesser-known martyrs whose bones symbolically reside beneath the altar. It opens daily from 8am to noon and 4 to 6pm, and admission is free.

Once you settle into town, with the aid of a map you'll be able to figure out ways to use handy **escalators** to avoid steep uphill climbs; hotel staff will also usually help you plot a level course. **Piazza del Mercato,** the probable site of the old Roman forum, is a bustling spot in the Upper Town lined with grocers and fruit vendors' shops.

Casa Romana ★ HISTORIC HOME As a stop on the busy Via Flaminia route and an important wine supplier, Spoletium was fairly prosperous in the Roman world. Enough of this patrician's home remains, including frescoes and mosaics, to give an idea of what the good life was like for a Roman occupant in the 1st century A.D. The resident was obviously well-to-do, though there's no proof for the claim that it was Vespasia Polla, the mother of the Emperor Vespasian.

Via di Visiale. © **0743/234350.** Admission 2.50€ adults, 2€ ages 15–25 and seniors 65 and over, 1€ children 7–14, free for children 6 and under. Daily 10:30am–5:30pm.

Cattedrale di Santa Maria dell'Assunta ★★ CATHEDRAL Spoleto's almost playfully picturesque cathedral was consecrated in 1098, barely 40 years after Frederick Barbarossa, Holy Roman Emperor, razed the entire town in retaliation for the citizens' lack of support in his ongoing wars against the papacy. The church seems to defy the brutality of that catastrophe, serenely set in a broad piazza at the bottom of a flight of monumental steps. White marble and golden mosaics on the dazzling facade are framed against a gentle backdrop of a forested hill. Inside, the apse is graced with frescoes of the "Life of the Virgin" that are largely from the brush of Filippo Lippi, one of the more colorful characters of his time. An ordained priest, Filippo shirked his duties to draw and was eventually given permission to paint full time. Though he worked frequently and was a favorite of the Medicis, he was chronically impoverished, supposedly because he spent so much money on women. The commission to come to Spoleto must have been a plum for the artist, then close to 60. His delicate and engaging scenes of the elegant Virgin being visited by the Archangel and holding her very sweet-looking infant betray nothing of the turbulence in his life, as he was fighting to get dispensation to marry a young nun, Lucrezia Buti, whom he had seduced and who had borne his son, Filippino Lippi (who would soon match his father's greatness as a painter). Both Lippis appear in the Domition

Spoleto's Big Bash

Spoleto's be-all and end-all annual event bridges the end of June and early July. The **Spoleto Festival** (www.festivaldispoleto.it) offers 3 weeks of world-class drama, music, and dance held in evocative spaces like an open-air restored Roman theater and the pretty piazza fronting the Duomo. A secondary **Spoleto Estate** season of music, art, and theater runs from just after the festival ends through September.

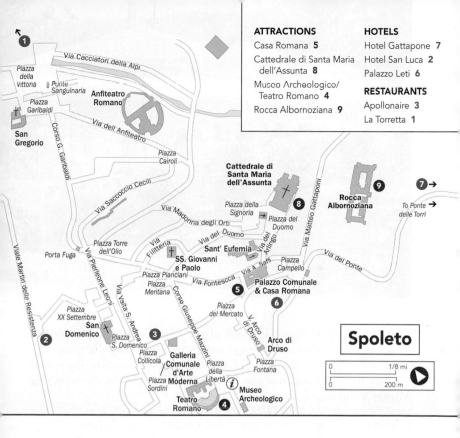

ATTRACTIONS
Casa Romana **5**
Cattedrale di Santa Maria dell'Assunta **8**
Museo Archeologico/ Teatro Romano **4**
Rocca Albornoziana **9**

HOTELS
Hotel Gattapone **7**
Hotel San Luca **2**
Palazzo Leti **6**

RESTAURANTS
Apollonaire **3**
La Torretta **1**

Spoleto

of the Virgin scene, Filippo wearing a white habit with young Filippino, as an angel, in front of him. Fillippo died before he completed the frescoes, and his assistants finished the task. The cause of his death was suspected to be poison, perhaps administered by Lucrezia's family or yet another paramour. He is buried beneath a monument on the right side of the transept, which his son Filippino designed at the request of Lorenzo de' Medici, Filippo's patron, who tried in vain to get the body back to Florence. In the Cappella delle Reliquie (Reliquary Chapel), on the left aisle, is a rare treasure—a letter written and signed by St. Francis. (Assisi has the only other bona fide signature.)

Piazza del Duomo. *©* **0743/231063.** Free admission. Daily 8:30am–12:30pm and 3:30–5:30pm (until 7pm Apr–Oct).

Museo Archeologico/Teatro Romano ★ MUSEUM/RUINS
Spoleto had the good fortune to more or less flourish through the Dark Ages and the Middle Ages, and as a consequence most of the Roman city was quarried or built over. The monastery of St. Agata was built atop this splendid theater that wasn't recognized until 1891. After a thorough restoration in the 1950s, the theater is the evocative venue for performances

Café in Spoleto.

during the Spoleto Festival. Much of the original orchestra flooring is intact, as is an elaborate drainage system that was allegedly quite efficient in flushing out the blood of slain animals and martyrs. Busts and statuary that once adorned the theater are on display in the adjoining Museo Archeologico.

Via di Sant'Agata 18A. (✆ **0743/223277.** Admission 4€ adults, 2€ ages 18–25, free for children 17 and under and seniors 65 and over. Daily 8:30am–7:30pm.

Rocca Albornoziana ★★ CASTLE Cardinal Albornoz, a power-hungry zealot tasked with rebuilding and strengthening the papal states, arrived in Spoleto in the mid-14th century and commissioned the Umbrian architect Matteo Gattapone to build a fortress. The site was perfect—atop a high hill above the town and, as history would prove, virtually impregnable. The walled-and-moated castle became famous in the 20th century as one of Italy's most secure prisons, where members of the Red Brigades terrorist organization were routinely incarcerated. The fortunate ones might have had a view through their cell windows of the majestic **Ponte delle Torri**, a 232m (760 ft.) long aqueduct built in the 13th century on Roman foundations. Its arches span a deep, verdant gorge, 90m (295 ft.) above the Tessino river, a scene that so impressed Wolfgang von Goethe on a 1786 visit to Spoleto that he dedicated an entire page of his "Italian Travels" to the spectacle. The current occupant of the fortress is the **Museo Nazionale del Ducato di Spoleto** (✆ **0743/223055**), with a benumbing collection of sarcophagi, mosaics, and religious statuary that you needn't feel guilty about not seeing (and a visit is costly as well). The views of the town and Umbrian countryside from the grounds are free, however, and well worth the ride up, via a series of escalators and elevators.

Piazza Campello. ℂ **0743/224952.** Admission 7.50€ adults, 6.50€ ages 15–25, 3.50€ children 7–14, free for children 6 and under. Tues–Sun 8:30am–7:30pm (last ticket 6:45pm).

Where to Stay

Accommodations are tight during the Spoleto Festival; reserve by March if you want to find a good, central room.

Hotel Gattapone ★   From the street, this completely unexpected retreat beneath the Rocca Albornozina seems like a relatively modest 19th-century villa. But step inside, and it's all polished wood, curved free-floating staircases, and leather couches facing window walls overlooking the Ponte dei Torre and green Monteluco hillsides. There's a cinematic, 1960s Antonioni-film quality to the place. In the guest rooms, slightly dated but well-maintained contemporary furnishings mix with traditional pieces, and huge bay windows hang over the same stunning views; rooms in the newer wing have sitting areas facing the views. Some guests comment that the air-conditioning is vintage, too, and anyone with mobility issues should keep in mind that there's no elevator and rooms and lounges flow for several floors down the hillside. But a flowery terrace at the bottom is one of many quirky charms.

Via del Ponte 6. www.hotelgattapone.it. ℂ **0743/223447.** 15 units. From 90€ double. Rates include buffet breakfast. **Amenities:** Bar; Wi-Fi (free).

Hotel San Luca ★★   A 19th-century tannery at the far edge of the city next to the Roman walls lends itself well to its current incarnation as an atmospheric and gracious hotel. A book-lined lounge, where canaries chirp in an antique cage and a fire crackles in colder months, faces a large courtyard, as do many of the rooms—others overlook a rose garden to the side. The unusually large quarters are all different and individually furnished with a mix of traditional and contemporary pieces and a smattering of antiques chosen by the owner—whose experience in the bath fixture business accounts for the extremely large and well-equipped windowed marble bathrooms. Sights and restaurants are about a 5-minute walk away, and the attentive staff will map out a route that involves the least amount of climbing. Among the many amenities is an easy-to-reach in-house garage, a real rarity in Spoleto.

Via Interna delle Mura 21. www.hotelsanluca.com. ℂ **0743/223399.** 35 units. From 90€ double. Rates include buffet breakfast. Garage parking (13€ per day). **Amenities:** Bar; babysitting; bikes; concierge; room service (bar); Wi-Fi (fee).

Palazzo Leti ★★   An entrance through a Renaissance garden that opens at one side to the Tessino gorge announces the air of enchantment that pervades this beautifully restored 13th-century palace of the Leti family. Views of the gorge and green Monteluco hills are the focal point of most of the guest rooms, though a few overlook a medieval alley that has a charm all its own; all have handsome period furnishings and rich fabrics, as well as welcoming couches and armchairs in the larger rooms. Exposed beams, granite hearths, and vaulted ceilings throughout enhance the historic surroundings. Anna Laura and Giampolo, who restored the palace from a dilapidated pile, are a friendly presence and provide all sorts of advice, including how to negotiate the narrow surrounding lanes in a car. Via degli Eremiti 10. www.palazzoleti.com. © 0743/224930. 12 units. 140€–200€ double. Rates include breakfast. Free parking. **Amenities:** Bar; babysitting; bikes; spa; Wi-Fi (free).

Where to Eat

For some gastro-shopping, visit **Bartolomei Orvieto** at 97 Corso Cavour (www.oleificiobartolomei.it; © 0743/344550), where you can taste and drink the products before buying. **Colder Gelateria** (© 0743/235015;** daily 12:30pm–midnight) serves some of the best gelato (notably the "bread and chocolate" flavor) in Umbria, created by local artisans Crispini.

Apollonaire ★ UMBRIAN   The low wood ceilings, stone walls, and beams are traditional holdovers from a 12th-century Franciscan monastery, but the menu is innovative and adventurous—contemporary Spoletan, if the food world has invented such a term. Dishes rely on fresh local ingredients and traditional Umbrian recipes but have that extra twist: *Strangozzi* (local long, rectangular wheat pasta) is topped with a pungent sauce of cherry tomatoes and mint, herb-roasted rabbit is served with black olive sauce, and pork filet mignon is topped with a sauce of pecorino cheese and pears soaked in Rosso di Montefalco. Via Sant'Agata 14 (near Piazza della Libertà). www.ristoranteapollinare.it. © 0743/225676. Main courses 12€–24€. Thurs–Tues noon–3pm and 7pm–midnight. Closed Feb.

La Torretta ★★ UMBRIAN   Comprising two welcoming rooms in a medieval tower converted to a wine cellar, just off an airy little piazza in a quiet corner of the old town, La Torretta is the place to settle in for a relaxed meal. Brothers Stefano and Elio Salvucci extend a genuine welcome and present a nice selection of Umbrian dishes with a focus on truffles, beginning with the *tris di antipasti al tartufo estivo* (trio of truffle-based appetizers) and working up to a choice of beautifully seasoned pork and beef grilled over a wood fire. The kitchen also makes a light-as-air truffle omelet, a memorable break from heavier *secondis*. Outdoor seating in summer. Via Filitteria 43. www.trattorialatorretta.com. © 0743/44954. Main courses 9€–16€. Wed–Mon 12:30–2:30pm and 7:45–10:45pm (closed Sun evening).

A Side Trip to Todi

45 km (28 miles) northwest of Spoleto

For sheer picturesqueness, few hilltowns in Umbria can match somber and proud Todi. What's more, at the top of the town is the finest square in Umbria, the **Piazza del Popolo**, a remarkable assemblage of 12th- to 14th-century palaces and the duomo. Its belvederes provide eagle's eye views of the rolling Umbrian countryside and the Tiber Valley below. Standing in this square and exploring the little lanes that run off it is the reason to be in Todi, where there's not much to see but a lot of ambience to soak in.

GETTING THERE   It's easy by car: Follow scenic S418 west out of Spoleto to Acquasparta, where you then take E45 northwest to Todi. By train, travel north from Spoleto to Perugia and change there for Todi; but you'll have to switch from the main station to Sant'Anna, in Piazzale Bellucci, and be sure to time the trip carefully so you don't wait hours for a connection.

VISITOR INFORMATION   The central **tourist office** is under the arches of the Palazzo del Capitano at Piazza del Popolo 38/39 (www.comune. todi.pg.it; ✆ **075/894-2526**). It's open Monday to Saturday 9:30am to 1pm and 3:30 to 7pm, Sunday 10am to 1pm and 3:30 to 7pm (to 6pm in winter when it's also closed Sun afternoons).

EXPLORING TODI

Piazza del Popolo is home to three harmonious public buildings from the 13th and 14th centuries that lend the square its austere dignity; the **Palazzo del Capitano**, where the tourist office is located, the **Palazzo dei Priori**, with its curious trapezoidal tower, and oldest of the three, the **Palazzo del Popolo** from 1213. Todi's **Duomo** is simple and elegant, graced with a rose window added to the 12th-century structure in 1500.

These medieval stones are quite recent in the scheme of the town's past, however, which is said to stretch to at least the 7th century B.C. Legend has it that Hercules founded the town a century or so earlier than that, and it was here that he killed Cacus, the fire-breathing dragon. It's known that the Romans usurped an Etruscan outpost sometime around 217 B.C., and their walls are still part of the town's massive fortifications.

WHERE TO EAT

Ristorante Umbria ★ UMBRIAN   For many visitors, the main reason to come to Todi is to enjoy a meal at this decades-old dining room just off Piazza del Popolo. *Palombaccio* (a type of wild dove), steaks, and other meats are grilled over an open fire, and often accompanied by truffles. The other pleasure of dining here is to sit on the terrace, from which all of Umbria seems to unfold at your feet like a vast green checkerboard (be sure to reserve an outside table in advance).

Via San Bonaventura 13. ✆ **075/894–2737.** Main courses 10€–18€. Wed–Mon 11am–3pm and 7–10:30pm.

ORVIETO ★★

87km (54 miles) W of Spoleto, 86km (53 miles) SW of Perugia

Walking through the streets of Orvieto, you might be delighted to discover that nothing much has changed in the past 500 years. Adding to the magic is, off to one side of town, what might be Italy's most beautiful cathedral, covered in dazzling mosaics and statuary and rising above an airy piazza. The final coup de grace is the fact that the entire town is set atop a volcanic outcropping some 315m (1,033 ft.) above the green countryside. This impenetrable perch ensured that Etruscan "Velzna" was among the most powerful members of the *dodecapoli* (Etruscan confederation of 12 cities) and the aerie-like positioning continues to make Orvieto seem a world apart.

Essentials

GETTING THERE Fourteen **trains** on the main **Rome-Florence** line stop at Orvieto daily (1 hr., 45 min. from Florence; 1 hr., 20 min. from Rome). From **Perugia,** take the train to Terontola (16 trains daily) to transfer to this line heading south toward Rome (1¼ hr. total train time).

Orvieto's **station** is in Orvieto Scalo in the valley. To reach the city, cross the street and take the **funicular** (www.atcterni.it; every 10 min. from 7:20am–8:30pm).

Orvieto is easy to reach by **car,** especially from southern Tuscany: It's right by the A1. The main link to the rest of Umbria is the SS448 to Todi (40 min.). You can leave your car in the large pay lot behind the train station off Piazza della Pace and take the funicular up to town or, if you want to get a bit closer, in the garage at Campo della Fiera, just outside the Porta Romana. From there you can take an elevator/escalator system up to Piazza San Giovanni or Piazza Ranieri.

VISITOR INFORMATION The **tourist office** is opposite the Duomo at Piazza Duomo 24 (www.comune.orvieto.tr.it; © **0763/341772**). It's open Monday to Friday 8:15am to 1:50pm and 4 to 7pm, Saturday 10am to 1pm and 3:30 to 7pm, and Sunday from 10am to noon and 4 to 6pm.

Exploring Orvieto

Duomo ★★ CATHEDRAL Orvieto's pièce de résistance is a mesmerizing assemblage of spikes and spires, mosaics and marble statuary—and that's just the facade. The rest of the bulky-yet-elegant church is banded in black and white stone and seems to perch miraculously on the edge of the cliffs that surround the town. You might notice that it is wider at the front than at the back, designed so to create the optical illusion upon entering that it is longer than it actually is. The facade has been compared to a medieval altarpiece, and it reads like an illustrated Catechism. On the four broad marble panels that divide the surface, Sienese sculptor and architect Lorenzo Maitani (who also more or less designed

Orvieto

Piazza XXIX Marzo

Piazza del Popolo

Piazza della Repubblica

Via G. Carducci

Viale Crispi

Via Roma

Corso Cavour

Via F. Cavallotti

Via Angelo Orvieto

Via S. Stefano

Via S. Porcari

Via dell'Olmo

Via Malabranca

Via Filippeschi

Via del Popolo

S. Leonardo

Corso Cavour

Via Maurizio

Via della Cava

Via Garibaldi

Via Albani

Via del Duomo

Via I. Scalza

Via Ripa Serancia

Via Maitani

Piazza del Duomo

Via Alberici

Via I. Scalza

PORTA MAGGIORE

Pozzo di San Patrizio

Piazza Cahen

FUNICOLARE

Duomo

Information ⓘ

0 — 200 yds
0 — 200 m

Florence

TUSCANY

UMBRIA

Orvieto

ATTRACTIONS
Duomo **5**
Grotte della Rupe
  (Etruscan Orvieto Underground) **7**
Museo Claudio Faina e Civico **6**
Pozzo di San Patrizio
  (St. Patrick's Well) **8**

HOTELS
Hotel Duomo **4**
Palazzo Piccolomini **2**

RESTAURANTS
Le Grotte del Funaro **1**
Trattoria Palomba **3**

the church) and others carved scenes from the Old and New Testament. On the far left is the story of creation, with Eve making an appearance from Adam's rib; on the far right, Christ presides over the Last Judgment, as the dead shuffle out of their sarcophagi to await his verdict. Prophets and the Apostles surround a huge rose window, and Mary appears in lush mosaics inlaid in fields of gold; she ascends to heaven in a triangular panel above the main portal, and she is crowned Queen of Heaven in the gable at the pinnacle of the facade.

Capella del Coporale   In 1263, a Bohemian priest, Peter of Prague, found himself doubting transubstantiation, the sacrament in

315

which the communion bread, or host, is transformed into the body of Christ during mass. He went to Rome to pray on St. Peter's tomb that his faith be strengthened and, stopping in Bolsena, just below Orvieto, was saying mass when the host began to bleed, dampening the corporal, or altar cloth. Pope Urban IV, who was in Orvieto at the time, had the cloth brought to him, and a few decades later, Pope Nicholas IV ordered the cathedral built to house the relic. Frescoes in the chapel tell the story of the miracle, and the exquisite enamel reliquary that once held the cloth remains in place.

Cappella San Brizio   The cathedral's other treasure is one of the Renaissance's greatest fresco cycles. The themes are temptation, salvation, damnation, and resurrection, though the scenes are rich in everyday humanity and allegedly inspired Michelangelo, who came to Orvieto and filled sketchbooks before beginning work on the Sistine Chapel. (In subsequent centuries church authorities had workers scramble over the frescoes and put sashes on the male nudes that Michelangelo so admired, though subsequent restorations have removed most of them.) Fra' Angelico (the "Angelic Friar," who learned his craft illuminating manuscripts) began the series in 1447 and Luca Signorelli completed the works that have come to be considered his masterpiece in 1504. Both artists appear in a magnificent panel of the "Sermon of the Antichrist," in which the devil coaxes a Christ impostor to lure the faithful to damnation. Signo-

relli looks handsome and proud, with his long blonde hair, and he gets a bit of revenge on the mistress who had jilted him, portraying her as the worried recipient of funds from a moneylender (or, according to some interpretations, she's a prostitute being paid for her services).

To the right of the altar is "The Entrance to Hell" and "The Damned in Hell," in which devils torment their victims, a man raises his fists to curse God as he sees Charon rowing across the Styx for him, and bodies writhe and twist for eternity. Signorelli gets his revenge again in his depiction of a winged devil leering toward a terrified blonde on his back—the ex-mistress, of course. Should a bit of relief be in order after all this misery, you need only look at the "Elect

Luca Signorelli's fresco cycle in Orvieto's cathedral.

in Heaven," where those who have been saved look quite content, even smug, in their assurance of eternal salvation.

Piazza del Duomo. www.museomodo.it. ✆ **0763/341167.** Admission 3€ including Cappella di San Brizio, free for children 10 and under. Apr–Oct Mon–Sat 9:30am–7pm, Sun 1–5:30pm (to 6:30pm July–Sept); Nov–Mar Mon–Sat 9:30am–1pm and 2:30–5pm (Sun to 5:30pm).

Grotte della Rupe (Etruscan Orvieto Underground) ★★

HISTORIC SITE   More than 1,200 artificial and natural caverns have been found in the *pozzolana* (a volcanic stone powdered to make cement mix) and *tufa* rock upon which Orvieto rests. Guided tours take in two of them here, 15m (45 ft.) below Santa Chiara convent, reached by a steep climb up and down 55 steps, along a narrow rock-hewn passage. The caverns have variously been used as Etruscan houses, water wells, ceramic ovens, pigeon coops, quarries, and cold storage (the temperature is a constant 14°C/58°F). Residents took shelter in them during World War II Allied bombings, but most unwisely—a direct hit would have annihilated the soft rock.

To look at Orvieto's tufa foundations from the outside, take a hike along the rupe, a path that encircles the base of the cliff. A landmark along the way is the **Necropoli Etrusca di Crocifisso del Tufo** (Etruscan Necropolis), where ancient Etruscan tombs are laid in a streetlike grid in subterranean caverns (3€; daily 8:30am–5:30pm). The tourist office can supply a map, Anello delle Rupe.

Grotte della Rupe: Piazza Duomo 23 (next to the tourist info office; open daily 10:30am–5:30pm). www.orvietounderground.it. ✆ **0763/344891.** Admission (by guided tour only, 45 min.–1 hr.) 6€ adults, 5€ students and seniors. Tours daily at 11am and 12:15, 3, 4, and 5:15pm (other times can be arranged); tours only Sat–Sun in Feb. English tours usually at 11:15am, but check in advance.

Museo Claudio Faina e Civico ★ MUSEUM   A palace next to the

cathedral houses what began as private collection in 1864. Interestingly, some of the most stunning pieces are not Etruscan, but Greek—Attic black-figure (6th-c.-B.C.) and red-figure (5th-c.-B.C.) vases and amphorae from Athenian workshops (including some by Greek master Exekias from 540 B.C.) that were bought by discriminating Etruscan collectors. You'll see the resemblance to Etruscan black *bucchero* ware from the 6th and the 5th century B.C.

Piazza del Duomo 29. www.museofaina.it. ✆ **0763/341-11** or 0763/341216. Admission 4.50€ adults; 3€ ages 7–12, seniors 65 and over, and families of 4 or more. Apr–Sept daily 9:30am–6pm; Oct–Mar daily 10am–5pm (closed Mon Nov–Mar).

Pozzo di San Patrizio (St. Patrick's Well) ★ HISTORIC SITE

Orvieto's position atop a rocky outcropping made it a perfect redoubt in time of siege, easy to defend but with one big drawback—a lack of water. When Pope Clement VII decided to hole up in Orvieto in 1527 to avoid turbulence in Rome, he hired Antonio Sangallo the Younger to dig a new well. Sangallo's design was unique: He dug a shaft 53m (175-ft.) deep and 14m (45-ft.) wide, accessible via a pair of wide spiral staircases that form a double helix and are lit by 72 internal windows. Mule-drawn carts could descend on one ramp and come back up the other without colliding. You can climb down, too, though it's a trek up and down 496 steps, and there's nothing to see at the bottom but, well, a well. A few steps up and down will introduce you to the concept, and give you time to contemplate the name. It's a reference to St. Patrick's Purgatory, a pilgrimage site in Ireland where Christ allegedly showed St. Patrick a cave and told him it was an entrance to hell.

Viale San Gallo (near the funicular stop on Piazza Cahen). ℂ **0763/343768.** Admission 5€ adults, 3.50€ students. May–Aug daily 9am–7:45pm; Mar–Apr and Sept–Oct daily 9am–6:45pm; Nov–Feb daily 10am–4:45pm.

Where to Stay

The upper town does not have many places to stay, so be sure to book ahead—especially on weekends, when many Romans come up to Orvieto for a small-town getaway.

Hotel Duomo ★★   These snug quarters just a few steps from the Duomo (viewable from some rooms with a lean out of the window) are not only extremely comfortable—with lots of modern built-in wood furnishings and excellent lighting (a rarity in Italian hotels in this price range)—but are also surprisingly quirky. A local artist, Livio Orazio Valentini, did the decor and hung his surrealistic paintings in the hallways, lounges, and rooms, complementing them with colorful upholstery and carpets to match the tones. He also created sculptural light fixtures that hang over many of the desks. The effect is slightly bohemian and quite homey, and the ambience is topped off nicely with a pleasant garden to one side of the hotel.

Vicolo dei Maurizio 7. www.orvietohotelduomo.com. ℂ **0763/341887.** 18 units. 100€–130€ double. Rates include breakfast. **Amenities:** Wi-Fi (free).

Palazzo Piccolomini ★★ Orvieto's most luxurious and character-filled accommodations are in a 16th-century *palazzo* that was resurrected from a dilapidated wreck 25 years ago. The stone and vaulted subterranean breakfast room and a couple of frescoed salons whisk you into the past, but most of the guest rooms are done in contemporary Umbrian chic—wood and tile floors, dark, simple furnishings, and crisp white walls with neutral-tone accents here and there, all very soothing. Some rooms have sitting areas, or open to terraces, or are two-level, though the real prize here is a room of any size with a countryside view (only those on the upper floors have them).

Piazza Ranieri 36 (2 blocks down from Piazza della Repubblica), 05018 Orvieto. www.palazzopiccolomini.it. *©* **0763/341743.** 32 units. From 100€ double. Rates include breakfast. Parking 15€ a day in next door lot. **Amenities:** Restaurant; babysitting; concierge; room service; Wi-Fi (free in public areas).

Where to Eat

Orvieto's unofficial pasta is *umbrichelli,* simple flour-and-water spaghetti rolled out unevenly by hand and somewhat chewy—similar to the *pici* of southern Tuscany, but not as thick. To sample a glass (or buy a bottle) of Orvieto Classico (accompanied by a *panino*), drop by the **Cantina Foresi,** Piazza Duomo 2 (*©* **0763/341611**). Ask to see the small, moldy cellar carved directly into the *tufa.*

Le Grotte del Funaro ★ UMBRIAN A *funaro* (rope maker) had his workshop in these grottoes carved into the cliff's *tufa* at the edge of town almost a thousand years ago, and you can almost see him at work in the shadowy recesses of the multilevel, cavelike rooms. You can sit outside in front and enjoy the sweep of green countryside far below the town, or better yet—so you don't miss all the atmosphere inside—ask for one of the few window seats. Wherever you sit, you'll dine simply and well on grilled meats, the house specialty (including a *grigliata mista* of suckling pig, lamb, sausage, and yellow peppers), as well as excellent pizzas.

Via Ripa Serancia 41 (at the west end of town near Porta Maggiore; well signposted). www.grottedelfunaro.it. *©* **0763/343276.** Main courses 10€–13€; pizza 5.50€–8.50€. Tues–Sun noon–3pm and 7pm–midnight. Closed 1 week in July.

Trattoria Palomba ★★ UMBRIAN This pleasant, white-walled room is the kind of place you'll want to linger, so settle in for a long lunch after a morning of seeing the sights or a comfy evening if you're spending the night in town—a meal here deserves long, leisurely appreciation. Black Umbrian truffles top many of the house-made pastas, most notably *umbrichelli al tartufo,* tossed with egg yolk and parmigiano. The house signature dish (*palomba,* Italian for wild dove) is roasted in a memorably delicious sauce of capers, rosemary, olives, and a hint of anchovies. Any of the meat dishes, including beef in a red wine sauce, are similarly satisfying, and accompanied by a nice selection of wines.

Via Cipirano Menente 16. *©* **0763/343395.** Main courses 10€–16€. Thurs–Tues noon–2pm and 7:30–10pm.

8

BOLOGNA
& EMILIA-
ROMAGNA

A lot of travelers zip through this northernmost stretch of central Italy as they hurry along the well-worn path between Florence and Venice. Which is good news for anyone wishing to slow down long enough to visit this region—you will find it's a little less crowded, and a little more engaged in everyday Italian life than other more popular stops on the Italian tourism circuit. While Emilia-Romagna's cities are certainly treasure troves of art and culture, this region has another delightful side to its personality: It's almost hedonistically devoted to fine food.

Bologna is one of Europe's largest remaining medieval enclaves, its old palaces are filled with art, and its stony piazzas host an animated street life revved up by students at Europe's oldest university. Parma proudly shows off its famous hams and cheeses, its musical traditions, and its art. Ravenna is awash in glittering Byzantine mosaics, and Ferrara is a time capsule of the Renaissance. It's easy to get from one place to the other by train—Bologna makes a handy base for exploring the entire region—and once you reach these old cities, the preferred mode of transport is bicycle.

BOLOGNA ★★

151km (94 miles) SW of Venice, 378km (234 miles) N of Rome

It's easy to love a city that's so enamored of food that it's nicknamed *La Grassa* (the Fat); so devoted to scholarship (home of Europe's oldest university, founded in 1088) that it's called *La Dotta* (the Learned); and so noted for its fiery libertine politics that it's known as *La Rossa* (the Red). There are plenty of other reasons to like Bologna, too. The lively working city of more than a million residents is built around one of the Europe's largest and best-preserved medieval cores, and an attractive swath of palaces and towers, grand piazzas and narrow lanes are all easily traversed on foot. Quirky museums and art-filled churches seem all the more appealing against a backdrop of animated street life and shop windows brimming with the region's famous hams and cheeses. You don't even have to carry an umbrella in Bologna, because 24 miles of sidewalks are covered with handsome loggias.

FACING PAGE: **Bulbs of garlic at Mercato delle Erbe food market in Bologna.**

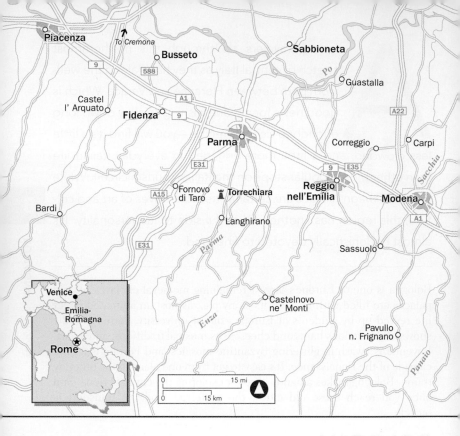

Essentials

GETTING THERE **By Plane** The international **Aeroporto Guglielmo Marconi** (www.bologna-airport.it; ☏ **051-6479615**) is 6km (3¾ miles) north of the city center and served by such domestic carriers as Alitalia and Meridiana; all the main European airlines also fly to this airport, including Ryanair (London-Stansted), EasyJet, and British Airways (both London-Gatwick), making flights from the U.K. especially competitive. A **bus** (marked aerobus) runs daily (6am–12:15am) every 15 to 30 minutes from the airport to Bologna's rail station (Stazione Centrale). A one-way ticket costs 6€ (pay the driver), and the trip usually takes 20 minutes.

By Train Bologna's **Stazione Centrale** is at Piazza Medaglie d'Oro 2 (☏ **892021**). High-speed trains arrive hourly from Florence (trip time: about 30 min.) and Milan (about 1 hr.) Regional trains connect Bologna with other cities in the region. Note that most service between Bologna and Florence and Milan is now via high-speed train, and only a very few slower and less expensive trains run on these routes. Bus nos. A, 25, and 30 run between the station and the historic core of

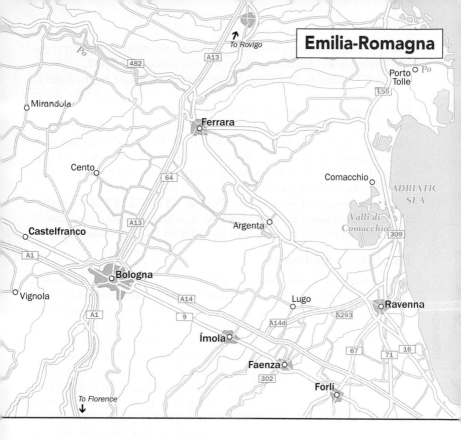

Bologna, Piazza Maggiore. Taxis use the meter, which starts at 3.15€—expect to pay around 6€ for trips into the center. You can make the walk easily in about 15 minutes, and it's mostly under covered loggias.

By Car If you are driving in from Florence, continue north along A1 until reaching the outskirts of Bologna, where signs direct you to the city center. From Milan, take A1 southeast along the Apennines. From Venice or Ferrara, follow A13 southwest. From Rimini, Ravenna, and the towns along the Adriatic, cut west on A14. See the note on p. 332 about driving and parking in Bologna; if you have a choice, it's much easier to arrive in Bologna without a car.

VISITOR INFORMATION The main **tourist office** (www.bolognawel come.com; ✆ **051-239660**) is at Piazza Maggiore in the Palazzo del Podestà, open daily 9am to 7pm. There is another office at the airport, in the arrivals hall (✆ **051-6472113**; open Mon–Sat 9am–7pm, and on Sun and holidays 9am–4pm).

GETTING AROUND Central Bologna is easy to cover on foot; most of the major sights are in and around Piazza Maggiore, and most of the sidewalks are famously covered. **City buses** leave for most points from

Piazza Nettuno or Piazza Maggiore, and the train station. Free city maps and bus maps are available at the storefront office of the **ATC** (Azienda Trasporti Comunali) at Piazza XX Settembre (www.atc.bo.it; ℭ **051-350111**). You can buy tickets at one of many booths and *tabacchi* in Bologna, or pay in machines on the buses. Tickets cost 1.50€ from a machine at stops or on the bus (no change), or 1.20€ if you buy in advance from a *tabacchi,* and are valid for 1 hour. A **day-ticket** valid until midnight on the day of validation cost 4€ and a **city pass**—a single ticket that allows 10 rides—costs just 11€. Once on board, you must validate your ticket or you'll be fined up to 150€.

Taxis are on 24-hour radio call at ℭ **051-372727** (Cooperativa Taxisti Bolognesiare) or ℭ **051-4590** (Consorzio Autonomo Taxisti). The meter starts at 3.10€ and goes up 1.05€ to 1.15€ per kilometer.

Exploring Bologna

A huge statue of a virile Neptune presides over the center of Bologna, facing the sweeping expanse of **Piazza Maggiore**, surrounded by crenellated 12th- and 13th-century *palazzi* and the enormous **Basilica di San Petronio.** Just about all the city's sights are within a few minutes' walk from the piazza. Before you set out, take a look at one of the more intriguing presences, the Palazzo di Rei Enzo, on the northeast side. Enzo (1218–1272) was king of Sardinia and the illegitimate son of German Emperor Frederick II. While Enzo was studying at the University of Bologna, the papal-supporting Guelphs defeated the Ghibellines, who supported the Holy Roman Empire. Enzo, aligned with the Ghibellines, was imprisoned in this grim looking palace until his death 23 years later. He didn't exactly languish in a dungeon—he was known for his lavish feasts, more than 150 romantic conquests, and a foiled escape attempt when his blonde hair, protruding from a basket, was a dead giveaway.

The Neptune statue on Piazza Maggiore.

Basilica di San Domenico ★★

CHURCH Spanish-born St. Dominic, founder of the Dominican order and patron saint of astronomers, lived only 3 years in Bologna, but he rests forever here in a shrine designed by the 13th

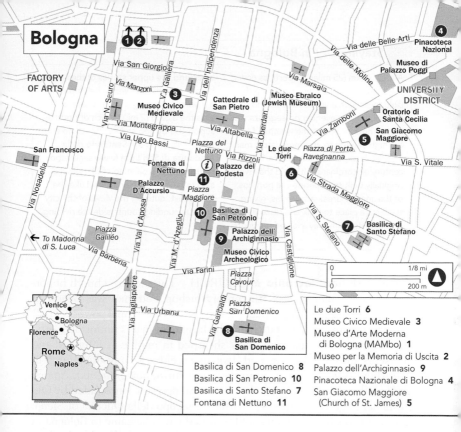

Bologna

FACTORY OF ARTS

Via San Giorgio

Via Manzoni

Via N. Sauro

Via Galliera

Via dell'Indipendenza

Via delle Belle Arti

Pinacoteca Nazional **4**

Via delle Moline

Via Marsala

Museo di Palazzo Poggi

UNIVERSITY DISTRICT

Cattedrale di San Pietro

3 Museo Civico Medievale

Via Montegrappa

Via Ugo Bassi

Via Altabella

Via Oberdan

Museo Ebraico (Jewish Museum)

Via Zamboni

Oratorio di Santa Cecilia

San Giacomo Maggiore **5**

Piazza del Nettuno

Via Rizzoli

Le due Torri

Piazza di Porta Ravegnanna

San Francesco

Via Nosadella

Fontana di Nettuno

i Palazzo del Podestà **11**

Palazzo D'Accursio

Piazza Maggiore

Via S. Vitale

Le due Torri **6**

Via Strada Maggiore

Piazza Galiléo

← To Madonna di S. Luca

Via Barberia

Via M. d'Azeglio

Via Val d'Aposa

10 Basilica di San Petronio

Palazzo dell' Archiginnasio **9**

Museo Civico Archeologico

Via S. Stefano

Via Castiglione

Basilica di Santo Stefano **7**

Via Farini

Piazza Cavour

Via Tagliapietre

Via Urbana

Piazza San Domenico

Via Garibaldi

Piazza Cavour

0   1/8 mi
0   200 m

Venice

Bologna

Florence

Rome ★

Naples

8 Basilica di San Domenico

Basilica di San Domenico **8**
Basilica di San Petronio **10**
Basilica di Santo Stefano **7**
Fontana di Nettuno **11**

Museo Civico Medievale **3**
Museo d'Arte Moderna di Bologna (MAMbo) **1**
Museo per la Memoria di Uscita **2**
Palazzo dell'Archiginnasio **9**
Pinacoteca Nazionale di Bologna **4**
San Giacomo Maggiore (Church of St. James) **5**

century's greatest sculptor, Nicola Pisano. Raised in wealth, Dominic aligned himself with the poor as a young student. To feed the starving he sold his belongings, including his manuscripts, saying, "Would you have me study off these dead skins, when men are dying of hunger?" In Bologna he encouraged his many followers "to have charity, to guard their humility, and to make their treasure out of poverty." The saint traveled from one end of Europe to the other before dying in 1221 on a bed of sackcloth; now he lies beneath elaborate carvings depicting his colorful life, the work of Arnolfo di Cambio. In the 15th century Nicolo di Bari added a canopy, carved with images of saints and evangelists, and was so proud of his work that he changed his name to Nicolo di Arca. A young Michelangelo, arriving in Bologna in 1495 when his patrons, the Medici, were expelled from Florence, added transcendent renderings of two other Bologna saints, Petronius and Proculus (who, though clothed, appears to be the prototype for his "David"). Bologna-born Guido Reni topped off the shrine in 1615 with a ceiling fresco depicting Dominic entering heaven amid legions of pious saints and swirling *putti*.

Piazza San Domenico 13. © **051-6400411.** Free admission. Mon–Sat 9am–noon and 3:30–6pm; Sun 3:30–5pm. Bus: A, 16, 30, 38, 39, or 59.

Staying Dry in Bologna

Almost 40km (25 miles) of porticos cover the sidewalks of Bologna, providing the Bolognese with a venue to stroll and strut during the evening *passeggiata,* no matter how inclement the weather. Most are high enough to accommodate a man on horseback, as mandated by a 14th-century city ordinance. It's said they were originally built to duplicate the porticos of the ancient Greek academies, giving students a place to walk and discourse; pragmatists claim they allowed residents to extend the upper stories of their homes over the sidewalks, helping ease a medieval housing crunch. Showiest of all is the 3.5km (2 mi.) stretch of porticos, supported by 666 arches, that climb a green hillside to the **Santuario della Madonna di San Luca** (www.sanlucabo. org). Inside is a painting of Mary that's said to have been painted by Luke the Evangelist; outside, the views of the city and surrounding countryside are riveting.

Basilica di San Petronio ★ CHURCH   The massive church honoring Bologna's patron, the 5th-century bishop Petronio, was begun in 1390, designed to be larger than St. Peter's in Rome. Papal powers cut off funding to protect their status and the basilica remains unfinished—the formidable brick walls were never sheathed in marble as intended and transepts are severely truncated (look down either side of the church to see where extensions end abruptly in the surrounding streets). Among the few flourishes are a magnificent central doorway surrounded by Old Testament figures rendered in marble by Jacopo della Quercia of Siena. The artist was in his 50s and well regarded when he came to Bologna in 1425 to undertake the commission; he finished just before his death in 1438, leaving a legacy that influenced many of the great artists of the Renaissance. Among them was Michelangelo, who claimed that della Quercia's rendering of the Creation of Adam here was the inspiration for his Genesis in the Sistine Chapel. In the Cappella Bolognini, the fourth on the left as you enter, Giovanni da Modena painted a fresco cycle between 1408 and 1420 that depicts scenes from the life of Petronio, along with scenes of Hell from Dante's Inferno—with a startling depiction of Satan eating and excreting doomed souls and Mohammed being devoured by devils in Hell (Al-Qaida operatives and other terrorists have twice in recent years tried to blow up the church in retaliation for the alleged defamation). The rather stark interior is enlivened ever so slightly at noon when a shadow indicating the day of the year makes an appearance on a meridian line in the left aisle; designed by Bologna's famous 17th-century astronomer Giovanni Domenico Cassini, the longest sundial in the world stretches for 70 meters (231 feet).

Piazza Maggiore. www.basilicadisanpetronio.it. ⓒ **051-225442.** Free admission; 2€ for Cappella Bolognini. Daily 7:45am–1pm and 3–6pm. Bus: A, 11, 13, 14, 17, 18, 19, 20, or 25.

Basilica di Santo Stefano ★★ CHURCH   Bologna's most storied religious site is actually seven churches, a stone maze of medieval apses, romantic porticos and courtyards awash in legend. Petronio, the 5th-century bishop of Bologna, allegedly founded the church on the remains of a Roman temple to the earth goddess Isis. He was originally laid to rest here in the **Church of the Sepulcher**, where pregnant Bolognese women would circle his tomb 33 times—once for every year of Christ's life—stopping at every turn to crawl through a low door to say a prayer before the saint's remains (his body has been since been reunited with his head in the Basilica di San Petronio, see above). The mothers-to-be moved on to the **Church of the Trinity** to pray before a fresco depicting a very pregnant Madonna stroking her belly. The **Church of Vitale and Agricola** is devoted to two other popular Bolognese saints and the city's first Christian martyrs, the 4th-century nobleman Agricola and his devoted slave; a cross near the tomb is said to be the one Agricola was holding when he was crucified, though it dates from much later. Similarly, a marble basin in the **Cortile di Pilato** (Courtyard of Pilate), alleged to be the one in which Pontius Pilate washed his hands after condemning Christ to death, actually dates to the 8th century; a statue atop a nearby column pays homage to the rooster who crowed three times when Peter denied knowing Jesus. It's said that Dante used to sit

A detail from San Domenico's tomb.

Public Indecency

Bologna's famous **Fontana di Nettuno** (Neptune Fountain) was designed in 1566 by a Belgian named Giambologna (the Italians altered his name), who gave the naked sea god many rippling muscles and surrounded him with erotic cherubs and sirens spouting water from their breasts. When the papal legate who occupied the Palazzo d'Accursio opposite protested that the spectacle was indecent, Giambologna got his revenge: If you approach the statue from its rear right side, you'll notice that the left arm is positioned in such a way to suggest an indecently large . . . well, walk around the statue and see for yourself.

in the lovely, two-tier Romanesque **cloister** and reflect during his exile in Bologna. Look at the carved capitals atop the pillars, with their luridly grotesque imagery of swiveling heads and men being crushed beneath boulders—most likely Dante found inspiration here for the hellish scenes of the *Divine Comedy*.

Via Santo Stefano 24. www.abbaziasantostefano.it. ℂ **051-223256.** Free admission. Daily 9am–noon and 3:30–6:30pm. Bus: 11, 13, 90, or 96.

Le due Torri ★★ MONUMENT/MEMORIAL   It's been estimated that in the 12th and 13th centuries as many as 100 stone towers rose above the rooftops of Bologna, reaching heights of 100m (330 ft.). They were probably built as places of refuge and for offensive purposes, and they implied no small amount of wealth, since it took as long as 10 years and enormous expense to erect such towers, which required successively thinner layers of stone and masonry on the upper levels. Some 20 towers remain, and the most famous are these two slender medieval skyscrapers that lean tipsily but poetically just east of Piazza Maggiore. The **Garisenda** rises 49m (162 ft.) and leans about 3m (11 ft.) from perpendicular; the **Asinelli** stands 102m (334 ft.) tall and inclines almost 2.5m (7½ ft.). Garisenda is off limits, but a climb up Asinelli's 500 steps reveals Bologna's finest aerial panorama, a sea of red-tile roofs and the green hills beyond.

Piazza di Porta Ravegnana. Admission 3€. Daily 9am–6pm (to 5pm in winter). Last entry 20 min. before closing. Bus: 11, 13, 14, 19, 25, or 27.

Museo Civico Medievale ★ MUSEUM   Treasures of medieval Bologna collected in the salons of the Palazzo Ghisilardi include priceless rare *codici miniati* (illuminated manuscripts) and gold vessels, but the most riveting pieces are a courtesan's shoes and other commonplace artifacts of everyday life in the Middle Ages. Ordinary funeral slabs provide such telling glimpses as a relief of a supine university professor with his hands resting on a book, as if he has fallen asleep while reading, while statues show off the haircuts and clunky headgear of the times. With a little imagination it's easy to think these are the men and women accompanying you on your wanderings through the loggias and squares of what is one of Italy's most intact medieval cities.

Palazzo Ghisilardi, Via Manzoni 4. ℂ **051-2193930.** Admission 4€ adults, 2€ students and children 15–17, free for children 14 and under. Tues–Fri 10am–3pm, Sat–Sun and holidays 10am–6:30pm. Bus: A, 11, 20, 27, or 28.

Museo d'Arte Moderna di Bologna (MAMbo) ★ MUSEUM A
former bread factory is the city's showcase for the avant-garde, with an emphasis on post–World War II art. Aside from the occasional blockbuster temporary exhibition, the standout is the collection of 85 works by Bolognese native artist Giorgio Morandi (1890-1964). He once said, "What interests me most is expressing what's in nature, in the visible world, that is"—somewhat of an understatement given his deceptively straightforward still lifes, which seem almost abstract in their minimalism. Some of Morandi's most pleasant works are landscapes of Grizzana, a village where he spent many lazy summers working and drawing. His studio has been reconstructed here, and you can also visit his apartment at Via Fondazza 36 (ℂ **051-649-6653;** by appointment; free admission), converted to stark galleries where his personal effects and the vases, utensils, and other objects he painted are on view. In the larger museum, another standout piece is Renato Guttuso's "I Funerali di Togliatti" (1972), awash in red flags, which depicts the funeral of the leader of the communist party, surrounded by images of other left-wing luminaries.

Via Don Minzoni 14. ℂ **051-6496611.** Admission 6€ adults, 4€ students and children 6–17, free for children 5 and under. Tues, Wed, and Fri noon–6pm; Thurs noon–10pm; Sat–Sun noon–8pm. Bus: A, 11, 20, 27, or 28.

Le Due Torri.

Museo per la Memoria di Uscita ★★ MUSEUM   In this haunting installation, artist Christian Boltanski commemorates the crash of a Bologna–Palermo flight off the eponymous Sicilian island on June 27, 1980, with reconstructed wreckage of the DC-9 and lighting and sound effects. Victims are commemorated with 81 lights blinking off and on against the black ceiling while from 81 speakers come snippets of ordinary conversation. Most effective of all is the shattered aircraft, allegedly shot down by an Italian military missile when it was mistaken for a Libyan spy plane. The incident was the subject of an extensive cover-up and investigation.

Via di Saliceto 3/22. (☏ **051-377680.** Free admission; Fri–Sun 10am–6pm.

Palazzo dell'Archiginnasio ★★ HISTORIC SITE   It's no accident that one of the grander buildings of Bologna University, completed in 1563, is adjacent to the basilica of San Petronio. Pope Pius IV deliberately commissioned a central hall to house the various university faculties on this site, in order to prevent the basilica from expanding and surpassing St. Peter's in Rome in size. Corridors and staircases decorated with the family crests of students lead to the **Teatro Anatomico,** a handsome lecture hall paneled in spruce where tiers of stiff wooden benches surround a marble slab. The Spellati, two skinless bodies carved in wood, support a canopy above the lecturer's chair, Apollo gazes down from the ceiling, and statues of Hippocrates and other august physicians line walls. A curious statue of a physician holding a nose pays homage to Gaspare Tagliacozzi, a pioneer of rhinoplasty (otherwise known as "a nose job"), a procedure that was much in demand in an era when noses were routinely cut off for punishment or revenge. The most looming presence, though, is a secret panel behind which sat a church inquisitor, spying on classes to make sure procedures did not waiver from church protocol for cadavers—all organs had to remain *in situ* and intact, ready for Judgment Day. Surrounding rooms, closed to the public, house some of the university's most priceless manuscripts.

Piazza Galvani. www.archiginnasio.it. (☏ **051-276811.** Free admission. Mon–Fri 9am–6:45pm; Sat 9am–1:45pm. Bus: A or 29B.

Pinacoteca Nazionale di Bologna ★★ MUSEUM   Beginning in the late 18th century, the former St. Ignatius monastery began to house altar pieces and other works gathered from religious institutions throughout Bologna. The collection grew considerably after 1815 when many works the French had sent off to the Louvre were returned to Bologna after the fall of the Napoleonic Empire. Among the great works from Bolognese churches is Raphael's "St. Cecilia in Estasi" (Gallery 15), in which the saint, patron of music, is portrayed holding a lute with other instruments strewn at her feet, rapturously listening to a heavenly choir. The museum's emphasis is on works by Emilian and Bolognese artists. Guido Reni (1575–1642), who was born and is buried in Bologna, dominates Gallery 24 with his "Massacre of the Innocents," a terrifying visualization of scripture in which two muscular, knife-wielding soldiers set upon a group of screaming women and children. An especially amiable presence is that of Bologna's own Carracci family in Gallery 23. The three artists—brothers Agostino and Annibale and their cousin Lodovico—opened a famous academy in Bologna in the 1580s, professing their belief in breaking away from mannerism to imbue painting with emotion and passion. Lodovico persevered with a career in art despite being mocked for his slow manner; though he became proficient, he is better known as a teacher than as an artist, as seen in the work of his cousins. Agostino's masterpiece is "The Communion of St. Jerome," but the work for which he became best known in some circles was "I Modi" (The Way), a highly erotic series of engravings. His brother Annibale was the greater and more passionate painter, as becomes clear in his darkly moving "Mocking of Christ."

Via delle Belle Arti 56. www.pinacotecabologna.beniculturali.it. (©) **051-4209411.** Admission 4€ adults, 2€ ages 18–25, free for children 17 and under. Tues–Thurs 3pm–7pm, Fri–Sun 10am–7pm. Closed holidays. Bus: 20, 28, 36, 37, 89, 93, 94, or 99 (to Porta San Donato).

San Giacomo Maggiore (Church of St. James) ★ CHURCH Members of Bologna's most powerful 15th-century family are laid to rest in the **Cappella Bentivoglio** (behind the altar to the left; you must insert .50€ to light the chapel). Their likenesses appear in frescoes by Lorenzo Costa, who came to Bologna in the 1480s from Ferrara before moving on to Mantua (see p. 456), where he achieved his greatest fame. "Madonna Enthroned" is an especially telling window into the lives of the family, who were continually plotting and plotted against and were finally expelled from Bologna under papal edict. Giovanni II Bentiviglio, who was eventually excommunicated and imprisoned in Rome, kneels with his wife next to the Madonna, as his children look on, the lot of them giving thanks for the discovery of a conspiracy to overthrow them. "Triumph of Death" shows a ghastly procession in which death, represented by a scythe-wielding skeleton, is seated on a chariot drawn by

---

A Liitle-Known Treasure

Nicolo dell'Arca, famous for his carvings on Bologna's tomb of St. Dominic, crafted another lesser-known but delightful work in the Church of Santa Maria della Vita, just off Piazza Maggiore at Via Clavature 8. His "Lamentation" is a set of life-size terracotta figures taking Christ from the cross; the expressions on the faces of the lamenters are etched in grief, and the grouping is one of the most humane and moving religious images you'll encounter—even though they're clumsily shored up with wood to prevent damage in an earthquake. The church is open daily (Mon–Sat 10am–noon and 3–7pm and Sun 3–7pm, but hours may vary), and admission is free.

oxen. Anton Galeazzo Bentivoglio, who fell out of favor with the papacy and was beheaded in 1435, lies in a tomb designed by Jacopo della Quercia, who labored so long over the doors to the **Basilica of San Petronio** (p. 326). For an eerie thrill, follow the left-side chapels about halfway down until you come to the one housing a terrifyingly realistic-looking effigy of the corpse of Christ, encased in glass and complete with lash marks, oozing wounds, and plenty of blood.

Piazza Rossini, Via Zamboni. ✆ **051-225970.** Free admission. Daily 7:30am–12:30 and 3:30–6:30pm (from 8:30am Sun). Bus: C.

Where to Stay

Bologna hosts four to six major trade fairs a year, during which times hotel room rates rise dramatically. You'll save a lot of money if you choose another time to visit (fair dates vary yearly; check with the tourist office). Bologna has a booming bed & breakfast scene, as well as many short-term rental apartments. A good place to browse offerings is **Airbnb.com**.

An important note on driving and parking: Much of central Bologna is closed to cars without special permits from 7am to 8pm daily (including Sun and holidays). When booking a room, be prepared to present your car registration number, which the hotel will then provide to the police to ensure that you are not fined for driving in a restricted area. Parts of the central city are entirely off limits to traffic on Sundays, so you will have to park outside the center. Ask when booking, and also ask about parking facilities (a hotel-issued parking permit is required in some areas) as well as the most efficient route to take to reach your hotel, because many streets are permanently closed to traffic. Best yet, come to this easily walkable city without a car.

MODERATE

Commercianti ★★   You can't stay any closer to San Petronio than you will at this atmosphere-rich *palazzo*—in the best of the rooms and suites, you can lay in bed, sit on a leafy terrace, or even soak in a deep tub while admiring the church's exquisite brickwork and statuary, so close you can almost reach out and touch it. Exposed timbers and fresco fragments lend a medieval aura to the distinctive decor, though many of the furnishings are plushly contemporary, with comfy armchairs and couches that invite you to relax after forays into the surrounding sights and markets. In the lower level breakfast room, a morning buffet is served beneath vaulted arches that betray the premise's 13th-century origins.

Via de' Pignattari 11. www.art-hotel-commercianti.it. ✆ **051-7457511.** 34 units. 136€–179€ double. Rates include buffet breakfast. Parking 28€ per day. Bus: 11, 13, 20, or 30. **Amenities:** Bar; babysitting; bikes (free); room service; Wi-Fi (free).

Hotel Porta San Mamolo ★★   Most of these rather romantic rooms surround a leafy courtyard, bringing the sense of a country retreat to the heart of Bologna—Piazza Maggiore is only a 15-minute walk away (or an easy ride on one of the bikes available for free). Nice-sized, tile-floored rooms are done in soothing creams and warm golds and reds, with light furnishings that are vaguely Florentine in style and offset with plenty of exposed beams, vaulted ceilings, and other architectural details. A few of the rooms have large terraces, others open directly into the garden, and breakfast is served in an airy, greenhouselike pavilion that seems summery even during the gray Bolognese winter.

Vicolo del Falconi 6–8. www.hotel-portasanmamolo.it. © **051-583056.** 43 units. 119€–172€ double. Rates include buffet breakfast. Parking 20€ per day. Bus: 29B or 52. **Amenities:** Bikes (free); room service; Wi-Fi (free).

Hotel Roma ★★ What this old Bologna fixture lacks in chic style it makes up for with plenty of old-school charm and hospitality and a wonderful location just off Piazza Maggiore. Downstairs lounges and a small bar are gracious and welcoming, and the plain, no-nonsense guest rooms upstairs are large and pleasantly done with brass beds and gleaming wooden floors; many open to small terraces overlooking the surrounding pedestrian streets, and many of the large tiled bathrooms are windowed. The excellent in-house restaurant, C'era Una Volta—which tellingly translates as Once Upon a Time—carries on the Roma's old-fashioned ways with Bolognese classics served by crispy uniformed waiters.

Via Massimo d'Azeglio 64. www.hotelroma.biz. © **051-226322.** 86 units. From 120€ double. Rates include buffet breakfast. Parking 20€ per day. Bus: 11, 13, 20, or 30. **Amenities:** Restaurant; bar; bikes (free); room service; Wi-Fi (free).

Il Convento dei Fiori di Seta ★★ The former "Silk Flowers Nunnery" is now a retreat as refined as the name implies. Enough of the 14th-century surroundings remain to remind you where you are—a crucifix looms over the chic balcony breakfast room, fresco fragments and exposed timbers offset crisply contemporary furnishings, and double-height rooms with curved walls are cleverly carved out of the former chapel. But the emphasis is clearly on worldly comforts, including fine linens, luxurious mosaic-tiled bathrooms, and a little spa where guests can soak and steam after a day of sightseeing.

Via Orfeo 34-4. www.ilconventodeifioridiseta.com. © **051-272039.** 10 units. 109€–139€ double; 220€–270€ suite. Rates include continental breakfast. Parking 25€. Bus: 11, 13, 32, or 33. **Amenities:** Bar; concierge; Jacuzzi; room service; sauna; Wi-Fi (free).

Metropolitan ★★★ This stylish haven is just a few steps off Via Independenzia but a world removed, an oasis of calm and comfort. Soothing whites and neutral shades offset Indonesian antiques and other Asian pieces in the lobby and breakfast room and extend to the contemporary guest rooms upstairs. All rooms have large mosaic-tiled bathrooms, and many have a small sitting room for a little extra space and privacy. Five airy, two-room suites open off a leafy roof terrace planted with olive trees; they're some of the most restful accommodations in the city center. Guests have access to a nearby swimming pool and spa/fitness facility, and the train station, Piazza Maggiore, and most city sights are an easy walk away. The hotel also rents out modern and well-equipped apartments near Piazza Maggiore; rates range from 100€ to 400€ per day depending on the size of the apartment and time of year.

Via Dell'Orso 6. www.hotelmetropolitan.com. ☏ **051-229393.** 50 units. 150€–170€ double. Rates include buffet breakfast. Free parking. Bus: A, 11, 20, 27, or 28. **Amenities:** Restaurant; bar; babysitting; room service; Wi-Fi (free).

INEXPENSIVE

Albergo delle Drapperie ★ This centuries-old guesthouse is smack dab in the middle of the bustling market streets and only steps from Piazza Maggiore. The four top-floor rooms, the largest and best, have vaulted ceilings, exposed wooden beams, gables, window seats that double as extra beds, and lots of other atmospheric touches. Rooms on the lower floors are considerably smaller and furnished with not much more than beds, though they're enlivened with homey iron bedsteads and the occasional fresco or coffered ceiling. You'll have to do some climbing to reach any of these guest quarters, as well as the lobby and breakfast room. The Drapperie also rents out apartments in a nearby building.

Via della Drapperie 5. www.albergodrapperie.com. ☏ **051-223955.** 21 units. 75€–85€ double. Rates include buffet breakfast. Bus: A, 11, 20, 27, or 28. **Amenities:** Wi-Fi (free).

Alberta D Bed and Breakfast ★★★ What must be some of the homiest lodgings in Bologna are scattered across two floors of a sophisticated and rambling home in a former medieval hospital complex. Three of the character-filled units face a tranquil inner courtyard, set up for warm-weather lounging, and three others, including a triple, are part of a separate, large upstairs apartment with shared kitchen (the apartment can also be rented in its entirety). Much of the furniture is antique or vintage, accompanied by chic accessories, and Alberta and her son, Pierfrancesco, are welcoming and helpful hosts. They serve a filling breakfast that includes Alberta's home-baked breads and cakes, homemade jams, fresh juices, and fine hams and cheeses.

Via Sant'Isaia 58. www.albertadbedandbreakfast.com. ☏ **051-333479.** 6 units. From 65€ double. Rates include breakfast. Bus: 21. **Amenities:** Sauna; Wi-Fi (free).

Hotel Accademia ★ The lobby and public rooms are a bit time-worn, but the Accademia, one of the few hotels in the university district, reveals some surprises upstairs. The large guest rooms have high ceilings and are spiffily up to date, with shiny wooden floors, blond contemporary furniture, tastefully muted colors, and shiny bathrooms—many with that ever-so-rare fixture in less-expensive Italian hotels, a bathtub. Clubs, bars, and affordable student-oriented *osterias* cram the surrounding streets—a plus that can be a late-night curse for guests in street-facing rooms, and a good reason to ask for a room facing the quiet courtyard in back.

Via delle Belle Arte 6. www.hotelaccademia.com. ☏ **051-232318.** 28 units. 89€–101€ double. Rates include buffet breakfast. Parking 15€ per day. Bus: A, 11, 20, 27, or 28. **Amenities:** Bikes (free); Wi-Fi (free).

Where to Eat

If there's one city in Italy where you really should indulge your appetite, it's Bologna. As capital of Italy's most productive agricultural region, Bologna has been a food center for centuries. Specialties include locally raised beef, exquisitely cured meats, fresh pastas, truffles, and hearty sauces—far more than just the rich meat sauce or the Americanized sandwich meat that was named after the city.

And if you've got room left after dinner, a favorite Bologna post-prandial attraction is **Gelatauro,** Via San Vitale 98 (www.gelatauro.com; ✆ **051-230049;** Mon 9am–8pm, Tues–Thurs 8:30am–11pm, Fri–Sat 8:30am–midnight, Sun 9:30am–11pm), run by three brothers and known for its organic gelato, including one divine concoction made from Sicilian oranges.

Caminetto d'Oro ★★ BOLOGNESE/ITALIAN Despite the sleekly contemporary appearance of the formal dining room and a more casual bistro to one side, the Carrati family has been feeding Bologna for 80 years, from premises that were once a bakery. They still use a decades-old oven to bake their own delicious breads, which are all made, along with their pasta, using wheat flour from a mill near Modena. Their *tagliatelle al ragu* is renowned—a favorite of many performers and theatergoers from the nearby Arena del Sole. This is also the best place in town for a steak, since their T-bones come from local Romagnola cattle and are seared on soapstone.

Via de'Falegnami 4. www.caminettodoro.it. ✆ **051-263494.** Main courses 8€–18€. Mon–Sat 12:30–2:30pm and 7:30–10:30pm. Bus: C.

Casa Monica ★★ BOLOGNESE/VEGETARIAN Tucked away in what looks like a converted garage in an alleylike street at the far western edge of the historic center is this pleasant, low-key dining room, an oasis of calm and refinement. Deep rose hues and subtly warm lamp light give the contemporary surroundings a welcoming, even romantic, glow, and the cuisine might be a sought-after break from heavier Bolognese fare. Many of the choices are vegetarian, including creamy risottos and an airy flan *di zucca* (squash), many of the main courses are fish, and even the homemade desserts are deceptively light. This transporting spot is only a 15-minute walk or a short cab or bus ride away from Piazza Maggiore.

Via San Rocco 16. www.casamonica.it. ✆ **051-522522.** Main courses 10€–18€. Daily 7:30–11pm. Bus: 13 or 96.

Drogheria della Rosa ★★★ BOLOGNESE/ITALIAN An old apothecary that looks much as it always has, except that now wine bottles are mixed in among the old-fashioned jars on the wooden shelves. Just as the premises once dispensed medicines, chef/owner Emanuele Addone dishes out warm hospitality and down-to-earth Bolognese cooking, with an emphasis on market-fresh ingredients. There's no menu, but a waiter, often Emanuele himself, will guide you through the daily offerings and suggest wines to match. A meal usually begins with a plate of prosciutto and a glass of prosecco. Tortellini are stuffed with zucchini blossoms or eggplant puree; filet mignon is roasted to perfection and drizzled with balsamic vinegar from Modena, guinea fowl is done beautifully with a honey sauce. Desserts, including a mascarpone with chocolate shavings, are sumptuous, but leave just a bit of room—some of the best gelato in Bologna is dispensed around the corner at **La Sorbetteria Castiglione,** at Via Castiglione 44.

Via Cartoleria 10. www.drogheriadellarosa.it. ℂ **051-222529.** Main courses 9€–18€. Mon–Sat 12:30–3pm and 8–10:30pm. Closed Aug 10–27 and 1st week of Jan. Bus: C, 11, or 13.

Il Rovescio ★ BOLOGNESE/VEGETARIAN   The name of this rustic-looking little room just off bar- and osteria-lined Via Pratello translates roughly as "upside down" or "backwards," and the concept applies to some unusual takes on traditional Bolognese cuisine. All the food is locally sourced, and the menu changes frequently to reflect what's fresh in season and, a real rarity in Bologna, often includes many vegetarian choices—grilled radicchio on a bed of polenta, or crepes filled with caramelized squash. Some of the meat presentations, such as little ginger-laced meatballs on a bed of pureed peas, can be surprising, too. Rovescio keeps very late hours, making it a good choice for night-owl diners.

Via Pietralata 28. ℂ **051-523545.** Main courses 10€–18€. Daily 7pm–3am. Bus: C, 11, or 13.

Montegrappa da Nello ★★ BOLOGNESE   This Bologna institution flows across several cozily paneled subterranean rooms just off Piazza Maggiore. Crisply uniformed waiters who seem to have been here since the place began serving in 1948 will lead you through the specialties, which include the house signature dish, *tortellini Montegrappa,* served in a cream-and-meat sauce, though the kitchen also prepares daily specials with some surprising variations of Bolognese standards, such as spinach tortellini with chicken filling. Funghi porcini and truffles appear in many of the classics, including a fragrant veal scallopine in truffle sauce. Meals should begin with a selection of buttery prosciutto and end with a selection of cheeses, all washed down with one of the fine wines from local vineyards. Even in good weather, forgo dining on the small terrace in the dreary lane out front and enjoy the ambience downstairs; to ensure a table down there, reserve for dinner.

Via Montegrappa 2. www.ristorantedanello.com. ℂ **051-236331.** Main courses 10€–17€. Daily noon–3pm and 7–11:30pm. Closed 1 week in Jan or Feb and all of Aug. Bus: A, 11, 20, 27, or 28.

Trattoria Anna Maria ★ BOLOGNESE   Photographs of Sophia Loren, Marcello Mastroianni, and legions of other film and music celebrities line the walls of these high-ceilinged, welcoming rooms, but everyone in Bologna knows that the real star is Anna Maria, who has been making what many consider to be the best pasta in town for 30 years. *Tortellini in brodo,* parcels of pasta filled with minced pork and floating in chicken broth, and *taglietelle* with a hearty Bolognese sauce are her signature dishes, but the meat and vegetable lasagnas are memorable, too. Anna Maria will probably find her way to your table at some point during your meal to make sure you've eaten every bite, but that won't be an issue.

Via Bella Arti 17/A. www.trattoriannamaria.com. ✆ **051-266894.** Main courses 9.50€–18€. Tues–Sat noon–3pm and 7–11pm. Bus: 11, 13, 20, 29B, 30, 38, or 39.

Trattoria dal Biassanot ★★★ EMILIAN   The wood beams, lace tablecloths, warm service, and other grace notes of this welcoming bistro (the name roughly means "night owl") do justice to the expertly prepared Bolognese classics that emerge from the kitchen. Light-as-a-feather *tagliatelle* with Bolognese sauce has a reputation as being some of the best in a city that's famous for the dish, but all of the handmade pastas and succulent sauces are excellent; even the bread is house made and delicious. You're best off putting yourself in the hands of the kitchen and opting for the very reasonably priced tasting menu, wine included. After a meal walk down Via Piella to see one of Bologna's lesser-known but more intriguing sights, the **Finestra,** a shuttered window that surprisingly opens to a view over a canal, one of many that once flowed through the city.

Via Piella 16a. www.dalbiassanot.it. ✆ **051-230644.** Main courses 8€–15€; fixed-price menu 25€. Tues–Sat noon–3pm and 7–11pm, Sun noon–3pm. Closed Aug. Bus: 19, 27, or 94.

Shopping

The shopping delights of Bologna revolve around—what else?—food.

The **Quadrilatero** is the gastronome epicenter of Bologna, where you can snack your way through a number of venerable food shops on a warren of lanes behind Piazza Maggiore. At **Tamburi,** one of Italy's most lavish food shops, Via Caprarie 1 (tamburini.com; ✆ **051-232-226**), a buffet selection of pastas, meats and fish, soups and salads, vegetables, and sweets is accompanied by 200 wines by the glass. **La Baita,** Via Pescherie Vecchie 3A (✆ **051-223-940**), lets you choose from a dizzying selection of hams and cheeses and enjoy them in a busy mezzanine dining room. **Eataly** (Via degli Orefici 19; www.eataly.it; ✆ **051-095-2820**), Bologna's outpost of the New York gourmet shop, sells books as well as cheese, hams, and other gourmet products and wine from ground-floor counters, consumed picnic-style at indoor and outdoor tables. The old covered **marketplace** across the way has been converted to house small bars and food stands, where you can purchase wine and cocktails along with light fare; in the evenings many offer free snacks to accompany drinks.

Osteria del Sole, Vicolo Ranocchi 1D (osteriadelsole.it; ✆ **348-225-6887;** closed Sun) is an invitingly rundown room with a novel twist on the bring-your-own policy—you bring the food, they supply the wine for 2€ a glass. Good places to shop for the accompanying meal are the enticing

A BREAK FROM THE ART circuit

Modena, 40km (25 miles) NW of Bologna, is in the center of what's known as La Terra dei Motori, the "Land of Motors." A car enthusiast who's been patiently traipsing through museums and churches might be delighted to learn that all of Italy's famed sports car manufacturers are located here—and open to the public. It's possible to make the pilgrimage by public transport, but not easily, and you certainly couldn't do the whole circuit in a day. Besides, a car buff will probably want to rent a car anyway, right? As an alternative, **Motorstars** (motorstars.org; ✆ **059-921667**) provides a full day of touring, with transport from Bologna and lunch, for 220€.

Museo Ferrari, Via Dino Ferrari 43 (www.ferrari.com; ✆ **0536-943204**), in Maranello (a suburb some 18km/11 miles from central Modena), pays homage to the magnificent cars that Enzo Ferrari began turning out in 1929; vintage and current models are on display. Admission is 13€ and it's open daily May to September from 9:30am to 7pm (until 6pm Oct–Apr). Tours run daily at 12:30 and

1:30pm, but you need to buy tickets in advance on the website.

Maserati, founded in Bologna in 1914, is now based in Modena, and 20 vintage models are parked permanently at the **Museo Panini** (www.paninimotormuseum.it), in the Modena suburb of Cittanova (on the SS9). Highlights include a rare Maserati Tipo 6CM from the 1930s and a Maserati A6G/54 from the 1950s. You must make an appointment to visit: The museum is open March to October (closed Aug), Monday to Friday from 9:30am to 12:30pm and from 3:30 to 6:30pm, and Saturday from 9:30am to 12:30pm. Admission is free.

A visit to the **Museo Lamborghini** (www.visit-lamborghini.com; ✆ **051-9597008**), Via Modena 12, in the company's hometown of Sant' Agata Bolognese, halfway between Bologna and Modena, can include a tour of the actual factory for 40€ (students 30€). Otherwise, to see the cars and other displays, admission is 13€ (students 10€). The museum is usually open Monday to Friday 10am to 12:30pm and 1:30 to 5pm, but call ahead to confirm.

Salumeria Simoni at Via Drapperie 5/2A (✆ salumeriasimoni.it; ✆ **051-231-880**) and **Enoteca Italiana,** Via Marsala 2/B (www.enotecaitaliana.it; ✆ **051-235-989**). You might want to add some bread and a pastry from **Atti,** Via Caprarie 7 (www.paoloatti.com; ✆ **051-220425**).

Bologna's central food market, **Mercato delle Erbe,** is a few blocks west of this district at Via Ugo Bassi 25 (www.mercatodelleerbe.it); it's open Monday to Wednesday 7am to 1:15pm and 5:30 to 7:30pm, Thursday and Saturday 7am to 1:15pm, and Friday 7am to 1:15pm and 4:30 to 7:30pm.

Maybe it's not too surprising that Bologna also has many famous chocolatiers. **Majani,** Via de' Carbonesi 5 (✆ **051-234302**), claims to be Italy's oldest sweets shop, having made and sold confections since 1796. **Roccati,** Via Clavature 17A (www.roccaticioccolato.com; ✆ **051-261-964**) is run by a husband-and-wife team that makes the *gianduja* (hazelnut and cognac-filled chocolate) their ancestors once concocted for the princes of Savoy.

Entertainment & Nightlife

Bologna's large student population keeps late hours in bars, clubs, and *osterias*, many clustered near the university on Via Zamboni and Via delle Belle Arti. Bolognese of all stripes, even those who plan to turn in early, stop at bars all over town for an *aperitivo,* when a glass of wine or a cocktail comes with snacks, usually served "all you can eat" buffet style.

CAFES, BARS & CLUBS

Camera a Sud ★   Three shabby-chic rooms in the Jewish ghetto are part coffee house, part wine bar and late-night hangout, and popular any time of the day. Via Valdonica 5. www.cameraasud.net. ☏ **051-0951448.** Mon–Sat noon–1am, Sun 5pm–1am.

Cantina Bentivoglio ★★   You'll hear some of the best jazz in Bologna in the cellars of a 16th-century *palazzo* near the university; unless you need to accompany your jazz with hard booze, select from one of the more than 500 labels that fill the wine racks. Via Mascarella 4B. www.cantina bentivoglio.it. ☏ **051-265416.** Daily 8pm–2am. Lunch Mon–Fri 12:15–2:45pm.

Le Stanze ★   Four chic rooms fill the nooks and crannies of a 17th-century chapel; come for lunch or coffee, and on weekend evenings begin with cocktails (accompanied by a terrific buffet) and hang around for the DJ sets. Via del Borgo di San Pietro www.lestanzecafe.com. ☏ **051-228767.** Mon–Sat 11am–1am.

Nu Lounge Bar ★★   Hip young professionals check each other out (and themselves in the huge mirrors) while enjoying martinis under the porticos in the Quadrilatero. Via dei Musei 6. www.nu-lounge.com. ☏ **051-222532.** Daily noon–2:30am.

Osteria de Poeti ★   Bologna's oldest *osteria*, feeding students since around 1600, not only dishes up cheap pastas and hearty *secondi* but live jazz and folk music as well, set against a mellow background of brick arches. Via Poeti 1. www.osteriadepoeti.com. ☏ **051-236166.** Tues–Fri 12:30–2:30pm and 7:30pm–2:30am, Sat–Sun 7:30pm–2:30am.

FERRARA ★★

52km (32 miles) N of Bologna, 100km (62 miles) SW of Venice

It's not that quiet, elegant Ferrara hasn't had some big moments. The powerful Este family held control of the city on the Po River for almost four centuries. Painters, composers, and poets came to town under their patronage and made Ferrara one of Europe's great capitals of culture. Lucrezia Borgia, notorious femme fatale of the Renaissance, arrived by ceremonial barge in 1502 to marry Prince Alfonso Este. They and the other Estes built pleasure pavilions and gardens and expanded their holdings into the Addizione, a model city of the Renaissance crisscrossed with straight, palace-lined avenues. By the end of the 16th century,

Ferrara by Bike

Ferrara is known in Italy as a *città della bicicletta*, because just about everyone in town, regardless of age, gets around on two wheels. The flat streets and squares lend themselves to easy pedaling, and the city's medieval walls are topped with trees, lawns, and a wide path that's ideal for cycling. Views of the city and surrounding farmlands are terrific, and if you want to go farther afield, well-marked bike paths lead into the Po Delta (the tourist office has a bike-path map). Many hotels offer guests free use of bikes, or you can rent them from the lot outside the train station (2.50€ an hour, 10€ a day).

however, the Estes were gone—and Ferrara has looked pretty much the same ever since. That, of course, is its appeal. It's like a Renaissance time capsule—the Estes' castle and palaces, the city's medieval quarters and encircling walls, and proud old convents and churches are the backdrop for everyday life in this attractive provincial city.

Essentials

GETTING THERE Ferrara is on the main **train** line between Bologna and Venice, with service to and from both cities twice an hour (30–45 min. from Bologna; 1–1½ hrs. from Venice). Ravenna is an hour away, with hourly departures all day. From the train station it's an easy 20-minute walk to the Duomo, but you can also take the frequent no. 2 bus to Piazza Travaglio (1.50€; pay on board with correct change). For more information, call ✆ **0532-599-411** (www.atc.bo.it). You may also rent a **bike** at the station and get around the way most locals do (see "Ferrara By Bike," above).

If you have a **car** and are coming from Bologna, take A13 north. From Venice, take A4 southwest to Padua and continue on A13 south to Ferrara.

VISITOR INFORMATION The helpful **tourist office** is inside the Castello Estense, Piazza del Castello (www.ferraraterraeacqua.it; ✆ **0532-299303**). It's open Monday to Saturday from 9am to 1pm and 2 to 6pm, Sunday 9:30am to 1pm and 2 to 5pm.

Exploring Ferrara

The **Castello Estense** is pretty much the center of town, with the **Cattedrale San Giorgio Martire** and twisting lanes of the medieval town just to the southeast. **Corso Ercole I d'Este,** flanked by beautiful *palazzi,* leads north into the Renaissance city and past **Palazzo dei Diamanti** to the city walls.

Castello Estense ★★ CASTLE With its moat, hefty brick walls, drawbridges, heavy gates, and four sturdy towers, the domain of the Este family still suggests power and might, just as it was intended to do.

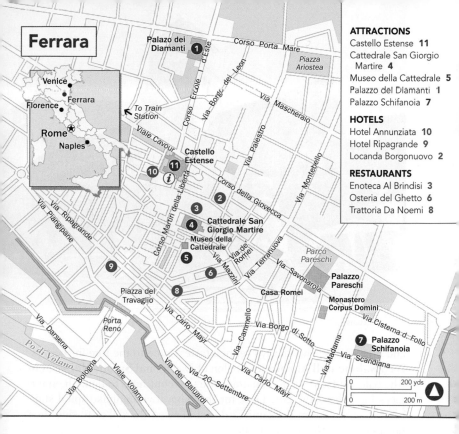

Ferrara

ATTRACTIONS

Castello Estense **11**
Cattedrale San Giorgio
   Martire **4**
Museo della Cattedrale **5**
Palazzo del Diamanti **1**
Palazzo Schifanoia **7**

HOTELS

Hotel Annunziata **10**
Hotel Ripagrande **9**
Locanda Borgonuovo **2**

RESTAURANTS

Enoteca Al Brindisi **3**
Osteria del Ghetto **6**
Trattoria Da Noemi **8**

Niccolò II d'Este ordered the castle built in 1385 as a place of refuge when his subjects became restless after a series of tax increases, and quite literally tore one of his officials to pieces. A long elevated gallery links the castle to the family's onetime residence, now the Palazzo Municipale, next door. Duke Niccolò d'Este III forever made the castle a place of infamy when, in 1425, he used a contrivance of mirrors to catch his 20-year-old wife, Parisina d'Este, in flagrante delicto with his illegitimate son, Ugolino. He promptly had the pair taken to the dungeons and beheaded; Robert Browning tells the story in his poem "My Last Duchess." (Ironically, Niccolò himself boasted of sleeping with 800 women and a popular rhyme of the time was "left and right of the river Po, everywhere there are children by Niccolò.") Young Lucrezia Borgia, with her reputation for adultery, incest, and a poisoning or two, took up residence in 1502 as the wife of Duke Alfonso d'Este, who kept his half-brother, Giulio, in the dungeons for 53 years for plotting to overthrow him. (Elderly Giulio allegedly created quite a stir when he finally emerged onto the streets of Ferrara in the clothing he had brought with him into his cell half a century before.) For all their perfidy, the Estes also hosted one of the finest courts in Europe and cultivated the Renaissance arts

341

Castello Estense.

and humanities. The family's refined tastes come to the fore in the frescoed **Salone dell'Aurora** (the Salon of Dawn) and **Salone dei Giochi** (the Salon of Games), and an orangerie that continues to flourish on terraces high above the city. Look for the innovative ramplike spiral staircase ascending from the courtyard that allowed the dukes to ride their horses right up to their quarters.

Largo Castello. www.castelloestense.it. ℰ **0532-299233.** Admission 8€ adults, 6.50€ children ages 11–18, free for ages 10 and under. Jan–May and Sept daily 9:30am–5:30pm; June daily 9:30am–1:30pm and 3–7pm; July–Aug Tues–Sun 9:30am–1:30pm and 3–7pm; Oct–Dec Tues–Sun 9:30am–5:30pm. Bus: 1, 7, 9, 11, or 21 from the train station.

Cattedrale San Giorgio Martire ★ CATHEDRAL The faithful did not even have to step beyond the magnificent 12th-century porch of Ferrara's cathedral to understand that salvation was a pretty dicey affair. In exquisite carvings above the entryway, the dead creep out of their tombs as an angel weighs sins and good deeds on a scale; as if to prove that the odds are against salvation, a devil mischievously tugs on the evil side so it skews toward sin. The saved, gloriously crowned and robed, proceed toward Heaven, where they are welcomed into the lap of Abraham; the naked damned slouch down to Hell to be tormented by sneering Devils. In the vast interior—redone in dark baroque style after an 18th-century fire—look for a fresco by Guercino ("the squinter") portraying the martyrdom of St. Lawrence. When Roman authorities demanded that Lawrence, an early church deacon, turn over ecclesiastic treasures, he brought them the poor, saying "Behold in these poor persons the treasures which I promised to show you." As punishment Lawrence was tied to a spit and burned over a roaring fire. After the good-natured saint roasted for a time, he allegedly said, "I'm well done, turn me over," a wisecrack that has earned him a place as patron of chefs and cooks. The **cathedral museum**, housed in the former San Romano church and monastery opposite the church, is well stocked with works by Ferrara's leading 15th-century painter of the Este court, Cosmé Tura. Most arresting among them is "St. George and the Princess," an especially intense portrayal of Ferrara's patron saint savagely trying to do away with a dragon to save a damsel in distress. The tale was a popular part of religious tradition as well as a romantic legend of chivalry, so it may well have satisfied both the Estes' spiritual and courtly aspirations.

Piazza della Cattedrale. (C) **0532-207449.** Free admission. Mon–Sat 7:30am–noon and 3–6:30pm; Sun 7:30am–12:30pm and 3:30–7:30pm. Museum: Admission 6€ adults, 3€ for students, children 17 and under free; 7€ joint admission with Palazzo Schifanoia. Tues–Sun 9am–1pm and 3–6pm. Bus: 11 from the train station.

Palazzo dei Diamanti ★ MUSEUM   The facade of the Estes' most remarkable residence comprises 8,500 spiky, diamond-shaped, white marble blocks, creating an architectural spectacle that shimmers in the light and seems to be constantly in movement. The *palazzo* stands at the intersection of two monumental avenues that were the main thoroughfares of the Addizione that Ercole d'Este laid out in the late 15th century, doubling the size of Ferrara and making the city into a Renaissance showplace. The **Pinacoteca Nazionale** occupies the first floor of the *palazzo* (the ground floor hosts special exhibitions) and provides a handy overview of the School of Ferrara, especially the trio of old masters who flourished under the Estes—Cosmé Tura, Francesco del Cossa, and Ercole de' Roberti (whose brilliance comes to light in the excellent free audioguide tour). Pride of place belongs to Tura's "Martyrdom of St. Maurelius," in which the subject, an early bishop of Ferrara, calmly kneels as his executioner swings a sword above his neck and some decidedly cheerful-looking *putti* look on from a cloud.

Corso Ercole d'Este 21. www.palazzodiamanti.it. (C) **0532-205844** or 0532-244949. Admission to Pinacoteca 4€ adults, free for children 17 and under. Free audio guides. Mon–Thurs 9am–1pm and 2pm–5pm, Fri 9am–2pm. Bus: 3C, or 4C from the train station.

Palazzo Schifanoia ★★★ HISTORIC HOME   The Estes retreated for leisure to several pleasure palaces around Ferrara, including this one enlarged by Duke Borso d'Este between 1450 and 1471. Schifanoia translates roughly as "chasing away tedium," and the concept comes to the fore in the **Salone dei Mesi (Salon of the Months),** where a mesmerizing cycle of frescoes represents the 12 months—or did, as only a few remain intact. Each is divided into three horizontal bands: The lower bands show scenes from the daily life of courtiers and people, with Duke Borso frequently making an appearance astride a horse; the middle bands illustrate signs of the zodiac; and the upper sections depict gods and goddesses associated with the sign. In this collaboration of the masters of the Ferrarese school of painting—Francesco del Cossa, Ercole de' Roberti, and Cosmé Tura—characters of those distant times seem to come alive and step out of the scenes (one figure actually does, perching on the edge of the frame as if he's about to jump into the room). Men ride horses and run footraces, harvesters pick grapes, women do needlework and play lutes. The artists even dug some skeletons out of the Este closet: In a mythical scene depicting Mars and Venus caught in a net as they make love, their clothing is laid beside the bed in such a way as to suggest a decapitated man and woman—a sly reference to the fate of the adulterous Ugolino and Parisina d'Este (see Castello Estense, above).

Via Scandiana 23. ✆ **0532-244949.** Admission 6€ adults, 3€ for students, free for 17 and under; 7€ joint admission with Museo della Cattedrale. Tues–Sun 9am–6pm. Bus: 1, 7, 9, or 21 from the train station.

Where to Stay

Hotel Annunziata ★★   The setting, across from Castello Estense, is medieval, and Casanova spent the night here when the place was a simple inn. Once inside the doors, though, you'll feel like you've been transported from old Ferrara into a Milanese showroom for contemporary style. The minimalist white color scheme strays into grays and beige here and there, even the occasional burst of red or orange, but for the most part this place is all about sleek lines, soothing neutrals, and minimalist calm, and it's all extremely comfortable and relaxing. In the large and bright guest rooms, the best with castle views, high-tech lighting and snowy linens contrast beautifully with wood floors and the occasional timbered ceiling, and bathrooms are sleekly luxurious. Six similarly stylish apartments with kitchenettes are located in a nearby 14th-century annex.

Piazza Repubblica 5. www.annunziata.it. ✆ **0532-201111.** 27 units. 89€–109€ double. Rates include buffet breakfast. Bus: 1, 7, 9, 11, or 21. **Amenities:** Restaurant; bar; babysitting; bikes (free); room service; Wi-Fi (free).

Hotel Ripagrande ★   A 15th-century *palazzo* retains enough arches and beams, striking medieval furnishings, and rich carpets and tapestries to suggest that it might still be the home of a count, as it was for many centuries. A breakfast room and lounge full of polished antiques and oil paintings wraps around a lovely courtyard, and upstairs the gracious, traditionally furnished guest rooms are suitably grand, though a wee bit threadbare in places—perhaps as befits faded royalty. Many sprawl over two and three levels, so if you don't like the idea of climbing up and down stairs to reach the bathroom in the middle of the night, ask for one of the enormous one-floor rooms.

Via Ripagrande 21. www.ripagrandehotel.it. ✆ **0532-765250.** 40 units. 59€–70€ double. Rates include breakfast. Bus: 1, 7, 9, 11, or 21. **Amenities:** Babysitting; bikes (free); room service; Wi-Fi (free).

Lucrezia Borgia, A Woman Misjudged?

With their lust for power and penchant for murder, the Borgias are still one of history's most notoriously dysfunctional families, 500 years after their Renaissance heyday. Lucrezia was born into the clan in 1480, the illegitimate daughter of Cardinal Rodrigo Borgia, soon to be Pope Alexander VI. By the time she was 20, she had a child, allegedly fathered by her brother Cesare, and had been married twice—one husband fled for his life when the Pope decided Lucrezia needed to make a more politically advantageous alliance, another was strangled as he lay recovering from knife wounds (both attacks arranged by Cesare). With this less-than-sterling reputation, Lucrezia got a chilly reception when she arrived in Ferrara in 1500 as the new bride of Duke Alfonso d'Este. Soon, however, she proved herself to be cultured, a brilliant conversationalist, and an ardent patron of the arts. She is said to have carried on a passionate affair with the poet Pietro Bembo, but she was also known to be pious, a loving wife and attentive mother. She died just short of her 39th birthday after giving birth to her fifth child.

Locanda Borgonuovo ★★★ This lovely old house, converted from a 17th-century convent and just down a cobblestone street from the *castello,* could set the gold standard for B&Bs everywhere. The four rooms are furnished with family pieces, including some serious antiques, and share a flowery courtyard and cozy library/sitting room; one especially large double has an extra bed and a kitchenette. An excellent breakfast is served in the family living room, and the gracious hosts lend bikes and dispense advice about the best ways to enjoy their beloved Ferrara.
Via Cairoli 21. www.borgonuovo.com. © **0532-211100.** 75€–100€. double. Rates include breakfast. Bus: 4C or 7. **Amenities:** Bikes (free); Wi-Fi (free).

Where to Eat

You'll get a good intro to Ferrara's gastronomic pleasures on a stroll down Via Cortevecchia, a narrow brick lane near the cathedral where traditional *salumerias* such as Marchetti at no. 35 (© **0532-204800**) sell the city's famous *salama da suga,* handmade sausages. The food stalls of the **Mercato Comunale,** at the corner of Via Santo Stefano and Via del Mercato, are also good grazing grounds. Look out for *coppia Ferrarese,* sourdough bread stretched into intertwining rolls that look like two sets of legs (hence the name, "the couple"). In restaurants, the pasta to try is *cappellacci di zucca*—round pasta stuffed with squash, served *al burro e salvia* (with butter and sage sauce) or *al ragu* (with meat sauce).

Enoteca Al Brindisi ★ FERRARESE It would be easy for this timbered, atmospheric little place—probably the oldest wine bar in the world, dating from 1435—to rest on its laurels. Titian was a regular, Copernicus is said to have lived upstairs while studying for his degree in 1503, and it looks like some of the dusty bottles stacked above the cramped tables have been around ever since. Locals (some of whom look

The Jews of Ferrara

Ferrara's Jewish heritage dates to the Middle Ages, with a Jewish community flourishing here when the Este family controlled the city in the 15th and 16th centuries. The social prominence of Ferrara's 20th-century Jews and their sad fate is the subject of Giorgio Bassani's novel *The Garden of the Finzi-Contini*, brought evocatively to the screen in director Vittorio de Sica's 1970 film of the same name. Ferrara's excellent

Jewish Museum, encompassing two synagogues in an old palazzo at Via Mazzini 95, was severely damaged in the earthquakes of 2012 and has been closed ever since, with a re-opening date still to be determined. Ferrara is also the future home of the **National Museum of Italian Jewry and the Shoah**, currently under development in a former prison at Via Piangipane 81.

like they've been around awhile, too) still pack the place, and waiters take earnest pride in recommending wines from throughout Italy, most available by the glass, accompanied by a short menu of *cappellacci di zucca* (squash ravioli) and a few other local specialties.

Via Adelardi 11. www.albrindisi.net. ℂ **0532-471225.** Main courses 7€–10€. Daily 11am–1am. Bus: 11 from the train station.

Osteria del Ghetto ★ FERRARESE/SEAFOOD   From a simple storefront on the narrow cobblestone lanes of Ferrara's centuries-old Jewish ghetto, a staircase leads to two homey upstairs rooms, enlivened with colorful murals. A small section of pasta and meat dishes are available, but clearly the kitchen's passion is for fish and seafood—a fresh catch is usually on the menu, and a large selection of fried calamari and shrimp, rich fish soup, *spaghetti alle vongole,* seafood salads, and other selections will tempt you away from the region's meat-heavy staples.

Via Vittoria 26/28. www.osteriadelghetto.it. ℂ **0532-764-936.** Main courses 8€–16€. Tues–Sun 12:30–2:30pm and 7:30–10:30pm. Bus: 2 from the train station.

Trattoria Da Noemi ★★ FERRARESE   The surroundings date to 1400, with a pleasant old-world decor that befits the provenance and gracious service to match, and the menu leans to old Ferrarese classics—some residents say no one does them better. This is the place to become acquainted with *cappellacci di zucca,* the city's signature dish, little pockets of light egg pasta stuffed with the pulp of roasted butternut squash with hints of nutmeg and parmigiano. Much of the meat-heavy *secondi* features local beef grilled over a wood fire. The house *semifreddo,* a delicious half-frozen custard with pistachio and walnuts or mint, is the perfect finish.

Via Ragno 31. www.trattoriadanoemi.it. ℂ **0532-769-070.** Main courses 8€–24€. Wed–Mon 12:15–2:30pm and 7–11pm. Bus: 2 or 11 from the train station.

RAVENNA ★★

74km (46 miles) E of Bologna, 145km (90 miles) S of Venice, 130km (81 miles) NE of Florence

It's hard to believe that little, off-the-beaten track Ravenna was the epi-center of the Western World for a brief spell, when it was the capital of the Western Roman Empire from A.D. 402 to A.D. 476. Those rulers and the fathers of the early Christian church, and then the Goths and Byzantines who followed them, carpeted Ravenna's churches and monuments in glittering mosaics to create an artistic legacy that rivals the splendors of Venice and Istanbul. (The great poet Dante, who's buried here, described Ravenna's mosaics as "the sweet color of Oriental sapphires.") Set amid the marshy landscapes of Emilia-Romagna's coastal plain, this once glamorous and powerful city is well worth the trip.

Essentials

GETTING THERE   With hourly **trains** that take only 1 hour 20 minutes from Bologna, Ravenna can easily be visited on a day trip. There's also frequent service from Ferrara (1 hr., 15 min.), which has connections to Venice. The train station is a 10-minute walk from the center at Piazza Fernini (ⓒ **892021**).

If you have a **car** and are coming from Bologna, head east along A14. From Ferrara, take the S16.

GETTING AROUND   Ravenna operates a useful bicycle rental scheme; get keys from the tourist office that provide unlimited access to bikes all over the city. Rates are 9.50€ per day for adults and 8.50€ for students (free for children 10 and under). If you need to take a local **bus** (as you will to visit the Basilica di Sant'Apollinare in Classe, see below), buy tickets (1.20€) in advance from any bar or *tabacchi*.

VISITOR INFORMATION   The **tourist office** is at Via Salara 8 (www.turismo.ravenna.it; ⓒ **0544-35404**). It's open Monday to Saturday 8:30am to 7pm, and Sunday from 10am to 6pm. Stop in here for a good map, bicycle rental, and combination tickets to the city's attractions. The office also books accommodations.

Exploring Ravenna

The elegant, Venetian-looking **Piazza del Popolo** was laid out in the late 15th century, when Venice ruled the city. From here you can easily walk to all of the sights, with the exception of Sant'Apollinare in Classe, for which you'll want to take a bus or drive.

Basilica di Sant'Apollinare in Classe ★★ CHURCH   What is now a landlocked suburb surrounded by pine groves about 6km (3¾ miles) south of the city was at one time the port of the capital of the Western Roman Empire. This huge 6th-century church—dedicated to

St. Apollinare, the first bishop and patron of Ravenna—befits the city's onetime importance. Apollinare allegedly landed in Ravenna sometime in the 2nd century and converted the locals. In a dazzling array of brilliantly hued mosaics, he is shown in prayer, surrounded by lambs (his flock) against a gentle background of rocks, birds, and plants, including the pines that still grow outside the church. (Lord Byron used to ride here with his Ravennese mistress, Teresa Guiccioli). Above Apollinaire is a depiction of the Transfiguration, when Christ became radiant and began shining with bright rays of light; he is represented as a golden cross on a starry blue background, while Peter, James, and John, the three disciples who were present at the event, are shown as lambs. Some especially touching mosaics on the right of the church shows three Old Testament figures who made sacrifices to God: Abel, Melchizedek, and Abraham.

Via Romea Sud 224, Classe. www.soprintendenzaravenna.beniculturali.it. © **0544-473569.** Admission 5€ adults, 2.50€ ages 18–25, free for children 17 and under. Daily 8:30am–7:30pm. Bus: 4 from rail station or Piazza Caduti (1.20€).

Basilica di Sant'Apollinare Nuovo ★★ CHURCH   The church that Emperor Theodoric built in the first part of the 6th century for followers of Arianism, a Christian sect, seems to be in perpetual motion. On the left side of the nave, reserved for women, 22 female saints and martyrs approach Mary and the Christ child as they receive gifts from the three magi, who sport natty leopard-skin leggings. On the right side, 26 male martyrs led by St. Martin approach a bearded Christ. Above these processions are 26 charmingly rendered scenes from the life of Christ, including one of Christ standing on shore and calling to Peter and Andrew in their small fishing boat, asking them to be his disciples. Mosaics near the door provide a picture-postcard view of the old city, including Theodoric's palace and other monuments and the port city of Classe. Look for the detached hand and forearm wrapped around a column of Theodoric's palace—it was once part of a portrait of Theodoric's court that was removed when the church became a Catholic basilica.

Via di Roma (between Via Carducci and Via Alberoni). www.ravennamosaici.it. © **0544-541688.** Admission 9.50€ adults, 8.50€ students, free for children 10 and under. Apr–Sept daily 9am–7pm; Mar and Oct daily 9:30am–5:30pm; Nov–Feb daily 10am–5pm.

Basilica di San Vitale ★★★ CHURCH   The emperor Justinian (who never visited Ravenna and ruled instead from Constantinople) completed this octagonal church—richly ornamented with intensely green, blue, and gold mosaics—in 540 as a symbol of his power. Endowed with a halo to indicate his role as head of church and state, Justinian stands next to a clean-shaven Christ, perched atop the world, flanked by saints and angels. Looking on are Justinian's two most important adjuncts, his empress, Theodora, and a bald Maximian, bishop of Ravenna. Theodora's presence suggests her immense influence and rapacious rise to power. Born into the circus, she became known for her beauty and was a famous

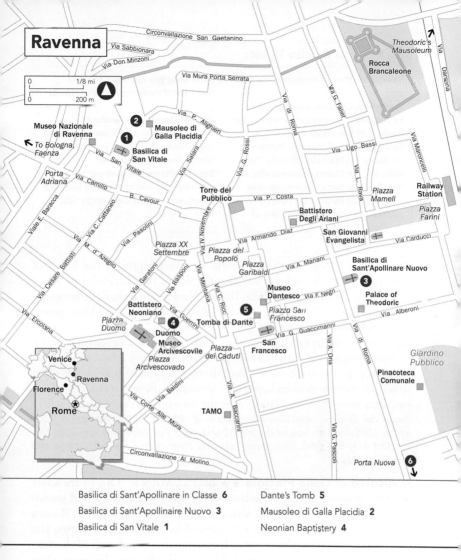

Ravenna

Theodoric's
Mausoleum

Rocca
Brancaleone

Via Sabbionara
Circonvallazione San Gaetanino
Via Don Minzoni
Via Mura Porta Serrata
Via P. Alighieri

Museo Nazionale
di Ravenna

Mausoleo di
Galla Placidia

Basilica di
San Vitale

← To Bologna,
Faenza

Porta
Adriana

Via Camillo

B. Cavour

Torre del
Pubblico

Via P. Costa

Battistero
Degli Ariani

San Giovanni
Evangelista

Via Carducci

Piazza
Mameli

Railway
Station

Piazza
Farini

Via di Roma
Via Ugo Bassi

Basilica di
Sant'Apollinare Nuovo

Viale E. Baracca

Via Pasolini

Piazza XX
Settembre

Via 4 Novembre

Via Armando Diaz

Piazza del
Popolo

Piazza
Garibaldi

Via A. Mariani

Museo
Dantesco

Via F. Negri

Palace of
Theodoric

Via Alberoni

Battistero
Neoniano

Piazza
Duomo

Duomo

Museo
Arcivescovile

Tomba di Dante

Piazza San
Francesco

San
Francesco

Piazza
dei Caduti

Venice

Ravenna

Florence

Rome

Via Corte Alle Mura

Via Baldini

TAMO

Via A. Baccarini

Circonvallazione Al Molino

Giardino
Pubblico

Pinacoteca
Comunale

Porta Nuova

actress and courtesan when she caught Justinian's eye. She became such a force in running the empire that in 532, not long before the completion of the church, she ordered that 30,000 insurgents be gathered up, brought to the Hippodrome in Constantinople, and slaughtered.

Via San Vitale 17. www.ravennamosaici.it. ✆ **0544-215193.** Admission 9.50€ adults, 8.50€ students, free for children 10 and under. Apr–Sept daily 9am–7pm; Mar and Oct daily 9am–5:30pm; Nov–Feb daily 9:30am–5pm.

Battistero Neoniano (Neonian Baptistery) ★ CHURCH Ravenna's oldest monument was erected by Bishop Ursus around 400, to accompany a long-ago destroyed basilica on the site of an ancient Roman

Ravenna Combo Tickets

Ravenna's system of museum cards can seem more Byzantine than the mosaics themselves. Church-run sites are covered by one card that covers admission to the **basilicas of San Vitale and Sant'Apollinare Nuovo,** the **Neonian Baptistry,** the **Mausoleo di Galla Placidia,** and the **Museo Arcivescovile,** all top sites. The card costs a reasonable 9.50€ and can be used for 7 days. In fact, you need this card to get into any of these sites; you can buy it at any of them. For state-sponsored sites, you can pay 8€ to see both the **Museo Nazionale** and the **Mausoleo di Teodorico** (worthy but not top of your list if you have only a day in Ravenna) or 10€ if you want to add to those the **Basilica di Sant'Apollinare in Classe**—although if that's the only one of the three you want to see, you can just buy a single ticket for that for 5€.

bath. The eight sides of this octagonal structure represent the 7 days of the week, as set out in Genesis, plus the day of the Resurrection, when Christ gave mankind eternal life. Bishop Neon embellished the structure at the end of the 5th century, adding the intensely colored blue, green, and gold mosaics that spread over the dome, showing John the Baptist baptizing Christ in the River Jordan, surrounded by a procession of the 12 Apostles carrying crowns as a sign of celestial glory. Many of the marble panels in the walls were taken from the Roman bathhouse—that structure, like the sunken baptistery, was originally at street level, which has risen more than 3m (10 ft.) over the intervening centuries.

Piazza del Duomo. www.ravennamosaici.it. (C) **0544-215201.** Admission 9.50€ adults, 8.50€ students, free for children 10 and under. Apr–Sept daily 9am–7pm; Mar and Oct daily 9:30am–5:30pm; Nov–Feb daily 10am–5pm. Closed Christmas and New Year's Day.

Mausoleo di Galla Placidia ★★ MONUMENT   One of the most powerful women of the Byzantine world was the daughter and grand-daughter of Roman emperors, sister of one ruler of the Western Roman Empire, and widow of another. Captured by the Visigoths during the sack of Rome in 410, she married King Athaulf, moved with his barbarian hordes to Barcelona, was traded back to the Romans for grain when Athaulf was murdered, and then married co-emperor Constantius, with whom she had a son, Valentinian III. When Constantius died and Valentinian became emperor at the age of 6, Galla acted as regent and in that capacity ruled the Western world for 12 years. Though she's most likely buried in Rome, her mausoleum here is crowned with a dome decorated with mosaics, vivid with hues of peacock blue, moss green, Roman gold, eggplant purple, and burnt orange. They're especially moving for their simplicity and spirituality—doves drink from fountains, as the faithful are nourished by God; a purple-robed Christ is surrounded by lambs, as the Heavenly king is surrounded by the faithful; and 570 tiny gold stars, suggesting life eternal, twinkle in the cupola. Soft light filtered by alabaster infuses the surroundings with an other-worldly luminosity.

Via Fiandrini Benedetto. www.ravenna mosaici.it. ☏ **0544-541688.** Admission 9.50€ adults, 8.50€ students (Mar to mid-June 2€ discount), free for children 10 and under. Apr–Sept daily 9am–7pm; Mar and Oct daily 9am–5:30pm; Nov–Feb daily 9:30am–5pm.

Dante's tomb.

Tomba di Dante (Dante's Tomb) ★ MONUMENT The author of the *Divine Comedy* settled in Ravenna in 1318, having traveled restlessly throughout Italy after he was exiled from his native Florence in 1302, when he fell out of political favor; he died of marsh fever here on September 14, 1321. This simple marble tomb, erected in 1780, is inscribed with a harsh reprimand to the Florentines, who are still clamoring for the body's return: "Here in this corner lies Dante, exiled from his native land, born to Florence, an unloving mother."

Via Dante Alighieri. ☏ **0544-33662.** Free admission. Daily 10am–6:30pm (Oct–Mar closes 4pm).

Where to Stay

Ravenna's hotels do a slow business off-season (anytime outside of summer); rates come down accordingly and are usually open to some negotiation.

Casa Masoli ★★★ Accommodations in Ravenna don't get any more atmospheric than they do in this beautiful 18th-century *palazzo* near the city center. Two splendid suites at the front of the house are especially grand and cavernous—one retains the original brick vaulting, another frescoes and a marble tub—but high ceilings, tall windows, and wood-veneered bathrooms lend all the rooms an aura of grandeur; those in the back face a surprisingly verdant garden. Scattered antiques, comfy lounge chairs and couches, and framed lithographs provide a homey familial ambience, as does the generous breakfast buffet with lots of homemade fare served in a frescoed salon.

Via Girolamo Rossi 22. www.casamasoli.it. ☏ **0544-217682.** 7 units. 70€–90€ double. Rates include buffet breakfast. **Amenties:** Wi-Fi (free).

Hotel Centrale Byron ★ From 1819 to 1821 Lord Byron shared a nearby palace with his lover, Contessa Teresa Guiccioli, and her husband, and Ravenna has been milking the incident ever since. This hotel—one of several establishments in town named for the Romantic poet—is a lot less evocative than its name suggests, but it is wonderfully located a stone's throw from most of the sights, a few steps from Piazza del Popolo, and an easy stroll from the train station. Constant updating has given the rooms a subtly contemporary patina more geared toward comfort than character, with some welcome touches that include sound-proofing and excellent lighting.

Via IV Novembre 14. www.hotelsravenna.it. ✆ **0544-212225.** 54 units. 70€–110€ double. Rates include buffet breakfast. Parking 15€. **Amenities:** Bar; room service; Wi-Fi (free).

Hotel Diana ★ Tucked away slightly off the beaten path at the edge of the city center, these large, bright, and simply furnished rooms (many with extremely large windowed bathrooms) are a good base for exploring and especially handy for motorists, with several easy-to-reach garages nearby. Downstairs, an English-speaking staff dispenses recommenda-tions with genuine enthusiasm, and a generous buffet breakfast is served on a large, glass-enclosed patio.

Via Girolamo Rossi 47. www.hoteldiana.ra.it. ✆ **0544-39164.** 33 units. 70€–92€ dou-ble. Rates include buffet breakfast. **Amenities:** Bikes (free); Wi-Fi (free).

Where to Eat

Ravenna's **Mercato Coperto** (near the center of town on Piazza Andrea Costa), once an attraction in itself, is closed for renovation and is slated to reopen in 2016. In the meantime, **Gastronomia Marchesini,** an elegant food store at Via Mazzini 2 (✆ **0544-212309**), is a good place to load up on regional hams and cheeses; it also operates a reasonably priced self-service restaurant upstairs, and a full service restaurant above that. **Profumo di Piadina**, 24 Via Cairoli, tops warm-from-the oven *piadina* (flatbread) with prosciutto, creamy *squaquerone* (cheese), and other locally produced ingredients.

Ca' de Ven ★★ ROMAGNOLA   A 16th-century guesthouse and for-mer spice warehouse with frescoed ceilings and lots of paneling and exposed timbers makes a delightful stop for lunch or a light dinner. Heavier fare is offered, but the emphasis here is on *piadina,* the local flatbread, and that's the way to go. It's served with a dozen or so fillings or, even better, by itself warm from the oven with a selection of cured meats and *squaquerone,* a delicate soft cheese. There's also a huge selection of wine by the glass. At lunch and in early evening you'll rub elbows at communal tables with what seems like half the population of Ravenna, so enjoy the familiar atmosphere and ignore the sometimes-brusque service.

Via Corrado Ricci 24. www.cadeven.it. ✆ **0544-30163.** *Piadine* about 4€, main courses 11€–15€. Tues–Sun 11am–11pm.

Cinema Alexander ★ ITALIAN/SEAFOOD   Vintage film posters play up the location in a former movie house, complete with balcony seating, and help provide a sophisticated setting for refined dishes that emerge from the kitchen. Ravenna's proximity to the sea comes to the fore in beautifully sauced fresh fish, and in some nice combinations like fusilli with tuna and pork or calamari couscous; meat dishes lean toward perfectly roasted game birds and some unusual local preparations, such as veal cheeks with potato and lemon puree. Service is friendly and attentive, as soft jazz and mellow renditions of movie themes float through the space.

Via Bassa del Pignataro 8. www.ristorantealexander.it. © **0544-212967.** Main courses 15€–28€. Tues–Sun 12:30–2:30pm and 7:30–11:30pm (closed Sun in summer).

La Bella Venezia ★ ROMAGNOLA   The name suggests a certain airy elegance, and the cream-colored walls and light, starched table-cloths in this small room off the Piazza della Popolo deliver on the promise. Despite the name, don't expect Venetian specialties: this restaurant's menu is for the most part typically and deliciously Romagnolese. The kitchen is much respected for its *cappelletti alla romagnola* (cap-shaped pasta stuffed with ricotta, roasted pork loin, chicken breast, and nutmeg, and served with meat sauce) and other homemade pastas, including simple ravioli with butter and sage and risotto with fresh seasonal vegetables. Other specialties are *cotoletta alla Bisanzio* (a fried veal cutlet topped with cherry tomatoes and arugula) and a rich fish soup, but everything on the small menu is prepared with finesse and served with old-world flair that keeps a local clientele coming back.

Via IV Novembre 16. www.bellavenezia.it. © **0544-212-746.** Main courses 10€–15€. Mon–Sat 12:15–2:15pm and 7:30–10:15pm.

PARMA ★

457km (283 miles) NW of Rome, 97km (60 miles) NW of Bologna, 121km (75 miles) SE of Milan

This prosperous little city on the Roman Via Emilia, about an hour north of Bologna, delivers a slice of the good life. Residents are surrounded by art-filled palaces and churches bestowed upon them by the Renaissance Farnese family and later Marie-Louise, wife of Napoleon. They enjoy the music of their own Giuseppe Verdi in a grand opera house, and when it comes to food—suffice it to say that elegant Parma has given the world some of the finest hams and cheeses ever. You could easily fill a very satisfying day or two here, enjoying the beautiful monuments, maybe listening to some music, stepping in and out of tempting food shops, and sitting down to some memorably delicious meals.

Essentials

GETTING THERE   Parma is served by the Milan-Bologna **rail** line, with hourly trains arriving from Milan (trip time: 45 min. on frequent fast trains, 1½ hr. on the less-frequent but less-expensive slower trains).

From Bologna, trains depart for Parma every 30 minutes or so (around 1 hr.). There are two or three direct trains a day from Florence (2 hr.); most journeys will require a change in Bologna. For information and schedules, call © **892021.**

If you have a **car** and are starting out in Bologna, head northwest along A1. Don't drive into the old town without first contacting your hotel—without a special pass you'll be fined 90€. You can park on the street, outside the restricted area, where you see blue lines (not blue and white lines), or aim for the official parking lots: Goito, Toschi, Duc, Dus, and Via Abbeveratoia (around 1€–1.70€ per hour).

VISITOR INFORMATION   The **tourist office** at Via Melloni 1A (www. turismo.comune.parma.it; © **0521-218889**) is open Monday 9am to 1pm and 3 to 7pm, Tuesday to Saturday 9am to 7pm, and Sunday 9am to 1pm.

Exploring Parma

It's easy to explore Parma on foot, as most of the sights surround Piazza Duomo and Palazzo della Pilotta and are within easy walking distance of the train station.

Battistero (Baptistery) and Duomo ★★★ CATHEDRAL   The moment you walk into the piazza del Duomo, you're in for a wallop of delightful visual storytelling. To one side rises the elegant **baptistery**, primarily the work of Italy's great Romanesque master Benedetto Antelami and begun in 1196. Octagonal in shape, it has four open loggias and tiers of 16 slender columns—all playing off the number eight, the sign of the Resurrection. Alternating bands of white and pink marble represent purity and the blood of Christ; carvings above the entrance are scripture in stone (look for the engaging sequence depicting King Herod pulling his beard in rage, Salome dancing, and St. John losing his head next to the baptistery itself). Inside, 13th-century frescoes depict the zodiac, the months and seasons, and the life of Christ with an overwhelming explosion of color and complex medieval iconography; there are some remarkably tender scenes, too, including one in which the Virgin Mary shields children huddled below her with her robe.

Two stone lions guard the entrance to the adjacent **Duomo**, one crushing a serpent (the devil), the other a lamb (symbol of sacrifice) under their paws. Inside are two of Parma's greatest treasures. Correggio, the master of light and color, spent 8 years painting the octagonal cupola; after finishing in 1530, he took his payment in a sack full of small change, went home, and died of fever at the age of 40. He presents the "Assumption of the Virgin" as a sea of free-floating angels, swirling limbs, and billowing clouds. A leggy Christ tumbles in a free fall out of the celestial light to meet his ascending mother, whose arms are outstretched toward her son. A contemporary compared the effect to a "hash of frogs' legs" and Charles Dickens commented that this was a scene that "no operative

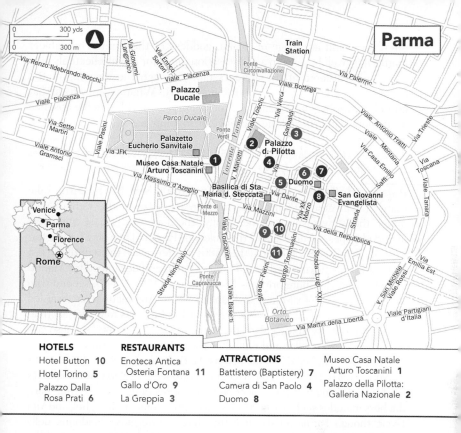

HOTELS

Hotel Button **10**

Hotel Torino **5**

Palazzo Dalla
Rosa Prati **6**

RESTAURANTS

Enoteca Antica
Osteria Fontana **11**

Gallo d'Oro **9**

La Greppia **3**

ATTRACTIONS

Battistero (Baptistery) **7**

Camera di San Paolo **4**

Duomo **8**

Museo Casa Natale
Arturo Toscanini **1**

Palazzo della Pilotta:
Galleria Nazionale **2**

surgeon gone mad could imagine in his wildest delirium." Church
authorities supposedly approached Titian to redo the dome in more conventional fashion, but the artist responded that the work was so masterful, they should have filled the structure with gold and presented it to
Correggio. In the transept to the right is a somber bas-relief of "The
Deposition from the Cross," by Antelami, creator of the baptistery next
door. Christ, his face bathed in sadness, stretches his elongated arms
over two groups, Mary and pious converts to one side, the unenlightened
on the other—including a group of Roman soldiers playing cards.

Piazza del Duomo 1. www.cattedrale.parma.it. ⓒ **0521-235886.** Free admission.
Daily 7:30am–12:30pm and 3–7pm. Battistero: Admission 6€ adults, 7€ with Museo
Diocesano; 4€ students, 5€ with Museo Diocesano. Daily 9am–12:30pm and
3–6:45pm.

Camera di San Paolo ★★ CONVENT   San Paolo was one of many
well-endowed convents where women of means who, for one reason or
another, could not marry spent their lives in relative comfort. When,
around 1519, the cultured abbess Giovanna di Piacenza wanted to fresco
her private dining room, she had the means to hire Correggio, who presented her with vivid mythological scenes, cherubs, astrological

references, and an image of Diana, goddess of the hunt. The subject matter may well have been a conversation piece for the intellectuals who frequently gathered at the abbess's table, though the meaning of the delightful representations remains a mystery. What is known is that church authorities later sealed off the chamber, considering the absence of religious subjects and the presence of so many bare-bottomed *putti* to be profane.

Via Melloni 3 (off Strada Garibaldi). ℰ **0521-533221.** Admission 2€ adults, 1€ ages 18–25, children 17 and under free. Tues–Sun 8:30am–noon and 2–6pm.

Palazzo della Pilotta: Galleria Nazionale ★★ MUSEUM   Like many Italian cities, Parma became a great center of the Renaissance under the stewardship of one family, the Farneses, whose members included popes, cardinals, and the dukes of Parma. They began their fortresslike Palazzo della Pilotta in the 1580s and remained there until the last heiress, Elisabetta, married King Philip of Spain and decamped for Madrid in 1714. The Hapsburg princess Marie-Louise (1791–1847), second wife of Napoleon and great-niece of France's Marie-Antoinette, was awarded the duchy a century later, and she made it her business to gather art treasures from the city in the palace the Farneses had left empty; she also collected works from villas and churches throughout Italy, confiscated when her husband marched down the peninsula. Badly damaged by Allied bombs in World War II, the restored palace now houses the Galleria Nazionale. It's not too surprising that the collection with connections to the Vienna-born duchess includes such northern artists as Hans Holbein, Brueghel, and Van Dyck, though Parma artists steal the show. Correggio's "Madonna della Scodella (With a Bowl)" portrays Joseph as an elderly, caring man and the Madonna as a young woman looking adoringly at her infant son; "St. Jerome with the Madonna and Child" also represents age, youth, and love—a gentle ode to tenderness. Napoleon supposedly wanted to cart these delightful canvases off to the Louvre, but Marie-Louise insisted they remain in Parma. Parmigianino's alluring "Turkish Slave" is clearly the portrait of a well-kept young woman, dressed in gold-threaded finery, and everything about her— turban, cheeks, eyes, breasts—is beautifully rounded. "La Scapigliata" (aka the "Female Head") is one of the most celebrated works by the Italian master of the Renaissance, Leonardo da Vinci; allegedly the artist presented it to a young man from Parma who modeled his hands for the "Last Supper." The palace's other treasure is the **Teatro Farnese,** a wooden theater the Farneses had built, along the lines of Palladio's theater at Vicenza, to impress the Medicis. It's been used only nine times, including an inaugural event in 1639 when the section in front of the stage was flooded for mock naval battles.

Piazzale della Pilotta 15. www.gallerianazionaleparma.it. ℰ **0521-233309.** Admission 6€ adults, 3€ ages 18–25, free for children 17 and under; includes Teatro Farnese. Galleria Nazionale Tues–Sat 8:30am–7pm, Sun 8:30am–2pm; Teatro Farnese Tues–Sun 8:30am–2pm.

Where to Stay

Hotel Button ★★   The Cortesa family has been welcoming guests to this city-center, 17th-century *palazzo* for more than 40 years, providing lots of advice and dispensing excellent coffee from the small lobby bar. The premises have long ago been stripped of any of their historic provenance, and the current reincarnation, with faded floral wallpaper and dark furnishings, seems like a relic from the middle of the 20th century. You might be charmed by the extra-large rooms and old-fashioned ambience (as we are) or find the place to be a bit stuffy and out of date, but you can't quibble with the excellent location in the heart of old Parma just off Piazza Garibaldi.

Borgo delle Salina 7. www.hotelbutton.it. ✆ **0521-208039.** 40 units. 100€ double. Rates include buffet breakfast. **Amenities:** Babysitting; bar; Wi-Fi (free).

Hotel Torino ★   A couple of handsome and homey lounges off the lobby and a sprightly, patio-like breakfast room do justice to one of Parma's best lodging locations, in the old center just down the street from Piazza del Duomo. Guest rooms are a bit more banal, though the muted tones and neutral furnishings are soothing, and the small spaces are streamlined with lots of handy built-ins for stashing gear; some of the singles closely resemble ships' cabins. Parking in a small garage handily tucked beneath the hotel is available for a small fee.

Borgo Angelo Massa. www.hotel-torino.it. ✆ **0521-281046.** 39 units. From 92€ double. Rates include buffet breakfast. In-house garage parking (fee). **Amenities:** Bar; Wi-Fi (free).

Palazzo Dalla Rosa Prati ★★★   Not to sound too clichéd, but you'll be living like royalty here in this magnificent *palazzo* on a corner of the Piazza Del Duomo, sharing quarters with the Marquis Dalla Rosa Prati and his family, who still occupy part of the premises. They have converted one wing of the palace to seven sprawling, handsomely furnished suites, all with kitchenettes, and another section to 10 large apartments. In the suites, huge wooden bedsteads, massive armoires, and other polished antiques augment the largely 18th-cenutry surroundings; the real scene stealers are the pink baptistery next door, practically abutting some of the tall windows, and the stone expanses of the piazza. Apartments are done tastefully but more functionally, have one or two bedrooms, and provide travelers with generous space to spread out. Suites are accessible by elevator, while reaching the apartments requires a climb up a grand but long staircase.

Strada al Duomo 7. www.palazzodallarosaprati.com. ✆ **0521-386429.** 17 units. From 150€ double. **Amenities:** Bar; cafe; Wi-Fi (free).

Where to Eat

Topping the tasting list in Parma is *parmigiano* cheese, made from the milk of cows raised just outside town and aged for at least 12 months. A meal often begins and ends with a small wedge, and it's grated over pastas and fresh vegetables, used as a filling in crepes, and in other ways makes its way into almost every course. Then there's ham. Parma gourmands do not settle for any old *prosciutto.* The cut of choice is *culatello,* from the right hind leg—if you observe a pig sitting down, you'll see this part carries less weight, and hence becomes less sinewy. *Culatello* is the antipasto of choice. You can purchase ham and cheese all over town; an especially attractive and aromatic shop is **Salumeria Garibaldi,** Via Garibaldi 42 (www.specialitadiparma.it; ℂ **0521-235606;** Mon–Sat 8am–8pm). You might also want to visit the cheese production operations at **Consorzio del Parmigiano Reggiano** (www.parmigiano reggiano.com; ℂ **0521-2927000**), at Via Gramsci 26; call or email to make an appointment.

Enoteca Antica Osteria Fontana ★ PARMIGIANA   Cheap nibbles and a huge selection of wine by the glass draw a local crowd to this plain room with a long bar and battered wooden communal tables. Grilled *panini* (sandwiches) are on offer, but the real treats are the morsels of parmigiano with a dribble of balsamic vinegar from nearby Modena, slices of buttery prosciutto, and *crostini*, pieces of bread topped with everything from pesto to chicken livers.
Via Farini 24. ℂ **0521-286037.** Sandwiches and snacks from 4€. Tues–Sat noon–2:30pm and 8–10:30pm.

Gallo d'Oro ★ PARMIGIANA   Parma's formidable food scene becomes decidedly more relaxed at this almost bohemian, bric-a-brac-filled trattoria just off Piazza Garibaldi. A young crowd seems to appreciate the old local traditions: Lambrusco, a slightly sparkling red, is the

Cheese and sausage for sale at Salumeria Garibaldi, Parma.

HITTING THE high NOTES

Duchess Marie-Louise, who beneficently ruled Parma from 1814 to 1847, built the **Teatro Reggio,** Via Garibaldi 16, near Piazza della Pace (www.teatroregio parma.org; ✆ **0521-039399**). Opened in 1829, it is still considered one of the world's finest music theaters, and it hosts an opera season that rivals Milan's. Most appreciated are the works of **Giuseppe Verdi,** composer of "Il Trovatore" and "Aïda" and other perennially popular classics. Verdi was born outside Parma in 1813 in the little village of Roncole and later settled with his mistress, the soprano Giuseppina Strepponi, in the **Villa Verdi di Sant'Agata,** in nearby

Busseto; the villa shows off their personal effects, pianos, portraits, and the bed upon which the maestro died in Milan in 1901 (✆ **0523-830210;** Tues–Sun 9:30–11:45am and 2:30–6:15pm/2–4:30pm Nov–Mar). **Arturo Toscanini,** the greatest orchestral conductor of the first half of the 20th century, was born in Parma in 1867. The rooms of his birthplace, **Museo Casa Natale Arturo Toscanini,** Via Rodolfo Tanzi 13, are filled with his scores, photos, and other personal effects (www.museotoscanini.it; ✆ **0521-285-499;** admission 2€; Wed–Sat 9am–1pm and 2–6pm; Sun 2–6pm).

wine of choice, and *cavallo* (horse) and *coniglio* (rabbit) are served a few different ways. Those who want to sample the local cuisine a bit less adventurously can work their way through *tortelli ripieni* (pasta stuffed with cheese and vegetables), *ravioli alla zucca* (pumpkin), and a long list of other delicious local pastas, all homemade.

Borgo della Salina 3. www.gallodororistorante.it. ✆ **0521-208846.** Main courses 8.50€–11€. Mon–Sat noon–3pm and 7–midnight; Sun noon–3pm.

La Greppia ★★★ PARMIGIANA/ITALIAN   Looking toward the window at one end of the simple dining room, across a sea of crisp linen, you'll see into the kitchen and notice that the staff is entirely female. In the *donnas*' hands you'll be treated to exquisite dishes, some of which you've probably never encountered before—pears poached in red wine with a dense cream sauce is the house-specialty antipasto, the pastas are all homemade and often filled with the freshest local vegetables, and the secondi menu is heavy with slow-cooked goat, *trippa alla parmigiana* (tripe) and other regional favorites. The homemade tortas, delicately filled with marmalade and a miraculous mélange of other ingredients, are irresistible. Service does the cuisine justice.

Via Garibaldi 39. ✆ **0521-233686.** Main courses 18€–28€. Wed–Sun noon–2:30pm and 7:30–10:30pm.

9

VENICE

N o place in the world quite looks like Venice. This vast, floating city of grand *palazzos*, elegant bridges, gondolas, and canals is a magnificent spectacle, truly magical when approached by sea for the first time, when its golden domes and soaring bell towers seem to emerge straight from the ocean. While it can sometimes appear that Venice is little more than an open-air museum, where tourists always outnumber the locals— by a large margin—it is still surprisingly easy to lose the crowds. Indeed, the best way to enjoy Venice is to simply get lost in its labyrinth of narrow, enchanting streets, stumbling upon a quiet *campo* (square), market stall, or cafe far off the beaten track, where even the humblest medieval church might contain masterful work by Tiepolo, Titian, or Tintoretto.

The origins of Venice are as muddy as parts of the lagoon it now occupies, but most histories begin with the arrival of refugees from Attila the Hun's invasion of Italy in 453. By the 11th century, Venice had already emerged as a major trading city, with special dispensation from Byzantine taxes granted in 1082, and by the 13th century a seaborne empire (which included Crete, Corfu and Cyprus) was created by a huge navy and commercial fleet. Despite being embroiled with wars against Genoa and the Turks, the next few centuries were golden years for Venice, when booming trade with the Far East funded much of its grand architecture and art. Although it remained an outwardly rich city, by the 1700s the good times were over, and in 1797 Napoleon dissolved the Venetian Republic. You'll gain a sense of some of this history touring **Piazza San Marco** and **St. Mark's Basilica,** or by visiting the **Accademia,** one of Italy's great art galleries, but only when you wander the back *calli* (streets), will you encounter the true, living, breathing side of Venice, still redolent of those glory days.

ESSENTIALS
Getting There

BY PLANE   You can fly to Venice nonstop from North America via **Delta Airlines** (www.delta.com) from Atlanta (June–Aug only), via **United Airlines** (www.united.com) from Newark, or via **US Airways** (www.

FACING PAGE: **A quiet corner of the Piazza San Marco at evening.**

usairways.com) from Philadelphia; connecting flights through Rome are available via **Alitalia** or a number of other airlines year-round. You can also connect through several major European cities with European carriers. No-frills **easyJet** (www.easyjet.com) flies direct from Berlin, London-Gatwick, Manchester, and Paris much cheaper than the major airlines, though rival budget carrier **Ryanair** (www.ryanair.com) uses the airport in nearby Treviso (a 1-hr. bus ride to Venice).

Flights land at the **Aeroporto di Venezia Marco Polo,** 7km (4¼ miles) north of the city on the mainland (www.veniceairport.it; ℮ **041-2609260**). There are two bus alternatives for getting into town. The **ATVO airport shuttle bus** (www.atvo.it; ℮ **0421-594672**) connects with Piazzale Roma not far from Venice's Santa Lucia train station (and the closest point to Venice's attractions accessible by car or bus). Buses leave for/from the airport about every 30 minutes, costing 6€ (11€ roundtrip); the trip takes about 20 minutes. Buy tickets at the automatic ticket machines in the arrivals baggage hall, or the Public Transport ticket office (daily 8am–midnight). The local **ACTV bus no. 5** (www.actv.it; ℮ **041-2424**) also costs 6€, takes 20 minutes, and runs two to four times an hour depending on the time of day; the best option here is to buy the combined ACTV and "Nave" ticket for 12€, which includes your first *vaporetto* ride at a slight discount (the "vaporetto" is the seagoing streetcar of Venice, which goes to all parts of the city). Buy tickets at machines just outside the terminal. With either bus, you'll have to walk to or from the final stop at Piazzale Roma to the nearby *vaporetto* (water bus) stop for the final connection to your hotel. (See *vaporetto* advice under "By Train," below). It's rare to see porters around who'll help with luggage, so pack light.

A **land taxi** from the airport to Piazzale Roma (where you get the *vaporetto*) will run about 45€ (the meter starts at 15€).

The most evocative and traditional way to arrive in Venice is by sea. For 15€, 14€ if you buy online, the **Cooperative San Marco/Alilaguna** (www.alilaguna.it; ℮ **041-2401701**) operates a large *motoscafo* (shuttle boat) service from the airport (with stops at Murano), arriving after about 1 hour and 15 minutes in Piazza San Marco. The *Linea Blu* (blue line) runs almost every 30 minutes from about 6am to midnight. The *Linea Arancio* (orange line) has the same frequency, costs the same, and takes the same amount of time to arrive at San Marco, but gets there through the Grand Canal, which is much more spectacular and offers the possibility to get off at one of the stops along the way. This might be convenient to your hotel and could save you from having to take another means of transportation. The *Linea Rossa* (red line) runs to the Lido and Murano (8€). If you arrive at Piazza San Marco and your hotel isn't in the area, you'll have to make a connection at the *vaporetto* launches. (If you're booking a hotel in advance, ask for specific advice how to get there.)

A good alternative is **Venice Shuttle** (www.venicelink.com; daily 8am–10pm; minimum 2 people for reservations), a shared water taxi

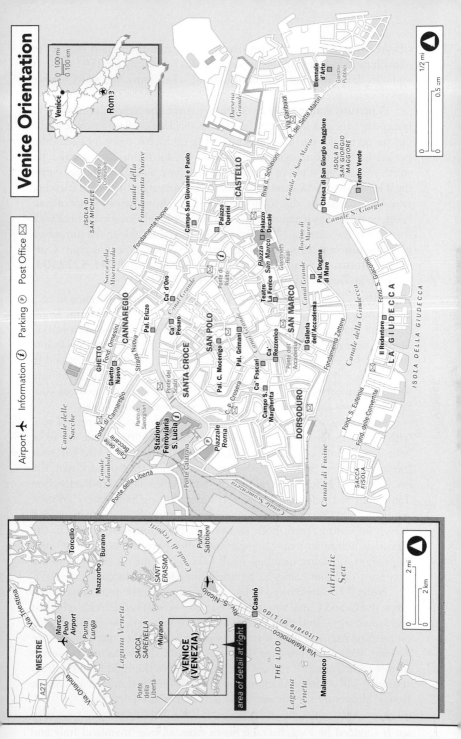

Venice Orientation

Airport ✈   Information ⓘ   Parking ℗   Post Office ✉

(they carry 6–8 people) that will whisk you from the airport directly to many hotels and most of the major locations in the city for 25€ to 30€. It operates daily from 8am to 10pm (add 6€ after 9pm). You must reserve online in advance.

A **private water taxi** (20–30 min. to/from the airport) is convenient but costly—there is a 110€ fee (discounts available on-line) to arrive in the city for up to four passengers with one bag each (20€ more for each extra person up to a maximum of 8, and another 10€ for 10pm–8am arrivals). It's worth considering if you're pressed for time, have an early flight, are carrying a lot of luggage (a Venice no-no), or can split the cost with a friend or two. The taxi may be able to drop you off at the front (or side) door of your hotel, or as close as it can maneuver given your hotel's location (check with the hotel before arriving). Your taxi captain should be able to tell you before boarding just how close he can get you. Try www.venicelink.com, **Corsorzio Motoscafi Venezia** (www.motoscafivenezia.it; ℭ **041-5222303**) or **Venezia Taxi** (www.veneziataxi.it; ℭ **041-723112**).

BY TRAIN   Trains from Rome (3¾ hr.), Milan (2½ hr.), Florence (2 hr.), and all over Europe arrive at the **Stazione Venezia Santa Lucia.** To get there, all must pass through (although not necessarily stop at) a station marked Venezia-Mestre. Don't be confused: Mestre is a charmless industrial city that's the last stop on the mainland. Occasionally trains end in Mestre, in which case you have to catch one of the frequent 10-minute shuttles connecting with Venice; it's inconvenient, so when you book your ticket, confirm that the final destination is Venezia Santa Lucia.

On exiting, you'll find the Grand Canal immediately in front of you, with the docks for a number of *vaporetti* lines (the city's public ferries or "water buses") to your left and right. Head to the booths to your left, near the bridge, to catch either of the two lines plying the Grand Canal: the no. 2 express, which stops only at the San Marcuola, Rialto Bridge, San Tomà, San Samuele, and Accademia before hitting San Marco (26 min. total); and the slower no. 1, which makes 13 stops before arriving at San Marco (a 33-min. trip). Both leave every 10 minutes or so, but in the mornings before 9am and the evenings after 8pm the no. 2 sometimes stops short at Rialto, meaning you'll have to disembark and hop on the next no. 1 or 2 that comes along to continue to San Marco.

Note: The *vaporetti* go in two directions from the train station: left down the Grand Canal toward San Marco—which is the (relatively) fast and scenic way—and right, which also eventually gets you to San Marco (at the San Zaccaria stop) if you are on the 2, but takes more than twice as long because it goes the long way around Dorsoduro (and serves mainly commuters). If you get the no. 1 going to the right from the train station, it will go only one more stop before it hits its terminus at Piazzale Roma. Make sure the *vaporetto* you get on is heading left.

BY BUS   Although rail travel is more convenient and commonplace, Venice is serviced by long-distance buses from all over mainland Italy and some international cities. The final destination is Piazzale Roma, where you'll need to pick up *vaporetto* no. 1 or no. 2 (as described above) to connect you with stops in the heart of Venice and along the Grand Canal.

BY CAR The only wheels you'll see in Venice are those attached to luggage. Venice is a city of canals and narrow alleys. **No cars are allowed,** or more to the point, no cars could drive through the narrow streets and over the footbridges—even the police, fire department, and ambulance services use boats. You can drive across the Ponte della Libertà from Mestre to Venice, but you can go no farther than Piazzale Roma at the Venice end, where many garages eagerly await your euros (and in high season, they're often full). The public **AVM garage** (www.avmspa.it; ✆ **041-2727301**) charges 26€ for a 24-hour period, while private outfit **Garage San Marco** (www.garagesanmarco.it; ✆ **041-5232213**) costs 30€ for 24 hours. From Piazzale Roma, you can catch *Vaporetti* lines 1 and 2, described above, which go down the Grand Canal to the train station and, eventually, Piazza San Marco.

Visitor Information

TOURIST OFFICES The main office is in the Palazzetto Carmagnani, San Marco 2637, 10 minutes from Piazza San Marco (www.turismov enezia.it; ✆ **041-5298711**; *vaporetto:* Giglio). It's open daily from 9am to 7pm. A more convenient office lies in the arcades off Piazza San Marco at Calle de l'Ascension 71/f (daily 8:30am–7pm), and there are smaller offices at the Piazzale Roma garages (daily 8am–2:30pm), Stazione Venezia Santa Lucia (daily 9am–7:30pm), in the arrivals hall at Marco Polo Airport (daily 9am–7:30pm), and at the Venice Pavilion inside the Giardinetti Reali (daily 8:30am–7pm), near Piazza San Marco.

The tourist office's map (2.50€) helps you find *vaporetto* lines and stops. More useful is the info-packed monthly (every 2 weeks in summer), *Un Ospite di Venezia* (www.unospitedivenezia.it); most hotels have free copies. Also very useful is *VeneziaNews* (www.venezianews.it), published monthly and sold at newsstands all over the city.

City Layout

Even armed with the best map or a hefty smartphone data plan, expect to get a little bit lost in Venice, at least some of the time (GPS directions are notoriously unreliable here). Just view it as an opportunity to stumble across Venice's most intriguing corners and vignettes. Keep in mind as you wander seemingly hopelessly among the *calli* (streets) and *campi* (squares) that the city wasn't built to make sense to those on foot, but rather to those plying its canals.

Venice lies 4km (2½ miles) from terra firma, connected to the mainland burg of Mestre by the Ponte della Libertà, which leads to Piazzale Roma. Snaking through the city like an inverted *S* is the **Grand Canal,** the wide main artery of aquatic Venice. Central Venice refers to the built-up block of islands in the lagoon's center, the six main *sestieri* (districts) that make up the bulk of the tourist city. Greater Venice includes all the inhabited islands of the lagoon—central Venice plus Murano, Burano, Torcello, and the Lido.

The Neighborhoods in Brief

SAN MARCO   The central *sestiere* is anchored by the magnificent Piazza San Marco and St. Mark's Basilica to the south and the Rialto Bridge to the north; it's the most visited (and, as a result, the most expensive) of the *sestieri*. This is the commercial, religious, and political heart of the city and has been for more than a millennium. Although you'll find glimpses and snippets of the real Venice here, ever-rising rents have nudged resident Venetians to look for housing in the outer neighborhoods: You'll be hard-pressed to find a grocery store or dry cleaner, for example. This area is laced with first-class hotels—but we'll give you some suggestions for staying in the heart of Venice without going broke.

CASTELLO   This quarter, whose tony waterside esplanade Riva degli Schiavoni follows the Bacino di San Marco (St. Mark's Basin), begins just east of Piazza San Marco, skirting Venice's most congested area to the north and east. Riva degli Schiavoni can sometimes get so busy as to seem like Times Square on New Year's Eve, but if you head farther east in the direction of the Arsenale or inland away from the *bacino,* the crowds thin out, despite the presence of such major sights as Campo SS. Giovanni e Paolo and the Scuola di San Giorgio.

DORSODURO   You'll find the residential area of Dorsoduro on the opposite side of the Accademia Bridge from San Marco. Known for the Accademia and Peggy Guggenheim museums, it is the largest of the *sestieri* and was known as an artists' haven until escalations of rents forced much of the community to relocate elsewhere. Good neighborhood restaurants, a charming gondola boatyard, the lively Campo Santa Margherita, and the sunny quay called le Zattere (a favorite promenade and gelato stop) all add to its character and color.

SAN POLO   This mixed-bag *sestiere* of residential corners and tourist sights stretches northwest of the Rialto Bridge to the church of Santa

9

Essentials

VENICE

Maria dei Frari, and the Scuola di San Rocco. The hub of activity at the foot of the bridge is due in large part to the Rialto Market—some of the city's best restaurants have flourished in the area for generations, alongside some of its worst tourist traps. The spacious Campo San Polo is the main piazza of Venice's smallest *sestiere.*

SANTA CROCE   North and northwest of the San Polo district and across the Grand Canal from the train station, Santa Croce stretches all the way to Piazzale Roma. Its eastern section is generally one of the least-visited areas of Venice—making it all the more desirable for curious visitors. Less lively than San Polo but just as authentic, it feels light-years away from San Marco. The quiet and lovely Campo San Giacomo dell'Orio is its heart.

CANNAREGIO   Sharing the same side of the Grand Canal with San Marco and Castello, Cannaregio stretches north and east from the train station to include the old Jewish Ghetto. Its outer reaches are quiet, unspoiled, and residential; one-quarter of Venice's ever-shrinking population of 60,000 lives here. Most of the city's one-star hotels are clustered about the train station—not a dangerous neighborhood but not one known for its charm, either. The tourist store–lined Lista di Spagna, which starts just to the left as you leave the train station, morphs into Strada Nova and provides an uninterrupted thoroughfare to the Rialto bridge.

LA GIUDECCA   Located across the Giudecca Canal from the Piazza San Marco and Dorsoduro, La Giudecca is a tranquil working-class residential island where you'll find a youth hostel and a handful of hotels (including the deluxe Cipriani, one of Europe's finest).

Venice's Castello neighborhood.

LIDO DI VENEZIA This slim, 11km-long (6¾-mile) island, the only spot in the Venetian lagoon where cars circulate, is the city's beach and separates the lagoon from the open sea. The landmark hotels here serve as a base for the annual Venice Film Festival.

Getting Around

Aside from traveling by boat, the only way to explore Venice is by walking—and by getting lost repeatedly. You'll navigate many twisting streets whose names change constantly and don't appear on any map, and streets that may very well simply end in a blind alley or spill abruptly into a canal. You'll also cross dozens of footbridges. Treat getting bewilderingly lost in Venice as part of the fun, and budget more time than you'd think necessary to get wherever you're going.

STREET MAPS & SIGNAGE The map sold by the tourist office and free maps provided by most hotels don't always show—much less name or index—all the *calli* (streets) and pathways of Venice. For that, pick up a more detailed map (ask for a *pianta della città* at news kiosks—especially those at the train station and around San Marco or most bookstores). The best (and most expensive) is the highly detailed Touring Club Italiano map, available in a variety of forms (folding or spiral-bound) and scales. Almost as good, and easier to carry, is the simple and cheap 1:6,500 folding map put out by Storti Edizioni (its cover is blue).

Still, Venice's confusing layout confounds even the best maps and navigators. You're often better off just stopping every couple of blocks and asking a local to point you in the right direction (always know the name of the *campo*/square or major sight closest to the address you're looking for, and ask for that).

As you wander, look for the ubiquitous yellow signs (well, *usually* yellow) whose destinations and arrows direct you toward five major landmarks: **Ferrovia** (the train station), **Piazzale Roma** (the parking garage), **Rialto** (one of the four bridges over the Grand Canal), **San Marco** (the city's main square), and the **Accademia** (the southernmost Grand Canal bridge).

BY BOAT The various *sestieri* are linked by a comprehensive *vaporetto* (water bus/ferry) system of about a dozen lines operated by the **Azienda del Consorzio Trasporti Veneziano** (**ACTV;** www.actv.it; © **041-5287886**). Transit maps are available at the tourist office and most ACTV stations. It's easier to get around on foot, as the *vaporetti* principally serve the Grand Canal, the outskirts, and the outer islands. The crisscross network of small canals is the province of delivery vessels, gondolas, and private boats.

A ticket valid for 1 hour of travel on a *vaporetto* is a steep 7€, while the 24-hour ticket is 20€. Most lines run every 10 to 15 minutes from 7am to midnight, and then hourly until morning. Most *vaporetto* docks (the only place you can buy tickets) have timetables posted. Note that

CRUISING THE canals

A leisurely cruise along the **Grand Canal** ★★★ (p. 377) from Piazza San Marco to the train station (Ferrovia)—or the reverse—is one of Venice's must-dos. It's the world's most unusual Main Street, a watery boulevard whose *palazzi* have been converted into condos. Lower water-lapped floors are now deserted, but the higher floors are still coveted by the city's titled families, who have inhabited these glorious residences for centuries; others have become the summertime dream homes of privileged expats, drawn here as irresistibly as the romantic Venetians-by-adoption who preceded them—Richard Wagner, Robert Browning, Lord Byron, and (more recently) Woody Allen.

As much a symbol of Venice as the winged lion, the **gondola** ★★★ is one of Europe's great traditions, incredibly and inexplicably expensive but truly as romantic as it looks (detractors who write it off as too touristy have most likely never tried it). The official, fixed rate is 80€ for a 40-minute gondola tour for up to six passengers. The rate bumps up to 100€ from 7pm to 8am, and it's 40€ for every additional 20 minutes (50€ at night). That's not a typo: 150€ for a 1-hour evening cruise. **Note:** Although the price is fixed by the city, a good negotiator at the right time of day (when business is slow) can sometimes grab a small discount, for a shorter ride. And at these ridiculously inflated prices, there is no need to tip the gondolier. You might also find discounts online.

Aim for late afternoon before sun down, when the light does its magic on the canal reflections (and bring a bottle of prosecco and glasses). If the gondola price is too high, ask visitors at your hotel or others lingering about at the gondola stations if they'd like to share it. Though the price is "fixed," before setting off establish with the gondolier the cost, time, and route (back canals are preferable to the trafficked and often choppy Grand Canal). They're regulated by the **Ente Gondola** (www.gondolavenezia.it; ✆ **041-5285075**), so call if you have questions or complaints.

And what of the serenading gondolier immortalized in film? Frankly, you're better off without. But if warbling is de rigueur for you, here's the scoop. An ensemble of accordion player and tenor is so expensive that it's shared among several gondolas traveling together. A number of travel agents around town book the evening serenades for around 35€ per person.

There are 12 gondola stations around Venice, including Piazzale Roma, the train station, the Rialto Bridge, and Piazza San Marco. There are also a number of smaller stations, with *gondolieri* in striped shirts standing alongside their sleek 11m (36-ft.) black wonders looking for passengers. They all speak enough English to communicate the necessary details. Remember, if you just want a quick taste of being in a gondola, you can take a cheap *traghetto* across the Grand Canal.

not all docks sell tickets. If you haven't bought a pass or extra tickets beforehand, you'll have to settle up with the conductor onboard (you'll have to find him—he won't come looking for you) or risk a stiff fine of at least 52€, no excuses accepted. Also available are 48-hour tickets (30€) and 72-hour tickets (40€). If you're planning to stay in Venice for a week and intend to use the *vaporetto* service a lot, it might make sense to pick up a Venezia Unica city pass (see "Venice Discounts," on p. 381), with

Come hell or high water

During the tidal *acqua alta* (high water) floods, Venice's lagoon rises until it engulfs the city, leaving up to 1.5 to 1.8m (5–6 ft.) of water in the lowest-lying streets. Piazza San Marco, as the lowest point in the city, goes first. As many as 50 floods a year have been recorded since they first started in the late 1700s.

Significant *acqua alta* can begin as early as late September or October, but usually takes place November to March. The waters usually recede after just a few hours. Walkways are set up around town, but wet feet are a given and locals tend to wear high-topped wading boots.

A complex system of hydraulic dams is being constructed out in the lagoon to cut off the highest of these high tides (a controversial project due to its environmental impact), but while the project is well underway, it won't be operational for years. **Tip:** If you are curious to see *acqua alta* (and it is indeed a wonderful spectacle), but aren't in Venice at the right time, you can still get lucky as very minor occurrences can happen all year round.

which you can buy 1-hour *vaporetto* tickets for 1.30€. All tickets must be validated in the yellow machines before getting on the *vaporetto*.

Just four bridges span the Grand Canal, and to fill in the gaps, *traghetti* skiffs (oversize gondolas rowed by two standing *gondolieri*) cross the Grand Canal at several intermediate points (during daylight hours only). Stations are located at the end of streets named Calle del Traghetto on your map (though not all of them have active ferries today; ask a local before walking to the canal), and are indicated by a yellow sign with the black gondola symbol. The fare is .70€ for locals and 2€ for visitors, which you hand to the gondolier when boarding. Most Venetians cross standing up. For the experience, try the Santa Sofia crossing that connects the Ca' d'Oro and the Pescheria fish market, opposite each other on the Grand Canal just north of the Rialto Bridge—the gondoliers expertly dodge water traffic at this point of the canal, where it's the busiest and most heart-stopping.

BY WATER TAXI *Taxi acquei* (water taxis) charge high prices and aren't for visitors watching their euros. The meter starts at a hefty 15€ and clicks at 2€ per minute. Each trip includes allowance for up to four to five pieces of luggage—beyond that there's a surcharge of 3€ to 5€ per piece (rates differ slightly according to company and how you reserve your trip). Plus there's a 10€ supplement for service from 10pm to 7am, and a 5€ charge for taxis on-call. Those rates cover up to four people; if any more squeeze in, it's another 5€ to 10€ per extra passenger (maximum 10 people). Taking a water taxi from the train station to Piazza San Marco or any of the hotels in the area will put you back about 65€ (the Lido is 85€), while there is a fixed 100€ fee (for up to four people) to go or come from the airport. Taxis to Burano or Torcello will be at least 120€. Note that only taxi boats with a yellow strip are the official operators sanctioned by the city. You can book trips with Consorzio Moscafi Venezia online at **www.motoscafivenezia.it** or call ℂ **041-5222303.**

Six water-taxi stations serve key points in the city: the Ferrovia, Piazzale Roma, the Rialto Bridge, Piazza San Marco, the Lido, and Marco Polo Airport.

BY GONDOLA   If you come all the way to Venice and don't indulge in a gondola ride, you might still be kicking yourself long after you have returned home. Yes, it's touristy, and, yes, it's expensive (see "Cruising the Canals" box on p. 369), but only those with a heart of stone will be unmoved by the quintessential Venetian experience. Do not initiate your trip, however, until you have agreed upon a price and synchronized watches. Oh, and don't ask them to sing.

[FastFACTS] VENICE

Consulates   See chapter 14.

Doctors & Hospitals   The **Ospedale Civile Santi Giovanni e Paolo** (© **041-5294111**), on Campo Santi Giovanni e Paolo, has English-speaking staff and provides emergency service (go to the emergency room, *pronto soccorso*), 24 hours a day (*vaporetto*: San Tomà).

Emergencies   The best number to call in Italy (and the rest of Europe) with a **general emergency** is © **112;** this connects you to the military trained (and English-speaking) **Carabinieri** who will transfer your call as needed. For the **police,** dial © **113;** for a medical emergency and to call an **ambulance,** the number is © **118;** for the **fire department,** call © **115.** All are free calls.

Internet Access   Venice has traditionally lagged behind the rest of Italy when it comes to Internet speeds and access, though many hotels, hostels, and bars now offer free Wi-Fi, and in 2009 Venice was one of the first cities in the nation to offer citywide Wi-Fi through a network of 200 hotspots. Visitors can buy packages online via www.veneziaunica.it: 5€ for 24 hr., 15€ for 3 days or 20€ for 7 days. Access codes are sent to your e-mail address; once in Venice look for the VeniceConnected network. Alternatively, there are plenty of "Internet points" dotted around the city, particularly in the busy areas around the Rialto, Piazza San Marco, and the railway station. Most charge 6€ to 8€ per hour. Try **ABColor-Internet Point** (© **041-5244380**), Lista di Spagna 220 in Cannaregio (a 3-min. walk from the train station), open daily 10am to 8pm, or **Venetian Navigator** (© **041-2771056**), Calle Casselleria 5300 in Castello (a 3-min. walk from Piazza San Marco), open daily 10am to 10pm.

Mail   The most convenient post offices are: **Venezia Centro** at Calle de la Acque, San Marco (© **041-2404149;** open Mon–Fri 8:25am–7:10pm and Sat 8:25am–12:35pm); **Venezia 4** at Calle de l'Ascension 1241, off the west side of Piazza San Marco (© **041-2446711,** open Tues–Fri 8:25am–1:35pm, Sat 8:25am–12:35pm); and **Venezia 3** at Campo San Polo 2012 (© **041-5200315;** same hours as Venezia 4).

Pharmacies   Venice's pharmacies take turns staying open all night. To find out which one is on call in your area, ask at your hotel or check the rotational duty signs posted outside all pharmacies.

Safety   Be aware of petty crime like pickpocketing on the crowded *vaporetti,* particularly the tourist routes, where passengers are more intent on the passing scenery than on watching their bags. Venice's deserted back streets are virtually crime-free, though occasional tales of theft have circulated. Generally speaking, Venice is one of Italy's safest cities.

371

EXPLORING VENICE

Venice is notorious for changing and extending the opening hours of its museums and, to a lesser degree, its churches. Before you begin your exploration of Venice's sights, ask at the tourist office for the season's list of museum and church hours. During the peak months, you can enjoy extended museum hours—some places stay open until 7 or even 10pm—but unfortunately these hours are not released until some time around Easter each year. Even then, little is done to publicize the information, so you'll have to do your own research.

San Marco

Basilica di San Marco (St. Mark's) ★★★ CATHEDRAL   One of the grandest, and certainly the most exotic of all cathedrals in Europe, **Basilica di San Marco** is an imperious treasure-heap of Venetian art and all sorts of lavish booty garnered from the eastern Mediterranean. Legend has it that **St. Mark,** on his way to Rome, was told by an angel his body would rest near the lagoon that would one today become Venice. Hundreds of years later, the city fathers were looking for a patron saint of high stature, more in keeping with their lofty aspirations, and in 828 the prophecy was duly fulfilled when Venetian merchants stole the body of St. Mark from Alexandria in Egypt (the story goes that the body was packed in pickled pork to avoid the attention of the Muslim guards).

Modeled on Constantinople's Church of the Twelve Apostles, the shrine of St. Mark was consecrated in 832, but in 976 the church burned

Byzantine mosaics adorn the Basilica di San Marco.

Know Before You Go

down. The present incarnation was completed in 1094, then extended and embellished over subsequent years, serving as the personal church of the doge. Even today San Marco looks more like a Byzantine cathedral than a Roman Catholic church, with a cavernous interior exquisitely gilded with Byzantine mosaics added over some 7 centuries, covering every inch of both ceiling and pavement. For a closer look at many of the most remarkable ceiling mosaics and a better view of the Oriental carpet–like patterns of the pavement mosaics, pay the admission to go upstairs to the **Museo di San Marco** (the entrance to this is in the atrium at the principal entrance); this was originally the women's gallery, or *matroneum,* and also includes the outside Loggia dei Cavalli. Here you can mingle with the celebrated *Triumphal Quadriga* of four gilded bronze horses dating from the 2nd or 3rd century A.D.; originally set on the Loggia, the restored originals were moved inside in the 1980s for preservation. (The word *quadriga* actually refers to a car or chariot pulled by four horses, though in this case there are only the horses.) The horses were taken to Venice from Constantinople in 1204 along with lots of other loot from the Fourth Crusade. A visit to the outdoor **Loggia dei Cavalli** (where replicas of the horses now stand) is an unexpected highlight, providing a panoramic view of the piazza below.

The basilica's greatest treasure is the magnificent altarpiece known as the **Pala d'Oro (Golden Altarpiece),** a Gothic masterpiece encrusted with over 2,000 precious gems and 83 enameled panels. It was created in 10th-century Constantinople and embellished by Venetian and Byzantine artisans between the 12th and 14th centuries. It is located behind the main altar, whose green marble canopy on alabaster columns covers the tomb of St. Mark (skeptics contend that his remains burned in the fire of 976). Also worth a visit is the **Tesoro (Treasury),** with a collection of the crusaders' plunder from Constantinople and other icons and relics amassed by the church over the years. Much of the loot has been incorporated into the interior and exterior of the basilica in the form of marble, columns, capitals, and statuary. Second to the Pala d'Oro in importance is the 10th-century **"Madonna di Nicopeia,"** a

Venice Attractions

CANNAREGIO

Pal. Giovanelli
S. Felice
Pal. Fontana
Ca' d'Oro **10**
Pal. Brandolin
Pescaria
Ca' d'Oro
S. Sofia
Strada Nuova
Pal. Sagredo
Pal. Mangilli
Ca' da Mosto
Pal. Falier
Fábbriche Nuove
S. Giovanni Crisostomo
Teatro Málibran
Ss. Apóstoli
S. Canciano
Rio di Santi
Rio di S.G. Crisostomo
Pal. Widman
Pal. Grifalconi
C. larga G. Gallina
Pal. Soranzo-Van Axel
Pal. Pisani
S. Maria d. Miracoli
Pal. Soranzo-Van Axel
Ospedale Civile
H
S. Maria d. Pianto
23
Ss. Giovanni e Paolo (S. Zanipolo)
Pal. Morosini
Pal. Muazzo
Fónt. d. Mendicanti

Pal. Aponal
S. Silvestro
Palazzo Dieci Savi
Fóndaco d. Tedeschi
Pal. Cavazza-Foscari
11
Rialto
Ponte di Rialto
Rio di S. Marina
Campo S. Marina
Palazzo Ruzzini
Pal. Donà
Pal. Cavignis
Pal. Donà
Palazzo Cappello
S. Lorenzo
22 →

Riva del Vin
Riva del Carbon
S. Silvestro
S. Bartolomeo
Palazzo Dolfin-Manin
Pal. Bembo
Ca' Farsetti
Palazzo Grimani
S. Luca
C. Stagneri
M. S. Salvador
S. Salvador
Pal. Tasca Papatava
C. Guerra
Salizzada S. Lio
C. Bande
S. Lio
S. Maria della Fava
Campo S. Maria Formosa
S. Maria Formosa
Pal. Querini Stampalia
Ruga Giuffa
Questura
CASTELLO
Pal. Priuli
Pal. Zorzi
S. Giorgio dei Greci

Cinema Rossini
Campo Manin
Palazzo Contarini d. Bovolo
Mándola
Ateneo Véneto
Pisc. di Frezzería
Teatro La Fenice
S. Fantin
C. Larga XXII Marzo
Calle C. Goldoni
C. del Teatro
Fábbri
C. Flubera
S. Zulián
Merc. Orologio
C. Spadaria
C. Fiubera
C. Canonica
C. Speechieri
S. Gallo
Palazzo Soranzo
Palazzo Novo
S. Giovanni Novo
Palazzo Trevisan-Cappello
S. Zaccaria
Convento
S. Giorgio dei Greci
La Pietà

Palazzi Contarini
Pal. Gritti
Palazzo Tiépolo
Palazzo Treves d. Bonfili
Museo Correr **14**
Piazza San Marco
15
16
17
18 **Basilica di San Marco**
19 **Palazzo Ducale (Doge's Palace)**
20 Pal. d. Prigioni
Ponte d. Socpiri (Bridge of Sighs)
Piazzetta
Molo
Riva
d. Schiavoni
S. Zaccaria
21 →

S. Moisè
S. S. Moisè
C. Vallaresso
Giardini ex Reali
Capo di Porto
S. Marco
Ex Ospizio
Pal. Genovese
12
S. Maria d. Salute
Seminario Patriarcale
Dogana da Mar
13
Punta d. Dogana

Bacino di San Marco

S. Giorgio Maggiore
Isola di S. Giorgio Maggiore

0 1/8 mi
0 200 m

Vaporettos ply Venice's main canals.

bejeweled icon also purloined from Constantinople and exhibited in its own chapel to the left of the main altar.

In July and August (with much less certainty the rest of the year), church-affiliated volunteers lead free tours Monday to Saturday, four or five times daily, beginning at 10:30am (note that not all tours are in English). Groups gather in the atrium, where you'll find posters with tour schedules.

Piazza San Marco. www.basilicasanmarco.it. © **041-2708311.** Basilica free admission; Museo di San Marco (includes Loggia dei Cavalli) 5€, Pala d'Oro 2€, Tesoro (Treasury) 3€. Basilica, Tesoro, and Pala d'Oro Mon–Sat 9:45am–5pm (Tesoro and Pala d'Oro close at 4pm Nov–Easter), Sun 2–5pm (Nov–Easter all close Sun at 4pm). Museo di San Marco daily 9:45am–4:45pm. *Vaporetto:* San Marco.

Campanile di San Marco (Bell Tower) ★★★ ICON An elevator will whisk you to the top of this 97m (318-ft.) brown brick bell tower where you get an awe-inspiring view of St. Mark's cupolas. With a gilded angel atop its spire, it is the highest structure in the city, offering a pigeon's-eye panorama that includes the lagoon, its neighboring islands, and the red rooftops and church domes and bell towers of Venice—and, oddly, not a single canal. Originally built in the 9th century, the bell tower was then reconstructed in the 12th, 14th, and 16th centuries, when the pretty marble loggia at its base was added by Jacopo Sansovino. It collapsed unexpectedly in 1902, miraculously hurting no one except a cat. It was rebuilt exactly as before, using most of the same materials, even rescuing one of the five historical bells that it still uses today (each bell was rung for a different purpose, such as war, the death of a doge, religious holidays, and so on).

Piazza San Marco. www.basilicasanmarco.it. © **041-2708311.** Admission 8€. Easter to June and Oct daily 9am–7pm; July–Sept daily 9am–9pm; Nov–Easter daily 9:30am–3:45pm. *Vaporetto:* San Marco.

Canal Grande (Grand Canal) ★★★ NATURAL ATTRACTION   A leisurely cruise along the "Canalazzo" from Piazza San Marco to the Ferrovia (train station), or the reverse, is one of Venice's (and life's) must-do experiences. (See box p. 369.) Hop on the **no. 1** *vaporetto* in the late afternoon (try to get one of the coveted outdoor seats in the prow), when the weather-worn colors of the former homes of Venice's merchant elite are warmed by the soft light and reflected in the canal's rippling waters, and the busy traffic of delivery boats, *vaporetti,* and gondolas that fills the city's main thoroughfare has eased somewhat.

Best stations to start/end a tour of the Grand Canal are Ferrovia (train station) or Piazzale Roma on the northwest side of the canal and Piazza San Marco in the southeast. Tickets 7€.

Palazzo Ducale and Ponte dei Sospiri (Doge's Palace and Bridge of Sighs) ★★★ PALACE   The pink-and-white marble Gothic-Renaissance **Palazzo Ducale,** residence of the doges who ruled Venice for more than 1,000 years, stands between the Basilica di San Marco and the sea. A symbol of prosperity and power, it was destroyed by a succession of fires, with the current building started in 1340, extended in the 1420s, and largely redesigned again after a fire in 1483. Forever being expanded, it slowly grew to be one of Italy's greatest civic structures. If you want to understand something of this magnificent place, the fascinating history of the 1,000-year-old maritime republic, and the intrigue of the government that ruled it, take the **Secret Itineraries tour** ★★★ (see "Secrets of the Palazzo Ducale," p. 379). Failing that, at least download the free iPhone/Android app (see the website) or shell out for the infrared audioguide tour (available at entrance, 6€) to help make sense of it all. Unless you can tag along with an English-speaking

Plaques along the Grand Canal mark the homes of famous residents.

tour group, you may otherwise miss out on the importance of much of what you're seeing.

The 15th-century **Porta della Carta (Paper Gate)** opens onto a splendid inner courtyard with a double row of Renaissance arches (today visitors enter through a doorway on the lagoon side of the palace). The self-guided route through the palace begins on the left side of the main courtyard, where the **Museo dell'Opera** contains assorted bits of masonry preserved from the Palazzo's exterior. Beyond here, the first major room you'll come to is the spacious **Sala delle Quattro Porte (Hall of the Four Doors),** with a worn ceiling by Tintoretto. The **Sala dell'Anticollegio,** the next main room, is where foreign ambassadors waited to be received by the doge and his council. It is covered in four works by Tintoretto, and Veronese's **"Rape of Europa"** ★★, considered one of the *palazzo's* finest. It steals some of the thunder of Tintoretto's "Mercury & the Three Graces" and **"Bacchus and Ariadne"** ★★—the latter considered one of his best by some critics. The highlight of the adjacent **Sala del Collegio** (the Council Chamber itself) is the spectacular cycle of **ceiling paintings** ★★ by Veronese, completed between 1575 and 1578 and one of his masterpieces. Next door lies the most impressive of the interior rooms, the richly adorned **Sala del Senato (Senate Chamber),** with Tintoretto's ceiling painting "The Triumph of Venice." Here laws were passed by the Senate, a select group of 200 chosen from the Great Council. After passing again through the Sala delle Quattro Porte, you'll come to the Veronese-decorated **Stanza del Consiglio dei Dieci (Room of the Council of Ten,** the Republic's dreaded security police), of particular historical interest. It was in this room that justice was dispensed and decapitations ordered. Formed in the 14th century to deal with emergency situations, the Ten were considered more powerful than the Senate and feared by all. Just outside the adjacent chamber, in the **Sala della Bussola (the Compass Chamber),** notice the **Bocca dei Leoni (Lion's Mouth),** a slit in the wall into which secret denunciations and accusations of enemies of the state were placed for quick action by the much-feared Council.

The Bridge of Sighs.

secrets OF THE PALAZZO DUCALE

The **Itinerari Segreti (Secret Itineraries)** ★★★ guided tours of the Palazzo Ducale are a must-see for any visit to Venice of more than one day. The tours offer an unparalleled look into the world of Venetian politics over the centuries and are the only way to access the otherwise restricted quarters and hidden passageways of this enormous palace, such as the doges' private chambers and the torture chambers where prisoners were interrogated. It is highly advisable to reserve in advance via the website (www.palazzoducale.visitmuve.it), by phone (toll-free within Italy ✆ **848-082-000**, or from abroad 041-4273-0892), or in person at the ticket desk. Tours often sell out at least a few days ahead, especially from spring through fall. Tours in English are daily at 9:55am and 11:35am, and cost 20€ for adults, 14€ for children ages 6 to 14 and students ages 15 to 25. There are also tours in Italian at 9:30am and 11:10am, and French at 10:20am and noon. The tour lasts about 75 minutes.

The main sight on the next level down—indeed, in the entire palace—is the **Sala del Maggior Consiglio (Great Council Hall).** This enormous space is animated by Tintoretto's huge **"Paradiso"** ★ at the far end of the hall above the doge's seat. Measuring 7×23m (23×75 ft.), it is said to be the world's largest oil painting; together with Veronese's gorgeous **"Il Trionfo di Venezia" ("The Triumph of Venice")** ★★ in the oval panel on the ceiling, it affirms the power emanating from the council sessions held here. Tintoretto also did the portraits of the 76 doges encircling the top of this chamber; note that the picture of the Doge Marin Falier, who was convicted of treason and beheaded in 1355, has been blacked out—Venice has never forgiven him. Tours culminate at the enclosed **Ponte dei Sospiri (Bridge of Sighs),** built in 1600, which connects the Ducal Palace with the grim **Palazzo delle Prigioni (Prison).** The bridge took its current name only in the 19th century, when visiting northern European poets romantically imagined the prisoners' final breath of resignation upon viewing the outside world one last time before being locked in their fetid cells. Some attribute the name to Casanova, who, following his arrest in 1755 (he was accused of being a Freemason and spreading antireligious propaganda), crossed this very bridge. One of the rare few to escape, he did so 15 months after his imprisonment began; it was 20 years before he dared return to Venice. Some of the stone cells still have the original graffiti of past prisoners, many of them locked up interminably for petty crimes.

San Marco, Piazza San Marco. www.palazzoducale.visitmuve.it. ✆ **041-2715911.** Admission only with San Marco Museum Pass (17€; see "Venice Discounts," p. 381). For an Itinerari Segreti (Secret Itineraries) guided tour in English, see "Secrets of the Palazzo Ducale," p. 379. Daily 8:30am–7pm (Nov–Mar until 5:30pm). *Vaporetto:* San Marco.

Rialto Bridge ★★ ICON   This graceful arch over the Grand Canal, linking the San Marco and San Polo districts, is lined with overpriced boutiques and teems with tourists. Until the 19th century, it was the only bridge across the Grand Canal, originally built as a pontoon bridge at the canal's narrowest point. Wooden versions of the bridge followed; the 1444 incarnation was the first to include shops, interrupted by a draw-bridge in the center. In 1592, this graceful stone span was finished to the designs of Antonio da Ponte (whose last name fittingly enough means bridge), who beat out Sansovino, Palladio, and Michelangelo with his plans that called for a single, vast, 28m-wide (92-ft.) arch in the center to allow trading ships to pass.

Ponte del Rialto. *Vaporetto:* Rialto.

Torre dell'Orologio (Clock Tower) MONUMENT   As you enter the magnificent **Piazza San Marco,** it is one of the first things you see, standing on the north side, the centerpiece of the stately white **Procu-ratie Vecchie** (the ancient administration buildings for the Republic). The Renaissance **Torre dell'Orologio** was built between 1496 and 1506, and the clock mechanism still keeps perfect time (although most of the original workings have been replaced over the years). On the top, two bronze figures, known as "Moors" because of the dark color of the bronze, pivot to strike the hour. Visits are by guided tour only (included in the price of admission).

Piazza San Marco. www.torreorologio.visitmuve.it. ℂ **848-082000** or 041-42730892. Admission 12€, 7€ for children ages 6–14 and students ages 15–25; ticket also good for admission to the Museo Correr, the Museo Archeologico Nazionale, and the Biblioteca Nazionale Marciana (but not Palazzo Ducale). Tours in English Mon–Wed 10am and 11am, Thurs–Sun 2pm and 3pm (must be reserved in advance); tours start at the Museo Correr ticket office. There are also tours in Italian and French. *Vapo-retto:* San Marco.

Castello

Basilica SS. Giovanni e Paolo ★ CHURCH   This massive Gothic church was built by the Dominican order from the 13th to the 15th cen-tury and, together with the Frari Church in San Polo, is second in size only to the Basilica di San Marco. An unofficial Pantheon where 25 doges are buried (a number of tombs are part of the unfinished facade), the church, commonly known as Zanipolo in Venetian dialect, is also home to many artistic treasures.

The brilliantly colored "**Polyptych of St. Vincent Ferrer**" (ca. 1465), attributed to a young Giovanni Bellini, is in the right aisle. You'll also see the foot of St. Catherine of Siena encased in glass near here. Visit the **Cappella del Rosario** ★ through a glass door off the left tran-sept to see the three restored ceiling canvases and one oil painting by Paolo Veronese, particularly "The Assumption of the Madonna."

VENICE discounts

Venice offers a somewhat bewildering range of passes and discount cards. We recommend buying an **ACTV travel card** (www.actv.it) and combining that with one of the first two museum passes listed below: The more complex Venice Card scheme is convenient once you've worked out what you want online, but doesn't save you much money and its main components are only valid for 7 days. However, the Venice Card website (www.veneziaunica.it) is now also a one-stop shop for all the passes listed below.

The **Museum Pass** (www.vivaticket.it) grants admission to all the city-run museums over a 6-month period. That includes the museums of St. Mark's Square—Palazzo Ducale, **Museo Correr,** Museo Archeologico Nazionale, and the Biblioteca Nazionale Marciana—as well as the Museo di Palazzo Mocenigo (Costume Museum), the Ca' Rezzonico, the Ca' Pesaro, the Museo del Vetro (Glass Museum) on Murano, and the Museo del Merletto (Lace Museum) on Burano. The Museum Pass is available online or at any of the participating museums and costs 24€ for adults, and 18€ for students under 30 and kids aged 6–14. There is also a **San Marco Museum Pass** (valid for 3 months) that lets you into the four museums of Piazza San Marco for 17€, and 10€ for students under 30 and kids aged 6–14. The **Chorus Pass** (www.chorusvenezia.org) covers every major church in Venice, 16 in all, for 12€ (8€ for students under 30), for up to 1 year. For 24€, the **Chorus Pass Family** gives you the same perks for two adults and their children up to 18 years old.

The **Venice Card** or Venezia Unica City Pass (www.veneziaunica.it) combines the above passes, transport, discounts and even Internet access on one card via a "made-to-order" online system, where you choose the services you want. The most useful option is the **Tourist City Pass**, which combines the Museum Pass and Chorus Pass plus free entry to the Jewish Museum and discounts on temporary exhibits for 40€ for 7 days (30€ for ages 6–29). You can also buy various transportation packages and Wi-Fi access (from 5€ for 24hr.). Once you've paid you'll be able to simply print out a voucher to use at museums and sights in Venice; to use public transport you must collect tickets by entering your booking code at one of the ACTV automatic ticket machines or by visiting one of the official Points of Sale in in the city (there's one in the train station open 7am to 9pm, as well as at the Rialto *vaporetto* stop open 7am to 11pm).

Also, for tourists between the ages of 14 and 29, there is the **Rolling Venice** card (also available at www.veneziaunica.it). It's valid until the end of the year in which you buy it, costs just 4€, and entitles the bearer to significant (20%–30%) discounts at participating restaurants (but only applies to cardholder's meal), and a similar discount on ACTV travel cards (20€ for 3 days). Holders of the Rolling Venice card also get discounts in museums, stores, language courses, hotels, and bars across the city (it comes with a thick booklet listing everywhere that you're entitled to get discounts).

Anchoring the large and impressive *campo* outside, a popular crossroads for this area of Castello, is the **statue of Bartolomeo Colleoni ★★**, the Renaissance condottiere who defended Venice's interests at the height of its power and until his death in 1475. The 15th-century work is by the

Florentine **Andrea Verrocchio;** it is considered one of the world's great equestrian monuments and Verrocchio's best.

Campo Santi Giovanni e Paolo 6363. www.basilicasantigiovanniepaolo.it. ℂ **041-5235913.** Admission 2.50€. Mon–Sat 9am–6pm, Sun noon–6pm. *Vaporetto:* Rialto.

Scuola di San Giorgio degli Schiavoni ★★ MUSEUM   One of the most mesmerizing spaces in Europe, the tiny main hall of the Scuola di San Giorgio degli Schiavoni once served as a meeting house for Venice's Dalmatian community (*schiavoni,* literally "Slavs"), built by the side of their church, San Giovanni di Malta, in the early 16th century. The main reason to visit is to admire the awe-inspiring narrative painting cycle on its walls, created by Renaissance master **Vittore Carpaccio** between 1502 and 1509. The paintings depict the lives of the Dalmatian saints George (of dragon-slaying fame), Tryphon, and Jerome, while in the upper hall (Sala dell'Albergo), there's Carpaccio's masterful "Vision of St. Augustine."

Calle dei Furlani 3259A. ℂ **041-5228828.** Admission 5€. Mon 2:45–6pm, Tues–Sat 9:15am–1pm and 2:45–6pm, Sun 9:15am–1pm. *Vaporetto:* Rialto.

Dorsoduro

Gallerie dell'Accademia (Academy Gallery) ★★★ MUSEUM
Along with San Marco and the Palazzo Ducale, the **Accademia** is one of the highlights of Venice, a magnificent collection of European art and especially Venetian painting from the 14th to the 18th centuries. Visitors are currently limited to 300 at one time, so lines can be long in high season—advance reservations are essential. There's a lot to take in here, so buy a catalog in the store if you'd like to learn more—the audioguides are a little muddled and not worth 6€. Note also that Da Vinci's iconic **Vitruvian Man** ★★★, one of the museum's prize holdings, is an extremely fragile ink drawing and rarely displayed in public.

Rooms are laid out in rough chronological order, though the ongoing renovation means some rooms may be closed when you visit (call ahead or check the website to see if any galleries are closed). Room 2 includes Carpaccio's grim "Crucifixion & Glorification of the Ten Thousand Martyrs of Mount Ararat" and his much lighter "Presentation of Jesus in the Temple," but the real showstoppers of the collection reside in rooms 4 and 5, with a gorgeous "St. George" by Mantegna and a series of Giovanni Bellini "Madonnas." Pride of place goes to Giorgione's enigmatic and utterly mystifying **"Tempest"** ★★.

Rooms 6 to 8 feature Venetian heavyweights Tintoretto, Titian, and Lorenzo Lotto, while Room 10 is dominated by Paolo Veronese's mammoth **"Feast in the House of Levi"** ★★. Tintoretto canvases make up the rest of the room, including his three legends of St. Mark. Opposite is Titian's last painting, a "Pietà" intended for his own tomb. Room 11 contains work by Tiepolo, the master of 18th-century Venetian painting, but also Tintoretto's "Madonna dei Tesorieri." The next rooms contain a relatively mediocre

The sculpture garden at the Peggy Guggenheim Collection.

batch of 17th- and 18th-century paintings, though Canaletto's **"Capriccio: A Colonnade"** ★ (Room 17), which he presented to the Academy when he was made a member in 1763, certainly merits a closer look for its elegant contrast between diagonal, vertical, and horizontal lines.

Room 20 is filled by Gentile Bellini's cycle of **"The Miracles of the Relic of the Cross"** ★, painted around 1500. The next room contains the monumental cycle of pictures by Carpaccio illustrating the **Story of St. Ursula** ★★. Finally, in room 24, there's Titian's "Presentation of the Virgin," actually created to hang in this space along with a triptych by Antonio Vivarini and Giovanni d'Alemagna.

Campo della Carità 1050, at foot of Ponte dell'Accademia. www.gallerieaccademia. org. ✆ **041-5200345.** Admission 11€ adults (includes Palazzo Grimani); free on Sundays (check in advance). Reservations by phone or online incur a 1.50€ charge. Daily 8:15am–7:15pm (Mon until 2pm). *Vaporetto:* Accademia.

Peggy Guggenheim Collection ★★ MUSEUM Though the **Peggy Guggenheim Collection** is one of the best museums in Italy when it comes to American and European art of the 20th century, you might find the experience a little jarring given its location in a city so heavily associated with the High Renaissance and the baroque. Nevertheless, art aficionados will find some fascinating work here, and the galleries occupy Peggy Guggenheim's wonderful former home, the 18th-century Palazzo Venier dei Leoni, right on the Grand Canal. Guggenheim purchased the mansion in 1949 and lived here, on and off, until her death in 1979. Highlights include Picasso's extremely abstract "Poet," and his more gentle "On the Beach," several works by Kandinsky ("Landscape with Red Spots No. 2" and "White Cross"), Miró's expressionistic "Seated Woman II," Klee's mystical "Magic Garden," and some unsettling works by Max Ernst ("The Kiss," "Attirement of the Bride"), who was briefly married to Guggenheim in the 1940s. Look out also for Magritte's "Empire of Light," Dalí's typically surreal "Birth of Liquid Desires," and a couple of gems from Pollock: his early "Moon Woman," which recalls Picasso, and "Alchemy," a more typical "poured" painting. The Italian Futurists are also well represented here, with a rare portrait from Modigliani ("Portrait of the Painter Frank Haviland").

Calle San Cristoforo 701. www.guggenheim-venice.it. ⓒ **041-2405411.** Admission 15€ adults; 12€ 65 and over, and for those who present an Alitalia ticket to or from Venice dated no more than 7 days previous; 9€ students 26 and under and children ages 10–18. Wed–Mon 10am–6pm. *Vaporetto:* Accademia (walk around left side of Accademia, take 1st left, and walk straight ahead following the signs).

San Sebastiano ★★ CHURCH   Lose the crowds as you make a pilgrimage to this monument to **Paolo Veronese,** his parish church and home to some of his finest work. Veronese painted the ceiling of the sacristy with the "Coronation of the Virgin" and the "Four Evangelists," while he graced the nave ceiling with "Scenes from the Life of St. Esther." He also decorated the organ shutters and panels around the high altar in the 1560s with scenes from the life of St. Sebastian. Although Veronese is the main event here, don't miss Titian's sensitive "St. Nicholas" (left wall of the first chapel on the right).

Campo San Sebastiano. ⓒ **041-2750462.** Admission 3€. Mon–Sat 10am–5pm. *Vaporetto:* San Basilio.

Santa Maria della Salute (Church of the Virgin Mary of Good Health) ★ CHURCH   Generally referred to as "La Salute," this crown jewel of 17th-century baroque architecture proudly reigns at a commercially and aesthetically important point, almost directly across from the Piazza San Marco, where the Grand Canal empties into the lagoon.

The first stone was laid in 1631 after the Senate decided to honor the Virgin Mary for delivering Venice from a plague that had killed around 95,000 people. They accepted the revolutionary plans of a young, relatively unknown architect, Baldassare Longhena (who would go on to design, among other projects, the Ca' Rezzonico). He dedicated the next 50 years of his life to overseeing its progress (he would die one year after its inauguration but five years before its completion). Today the dome of the church is an iconic presence on the Venice skyline, recognized for its exuberant exterior of volutes, scrolls, and more than 125 statues. The most revered image inside is the **Madonna della Salute,** a rare

---

The Biennale

Venice hosts the latest in contemporary art and sculpture from dozens of countries during the prestigious **Biennale d'Arte** ★★★ (www.labiennale.org; ⓒ **041-5218711**), one of the world's top international art shows. It fills the pavilions of the **Giardini** (public gardens) at the east end of **Castello** and at the **Arsenale**, as well as in other spaces around the city from May to November every odd-numbered year (usually open Tues–Sun 10am–6pm). Tickets cost 25€, 20€ for those 65 and over, and 15€ for students and all those 26 and under.

black-faced sculpture of Mary brought back from Candia in Crete in 1670 as war booty. The otherwise rather sober interior is livened by the sacristy, where you will find a number of important ceiling paintings and portraits of the Evangelists and church doctors by **Titian.** On the right wall of the sacristy, which you have to pay to enter, is Tintoretto's **"Marriage at Cana"** ★, often considered one of his best paintings.

Campo della Salute 1. (?) **041-5225558.** Free admission to church; sacristy 3€. Daily 9am–noon and 3–6pm. *Vaporetto:* Salute.

Scuola Grande dei Carmini ★★ CHURCH   The former Venetian base of the Carmelites, finished off in the 18th century, is now a shrine of sorts to **Giambattista Tiepolo,** who painted the ceiling of the upstairs hall between 1739 and 1744. It's truly a magnificent sight, Tiepolo's elaborate rococo interpretation of "Simon Stock Receiving the Scapular" now fully restored along with various panels throughout the building.

Campo San Margherita 2617. www.scuolagrandecarmini.it. (?) **041-5289420.** Admission 5€. Daily 11am–4pm. *Vaporetto:* San Basilio.

Squero di San Trovaso ★★ HISTORIC SITE   One of the most intriguing sights in Venice is this small *squero* (boatyard), which first opened in the 17th century. Just north of the Zattere (the wide, sunny walkway that runs alongside the Giudecca Canal in Dorsoduro), the boatyard lies next to the Church of San Trovaso on the narrow Rio San Trovaso (not far from the Accademia Bridge). It is surrounded by Tyrolean-looking wooden structures (a true rarity in this city of stone built on water) that are home to the multigenerational owners and original workshops for traditional Venetian boats. Aware that they have become a tourist site themselves, the gondoliers don't mind if you watch them at work from across the narrow Rio di San Trovaso, but don't try to invite yourself in.

Dorsoduro 1097 (on the Rio San Trovaso, southwest of the Accademia). *Vaporetto:* Zattere.

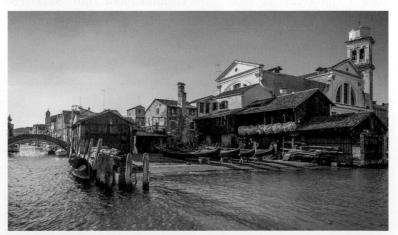

Gondola Boatyard.

San Polo & Santa Croce

Basilica Santa Maria Gloriosa dei Frari ★★ CHURCH Known simply as "i Frari," this immense 14th-century Gothic church was built by the Franciscans and is the largest church in Venice after San Marco. It houses a number of important works, including two Titian masterpieces: the **"Assumption of the Virgin"** ★★ over the main altar, painted when the artist was only in his late 20s, and his "Virgin of the Pesaro Family" in the left nave. For the latter work, commissioned by one of Venice's most powerful families, Titian's wife posed for the figure of Mary (and then died soon afterward in childbirth). Don't miss Giovanni Bellini's **"Madonna & Child"** ★★ over the altar in the sacristy; novelist Henry James was struck dumb by it, writing "it is as solemn as it is gorgeous." The grand **mausoleum of Titian** is on the right as you enter the church, opposite the oddly incongruous 18th-century monument to sculptor **Antonio Canova**, shaped like a pyramid—designed by Canova himself, this was originally supposed to be Titian's tomb.

Campo dei Frari 3072. www.basilicadeifrari.it. ℭ **041-2728611.** Admission 3€, audioguide 2€. Mon–Sat 9am–6pm; Sun 1–6pm. *Vaporetto:* San Tomà (walk straight ahead on Calle del Traghetto and turn right and immediately left across Campo San Tomà; walk straight ahead, on Ramo Mandoler then Calle Larga Prima, and turn right when you reach beginning of Salizada San Rocco).

Scuola Grande di San Rocco (Confraternity of St. Roch) ★★★ MUSEUM Like many medieval saints, French-born St. Rocco (St. Roch) died young, but thanks to his work healing the sick in the 14th century, his cult became associated with the power to cure the plague and other serious illnesses. When the saint's body was brought to Venice in 1485, this *scuola* began to reap the benefits, and by 1560 the current complex was completed, work beginning soon after on more than 50 major paintings by Tintoretto. Today the *scuola* is primarily a shrine to the skills of **Tintoretto.** You enter in the **Ground Floor Hall (Sala Terrena)**, where the paintings were created between 1583 and 1587, led by one of the most frenzied "Annunciations" ever made, while "The Flight into Egypt" is undeniably one of Tintoretto's greatest works. Upstairs is the **Great Upper Hall (Sala Superiore),** where Old Testament scenes

---

THE film FESTIVAL

The **Venice International Film Festival** ★, in late August and early September, is the most respected celebration of celluloid in Europe after Cannes. Films from all over the world are shown in the **Palazzo del Cinema** on the Lido as well as at various venues—and occasionally in some of the *campi*. Ticket prices vary, but those for the less-sought-after films are usually modest. Visit www.labiennale.org/en/cinema for more details.

such as "Moses Striking Water From the Rock" cover the ceiling. The paintings around the walls, based on the New Testament, are generally regarded as a master class of perspective, shadow, and color. Off this main hall is the **Sala dell'Albergo,** where an entire wall is adorned by Tintoretto's mind-blowing "Crucifixion" (as well as his "Glorification of St. Roch," on the ceiling, the painting that actually won him the contract to paint the *scuola*). Way up in the loft, the newly opened **Tesoro** (Treasury) is a tiny space dedicated primarily to gold reliquaries containing venerated relics such as the fingers of St. Peter and St. Andrew, and one of the thorns that crowned Christ during the cruxifixion.

Campo San Rocco 3052, adjacent to Campo dei Frari. www.scuolagrandesanrocco. it. ✆ **041-5234864.** Admission 10€ adults (price includes audioguide); 8€ ages 18–26; 18 and under free. Daily 9:30am–5:30pm. *Vaporetto:* San Tomà (walk straight ahead on Calle del Traghetto and turn right and immediately left across Campo San Tomà; walk straight ahead on Ramo Mandoler, Calle Larga Prima, and Salizada San Rocco, which leads into the *campo* of the same name—look for crimson sign behind Frari Church).

Cannaregio

Galleria Giorgio Franchetti alla Ca' d'Oro ★★ MUSEUM   This magnificent *palazzo* overlooking the Grand Canal, the "golden house," was built between 1428 and 1430 for the noble Contarini family. Baron Giorgio Franchetti bought the place in 1894, and it now serves as an atmospheric art gallery for the exceptional collection he built up throughout his lifetime. The highlight here is **"St. Sebastian" ★★** by Paduan artist Andrea Mantegna, displayed in its own marble chapel built by the overawed baron. The so-called "St. Sebastian of Venice" was the third and final painting of the saint by Mantegna, created around 1490 and quite different to the other two (in Vienna and Paris, respectively); it's a bold, deeply pessimistic work, with none of Mantegna's usual background details to detract from the saint's suffering.

Strada Nuova 3932. www.cadoro.org. ✆ **041-520-0345.** Admission 6€, plus 1.50€ reservation fee (price increases during special exhibitions). Mon 8:15am–2pm; Tues–Sun 8:15am–7:15pm. *Vaporetto:* Ca' d'Oro.

Canal entrance to Ca' d'Oro.

Museo Ebraico di Venezia (Jewish Museum of Venice) ★

MUSEUM/SYNAGOGUE In the heart of the Ghetto Nuovo, the Jewish Museum contains a small but precious collection of artifacts related to the long history of the Jews in Venice, beginning with an exhibition on Jewish festivities in the first room; chandeliers, goblets, and spice-holders used to celebrate Shabbat, Shofàrs (ram's horns) and a Séfer Torà (Scroll of Divine Law). The second room contains a rich collection of historic textiles, including Torah covers, and a rare marriage contract from 1792. A newer exhibition area explores the immigration patterns of Jews to Venice, and their experiences once here. For many the real highlight, though, is the chance to tour three of the area's five historic synagogues (ladies must have shoulders covered and men must have heads covered; no photos): German (Scuola Grande Tedesca), founded in 1528; Italian (Scuola Italiana), founded in 1575; Sephardic (Scuola Levantina), founded in 1541 but rebuilt in the second half of 17th century; Spanish (Scuola Spagnola), rebuilt in the first half of 17th century; and the baroque-style Ashkenazi (Scuola Canton), largely rebuilt in the 18th century. It's difficult to predict which three you'll visit on any given day, as it depends on which synagogues are being used (and on the whim of your guide); the Levantina and the Spanish are the most lavishly decorated, with one usually included on the tour.

Cannaregio 2902B (on Campo del Ghetto Nuovo). www.museoebraico.it. Ⓒ **041-715359.** Museum 4€ adults, 3€ children; museum and synagogue tour 10€ adults, 8€ children. Museum Sun–Fri 10am–7pm (Oct–May until 5:30pm); synagogue guided tours in English hourly 10:30am–5:30pm (Oct–May last tour 4:30pm). Closed on Jewish holidays. *Vaporetto:* Guglie.

Giudecca & San Giorgio

Il Redentore ★★ CHURCH Perhaps the masterpiece among Palladio's churches, Il Redentore was commissioned by Venice to give thanks for being delivered from the great plague (1575–77), which claimed over a quarter of the population (some 46,000 people). The doge established a tradition of visiting this church by crossing a long pontoon bridge made up of boats from the Dorsoduro's Zattere on the third Sunday of each July, a tradition that survived the demise of the doges and remains one of Venice's most popular festivals.

The interior is done in grand, austere, painstakingly classical Palladian style. The artworks tend to be workshop pieces (from the studios or schools, but not the actual brushes, of Tintoretto and Veronese), but there is a fine "Baptism of Christ" by Veronese himself in the sacristy, which also contains Alvise Vivarini's "Madonna with Child & Angels" alongside works by Jacopo da Bassano and Palma il Giovane, who also did the "Deposition" over the right aisle's third chapel (be warned, however, that the sacristy is often closed).

Campo del Redentore 195, La Giudecca. Ⓒ **041-523-1415.** Admission 3€. Mon–Sat 10am–5pm. *Vaporetto:* Redentore.

Il Redentore.

San Giorgio Maggiore ★★ CHURCH   This church sits on the little island of San Giorgio Maggiore across from Piazza San Marco. It is one of the masterpieces of Andrea Palladio, the great Renaissance architect from nearby Padua. Most known for his country villas built for Venice's wealthy merchant families, Palladio designed this church in 1565 and it was completed in 1610. To impose a classical front on the traditional church structure, Palladio designed two interlocking facades, with repeating triangles, rectangles, and columns that are harmoniously proportioned. Founded as early as the 10th century, the church had its interior reinterpreted by Palladio with whitewashed stucco surfaces, stark but majestic, an unadorned but harmonious space. The main altar is flanked by two epic paintings by an elderly Tintoretto, "The Fall of Manna," to the left, and the more noteworthy **"Last Supper"** ★★ to the right, famous for its chiaroscuro. Through the doorway to the right of the choir leading to the Cappella dei Morti (Chapel of the Dead), you will find Tintoretto's "Deposition." To the left of the choir is an elevator that you can take to the top of the campanile—for a charge of 6€—to experience an unforgettable view of the island, the lagoon, and the Palazzo Ducale and Piazza San Marco across the way.

On the island of San Giorgio Maggiore, across St. Mark's Basin from Piazza San Marco. ℭ **041-5227827.** Free admission. Mon–Sat 9:30am–12:30pm; daily 2:30–6pm (Oct–Apr to 4:30pm). *Vaporetto:* Take the Giudecca-bound *vaporetto* (no. 2) on Riva degli Schiavoni (San Marco/San Zaccaria) and get off at the 1st stop, San Giorgio Maggiore.

Exploring Venice's Islands

Venice shares its lagoon with three other principal islands: Murano, Burano, and Torcello. Guided tours of the three are operated by a dozen agencies with docks on Riva degli Schiavoni/Piazzetta San Marco (all interchangeable). The 3- and 4-hour tours run 25€ to 35€, usually include a visit to a Murano glass factory (you can easily do that on your own, with less of a hard sell), and leave daily around 9:30am and 2:30pm (times change; check in advance).

You can also visit the islands on your own conveniently and easily using the *vaporetti*. Line nos. 4.1 and 4.2 make the journey to Murano from Fondamente Nove (on the north side of Castello). For Murano, Burano, and Torcello, Line no. 12 departs Fondamente Nove every 30 minutes; for Torcello change to the shuttle boat (Line 9) that runs from Burano, timed to match the arrivals from Venice. The islands are small and easy to navigate, but check the schedule for the next island-to-island departure (usually hourly) and your return so that you don't spend most of your day waiting for connections.

MURANO ★★

The island of Murano has long been famous throughout the world for the products of its glass factories. A visit to the **Museo del Vetro (Museum of Glass),** Fondamenta Giustinian 8 (www.museovetro.visitmuve.it; ✆ **041-739586**), provides context, charting the history of the island's glassmaking and definitely worthwhile if you intend to buy a lot of glassware. Daily hours are 10am to 6pm (Nov–Mar to 5pm), and admission is 10€ for adults and 5.50€ children 6 to 14 and students 30 and under.

Dozens of *fornaci* (kilns) offer free shows of mouth-blown glassmaking almost invariably hitched to a hard-sell tour of their factory outlet store. These retail showrooms of delicate glassware can be enlightening or boring, depending on your frame of mind. Almost all the places will ship their goods, but that often doubles the price. On the other hand, these pieces are instant heirlooms.

Murano also has two worthy churches (both free): the largely 15th-century **San Pietro Martire ★** (Mon–Sat 9am–5:30pm, Sun noon–5:30pm), with its paintings by Veronese and Giovanni Bellini, and the ancient **Santa Maria e Donato ★** (Mon–Sat 9am–6pm, Sun 12:30–6pm), with its intricate Byzantine exterior apse, 6th-century pulpit, stunning mosaic of Mary over the altar, and a fantastic 12th-century inlaid floor.

BURANO ★★★

Lace is the claim to fame of tiny, historic Burano, a craft kept alive for centuries by the wives of fishermen waiting for their husbands to return from the sea. Sadly, most of the lace sold on the island these days is made by machine elsewhere. It's still worth a trip if you have time to stroll the back streets of the island, whose canals are lined with the brightly colored, simple homes of the Buranesi fishermen—it's quite unlike anything in Venice or Murano. The local government continues its attempt to keep its centuries-old lace legacy alive with subsidized classes.

Visit the **Museo del Merletto (Museum of Lace Making),** Piazza Galuppi 187 (www.museomerletto.visitmuve.it; ✆ **041-730034**),

Jews began settling in Venice in great numbers in the 15th century (originally on the island of Giudecca, thought to be named after a corruption of the Latin "Judaica"), and the Republic soon came to value their services as moneylenders, physicians, and traders. In 1516, however, fearing their growing influence, the Venetians forced the Jewish population to live on an island where there was an abandoned 14th-century foundry (ghetto is old Venetian dialect for "foundry"), and drawbridges were raised to enforce a nighttime curfew. By the end of the 17th century, as many as 5,000 Jews lived in the Ghetto's cramped confines. Napoleon tore down the Ghetto gates in 1797, but it wasn't until the unification of Italy in 1866 that Jews achieved equal status with their fellow citizens. It remains the spiritual center for Venice's ever-diminishing community of Jewish families, with two synagogues and Chabad House; although accounts vary widely, it's said that anywhere from 500 to 2,000 Jews live in all of Venice and Mestre, though very few live in the Ghetto. Aside from its historic interest, this is also one of the less touristy neighborhoods in Venice (although it has become something of a nightspot) and makes for a pleasant and scenic place to stroll. Venice's first kosher restaurant, **Gam Gam,** opened near here in 1996, at 1122 Ghetto Vecchio right on the canal (www.gamgamkosher.com; © **366-2504505**), close to the Guglie *vaporetto* stop. Owned and run by Orthodox Jews, it is open Sunday to Thursday noon to 10pm, noon to 2 hours before Shabbat (sunset on Fri evening), and on Saturday from 1 hour after Shabbat, until 11pm (excluding summer).

to understand why something so exquisite should not be left to fade into extinction. It's open Tuesday to Sunday 10am to 6pm (Nov–Mar to 5pm), and admission is 5€ adults, 3.50€ children 6 to 14 and students 29 and under.

TORCELLO ★★

Torcello is perhaps the most charming of the islands, though today it consists of little more than one long canal leading from the *vaporetto* landing to a clump of buildings at its center.

Torcello boasts the oldest Venetian monument, the **Basilica di Santa Maria dell'Assunta ★★★**, whose foundation dates from the 7th century (© **041-2702464**). It's famous for its spectacular 11th- to 12th-century Byzantine mosaics—a "Madonna and Child" in the apse and a monumental "Last Judgment" on the west wall—rivaling those of Ravenna's and St. Mark's basilicas. The cathedral is open daily 10:30am to 6pm (Nov–Feb to 5pm), and admission is 5€ (audioguide an extra 2€). Also of interest is the adjacent 11th-century church of **Santa Fosca** (free admission), though it's a simple, Byzantine brick church with a plain interior, and the **Museo di Torcello** (© **041-730761**) with two small galleries showcasing archeological artifacts from the Iron Age to medieval period, many found on the island. The church closes 30 minutes before the basilica, and the museum is open Tuesday to Sunday 10:30am to 5:30pm (Nov–Feb to 5pm). Museum admission is 3€. You must buy tickets for all attractions at the Basilica entrance.

carnevale A VENEZIA

Carnevale traditionally was the celebration preceding Lent, the period of penitence and abstinence prior to Easter; its name is derived from the Latin *carnem levare*, meaning "to take meat away." Today Carnevale in Venice builds for 10 days until the big blowout, Shrove Tuesday (Fat Tuesday), when fireworks illuminate the Grand Canal, and Piazza San Marco is turned into a giant open-air ballroom for the masses. The festival is a harlequin patchwork of musical and cultural events, many of them free of charge, which appeals to all ages, tastes, nationalities, and budgets. Musical events are staged in some of the city's dozens of *piazze*—from reggae and zydeco to jazz and baroque. Special art exhibits are mounted at museums and galleries. Book your hotel months ahead, especially for the 2 weekends prior to Shrove Tuesday. Check **www.carnevale venezia.com** for details on upcoming events.

Peaceful Torcello is uninhabited except for a handful of families (plus a population of feral cats), and is a favorite picnic spot. You'll have to bring the food from Venice—there are no stores on the island and only a handful of bars/trattorias plus one rather expensive restaurant, the **Locanda Cipriani** (Wed–Mon noon–3pm; closed Jan–Feb; www.locandacipriani.com) of Hemingway fame, which opened in 1935 and is definitely worth a splurge. Once the tour groups have left, the island offers a very special moment of solitude and escape.

THE LIDO

Although a convenient 15-minute *vaporetto* ride away from San Marco, Venice's **Lido beaches** are not much to write home about and certainly no longer a chic destination. For bathing and sun-worshipping there are much better beaches nearby—in Jesolo, to the north, for example. But the parade of wealthy Italian and foreign tourists (plus a good number of Venetian families with children) who still frequent this coastal area throughout summer is an interesting sight indeed, although you'll find many of them at the elitist beaches affiliated with such deluxe hotels as the legendary Excelsior (in a sign of the times, the equally storied De Bains Hotel went out of business in 2010 to be converted into luxury apartments).

There are two main beach areas at the Lido. **Bucintoro** is at the opposite end of Gran Viale Santa Maria Elisabetta (referred to as the Gran Viale) from the *vaporetto* station Santa Elisabetta. It's a 10-minute stroll; walk straight ahead along Gran Viale to reach the beach. **San Nicolò,** about 1.5km (1 mile) away, can be reached by bus B. Renting loungers and parasols can cost from 10€–20€ per person (per day) depending on the time of year (it's just 1€ to use the showers and bathrooms). Keep in mind that if you stay at any of the hotels on the Lido, most of them have some kind of agreement with the different *bagni* (beach establishments).

Vaporetto line nos. 1, 2, 5.1, 5.2, and LN cross the lagoon to the Lido from the San Zaccaria–Danieli stop near San Marco. Note that the Lido becomes chilly, windswept and utterly deserted between October and April.

Organized Tours

Because of the sheer number of sights to see in Venice, some first-time visitors like to start out with an organized tour. Although few things can really be covered in any depth on these overview tours, they're sometimes useful for getting your bearings. **Avventure Bellissime** (www.tours-italy.com; ✆ 041-970499) coordinates a plethora of tours (in English), by boat and gondola, though the walking tours are the best value, covering all the main sights around Piazza San Marco in 2 hours for 25€ (discounts available on-line). For something with a little more bite, try **Urban Adventures** (www.urbanadventures.com; ✆ 348-9808566), which runs enticing *cicchetti* tours (2.5 hr.) for 75€.

For those with more energy, learn to "row like a Venetian" (yes, literally standing up), at **Row Venice** (www.rowvenice.com; ✆ 347-7250637), where 1½-hour lessons take place in traditional, hand-built "shrimp-tail" or *batele coda di gambero* boats for 80€ for up to 2 people. Or you could abandon tradition altogether and opt for a **Venice Kayak** tour (www.venicekayak.com; ✆ 346-4771327), a truly enchanting way to see the city from the water. Day trips are 120€ per person for 2 to 6 persons with guide (10am–4 or 5pm).

Especially for Kids

It goes without saying that a **gondola ride** (p. 369) will be the thrill of a lifetime for any child (or adult). If that's too expensive, consider the convenient and far cheaper alternative: a **ride on the no. 1** *vaporetto* (p. 377).

Judging from the squeals of delight, **feeding the pigeons in Piazza San Marco** (purchase a bag of corn and you'll be draped in pigeons in a nanosecond; could be the high point of your child's visit to Venice, and it's the ultimate photo op. Be sure your child won't be startled by all the fluttering and flapping.

A jaunt to the neighboring **island of Murano** (p. 390) can be as educational as it is recreational—follow the signs to any *fornace* (kiln), where a glassblowing performance of the island's thousand-year-old art is free entertainment. But be ready for the guaranteed sales pitch that follows.

Before you leave town, take the elevator to the **top of the Campanile di San Marco** (the highest structure in the city; p. 376) for a scintillating view of Venice's rooftops and church cupolas, or get up close and personal with the four bronze horses on the facade of the Basilica San Marco. The view from its **outdoor loggia** is something you and your children won't forget. Scaling the **Torre dell'Orologio** (p. 380) or the bell tower at **San Giorgio Maggiore** (p. 389) should also be lots of fun.

The **winged lion,** said to have been a kind of good luck mascot to St. Mark, patron saint of Venice, was the very symbol of the Serene Republic and to this day appears on everything from cafe napkins to T-shirts. Keep a running tab of who can spot the most flying lions—you'll find them on facades, atop columns, over doorways, as pavement mosaics, on government stamps, and on the local flag.

WHERE TO STAY

Few cities boast as long a high season as that of Venice, which begins with the Easter period. May, June, and September are the best months weather-wise and, therefore, the most crowded. July and August are hot (few of the one- and two-star hotels offer air-conditioning; when they do, it usually costs extra). Like everything else, hotels are more expensive here than in any other Italian city, with no apparent upgrade in amenities. The least special of those below are clean and functional; at best, they're charming and thoroughly enjoyable, with the serenade of a passing gondolier thrown in for good measure. Some may even provide you with your best stay in all of Europe.

It's highly advisable to reserve in advance, even in the off-season. If you haven't booked, come as early as you can on your arrival day, definitely before noon. Another alternative to reserve upon your arrival is through the **A.V.A.** (Venetian Hoteliers Association), online at www. veneziasi.it or ⓒ **041-5222264.** Simply state the price range you want to book, and they'll confirm a hotel while you wait. There are offices at the train station, in Piazzale Roma garages, and in the airport.

SEASONAL CONSIDERATIONS Most hotels observe high- and low-season rates and the high-end hotels generally adapt their prices to availability. In the prices listed below, **single figures represent rack rates,** because the price varies too widely depending on availability, and you can usually get a room for much less, even in high season.

Self-Catering Apartments

Anyone looking to get into the local swing of things in Venice should stay in a short-term rental apartment. For the same price or less than a hotel room, you could have your own one-bedroom apartment with a washing machine, A/C, and a fridge to keep your wine in. Properties of all sizes, styles, and price ranges are available for stays of 3 nights to several weeks.

It's standard practice for local rental agencies to collect 30% of the total rental amount upfront to secure a booking. When you get to Venice and check in, the balance of your rental fee is normally payable in cash only, so make sure you have enough euros before you leave home. Upon booking, the agency should provide you with detailed "check-in" procedures. Normally, you're expected to call a cell or office phone when you arrive in Venice, and then the keyholder will meet you at the front door of the property at the agreed-upon time. Before the keyholder disappears, make sure you have a few numbers to call in case of an emergency. Otherwise, most apartments come with a list of neighborhood shops and services. Beyond that, you're on your own, which is what makes an apartment stay a great way to do as the Venetians do.

RECOMMENDED AGENCIES

Airbnb (www.airbnb.com) is now a major player in Venice, with over 1000 properties listed from just 30€ per night. **Couchsurfing** (www.couchsurfing.com) is also popular and generally safe in Venice, though take the usual precautions using the apartment-swapping service. **Cities Reference** (www.citiesreference.com; ✆ 06-48903612) is the best traditional apartment rental agency for Venice, with over 250 properties listed. The company's no-surprises property descriptions come with helpful information and lots of photos. **Cross Pollinate** (www.crosspollinate.com; ✆ 06-99369799) is a multi-destination agency but with a decent roster of personally inspected apartments and B&Bs in Venice, created by the American owners of the Beehive hotel in Rome. **Go withOh** (www.gowithoh.com; ✆ 800/567-2927 in the U.S.) is a hip rental agency that covers 12 European cities, including Venice. The website is fun to navigate, offers money-saving tips, and lists more than 200 apartments for rent in the city. **Rental in Venice** (www.rentalinvenice.com; ✆ 041-718981) has an alluring website—with video clips of the apartments—and the widest selection of midrange and luxury apartments in the prime *San Marco* zone (there are less expensive ones, too).

San Marco

EXPENSIVE

Corte Di Gabriela ★★★   This gorgeous boutique hotel just a short walk from Piazza San Marco combines contemporary design and classical Venetian style—ceiling murals, marble pillars, and exposed brick blend with designer furniture and appliances (including free use of iPads, strong Wi-Fi, and hundreds of satellite TV channels). The fully renovated property dates from 1870, once serving as the home and offices of Venetian lawyers. It's the attention to detail that makes a stay here so memorable, with breakfast one of the highlights and well worth lingering over: fresh pastries made by the owners the night before, decent espresso, and a spread of crepes and omelets made on request.

Calle degli Avvocati 3836. www.cortedigabriela.com. ✆ **041-5235077.** 10 units. 320€–420€ double. Rates include buffet breakfast. *Vaporetto:* Sant' Angelo. **Amenities:** Bar; babysitting; concierge; room service (limited hours); Wi-Fi (free).

MODERATE

Locanda Fiorita ★★   Hard to imagine a more picturesque location for this little hotel, a charming, quiet, *campiello* draped in vines and blossoms—no wonder it's a favorite of professional photographers. Most of

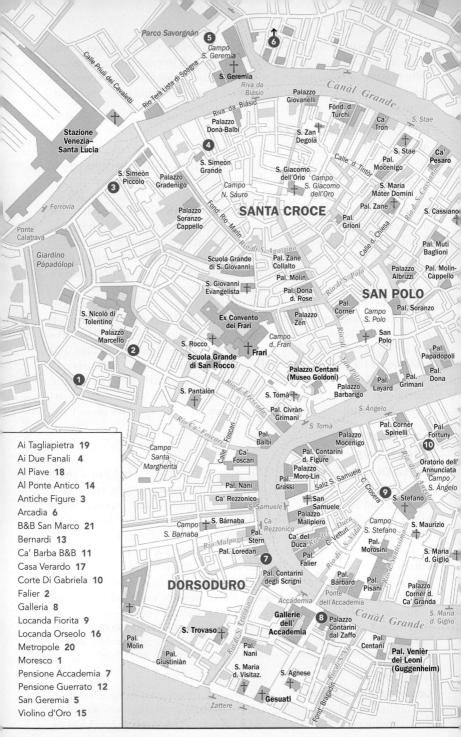

Venice Hotels

CANNAREGIO

Pal. Giovanelli
S. Felice
Pal. Fontana
Ca' d'Oro
Pal. Sagredo
S. Sofia
Strada Nuova
Calle d. Vele
Rio ter. d. SS. Apostoli
Ss. Apóstoli
S. Canciano
Pal. Widman
Calle d. Fumo
Calle d. Squero
Ospedale Civile
H
S. Maria d. Pianto
Pal. Brandolin
Pal. Botteri
Ca d'Oro
Pescaria
Pal. Mangilli
Ca' da Mosto
Pal. Falier
Rio d. Santi
S. Giovanni Crisostomo
Rio d. SG. Crisóstomo
S. Maria d. Miracoli
Pal. Soranzo-Van Axel
Pal. Pisani
Pal. Grifalconi
C. larga G. Gallina
Fond. d. Mendicanti
Ss. Giovanni e Paolo (S. Zanipolo)
Pal. Morosini
Pal. Muazzo
Fábbriche Nuove
Calle d. Beccarie
Rio di S. Marina
Ponte d.
Rialto
Palazzo Dieci Savi
Fóndaco d. Tedeschi
Pal. Cavazza-Foscari
Campo S. Marina
Palazzo Ruzzini
Pal. Donà
Pal. Cavignis
Pal. Donà
Palazzo Cappello
S. Lorenzo
S. Aponàl
Riva del Vin
Rialto
Teatro Málibran
Pal. Dolfin-Manin
S. Bartolomeo
C. Stagneri
S. Lio
S. Maria della Fava
Salizada S. Lio
Campo S. Maria Formosa
S. Maria Formosa
Questura
CASTELLO
S. Silvestro
Riva del Carbon
Pal. Bembo
C. del Teatro
M. S. Salvador
S. Salvador
Pal. Tasca Papafáva
C. Bande
Pal. Querini Stampalia
Ruga Giuffa
S. Silvestro
Palazzo Grimani
Ca' Farsetti
C. del Teatro
Calle d.
C. Guerra
Palazzo Soranzo
Pal. Priuli
Pal. Zorzi
S. Luca
Campo Manìn
Calle C. Goldoni
S. Zuliàn
C. Spadaria
Palazzo Trevisan-Cappello
S. Giovanni Novo
S. Giorgio dei Greci
Cinema Rossini
Palazzo Contarini d. Bovolo
Fabbri
C. Fiubera
Merc. Orologio
C. Speziali
C. Canonica
S. Zaccaria
C. d. Mandola
Ateneo Véneto
Frezzeria
S. Gallo
Torre d. Orologio
Basilica di San Marco
Convento
La Pietà
SAN MARCO
Pisc. di Frezzeria
Campanile
Piazza San Marco
Palazzo Ducale (Doge's Palace)
Pal. d. Prigioni
Teatro La Fenice
S. Fantin
S. Moisè
Museo Corrèr
Giardini ex Reali
Molo
Ponte d. Sospiri (Bridge of Sighs)
Riva
d. Schiavoni
S. Zaccaria
C. Larga XXII Marzo
S. S. Moisè
C. Vallaresso
S. Ricotto
Piazzetta
Palazzi Contarini
Palazzo Tiépolo
Capo di Porto
S. Marco
Pal. Gritti
Palazzo Treves d. Bonfili
Bacino di San Marco
Pal. Genovese
Salute
Punta d. Dogana
Dogana da Mar
S. Maria d. Salute
Seminario Patriarcale
Ex Ospizio

0   1/8 mi
0   200 m

Isola di S. Giorgio Maggiore

the standard rooms are small (bathrooms are tiny), but all are furnished in an elegant 18th-century style, with wooden floors, shuttered windows, and richly patterned fittings (A/C and satellite TV are included). The helpful staff more than make up for any deficiencies, and breakfast is a real pleasure, especially when taken outside on the *campiello*.

Campiello Novo 3457a. www.locandafiorita.com. ℂ **041-5234754.** 10 units. 80€–160€ double. Rates include continental breakfast. *Vaporetto:* Sant'Angelo (walk to the tall brick building and go around it, turning right into Ramo Narisi; at a small bridge turn left and walk along Calle del Pestrin until you see a small piazza on your right [Campiello Novo]; the hotel is immediately opposite). **Amenities:** Babysitting; concierge; room service; Wi-Fi (free).

Locanda Orseolo ★★★   This enticing inn comprises three elegant guesthouses operated by the friendly Peruch family and located right behind Piazza San Marco. The place oozes character, with exposed wood beams and heavy drapes giving a medieval feel and rooms lavishly decorated with Venetian-style furniture and tributes to the masks of the Carnevale—a cross between an artist's studio and Renaissance palace. Lounge with an aperitif on the terrace overlooking the Orseolo canal, and enjoy eggs and crepes made to order at breakfast, while watching the gondolas glide by.

Corte Zorzi 1083. www.locandaorseolo.com. ℂ **041-5204827.** 15 units. 150€–220€ double. Rates include buffet breakfast. *Vaporetto:* San Marco. **Amenities:** Babysitting; concierge; Wi-Fi (free).

Violino d'Oro ★★   The relatively spacious rooms in this handsome 18th-century building have been traditionally adorned in a neoclassical Venetian style with exposed wooden beams, crystal chandeliers, and heaps of character. Most rooms also overlook the romantic San Moisè canal, and Piazza San Marco is just a 5-minute stroll away. At this price point (with incredible deals in low season), it's reassuring to know you get proper air-conditioning, satellite TV, and a decent elevator. Breakfast is an event, with a vast spread of homemade cakes, savory pies, and muffins complementing one of the best cappuccinos in the city.

Calle Larga XXII Marzo 2091. www.violinodoro.com. ℂ **041-2770841.** 26 units. 69€–204€ double. Rates include buffet breakfast. *Vaporetto:* San Marco–Vallaresso (walk straight up Calle di Ca' Vallaresso, turn left on Salizada San Moisè, and cross the footbridge; the hotel is across the *campiello* on the left). **Amenities:** Bar; concierge; room service; Wi-Fi (free).

Castello

EXPENSIVE

Metropole ★★★   This five-star behemoth with a prime location on the water is part luxury hotel, part eclectic art museum, with antiques, Asian artworks, and exhibits of ancient fans, corkscrews, and tapestries dotted throughout. It's no dusty grand dame, however; on the contrary, the hotel is a chic boutique with rooms furnished with a classic Oriental theme. The building has an incredible history, beginning life in the Middle Ages as the Ospedale della Pietà, serving as a charitable institution for orphans and abandoned girls, and later a music school (Vivaldi taught violin here in the early 18th c.). After it was converted into a hotel in 1895, Sigmund Freud was an early guest, along with Thomas Mann in 1900, who allegedly wrote parts of *Death in Venice* here.

Riva degli Schiavoni 4149. www.hotelmetropole.com. © **041-5205044.** 67 units. 202€–316€ double. Buffet breakfast 30€ (sometimes included). *Vaporetto:* San Zaccaria (walk along Riva degli Schiavoni to the right; the hotel is next to La Pietà church). **Amenities:** Restaurant; bar; babysitting; concierge; room service; Wi-Fi (free).

MODERATE

Al Piave ★★　Al Piave is a cozy, old-fashioned family-run hotel just 5 minutes from Piazza San Marco. Rooms are simply but attractively furnished with richly woven rugs and carpets, marble floors, and some of the original wood beams exposed (some come with a terrace, while the family suites are a good value for groups). Bathrooms are relatively big, and the A/C a welcome bonus in the summer, but there are no elevators, so be prepared if you get a higher floor. Outside of peak months (July, Sept), Piave is an exceptionally good value, given its proximity to the *piazza*.

Ruga Giuffa 4838. www.hotelalpiave.com. © **041-5285174.** 20 units. 130€–210€ double. Rates include continental breakfast. Closed Jan 7 to Carnevale. *Vaporetto:* San Zaccaria (find Calle delle Rasse beyond Palazzo Danieli, and walk to the end of the street; turn left and then immediately right; continue straight until you get to tiny Ponte Storto, cross and continue until you reach Ruga Giuffa—the hotel is on the left). **Amenities:** Babysitting; concierge; Wi-Fi (free).

Casa Verardo ★★★　Tucked away across a small bridge in the warren of central Castello, this enchanting hotel occupies a 16th-century *palazzo*, though it's been a hotel since 1911. Rooms (over four floors, with an elevator) sport an old-fashioned Venetian style, with Florentine furniture, hand-painted beds, and colorful textiles (there are precious antiques and paintings scattered throughout the property), but updated with air-conditioning and satellite TV. Some rooms have a view over a canal, others over the shady courtyard and the city. Don't miss the top floor, where the panoramic terrace is a pleasant spot for an aperitif. They'll also take you to Murano for free, but you have to find your own way back.

Calle Drio La Chiesa 4765 (at foot of Ponte Storto). www.casaverardo.it. © **041-5286138.** 25 units. 140€–225€ double. Rates include buffet breakfast. *Vaporetto:* San Zaccaria (walk straight on Calle delle Rasse to Campo SS. Filippo e Giacomo; continue straight through the *campo* to Calle della Sacrestia, then Calle Drio La Chiesa until you reach Ponte Storto, and look for the hotel on the left). **Amenities:** Bar; babysitting; concierge; room service; Wi-Fi (free).

INEXPENSIVE

Ai Tagliapietra ★★★　This cozy B&B is run by the amicable Lorenzo (who will bend over backward to make your stay a memorable one), and a real bargain in this part of town. Rooms are basic, but spotless, modern, and relatively spacious with private showers. The small, shared kitchenette is available for guests' use (with refrigerator and free tea). Lorenzo will usually meet you at San Zaccaria, give you a map, print your boarding passes, and generally organize your trip if you desire, making this an especially recommended budget option for first-time visitors.

Salizada Zorzi 4943. www.aitagliapietra.com. ℂ **347-3233166.** 4 units. 75€–100€ double. Rates include breakfast. *Vaporetto:* San Zaccaria (walk straight on Calle delle Rasse to Campo SS. Filippo e Giacomo; continue straight through the *campo* to Calle della Sacrestia, then take the first left; cross Salita Corte Rotta and continue on to Salizada Zorzi). **Amenities:** Wi-Fi (free).

B&B San Marco ★★★   With just three rooms, this exquisite B&B in a peaceful, residential neighborhood fills up fast, so book ahead. It's a comfortable, charming yet convenient option, the kind of place that makes you feel like a local, but not too far from the main sights. Your hosts are the bubbly Marco and Alice Scurati, who live in the attic upstairs, happy to provide help and advice. Rooms overlook the Scuola di San Giorgio degli Schiavoni and offer wonderful views of the canal and streetscapes nearby, and are furnished with original antique family furniture. Two rooms share a bathroom; the third has a private shower. Breakfast is self-service in the shared kitchen; yogurts, croissants, pastries, punchy espresso, cappuccino, juice, and tea.

Fondamenta San Giorgio dei Schiavoni 3385. www.realvenice.it. ℂ **041-5227589.** 3 units. 70€–125€ double. Rates include breakfast. *Vaporetto:* San Zaccaria (walk straight on Calle delle Rasse to Campo SS. Filippo e Giacomo; continue straight through the *campo* to Calle della Sacrestia, cross the canal and take a left at Campo S Provolo along Fondamenta Osmarin; turn left where the canal ends at a larger canal, and walk up to the bridge that connects to Calle Lion; at the end of the street turn left along the canal; this is Fondamenta San Giorgio dei Schiavoni). **Amenities:** Wi-Fi (free).

Dorsoduro
MODERATE

Galleria ★★   Just around the corner from the Accademia, right on the Grand Canal, this hotel occupies a 19th-century *palazzo* in one of the most inviting locations in the city. It's been a hotel since the 1800s, hosting poet Robert Browning in 1878, and maintains a Venetian 18th-century theme in the rooms, with wood furniture and rococo decor. Hosts Luciano and Stefano serve a simple breakfast in your room. Note that the smallest rooms here really are tiny, and there is no A/C (rooms are supplied with fans when it gets hot), but the fridge of free water and sodas is a lifesaver in summer.

Dorsoduro 878a (at foot of Accademia Bridge). www.hotelgalleria.it. ℂ **041-5232489.** 9 units, 6 with bathroom. 110€–220€ double. Rates include continental breakfast. *Vaporetto:* Accademia (with Accademia Bridge behind you, hotel is just to your left). **Amenities:** Babysitting; concierge; room service; Wi-Fi (free in public areas).

Moresco ★★★   An incredibly attentive staff, a decadent breakfast that includes prosecco (to mix with orange juice, ahem), and a lavish 19th-century Venetian decor away from the tourist hubbub make this a justly popular choice. Rooms seamlessly blend Venetian style with modern design. Some rooms have a terrace (with views over the canal or garden), while others have a spa bathtub; all have flatscreen TVs with satellite channels. If the weather cooperates, take breakfast in the courtyard garden to really soak up the ambience. The hotel is just a 5- to 10-minute walk from Piazzale Roma and the train station, but note that there are a number of bridges and stairs to negotiate along the way.

Fondamenta del Rio Novo 3499, Dorsoduro. www.hotelmorescovenice.com. ℰ **041-2440202.** 23 units. 165€–226€ double. Rates include continental buffet breakfast. *Vaporetto:* Ferrovia/Piazzale Roma (from the train station walk south west along Fondamenta Santa Lucia, cross Ponte della Costituzione and turn left onto Fondamenta Santa Chiara; cross Ponte Santa Chiara and turn right onto Fondamenta Papadopoli, continuing across Campiello Lavadori then along Fondamenta del Rio Novo). **Amenities:** Bar; concierge; free trips to Murano; room service; Wi-Fi (free).

Pensione Accademia ★★ This spellbinding hotel with a tranquil blossom-filled garden has a fascinating history. The Gothic-style Villa Maravege was built in the 17th century as a family residence, but served as the Russian Embassy between World Wars I and II before becoming a hotel in 1950. If that's not enticing enough, the rooms are fitted with Venetian-style antique reproductions, classical hardwood furnishings, handsome tapestries, and A/C, with views over either the Rio San Trovaso or the gardens. Breakfast is served in your room, in the dining hall, or on the garden patio.

Fondamenta Bollani 1058. www.pensioneaccademia.it. ℰ **041-5210188.** 27 units. 140€–300€ double. Rates include buffet breakfast. *Vaporetto:* Accademia (turn right down Calle Gambara, which doglegs 1st left and then right; it becomes Calle Corfu, which ends at a side canal; walk left to cross over the bridge, and then turn right back toward the Grand Canal and the hotel). **Amenities:** Bar; babysitting; concierge; room service; Wi-Fi (free).

San Polo

MODERATE

Ca' Barba B&B ★★ What you'll remember most about Ca' Barba may well be the host, Alessandro, who will usually meet guests at the Rialto *vaporetto* stop; inspire daily wanderings with tips, maps, and books; and provide fresh breads and pastries from the local bakery for breakfast. Of the four rooms (advance reservations are essential), no. 201 is the largest and brightest, with a Jacuzzi tub (202 also has one). All rooms come with antique furniture, 19th-century paintings of Venice, wood-beamed ceilings, LCD TVs, air conditioning, and strong Wi-Fi.

Calle Campanile Castello 1825. www.cabarba.com. ℰ **041-5242816.** 4 units. 140€–180€ double. Rates include breakfast. *Vaporetto:* Rialto (walk back along the Grand Canal, and turn left when you reach Calle Campanile Castello). **Amenities:** Concierge; Wi-Fi (free).

Pensione Guerrato ★★★ Dating, incredibly, from 1227, it's definitely one of the city's most historic places to lay your head. The building's long and complicated history—it was once the "Inn of the Monkey," run by nuns, the original mostly destroyed by fire in 1513—is well worth delving into (the owners have all the details). Rooms are simply but classically furnished, with wood floors, exposed beams, air conditioning, and private bathrooms—some rooms still contain original frescos, possibly dating from the medieval inn. Note that some rooms are on the sixth floor—and there's no elevator.

Calle Drio La Scimia 240a (near the Rialto Market). www.pensioneguerrato.it. © **041-5227131.** 19 units. 100€–145€ double. Rates include buffet breakfast. Closed Dec 22–26 and Jan 8–early Feb. *Vaporetto:* Rialto (from the north side of the Ponte Rialto, walk straight through the market until the corner with the UniCredit Banca; go 1 more short block and turn right; the hotel is halfway along Calle Drio La Scimia). **Amenities:** Babysitting; concierge; Wi-Fi (free).

Santa Croce

MODERATE

Antiche Figure ★★★ The most convenient luxury hotel in Venice lies directly across the Grand Canal from the train station, a captivating 15th-century *palazzo* adjacent to an ancient gondola workshop (seriously). History aside, this is a very plush choice, with rooms decorated in a traditional neoclassical Venetian style, with gold leaf, antique furniture, red carpets, silk tapestries, and aging Murano glass and chandeliers, but also LCD satellite TVs and decent Wi-Fi. With the soothing nighttime views across the water it's certainly a romantic choice, and the staff is worth singling out—friendly and very helpful. There is an elevator, just in case you were wondering.

Fondamenta San Simeone Piccolo 687. www.hotelantichefigure.it. © **041-2759486.** 22 units. 105€–264€ double. Rates include buffet breakfast. *Vaporetto:* Ferrovia (from the train station you just need to cross the Scalzi bridge on your left and take a right). **Amenities:** Restaurant; bar; babysitting; concierge; room service; Wi-Fi (free).

INEXPENSIVE

Ai Due Fanali ★★ Originally a wooden oratory frequented by fishermen and farmers (later rebuilt), this beguiling hotel features small but artsy rooms, even for Venice: Headboards have been hand-painted by a local artist, exposed wood beams crisscross the ceiling, vintage drapes and curtains add a cozy feel, and work by 16th-century Mannerist painter Jacopo Palma the Younger adorns the public areas. The bathrooms are embellished with terracotta tiles and Carrera marble. The location is close to the train station, and the roof terrace is the best place to soak up a panorama of the city (breakfast is served up here). It's incredibly popular—book months ahead.

Campo San Simeon Profeta 946. www.aiduefanali.com. © **041-718490.** 16 units. 95€–125€ double. Rates include buffet breakfast. Closed most of Jan. *Vaporetto:* Ferrovia (cross the Scalzi bridge over the Grand Canal; once you are to the other side, continue straight, taking the 2nd left and keep walking to the Campo San Simeon Profeta). **Amenities:** Bar; concierge; room service; Wi-Fi (free).

Falier ★   This tranquil budget hotel is set in a quiet neighborhood, next to the Frari Church and just a 10-minute walk from the train station. Rooms are fairly compact (potentially cramped for some), but par for this price point in Venice, and all are air-conditioned. The elegant garden is a great place for the continental breakfast (you can also have it in the dining room), featuring warm croissants, cheese, a selection of yogurts and cereals, plus teas, coffee, and fruit juices. The hotel provides free entrance to the Venice casino and a free tour of a Murano glass factory, but the friendly English-speaking staff will also set you up with all manner of other tour options.

Salizada San Pantalon 130. www.hotelfalier.com. © **041-710882.** 19 units. 85€–160€ double. Rates include continental breakfast. *Vaporetto:* Ferrovia. (From the train station, cross the Scalzi Bridge, turn right along the Grand Canal an walk to the first footbridge; turn left before crossing the bridge and continue along the smaller canal to Fondamenta Minotti; turn left here, and the street becomes Salizada San Pantalon.) **Amenities:** Concierge; Wi-Fi (free).

Cannaregio
EXPENSIVE

Al Ponte Antico ★★★   Yes it's expensive, but this is one of the best, most exclusive hotels in Venice, steps from the Rialto Bridge, with a private wharf on the Grand Canal—forget those giant five-stars, to indulge your James Bond fantasy, look no further. Part of the attraction is size—there are only seven rooms—but the attention to lavish detail is astounding, with opulent rooms and bright, rococo wallpaper, rare tapestries, elegant beds, and Louis XV–style furnishings that make this place seem like Versailles on the water. The building was originally a 16th-century *palazzo;* don't miss the charming balcony where breakfast is served, and where fabulous Bellinis are offered in the evenings.

Calle dell'Aseo 5768. www.alponteantico.com. © **041-2411944.** 7 units. 240€–430€ double. *Vaporetto:* Rialto (walk up Calle Large Mazzini, take the 2nd left and then continue to walk through Campo San Bartolomio; continue north along Salizada S.G. Grisostomo until you see Calle dell'Aseo on the left). **Amenities:** Bar; concierge; room service; Wi-Fi (free).

Arcadia ★★★   This sensational, modestly advertised boutique set in a 17th-century *palazzo* has an appealing blend of old and new: The theme is Byzantium east-meets-west, combining elements of Venetian and Asian style, but the rooms are full of cool, modern touches—rainforest showers, A/C, flatscreen TVs, bathrobes, slippers, and posh toiletries, with a lobby crowned with a Murano glass chandelier. It's a 5-minute walk from the train station.

Rio Terà San Leonardo 1333, Cannaregio. www.hotelarcadia.net. © **041-717355.** 17 units. 130€–300€ double. Rates include continental buffet breakfast. *Vaporetto:* Guglie (take a left into the main street Rio Terà San Leonardo; Arcadia is just 30m [98 ft.] on the left). **Amenities:** Bar; concierge; room service; Wi-Fi (free).

INEXPENSIVE

Bernardi ★★   This hotel is an excellent deal, with small, basic but spotless rooms in a 16th-century *palazzo* (the superior rooms are bigger), owned and managed by the congenial (and English-speaking) Leonardo and his wife, Teresa. Most rooms come with one or two classical Venetian touches: Murano chandeliers, hand-painted furniture, exposed wood beams and tapestries. The shared showers are kept very clean (11 rooms have private bathrooms), and fans are provided in the hot summer months for the cheaper rooms (no A/C). Breakfast is very basic, however, and note that the more spacious annex rooms, which have air-conditioning (nearby the main building) don't appear to get good Wi-Fi coverage.

Calle de l'Oca 4366. www.hotelbernardi.com. ✆ **041-5227257.** 18 units, 11 with private bathroom. 60€–94€ double. Rates include breakfast. *Vaporetto:* Ca' d'Oro (walk straight to Strada Nova, turn right toward Campo SS. Apostoli; in the square, turn left and take the 1st side street on your left, which is Calle de l'Oca). **Amenities:** Concierge; room service; Wi-Fi (free).

San Geremia ★   An excellent budget option just 10 minutes from the train station. Rooms are small and simple but adequate, with most featuring air-conditioning and views across the canal or *campo*. Note that there is no elevator (some rooms are up 3 flights of stairs), and breakfast is not provided (but you get 50% off breakfast next door). There are no TVs in the rooms but there is strong Wi-Fi. The dorm rooms are a good deal at just 21€ to 25€ per night (for guests under 35 only). Cash only.

Campo San Geremia 283. www.hotelsangeremia.com. ✆ **041-715562.** 20 units, 14 with private bathroom. 46€–100€ double. Closed the week of Christmas. *Vaporetto:* Ferrovia (exit the train station, turn left onto Lista di Spagna, and continue to Campo San Geremia). **Amenities:** Babysitting; concierge; room service; Wi-Fi (free).

WHERE TO EAT

Eating cheaply in Venice is not easy, though it's by no means impossible. The city's reputation for mass-produced menus, bad service, and wildly overpriced food is, sadly, well warranted, and if you've been traveling in other parts of the country, you may be a little disappointed here. Having said that, everything is relative—this is still Italy after all—and there are plenty of excellent options in Venice (see below). As a basic rule, value for money tends to increase the further you travel from Piazza San Marco, and anything described as a *menù turistico,* while cheaper than a la carte, is rarely any good in Venice (exceptions noted below). Note also that compared with Rome and other points south, Venice is a city of early meals: You should be seated by 7:30 to 8:30pm. Most kitchens close at 10 or 10:30pm, even though the restaurant may stay open until 11:30pm or midnight.

While most restaurants in Italy include a cover charge (*coperto*) that usually runs 1.50€ to 3€, in Venice they tend to instead tack on 10% to 12% to the bill for "taxes and service." Some places in Venice will very annoyingly charge you the cover and still add on 12%. A menu should state clearly what extras the restaurant charges (sometimes you'll find it in miniscule print at the bottom) and if it doesn't, take your business elsewhere.

San Marco

EXPENSIVE

Bistrot de Venise ★★★ VENETIAN   Though it looks a bit like a wood-paneled French bistro, the menu here is primarily old-school Venetian, specializing in rare wines and historical recipes from the 14th to 18th centuries. It's gimmicky, but it works; think old-fashioned fennel soup, an incredible shrimp pie, and cod fillet with almonds in a light ginger and saffron sauce, served with wild berries and garlic pudding. The "historical" tasting menu is a splurge, but we recommend it as the best introduction. Whatever you opt for, expect service to be top-notch.

4685 Calle dei Fabbri. www.bistrotdevenise.com. © **041-5236651.** Main courses 26€–34€; classic Venetian tasting menu 65€; historical 5-course Venetian menu 95€. Daily: bar 10am–midnight, restaurant noon–3pm and 7pm–midnight. *Vaporetto:* Rialto (turn right along canal, cross small footbridge over Rio San Salvador, turn left onto Calle Bembo, which becomes Calle dei Fabbri; Bistrot is about 5 blocks ahead).

Da Fiore ★★ TRATTORIA/VENETIAN   Classy but laid-back Venetian trattoria (not to be confused with the posher *osteria* with the same name). The menu features typical Venetian dishes like squid ink pasta, but the specials here are the most fun, with *moeche* (local soft shell crab) a particular treat (the two main seasons are Mar–Apr and Oct–Nov). Desserts are another specialty, with all sorts of sugary *golosessi* on offer, from *buranelli* to *zaletti* (cornmeal cookies, typically eaten dipped in sweet wine or chocolate), and an exceptional *sgroppino al limone* (lemon sherbet). Make sure you visit the associated bar and *cicchetteria* next door, the **Bacaro di Fiore** (Wed–Mon 9am–10pm), which has been around since 1871, serving cheap wine and snacks like fried fish, fried vegetables (zucchini, pumpkin flowers, and artichokes), and crostini with creamed cod.

Calle delle Botteghe 3461, off Campo Santo Stefano. www.dafiore.it. © **041-5235310.** Main courses 16€–28€. Wed–Mon noon–3pm and 7–10pm. Closed 2 weeks in Jan and 2 weeks in Aug. *Vaporetto:* Accademia (cross bridge to San Marco side and walk straight ahead to Campo Santo Stefano; as you are about to exit the *campo* at northern end, take a left onto Calle delle Botteghe; also close to Sant'Angelo *vaporetto* stop).

MODERATE

Rosticceria San Bartolomeo ★★ DELI/VENETIAN   Also known as Rosticceria Gislon, this no-frills spot has a cheap canteen section popular with locals and a more expensive upstairs sit-down dining room, but don't be fooled by appearances—the downstairs section is just as good, with a range of grilled fish and seafood pastas on offer (lots of scampi, clams, and mussels), a tasty "mozzarella in carrozza" (fried cheese sandwich; 1.70€), and there is a discount if you order to take out. Otherwise just sit at the counter and soak up the animated scene, as the cooks chop, customers

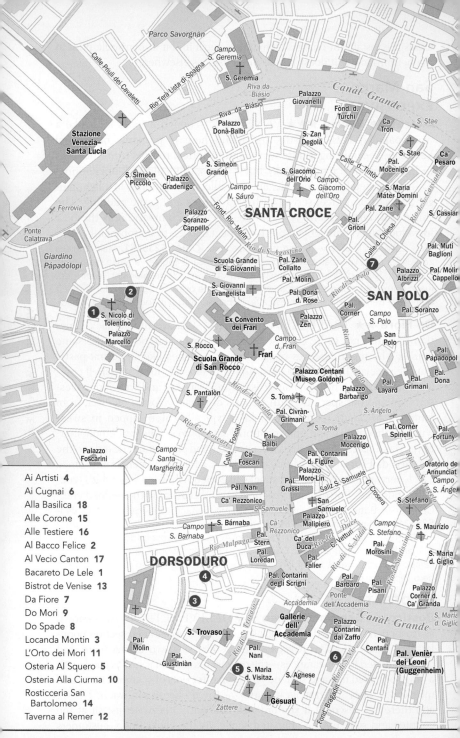

Venice Restaurants

CANNAREGIO

Pal. Giovanelli

S. Felice

Pal. Fontana

Ca' d'Oro

Pal. Sagredo

S. Sofia

Ss. Apóstoli

Pal. Widman

Pal. Brandolin

Pescaria

Pal. Mangilli

Ca' da Mosto

Pal. Falier

S. Canciano

C. larga G. Gallina

Pal. Grifalconi

Ospedale Civile

S. Maria d. Pianto

Fábbriche Nuove

S. Maria d. Miracoli

Pal. Soranzo-Van Axel

Ss. Giovanni e Paolo (S. Zanipolo)

S. Giovanni Crisostomo

Teatro Málibran

Pal. Pisani

Pal. Dieci Savi

Fóndaco d. Tedeschi

Pal. Cavazza-Foscari

Campo S. Marina

Palazzo Ruzzini

Pal. Donà

Pal. Cavignis

Pal. Morosini

Pal. Muazzo

S. Aponàl

S. Silvestro

Riva del Vin

S. Lio

Campo S. Maria Formosa

Pal. Donà

Palazzo Cappello

S. Lorenzo

S. Bartolomeo

Palazzo Dolfin-Manin

S. Maria della Fava

S. Maria Formosa

Questura

Riva del Carbon

Pal. Bembo

M. S. Salvador

Pal. Tasca Papafáva

Pal. Querini Stampalia

CASTELLO

Palazzo Grimani

Ca' Farsetti

S. Salvador

Palazzo Soranzo

Pal. Priuli

Pal. Zorzi

S. Luca

S. Zulián

Palazzo Trevisan-Cappello

S. Giovanni Novo

S. Giorgio dei Greci

Cinema Rossini

Campo Manin

Palazzo Contarini d. Bovolo

C. Frubera

C. Canonica

S. Zaccaria

Mandola

Ateneo Véneto

S. Gallo

Mercerie Orologio

Torre d. Orologio

Convento

La Pietà

Teatro La Fenice

S. Fantin

Pisc. di Frezzeria

Frezzeria

Campanile

Basilica di San Marco

Palazzo Ducale (Doge's Palace)

Pal. d. Prigioni

S. Zaccaria

C. Larga XXII Marzo

S. Moisè

S.S. Moise

Museo Corrèr

Piazza San Marco

Molo

Riva d. Schiavoni

Ponte d. Sospiri (Bridge of Sighs)

Palazzi Contarini

Palazzo Tiépolo

Palazzo Treves d. Bonfili

Giardini ex Reali

Capo di Porto

S. Marco

Pal. Gritti

Pal. Genovese

Salute

Dogana da Mar

Punta d. Dogana

Bacino di San Marco

S. Maria d. Salute

Seminario Patriárcale

Ex Ospizio

0 ___ 1/8 mi
0 ___ 200 m

S. Giorgio Maggiore

Isola di S. Giorgio Maggiore

chat, and people come and go. Order the roast chicken, salt cod, or polenta—typical Venetian fare without all those extra charges.

Calle della Bissa 5424. ✆ **041-5223569.** Main courses 10€–22€. Daily 9:30am–9:30pm (Mon until 3:30pm). *Vaporetto:* Rialto (with bridge at your back on San Marco side of canal, walk straight to Campo San Bartolomeo; take underpass slightly to your left marked sottoportego della bissa; the *rosticceria* is at the 1st corner on your right; look for gislon above the entrance).

Castello

EXPENSIVE

Alle Corone ★★★ SEAFOOD/VENETIAN   One of Venice's finest restaurants, an elegant 19th-century dining room located inside the Hotel Ai Reali and overlooking the canal. Start with a selection of classic Venetian cicchetti (21€) before moving on to gnocchi with squid and wild asparagus (19€) or main courses such as baked turbot with black olives, seared tuna with poppy seeds, or roast rack of lamb with thyme, potatoes, and artichokes. To finish, the rosemary panna cotta with apple and ginger jam is spectacular (9€). Reservations recommended.

Campo della Fava 5527 (Hotel Ai Reali). www.hotelaireali.com. ✆ **041-2410253.** Main courses 28€–32€. Daily noon–2:30pm and 7–10:30pm. *Vaporetto:* Rialto (walk east along Calle Larga Mazzini, turn left Merceria then right on Calle Stella until you reach the hotel).

Alle Testiere ★★★ ITALIAN/VENETIAN   This tiny restaurant (with only nine tables, seating for around 22), is the connoisseur's choice for fresh fish and seafood, with a menu that changes daily and a shrewd selection of wines. Dinner is served at two seatings (reservations are essential), where you choose from appetizers such as scallops with cherry tomatoes and orange, and clams that seem to have been literally plucked straight from the sea. The John Dory fillet with aromatic herbs is always an exceptional main choice, but the pastas—ravioli with eggplant and pesto, or the ricotta with prawns—are all superb. Finish off with home-made peach pie or chestnut pudding. In peak season, plan to make reservations at least 1 month in advance, and note that you'll have a less rushed experience in the second seating.

Calle del Mondo Novo 5801 (off Salizada San Lio). www.osterialletestiere.it. ✆ **041-5227220.** Main courses 26€, but many types of fish sold by weight. Tues–Sat noon–3pm and 2 seatings at 7 and 9:30pm. *Vaporetto:* Equidistant from either the Rialto or San Marco stops. Look for store-lined Salizada San Lio (west of the Campo Santa Maria Formosa), and from there ask for the Calle del Mondo Novo.

MODERATE

Al Vecio Canton ★ ITALIAN/PIZZA   Venice is not known for pizza, partly because fire codes restrict the use of traditional wood-burning ovens, but the big, fluffy-crusted pies here—made using natural mineral water—are the best in the city. They also do a mean T-bone steak, cooked tableside on a granite slab, accompanied by truffle or red pepper sauce, and some of the pastas are pretty good, too—stick with seafood versions like cuttlefish,

BACARI & CICCHETTI

One of the essential culinary experiences of Venice is trawling the countless neighborhood bars known as **bacari,** where you can stand or sit with *tramezzini* (small, triangular white-bread half-sandwiches filled with everything from thinly sliced meats and tuna salad to cheeses and vegetables), and **cicchetti** (tapaslike finger foods, such as calamari rings, speared fried olives, potato croquettes, or grilled polenta squares), traditionally washed down with a small glass of wine, Veneto prosecco or spritz (a fluorescent cocktail of prosecco and orange-flavored Aperol). All of the above will cost approximately 1.50€ to 6€ if you stand at the bar, as much as double when seated. Bar food is displayed on the countertop or in glass counters and usually sells out by late afternoon, so though it can make a great lunch, don't rely on it for a light dinner. A concentration of popular, well-stocked bars can be found along the **Mercerie** shopping strip that connects Piazza San Marco with the Rialto Bridge, the always lively **Campo San Luca** (look for Bar Torino, Bar Black Jack, or the character-filled Leon Bianco wine bar), and **Campo Santa Margherita**.

and the seasonal *moeche* (soft-shell crabs fried in batter) and *schie,* small gray shrimp caught in the lagoon. Wash it all down with the drinkable house wine, or for a change, tasty craft beers from Treviso-based 32 Via dei Birrai. Castello 4738a (at the corner of Calle Ruga Giuffa). www.alveciocanton.it. $\mathcal{C}$ **041-5287143.** Main courses 13€–20€. Wed–Mon 11:30am–3pm and 6–10:30pm. *Vaporetto:* San Zaccaria (head down the road that flanks the left side of the Hotel Savoia e Jolanda to Campo San Provolo; take Salizada San Provolo on the north side of the *campo,* cross the 1st footbridge on your left, and the pizzeria is on the 1st corner on the left).

INEXPENSIVE

Alla Basilica ★★ VENETIAN   Considering this restaurant is just around the corner from the Doge's Palace and St. Mark's, lunch here is a phenomenally good deal. Don't expect romance—it's a large, noisy, canteenlike place—but the simple, freshly prepared meals comprise a pasta course like creamy lasagna or *spaghetti con ragu,* a meat or fish main (think grilled pork chops or *dentice al vapore con zucchini grigliate,* steamed red snapper with grilled zucchini), and mixed vegetables for just 14€, with bread and bottled water. Add a liter of extremely drinkable house wine for just 10€. Basilica is a favorite of local workers and English is rarely spoken, so you'll need to practice your Italian skills here. Calle degli Albanesi 4255, Castello. www.allabasilicavenezia.it. $\mathcal{C}$ **041-5220524.** Lunch set menu 14€. Tues–Sun noon–3pm. *Vaporetto:* San Marco (as you disembark, the entrance to Calle degli Albanesi is a short walk to the left).

Dorsoduro
EXPENSIVE

Ai Artisti ★★★ VENETIAN   This unpretentious, family-owned *osteria* and *enoteca* is one of the best dining experiences in Venice, with a menu that changes daily according to what's available at the market (because the fish market is closed on Monday, no fish is served that day). Grab a table by the canal and feast on stuffed squid, pan-fried sardines, and an amazing, buttery veal *scallopini,* or opt for one of the truly wonderful pastas. The tiramisu and chocolate torte are standouts for dessert. Something that's likely to stay with you in addition to the food is the impeccable service; servers are happy to guide you through the menu, and offer brilliant suggestions for wine pairing. Reservations recommended—it's a tiny place, with seating for just 20.

Fondamenta della Toletta 1169A. ✆ **041-5238944.** Main courses 22€–30€. Mon–Sat noon–4pm and 7–10pm. *Vaporetto:* Accademia (walk around Accademia and turn right onto Calle Gambara; when this street ends at Rio di San Trovaso, turn left onto Fondamenta Priuli; take the 1st bridge over the canal and onto a road that soon leads into Fondamenta della Toletta).

Locanda Montin ★★ VENETIAN   Montin was the famous ex-hangout of Peggy Guggenheim in the 1950s, and was frequented by Jimmy Carter, Robert De Niro, and Brad Pitt, among many other celebrities, but is the food any good? Well, yes. Grab a table in the wonderfully serene back garden (completely covered by an arching trellis), itself a good reason to visit, and sample Venetian classics such as sardines in "soar" (a local marinade of vinegar, wine, onion, and raisins), and an exquisite *seppie in nero* (cuttlefish cooked in its ink). For a main course, it's hard to beat the crispy sea bass *(branzino)* or legendary monkfish, while the lemon sorbet with vodka is a perfect, tangy conclusion to any meal.

Seafood, a Venice specialty.

Fondamenta di Borgo 1147. www.locandamontin.com. ✆ **041-5227151.** Main courses 22€–30€. Daily 12:30–2:30pm and 5pm–midnight. *Vaporetto:* Ca'Rezzonico (walk straight along Calle Lunga San Barnaba for around 1,000 ft., then turn left along Fondamenta di Borgo).

MODERATE

Ai Cugnai ★★ VENETIAN The name of this small trattoria means "at the in-laws," and in that spirit the kitchen knocks out solid, home-cooked Venetian food, beautifully prepared and very popular with locals and hungry gondoliers. The classics are done especially well: The *spaghetti vongole* here is crammed with sea-fresh mussels and clams, the *caprese* and baby octopus salad perfectly balanced appetizers, and the house red wine is a top value. Our favorite, though, is the sublime spaghetti with scallops, a slippery, salty delight. There are just two small tables outside, so get here early if you want to eat alfresco. Calle Nuova Sant'Agnese 857. © **041-5289238.** Main courses 13€–25€. Tues–Sun noon–3:30pm and 7–10pm. *Vaporetto:* Accademia (head east of bridge and Accademia in direction of Guggenheim Collection; restaurant will be on your right, off the straight street connecting the 2 museums).

INEXPENSIVE

Osteria Al Squero ★★★ WINE BAR/VENETIAN   Enticing *osteria* with perhaps the most beguiling view in Venice, right opposite the Squero di San Trovaso (p. 385). Sip coffee and nibble *cicchetti* (from around 1.20€), while observing the activity at this medieval gondola boatyard and workshop, on the other side of the Rio di San Trovaso. It's essentially a place for a light lunch or *aperitivi* rather than a full meal, snacking on delights such as Carnia smoked sausage, baccalà crostini (cod), anchovies, blue cheese, tuna, and sardines in saor for a total of around 15€ per person. House wine from 1.50€.

Fondamenta Nani 943–944. © **335-6007513.** *Cicchetti* 1.20€ per piece. Tues–Sun 7am–8pm. *Vaporetto:* Zattere (walk west along the waterside to the Rio di San Trovaso and turn right up Fondamenta Nani).

San Polo

MODERATE

Do Spade ★ VENETIAN   It's tough to find something so authentic and local this close to the Rialto Bridge these days, but Do Spade has been around since 1415. Most locals come here for the *cicchetti* (you can sit on benches outside if it's too crowded indoors), typical Venetian small plates such as fried calamari, meatballs, mozzarella, salted cod (1–3€), and decent wines (3€ a glass). The more formal restaurant section is also worth a try, with seafood highlights including a delicately prepared monkfish, scallops served with fresh zucchini, and rich seafood lasagna, though the seasonal pumpkin ravioli is one of the best dishes in the city.

Sottoportego do Spade 860. www.cantinadospade.com © **041-5210574.** Main courses 14€–22€. Daily 10am–3pm and 6–10pm. *Vaporetto:* Rialto Mercato (with your back to Grand Canal, walk straight up Ruga Vecchia San Giovanni and turn right on Ruga dei Spezieri; at the end turn left on Calle de le Beccarie O Panataria, and then take 2nd right onto covered Sottoportego do Spade).

INEXPENSIVE

Do Mori ★★★ WINE BAR/VENETIAN   Serving good wine and *cicchetti* since 1462 (check out the antique copper pots hanging from the ceiling), Do Mori is above all a fun place to have a genuine Venetian experience, a small, dimly lit *bàcari* that can barely accommodate ten people standing up. Sample the baby octopus and ham on mango, lard-smothered *crostini,* and pickled onions speared with salty anchovies, or opt for the *tramezzini* (tiny sandwiches). Local TV (and BBC) star Francesco Da Mosto is a regular, but note that this institution is very much

EATING cheaply IN VENICE

You don't have to eat in a fancy restaurant to enjoy good food in Venice. Prepare a picnic, and while you eat alfresco, you can observe the life in the city's *campi* or the aquatic parade on its main thoroughfare, the Grand Canal.

Mercato Rialto

Venice's principal open-air market has two parts, beginning with the produce section, whose many stalls, alternating with those of souvenir vendors, unfold north on the San Polo side of the Rialto Bridge. The vendors are here Monday to Saturday 7am to 1pm, with some staying on in the afternoon. Behind these stalls are a few permanent food stores that sell delicious cheese, cold cuts, and bread selections. At the market's farthest point, you'll find the covered **fish market,** still redolent of the days when it was one of the Mediterranean's great fish bazaars. The fish merchants take Monday off and work mornings only.

Campo Santa Margherita

On this spacious *campo* in Dorsoduro, Tuesday through Saturday from 8:30am to 1pm, a number of open-air stalls set up shop, selling fresh fruit and vegetables. There's also a conventional supermarket, **Punto SMA,** just off the *campo* in the direction of the quasi-adjacent *campo* San Barnaba, at no. 3019.

San Barnaba

This is where you'll find Venice's heavily photographed **floating market** (mostly fruit and vegetables) operating from a boat moored just off San Barnaba at the Ponte dei Pugni in Dorsoduro. This market is open daily from 8am to 1pm and 3:30 to 7:30pm, except Wednesday afternoon and Sunday.

The Best Picnic Spots

Given its aquatic roots, you won't find much in the way of green space in Venice (if you are desperate for green, walk 30 min. past San Marco along the water, or take a *vaporetto,* to the **Giardini Pubblici,** Venice's only green park, but don't expect anything great). A much more enjoyable alternative is to find some of the larger *campi* that have park benches, such as Campo San Giacomo dell'Orio (in the quiet *sestiere* of Santa Croce). The two most central are **Campo Santa Margherita** (*sestiere* of Dorsoduro) and **Campo San Polo** (*sestiere* of San Polo).

For a picnic with a view, scout out the **Punta della Dogana (Customs House)** near La Salute Church in Dorsoduro for a prime viewing site at the mouth of the Grand Canal. Pull up on a piece of the embankment here and watch the flutter of water activity against a canvaslike backdrop deserving of the Accademia Museum. In this same area, another superb spot is the small **Campo San Vio** near the Guggenheim, which is directly on the Grand Canal (not many *campi* are) and even boasts two benches as well as the possibility to sit on an untrafficked small bridge.

To go a bit farther afield, you can take the *vaporetto* out to Burano and then no. 9 for the 5-minute ride to the near-deserted island of **Torcello.** If you bring a basketful of bread, cheese, and wine you can do your best to reenact the romantic scene between Katharine Hepburn and Rossano Brazzi from the 1955 film *Summertime.*

on the well-trodden tourist trail—plenty of *cicchetti* tours stop by in the early evening. Local wine runs around 3€ to 4€ per glass.

Calle Do Mori 429 (also Calle Galeazza 401). ✆ **041-5225401.** *Tramezzini* and *cicchetti* 1.80€–3€ per piece. Mon–Sat 8am–8pm (June–Aug closed daily 2–4:30pm). *Vaporetto:* Rialto Mercato (with your back to Grand Canal, walk straight up Ruga Vecchia San Giovanni and turn right on Calle Galeazza).

Osteria Alla Ciurma ★★★ WINE BAR/VENETIAN   With a dining room decked out like a traditional Venetian boat, this *cicchetteria* offers some of the freshest seafood snacks in the city, washed down with quality wines, Spritz and prosecco—they source their fresh fish from the daily market, just around the corner. Mouth-watering *cicchetti* include cod fillets, fried zucchini flowers, fried artichokes and shrimp wrapped in bacon. More substantial sandwiches (from 3.50€) and lunch specials (noon–3pm) from 5€ are also available.

Calle Galeazza 406. www.osteriaciurma.it. ℂ **340-6863561.** *Cicchetti* 1.50€–2€ per piece. Mon–Sat 9am–3pm and 5:30–9pm; Sun 10:30am–3pm (May–Sep only). *Vaporetto:* Rialto Mercato (with your back to Grand Canal, walk straight up Ruga Vecchia San Giovanni and turn right on Calle Galeazza).

Santa Croce
MODERATE

Al Bacco Felice ★ ITALIAN   This quaint, friendly neighborhood restaurant is convenient for the train station and popular with locals, with a real buzz most evenings. Stick with the basics and you won't be disappointed—the pizzas, pastas, and fish dishes are always outstanding, with classic standbys *spaghetti alle vongole,* pasta with spicy *arrabbiata,* and *carpaccio* of swordfish especially well done. The meal usually ends with complimentary plates of Venetian cookies, a nice touch.

Santa Croce 197E (on Corte dei Amai). ℂ **041-5287794.** Main courses 15€–30€. Mon–Fri noon–3:30pm and 6:30–11pm, Sat and Sun noon–11:30pm. *Vaporetto:* Piazzale Roma (you can walk here in 10 min. from the train station; from the Piazzale Roma *vaporetto* stop keep the Grand Canal on your left and head toward the train station; cross the small canal at the end of the park and immediately turn right onto Fondamenta Tolentini; when you get to Campo Tolentini turn left onto Corte dei Amai).

INEXPENSIVE

Bacareto Da Lele ★★★ WINE BAR/VENETIAN   This tiny hole-in-the-wall *bacaro* is worth seeking out for its fresh snacks, sandwiches and *cicchetti.* Tiny glasses or *'ombras'* of wine and prosecco are just 0.60€–1€)—there are no seats, so do as the locals do and grab a space on the nearby church steps, outside by the canal, while you sip and nibble. Opt for a tiny porchetta and mustard or the bacon and artichoke panini (around 1€–2€), antipasti plates for 1.20€ (cheese and salami) or a simple, freshly baked crostini for 1€–1.60€. Expect long lines here in peak season—the secret is definitely out.

Campo dei Tolentini 183. No phone. *Cicchetti* 1€–2€ per piece. Mon–Fri 6am–8pm, Sat 6am–2pm. *Vaporetto:* Piazzale Roma (walk left along the Grand Canal, past the Ponte della Costituzione, into the Giardino Papadopoli; turn right along Fonadmenta Papadopoli then turn left and cut across the park at the 1st bridge; the next canal you hit should be the Rio del Tolentini, with the campo across the bridge and Bacareto Da Lele on the southwest corner).

Cannaregio

EXPENSIVE

L'Orto dei Mori ★★ VENETIAN   Traditional Venetian cuisine is cooked up by a young Sicilian chef, so expect some subtle differences to the usual flavors and dishes. Everything on the relatively small menu is exceptional—the *baccalà* (salted cod) especially so—and the setting next to a small canal is enhanced by candlelight at night. This place can get very busy—the waiters are normally friendly, but be warned, expect brusque treatment if you turn up late or early for a reservation. Don't be confused: The restaurant prefers to serve dinner, broadly, within two seatings, one early (7–9pm) and one late, so that's why waiters will be reluctant to serve those that arrive early for the second sitting—even if there's a table available, you'll be given water and just told to wait.

Campo dei Mori 3386. www.osteriaortodeimori.com. ✆ **041-5243677.** Main courses 19€–25€. Wed–Mon 12:30–3:30pm and 7pm–midnight, usually in 2 seatings (July–Aug closed for lunch Mon–Fri). *Vaporetto:* Madonna dell'Orto (walk through the *campo* to the canal and turn right; take the 1st bridge to your left, walk down the street and turn left at the canal onto Fondamenta dei Mori; go straight until you hit Campo dei Mori).

INEXPENSIVE

Taverna al Remer ★★ VENETIAN   Eating on a budget in Venice doesn't always mean panini and pizza slices. This romantic *taverna* overlooks the Grand Canal from a small, charming piazza, and while the a la carte options can be pricey, the secret is to time your visit for the buffets. The 20€ lunch is a fabulous deal, with a choice of two fresh pastas plus a buffet of antipasto which includes seasonal vegetables, salads, cold cuts, a choice of two or three quality hot dishes (such as Venice-style liver with polenta, or pan-fried squid), a choice of two or three desserts, and coffee, water, and quarter liter of wine (per person), all included. The evening *aperitivo* is an even better deal, from just 7€ for as much smoked meats, sausage, salads, seafood risotto and pasta as you can eat, plus one Aperol spritz, bellini, vino, or prosecco. Normal service resumes after the buffet is cleared (main courses 16–25€), with live music (Latin, soul, jazz) most nights at 8:30pm, but as long as you order a few drinks it's fine to stick around and take in the scene.

Cannaregio 5701 (off Salizada S. Giovanni Grisostomo). www.alremer.it. ✆ **041-5228789.** Lunch buffet 20€; aperitivo (5:30–7:30pm) from 7€. Mon, Tues, and Thurs–Sat noon–2:30pm and 5:30pm–midnight; Sun 5:30pm–midnight. *Vaporetto:* Ca' d'Oro or Rialto; (heading south on Salizada S. Giovanni Grisostomo, look for a narrow passage on the right, just beyond the Ponte S. Giovanni footbridge).

Gelato

Is the gelato any good in Venice? Italians might demur, but by international standards, the answer is most definitely yes. As always, though, remember that gelato parlors aimed exclusively at tourists are notorious for poor quality and extortionate prices, especially in Venice. Try to avoid places near Piazza San Marco altogether. Below are two of our favorite spots in the city. Each generally opens midmorning and closes late. Winter hours are more erratic.

Il Doge ★★ GELATO   Definite contender for best gelato in Venice, with a great location at the southern end of the *campo* since 1986. These guys use only natural, homemade flavors and ingredients, from their exceptional spicy chocolate to their specialty, "Crema de Doge," a rich concoction of eggs, cream, and real oranges. Look for refreshing *granitas* in summer.
Campo Santa Margherita 3058, Dorsoduro. ✆ **041-5234607.** Cones and cups from 1.50€–5.50€. *Vaporetto:* Ca'Rezzonico.

La Mela Verde ★★ GELATO   The popular rival to Il Doge for best scoop in the city, with sharp flavors and all the classics done sensationally well: pistachio, chocolate, *nocciola* and the mind-blowing lemon and basil. The overall champions: *mela verde* (green apple), like creamy, frozen fruit served in a cup, and the addictive tiramisu flavor.
Fondamenta de L'Osmarin, Castello 4977. ✆ **349-1957924.** Cones or cups from 1.50€. *Vaporetto:* Zaccaria.

SHOPPING

In a city that for centuries has thrived almost exclusively on tourism, remember this: **Where you buy cheap, you get cheap.** Venetians, centuries-old merchants, aren't known for bargaining. You'll stand a better chance of getting a good deal if you pay in cash or buy more than one item. In our limited space below, we've listed some of the more reputable places to stock up on classic Venetian items.

Shopping Streets & Markets

A mix of low-end trinket stores and middle-market-to-upscale boutiques line the narrow zigzagging **Mercerie** running north between Piazza San Marco and the Rialto Bridge. More expensive clothing and gift boutiques make for great window-shopping on **Calle Larga XXII Marzo,** the wide street that begins west of Piazza San Marco and wends its way to the expansive Campo Santo Stefano near the Accademia. The narrow **Frezzeria,** just west of Piazza San Marco and running north-south, offers a grab bag of bars, souvenir shops, and tony clothing stores like Louis Vuitton and Versace. There are few bargains to be had; the non-produce part of the **Rialto Market** is as good as it gets for basic souvenirs, where you'll find cheap T-shirts, glow-in-the-dark plastic gondolas, and tawdry glass trinkets. The **Mercatino dei Miracoli** (✆ **041-2710022**), held only six times a year in Campo Santa Maria Nova (Cannaregio), is a fabulous flea market with all sorts of bric-a-brac and antiques sold by ordinary Venetians—haggling, for once, is acceptable. It usually takes place on the second Saturday or Sunday of March, April, May, September, October, and December, from 8:30am to 8pm. The **Mercatino dell'Antiquariato** (www.mercatinocamposanmaurizio.it) is a professional antiques market in Campo San Maurizio, San Marco;

it takes place 4 to 5 times a year (usually Mar–Apr, May, Sept, Oct, and Dec; check the website for dates).

Arts & Crafts

Venice is uniquely famous for local crafts that have been produced here for centuries and are hard to get elsewhere: the **glassware** from Murano, the **delicate lace** from Burano, and the *cartapesta* **(papier-mâché) Carnevale masks** you'll find in endless *botteghe* (shops), where you can watch artisans paint amid their wares.

Art glass for sale at Venini.

Now here's the bad news: There's such an overwhelming sea of cheap glass gewgaws that buying Venetian glass can become something of a turnoff (shipping and insurance costs make most things unaffordable; the alternative is to hand-carry anything fragile). There are so few women left on Burano willing to spend countless tedious hours keeping alive the art of lace-making that the few pieces you'll see not produced by machine in China are sold at stratospheric prices; ditto the truly high-quality glass (although trinkets can be cheap and fun). The best place to buy glass is Murano itself—the **"Vetro Artistico Murano"** trademark guarantees its origin, but expect to pay as much as 60€ for just a wine glass.

Atelier Segalin di Daniela Ghezzo ★★   Founded in 1932 by master cobbler Antonio Segalin and his son Rolando, this old leather shoe store is now run by Daniela Ghezzo (the star apprentice of Rolando), maker of exuberant handmade shoes and boots, from basic flats to crazy footwear designed for Carnevale (shoes from 650€–1,800€). It's open Monday to Friday 10am to 1pm and 3pm to 7pm, and Saturday 10am to 1pm. Calle dei Fuseri 4365, San Marco. www.danielaghezzo.it. ✆ **041-5222115.** Vaporetto: San Marco.

Il Canovaccio ★   Remember the creepy orgy scenes in Stanley Kubrick's film *Eyes Wide Shut*? The ornate masks used in the movie were made by the owners of this vaunted store. All manner of traditional, feathered, and animal masks are knocked out of their on-site workshop. It's open daily 10am to 7:30pm. Calle delle Bande 5369 (near Campo Santa Maria Formosa), Castello. www.ilcanovaccio.com. ✆ **041-5210393.** Vaporetto: San Zaccaria.

Il Grifone ★★★   Toni Peressin's handmade leather briefcases, satchels, bound notebooks, belts, and soft-leather purses have garnered quite a following, and justly so—his craftsmanship is truly magnificent (he makes everything in the workshop out back). Items start at around 15€.

It's usually open Tuesday to Friday 9am to 12:30pm and 4 to 7:30pm, and Saturday 10am to noon. Fondamenta del Gaffaro 3516, Dorsoduro. www.ilgrifo nevenezia.it. ⓒ 041-5229452. Vaporetto: Piazzale Roma

La Bottega dei Mascareri ★★   High-quality, creative masks—some based on Tiepolo paintings—crafted by the brothers Sergio and Massimo Boldrin since 1984. Basic masks start at around 15€ to 20€, but you'll pay over 75€ for a more innovative piece. The original branch lies at the foot of the Rialto Bridge (San Polo 80; ⓒ **041-5223857**). Both locations tend to open daily 9am to 6pm. Calle dei Saoneri 2720, San Polo. www.mascarer.com. ⓒ **041-5242887.** Vaporetto: Rialto.

Marco Polo International ★   This vast showroom, just west of the Piazza San Marco, displays quality glass direct from Murano (although it's more expensive than going to the island yourself), including plenty of easy-to-carry items such as paperweights and small dishes. It opens daily 10am to 7pm. Frezzeria 1644, San Marco. www.marcopolointernational.it. ⓒ **041-5229295.** Vaporetto: San Marco.

Venini ★   Convenient, classy, but incredibly expensive, Venini has been selling quality glass art since 1921, supplying the likes of Versace and many other designer brands. Their **workshop** on Murano is at Fondamenta Vetrai 50 (ⓒ **041-2737211**). Both locations tend to open Monday to Saturday 9:30am to 5:30pm. Piazzetta Leoncini 314, San Marco. www. venini.it. ⓒ **041-5224045.** Vaporetto: San Marco.

Making a Carnevale mask.

ENTERTAINMENT & NIGHTLIFE

If you're looking for serious nocturnal action, you're in the wrong town—Verona and Padua are far more lively. Your best bet is to sit in the moonlit Piazza San Marco and listen to the cafes' outdoor orchestras, with the illuminated basilica before you—the perfect opera set—though this pleasure comes with a hefty price tag. Other popular spots to hang out include **Campo San Bartolomeo,** at the foot of the Rialto Bridge (although it is a zoo here in high season), and nearby **Campo San Luca.** In late-night hours, for low prices and low pretension, the absolute best place to go is **Campo Santa Margherita,** a huge open *campo* about halfway between the train station and the Accademia bridge.

Visit one of the tourist information centers for current English-language schedules of the month's special events. The monthly *Ospite di Venezia* is distributed free or online at **www.unospitedivenezia.it** and is extremely helpful but usually available only in the more expensive hotels.

Performing Arts & Live Music

Venice has a long and rich tradition of classical music, and there's always a concert going on somewhere; this was, after all, the home of Vivaldi. People dressed in period costumes stand around in heavily trafficked spots near San Marco and Rialto passing out brochures advertising classical music concerts, so you'll have no trouble finding up-to-date information.

Santa Maria della Pietà ★★   The so-called "Vivaldi Church," built between 1745 and 1760, holds concerts throughout the year; check the website for specific dates. Lauded ensemble **I Virtuosi Italiani** gives a concert series here every September. Tickets are usually around 25€. Riva degli Schiavoni 3701, Castello. www.chiesavivaldi.it. ℭ **041-5221120.** Vaporetto: San Zaccaria.

Teatro La Fenice ★★★   One of Italy's most famous opera houses (it officially ranks third after La Scala in Milan and San Carlo in Naples), La Fenice opened in 1836, but was rebuilt after a devastating fire and reopened in 2003. The opera season runs late November through June, but there are also ballet performances and classical concerts. Tickets are expensive for the major productions; around 70€ for the gallery, and 110€ to 220€ for a decent seat. Those on a budget can opt for obstructed-view seats (25€) or listening-only seats (15€). Campo San Fantin 1965, San Marco. www.teatrolafenice.it. ℭ **041-2424.** Vaporetto: Giglio.

Cafes

For tourists and locals alike, Venetian nightlife mainly centers on the many cafes in one of the world's most remarkable *piazze:* Piazza San Marco. It is also the most expensive and touristed place to linger over a Spritz or anything else for that matter, but it's a splurge that should not be dismissed too readily.

Caffè dei Frari ★★★   Established in 1870, the walls of this inviting bar and cafe overlooking the Friari church are still adorned with the

Interior of Teatro La Fenice.

original Art Nouveau murals, an antique wooden bar, and a wrought-iron balcony upstairs. The seafood is especially good here, and there are usually at least three excellent German beers on tap. The laid-back owner doubles as DJ Friday and Saturday evenings (he's pretty good). Open Tuesday to Saturday 9am to 10pm, and Sunday and Monday 9am to 4pm. Fondamenta dei Frari 2564, San Polo. ⓒ **041-5241877.** Vaporetto: San Tomà.

Caffè Florian ★★ Occupying prime *piazza* real estate since 1720, this is one of the world's oldest coffee shops, with a florid interior of 18th-century mirrors, frescoes, and statuary. Sitting at a table expect to pay 9€ for a cappuccino, 18.50€ for a Bellini (prosecco and fresh peach nectar in season) and 12.50€ for a Spritz—add another 6€ if the orchestra plays (Mar–Nov). Standing or sitting at the bar is much cheaper (5€ for a cappuccino, 8.50€ for a Bellini and so on). Open Mon–Thurs 10am 9pm, Fri & Sat 9am 11pm, and Sun 9am 9pm. Piazza San Marco 56. www.caffeflorian.com. ⓒ **041-5205641.** Vaporetto: San Marco.

Caffè Lavena ★★ Said to be Wagner's favorite cafe (look for the plaque inside), and the hangout of fellow composer Franz Liszt, Lavena lies on the opposite side of the *piazza* to Florian and was founded just a few decades later in 1750. Expect the same high prices and surcharges here (a famous case saw seven tourists charged 100€ for four coffees and three liqueurs), though as with Florian, if you stand and drink at the bar you'll pay much less than sitting at a table (coffee is just 1€). Open daily 9:30am–midnight (closed Tues in winter). Piazza San Marco 133–134. www. lavena.it. ⓒ **041-5224070.** Vaporetto: San Marco.

Il Caffè (aka Caffe Rosso) ★★★ Established in the late 19th century, Il Caffè has a history almost as colorful as its clientele, a mixture of students, aging regulars, and lost tourists. This is an old-fashioned, no-nonsense Venetian cafe/bar, with reasonably priced drinks and 419 sandwiches, and plenty of seating on the *campo*. Open Monday to Saturday 7am to 1am. Campo Santa Margherita 2963, Dorsoduro. www.cafferosso.it. ✆ **041-5287998.** Vaporetto: Ca'Rezzonico.

Birreria, Wine & Cocktail Bars

Although Venice boasts an old and prominent university, dance clubs barely enjoy their 15 minutes of popularity before changing hands or closing down (some are open only in the summer months). Young Venetians tend to go to the Lido in summer or mainland Mestre. Evenings are better spent lingering over a late dinner, having a pint in a *birreria*, or nursing a glass of prosecco in one of Piazza San Marco's or Campo Santa Margherita's overpriced outdoor bars and cafes. (**Note:** Most bars are open Mon–Sat 8pm–midnight.)

Al Prosecco ★★   Get acquainted with all things bubbly at this smart *enoteca*, a specialist, as you'd expect, in Veneto prosecco. It features plenty of tasty *cichetti* to wash down the various brands, and a gorgeous terrace from which to observe the *campo* below. Drinks run 3€ to 5€. Open Monday to Saturday 10am to 10:30pm (closes at 8pm in winter; closed Aug and Jan). Campo San Giacomo da l'Orio 1503, Santa Croce. www.alprosecco.com. ✆ **041-5240222.** Vaporetto: San Stae.

Caffè Centrale ★★   Not really a cafe but a super hip bar and restaurant (with iPad menus), this spot is located within the 16th-century Palazzo Cocco Molin, just a short walk from Piazza San Marco. It's got an intriguing selection of local and foreign beers (5.50€–7.50€), and a huge cocktail list (10€–12€)—Spritz is 7.50€ (cover is an extra 5€ per person). Get a table by the canal or lounge on one of the super comfy leather sofas. Open daily 7pm to 1am. Piscina Frezzeria 1659, San Marco. www.caffecentralevenezia.com. ✆ **041-8876642.** Vaporetto: Vallaresso.

Harry's Bar ★   Possibly the most famous bar in Venice (and now a global chain), Harry's was established in 1931 by Giuseppe Cipriani and frequented by the likes of Ernest Hemingway, Charlie Chaplin, and Truman Capote. The Bellini was invented here in 1948 (along with *carpaccio* 2 years later), and you can sip the signature concoction of fresh peach juice and prosecco for a mere 16€. Go for the history but don't expect a five-star experience—most first-timers are surprised just how ordinary it looks inside. It also serves very expensive food, but just stick to the drinks. Open daily 10:30am to 11pm. Calle Vallaresso 1323, San Marco. www.harrysbarvenezia.com. ✆ **041-5285777.** Vaporetto: Vallaresso.

Margaret DuChamp ★★   This popular student and *fashionista* hangout has plenty of chairs on the *campo* for people-watching, cocktails, and a spritz or two (most cocktails just 5–7€). It also serves decent panini (7€) and *tramezzini* (2€ at the table, or 1.50€ at the bar) and has free Wi-Fi. Open Wednesday to Monday 9am to 2am. Campo Santa Margherita 3019, Dorsoduro. ✆ **041-5286255.** Vaporetto: Ca' Rezzonico.

Paradiso Perduto ★★ "Paradise Lost" is the most happening bar in this neighborhood, crammed with students most nights and featuring the occasional live music set (full concerts every Mon and every first Sun of the month), great *cichetti* (piled in mountains at the bar), and cheap(ish) wine. Some people come to dine on the tasty seafood, but it's usually too busy and noisy to enjoy a proper meal here—stick to the drinks and the snacks. Open Thursday to Monday noon to midnight (closed Tues–Wed). Fondamenta della Misericordia 2540, Cannaregio. www.ilparadiso perduto.com. ℂ **041-720581.** Vaporetto: Madonna dell'Orto.

DAY TRIPS FROM VENICE

If you only have 3 days or so, you will probably want to spend them in the center of Venice. However, if you are here for a week—or on your second visit to the city—head over to the mainland to see some of the old towns that lie within the historic Veneto region.

Padua ★★★

40km (25 miles) W of Venice

Tucked away within the ancient heart of **Padua** lies one of the greatest artistic treasures in all Italy, the precious Giotto frescoes of the **Cappella degli Scrovegni.** Although the city itself is not especially attractive (it was largely rebuilt after bombing during World War II), don't be put off by the urban sprawl that now surrounds it; central Padua is refreshingly bereft of tourist crowds, a workaday Veneto town with a large student population and a small but intriguing ensemble of historic sights.

ESSENTIALS

GETTING THERE The most efficient way to reach Padua is to take the **train** from Santa Lucia station. Trains depart every 10 to 20 minutes, and take 25 to 50 minutes depending on the class (tickets range from 4.05€–13€ one-way). The main station is a short walk north up Corso del Popolo from the Cappella degli Scrovegni and the old city.

VISITOR INFORMATION The **tourist office** at the train station is usually open Monday to Saturday 9am to 7pm, and Sunday 9:15am to 12:30pm (www.turismopadova.it; ℂ **049-8752027**), while the office in the old city at Piazzetta Pedrocchi (ℂ **049-8767927**) is open Monday to Saturday 9am to 1:30pm and 3 to 7pm.

EXPLORING PADUA

The one unmissable sight in Padua is the **Cappella degli Scrovegni ★★★** (www.cappelladegliscrovegni.it; ℂ **049-2010020;** daily 9am–7pm) at Piazza Eremitani, an outwardly unassuming chapel commissioned in 1303 by Enrico Scrovegni, a wealthy banker. Inside, however, the chapel is gloriously decorated with an astonishing cycle of frescoes completed by Florentine genius **Giotto** two years later. The frescoes depict the life of the Virgin Mary and the life of Jesus, culminating with the Ascension and Last Judgment. Seeing Giotto's powerful work in the flesh is spine-tingling; this is where he makes the decisive break with Byzantine art, taking the first important steps toward the realism and humanism that would characterize the Renaissance in Italy.

Entrance to the chapel is limited, involving groups of 25 visitors spending 15 minutes in a climate-controlled airlock, used to stabilize the temperature, before going inside for another 15 minutes. To visit the chapel you must **make a reservation at least 24 hours in advance.** You must arrive 45 minutes before the time on your ticket. Tickets cost 13€ (6€ for kids ages 6–17 and students under 27).

If you have time, try and take in Padua's other historic highlights. The vast **Palazzo della Ragione** on Piazza del Erbe (Tues–Sun Feb–Oct 9am–7pm, Nov–Jan 9am–6pm; 4€) is an architectural marvel, completed in 1219, and decorated by frescoes completed by Nicola Miretto in the 15th century. Pay a visit also to the **Basilica di Sant'Antonio** (www.basilicadel santo.org; ☎ **049-8225652;** daily Apr–Sept 6:20am–7pm, Oct–Mar 6:20am–7:45pm; free admission) on the Piazza del Santo, the stately resting place of **St. Anthony of Padua,** the Portuguese Franciscan best known as the patron saint of finding things or lost people. The exterior is a bizarre mix of Byzantine, Romanesque, and Gothic styles (largely completed in the 14th c.), while the interior is richly adorned with statuary and murals. Don't miss **Donatello**'s stupendous equestrian statue of the Venetian *condottiere* **Gattamelata** (Erasmo da Narni) in the piazza outside, raised in 1453 and the first large bronze sculpture of the Renaissance.

Ancient statues in Padua.

WHERE TO EAT

Padua offers plenty of places to eat, and you'll especially appreciate the overall drop in prices compared to Venice. It's hard to match the location of **Bar Nazionale ★★**, Piazza del Erbe 40 (Mon–Sat 9am–11:30pm), on the steps leading up to Palazzo della Ragione, though it's best for drinks and snacks (excellent *tramezzini*) rather than a full meal. For that, make for **Osteria dei Fabbri ★**, Via dei Fabbri 13, just off Piazza del Erbe (www.osteriadeifabbri.it; ☎ **049-650336;** Mon–Sat noon–3pm and 7–11pm), which cooks up cheap, tasty pasta dishes for under 10€.

Verona ★★
115km (71 miles) W of Venice

The affluent city of **Verona,** with its gorgeous red and peach-colored medieval buildings and Roman ruins, is one of Italy's major tourist draws, though its appeal owes more to **William Shakespeare** than real history. He immortalized the city in his (totally fictional) *Romeo and Juliet, The Two Gentlemen of Verona*, and partly, *The Taming of the Shrew*. Though it does attract its fair share of tourism, Verona is not Venice; this is a booming trading center, with vibrant science and technology sectors.

ESSENTIALS

GETTING THERE   The best way to reach Verona from Venice is by **train.** Direct services depart every 30 minutes and take anywhere from 1 hour and 10 minutes to 2 hours and 20 minutes, depending on the type of train you catch (tickets range from 8.60€–23€ one-way). From Verona station (Verona Porta Nuova), it's a 15-minute walk to the historic center.

VISITOR INFORMATION   The **tourist office** is off Piazza Bra at Via Degli Alpini 9 (www.tourism.verona.it; ☎ **045-8068680;** Mon–Sat 9am–7pm, Sun 10am–4pm); stop there for maps, hotel reservations, discount cards, and guided tour information.

EXPLORING VERONA

"Two households, both alike in dignity, in fair Verona . . ." So go the immortal opening lines of *Romeo and Juliet,* ensuring that the city has been a target for lovesick romantics ever since. Though Verona is crammed with genuine historic goodies, one of the most popular sites is the ersatz **Casa di Giulietta,** Via Cappello 23 (Mon 1:30–7:30pm, Tues–Sun 9am–7:30pm; 6€), a 14th-century house (with balcony, naturally), said to be the Capulets' home. In the courtyard, the chest of a bronze statue of Juliet has been polished to a gleaming sheen, thanks to a legend claiming that stroking her right breast brings good fortune. **Juliet's Wall,** at the entrance, is quite a spectacle, covered with the scribbles of star-crossed lovers; love letters placed here are taken down and, along with 5,000 letters annually, are answered by the Club di

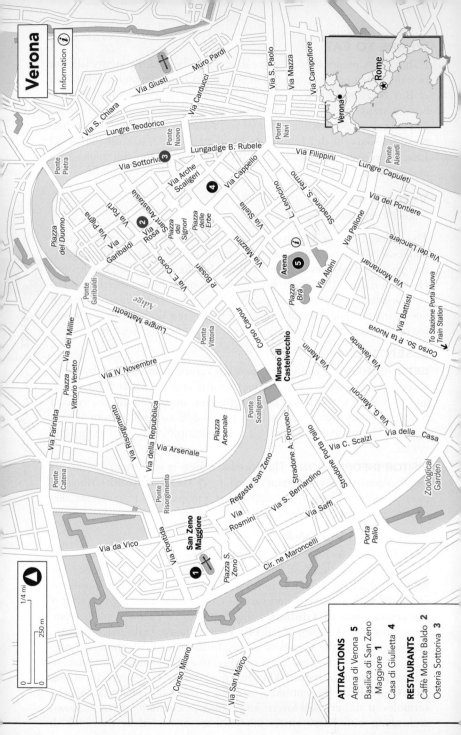

Verona

Information ⓘ

Rome

Verona ●

1/4 mi

250 m

Via Giusti

Muro Pardi

Via S. Chiara

Via Carducci

Lungre Teodorico

Via S. Paolo

Via Mazza

Via Campofiore

Ponte Nuovo

Lungadige B. Rubele

Ponte Navi

Via Sottoriva ❸

Via Arche Scaligeri

Via Cappello

Via Filippini

Lungre Capuleti

Ponte Aleardi

Ponte Pietra

Piazza del Duomo

Via Pigna

Via Forti

Sant'Anastasia

❷

Via Rosa

Piazza del Signori

Piazza delle Erbe

❹

Via Stella

Stradone S. Fermo

L. Leoncino

Via del Pontiere

Via Garibaldi

Via Mazzini

ⓘ

Via del Lanciere

Ponte Garibaldi

Via E. Corso

P. Bosari

Arena ❺

Piazza Brà

Via Alpini

Via Pallone

Via Montanari

Via Battisti

Adige

Lungre Matteotti

Ponte Vittoria

Corso Cavour

Via Manin

Via Valverde

To Stazione So. P.ta Nuova

Corso So. P.ta Nuova → Train Station

Piazza Vittorio Veneto

Via dei Mille

Via IV Novembre

Museo di Castelvecchio

Via G. Marconi

Via della   Casa

Via Farinata

Via Risorgimento

Via della Repubblica

Via Arsenale

Ponte Scaligero

Piazza Arsenale

Stradone Porta Palio

Via C. Scalzi

Ponte Catena

Ponte Risorgimento

Regaste San Zeno

Stradone A. Provolo

Via S. Bernardino

Via Saffi

Zoological Garden

Via da Vico

Via Pontida

San Zeno Maggiore ❶

Via Rosmini

Piazza S. Zeno

Cir. ne Maroncelli

Porta Palio

Corso Milano

Via San Marco

ATTRACTIONS

Arena di Verona **5**
Basilica di San Zeno
Maggiore **1**
Casa di Giulietta **4**

RESTAURANTS

Caffè Monte Baldo **2**
Osteria Sottoriva **3**

424

Piazza del Erbe in the center of Verona.

Giulietta (a group of locally based volunteers). There's not much to see inside the house.

Once you've made the obligatory Juliet pilgrimage, focus on some really amazing historic ruins. The 1st-century **Arena di Verona** (Roman Arena; Mon 1:30–7:30pm, Tues–Sun 9am–7:30pm; 6€), in the spacious Piazza Bra, is the third largest classical arena in Italy after Rome's Colosseum and the arena at Capua—it could seat some 25,000 spectators and still hosts performances today (see www.arena.it). To the northwest on Piazza San Zeno, the **Basilica di San Zeno Maggiore** (Mar–Oct Mon–Sat 8:30am–6pm, Sun 12:30–6pm; Nov–Feb Tues–Sat 10am–1pm and 1:30–5pm, Sun 12:30–5pm; 2.50€) is the greatest Romanesque church in northern Italy. The present structure was completed around 1135, over the 4th-century shrine to Verona's patron saint, St. Zeno (who died in 380). Its massive rose window represents the Wheel of Fortune, while the impressive lintels above the portal represent the months of the year. The highlight of the interior is "Madonna and Saints" above the altar, by Mantegna.

WHERE TO EAT

Even in chic Verona, you'll spend less on a meal than in Venice. The most authentic budget Verona restaurant is **Osteria Sottoriva,** Via Sottoriva 9 (☏ **045-8014323;** Thurs–Tues 11am–10:30pm), one of the most popular places in town for lunch or dinner; try the *trippa alla parmigiana* (braised tripe) or the hopelessly rich gorgonzola melted over polenta (main courses 8€–12€). The **Caffè Monte Baldo,** Via Rosa 12 (☏ **045-8030579**), is an old-fashioned cafe transformed into a trendy *osteria,* serving classic pastas and scrumptious *crostini* with wine in the evenings (many bottles from nearby vineyards).

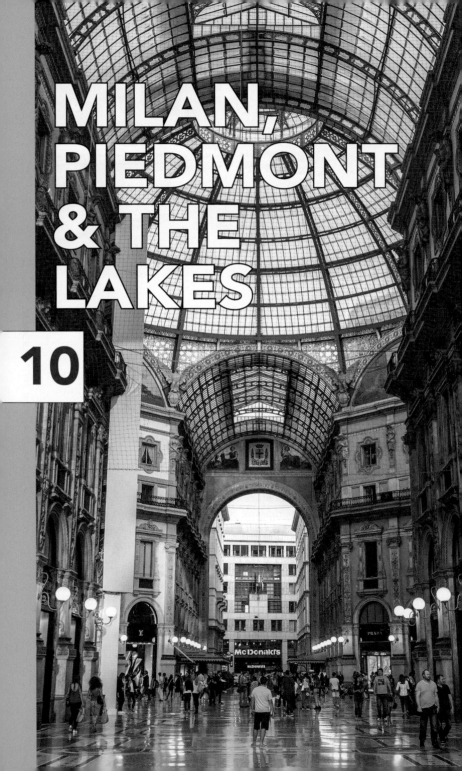

MILAN, PIEDMONT & THE LAKES

10

Lombardy and Piedmont are the powerhouses of northern Italy, thanks to the sprawling but charming cities of Milan and Turin, thriving on the industries that drive this region forward. Agriculture plays its part here also, from the rice fields of the fertile eastern Lombardy plains to the hilly vineyards and hazelnut groves of Piedmont. Then there's the beauty of the lake district between Milan and the Alps, which has been a source of inspiration for writers and artists over the centuries. Many of the lakes are within an hour or so of the city, making them a favorite destination for Milan city dwellers and tourists alike.

MILAN (MILANO) ★★★

552km (342 miles) NW of Rome, 288km (179 miles) NW of Florence, 257km (159 miles) W of Venice) 140km (87 miles) NE of Turin, 142km (88 miles) N of Genoa

Milan—or Milano, as the Italians say it—is elegant, chaotic, and utterly beguiling. Traffic chokes the streets, and it can be bitterly cold in winter and stiflingly hot in summer, yet its architecture is majestic and the robust Northern Italian cuisine warming. It's a world-class stop on the international fashion stage, the banking capital of Italy, a wealthy city of glamorous people and stylish shopping streets.

And Milan has history. As well as the Roman ruins, the soaring Duomo and its majestic piazza, the galleries are stuffed with priceless artworks, and there are ancient churches, medieval castles, Renaissance palaces, and amazing contemporary architecture to admire.

In 2015, Milan hosted the 6-month-long **Expo Milano 2015,** focused on the theme "Feeding the Planet. Energy for Life," in a suburban area northwest of the *centro storico*. Massive changes were made to the city in preparation, including a new cluster of buildings constructed in the CityLife district, featuring innovative towers by international archistars Arata Isozaki, Daniel Libeskind, and Zaha Hadid.

Essentials

GETTING THERE

BY PLANE   Both of Milan's major airports are operated by **SEA** (www.seamilano.eu; ✆ 02-232-323). **Milan Malpensa,** 45km (28 miles) northwest of the center, is Milan's major international airport. The **Malpensa Express** train (www.malpensaexpress.it; ✆ 02-7249-4949),

FACING PAGE: **Galleria Vittorio Emanuele II in Milan.**

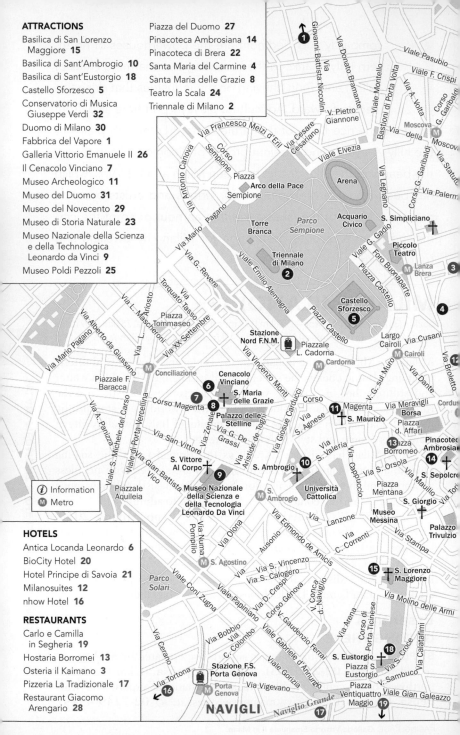

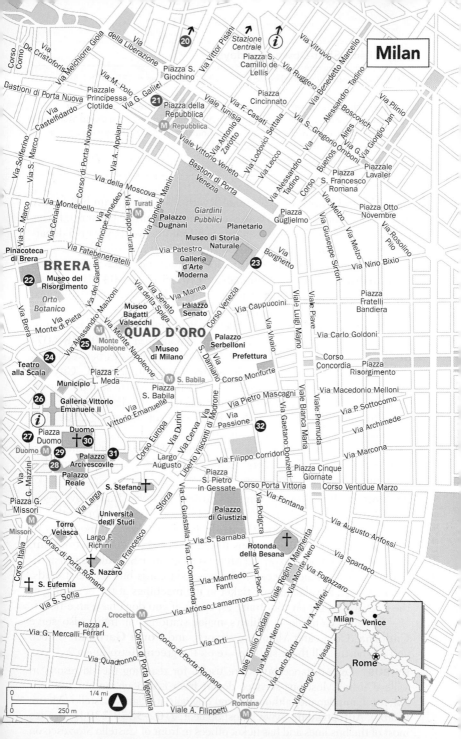

costs 12€ and leaves from Terminal 1 with a 30-minute run half-hourly to Cadorna train station, or hourly to Stazione Centrale (45 min). Buses also run directly to Stazione Centrale, a 50-minute journey, with 5 departures per hour, for 10€ per single journey or 16€ round-trip; they're operated by **Malpensa Shuttle** (www.malpensashuttle.it; ✆**02-5858-3185**) or **Autostradale** (www.autostradale.it; ✆ **02-5858-7304**). By taxi, the trip into town costs a wallet-stripping 90€ and takes about 50 minutes. It's the only option after midnight.

Milan Linate, 7km (4.5 miles) east of the center, handles European and domestic flights. **Air Bus** (www.atm-mi.it; ✆ **02-48-607-607**) makes the 25-minute trip by bus every 30 minutes between 6am and midnight from Linate to Milan's Stazione Centrale for 5€. City bus no. 73 leaves every 10 minutes for the San Babila Metro stop downtown (1.50€) and takes 25 minutes. The express no. X73 is faster and departs every 20 minutes between 7am and 8pm, with tickets costing 1.50€. The trip into town by taxi costs roughly 20€.

Malpensa Shuttle buses also connect Malpensa and Linate airports with five daily services between 9:30am and 6:20pm. The trip takes 90 minutes and costs 13€ (roundrip 26€).

BY TRAIN   Milan is one of Europe's busiest rail hubs. Trains travel every half-hour to Bergamo (1 hr.), Mantua (2 hr.), and Turin (1 hr. by the AV high-speed train). **Stazione Centrale** is a half-hour walk northeast of the center, with easy connections to Piazza del Duomo by Metro, tram, and bus. The station stop on the Metro is Centrale F.S. Multilingual automatic ticket machines accept cash and credit cards but *not* debit cards. You may need to validate your ticket in the machines at the beginning of the track as you get on your train, especially if you don't have an e-ticket.

Stazione Centrale is Milan's major station, but trains also serve **Cadorna** (Como and Malpensa airport), and **Porta Garibaldi** (Lecco and the north). All these stations are on the green Metro Linea 2.

BY BUS   Long-distance buses are useful for reaching the ski resorts in Valle d'Aosta. Most bus services depart from Lampugnano bus terminal (Metro: Lampugnano) although some originate in Piazza Castello (Metro: Cairoli). **Autostradale** (www.autostradale.it; ✆ **02-5858-7304**) operates most of the bus lines and has ticket offices in front of Castello Sforzesco on

Piazza Castello, open daily 9am to 6pm, and in front of the Duomo in Passageway 2 next to the TIM mobile phone store, open weekdays 8:30am to 6pm and weekends 9am to 4pm. **Savda** (www.savda.it; **0165-367-011**) runs five daily buses (more in the winter) between Milan Lampugnano and Aosta (2½ hr.; 17€) or Courmayeur (3½ hr.; 19.50€).

BY CAR The A1 autostrada links Milan with Florence (3 hr.) and Rome (6 hr.), while the A4 connects Milan with Verona (2 hr.) and Venice (2½ hr.) to the east and Turin (1 hr.) to the west.

GETTING AROUND

BY TRAIN Milan's most famous sights are within walking distance of each other, but the public transport system, an integrated system of **Metro, trams,** and **buses,** run by **ATM** (www.atm.it; ✆ **02-48-607-607**), is a cheap and effective alternative to walking. The Metro closes at midnight (Sat at 1am), but buses and trams run all night. Metro stations are well signposted; trains are speedy, clean, safe, and frequent—they run every couple of minutes during the day and about every 5 minutes after 9pm. Tickets for 90 minutes of travel on Metro, trams, or buses cost 1.50€. A 24-hour unlimited travel ticket is a better value at 4.50€ and a 2-day ticket goes for 8.25€. Tickets are available at newsstands and Metro stations (all machines have English-language options; the 24-hr. ticket option is listed under "Urban"). Stamp your ticket when you board a bus or tram—there is a 35€ fine (more if not paid on the spot) if you don't. For more information, visit the ATM information offices in the Duomo Metro, Stazione Centrale, and Cadorna, all open Monday to Saturday, 7:45am to 8pm.

Lines 1 (red, with stops at Cairoli for Castello Sforzesco and Duomo for Galleria Vittorio Emanuele II and the Duomo) and 3 (yellow, with a stop at Via Montenapoleone) are the most useful for sightseeing.

BY CAR Driving and parking in Milan are not experiences to relish. First of all, you'll have to pay the Area C congestion charge of 5€ to enter the *centro storico* Monday to Friday, 7:30am to 7:30pm. On top of that, the one-way system is complicated, some streets are reserved for public transport only, and there are many pedestrianized areas. Hotels will make parking arrangements for guests—take advantage of that.

BY TAXI Taxis are located in major *piazze* and by major Metro stops. There is a taxi stand in Piazza del Duomo and outside Castello Sforzesco; a journey between the two will cost around 7€. Hotel reception staff can call a taxi for you; otherwise, a reliable company is **Taxiblu** at ✆ **02-4040.** Meters start at 3.30€ and prices increase by 1.09€ per kilometer. Expect surcharges for waiting time, luggage, late-night travel, and Sunday journeys.

BY BIKE With the streets of the *centro storico* largely pedestrianized, Milan is a good city for cycling, with a handy bike-sharing program, **BikeMi.** The tariff for the pass is typically convoluted: For 2.50€ a day or 6€ a week, you can buy a pass that allows 30 minutes of free travel.

The next 2 hours are charged at 0.50€ per 30 minutes (or fraction of it) up until 2 hours, and thereafter your time is charged at 2€ per hour or fraction of it. Pick up one of the distinctive custard-yellow bikes at racks from outside Castello Sfozesco and the Duomo as well as at tram, bus, and metro stops. Buy your pass online (www.bikemi.com); at the **ATM Points** at Centrale, Cadorna, Garibaldi, and Duomo stations from 7:45am to 8pm; or by calling ✆ **02-48-607-607.**

ON FOOT The attractions of the *centro storico* are all accessible on foot. From Piazza del Duomo, Via Montenapoleone is a 10-minute walk through Piazza della Scala and along Via Manzoni, and it is a 10-minute walk to Castello Sforzesco. Santa Maria delle Grazie and "The Last Supper" are a 30-minute stroll from Piazza del Duomo.

VISITOR INFORMATION

The main **Azienda di Promozione Turistica (APT) tourist office** is in Galleria Vittorio Emanuele on the corner of Piazza della Scala (www.visitamilano.it; ✆ **02-8845-5555**). It's open Monday to Friday 9am to 7pm, Saturday 9am to 6pm, and Sunday 10am to 6pm. There is an office in **Stazione Centrale** (✆ **02-7740-4318**), after the police command station and track 21, open Monday to Friday 9am to 6pm and Saturday and Sun from 9am to 1:30pm and 2pm to 6pm.

CITY LAYOUT

Milan developed as a series of circles radiating out from the central hub, Piazza del Duomo. Within the inner circle are most of the churches, museums, and shops of the *centro storico*. **Parco Sempione** and Leonardo's "The Last Supper" are to the west in the well-heeled neighborhood of Magenta. The slightly grungy cafe-filled districts of **Porta Ticinese** and **Navigli** lie directly south, with genteel **Brera** and its classy stores and restaurants slightly to the north. The **Quadrilatero d'Oro (Golden Quadrilateral)** is the mecca of Milanese fashion shoppers and is northeast of the Duomo, although **Via Tortona** near the Navigli is quickly developing as a funky shopping option. A burgeoning new **financial district** is growing between Porta Garibaldi and Centrale stations, while the towers of **CityLife** have taken over the old fairgrounds area (the new fairgrounds are located in Rho).

Milano Discount Card

The **MilanoCard** (www.milanocard.it) offers a great deal on Milan sightseeing at just 6.50€ for 24 hours or 13€ for 3 days. You get a lot for your buck, including free travel on all public transportation, discounts in some stores and restaurants, and reduced entry to more than 20 museums and galleries. Each card is valid for one adult and a child under 10—a brilliant value for the money.

[FastFACTS] MILAN

ATMs/Banks Banks with multilingual ATMs are all over the city center. Opening hours are roughly Monday to Friday 8:30am to 1:30pm and 3 to 4pm, with major branches opening Saturday morning for a couple of hours. Central branches may also stay open through lunch.

Business Opening Hours
Most stores in central Milan are open Tuesday to Saturday, 9:30am to 7:30pm, with a half-day Monday (3:30–7:30pm). Most shops close on Sundays and some still close for lunch between 12:30pm and 3:30pm.

Consulates
U.S. Consulate is at Via Principe Amedeo 2/10 (✆ **02-290-351**), and is open Monday to Friday, 8:30am to noon for emergencies, otherwise by appointment (Metro: Turati). **Canadian Consulate** is at Piazza Cavour 3 (✆ 02-626-942-38); it's open Monday to Friday from 9am to 1pm. Appointment recommended. (Metro: Turati). **British Consulate** is at Via San Paolo 7 (✆ **02-723-001**), open Monday to Friday from 9am to 5pm. (Metro: Duomo). **Australian Consulate,** at Via Borgogna 2 (✆ **02-776-741**), is open from Monday to Thursday 9am to 5pm and on Fridays from 9am to 4:15pm (Metro: San Babila). **New Zealand Consulate** is at Via

Teraggio 17 (✆ **02-7217-0001**); office hours are Monday to Friday from 9am to 5pm (Metro: Cadorna).

Crime
For police emergencies, dial ✆ **112** (a free call). There is a police station in Stazione Centrale but the **Questura** is the main station, just west of the Giardini Pubblici at Via Fatebenefratelli 11 (✆ **02-62-261**; Metro: Turati).

Dentists
Excellence Dental Network at Via Mauro Macchi 38 near Stazione Centrale (www.excellencedentalnetwork.com; ✆ **02-7628-0498**) has English-speaking staff.

Doctors
Milan Medical Center at Via Angelo Mauri 3, near Cadorna station (www.milanmedicalcenter.it; ✆ **338-1651-324** for emergencies) has a multilingual staff.

Drugstores
Pharmacies rotate 24-hour shifts. Signs in most pharmacies post the schedule. The **Farmacia Stazione Centrale** (✆ **02-669-0735**) in Stazione Centrale is open 24 hours daily and the staff speaks English.

Emergencies
All emergency numbers are free. Call ✆ **112** for a **general emergency**; this connects to the **Carabinieri,** who will transfer your call as needed; for the **police,** dial ✆ **113;** for a

medical emergency or an ambulance, call ✆ **118;** for the **fire department,** call ✆ **115.**

Hospitals
The **Ospedale Maggiore Policlinico** (✆ **02-55-031**) is a 5-minute walk southeast of the Duomo at Via Francesco Sforza 35 (Metro: Duomo or Missori). Most of the medical personnel speak English.

Internet
The free **Open Wi-Fi Milano** network has hundreds of hotspots all over the city, with Internet access for phones, tablets, and laptops. In addition, many Milanese hotels, bars, and cafes offer free Wi-Fi. Throughout the city, branches of the **Arnold Coffee** (www.arnoldcoffee.it) American-style coffee bars offer free Wi-Fi.

Post Office
The main post office, **Poste e Telecommunicazioni,** is at Via Cordusio 4 (✆ **02-7248-2126;** Metro: Cordusio). It's open Monday to Friday 8am to 7pm and Saturday 8:30am to 1:50pm. The post office in Stazione Centrale is open Monday to Friday 8am to 5:30pm and Saturday from 8:15am to 3:30pm. Other branches are open Monday to Saturday 8:30am to 1:30pm.

Safety
Milan is generally safe, although public parks and the area around Stazione Centrale are best avoided at night.

Exploring Milan

Remember to dress modestly when visiting Milan's churches; no short shorts for either sex, women must have their shoulders covered, and skirts must be below the knee. The dress code at the Duomo is particularly strict.

Castello Sforzesco ★ MUSEUM Although it has lived many lives under several different occupiers and been restored many times, this fortified castle is the masterpiece of Milan's two most powerful medieval and Renaissance dynasties, the Visconti and the Sforza. The Visconti built the castle (and the Duomo) in the 14th century before the Sforzas married into their clan, eclipsed their power, and took their castle in the 1450s, turning it into one of the most gracious palaces of the Renaissance. Sforza *capo* Ludovico il Moro and his wife Beatrice d'Este also helped transform Milan into one of Italy's great centers of the Renaissance by commissioning works by Bramante, Michelangelo, and Leonardo da Vinci.

The castle's most recent restoration was at the hands of architect Luca Beltrami at the end of the 19th century; it opened as a museum in 1905. Today it contains a dozen museums and archives, known collectively as the Musei del Castello Sforzesco. Many of the Sforza treasures are on view in the miles of rooms that surround the castle's labyrinthine courtyards, stairways, and corridors. They include a *pinacoteca* with works by Bellini and Correggio plus Spanish Mannerists Ribera and Ricci. The extensive holdings of the Museo d'Arte Antica include the final work of 89-year-old Michelangelo; his evocative, unfinished "Pietà Rondanini" is found in the Sala degli Scarlioni.

On the second floor, the highlight of the decorative arts collection is the "Cassone del Tre Duchi," a chest commissioned by the Sforzas in 1494 and decorated with images of the dukes in full military regalia. The main attractions of the applied art galleries are the exquisite Trivulzio Tapestries by Bramantino in the Sala della Balla.

Piazza Castello. www.milanocastello.it. ✆ **02-8846-3700.** Castle courtyards: Free admission. Daily 7am–6pm (summer until 7pm). Musei del Castello Sforzesco: Admission 5€ (free Tues 2–5:30pm; Wed–Thurs and Sat–Sun 4:30–5:30pm). Tues–Sun 9am–5:30pm (last admission 30 min. before closing). Metro: Cairoli.

Duomo di Milano ★★★ CHURCH Although there has been a church here since at least A.D. 355, building started on the present exterior of Milan's magnificent Gothic Duomo in the late 14th century, to a design by Gian Galeazzo Visconti (1351–1402). Marble slabs for the facade were transported from quarries bordering Lake Maggiore into the city along the Navigli canals. It was consecrated in 1418, but the enormous dome wasn't added until the 16th century and the Duomo was not deemed complete until 1965, when the mammoth cast-bronze doors were finally finished.

Today the cathedral's facade has emerged sparkling from the scaffolding that had engulfed it since 2009 (although restoration work continues down its southern flank). Once again it dominates the vast, traffic-free

Aerial view of Milan.

Piazza del Duomo (see p. 439). Able to accommodate 40,000 people, it is one of the world's largest churches (St. Peter's in Rome, p. 75, takes the record), with an embellished triangular facade encrusted with flying buttresses plus around 2,300 statues and gargoyles. Pinnacles bristle on the domed roof, topped by a 5m (16-ft.) gilded figure of the Virgin Mary, known as **La Madonnina** and regarded as Milan's lucky mascot.

The interior of the Duomo is surprisingly subdued and serene, despite the hordes of tourists who pour in daily. The floors are of complex patterned marble reflecting patterns of sunlight as it streams through jewel-like stained-glass windows. Rows of 52 marble columns divide the space into five cavernous aisles, and the side chapels are dotted with Renaissance and Mannerist tombs.

In the crypt, the **Baptistero di San Giovanni alle Fonti** reveals the remains of the octagonal 4th-century foundations of the original church (ticket included in admission to the Museo del Duomo), which is almost certainly where Sant'Ambrogio, patron saint and Bishop of Milan in A.D. 374, christened the great missionary St. Augustine. Pride of place in the Treasury goes to the ornate **gilded tomb of Carlo Borromeo** (see p. 470), Archbishop of Milan and leader of the Counter-Reformation, who died in 1584.

Piazza del Duomo. www.duomomilano.it. ℂ **02-7202-2656.** Free admission. Daily 7am–7pm. Metro: Duomo.

Galleria Vittorio Emanuele II ★★ SHOPPING MALL   Milan's most elegant shopping arcade links the Piazza del Duomo with Piazza della Scala, site of the famous opera house. The gallery, which was spruced up during the preparations for Expo 2015, is entered through an enormous Neo-Classical triumphal archway leading to a shopping mall blessed with ornate marble flooring and a massive octagonal glass dome. Inside, the arcade is lined with genteel grand cafes such as Biffi and Il Savini, where

Take the trip up to the Duomo (www. duomomilano.it) roof for spine-tingling views across the rooftops of Milan and, on a clear day, to the Alps beyond. Elevators (12€) are found on the church's northeast corner, while stairs to the top (7€) are on the north flank. As well as the panorama, you can get up close to the Gothic pinnacles, saintly statues, and flying buttresses, as well as the spire-top gold statue of "**La Madonnina**" (the little Madonna), the city's beloved good-luck charm. The elevator is open daily 9am–6:30pm (last ticket sold at 6pm).

Other sneaky viewpoints over the Duomo include the food market on the top floor of classy department store **La Rinascente** (see p. 449) and the posh **Restaurant Giacomo Arengario** (see p. 448) at the **Museo del Novecento** (see p. 437). To look down on Parco Sempione and the crowds in the Triennale Design Museum, take the elevator up Torre Branca near the north end of the park (Viale Alemagna, open mid-May to mid Sept, hours vary).

the local elite gather to dine after a night at the opera. The designer stores here currently include Gucci, Versace, Prada, Louis Vuitton, and Swarovski.

Galleria Vittorio Emanuele II was the masterpiece of Bolognese architect Giuseppe Mengoni, who designed it in the 1870s to mark the unification of Italy under King Vittorio Emanuele II; note how the mosaic and fresco decorations incorporate patriotic symbols and coats of arms of various Italian cities. Unfortunately Mengoni never saw his magnus opus flourishing, as he died in a fall from scaffolding the day before it opened in 1878. Today giggling crowds gather under the soaring dome to spin around on one heel on the private parts of a little mosaic bull in the floor, a legendary good-luck ritual. At press time, the city was considering creating a panoramic terrace inside the galleria to offer visitors a birds-eye view of what is considered to be the "living room" of the Milanesi. Piazza del Duomo. Open 24 hours. Metro: Duomo.

Museo Archeologico ★★ MUSEUM Milan's beautifully curated archaeology museum is no dusty old relic but a vibrant, fascinating exhibition, a series of airy galleries housed among the cloisters, towers, and courtyards of the 8th-century convent of Monastero Maggiore of San Maurizio. Subdivided into eight themed exhibitions, including Ancient Milanese, Greek, and Etruscan displays, the museum is built around the remains of a villa and a section of the 4th-century Roman walls that once fortified Milan. Roman Milan was known as Mediolanum; this area of the city is particularly rich in ruins dating back to the time when it was capital of the Western Roman Empire. Most of the treasures exhibited were excavated locally.

The museum now incorporates a glimpse inside a third-century defense tower, with traces of medieval frescoes on its rounded walls; these portray Jesus showing his stigmata to St. Francis. Highlights of the collections include the 1st-century B.C. **mosaic pavement** unearthed nearby in 1913; the stunning, gleaming 4th-century **Trivulzio Diattreta Cup,** made of the finest hand-blown glass; and the busts of various emperors from Caesar onwards.

Corso Magenta 15. www.comune.milano.it. © **02-8844-5208.** Admission 5€ adults, 3€ reduced-price admission. Free Tues after 2pm. Tues–Sun 9am–5:30pm. Metro: Cadorna.

Museo del Duomo ★★★ MUSEUM   The new jewel in the crown of Milan's museums opened in November 2013 on the ground floor of the Palazzo Reale. Enter on the left of the courtyard, to the right of the Duomo as you look at the facade. Incredible treasures from the Duomo are displayed here in an imaginatively curated exhibition, leading visitors on a chronological journey through the life of both Milan and its cathedral. Highlights among the carved cherubs, angels, and Renaissance Madonnas include a room full of startling gargoyles, ethereal 15th-century stained-glass works, scale wooden models of the cathedral, and the original supporting structure of **"La Madonnina"** (see p. 435), who has adorned the Duomo rooftop since 1774. Perhaps the standout piece is **"Jesus and the Moneylenders"** by Tintoretto, rediscovered by happy accident in the Duomo sacristy after World War II.

Piazza del Duomo 12. http://museo.duomomilano.it. © **02-7202-2656.** Admission 6€, 4€ under 26 and seniors. Tues–Sun 10am–6pm. Metro: Duomo.

Museo del Novecento ★ MUSEUM   Opened in 2010, the futuristic building of the city's museum of 20th-century art forms a modern wing of the Palazzo Reale. You reach it via a circular concrete passageway, which winds up to the museum entrance on the third floor. The undisputed star of the collection is Giuseppe Pellizza da Volpedo's painting **"The Fourth Estate"** (1901), which is free for all to admire in the passageway outside the museum. Otherwise the collection showcases Italian modern art from Futurist to Arte Povera, making the case that Italy's contribution to the world of art did not halt with the Renaissance. There are some brilliant bursts of genius in the exhibition, such as the magnificent **"Philosopher's Troubles"** (1926) by Giorgio de Chirico and the moving **"Thirst"** (1934) by sculptor Arturo Martini, so stick with it. Temporary exhibitions in the Palazzo Reale are accessible by the exit from the museum, but be warned, the signage is confusing.

Palazzo dell'Argenario, Piazza del Duomo 12. www.museodelnovecento.org. © **02-7634-0809.** Admission 10€ adults, 8€ students and seniors. Mon 2:30–7:30pm, Tues–Sun 9:30am–7:30pm (Thurs, Sat until 10:30pm). Metro: Duomo.

Museo Nazionale della Scienza e della Tecnologica Leonardo da Vinci ★★ MUSEUM   This cavernous monolith's main building is constructed around the twin courtyards and three floors of the former monastery of San Vittore Olivetan, plus three modern additions and outdoor spaces. While recent renovations have made the exhibits more interactive and fun, the floor plan is still immensely confusing, and it's a big museum; pick up a brochure so you don't miss the highlights. These include a clutch of Leonardo's anatomical drawings and not-so-batty designs for flying machines on the top floor, a display of 20th-century technology that will shock teenagers for how rudimentary it is, and a mini-submarine ride (book in advance: ✆ **02-4855-5330**; Tues and Thurs after 1:30pm; 10€). The Air and Water Building has lots of full-size airplanes and boats to explore; there's a railway track full of locomotives, and interactive labs for kids to play around with basic experiments.

Via San Vittore 21. www.museoscienza.org. ✆ **02-485-551.** Admission 10€ adults, 7.50€ under 25, 4.50€ seniors. Guided tour of activities in English 65€ for 1 hour. Tues–Sun 9:30am–5pm. Metro: Sant'Ambrogio.

Museo Poldi Pezzoli ★★ ART GALLERY   This wonderfully eclectic art collection was the life's work of aristocrat Gian Giacomo Poldi Pezzoli, who donated his lifetime's investment in artwork and decorative arts to the city of Milan in 1879; it is now elegantly displayed in his luxurious former *palazzo*. The ornate rooms of the ground floor feature Oriental rugs, weapons, ancient armor, and rare books. Up the carved marble stairs the riches continue, through extravagant rooms hung with family portraits, displaying hand-blown Murano glass and dainty Limoges china. Scenes from *The Divine Comedy* are featured in stained glass, and fine gilded pistols sit side by side with precious jewelry.

The stars of this wonderful show are the intricate **Armillary Sphere,** crafted by Flemish clockmaker Gualterus Arsenius in 1568 to illustrate contemporary theories of planetary movement, and the **Renaissance paintings** by Botticelli and Piero della Francesca in the Golden Room. And still the collection grows: Recent acquisitions include a set of gold-and-ivory netsuke and a curiously intimate set of lacy bonnets for babies dating from the 18th century.

Via Manzoni 12. www.museopoldipezzoli.it. ✆ **02-794-889.** Admission 10€ adults; 7€ seniors and students 11–18; free under 10. Audioguides 5€. Wed–Mon 10am–6pm, closed Tues. Metro: Montenapoleone.

cruising **THE CANALS**

Take Metro Line 2 to Porta Genova to explore Milan's Navigli area (*navigli* means canals), the perfect spot for a relaxed drink, people-watching, and a late-night supper. Crowded and full of life, these few streets are refreshingly casual in ambience after the dressy obsession of the city center—it's one of the few places in Milan where you will see punks, hippies, and Goths, or find vintage stores.

Building started in the late 13th century on the Navigli canals, designed initially to transport marble slabs from quarries along Lake Maggiore (see p. 467) into the city to build the Duomo. The Naviglio Grande was Europe's first major canal and is one of the great engineering marvels of the medieval era. Used to import food, commodities, and trade goods, the canals were crucial to Milan's infrastructure until the 1970s, when road transport won out and several waterways were filled in. Take a boat tour of the canals to peek into Milan's industrial heritage; **Navigli Lombardi** (www.naviglilombardi.it; ✆ **02-6679131**) runs daily tours.

Milan's Piazza del Duomo.

Piazza del Duomo ★★ PIAZZA
The Piazza del Duomo has been the beating heart of Milan since the city was settled by the Romans in 220 B.C. and known as Mediolanum. This vast traffic-free piazza sees local life passing to and fro daily, added to by the bustle of tourists peering up at the majestic Duomo while dodging pigeons and street sellers pushing cheap souvenirs. From here a tangle of narrow streets branch off in all directions through the city's *centro storico* (historic center). The square took on its present form following the Unification of Italy in 1861, when the medieval buildings were replaced by splendid neoclassical buildings designed by Giuseppe Mengoni (1829–1877), also architect of the **Galleria Vittorio Emanuele II** (see p. 435) and the sculptor of the equestrian statue of Vittorio Emanuele II in the middle of the square.

The piazza is home to the superb **Museo del Duomo** (see p. 437), temporary art exhibitions in the **Palazzo Reale** (www.comune.milano. it; ✆ **02-0202**), and the 20th-century Italian art in the **Museo del Novecento** (see p. 439).
Metro: Duomo.

Pinacoteca Ambrosiana ★★ ART GALLERY   Founded in 1609 to display the private collections of the pious Cardinal of Milan Federico Borromeo, this gallery is housed in the world's second-oldest public library (after the Bodleian in Oxford, U.K.). While the emphasis is on Italian art from the 15th to early 20th centuries, some Dutch work is also exhibited.

Despite the confusing layout encompassing courtyards, passageways, stairwells, and any number of tiny exhibition rooms, the gallery is well worth visiting for four outstanding works of art: the fine portrait of **"The Musician"** by Leonardo da Vinci (1490); the cartoon for **"The School of Athens"** by Raphael (1510); Caravaggio's cute **"Basket with Fruit,"** painted around 1599; and Titian's **"Adoration of the Magi"** (ca. 1550).

Leonardo's original "Codex Atlanticus" is in the Biblioteca Ambrosiana next door along with other rare manuscripts; drawings from the "Codex" can be seen in the Sacristy of Bramante in Santa Maria della Grazie.
Piazza Pio XI. www.ambrosiana.eu. ✆ **02-806-921.** Admission to pinacoteca and sacristy 20€ adults, 15€ children 13 and under. Pinacoteca only 10€. Tues–Sun 10am–6pm. Metro: Duomo or Cordusio.

10

MILAN, PIEDMONT & THE LAKES

Milan (Milano)

MILAN'S time-travel CHURCHES

Milan has been an important center of Christianity since Emperor Constantine sanctioned the faith in A.D. 313. There are more than 100 churches in Milan and, like the Duomo, many of them lie on pagan foundations. In these, layer upon layer of history can be stripped back to their early remains.

Two such churches are on Corso di Porta Ticinese. **The Basilica di San Lorenzo Maggiore** was built in the 4th century, using rubble removed from the amphitheater nearby, at the same time as the 16 Corinthian columns standing outside. The church now has a 16th-century facade, but inside, fragments of the original building survive: The octagonal, white-washed Cappella di Sant'Aquilino retains pieces of the 4th-century gold mosaic that once covered all the walls, and to the right of this stairs lead down to the foundations of the first basilica.

A step further along Corso di Porta Ticinese, the **Basilica di Sant'Eustorgio** has undergone many facelifts. The foundations of the original 4th-century

church are behind the altar in the basilica, although the present Neo-Romanesque facade dates from 1865. The ornate Cappella Portinari dates from the 15th century, built as a memorial to St. Peter.

In Piazza Sant'Ambrogio you'll find the sublime Lombard Romanesque **Basilica di Sant'Ambrogio.** Built over a Roman cemetery, the church was extensively remodeled from the 8th to 11th centuries, and it is here that the remains of Milan's patron saint, Ambrogio, are housed. The glittering mosaics in the apse and wall frescoes in the side chapels show scenes from the life of the saint, and a great gold altar constructed in the 9th century holds his remains.

The Baroque church of **Santa Maria del Carmine** in Brera was built over the remains of a Romanesque basilica and partly remodeled in 1400; most of its present incarnation dates from 1447. The Gothic-Lombard facade was added in 1880, making the church a true mishmash of styles.

Pinacoteca di Brera ★★★ ART GALLERY   Milan's, and indeed Lombardy's, premier art collection resides over an art school in a 17th-century Jesuit college, wrapped around a two-story arcaded courtyard. This peerless collection romps in a circular tour through Italian art from medieval to Surrealism in 38 roughly chronological rooms. Along the way there are splendid Renaissance altarpieces, Venetian School and Baroque paintings, gloomy Mannerist works, and, thanks to recent donations, the odd piece by Picasso and Umberto Boccioni to enjoy.

Although the collection is not immense, it is of exquisite quality; just some of the breathtaking highlights include Piero della Francesca's sublime **Montefeltro Altarpiece** (1474); the ethereal **"Cristo Morto"** by Andrea Mantegna (1480); Caravaggio's superb, if mournful, 17th-century **"Supper at Emmaus"** (1601); and Raphael's **"Marriage of the Virgin"** (1504), which was beautifully restored in the glass-walled, temperature-controlled restoration rooms that are open to the public.

Of the secular work in the gallery, standout pieces include Francesco Hayez's **"The Kiss"** (1859) and artist Giovanni Fattori's pastoral scenes, which lead the way for the Macchiaioli School of Italian Impressionists from the late 19th century. Bringing the collection all the more up to date are donations including a clutch of works by Italian playboy artist Amedeo Modigliani and the sculptor Marino Marini.

Via Brera 28. www.brera.beniculturali.it. ✆ **02-722-632-64.** Admission 10€ adults, 7€ seniors and students under 18. Audioguide 5€. Tues–Sun 8:30am–7:15pm. Metro: Lanza.

Santa Maria delle Grazie ★★ CHURCH The delightful Lombard Renaissance church of Santa Maria delle Grazie is often ignored in the mad scramble to see Leonardo da Vinci's world-renowned "Last Supper" in the *cenacolo* (refectory) of the Dominican convent attached to the church. Started in 1465–1482 by Gothic architect Guiniforte Solari (ca. 1429–1481), the church was subsequently enlarged when the Sforza duke Ludovico il Moro (see p. 434) decided to make it his family mausoleum. He commissioned Leonardo da Vinci to paint the "Last Supper," and asked Donato Bramante, the leading light of the Lombard Renaissance who also had a hand in the design of St Peter's in Rome, to add the terracotta-and-cream arcaded apse in 1492. Inside the church itself, a clash of styles is evident between Solari's heavily frescoed Gothic nave and Bramante's airy, somber apse.

Piazza Santa Maria delle Grazie. www.grazieop.it. No phone. Free admission. Mon–Sat 7am–noon, 3–7:15pm; Sun 7:30am–12:30pm, 3:30pm–9pm. Metro: Cadorna or Conciliazione.

Santa Maria delle Grazie, Il Cenacolo Vinciano ★★★ CHURCH Milan's greatest art treasure is also one of the most famous on earth, largely thanks to Dan Brown's blockbuster novel *The Da Vinci Code*. Painted for Milanese ruler Ludovico il Moro by Leonardo da Vinci between 1495 and 1497, "The Last Supper" adorns the back wall of the refectory in the Dominican convent attached to the church of Santa

---

Seeing "The Last Supper"

Unsurprisingly, Leonardo's "The Last Supper" is on almost every tourist's itinerary of Milan. And with only 30 people allowed in to the Cenacolo Vinciano at a time, it is a challenge to get a ticket if you don't book well in advance. Try the official website first, www.cenacolo vinciano.net, or call ✆ **02-9280-0360** (tickets are 6.50€ from the website, plus a 1.50€ booking fee) **3 months** before you are due to visit. Tickets are sold online for visits 3 months ahead. Present your e-tickets at the booking office

outside the Cenacolo in Piazza Santa Maria delle Grazie at least 20 minutes before your allotted time slot. And remember that the Cenacolo is not in the church of Santa Maria delle Grazie itself, but in the refectory behind it, with a separate entrance of its own.

If you've missed the opportunity to snag a ticket in advance, many tour companies guarantee admission to "The Last Supper" as part of their guided tours of the city, which range from 40€ to 70€ (see "Organized Tours," below).

Maria delle Grazie (see p. 441). Leonardo's masterpiece depicts Christ revealing that one of his disciples will soon betray him; horror and disbelief are etched on every face, while Jesus remains calm and resigned. As we look at the fresco, Judas sits to the left of Jesus, leaning away from him with the bag of silver clearly visible in his right hand. Is it Mary Magdalene sitting between him and Jesus? Wherever you stand on the controversy, there is no doubt that "The Last Supper" is one of the world's most poignant and beautiful works of art.

Due to da Vinci experimenting with his painting technique and applying tempera straight on to the walls of the refectory, his sublime fresco began to deteriorate virtually on completion. It suffered several ham-fisted restoration attempts in the 18th and 19th centuries and survived target practice by Napoleon's troops, not to mention a period exposed to the open air after Allied bombing in WWII. The latest cleanup of the fresco was completed in 1999, and while the colors are muted, they are thought to resemble Leonardo's original fresco. The famous fresco is now climate-controlled for preservation, and groups of only 30 at a time are allowed in to view it, in pre-allocated periods of 15 minutes.

Piazza Santa Maria delle Grazie 2. www.cenacolovinciano.net, ✆ **02-9280-0360.** Admission 6.50€ adults, 3.25€ ages 4–17 and seniors. 1.50€ booking fee applies to all tickets. Tues–Sun 8:15am–7pm. Metro: Cadorna or Conciliazione.

Triennale di Milano ★★★ MUSEUM   Opened in 2007, this sleek, white temple of cool is dedicated to contemporary design, and as you'd expect in this city of stylistas, it's busy day and night. Located at the north end of Parco Sempione just by the Torre Branca (see p. 436), it features on-trend temporary exhibits, anything from black-and-white photography to retrospectives on Italian design icons. On the second floor an internal bridge, designed by Michele de Lucchi from sheets of bamboo, leads from the exhibition spaces into the Triennale Design Museum (separate entry fee), which has oft-changed displays of modern Italian design classics, well signposted in English. The Agora Theater puts on innovative shows and the bookstore is *the* place to pick up beautifully produced full-color coffee-table tomes. A lovely spot with views over Parco Sempione, the DesignCafé and Restaurant is the venue of choice on Sundays for smart Milanese and their immaculately turned-out offspring.

Viale Alemagna 6. www.triennale.it. ✆ **02-724-341.** Admission to Design Museum 8€ adults, 6€ students 25 and under, seniors 65 and over. Temporary exhibits range from free to 8€. Tues–Wed and Fri–Sun 10:30am–8:30pm; Thurs 10:30am–11pm. Metro: Cadorna or Cairoli.

Organized Tours

Among the scores of companies offering guided tours of Milan and Lombardy, here are three of the best. **Viator** (www.viator.com; U.S. ✆ **702-648-5873**) offers private guided tours of Milan with hotel pick-ups as well as sightseeing tours by Segway, plus jaunts out to the lakes Como and

Maggiore. **Zani Viaggi** (www.zaniviaggi.it; ✆ **02-867-131**) leads specialist tours to the revered turf of San Siro Stadium (see below) and the shopping outlets of northern Lombardy, while **Local Milan Tours** (www.localmilantours.com; U.S. ✆ **866/663-7017**) can organize trips around La Scala (see p. 451) and day trips as far afield as Venice.

Outdoor Activities

Milan is a densely populated urban sprawl where green space is rare and precious. The largest park is the 47-hectare (116-acre) expanse of **Parco Sempione** behind Castello Sforzesco. It is the lungs of the city, the favorite place of well-heeled Milanese to walk their dogs along shady pathways sheltered by giant chestnuts; it is here that lovers come to moon around the ornamental lakes designed in English Romantic fashion by Emilio Alemagna in the early 1800s. The **Giardini Pubblici** on Bastioni di Porta Venezia is another haven, a firm favorite with families at the weekend for its little fair. Joggers circuit the park, and in winter there's ice-skating on the ornamental ponds. **Parco Solari** and **Gardaland Waterpark** (see p. 444) have swimming pools, and **Idroscalo** (see p. 444) at Linate offers every outdoor activity from sailing and swimming to climbing or tennis. The **Lombardy lakes** all offer the chance for watersports, cycling, and hiking. For sports fanatics, San Siro Stadium (www.sansiro.net; ✆ **02-4879-8201**) and **Monza F1 racetrack** (see p. 445) are open for tours.

Especially for Kids

Despite being world-renowned as a hub of high finance, fashion, and design, Milan is after all an Italian city and all Italians dote on children. The city's rather formal facade belies its many family-friendly attractions, museums, *gelaterie*, and play parks, and everywhere you go, your *bambini* will be worshipped, hugged, and multilaterally adored.

Where to start? Chief among attractions that all kids will love is the ride up to the **Duomo rooftop** (see p. 434) for views across the red roof tops of the city to the Alps. The basement level of the **Museo Nazionale della Scienza e della Tecnologica Leonardo da Vinci** (see p. 437) is stuffed full of fun, interactive activities for kids. Children ages 4 to 11 can be distracted by the play area Sforzinda in the **Castello Sforzesco's** (see p. 434) 14th-century dungeons while parents explore the decorative arts. A picnic lunch and a run around in the adjoining **Parco Sempione** is a welcome respite from cultural overload.

The new **Museo dei Bambini** (Via Enrico Besana 12; www.muba.it; ✆ **02-4398-0402**) doesn't have a permanent collection, but offers creative and educational workshops for children ages 2 and up. Opening times and cost of workshops vary, but tend to run around 10 euros. The museum also has a café and a large garden around the historic circular structure, the late-Baroque Rotonda della Besana, which has been everything from a cemetery for the poor to a stable to a home for the chronically ill.

Italy's version of Disneyland, **Gardaland**, is located a couple of hours from Milan in Castelnuovo del Garda (see p. 473), but there are plenty of options closer to the city. Located on the far western outskirts of town, the Milan offshoot of Gardaland, **Gardaland Waterpark** (Via Gaetano Airaghi 61; www.gardalandwaterpark.it; ✆ **02-4820-0134**), has splashy water slides, fun rides, and picnic areas. It typically opens at the end of May and stays open until the end of August. To get there, take the red subway line (direction Rho Fieramilano) to the Lotto stop, then bus 423 (direction Settimo Milanese) to Via Airaghi. The park is open daily 10am to 7pm. Admission is free but you pay by activity; an all-day ticket costs 18€ adults and 12€ for children under 12 (on Sundays, adult tickets are 20€). Enter after 2:30 p.m. for slightly reduced tickets. Swimming pools are 8€ on the weekend, and parking is 2€.

About 30 minutes northeast of Milan in the direction of Bergamo, the **Leolandia** amusement park (Via Vittorio Veneto 52, Capriate San Gervasio; www.leolandia.it) has rides and games for kids of all ages, as well as the delightful Minitalia, a replica of all of the major cities and monuments in Italy. More compact and manageable than the main Gardaland, it may be better suited to smaller children, with features such as Peppa Pig World, opened in 2015 as a draw for the toddler set. Full-price tickets purchased at the park cost 31.50€, but can be had for half that online. Children up to 89 cm (about 3 feet) enter free. Leolandia opens in April and stays open through Halloween (in fact, the park has special Halloween celebrations, which is unusual—Halloween isn't widely celebrated in Italy). In early spring and fall, it's open only weekends, in June and July it's open Wednesday to Sunday, and it's open daily in August. The Z301 bus from Milan to Bergamo, managed by **Nord Est Trasporti** (www.nordesttrasporti.it; ✆ **800-905-150**), stops near Leolandia, at Capriate San Gervasio.

Another great green public space is the **Giardini Pubblici** (see p. 443) Here there are playgrounds, roundabouts, and a little electric train that chugs around the park. The Corso Venezia side of the park is home to the **Museo di Storia Naturale** (www.comune.milano.it; ✆ **02-8846-3337**; Tues–Sun 9am–5:30pm; admission 5€), where you can take the kids to see the dinosaur skeletons and the carcasses of massive bugs. As for swimming pools in the city, there's a municipal swimming pool in **Parco Solari** (Via Montevideo 20).

Near the Linate airport, just east of the city center, the **Idroscalo** park (Via Circonvallazione Idroscalo 29, Segrate; www.idroscalo.info; no phone) features a manmade lake that was originally created for seaplanes to land. This area has now been turned into a park open daily (summer 7am–9pm; winter 7am–5pm) and offers loads of sporting activities from sailing and swimming to climbing and ping-pong. There are also a couple of clubs and restaurants in the park where one can have a lounge-y, leisurely brunch on Sundays (try Le Jardin Au Bord du Lac, for example: www.lejardinauborddulac.com, Via Circonvallazione 51). Take the ATM

Milan (Milano)

MILAN, PIEDMONT & THE LAKES

Line 73 bus to Linate airport, then ATM Line 183 or 923 to Idroscalo. At night it is best to take a taxi as public transportation runs less frequently.

Most restaurants will happily rustle up a child's portion of pasta and tomato sauce, and if all else fails, it's usually easy to bribe any child with a visit to one of Milan's delicious ice cream shops; try **Biancolatte** (Via Turati 30; ☏ **02-6208-6177**) for dark-chocolate ice-cream cakes and **Rinomata Gelateria** (Ripa di Porta Ticinese 1; ☏ **02-5811-3877**) in Navigli for the most traditional ice-cream cones in town.

Outlying Attractions

Autodromo Nazionale Monza ★★ RACING CIRCUIT   Sprawled along the River Lambro in Lombardy, and 15km (10¼ miles) northeast of Milan, Monza is an appealing city with a central core reminiscent of a mini-Milan; it has a majestic early-Gothic Duomo and photogenic piazzas backed by lots of greenery. Sadly, the centro storico is usually bypassed in favor of the 10km (6.2-mile) Formula One racetrack that is the epicenter of car-mad Italy's hopes and dreams. The home of the Italian Grand Prix since 1922, Monza track is now open to all aspiring speed demons that fancy being a racing driver for the day. Race training sessions are held daily, with half-hour slots available for would-be champions to try out their skills on the track. Rallies, endurance races, and special events take place all year around while the Italian Formula One Grand Prix is held in September in front of hundreds of thousands of fans. Check the website for tickets and event details.

Via Vedano 5, Monza. www.monzanet.it. ☏ **039-2482-239.** Accessible by train (15 min.) from Centrale and Garibaldi stations.

Certosa di Pavia ★★★ CHURCH   Located a few miles north of the town of Pavia, this awesome Carthusian monastery is well worth a day trip. It was originally commissioned in 1396 as a mausoleum for Milan's ruling family the Viscontis (see p. 434), but after the Viscontis' dynastic downfall, the Sforza family took over, refurbishing the monastery according to their exorbitant tastes. The result is a highly intricate Renaissance façade, the swansong of master 15th-century architect Giovanni Antonio Amadeo, who also worked on the **Basilica di Santa Maria Maggiore in Bergamo** (see p. 454). The monastery contains the ornate tomb (but not the bodies) of Ludovico del Moro and his wife Beatrice, who together shaped the Milanese Renaissance (see p. 434). A tour takes in the peaceful cloisters, monks' cells, and refectory, but the highlight of this lovely place is the decorative church, its swaths of frescoes, the *pietra dura* altar, and the massive **mausoleum** of Gian Galeazzo Visconti.

Via Del Monumento 4, Certosa di Pavia. www.comune.pv.it/certosadipavia. ☏ **0382-925-613.** Admission and guided tours by donation. Open Tues–Sun. May–Aug 9–11:30am, 2:30–6pm; Mar–Apr, Sept 9–11:30am, 2:30–5:30pm; Oct 9–11:30am, 2:30–5pm; Nov–Feb 9–11:30am, 2:30–4pm. Accessible by train from Milan Stazione Rogoredo (Metro Line 3) to Certosa (3.60€), then a 15-minute walk.

Where to Stay

Milan is northern Italy's biggest commercial center, big on banking and industry, and for years its hotels have tended to chase expense-account customers, often to the detriment of tourists and families. The winds of change are blowing, however. A recent wave of cozy, independent *locandas* and *albergos,* as well as design-conscious boutique hotels, have come along to complement the grand old institutions.

Note that prices are often higher during the week than on the weekend, and room rates really soar when the fashion crowd hits town (late Feb and late Sept).

EXPENSIVE

Hotel Principe di Savoia ★★   This lovely, grand Beaux Arts institution is now part of the Dorchester Collection, which has busily been collecting famous hotels in Europe and on the west coast of the U.S. There's still nowhere better for a truly luxurious stay in Milan than this five-star respite from the urban intensity, where every conceivable guest whim is swiftly addressed. Guests have access to serene gardens, a soothing top-floor spa, a quality restaurant, an elegant bar, and opulent, suitably swagged rooms and suites. Former guests include George Clooney, Madonna, and the boys of One Direction, among others. Not surprisingly this luxury comes at a price, but for a bit of old-fashioned glamour, there's nowhere else like it.

Piazza Della Repubblica 17. www.dorchestercollection.com/en/milan/hotel-principe-di-savoia. ✆ **02-623-01.** 301 units. 250€–510€ double; 310€–4,700€ suite. Free parking valet service extra. Metro: Repubblica. **Amenities:** 1 restaurant; bar; concierge; room service; babysitting; spa; gym; indoor pool; Wi-Fi (free/high-speed service 9€ per day).

Milanosuites ★★★   Long considered one of the best-kept secrets in Milan, the former Antica Locanda dei Mercanti had a thorough facelift and re-emerged as the elegant, light-filled Milanosuites, set in a charming 18th-century townhouse tucked away in the appealing rabble of streets between the Castello Sforzesco and Piazza del Duomo. The number of guest rooms was reduced, making way for glamorous suites graced with parquet floors and simple white furnishings. All have living rooms and some have kitchenettes. Families can book a suite with two bedrooms.

Via San Tomaso 8. www.milanosuites.it. ✆ **02-8909-6849.** 5 units. 280€–320€ suite. Metro: Cordusio or Cairoli. **Amenities:** Concierge; room service; Wi-Fi (free).

nhow Milan ★★   A boutique hotel that is currently the darling of the fashion set, the nhow is part of a chain intent on providing stylish, well-priced accommodation, but somehow it feels a bit soulless. The sleek reception area sets the scene with an orange color scheme straight from the 1960s, only to be outdone by the lime-green furnishings in the minimalist bar, usually inhabited by gossiping models. Glass elevators whiz up to rooms decorated in white and slashes of bright color; the standard rooms are compact with walk-in showers. The fourth floor is the preserve of stylish, loft-style suites with views over Milan's burgeoning Zona Tortona fashion district. Porta Genova Metro station is close by.

Via Tortona 35. www.nhow-milan.com. ✆ **02-489-8861.** 246 units. 189€–289€ double; 419€–2,200€ suite. Rates include breakfast. Parking 24€ per day. Metro: Porto Genova. **Amenities:** Restaurant; bar; spa; gym; Wi-Fi (free).

MODERATE

Antica Locanda Leonardo ★★★ This lovely old-school *albergo* in snooty Corso Magenta looks inward on a surprisingly tranquil courtyard garden. It's like stepping into a family home; the rooms have been extensively revamped but still retain their wonderfully traditional feel, with heavy antique headboards and dressers, gilt mirrors, and elegant draperies. The bathrooms have also been dragged into the 21st century, but the cozy lounge and breakfast room remain delightfully of a former age. The pricier courtyard facing rooms, most of which have tiny wrought-iron balconies, deflect the late-night noise on Corso Magenta.

Corso Magenta 78. www.anticalocandaleonardo.com. ✆ **02-4801-4197.** 16 units. 100€–320€ double (garden side are more expensive). Rates include breakfast. Parking 28€ per day. Metro: Concilliazione, Cardorna. **Amenities:** Concierge; Wi-Fi (free).

INEXPENSIVE

BioCity Hotel ★★★ This fab little *albergo* offers the best value for accommodation in Milan. It's all a budget hotel should be: small and pristine, with a miniscule bar and breakfast room and a tiny terrace out back—*and* it's eco-friendly. Guest rooms are stylish, with big bathrooms that would enhance a four-star hotel. The reception area manages to squeeze in a little lounge that's furnished with edgy pieces. Plus there's even a tiny shop selling organic goodies. Operated by genial, well-informed owners, the BioCity is a few minutes' walk from Stazione Centrale in an area kindly referred to as "up and coming." It's close to Metro Linea 3, which zips straight into the *centro storico.*

Via Edolo 18. www.biocityhotel.it. ✆ **02-6670-3595.** 17 units. 72€–90€ double. Rates include breakfast. Street parking free; covered parking 20€ per day. Metro: Sondrio. **Amenities:** Bar; Wi-Fi (free).

Where to Eat

There are thousands of eateries in Milan, from pizzerias to grand old cafes, gourmand Michelin-starred restaurants in highfalutin surroundings to corner bars with a great selection of *aperitivo*-time tapas, *gelaterie* to traditional *osterie.* Avoid the obvious tourist traps along Via Dante or indeed any place that has a menu showing photos of the dishes and you can't go far wrong.

Cocktail hour starts at around 6:30pm. Around that time, a tapaslike spread of olives, crudités, cold pasta dishes, rice, salads, salamis, and breads make its appearance in every city bar worth its salt. This is when the Milanese appear as if by magic, from shopping or work, to meet up for cocktails, a bitter Campari, or a glass of prosecco. By the time *aperitivo* hour is over, thoughts turn towards supper and the restaurants start to fill up. This phenomenon takes place all over Milan. Every night.

EXPENSIVE

Carlo e Camilla in Segheria ★★ MODERN ITALIAN   Celebrated chef Carlo Cracco's latest venture, in an old sawmill outside the *centro storico,* offers up an innovative new concept. The restaurant and cocktail bar has a sparse yet warm post-industrial feel with one long communal table for up to 65 people and large chandeliers hanging from the ceiling. Come for a truly unique cocktail from head mixologist Filippo Sisti (some say these are the best drinks in town) or stay for dinner with modern Italian food that is clean, fresh, and "not too cerebral." The menu features dishes like spaghetti with anchovies, lime, and coffee, or the salmon "cube" with a yogurt and lemongrass sauce.

Via G. Meda 24. www.carloecamillainsegheria.it. ✆ **02-837-3963.** Dishes range from 15€–25€. Mon–Sun. 6pm–2am. Metro: Romolo though Tram 3 from the Duomo gets you closer to the restaurant as it passes right outside.

Restaurant Giacomo Arengario ★★★ NORTHERN ITALIAN Deserving of three stars just for its views of the Duomo, this super-hot spot is currently the number-one choice for smartly attired Milanese business lunchers and it's just as popular with tourists for the view. There's a smart little bar reminiscent of a Marrakesh casbah on acid where *aperitivi* are served early in the evening, but the real point here is to get seated by those plate-glass windows and gawk at the Duomo. The menu is a gourmet take on Milanese specialties; *fritto misto* comes fried in a lighter-than-light batter and is simply delicious accompanied by a spicy rocket salad, while the risotto comes perfectly prepared and slips down a treat with a glass of prosecco. There's a cover charge of 5€.

Via Guglielmo Marconi 1. www.giacomoarengario.com. ✆ **02-72-093-814.** Main courses 18€–50€. Daily noon–midnight. Metro: Duomo.

MODERATE

Hostaria Borromei ★★ LOMBARDY   This stalwart Milanese favorite with a delicious down-home vibe and hearty Lombardian gastronomy needs booking in advance for weekend dining, especially on the vineyard terrace for summer dining. The menu features polenta, thick homemade noodle pastas, saffron-flavored risotto, the famed veal shank dish *osso bucco*, and plenty of seafood. Seasonal cheeses and traditional puddings such as *tiramisu* and *panna cotta* round off a warming dining experience in lively surroundings.

Via Borromei 4. www.hostariaborromei.com. ✆ **02-8645-3760.** Main courses 18€–44€. Mon–Fri 12:30–2:45pm and 7:30–10:45pm; Sat–Sun 7:30–10:45pm. Metro: Cordusio or Duomo.

Osteria il Kaimano ★★ NORTHERN ITALIAN A good pick among the buzzing restaurants and bars of Brera, this casual, gently chaotic *osteria* is just the job for people-watching, Saturday lunchtime or a late-night dinner. The menu of pasta and pizza staples may not be vastly different from the other Brera dining options—**Sans Egal** (Vicolo Fiori 2; www.sansegal.it; ✆ 02-869-3096) and **Nabucco** (Via Fiori Chiari 10; www.nabucco.it; ✆ 02-860-663) are also good choices—but here the atmosphere and service shine. Strong choices include the zucchini flowers stuffed with ricotta for starters (12€) and vast pizzas that continually pile out of the wood-burning oven. There's a little terrace on the street for summer eating, but in winter the smokers are all relocated here.
Via Fiori Chiari 20. ✆ **02-8050-2733.** Main courses 15€–40€. Daily noon–2:30pm, 6–11:30pm. Metro: Lanza Brera.

Pizzeria Tradizionale ★★ PIZZERIA One of the busiest pizzerias in Milan is found down at the Navigli; it's a simple affair, with checked tablecloths. Tradizionale is always crammed with happy families devouring enormous crispy pizzas piled high with local salamis and mozzarella as well as vast bowls of garlic-infused spaghetti alle *vongole* (clams). The house wines can be a bit rough but there are decent Chiantis and Soaves on the wine list. There's always plenty of backchat between waiting staff and guests and the noise really ratchets up as the night goes on. Altogether a fun night out.
Ripa di Porta Ticinese 7. www.pizzeriatradizionale.com ✆ **02-839-5133.** Main courses 8.50€–18€. Open daily noon–2:30pm and 7pm–1am except Wednesdays (only open for dinner). Metro: Porta Genova.

Shopping

Milan *is* shopping. And Milan is expensive.

Milan is known the world over as one of the temples of high fashion, with the hallowed streets **Montenapoleone** and **Spiga** in the **Quadrilatero d'Oro** the most popular place of worship. Here D&G, Prada, Gucci, Hermès, Louis Vuitton, Armani, Ralph Lauren, Versace, and Cavalli all jostle for customers among Milan's minted fashionistas. More reasonable shopping areas include **Via Torino** and **Corso Buenos Aires,** where mid-range international brands proliferate; if you're clever you can also pick up a designer bargain at outlet store **Il Salvagente** (Via Fratelli Bronzetti 16; ✆ **02-7611-0328**).

Fashion is one Milanese obsession, food is another, and the *centro storico* has many superb delis from which to purchase the purest of olive oils and fine cheeses. **Peck** (Via Spadari 9; ✆ **02-802-3161**) is still the number-one gourmet spot, although competition is keen from **Buongusto** (Via Caminadella 2; ✆ **02-8645-2479**) for the freshest of pasta in many guises, and the huge new **Eataly** megastore in Piazza XXV Aprile (www.eataly.it) for all comestibles Italian. The **top floor of La Rinascente department store** in Piazza del Duomo (see below) is another

Upscale shopping in Milan.

haven for foodies, with its Obika mozzarella bar and fine selection of packaged Italian goods (as an added bonus, you get a close-up view of the Duomo).

English-language books are sold at **Feltrinelli Librerie**, **Mondadori Multicenter,** and **Rizzoli** (all in and around Piazza del Duomo or inside the galleria) along with mobile and camera accessories. English-language newspapers can be found on most major newsstands around the *centro storico*.

MILANO MARKETS

Everybody loves a bargain, and there's no better place to find one than at the colorful, chaotic **Viale Papiniano market** (Metro: Sant'Agostino). Its sprawl of stalls are open Tuesday and Saturday; some flog designer seconds, others leather basics. **Flea markets** spring up on Saturdays along Alzaia Naviglio Grande (Metro: Porta Genova) and Fiera di Sinigaglia (Metro: Porta Genova), and on Sundays at San Donato Metro stop. The most historic is the Christmas extravaganza **Oh Bej! Oh Bej!** (roughly, Oh so nice! Oh so nice!), which seasonally takes over the *centro storico* around Sant'Ambrogio and Parco Sempione, selling everything from leather bags to handcrafted jewelry. A large **food market** at the Piazza Wagner metro stop is open every morning except Sunday. One Saturday a month, a Slow Food outdoor market is held in the courtyard of **Fabbrica Vapore** in north Milan (Via Procaccini 4; www.fabbricadel vapore.org).

Nightlife & Entertainment

Unless you're heading for the Ticinese and Navigli, Milan is a dressy city and generally looks askance at scruffy jeans and sneakers after dark. When most people don't dine until well after 10pm, it's not surprising that clubs and bars stay open until the very wee hours.

Milan has its share of glitzy clubs and cocktail bars, but most explode on the scene and disappear just as quickly. A few spots that appear to be in for the long haul include the vine-covered cocktail terrace

What's on When in Milan

To keep up with Milan's ever-changing nightlife, check out **"Hello Milano"** (www.hello milano.it/hm), which is published monthly and available in most hotels.

at **10 Corso Como** (www.10corsocomo.com; ☎ **02-2901-3581**), the evergreen dance club **Hollywood** (www.discotecahollywood.it; ☎ **02-6555-318**), and mega-club **Plastic** at Via Gargano 15 (no phone). A new kid on the block, **Ceresio 7 Pools & Restaurant** (www.cere sio7.com; ☎ **02-310-392-21**) offers a novel setup: a chic, sleek rooftop lounge with two pools where one can enjoy a cocktail while enjoying amazing views of the city.

North of Parco Sempione, **Chinatown** is a great area to explore for the dim sum restaurants concentrated around Via Paolo Sarpi. Just north of there, the **Fabbrica del Vapore** (Steam Factory; Via Procaccini 4, www.fabbricadelvapore.org; no phone) is an exciting arts venue featuring concerts and exhibition such as the visually stunning 2014 show "Van Gogh Live."

A venerable Milan institution, the **Conservatorio di Musica Giuseppe Verdi** has two stages for classical concerts, at Via Conservatorio 12 (www.consmilano.it; ☎ **02-762-110;** box office open Mon–Fri 8am–8pm). Yet Milan is forever associated with the grand old dame of opera, **Teatro Alla Scala,** perhaps the world's favorite opera house. La Scala is all decked out with sumptuous red seats, boxes adorned with gilt, and chandeliers dripping crystal. Tickets are hard to come by, so book well in advance of the opera season, kicking off on December 7 each year. Book online at www.teatroallascala.org, pay by phone with a credit card (☎ **02-861-778**), or go to La Scala's booking office in the Galleria del Sagrato, Piazza del Duomo, which is open from noon to 6pm daily (closed Aug). The ticket office at the opera house (Via Filodrammatici 2) releases 140 last-minute tickets for that evening's performance 2½ hours before the curtain goes up; get there promptly if you want a ticket.

BERGAMO ★★

47km (29 miles) northeast of Milan.

Bergamo is a city of two distinct characters. The ancient **Città Alta** is a beautiful medieval and Renaissance town perched on a green hill. **Città Bassa,** mostly built in the 19th and 20th century, sits at the feet of the upper town and concerns itself with getting on with 21st-century life. Visitors tend to focus on the historic upper town, which is largely a place for wandering, soaking in its rarified atmosphere, and enjoying the lovely vistas from its belvederes.

Essentials

GETTING THERE   **Trains** arrive from and depart for Milan Stazione Centrale hourly (50 min.; 5.50€).

Bus services to and from Milan are run by **Nord Est Trasporti** (www.nordesttrasporti.it; ✆ **800-905-150**) and run at least hourly, with more services at commuter times; journey time is an hour and fares are 5.65€. The Z301 bus leaves from the Beltrami-Cairoli stop near Piazza Cadorna.

If you are driving, Bergamo is linked to Milan via the A4. The trip takes under an hour if traffic is good. Note: It's difficult to park in the largely pedestrianized Città Alta—park instead in Città Bassa and take the funicular (see below) up to the historic area.

VISITOR INFORMATION   The **Città Bassa tourist office** is close to the train and bus stations at Viale Papa Giovanni XXIII 57 (✆ **035-210-204**); it's open daily 9am to 12:30pm and 2 to 5:30pm. The **Città Alta office** is at Via Gombito, 13 (✆ **035-242-226**), right off Via Colleoni, and is open daily 9am–5:30pm. The **Bergamo Card** costs 10€ for 24 hours or 15€ for 2 days, but only makes sense if you plan to visit all the museums, as the churches are all free to enter. Check the website **www.comune.bergamo.it** for more information.

CITY LAYOUT   Piazza Vecchia, the Colleoni Chapel, and most major sights are in the **Città Alta,** which is dissected by **Via Colleoni.** To reach **Piazza Vecchia** from the funicular station at **Piazza Mercato delle Scarpi,** it's a 5-minute stroll along **Via Gombito.** The Accademia Carrara is in the Città Bassa.

GETTING AROUND   Bergamo has an efficient **bus system** that runs throughout the Città Bassa and to points around the Città Alta; tickets are 1.30€ for 90 minutes of travel and are available from the machines at the bus stops outside the train station or at the bus station opposite.

To reach the Città Alta from the train station, take bus no. 1 or 1A (clearly marked Città Alta on the front) and make the free transfer to the **Funicolare Bergamo Alta,** run by ATB Bergamo (Largo Porta Nuova; www.atb.bergamo.it; ✆ **035-236-026**), connecting the upper and lower cities. It runs every 7 minutes from 7am to 1:20am.

Exploring the Città Bassa

Most visitors scurry through Bergamo's lower, newer town on their way to the Città Alta, but you may want to pause long enough to explore its main thoroughfare, **Corso Sentierone,** with its mishmash of architectural styles (16th-century porticos, the Mussolini-era Palazzo di Giustizia, and two mock Doric temples); it's a pleasant place to linger over espresso in a pavement cafe. The **Accademia Carrara** (Piazza Giacomo Carrara 82, www.lacarrara.it; ✆ **035-234396**) is worth a peek for its fine collection of Raphaels, Bellinis, Botticellis, and Canolettos. Città Bassa's

Lombardy & the Lake District

453

19th-century **Teatro Gaetano Donizetti** (Piazza Cavour 14) is the hub of Bergamo's lively cultural scene, with a fall opera season and a winter-to-spring season of dramatic performances; for details, call the theater at ☎ **035-416-0611** (www.teatrodonizetti.it).

Exploring the Città Alta

Crammed with *palazzi,* monuments, and churches, the Città Alta centers on two hauntingly beautiful adjoining squares, **the piazzas Vecchia** and **del Duomo.** Bergamasco strongman Bartolomeo Colleoni (see below) gave his name to the Città Alta's delightful main street, cobble-stoned and so narrow you can almost touch the buildings on either side in places. It's lined with gorgeous shoe shops, posh delis, and classy confectioners.

The **Piazza Vecchia** looks like something out of one of local hero Gaetano Donizetti's opera sets; this hauntingly beautiful square was the hub of Bergamo's political and civic life from medieval times. The 12th-century **Palazzo della Ragione** (Court of Justice) was built by the Venetians, and its three graceful ground-floor arcades are embellished with the Lion of Saint Mark, symbol of the Venetian Republic, visible above the tiny 16th-century balcony and reached by a covered staircase to the right of the palace. Across the piazza, there's the **Biblioteca Civica (Public Library)**.

Walk through the archways of the Palazzo della Ragione to reach **Piazza del Duomo** and the **Basilica di Santa Maria Maggiore ★★**, (www.fondazionemia.it/basilica_s_maria_maggiore_bergamo/index.asp; ☎ **035-223-327**). The basilica itself is entered through an ornate portico supported by Venetian lions; the interior is a masterpiece of ornately Baroque giltwork hung with Renaissance tapestries. Bergamo native son Gaetano Donizetti, the popular opera composer, is entombed here in a marble sarcophagus that's as excessive as the rest of the church's decor. An octagonal Baptistery in the piazza outside was originally inside the church but was removed and reconstructed in the 19th century. The oft-forgotten Tempietto of Santa Croce, tucked to the left of the basilica entrance, is worth seeking out for its endearing fragments of fresco of "The Last Supper." From April through October the basilica is open Tuesday to Saturday 9am to 12:30pm and 2:30 to 6pm, and Sunday 9am to 1pm and 3 to 6pm; November through March it's open Tuesday through Saturday 9am to 12:30pm and 2:30 to 5pm. Admission is free.

Most impressive, however, is the **Cappella Colleoni ★★★** (Piazza del Duomo; ☎ **035-210-061;** free admission), found to the right of the basilica doors and entered through a highly elaborate pink-and-white marble facade. Bartolomeo Colleoni was a Bergamasco *condottiero* (mercenary) who fought for the Venetians; as a reward for his loyalty he was given Bergamo as his own private fiefdom in 1455. His elaborate funerary chapel was designed by Giovanni Antonio Amadeo, who created the Certosa di Pavia (see p. 445). Colleoni lies beneath a ceiling frescoed by Tiepolo and surrounded by statuary, Cappella Colleoni is open March to October daily from 9am to 12:30pm and 2 to 6:30pm; and November to February Tuesday to Sunday 9am to 12:30pm and 2 to 4:30pm.

Where to Stay & Eat

The charms of Bergamo's Città Alta are no secret and hotel rooms are in great demand over the summer, so make reservations well in advance. If you're staying in Milan, the city is an easy hour's journey from Stazione Centrale, making a perfect day trip.

Caffè della Funicolare ★ CAFE   In the upper terminal of the funicular, this simple spot serves coffee, wine, beer, basic snacks, and now even more elaborate meals. Bag a table on the terrace looking straight down over Bergamo Bassa, for some of the best views in the upper town. Via Porta Dipinta 1. www.caffedellafunicolare.it. *©* **035-210-091.** Main courses 10€–15€, sandwiches 5€ and up. Daily 8am–2am.

Caffè del Tasso ★ CAFE   On the Città Alta's atmospheric main piazza, this charming spot began life as a tailor's shop, but it's been a cafe since 1581. Today it has the gently jaded, rather cozy air of a 1950s teashop, but service is smart and they're generous with their *aperitivo* snacks. Next door the gelateria does brisk trade in summer, while an early evening drink on the terrace in summer is just a step away from heaven. Piazza Vecchia 3. *©* **035-237-966.** Main courses 10€–18€. Open daily 8am–midnight.

Hotel Piazza Vecchio ★★   Just steps from the Piazza Vecchio in the historic Città Alta, this ancient townhouse has stone walls and beamed ceilings. The rooms are all simply furnished, but each has a sleek new bathroom. The quieter rooms are at the back of the hotel looking over a labyrinth of alleyways and rooftops. Via Colleoni 3. www.hotelpiazzavecchia.it. *©* **035-253-179.** 13 units. 120€–200€ double. Rates include breakfast. **Amenities:** Wi-Fi (free).

Osteria della Birra ★★ ORGANIC BREWPUB   A great find in the Città Alta, this microbrewery restaurant offers a simple menu of *piadine* (flatbread) and *panini* stuffed full of local cured hams and artisanal cheeses. The *raison d'etre*, however, is the beer (no wine here). Part of the Elav microbrewery, this spot is run by a bunch of enthusiastic youngsters keen to promote their organic brew along with their largely organic produce. Piazza Masheroni 1/c. www.elavbrewery.com/en/pubs/osteria-della-birra. *©* **035-242-440.** Main courses 8€–15€. Mon–Fri noon–3pm, 6pm–2am; Sat–Sun noon–2am.

MANTUA (MANTOVA) ★★★

158km (98 miles) E of Milan, 62km (38 miles) N of Parma, 150km (93 miles) SW of Venice

One of Lombardy's best-kept secrets, Mantua is in the eastern reaches of the region, making it an easy side trip from Milan. Like its neighboring cities in Emilia-Romagna, Mantua owes its beautiful Renaissance monuments to one family, in this case the Gonzagas, who conquered the city in 1328 and ruled benevolently until 1707. They were avid collectors of art and ruled through the greatest centuries of Italian art; encounter the treasures they collected in the massive **Palazzo Ducale**; in their summer retreat, the **Palazzo Te**; and in the churches and piazzas that grew up around their court.

The Palazzo Ducale, the **Galleria Museo Palazzo Valenti Gonzaga**, and other monuments were recently restored, while Mantegna's famous **Camera degli Sposi** reopened in 2015 following earthquake damage in 2012 (see p. 458).

Essentials

GETTING THERE Six direct **trains** depart daily from Milan Stazione Centrale (1 hr. 50 mins.; 11.50€). There are nine daily trains from Verona (30–40 min.; 3.75€).

The speediest highway connections from Milan are via the A4 autostrade to Verona, then the A22 from Verona to Mantua (about 2 hrs.).

VISITOR INFORMATION The **tourist office** at Piazza Mantegna 6 (www.turismo.mantova.it; © **0376-432-432**) is open on weekends from 9am–5pm; during the week, the office is open 9am–1:30pm and 2:30–5pm (until 6pm in spring and summer). It's just to the right of the entrance to the basilica of Sant'Andrea.

CITY LAYOUT Mantua is tucked onto a fat finger of land surrounded on three sides by the **Mincio River,** which widens into a series of lakes, named prosaically **Lago Superiore, Lago di Mezzo,** and **Lago Inferiore.** Most of the sights are within an easy walk of one another within the compact center, which is a 15-minute walk northwards from the lakeside train station.

Exploring Mantua

Mantua is a place for wandering along arcaded streets and through cobbled squares with handsomely proportioned churches and *palazzi*.

The southernmost of these squares is **Piazza delle Erbe (Square of the Herbs)** ★, so named for its produce-and-food market. Mantua's civic might is clustered here in a series of late-medieval and early Renaissance structures that include the **Palazzo della Ragione (Courts of Justice)** and **Palazzo del Podestà (Mayor's Palace)** from the 12th and 13th centuries, and the **Torre dell'Orologio,** topped with a

14th-century astrological clock. Also on this square is Mantua's earliest religious structure, the **Rotunda di San Lorenzo,** a miniature round church from the 11th century (all of its building were closed for restoration and covered with scaffolding at the time of writing). The city's Renaissance masterpiece, **Basilica di Sant'Andrea** (see below), is off to one side on Piazza Mantegna.

To the north, Piazza delle Erbe transforms into **Piazza Broletto** through a series of arcades; here a statue commemorates the poet Virgil, who was born in Mantova in 70 B.C. The next square, **Piazza Sordello,** is vast, cobbled, rectangular, and lined with well-restored medieval *palazzi* and the 13th-century Duomo. Most notable is the massive hulk of the **Palazzo Ducale** (see below) that forms the eastern wall of the piazza. To enjoy Mantua's lakeside views and walks, follow Via San Giorgio from the **Piazza Sordello** and turn right on to Lungolago dei Gonzaga, which leads back into the town center.

Tip: The **Mantua Museum Card** costs 15€ and allows access to five city museums for 15€, allowing a saving of several euros on normal admission charges. Visit **www.mantovaducale.beniculturali.it** for more details.

Basilica di Sant'Andrea ★★ CHURCH

A graceful Renaissance facade fronts this 15th-century church by star architect Leon Battista Alberti. The grandest church in Mantua, it is topped by a dome added by Filippo Juvarra in the 18th century. Inside, the vast classically proportioned space is centered on the church's single aisle. Light pours in through the dome, highlighting the carefully crafted *trompe l'oeil* painting of the coffered, barrel-vaulted ceiling. The Gonzagas' court painter Andrea Mantegna—creator of the Camera degli Sposi in the **Palazzo Ducale** (see below)—is buried in the first chapel on the left. The crypt houses a reliquary containing the blood of Christ, which was allegedly brought here by Longinus, the Roman soldier who thrust his spear into Jesus's side; this is processed through town on March 18, the feast of Mantua's patron, Sant'Anselmo.

Piazza Mantegna. www.santandreainmantova.it. Free admission. Daily 8am–noon, 3–7pm.

Museo di Palazzo Ducale ★★ PALACE

The massive power base of the Gonzaga dynasty spreads over the northeast corner of Mantua, incorporating Piazza Sordello, the Romanesque-Gothic Duomo, the Castello San Giorgio, and the Palazzo Ducale. Together they form a private city connected by a labyrinth of corridors, ramps, courtyards, and staircases filled with Renaissance frescoes and ancient Roman sculptures. Behind the walls of this massive fortress-cum-family palace lies the history of Mantua's most powerful family and what remains of the treasure trove they amassed over the centuries. Between their skills as warriors and their penchant for marrying into wealthier houses, the

Gonzagas acquired power, money, and the services of some of the top artists of the time, including Pisanello, Titian, and Andrea Mantegna.

The most fortunate of many opportunistic unions was in 1490, between Francesco II Gonzaga and aristocratic Isabella d'Este from Ferrara. It was she who commissioned many of the complex's art-filled apartments, including the incomparable **Camera degli Sposi** in the north tower of the Castello San Giorgio. This is the undoubted masterpiece of Andrea Mantegna, taking 9 years to complete. It provides a fascinating glimpse into late 15th-century courtly life.

The Palazzo Ducale offers up a glorious maze of gilded, frescoed, marble-floored rooms, passageways, corridors, secret gardens, follies, and scattered pieces of elaborate *intaglio* furniture. Standouts among all the excess include the Arturian legends ornamenting walls of **the Sala del Pisanello**, painted by Pisanello between 1436 and 1444; the **Sale degli Arazzi** (Tapestry Rooms) hung with copies of Raphael's tapestries in the Vatican; the **Galleria degli Specchi** (Hall of Mirrors); the low-ceilinged **Appartamento dei Nani** (Apartments of the Dwarfs), where a replica of the Holy Staircase in the Vatican is built to miniature scale; and the **Galleria dei Mesi** (Hall of the Months).

Piazza Sordello, 40. www.mantovaducale.beniculturali.it. ℗ **0376-224-832** for ticket info. Admission 6.50 € for the Palazzo Ducale Museum; 12€ for the Castello San Giorgio + Corte Vecchia + Freddi Collection; 6.50€ for the Corte Vecchia + apartment of Isabella d'Este. Free admission to all on the first Sunday every month. Tues–Sun 8:15am–7:15pm. Last entrance at 6:20pm.

Palazzo Te ★★ PALACE   This glorious summer palace, designed by Giulio Romano between 1525 and 1535, took a decade to complete. Built for Federico II Gonzaga, the sybaritic son of Isabella d'Este (see above), this splendid Renaissance palace was his retreat from court life, and it was designed to indulge his obsessions. A tour leads through a series of evermore-lavishly adorned apartments, decorated by the best artists of the day. Gonzaga's enthusiasms for love and sex, astrology, and horses are evident throughout, from the almost 3-D effect in the **Hall of the Horses** to the sexually overt frescoes by Romano in the elaborate **Chamber of Amor and Psyche.** The greatest room in the palace, however, is a metaphor for Gonzaga power: In the **Sala dei Giganti (Room of the Giants),** Titan is overthrown by the gods in a dizzying display of architectural *trompe l'oeil* that gives the illusion that the ceiling is falling inwards. The Palazzo Te is also home of the **Museo Civico**, whose permanent collections on the upper floors include the Gonzaga family's coins, medallions, 20th-century family portraits by Armando Spadini, and a few Egyptian artifacts.

Viale Te 13. www.palazzote.it. ℗ **0376-323-266.** Admission 10€ adults, 7€ seniors, 3.50€ ages 12–18 and students, free for under 12. Mon 1–6pm; Tues–Sun 9am–6pm. Audioguide 5€. Palazzo Te is a 20-minute walk from the center of Mantua along Via Principe Amedeo.

Frescoed ceilings in Mantua's Palazzo Te.

MORE MANTUA MUSEUMS

En route from the center of town to Palazza Te, you'll pass **Casa del Mantegna ★,** the house and studio of Andrea Mantegna, which is now an art gallery (Via Acerbi 47, ℭ **0376-360-506;** Tues–Sun 10am–12:30pm, Tues–Wed 3–5pm, Sat–Sun 3–6pm; admission free). Close by in the stark white Palazzo Sebastiano, the **Museo della Città ★** (Largo XXIV Maggio 12; www.museodellacitta.mn.it; ℭ **0376-367-087**; Mon 1–6pm, Tues–Sun 9am–6pm; admission 12€) gallops through the history of Mantua. Among its many architectural fragments and columns is an impressive bust of Francesco Gonzaga, who commissioned the palace in 1507.

Just to the left of the Palazzo Ducale's main entrance, in the old markethall at the corner of Piazza Sordello, the **Museo Archeologico Nazionale di Mantova** houses in one giant space all sorts of local discoveries of Bronze Age, Greek, Etruscan, and Roman pottery, glassware, and utensils (www.museoarcheologicomantova.beniculturali.it; ℭ **0376-320-003;** admission 4€, age 17 and under free; Nov–Mar Tues–Sun 8:30am–1:30pm; Apr–Oct Tues, Thurs, Sat 1:30–7pm, Wed, Fri, Sun 8:30am–1:30pm.).

The lovely Baroque interior of the **Teatro Bibiena ★★** is also worth a peek for its rows of luxurious boxes. Find it at Via Accademia 47 (ℭ **0376-327-653;** admission 2€, 17 and under free; Tues–Sun 10am–1pm and 3–6pm, except Sat–Sun 10am–6pm mid-Mar to mid-Nov.)

For a change of pace—if you can catch it open, which is usually on weekends—the **Galleria Storica dei Vigili del** Fuoco (Fire Engine Museum) ★ at Largo Vigili del Fuoco 1 (www.vigilfuoco.it; ℭ **0376-227-71**) has plenty of historic engines to distract from ancient art. Call beforehand to check opening times.

Where to Eat & Stay

Like Milan, Mantua sees many expense-account business travelers during the week, with families and tourists flocking in for the weekends and over summer, so book rooms in the town center well ahead of time.

Caffè Caravatti ★ CAFE   Join the Mantovese for a lunchtime pick-me-up after a morning of shopping in the gorgeous arcaded streets of the old city. The old-fashioned brass and wood bar is lined with mysterious local liqueurs while glasses of prosecco and Campari cocktails are dispensed at the speed of light.
Via Broletto 16. ✆ **0376-327-826.** Mon–Thurs 7am–8:30pm, Fri–Sat 7am–midnight.

Caffè Modi ★ ITALIAN   Named for louche artist Amedeo Modigliani, whose moody portrait dominates the restaurant, Modi is a casual and friendly stop on the tourist circuit around Piazza Sordello. Chill music plays and threadbare armchairs lend a bohemian charm to the place. The menu is predictable in its selection of local pasta dishes and vast mountains of salad, but they are all well presented and tasty. If the place is quiet, the lovely laidback owner will come and chat—mostly about her enthusiasm for the works of Modigliani. Concerts and recitals are held here from time to time.
Via San Giorgio 4. ✆ **0376-181-0111.** Main courses 8€–15€. Wed–Mon noon–3pm, 7:15pm–midnight.

Il Scalco Grasso ★★ MODERN ITALIAN   This contemporary bistro with a minimalist black-and-red decor is owned by a young chef keen to push boundaries. Expect beautifully created vegetarian dishes—local pasta stuffed with marrow squash, delicate risotto, or perhaps a superb chickpea soup flavored with squid—alongside menu items like tartare of veal, pike, beef cheek, and local delicacy stracotto d'asino (donkey stew). Some lovely Lugano wines are available by the glass or bottle, and little bites of delicacies are happily produced for guests to sample before ordering. A sophisticated choice, with reservations recommended for weekends.
Via Trieste 55. www.scalcograssomantova.it. ✆ **349-374-7958.** Main courses 18€–30€. Daily noon–2:30pm and 7:30–10pm (until 11:30pm Fri–Sat); except no lunch Mon, no dinner Sun.

Osteria dell'Oca ★★★ LOMBARDY   The restaurant "of the duck" is crammed nightly with locals enjoying vibrant local cooking at truly amazing prices. This is an Italian family-run restaurant at its very best: noisy, happy, and joyous. The best *primi* are the sharing plates of *peccati di gola*, local salamis and pancetta accompanied by a thick wedge of creamy polenta, lard, and beetroot salsa. Other specialties are ravioli stuffed with marrow and pike pulled fresh from the lakes surrounding the city. Only three wines are served, in chunky carafes. Opt for the white from local vineyards rather than the *lambrusco*, which is overly sweet. This generous outpouring of food is rounded off with complimentary coffees and the thick, treacle-like hazelnut *digestivo della casa*. Book ahead for a weekend table.

Via Trieste 10. www.osteriadellocamantova.com. © **0376-327-171.** Main courses 12€–17€. Wed–Sat and Mon noon–3pm and 7:15–11:30pm, Sun noon–3pm.

Casa Poli ★★★   Hidden behind the facade of a 19th-century mansion, this bijou boutique hotel is packed night after night with both business travelers and holidaymakers. It's easy to see why. Guest rooms are spotless and stylishly pared down in contemporary style, with funky lights, bright splashes of color, and equally cool bathrooms. The lounge is full of arty books, and the pretty summer courtyard is a great spot to while away an hour over an evening *aperitivo*. But it's the staff that really makes this place shine; they're chatty and informal, and all willing to go that extra mile to accommodate guest requests.

Corso Garibaldi 32. www.hotelcasapoli.it. © **0376-288-170.** 27 units. 118€–170€ double. Rates include continental breakfast. Free street parking. **Amenities:** Bar; concierge; Wi-Fi (free).

Residenza Bibiena ★★   Tucked away in a pretty corner of Mantua's *centro storico* 5 minutes from the Palazzo Ducale, this cozy B&B, located in a traditional terracotta townhouse, has a pleasing air of old-school charm. The rooms are very simply furnished with wooden furniture and tiled floors enlivened by warm color schemes and pretty bed linens. Vast family rooms are available, the en suites are all huge by Italian standards, and a couple of rooms have terraces. Breakfast is served in the bar across the road.

Piazza Arche, 5. www.residenzabibiena.it. © **0376-355-699.** 5 units. 80€ double. Rates include breakfast. Parking 15€. **Amenities:** Wi-Fi (free).

Shopping & Entertainment

The favored shopping streets in Mantua radiate off Piazza delle Erbe, a delightful cluster of cobbled and arcaded streets sheltering delis stuffed with local cheeses, hams, fresh pasta, and olive oils. **Corso Umberto, Via Verdi,** and **Via Oberdan** are lined with classy boutiques, smart shoe shops, and bookstores. There's a **farmers' market** on Lungorio IV di Novembre on Saturday, and come lunchtime the lines outside the delicatessens form as happy patrons leave with beautifully packaged goodies. It's perfect fodder for a picnic in the lakeside gardens along Lungolago dei Gonzaga.

Mantua is a cultured city well supplied with theater and classical concerts; there are regular recitals at cute little **Teatro Bibiena** (see p. 459) and a full program of films and concerts at **Mantova Teatro** in the Piazza Cavallotti (www.teatrosocialemantova.it). A chamber-music festival is held every May and the **Festivaletteratura literature festival** each September.

LAKE COMO ★★★

Como (town): 65km (40 miles) NE of Milan; Menaggio: 35km (22 miles) NE of Como and 85km (53 miles) N of Milan; Varenna: 50km (31 miles) NE of Como and 80km (50 miles) NE of Milan

Life is slower around the northern Italian lakes than in mega-paced Milan. The city of Como is an ideal base for drawing breath and kicking back. Sitting on the southwestern tip of Lake Como, the city is essentially a center of commerce with a miniscule medieval quarter and a pretty waterfront. Tourists flock here for its ancient heritage, fine churches, and lake views. From there, frequent ferry service hops around the lake, visiting its many romantic lakeshore villas and villages.

Essentials

GETTING THERE   **Trains** run from Milan's Stazione Central and Porta Garibaldi half-hourly to Como San Giovanni; the trip takes 1 hour and costs 4.80€. One-hour services from Milan Cadorna arrive at Como Nord Lago (just off the lakefront promenade, near the ferry point) and cost 4.80€.

VISITOR INFORMATION   The **regional tourist office** at Piazza Cavour 17 (www.lakecomo.com; ✆ **031-269-712**) dispenses a wealth of information on hotels, restaurants, and campgrounds around the lake. The office is open Monday to Saturday 9am to 1pm and 2 to 5pm. You'll also find tourist offices open in summer in several of the small towns around the lake; in **Tremezzo** at Via Regina 3 (✆ **0344-40-**493); in **Varenna** at Via IV Novembre 7 (www.varennaitaly.com; ✆ **0341-830-367**); and in **Bellaggio** at Piazza Mazzini (www.bellagiolakecomo.com; ✆ **0341-950-204**).

GETTING AROUND   Como is the jumping-off point for most adventures on Lake Como, which is criss-crossed by regular **ferry routes:** It takes 4 hours to travel from one end to the other and there are many stops along the way. The most popular are **Tremezzo, Menaggio, Bellagio,** and timeless **Varenna** (see p. 464). Single fares from Como are 10.40€ to Bellagio; a day pass costs 28€. Tickets cannot be purchased online. The ferry terminal, run by **Navigazione Lago di Como,** is on the lake esplanade at Via per Cernobbio 18 (www.navigazionelaghi.it; ✆ **031-579-211**).

Como ★★

Como's tiny *centro storico* is dominated by the flamboyant **Duomo ★★** (Piazza Duomo; www.cattedraledicomo.it; ✆ **031-331-2275**), which combines Gothic and Renaissance architecture for two very different facades; long, narrow windows and a Gothic stained-glass rose window mark the western end, with a seamless apse and Baroque dome added in 1744 by architect Filippo Juvarra (see p. 485) at the eastern end. The Duomo is open daily 10:30am to 5pm (visitors are welcome from 1pm to 4:30pm on Sundays after mass) and admission is free.

Two blocks south of the Duomo, the 12th-century **San Fedele ★** basilica (free admission; daily 8am–noon, 3:30–7pm), stands above a charming square of the same name. Parts of the five-sided church, including the altar, date from the 6th century, and there are some fine frescoes along the right-hand side aisle.

Como's main street, **Corso Vittorio Emanuele II,** cuts through the medieval quarter and has plenty of upmarket boutiques and classy delis. If you have time, take the 10-minute **funicular ride** from Lungo Lario Trieste up to hilltop **Brunate ★★,** which has a cluster of excellent restaurants and bars. The funicular runs up a steep cliff-side, with glorious views of Lake Como glinting below; at the top, you'll also find wooded hiking trails that lead up to Bellagio. The funicular ticket office is at Piazza de Gasperi 4 (www.funicolarecomo.it; © **031-303-608;** daily 8am–10:30pm; funicular runs until midnight on Saturdays and in summer). Tickets are 3€ adults, 2€ for kids under 12 (children under 110cm in height travel free). Trains depart both ends of line every 30 minutes.

Lake Como's Waterfront Villages

The romantic waterfront villages of Lake Como, with their cute clusters of yellow and pink houses, majestic *palazzos,* and lush lakeside gardens, are easily explored by ferry (see p. 462) or by car. Here are a few of the highlights, going clockwise round the lake.

LENNO ★★★   For centuries Lake Como was the playground of privileged Lombardian aristocrats (and quite honestly not much has changed); **Villa del Balbianello** at Lenno (Via Comoedia 5; http://eng.fondoambiente.it/beni/villa-del-balbianello-fai-properties.asp; © **0344-56-110**), is one of the best known of their fabulous villas, with ornate landscaped gardens and a 16th-century palace sitting high on its peninsula over the lake. (You may recognize it from its recent brush with fame in the Bond movie *Casino Royale.*) The interior is full of priceless French furniture complemented by eclectic artwork from the travels of its former owner, explorer Guido Monzino, who died in 1988 and left the villa to the Italian National Trust. Admission varies: Garden entrance only is 7€ adults, 3€ kids 4 to 12; garden and villa (with compulsory tour) is 13€ adults, 7€ children aged 4–12. (Tip: There's a discount if you reserve in advance.) Open mid-March to mid-November, 10am to 6pm, closed Monday and Wednesday.

TREMEZZO ★★   On the western side of Lake Como, Tremezzo was the prestigious 19th-century retreat of the Italian aristocracy; today it is lorded over by the exceptionally expensive **Grand Hotel Tremezzo** (www.grandhoteltremezzo.com; © **0344-42-491**) and its wonderfully stylish lido on the lake. The luxurious gardens, museum, and rich art collections of the ornate 17th-century **Villa Carlotta** are open to the public (Via Regina 2; www.villacarlotta.it; © **0344-404-05**). Admission is 9€ adults, 7€ seniors, 5€ students. Open late March to mid-October from 9am to 7:30pm (last entry 6pm); open late October to mid-March from 10am to 6pm (last entry 5pm).

The gardens of Villa Carlotta.

BELLANO ★   Most people stop in Bellano on the eastern shores of Lake Como to visit the **Orrido** (© **338-5246-716;** admission 3€ adults, 2.50€ seniors and under 14), a deep gorge cut out of the cliffs by the River Pioverna as it tears down the hillside. A nighttime trip down the floodlit gorge is a rare and eerie treat, and one that appears to be under threat from recent hydroelectric plans that will reduce the flow of the torrent. Opening times vary seasonally but are roughly: April to June and September 10am to 1pm and 2:30 to 7pm; July to August 10am to 7pm and 8:45 to 10pm.

VARENNA ★★★   Adorable Varenna gives Bellagio a run for its money as the prettiest village on Lake Como, with a tumble of pink and terracotta houses in a labyrinth of narrow, cobbled streets, and smart villas clustered around the shoreline. Its winding lakeside path hangs over the water, with bars, shops, and art galleries looking over the lake. Linger a while over a glass of prosecco and watch the sun go down over the glittering water.

BELLAGIO ★★★   Photogenic Bellagio is the most popular destination around Lake Como and has just about remained on the right side of overtly touristic. The shady lakefront promenade is lined with chic hotels, bars, and cafes. Pretty medieval alleyways ascend from the lake in steep steps and are lined with souvenir stores selling expensive hand-tooled leather accessories. Just don't expect too many bargains. Regardless of the multitude of tourists, this is still a lovely place to linger for lunch overlooking the lake.

Where to Eat & Stay

With Como's fame has come a paucity of decent moderately priced hotels, although there are still plenty of options around the lake. If you're looking for a splurge, Cernobbio is home to one of Italy's most exclusive and expensive hotels: the **Villa d'Este** (see below). The local cuisine draws heavily on the lake, and polenta is as popular here as pasta.

Da Pietro ★★ PASTA AND PIZZA There are several touristy restaurants on Como's gorgeous Piazza del Duomo, all in a row and fairly interchangeable, but Da Pietro has long had the edge for friendliness and smooth service. It's a perfect family pitstop for a lunch of decently cooked pasta or vast, crisp pizzas. You pay for the peerless view of the Duomo, but the atmosphere is buzzing night and day.
Piazza Duomo 16, Como. ℂ **031-264-005.** Main courses around 12€. Daily 10am–midnight.

The narrow streets of Bellagio.

Splendide Ristorante ★★★ REGIONAL ITALIAN There's not a prettier spot on the whole of Lake Como than this geranium-filled terrace belonging to the Hotel Excelsior Splendide in Bellagio. Hanging out over the shimmering waters of the lake, the restaurant concentrates on good local dishes, from polentas and pasta to giant prawns sizzled in garlic and fresh trout from the lake. There's also a delicious ice cream bar under the arcade across the street.
Via Lungo Lario Manzoni 28, Bellagio. www.hsplendide.com. ℂ **031-950-225.** Main courses 10€–40€. Mar–Nov noon–2:30pm.

La Polenteria ★★★ REGIONAL ITALIAN Vegetarians, be prepared to take pot luck, as the ethos behind La Polenteria is to utilize and cook whatever is in season; this could be anything from snails, venison, wild boar, and fish fresh from the lake to porcini mushrooms, or, in fall, pasta flavored with chestnuts. As the name suggests, the regional specialty polenta (cornmeal) accompanies many of the dishes. The rustic dining room has had a facelift; gone are the shelves of dusty bottles and farming implements hanging on the walls. Now they are a cheery, warming yellow. Booking is advisable and proceedings can get riotous in the evening.
Via Scalini, 66, Brunate. www.lapolenteria.it. ℂ **031-336-5105.** Main courses 8€–30€. Fri 7:15–10:30pm, Sat–Sun 12:15pm–2:30pm, 7:30–10:30pm.

Hotel du Lac ★★ With one entrance slap-bang on Varenna's charming waterfront and the other hidden away in its equally photogenic tangle of alleyways, the Hotel du Lac is housed in an elegant 19th-century villa offering prized views across Lake Como. It's now open for "light lunch," and the flower-filled terrace is the perfect spot for cocktails à deux as the sun sinks over the lake. The romantic theme continues inside with marble pillars and wrought-iron staircases, roomy (for Europe) bedrooms decked out in subtle shades of green, gold, and red, plus revamped bathrooms.

Via del Prestino 11, Varenna. www.albergodulac.com. ℂ **0341-830-238.** 16 units. Doubles 175€–260€. Rates include breakfast. Closed mid-Nov to Feb. Free parking. **Amenities:** Restaurant (lunch only); bar; Wi-Fi (free).

Hotel Paradiso sul Largo ★★★ This great *albergo* has had a total overhaul since it reopened in 2008 and is now powered by voltaic panels, making it the first eco-hotel around Lake Como. Right at the top of the village of Brunate above Como town, it's in a little *piazza* surrounded by restaurants and is on the edge of pleasingly untamed forested countryside. The rooms are simple, spotlessly clean, and functional, but the main selling points are the amazing hilltop views over Lake Como from the breakfast room, and the panoramic terrace with swimming pool and Jacuzzi. Be sure to book a room with lake views.

Via Scalini 74, Brunate San Maurizio. www.hotelparadisosullago.com. ℂ **031-364-099.** 12 units. 137€ double. Rates include breakfast. Free parking. **Amenities:** Pizza restaurant; bar; outdoor pool; shuttle service; Wi-Fi (free).

Nest on the Lake ★★ This cute little B&B is in a tranquil lakeside spot in Lezzeno, minutes from Bellagio (see p. 464). Bedrooms are all decked out in white, some with four-poster beds, and all have wrought-iron balconies. A decent self-service breakfast is offered, and the more-than-helpful Raffa and Tino are building quite a reputation for their hospitality; they are happy to recommend restaurants and organize tours. The minimum stay is 3 nights in summer.

Frazione Sostra 17/19, Lezzeno. www.nestonthelake.com. ℂ **031-914-372.** 5 units. 100–110€ double; 120–140€ apt. Parking 5€ per day. **Amenities:** Solarium; Wi-Fi (free).

Villa d'Este ★★ Set in an ornate Renaissance *palazzo* dating from 1568 and overlooking Lake Como amid verdant parklands, the Villa d'Este certainly adds to the lake's reputation as playboy central. It sees a constant procession of celebs and minor royalty arriving by speedboat or helicopter to luxuriate in the raft of sporting facilities, the array of fine dining options, and the refined rooms furnished with priceless antiques. As befits one of the most exclusive hotels in the world, two revamped private villas guarantee complete seclusion from the hoi polloi.

Via Regina 40, Cernobbio. www.villadeste.com. ℂ **031-3481.** 152 units. 440€–760€ double; 880€–970€ junior suite. Rates include breakfast. Free parking. Closed mid-Nov to mid-Mar. **Amenities:** 3 restaurants; 3 bars; nightclub; indoor and outdoor pools; spa; concierge; Wi-Fi (free).

LAKE MAGGIORE ★★

Stresa: 90km (56 miles) NW of Milan

Maggiore lies west of Como, a long, thin wisp of a lake protected by mountains and fed by the River Ticino, which flows on to Milan. Roughly a quarter of the northern section of the lake stands in Switzerland, including the city of Locarno and its delightful satellite resort of **Ascona.** **Stresa** is the largest town on the Italian part of the lake, a timeless resort on the western shoreline, famed for its position opposite the **Isole Borromee** islands. Regular **ferries** span Maggiore and there are frequent stops on the way from **Arona,** south of Stresa; the most popular include **Luino** for its massive market, and **Laveno** for cable-car rides up to mountain panoramas (see p. 469).

Essentials

GETTING THERE Stresa is linked with Milan Stazione Centrale and Porta Garibaldi by 20 **trains** a day. Journeys take around an hour and cost 8.30€.

Boats arrive at and depart from Piazza Marconi, Stresa. Many lakeside spots can be reached from Stresa, with most boats on the lake operated by **Navigazione Laghi** (www.navlaghi.it; ✆ **0322-233-200**). The lake's main ferry office, however, is at the lake's southern tip in **Arona,** at Viale Baracca 1; from there, ferries to Stresa take 40 minutes and cost 6.20€.

The A8 runs west from Milan to Sesto Calende, near the southern end of the lake; from there, follow Route SS33 up the western shore to Stresa. The trip takes just over an hour, but much longer on a summer weekend.

The Alps rise above Lake Maggiore.

VISITOR INFORMATION   Stresa's **tourist office** is at the ferry dock on Piazza Marconi (www.stresaturismo.it; ☎ **0323-30-150**) and is open daily 10am to 12:30pm and 3 to 6:30pm (mid-October to mid-March closed Sat afternoons and Sun). For hiking information, ask for the booklet "Percorsi Verdi."

Stresa & the Islands

The biggest town on the Italian side of Maggiore, elegant Stresa is the springboard to the Isole Borromee (Borromean Islands), the tiny Baroque jewels of the lake. Now a genteel tourist town, Stresa captured the hearts of 19th-century aristocracy, who settled in droves in grandiose villas strung along the promenade. Just back into the tangle of medieval streets, **Piazza Cadorna** is a mass of restaurants that spill out into the center of the square in summer. There's a food and craft market on summer Thursday afternoons along the promenade, and a lido and beach club on the lakefront.

The three Isole Borromee are named for the aristocratic Borromeo family who has owned them since the 12th century. Public **ferries** leave for the islands every half-hour from Stresa's Piazza Marconi outside the tourist office; a 16.90€ **daily pass** is the most economical way to visit the Bella, Pescatori, and Madre islands all in one day. For more information on the Borromean Islands, check out www.isoleborromee.it.

ISOLA DEI PESCATORI ★★   Pescatori is stuck in a medieval time warp, with ancient fishermens' houses clustered together on every inch of the tiny island. Wander the meandering cobbled streets as they reveal tiny churches, art galleries, souvenir shops, pizza and pasta restaurants, and, at every turn, a glimpse of the lake beyond. It's an entrancing place to explore, but be warned: the prices are extortionate and the crowds frustrating.

ISOLA BELLA ★★★   The minute islet of Bella is dominated by the massive Baroque **Palazzo Borromeo** (www.isoleborromee.it) with its formal Italianate gardens. It makes for an absorbing tour, with conspicuous displays of wealth evident in the rich decor and exquisite furnishings. The terraced gardens, restored in 2014, are dotted with follies and have spectacular views across Maggiore. Of special interest are the ornate grottoes underground where the Borromeos went to stay cool, or the painting gallery, hung with 130 of the most important artworks the Borromeos collected over the centuries. Admission is 15€ adults, 8.50€ for ages 6 to 15. Open mid-Mar to mid-Oct 9am–5:30pm.

ISOLA MADRE ★★   The largest and most peaceful of the islands is Isola Madre (30 min. from Stresa), overspread with exquisite flora in the 3.2-hectare (8-acre) **Orto Botanico.** Pick up a map at the ticket office to identify all the rhododendrons, camellias, and ancient wisteria. Many a peacock and fancy pheasant stalk across the lawns of another 16th-century **Borromeo palazzo** (www.isoleborromee.it), which is filled with family memorabilia and some interesting old puppet-show stages.

Isola Bella.

Admission to the garden and palace is 12€ adults, 6.50€ for ages 6 to 15. Open Mar–Oct 9am–5:30pm.

Around Lake Maggiore

Beyond Stresa, Maggiore offers natural beauty and architectural wonders as well as lively towns, markets, and cable-car rides up into the mountains.

Arona ★★   As well as having the lake's main ferry office (see p. 467) this sophisticated town at the southern end of Lake Maggiore is a shopping magnet, with its charming **Via Cavour** lined with elegant boutiques and expensive delicatessens. The giant bronze **statue of Carlo Borromeo** (see p. 470), who was born in Arona in 1538, is located just outside of town. It's so huge, you can even climb inside and gaze out at the lake through Carlo's eyes (ⓒ **0322-249-669;** admission 5€; mid-Mar to Oct daily 9am–noon and 2–6pm).

Luino ★★   On the western shore of Lake Maggiore just a few miles from the Swiss border, Luino is home of one of northern Italy's most popular **street markets**, with more than 350 stalls taking over the town every Wednesday. Here you'll find cheery sarongs, spices, piles of salami, grappas, olive oils, as well as the hand-tooled leather belts and bags for which the region is famous. Day visitors from Milan can catch the train directly to Luino from Milan's Stazione Centrale or Stazione Porta Garibaldi in under 2 hours (7.90€), while extra ferries serve the town every Wednesday. Check ferry timetables with www.navlaghi.it.

Sasso del Fero ★★★   East of the lakeshore town of Laveno, make for Laveno Mombello, where you can take the 16-minute **cable-car** trip (www.funiviedellagomaggiore.it; ⓒ **0332-668-012;** 10€ roundtrip) up the lush Val Cuvia to the Poggia Sant'Elsa viewpoint atop **Sasso del Ferro**, towering 1,062m (3,484 ft.) over Lake Maggiore. Here you'll find

The all-powerful Borromeo family were Lombardian aristocrats who played a major part in Milanese politics and religion for 200 years. They regarded the vast tracts of land around the southern end of Lake Maggiore as their own personal fiefdom, where they built castles, monuments, and palaces. The family spawned several archbishops of Milan, including Federico (1564–1631) and Carlo (1538–1584), a singularly wily and wealthy individual who was canonized in 1610 for his support of the Counter-Reformation against papal infallibility. A great bronze statue of Carlo stands in Arona, on a hillock looking out across the lake to his former family home, Rocca Borromeo at Angera.

truly breathtaking panoramas, looking west to the snow-capped Alps or south over the mini-lakes Varese, Monate, and Comabbio. If the conditions are right, there'll be plenty of paragliders to watch, and the hills are crisscrossed with scenic hiking trails. Leave time to relax over a prosecco in the **Ristorante Albergo Funivia** (see p. 471). Opening times vary according to weather conditions, but the cable car generally runs April to October (Mon–Fri 11am–6:30pm; Sat–Sun 11am–10:30pm).

Santa Caterina del Sasso Ballaro ★★★   Just south of Reno on the southeastern leg of Maggiore, beneath an inconspicuous car park in Piazza Cascine del Quiquio, an elevator descends to the magical hermitage of **Santa Caterina del Sasso Ballaro** (Via Santa Caterina 13, Leggiuno; www.santacaterinadelsasso.com; ✆ **0332-647-172**). Founded in the 13th century, this Dominican monastery sits photogenically against a sheer rock face, clinging to an escarpment 15m (49 ft.) above the lake. The serene complex of soft pink stone is embellished with Renaissance arches, a square bell tower, and pretty cobbled courtyards. Don't miss the 14th-century frescoes of biblical scenes in the chapel, which were hidden under lime during the Italian suppression of the monasteries in the 1770s and only rediscovered in 2003. The little gift shop sells honey, candles, and soaps made by the monks. Admission is free, but donations are accepted (open Apr–Oct 9am–noon and 2:30–6pm, Nov–Mar Sat–Sun 9am–noon and 2–5pm).

Where to Eat & Stay

There are many hotels scattered around Maggiore eager to grab the tourist dollar: some good, some bad, many indifferent. Here are two that are exceptional, at opposite ends of the price spectrum. Just like the hotels in the area, the standard of food can varies wildly; pick your restaurants in touristy Stresa with care.

Ristorante Piemontese ★★ NORTHERN ITALIAN   A cut above the myriad pasta/pizza places that haunt the town center, this is where all the Italian locals go to dine in Stresa. Here, the Bellossi family concentrates on producing serious cooking, offering excellent Barbera di Alba wines to round out your meal. Dishes such as porcini risotto and duck confit are proudly presented in elegant and romantic surroundings, with fish and game options changing according to season. Finish off with a cheeseboard of pungent local cheeses.

Via Mazzini 25, Stresa. www.ristorantepiemontese.com. ✆ **0323-302-35.** Main courses 8€–20€. Tues–Sun 7:30–10:30pm. Closed Dec–Jan.

Ristorante Verbano ★★ SEAFOOD Although many of the restaurants on the Isole Borromee are overpriced and underwhelming, Verbano is the exception (so you should probably book ahead on the weekends). For once on this touristy little island, the service is exemplary; you won't feel rushed and the waiting staff is courteous and informed. Not only is its position sublime, overlooking Isola Bella's Palazzo Borromeo (see p. 468) with lake waters lapping around the terrace—this would make a romantic proposal spot—but the food is pretty good, too. Chef Diego Pioletti specializes in cooking fish fresh from the lake as well as creating hearty homemade pasta dishes and traditional risottos; there's also a five-course gourmet menu option priced at 50€.

Via Ugo Ara 2, Isola Pescatori. www.hotelverbano.it. ✆ **0323-304-08.** Main courses 15€–30€. Daily noon–2:30pm and 7–10pm (winter closed Wed). Closed Jan.

Albergo Funivia ★★ This basic hotel up at the Poggia Sant'Elsa belvedere is only accessible by the Sasso del Ferro cable car (see p. 469). The upside—literally—is beautiful views over Lake Maggiore towards the Alps from the balconies in every room. It's best for summer visits when the weather can be almost guaranteed. The restaurant serves a simple local menu and the sun terrace is always crammed on sunny days. Little can beat sitting out there after dark and watching the lights around the lake glittering in the distance.

Via Tinelli, 15, Località Poggio Sant Elsa, Laveno Mombello. www.funiviedellago maggiore.it. ✆ **0332-610-303.** 12 units. Doubles 80€. Unguarded parking at foot of funicular. **Amenities:** Bar; restaurant; Wi-Fi (free).

Grand Hotel des Iles Borromee ★★★ The vast, over-the-top Belle Epoque exterior of this majestic old hotel in Stresa faces Lake Maggiore with its manicured and landscaped gardens. The interior lives up to the exterior, too, and with panache; all is hushed, ornate, marble, and gilded, opulent as a mini-Versailles. Rooms vary from doubles with garden views, which are (relatively) staidly decorated with plush marble bathrooms, to the fabulously glitzy Hemingway Suite, which consists of three bedrooms, a living room, four bathrooms, and a terrace overlooking the lake—it's almost blinding in its marble, silk, stucco, and gilt design. There's a blissful spa to chill out in and a gourmet restaurant with a lakeview terrace.

Corso Umberto I 67, Stresa. www.borromees.it. ✆ **0323-938-938.** 172 units. 185€–450€ double; 400€–3,300€ suite (higher prices are summer rates). Rates include breakfast. Valet parking. **Amenities:** Restaurant; bar; concierge; spa; sauna; indoor pool; 2 outdoor pools; personal trainer; gym; helicopter pad; Wi-Fi (free).

LAKE GARDA (LAGO DI GARDA) ★★

Sirmione: 130km (81 miles) E of Milan, 150km (93 miles) W of Venice; Riva del Garda: 170km (105 miles) NE of Milan, 199km (123 miles) NW of Venice, 43km (27 miles) S of Trent

Lake Garda is the largest and easternmost of the Northern Italian lakes, with its western flanks lapping against the flat plains of Lombardy and its southern extremes in the Veneto. In the north, its deep waters are backed by Alpine peaks. Garda's shores are green and fragrant with flowery gardens, groves of olives and lemons, and forests of pines and cypress.

Essentials

GETTING THERE Regular **trains** run from Milan Stazione Centrale and stop at Desenzano del Garda (fares start at 9.20€). From here it's a 20-minute bus ride to Sirmione; buses make the short hop every half hour for 1.90€).

Hydrofoils and ferries operated by **Navigazione Laghi** (www. navlaghi.it; ✆ **800-551-801**) ply the waters of the lake. One to two hourly ferries connect Sirmione with Desenzano del Garda in season (20 min. by ferry, 3€); less frequently October to April.

Sirmione is just off the A4 between Milan and Venice. From Venice the trip takes about 1½ hours, and from Milan a little over an hour. There's ample parking in Piazzale Monte Baldo.

VISITOR INFORMATION **Sirmione**'s tourist office is at Viale Marconi 8 (www.comune.sirmione.bs.it; ✆ **030-374-8721**). There is also a tourism kiosk at Viale Marconi 2 just before the bridge into the old part of town. Hours vary depending on the season. In **Riva del Garda**, the tourist office is on the lakefront at Largo Medaglie d'Oro al Valor Militare 5 (www.gardatrentino.it/en; ✆ **0464-554-444**). Hours vary depending on the season. There's also a tourist office in **Gardone Riviera** at Corso Repubblica 8 (✆ **0365-20-347**).

Sirmione

Perched on a promontory swathed in cypress and olive groves on the southernmost edge of Lake Garda, photogenic Sirmione has been a popular spot since the Romans first discovered hot springs here.

Lemon groves are abundant around Lake Garda.

Despite the onslaught of summer visitors, this historic little town manages to retain its charm. Sirmione has lakeside promenades and pleasant beaches and is small enough for everywhere to be accessible on foot. It is chiefly famous for its thermal springs, castle, and northern Italy's largest Roman ruins.

The moated, fortified **Rocca Scaligero ★★★** (*©* **030-916-468**) was built on the peninsula's narrowest point and today dominates the *centro storico*. Built in the late 13th century by the Della

Thermal baths in Sirmione.

Scala family, who ruled Verona and many of the lands surrounding the lake, the castle is worth a visit for its sweeping courtyards, turreted defence towers, dungeons, and views across Lake Garda from the battlements. It's open Tuesday to Saturday 8:30am to 7:30pm, and from 8:30am to 2pm on Sundays; admission is 4€, ages 18 to 25 2€.

From the castle, it's a 15-minute walk (or take the open-air tram from Piazza Piatti) along Via Vittorio Emanuele from the town center to the tip of Sirmione's peninsula and the **Grotte di Catullo ★★** (*©* **030-916-157**), romantically placed ruins with views across the lake. Built around A.D. 150, the remains are thought to represent two sizeable villas owned by aristocratic Roman families. A small museum of Roman artifacts found at the site includes jewelry and mosaic fragments (Piazzale Orti Manara 4; admission 6€ adults, 3€ 18–25; opening times vary, but are generally Apr–Sept Tues–Sat 8:30am–7:30pm, Sun 9:30am–6:30pm; Mar–Oct Tues–Sat 9am–5pm, Sun 8:30am–2pm).

The massive amusement park **Gardaland** (www.gardaland.it; *©* **045-6449-777**) is half an hour's drive east of Sirmione at Castelnuovo del Garda. This huge resort includes a hotel and an aquarium and is generally thronged during school vacation periods, but if Disneyland-type places are your thing, you may want to check it out.

Riva del Garda

The northernmost settlement on Lake Garda is a thriving Italian town, with medieval towers, a smattering of Renaissance churches and *palazzi*, and narrow cobblestone streets where everyday business proceeds in its alluring way. Note that Riva del Garda becomes a cultural oasis in July, when the town hosts the international **Largo di Garda Festival** of classical music (www.mrf-musicfestivals.com). Riva del Garda's **Old Town** is pleasant, although the only notable historic attractions are the 13th-century **Torre d'Apponale** in Piazza III Novembre, which is open in

Halfway up the western shore of Lake Garda, this little resort—easily accessible by ferry or bus from Desenzano del Garda—offers visitors a gorgeous backdrop for a little relaxation. Oleanders dot the paved promenade, and the charming *centro storico* (Gardone Sopra) is filled with enticing bars and restaurants.

Uphill from Gardone Sopra, the **Heller Garden** (Via Roma 2; www.hellergarden.com; © **0336-410-877**) is a tropical paradise founded by Arthur Hruska, a botanist who was also dentist to the ill-fated Tsar Nicholas II of Russia. Hruska planted this botanical haven in the 1900s, and 8,000 rare palms, orchids, and tree ferns now thrive here, thanks to the town's mild, sheltered climate. Today the gardens are curated by Austrian artist André Heller, whose sculptures can be found scattered among the water features, cacti, and bamboo copses. The garden is open March to October daily from 9am to 7pm; admission is 10€, 5€ for ages 6 to 11.

Gardone Riviera's other highlight is the **Vittoriale degli Italiani** (Via Vittoriale 12; www.vittoriale.it; © **0365-296-511**), the wildly ostentatious and bizarrely decorated villa home to Gabriele d'Annunzio, Italy's most notorious poet and sometime war hero. He bought this hillside estate in 1921 and died here in 1936; a visit pays tribute to d'Annunzio's hedonistic lifestyle rather than his fairly awful poetry. The claustrophobic rooms of this madcap mansion are stuffed with bric-a-brac and artifacts from his colorful life, including mementos of his long affair with actress Eleonora Duse. The patrol boat D'Annunzio commanded in World War I, a museum containing his biplane and photos, and the poet's pompous hilltop mausoleum are all found in the formal gardens that cascade down the hillside in luxuriant terraces. Summer concerts and plays are held at the amphitheater (www.anfiteatrodelvittoriale.it). The villa is open daily; in summer from 8:30am to 8pm and winter from 9am to 5pm. Admission ranges from 8€ to 16€, depending on which parts of the estate you choose to visit. Note that villa tours are available in Italian only.

summer for visitors to climb its 165 steps for views across the lake, and the moated lakeside castle, **La Rocca.** Part of the castle now houses an unassuming civic museum with changing exhibitions (© **0464-573-869**; open daily 10am–12:30pm and 1:30–6pm, closed on Mon Oct–June; admission 3€ adults, 1.40€ ages 15–26 and over 65, children 14 and under free).

Where to Eat & Stay

Sirmione and Riva del Garda have a choice of pleasant, moderately priced hotels, all of which book up quickly in July and August, when the rates increase. The local cuisine features fish from the lake and plenty of pasta.

Osteria Al Torcol ★★ ITALIAN   Consistently regarded as the standout restaurant in Sirmione, Torcol serves up good strong Italian cooking bursting with flavor, while managing to keep things moderately priced. This atmospheric place has an old-world wooden interior packed with bottles of local wines (many available by the glass) and a serving staff that really know what they are talking about. Signature dishes include fresh *tagliolini* (noodles) with pistachio and shrimp as well as a choice of fish of the day straight from the lake; it might be trout or pike. Book in advance if you want to eat outside on the rustic patio under the trees or at one of the lovely tables out front.

Via San Salvatore 30, Sirmione. ✆ **030-990-4605.** Main courses 13€–30€. Open May–Sept daily 12:30–3pm, 7:30–10:30pm; Oct–Jan Sat–Sun 12:30–3pm, 7:30–10:30pm; Feb–Apr Sat–Sun 7:30–10:30pm.

Trattoria Riolet ★ ITALIAN   As popular with Gardone locals as with summer visitors, the Riolet has unsurpassed views over Lake Garda from its hilltop aerie. Although the cuisine might be rustic—think pasta pesto, chicken kebabs cooked over the open fire and served with polenta, and lots of grilled fish—everything is freshly cooked and as fresh and tasty as could be. There's no menu, so take a leap of faith and follow your waiter's advice when ordering—and be sure to enjoy a carafe or two of the local wines.

Via Fasano Sopra 47, Gardone Riviera. ✆ **0365-205-45.** Thurs–Tues 7–10:30pm. Main courses 8€–25€.

Hotel du Lac et du Parc ★★★   Set in lush gardens, this massive, family-friendly resort has swimming pools, spas, and every conceivable luxury. Leading down to a little beach at the lake, the grounds are roomy enough to contain 33 bungalows and two luxurious blocks of apartments, still leaving ample space for the hotel. Somehow, despite the size of the operation, the service still feels personal and attention to detail is manifest everywhere. The gym, spas, and pools are spotless, the rooms are cheery and tasteful—ask for one overlooking the palm trees and rare plants of the park—and the breakfast buffet is five star. A tiny drawback is the over-fussy cuisine in the **La Capannina** restaurant, but there are plenty of dining options in Riva del Garda itself, a 15-minute walk away.

Via Rovereto 44, Riva del Garda. www.dulacetduparc.com. ✆ **0464-566-600.** 159 units in main hotel. 103€–229€ double; 170€–655€ suites. Rates include breakfast. Free parking. Closed Jan to mid-Apr. **Amenities:** 2 restaurants; 3 bars; 2 outdoor pools; indoor pool; gym; spa; sauna; gardens; babysitting; kids' club; water sports; concierge; room service; Wi-Fi (free).

Hotel Eden ★   Once home of American poet Ezra Pound, this pink-stucco lakeside hotel is in the heart of the action in Sirmione, a stone's throw from the picturesque *centro storico*. Inside, the hotel is decked out in a bright and modern way with jazzy public spaces and vivid wallpaper designs; the breakfast room leads out to a shady terrace overlooking the lake, and a swimming pier juts out over the water. The modern take on a '70s theme is continued in the bedrooms, which have walls of splashy wallpaper enlivening the simple furnishings. Ask for a lakeview room as it can get a little noisy at night at the back of the hotel.

Piazza Carducci 19, Sirmione. www.hoteledensirmione.it. ✆ **030-916-481.** 30 units. 139€–183€ double. Rates include breakfast. Free parking nearby; 10€ in garage. Closed Nov–Easter. **Amenities:** Restaurant; bar; concierge; room service; Wi-Fi (free).

out and about ON LAKE GARDA

Riva Del Garda's main attraction is the lake, lined with plush hotels and a waterside promenade that stretches for several miles past parks and pebbly beaches. The water is warm enough for swimming May to October, and air currents fanned by the mountains make Riva and neighboring Torbole the windsurfing capitals of Europe. Kitesurfing, kayaking, and sailing are all popular pastimes.

A convenient point of embarkation for a lake outing is the beach next to **La Rocca** castle (see p. 474), where you can rent rowboats or pedal boats for about 10€ per hour; from March through October, the concession is open daily 8am to 8pm.

Check out the sailing and windsurfing at **Sailing du Lac** at the luxurious **Hotel du Lac et du Parc** (see p. 475) where windsurf equipment can be rented for 47€ per day or 20€ for an hour. Lessons start at 49€ for 2 hours. Dinghy lessons are available from 75€ for 2 hours, rental from 25€ per hour. The school is open from mid-April to mid-October 8:30am to 6:30pm.

Lake Garda is also renowned for mountain biking; there are more than 80 routes around the waterside and up into the Alpine foothills. Rent bikes from **Happy Bike,** Viale Rovereto 72 (www.happy-bike.it; *©* **34-7943-1208**), open daily 9am to 1pm and 3 to 7pm; rent a mountain bike for 14€ per day, or grab an eco-friendly electric bike for 49€ per day.

TURIN ★★★

669km (415 miles) NW of Rome, 140km (87 miles) E of Milan

It's often said that Turin is the most French city in Italy. The reason is partly historical and partly architectural. From the late 13th century until Italy's unification in 1861, Turin was the capital of the **House of Savoy.** These aristocrats of extraordinary wealth were as French as they were Italian, with estates that extended well into the present-day French regions of Savoy, the Côte d'Azur, and Sardinia. Under the Savoys, Francophile 17th- and 18th-century architects razed much of the original city and its Roman foundations, replacing them with broad avenues, airy piazzas, and grandiose buildings. As a result, Turin is one of Europe's great baroque cities, as befitting the capital (albeit briefly) of a nation.

Thanks in part to the 2006 Winter Olympics, and another makeover for the 150th anniversary of Italian unification in 2011, Turin today has transformed itself from a former industrial power into a vibrant city full of museums, enticing cafes, beautiful squares, and designer stores. This elegant and sophisticated city is deservedly gaining a reputation as the go-to destination in northeast Italy.

Essentials

GETTING THERE   Domestic and international **flights** land at **Turin Airport** (www.aeroportoditorino.it; *©* **011-567-6378**), about 13km (8 miles) northwest of Turin. Direct trains (www.gtt.to.it) run from the airport to GTT Dora Railway Station every 30 minutes between 5am and

ATTRACTIONS

Basilica di Superga **13**

Duomo di San Giovanni Battista **5**

Mole Antonelliana **12**

Museo Egizio **10**

Museo Nazionale d'Automobile **15**

Museo Nazionale del Risorgimento Italiano **11**

Museo della Sindone **1**

Palazzo Madama **9**

Palazzo Reale **4**

HOTELS

Le Petit Hotel **6**

Townhouse 70 **8**

VitaminaM **14**

RESTAURANTS

Officine Bohemien **7**

Ruràl **2**

Trattoria Santo Spirito **3**

11pm, costing 3€; the trip takes 19 minutes. SADEM (www.sadem.it) buses run between the airport and the city's main train stations, Porta Nuova and Porta Susa (40 min.; 6.50€). **Taxis** into town take about 30 minutes and cost 30€ to 50€, depending on the time of day.

Turin's main **train** station is **Stazione di Porta Nuova** on Piazza Carlo Felice. There is regular daily Trenitalia (www.trenitalia.com; 𝄐 **89-20-21**) service from Milan. The fastest trains take 1 hour, with fares averaging 29€ (check advance-purchase fares, however, which can be as low as 9€). Slower trains take up to 2 hours, with fares of 12.20€ to 17€. **Stazione di Porta Susa** connects Turin with local Piedmont towns and is the terminus for the TGV service to Paris; four trains a day make the trip to Paris in under 6 hours for around 98€, but there are often specials in the off-season for as low as 29€ each way.

Turin's main **bus terminal** is **Autostazione Bus,** Corso Vittorio Emanuele II 131 (www.autostazionetorino.it). The ticket office is open daily 9am to 1pm and 3 to 7pm. Buses connect Turin to Courmayeur, Aosta, Milan, and many small towns in Piedmont. There is a 2-hour SADEM (www.sadem.it) bus service to Milan Malpensa Airport costing 22€.

Turin is at the hub of the autostrade network. The A4 connects Turin with Milan in 90 minutes. Journey time via the A5 to Aosta is also around 90 minutes.

GETTING AROUND   All the main sights of Turin are well within walking distance of each other. There's also a vast network of GTT trams and buses as well as one metro line (www.gtt.to.it; ✆ 011-57-641). The Linea 7 tourist tram trundles around a circular route from Piazza Castello. Tickets on public transportation are available at newsstands for 1.50€ and are valid for 90 minutes. All-day tickets are 5€ and last 24 hours. There is no need to drive in the city center.

You can find taxis at stands in front of the train stations and around Piazza San Carlo and Piazza Castello. To call a taxi, you can dial **Pronto** at ✆ 011-5737, but all hotel reception desks will order a taxi for you. Meters start at 3.50€ and prices increase by 1.25€ per kilometer; there are surcharges for waiting time, luggage, late-night travel, and Sunday journeys.

VISITOR INFORMATION   The **tourist office** on the corner of Via Garibaldi and Piazza Castello (www.turismotorino.org; ✆ 011-535-181), is open daily 9am to 6pm. There are also branches in **Stazione Porta Nuova** and at the airport (same phone; same hours).

The tourist offices on Piazza Castello and at Stazione Porta Nuova sell the bargain **Torino+Piemonte Card** for 26€. This is valid for one adult and one child up to age 12 for 48 hours and grants access to over 180 museums, monuments, castles, and royal palazzos, as well as free public transport within Turin, plus discounts on car rentals, ski lifts, theme parks, concerts, and sporting events (3- and 5-day versions are also available). Check www.turismotorino.org/card for details.

CITY LAYOUT   With the Alps as a backdrop to the north and the River Po threading through the city center, Turin has as its glamorous backbone the elegant arcaded **Via Roma**, lined with designer shops and grand cafes. Via Roma runs northwards through a series of ever-lovelier Baroque squares until it reaches **Piazza Castello** and the heart of the city around the palaces of the Savoy nobility.

From here, a walk west leads to the **Area Romano**, a mellow jumble of narrow streets that's the oldest part of the city. Its edge is marked by Via Garibaldi. Or turn east from Piazza Castello along Via Po to one of Italy's largest squares, the **Piazza Vittorio Veneto** and, at the end of this elegant expanse, the River Po and **Parco del Valentino.**

[FastFACTS] TURIN

ATMs/Banks There are banks with multilingual ATMs all over the city center. Opening hours are roughly Monday to Friday 8:30am to 1:30pm and 2:30 to 4:30pm.

Business Hours Stores are open Monday to Saturday from 9am–1pm and 4 to 7:30pm.

Consulates The consulates of the U.S., Canada, U.K., Australia, and New Zealand are in Milan (see p. 433).

Dentists Dr. Marco Capitanio at Via Treviso 24/G, (www.marcocapitanio. com; ☏ **34-7157-8802**), speaks fluent English.

Doctors The Medical Center at Corso Einaudi, 18/A (www.medical-center. it; ☏ **011-591-388**) has some English-speaking staff.

Drugstores A convenient late-night pharmacy is **Farmacia Boniscontro,** Corso Vittorio Emanuele 66 (☏ **011-538-271**); it is open all night but closes for lunch, 12:30 to 3pm, and is closed on Saturday and Sunday. The website **www. orari-di-apertura.it/farma cie-torino.htm** gives the opening hours of most of Turin's central pharmacies.

Emergencies All emergency numbers are free. Call ☏ **112** for a **general emergency**; this connects to the **Carabinieri,** who will transfer your call as needed; for the **police,** dial ☏ **113;** for a **medical emergency** or an ambulance, call ☏ **118;** for the **fire department,** call ☏ **115.**

Hospitals The **Ospedale Mauriziano Umberto I,** Largo Filippo Turati 62 (www.mauriziano.it; ☏ **011-508-1111**), offers a variety of medical services.

Internet Many Turin cafes, bars, restaurants, and hotels now have Wi-Fi. Try, for example, **Busters Coffee** (www.busterscoffee.it) at Via Cesare Battisti 7/L near Piazza Castello and the University of Turin. This café offers free Wi-Fi and serves up Italian coffee, tea, American-style beverage concoctions, panini, and salads. Open Mon to Fri 7:30am to 7:30pm and Sat to Sun 8:30am to 7:30pm

Police In an emergency, call ☏ **113;** this is a free call. The central police station (Questura Torino) is near Stazione di Porta Susa at Corso Vinzaglio 10 (☏ **011-558-81**).

Post Office Turin's **main post office,** just west of Piazza San Carlo at Via Alfieri 10 (☏ **011-506-0265**), is open Monday to Friday 8:30am to 6:30pm and Saturday from 8:30am to noon. A list of central post offices and opening times can be found at www. quartieri.torino.it/Elenco Poste.asp.

Safety Turin is a relatively safe city, but use the same precautions you would exercise in any large city. Specifically, avoid the riverside streets along the Po when the late-night crowds have gone home.

Exploring Turin

The stately arcades of **Via Roma,** Turin's premier shopping street, were designed in 1714 by Filippo Juvarra (see p. 483). This chic thoroughfare runs from the circular **Piazza Carlo Felice,** ringed with outdoor cafes and constructed around formal gardens, north into **Piazza San Carlo,** which is quite possibly Italy's most beautiful square. In summer Piazza San Carlo is Turin's harmonious outdoor *salone,* its arcaded sidewalks lined with big-name fashion stores and elegant cafes, including the genteel **Caffé Torino** (☏ **011-545-118**). In the center of the piazza prances a 19th-century equestrian statue of Duke Emanuele Filiberto of Savoy. A

Piazza San Carlo, Turin.

pair of 17th-century churches, **San Carlo** and **Santa Cristina**, face each other like bookends at the southern entrance to the square.

At the far north end of Via Roma, the **Piazza Castello** is dominated by **Palazzo Madama** (see p. 483), named for its 17th-century inhabitant, Christine Marie of France, who married into the Savoy dynasty in 1619. Further north still stands the massive complex of the **Palazzo Reale** (see p. 484), residence of the Savoy dukes from 1646 to 1865.

Duomo di San Giovanni Battista ★ CHURCH   One of the few pieces of Renaissance architecture in Baroque-dominated Turin, this otherwise uninspiring 15th-century cathedral tucked round the west flank of the Palazzo Reale is famous as the resting place of the **Turin Shroud** (see p. 481) when the shroud is not on display. The linen cloth is preserved in an aluminium casket specially manufactured by an Italian aerospace company in the temperature-controlled, air-conditioned **Cappella della Sacra Sindone** and closed off from human contamination with bulletproof glass. The shroud's casket is adorned with a crown of thorns; the faithful come in droves to worship at the chapel, which is the last one in the left-hand aisle. To learn all about the history of the shroud, head for the **Museo della Sindone** (see p. 483).

Piazza San Giovanni. www.visitatorino.com/duomo_torino.htm. 𝒞 **011-436-1540.** Free admission. Mon–Fri 7am–12:30pm, 3–7pm; Sat–Sun 8am–12:30pm, 3–7pm. Bus: 11, 12, 51, 55, 56, 61, 68. Trams: 4, 13, 15, 18.

Mole Antonelliana & Museo Nazionale del Cinema ★★★ MUSEUM   Turin's most peculiar building was once the tallest in Europe, begun in 1863 as a synagogue but then hijacked by the city fathers to become a monument to Italian unification (at the time, Italy was ruled by the House of Savoy from their powerbase in Turin). The Mole has a squat brick base supporting several layers of pseudo-Greek columns, topped by a steep cone-like roof and a skinny spire, all of it rising 167m (548 ft.) above the streets. It is now home to Italy's National Film Museum.

The museum recently underwent a facelift to haul it into the digital age, adding interactive displays, mobile tagging, digital captions, and augmented reality features. Wi-Fi is now offered free inside the museum all the way up to the panoramic terrace. The first exhibits track the intriguing development of moving pictures, from shadow puppets to risqué peep shows and flickering images of galloping horses filmed by Eadweard Muybridge in 1878. The rest of the display uses clips, stills, posters, and props to illustrate the major aspects of movie production, from *The Empire Strikes Back* storyboards to the creepy steady-cam work in *The Shining*. There are plenty of buttons to push and lots of interactive action to keep kids happy.

The highlight of a visit is the ascent through the roof of the museum's vast atrium and up 85 m (279 ft.) inside the tower to the 360-degree observation platform at the top, an experience that affords a stunning view of the gridlike streets of Turin and its backdrop of snowy Alpine peaks. At the end of a tour, a giant movie screen plays films on a loop outside the stylish Cabiria Café.

Via Montebello 20. www.museocinema.it. *©* **011-8138-511.** Museum and panoramic lift: admission 14€, 11€ seniors and students up to age 26, 8€ ages 6–18, free under 5. Museum only: admission 10€, 8€ seniors and students up to age 26, 3€ ages 6–18, free under 5. Panoramic lift only: 7€; 5€ students, seniors, and ages 6–18. Open Tues–Fri & Sun 9am–8pm, Sat 9am–11pm. Multilingual guided tours by advance booking. Bus: 18, 55, 56, 61, 68. Tram: 13, 15, 16.

Museo Egizio (Egyptian Museum) ★★ MUSEUM   Turin's magnificent Egyptian collection is one of the world's largest—no surprise, since it was also the world's *first* Egyptian museum, thanks to the Savoy kings and their explorers Bernardino Drovetti and Ernesto Schiaparelli, who voraciously amassed Egyptian ephemera until the early 20th century, when attitudes reversed against such cultural plundering. At the

---

History of the Turin Shroud

The Turin Shroud is allegedly the linen cloth in which Christ was wrapped when he was taken from the cross—and to which his image was miraculously affixed. The image on the cloth is of a bearded face—remarkably similar to the depiction of Christ in Byzantine icons—and a body marked with bloodstains consistent with a crown of thorns, a slash in the rib cage (made by the Roman centurion Longinus, see p. 457), what appear to be nail holes in the wrists and ankles, and scourge marks on the back from flagellation.

Carbon dating results are confusing; some have suggested that the shroud was manufactured around the 13th or 14th centuries, while other tests imply that those results were affected by the fire that all but destroyed it in December 1532. Regardless of scientific skepticism, the shroud continues to entice hordes of the faithful to worship at its chapel in the Duomo di San Giovanni Battista and the mystery remains unsolved—just how was that haunting image impregnated onto the cloth?

---

point of writing, this museum was a *lavoro in corso* (work in progress), as a flashy new museum was due to open any day. The collection contains artifacts squirreled together from all eras of ancient Egypt, including a papyrus "Book of the Dead" and funerary objects. The most captivating exhibits are the exquisitely painted wooden sarcophagi and mummies of Kha and Merit, an aristocratic couple whose tomb was discovered in 1906, along with more than 500 funerary items. The new museum will feature an innovative system of escalators to lead visitors seemingly on a path along the Nile. There will also be a library, café, classrooms, and rooftop garden in the new four-level, 10,000-square-meter museum.

Via Accademia delle Scienze 6. www.museoegizio.it. ✆ **011-440-6903.** Admission 13€ adults, 9€ ages 15–18, 1€ ages 6–14, free for children 5 and under. Open Mon 9am–2pm, Tues–Sun 8:30am–7:30pm. Bus: 55, 56. Tram: 13.

Museo Nazionale dell'Automobile ★★★ MUSEUM

Not surprisingly in a city that spawned Fiat, the car is king at this whizzy, innovative museum. Alfa Romeos and lots of bright-red Ferraris feature heavily among the displays, which start with vintage cars from the days when road travel was only for the very wealthy and progress through to factory-line car production for the masses. A note of social responsibility is struck by displays that highlight the social, financial, and environmental effects that combustion engines have had on the planet. More than anything, you get to gaze at gorgeous cars. You don't need to be a car buff to appreciate the lovely lines of a Maserati, and this is the perfect place to bring kids who have traipsed around one too many Baroque *palazzo*.

Corso Unità d'Italia 40. www.museoauto.it. ✆ **011-677-666.** Admission 12€ adults, 8€ children 6–18 and seniors, free for children under 6. Open Mon 10am–2pm; Tues 2–7pm; Wed–Thurs, Sun 10am–7pm; Fri–Sat 10am–9pm. Metro: Lingotto.

Vintage cars at the Museo Nazionale dell'Automobile.

Museo Nazionale del Risorgimento Italiano (National Museum of the Risorgimento) ★★★ MUSEUM   On the Piazza Carignano—one of the most majestic in a city full of splendid corners—the equally handsome redbrick *palazzo* of the same name acquired huge national importance as the sometime home of Italy's first king following the country's Unification in 1861. Originally built between 1679 and 1685 by Baroque maestro Guarino Guarini, the palace now houses the Museo del Risorgimento; at its heart is the ornate circular chamber where Italy's first parliament met. For an Italian museum, this is incredibly well organized, with clear, timed itineraries suggested in literature at the door as well as online. More than 30 artfully decorated rooms detail the military campaigns that led to Unification, both from an Italian and a European perspective; even non-Italians can easily appreciate the stirring drama of these years. Displays of uniforms, vivid warlike paintings, weapons, maps, and correspondence reveal feats of great derring-do as we are led through the Italy of the 19th century from Napoleon to Garibaldi. There's a refreshing amount of multilingual signage and labelling; this fascinating exhibition should be used as an example to some other Italian museums.

Via Accademia delle Scienze 5. www.museorisorgimentotorino.it. ✆ **011-562-1147.** Admission 10€ adults, 8€ seniors, 5€ students; 4€ high-school students, 2.50€ primary school, free 6 and under. Tues–Sun 10am–6pm. Bus: 11, 12, 27, 51, 51/, 55, 56, 57. Tram: 13, 15.

Museo della Sindone (Holy Shroud Museum) ★★ MUSEUM There are no Disneyesque special effects in this curiously endearing little museum, which is refreshing considering the Turin Shroud's hefty status as one of the world's most famous religious relics. A visit kicks off with a 15-minute film about the shroud, its provenance, and the various theories and mysteries surrounding it; then it's down to a series of rooms chronicling its history from the first firm mention in 1204, to the fire that nearly destroyed it in Chambéry in 1532, to its arrival in Turin with the House of Savoy in 1578, and the modern-day carbon-testing sagas. The tour finishes in the richly ornamented chapel of Santo Sudario, private place of worship for the Savoy dukes, where a copy of the shroud is displayed over the gleaming, gilded altar. The shroud itself is not displayed here (it is in the royal chapel of the Duomo, see above), and is only taken out periodically. Check www.sindone.org to find out when the shroud will next be displayed in the Duomo; advance reservations are usually required to see the shroud in its brief public displays.

Via San Domenico 28. www.sindone.it. ✆ **011-436-5832.** Admission 6€ adults, 5€ students, aged 12 and under, and seniors. Daily 9am–noon and 3–7pm.

Palazzo Madama—Museo Civico di Arte Antica (Civic Museum of Ancient Art) ★ MUSEUM   Looking like two buildings sandwiched together, Palazzo Madama dominates Piazza Castello; its medieval facade looks eastward, while the westward face is its Baroque addition, created by the architect Filippo Juvarra in the 18th century, when he was giving Turin its elegant arcaded facelift. Once inside this massive structure, you'll discover it incorporates a Roman gate and tower; courtyards, apartments, and towers from the medieval castle; and several Renaissance additions. Juvarra also added a monumental marble staircase to the interior, most of which is given over to the all-encompassing collections of the Museo Civico di Arte Antica. The holdings cover four mammoth floors and focus on the medieval and Renaissance periods, which are shown off well against the castle's austere, stony medieval interior. On the top floor you'll find one of Italy's largest collections of ceramics, but it's all rather disorganized in layout. The star of the show here is Antonello da Messina's sublime "Portrait of a Man," hidden away in the Treasure Tower at the back of the building.

Piazza Castello. www.palazzomadamatorino.it. ☎ **011-443-3501.** Admission 10€ adults, 8€ student and seniors, free under 18. Free admission for all on the first Tuesday of the month. Tues–Sat 10am–6pm; Sun 10am–7pm. Bus: 11, 12, 51, 55, 56, 61, 68; Trams: 4, 13, 15, 18.

Palazzo Reale (Royal Palace) & Armeria Reale (Royal Armory)

★ PALACE   Overshadowing the north side of the Piazza Castello, the residence of the House of Savoy was begun in 1646; the family lived here up until 1865. Designed by the architect Amedeo di Castellamonte, the palace reflects the ornately Baroque tastes of European ruling families of the time, while its sheer size gives some indication of the wealth of these medieval oligarchs. This Savoy palace gives the ostentatious frippery of Versailles a run for its money; there are throne rooms, dining rooms, ballrooms, bedrooms, Chinese rooms, and apartments hung with priceless Gobelins tapestries, all lavishly adorned with silk walls, sparkling chandeliers, ornate wooden floors, and delicate gilded furniture.

The east wing of the *palazzo* houses the **Armeria Reale,** one of the most important arms and armor collections in Europe, especially of weapons from the 16th and 17th centuries. It's also unusual for its collection of stuffed horses, which look ready to leap into battle at any moment.

Behind the palace are the formal **Giardini Reali (Royal Gardens),** laid out by André Le Nôtre, who designed the Tuileries in Paris and the gardens at Versailles.

The Savoy royal family had an even keener eye for paintings than for Baroque décor, amassing an impressive collection of 8,000 works of art. Currently awaiting a new home, the collection's highlights are on show in temporary accommodation in the **Galleria Sabauda** on the ground floor of the Palazzo Reale's New Wing. (This is a few minutes' walk from the main *palazzo,* past the Duomo, see p. 480). The exhibition kicks off with early Piedmont and Dutch religious works works, plus a moody Rembrandt self-portrait and two massive paintings by van Dyck: "The Children of Charles I" (1637) and a magnificent equestrian portrait of Prince Thomas of Savoy (ca. 1634).

Now permanently housed n the basement beneath the Galleria Sabauda, the **Museo Archeologico** provides a thoughtfully designed exhibition, which tells the story of Turin's development from Roman through medieval times. Incorporated into the museum is a section of Roman wall, remnants from the theater nearby, and a mosaic only discovered in 1993.

The **Biblioteca Reale** (Royal Library) is also part of the Palazzo Reale complex; it's free to enter and you'll find it (eventually) on the right of the main entrance. Founded in 1831, its scholarly wooden interior houses 200,000 rare volumes as well as ancient maps and prints. On the opposite side of the gates is the fine **church of San Lorenzo,** designed by Baroque master-architect Guarino Guarini in 1666. Its plain facade belies the lacy dome and frothy interior.

Piazzetta Reale 1. www.ilpalazzorealeditorino.it. ✆ **011-436-1455.** Palazzo and all exhibitions: admission 12€ adults, 6€ ages 18–25, free for children and seniors. Free admission for all on the first Sunday of the month. Tues–Sun 8:30am–7:30pm; last admission 6pm. Museo Archeologico closed Sun morning. Bus: 11, 12, 51, 55, 56, 61, 68; Trams: 4, 13, 15, 18.

Outlying Attractions

Basilica di Superga ★★ CHURCH Half the fun of a visit to this lovely basilica is the 6.5km (4-mile) journey northeast of the city center on a narrow-gauge railway through the lush countryside of the Parco Naturale della Collina di Superga. The church was built as thanksgiving to the Virgin Mary for Turin's deliverance from the French siege of 1706. Prince Vittorio Amedeo II commissioned Filippo Juvarra, the Sicilian architect who designed much of Turin's elegant center, to build the magical Baroque confection on a hill high above the city. The eye-catching exterior, with its beautiful colonnaded portico, elaborate dome, and twin bell towers, is actually more visually appealing than the ornate but gloomy interior, a circular chamber ringed by six chapels. Many scions of the House of Savoy are buried here in the Crypt of Kings beneath the main chapel. Tours of the royal apartments are available in slots of 45 minutes, with a maximum of 15 people.

Strada della Basilica di Superga, 75, www.basilicadisuperga.com. ✆ **011-899-7456.** Basilica: free admission. Appartamento Reale: admission 5€, open summer Tues–Sun 9:30am–7pm, winter Sat–Sun 10am–6pm. Trains leave from Stazione Sassi (4€ roundtrip) and stop at Piazza Gustavo Modena; from there, follow Corso Casale on east side of the River Po. Bus: 61 from side of Ponte Vittorio Emanuele I opposite Piazza Vittorio Veneto.

Palazzina di Caccia di Stupinigi ★ PALACE Yet another Savoy family home is found at Stupinigi, just a few miles southwest from Turin. More great work commissioned in 1729 from the architect Filippo Juvarra resulted in a sumptuous, ornately decorated hunting lodge surrounded by royal forests. Built on a humungous scale, the palace's wings fan out from the main house, topped by a domed pavilion on which a large bronze stag is featured. Every bit as lavish as the apartments in the Savoys' city residence, Palazzo Reale (see p. 484), the interior is stuffed with furniture, paintings, and bric-à-brac assembled from their myriad residences, forming the **Museo d'Arte e Ammobiliamento (Museum of Art and Furniture).** Wander through the acres of apartments to understand why Napoleon chose this for his brief sojourn in Piedmont in 1805 while on his way to Milan to be crowned emperor. Outstanding among the many, many frescoes are the scenes of a deer hunt in the King's Apartment and the triumph of Diana in the grand salon. The elegant gardens and surrounding forests provide lovely terrain for a jaunt. At the time of writing, the palace is under extensive restoration, although still open to the public.

Piazza Principe Amedeo 7, Stupingi, Nichelino. http://www.ordinemauriziano.it/tesori.html. 📞 **011-358-1220**. Admission 12€, seniors 8€, children 6–14 5€. Tues–Fri 10am–5:30pm, Sat 10am–6:30pm. 8.5km (5¼ miles) southwest of the city center.

Reggia di Venaria Reale ★★★ PALACE   Completing the triumvirate of glitzy Savoy households around Turin, the Venaria was constructed in the mid–17th century to a design by Amedeo di Castellamonte, but sure enough Filippo Juvarra also had a hand in the design. This massive complex, its stables, and its awesome formal gardens are now on the UNESCO World Heritage Sites list. Reopened in 2011 after decades of work, Venaria now offers a great, family-oriented day out with loads of outdoor summer activities as well as a glimpse into the extraordinarily privileged lives of the Savoy family. The Fountain of the Stag dances to music in the lake outside the *palazzo*; in the grounds, there are follies aplenty and the mock-Roman Fountain of Hercules to discover. Permanent exhibitions in the house include the Peopling the Palaces lightshow conceived by film director Peter Greenaway, who also had a hand in the exhibitions at the Museum of Cinema (see p. 480) in Turin.

Piazza della Repubblica 4, Venaria Reale (10km/6¼ mi northwest of the city center). www.lavenaria.it. 📞 **011-499-2333**. Admission varies from 25€ for palace, gardens, and activities to 5€ for gardens only, with many price options in between. Tues–Fri 9am–5pm, Sat–Sun 9:30am–7:30pm (last admission 1 hour before closing). Bus: 11 from Piazza Repubblica. A Venaria Express bus runs Tues–Sun (40 min.), with stops at Stazione Porta Nuova, on Via XX Settembre, and at Stazione Porta Susa.

Organized Tours

Several tour companies run trips around Turin and Piedmont. **Viator** (www.viator.com; U.S. ✆ 702-648-5873) offers an intriguing underground tour of the city's catacombs and hosts guided tours of the Barolo region (see p. 492). A hop-on, hop-off bus service circles the major attractions and is run by **Torino City Sightseeing** (www.torino.city-sightseeing.it; ✆ 011-535-181), while **Delicious Italy** (www.delicious italy.com) showcases the food stores and restaurants that have given Turin its gourmet reputation.

Where to Stay

Turin has seen a recent injection of private capital into the hotel scene, and as a result, many boutique hotels have opened, giving travelers an alternative to the faceless frumpery of many of the city's older hotels.

Le Petit Hotel ★★   Unassuming from the front, the Petit Hotel has had a brush-up inside and offers very simple bedrooms with spotless, functional bathrooms. There's not much luxury but prices are very reasonable and the address is central. A casual restaurant offers pizza and pasta staples, though there are better places to eat within a couple minutes' walk. In summer the Marechiaro restaurant moves outdoors, offering a great spot for an early evening drink. The breakfast room has been upgraded and now offers a buffet of breads, cheeses, fruit, and pastries. The hotel also offers some smartly furnished self-catering apartments.
Via San Francesco d'Assisi 21. www.lepetithotel.it. ✆ **011-561-2626.** 79 units. Doubles 89€–129€; apartments 150€–220€. Rates include breakfast. Free parking. **Amenities:** Restaurant; Wi-Fi 5€ for 3 hours.

Townhouse 70 ★★★   Part of a luxury chain that also has hotels in Milan, the Townhouse could not be better placed for sightseers, just steps away from Piazza Castello and the Palazzo Reale (see p. 484). It is a smooth, urbane hotel, with a tiny *aperitivo* bar tucked in one corner of reception and a breakfast room sporting one massive table, where smart businessmen and families all sit down together. Rooms are spacious for a city-center hotel, and decorated in soothing dark colors. The comfy beds have statement headboards; bathrooms have massive showers. The quieter bedrooms look over an internal courtyard, but keep in mind that there is a bit less privacy when your shutters are open.
Via XX Settembre 70. www.townhouse.it. ✆ **011-1970-0003.** 48 units. Doubles 112€–170€. Rates include breakfast. Parking in ZTL traffic-limited zone (fee). **Amenities:** Bar; concierge; room service (7–10am); Wi-Fi (free).

VitaminaM ★★★   This tiny B&B with just two rooms has a funky interior design full of arty offerings from up-and-coming Torino designers. The rooms are flooded with light, with silver and red color schemes, and the bathrooms are surprisingly luxurious, with full-length baths.

Book well ahead as this is one of the hottest tickets in town; the only drawback is that the B&B is four floors up with no elevator.

Via Belfiore 18. www.vitaminam.com. © **347-1526-130.** 2 units. 100€–120€ double. Rates include breakfast. Underground parking nearby 15€ per day. **Amenities:** Wi-Fi (free).

Where to Eat

Turin's gourmet reputation outshines other Italian cities renowned for their gastronomy. Many restaurants are strong advocates of the Slow Food movement, and even a cursory glance at a menu will tell you whether ingredients are local; look for porcini mushrooms and truffles in season. Wine lists should feature Barolo, Barbera, and Barbaresco reds and sparkling Asti whites. Turin is also home to the world's largest food and wine fair, the **Salone del Gusto** (www.salonedelgusto.it), which runs every two years in October.

Officine Bohemien ★★ PIEDMONT This offbeat, low-key restaurant down a side street resembles a St-Tropez cafe circa 1950s, with walls covered with black-and-white posters. It's casual and slightly edgy, run by a young, delightful staff. There's a laidback bar selling Piedmont wines and fancy cocktails while jazz plays in the background; frequent live-music events are held here. Lunch sees offerings of staple pasta dishes such as *spaghetti pomodoro e basilica* or big salads at really good prices; dinner is a little more sophisticated, with menus changing daily according to what's available. Great platters of grilled and smoked meats, regional cheeses, chutneys, and fruits and vegetables are all sourced locally; bread is made daily in the kitchens.

Via San Camillo de Lellis (was Via Mercanti) 19. www.officinebohemien.it. © **011-764-0368.** Main courses 8€–12€. Tues–Fri noon–3pm, 7:30–10:30pm; Sat 7:30–10:30pm.

Ruràl ★★★ MODERN PIEDMONT One to watch, Ruràl is an award-winning proponent of the Slow Food ethos (born in nearby Bra), with a menu that is currently taking Turin to the top of the gastronomic charts. Its deceptively simple white and blond-wood interior strikes a classy note; the clientele is smart and the service friendly and informed. Chefs, under the auspices of Piero Bergese, emerge from the open-plan kitchen to discuss the dishes with customers. A great sharing plate of rabbit, "tonnato" (a creamy sauce flavored with tuna) meats, veal sausage, carpaccio, and tartare showcases typical Piedmont specialties,

---

Shaken, not Stirred

Turin gave the world the aperitif vermouth, which was invented in 1786 by Antonio Benedetto Carpano; the brands Martini and Cinzano are still made in the Piedmont region. Order a glass at the gorgeous **Art Nouveau Caffè Mulassano** at Piazza Castello 15 (www.caffemulassano.com; © **011-547-990**), or come early to enjoy coffee and tempting cannoli or dainty fruit tarts at the ornate marble counter.

and the wine list offers plenty of decent regional reds and whites. It's obvious that everybody involved in this project is obsessive about food and proud to present the best of Piedmontese rural gastronomy.

Via San Dalmazzo 16. www.ristoranterural.it. ℂ **011-2478-470.** Main courses 15€–30€. Tues–Sat 12:30pm–2:30pm and 7:30–11pm, Sun 12:30pm–2:30pm.

Trattoria Santo Spirito ★★ SEAFOOD   In a bustling piazza a few minutes' walk from Palazzo Reale in the heart of the Area Romana, Santo Spirito is well loved for its vast platters of mussels, tuna carpaccio, simply grilled fish, and delicious fettucine served with lobster. Portions are huge, so don't be tempted to over-order, especially at lunchtime. It is testament to the standard of cooking here that this place has thrived since 1975 in a city where restaurants open and close every day; it's not haute cuisine but great rustic cooking with fresh ingredients and plenty of strong flavors. In summer, tables spread out onto the piazza; in winter there's a cozy fire inside and heaters warm the loggia.

Largo IV Marzo 11. www.trattoriaspiritosanto.com. ℂ **011-4360-877.** Daily 12:30–3:30pm, 7:30pm–midnight. Main courses 9€–25€, separate land and sea tasting menus available for 40€.

Outdoor Activities

Turin's beautiful playground is **Parco del Valentino,** which cradles the left bank of the River Po between the Ponte Umberto I and the Ponte Isabella. Its first incarnation was in 1630, when it was the private garden of the Savoy dukes, but the park was much extended in romantic English-landscape style in the 1860s and opened to the public. It's a

Rowers on the River Po, flowing through Turin.

romantic place to stroll among the botanical gardens, flowerbeds, and manicured lawns. The massive **Castello del Valentino**, built in 1660, was the pleasure palace of Christine Marie of France (see p. 480); it is closed to the public. The castle forms an incongruous backdrop to the **Borgo Medievale** (see below), a riverside replica of a 15th-century Piedmontese village. It's a pleasant walk back into the city center along Corso Emanuele Vittorio II, or Tram 9 takes you back to Porta Nuova.

There are half a dozen rowing clubs on the Po; Reale Societa Canottieri Cerea (www.canottiericerea.it) is the oldest. Jogging and cycling routes follow the riverside pathways.

A little further afield, it takes around an hour to reach the hiking trails of the **Gran Paradiso** national park (see p. 499). Turin is also an hour away from the ski resorts of **Valle d'Aosta** (see p. 497) in the Alps, and it's just a little further to the sandy beaches of the **Riviera delle Palme** to the south.

Especially for Kids

There's plenty for kids to do in Turin. There are the open spaces of **Parco del Valentino** (see above) to run around in, plus free admission to the open-air **Borgo Medievale,** a mock-Piedmontese village built for the Italian General Exposition in 1884 (Viale Virgilio 107; www.borgomedioe valetorino.it; ✆ **011-4431-701**; open 9am–7pm [8pm in summer]). Most youngsters will be intrigued by the **Museum of Cinema** at the Mole Antonelliana (see p. 480), or at least the trip up the Mole's tower to see the city lying far below.

The **Museo Nazionale dell'Automobile** provides a modern antidote to Turin's baroque attractions, as does a trip south of the city center to the **Olympic stadium** (www.olympicstadiumturin.com), built for the 2006 winter games and now home to rival Serie A Italian football teams Torino and Juventus. Both the stadium and its sports museum are open for guided tours (Tues–Sun 2–6pm; tours 10€ adults, 8€ under 16, seniors, students).

And if all else fails, pop into **Caffè Fiorio** (Via Po 8; ✆ **011-8173-225**) for some delicious ice cream.

Shopping & Nightlife

Turin's high-end shopping area is quite simply one of the most beautiful in the world. The arcaded **Via Roma** does full justice to the exquisite fashions on sale in Gucci, Armani, Ferragamo, Max Mara, and so on. At the end of Via Roma, the glass-roofed **Galleria Subalpina**, which links Piazza Castello with Piazza Carlo, competes with Milan's Galleria Vittorio Emanuele II for sheer opulence in its three levels of art galleries, antiquarian bookstores, and cafes. For those whose pockets may not be quite so deep, **Via Garibaldi, Corso XX Settembre,** and the surrounding streets together offer mid-range international brands at reasonable prices.

The windows of Italian food shops are always a thing of joy, and the specialist delis and confectioners of Turin are no exceptions. **Confetteria Stratta** (Piazza San Carlo 191; ✆ **011-547-920**) and **Pasticceria Gerla** (Corso Vittorio Emanuele 11) are thronged daily for their extravagant pastries, cakes, and *gianduiotti* (chocolate with hazelnuts). Turin is famous for its quality confectionery—the city produces 40% of Italy's **chocolate** and celebrates it with its own festival, CioccolaTO (www.cioccola-to.it; dates change annually). Turin also has a branch of **Eataly** (see p. 151), the current top tip for gourmet Italian produce, at Via Nizza 230, a little out of the center in Lingotto.

Most newsagents in Turin have English-language newspapers, and the two branches of **Feltrinelli** (Piazza Castello 19, ✆ **011-541-627** or Stazione Porta Nuova ✆ **011-563-981**) sell multilingual books.

Nightlife in the city that invented the vermouth *aperitivo* is sophisticated and, as in Milan, it starts in the cafes and bars and finishes very, very late. Squeeze in with the Torinese at the bar of **Caffè Platti** (Corso Vittorio Emanuele II 72; ✆ **011-506-9056**) for a vermouth, and pick from the plates of enticing little pizzas made on the premises. Choose a Slow Food (see p. 488) restaurant for dinner, and then join models and footballers to dance at **Kogin's** (Corso Sicilia 6; ✆ **011-661-0546**). In summer, head for the Murazzi embankment along the River Po for live bands and DJs in late-night dance clubs.

Dance, opera, theater, and musical performances (mostly classical) are on the agenda all year around—check the website www.visitatorino.com—but September is the month to really enjoy classical music in Turin, when more than 60 classical concerts are staged around the city during the month-long **Settembre Musica** festival (www.mitosettembremusica.it; ✆ **011-442-4787**), which is hosted jointly with Milan. Beyond the festivals you'll find classical concerts at **Auditorium della RAI,** Via Rossini 15 (www.orchestrasinfonica.rai.it; ✆ **011-810-4653**) and dance performances, and operas staged at the city's venerable **Teatro Regio** (www.teatroregio.torino.it, ✆ **011-8815-241**; tickets at Piazza Castello 215).

The Markets of Turin

The **produce market** in and around Porta Palazzo takes over the gigantic Piazza della Republica Monday to Friday 8:30am to 1:30pm and Saturday until 6:30pm. A bustling **flea market** takes place in the warren of streets behind the Porta Palazzo every Saturday, among the antique shops on Via Borgo Dora. The second Sunday of every month, the same spot is the scene of an **antiques market,** the **Gran Balon** (www.balon.it), where more than 200 dealers from across northern Italy display their wares. Come December, a **Christmas market** sets out its stalls in Via Borgo Dora. Turin has many stores specializing in rare books and old prints, and these also sell their wares from stalls along the Via Po.

THE PIEDMONT WINE COUNTRY ★★

South of Turin, the Po valley rises into the rolling hills of Langhe and Roero, flanked by orchards and vineyards. You'll recognize the region's place names from the labels of its first-rate wines, among them **Asti Spumanti, Barbaresco,** and **Barolo.** And vines are not all that flourish in this fertile soil—truffles top the list of the region's gastronomic delights, along with rabbit and game plus excellent cheeses.

Asti ★★★

Asti: 60km (37 miles) SE of Turin, 127km (79 miles) SW of Milan

The Asti of sparkling-wine fame is a bustling working city, but it has many treasures to uncover in its history-drenched *centro storico*—medieval towers (120 are still standing), Renaissance palaces, and piazzas provide the perfect setting in which to sample the town's most famous product, which flows readily in the local *enoteche* and cantinas.

ESSENTIALS

GETTING THERE   Up to four **trains** per hour link Asti with **Turin Porta Nuova** (35 min; 5.25€) via **Trenitalia** (www.trenitalia.com; ✆ **89-20-21**). **Arfea** (www.arfea.it; ✆ **0131-225-180**) runs **buses** from Turin Autostazione to Asti; the trip takes 1 hour. By car, Asti can be reached in less than an hour from Turin via Autostrada 21.

VISITOR INFORMATION   The **APT tourist office** is near the train station at Corso Vittorio Alfieri 34 (✆ **0141-530-357**). It's open Monday to Saturday 9am to 1pm and 2:30 to 6:30pm; Sunday 9am to 1pm and 1:30pm to 5:30pm.

EXPLORING ASTI

Asti's historic heart is centered on three adjoining squares: **Piazza Libertá,** the vast **Campo del Palio,** and the grand arcaded **Piazza Alfieri.** Every year on the third Sunday of September, this area is mobbed for Asti's annual horse race, the **Palio** (www.palio.asti.it; ✆ **0141-399-482**), now held in Piazza Alfieri (originally it was in Campo del Palio). Like the similar race in the Tuscan city of Siena (see p. 36), Asti's Palio begins with a colorful medieval pageant through the town and ends with a wild bareback ride around the triangular Piazza Alfieri. First staged in 1273, the race coincides with Asti's other great festival, the **Douja d'Or** (www.doujador.it), a weeklong bacchanal celebrating the successful grape harvest.

Behind **Piazza Alfieri** stands the Romanesque-Gothic redbrick **Collegiata di San Secondo** (www.comune.asti.it; ✆ **0141-530-066;** daily 10:45am–noon, 3:30–5:30pm, Sun morning for Mass only). This church has two distinctions: it houses the Palio Astigiano, the prestigious banner awarded to the winning jockey at the Palio, and it also contains the tomb of St. Secondo, patron saint of both the horse race and the

town. A Roman officer who converted to Christianity in A.D. 119, Secondo was martyred for his faith, beheaded in roughly the spot where his tomb now stands.

From Piazza Alfieri, the charming and largely pedestrianized **Corso Alfieri** bisects the old town and is lined with Renaissance *palazzi*. At the eastern end is the church of **San Pietro in Consavia** (© **0141-399-489;** Tues-Sun 10am–1pm, 3–6pm, or until 7pm in summer) with a 10th-century Romanesque baptistery that was once a place of worship for the Knights of the Order of St. John. At the opposite, western extreme of Corso Alfieri you'll find the rotund **church of Santa Caterina,** abutting the medieval red-and-white brick-topped **Torre Rossa**.

Asti's 15th-century **Cattedrale di Santa Maria Assunta** (☎ **0141-592-924;** daily 9am–noon, 3–6pm) is also at the western end of town in Piazza Cattedrale. Its austere exterior hides the gaudy excesses of the interior; every inch of the church is festooned with frescoes by late 15th-century artists, including Gandolfino d'Asti.

Being the agricultural and gourmet hotspot that it is, Asti is blessed with two **food markets.** The larger is held Wednesdays and Saturdays (7:30am–1pm) in the Campo del Palio and spills over into piazzas Della Libertà and Alfieri, with stalls selling cheeses, herbs, flowers, oils, and wines. The undercover **Mercato Coperto** on Piazza della Libertà is open daily except Sunday (Mon–Wed and Fri 8am–1pm, 3:30–7:30pm; Thur 8:30am–1pm; Sat 8am–7:30pm). Look for white truffles, *bagna cauda* (a fondue-like dip served warm and made with ingredients like olive, oil, butter, garlic, and anchovies), robiola cheeses, almond-flavored *amaretti* biscuits, and *nocciolata* (hazelnut and chocolate spread). The region's famous Asti Spumante DOCG sparkling wines can be bought from *cantinas* and *enoteche* in the town center and direct from some vineyards—a list is available from the **tourist office** at Corso Vittorio Alfieri 34 (see p. 492).

Visiting the Wine Villages

Gastro-destination **Alba** ★★ (60km/37 miles south of Turin; 155km/96 miles southwest of Milan) is the jumping-off point for visiting the many vineyards of the Barolo wine-producing region. While it's a pleasure to walk along the Via Vittorio Emanuele and the narrow streets of the old town center, wine and food are what Alba's all about. Wherever you go, you'll end up peering into store windows to admire displays of wines, truffles, and the calorific but enticing *nocciolata* cake made of hazelnuts and chocolate. The streets are crammed with enough enticing restaurants to make gourmands very happy indeed (see p. 495).

Just to the south of Alba lie some of the Piedmont's most enchanting wine villages, sitting on hilltops among orderly rows of vines. The best way to see these villages is to drive; hire cars in Turin from **Avis,** Via Lessona Michele 30 (www.avis.com; ☎ **011-774-1962**), **Hertz,** at Corso Turati 37 (www.hertz.it; ☎ **011-502-080**), or **Sixt,** at Via Mongrando 48 (www.sixt.it; ☎ **011-888-768**). Before you head out on the small country roads, provide yourself with a good map and a list of vineyards from the tourist office in Asti (see p. 492).

The main road through the wine region is the SS231, which runs between Alba and Asti. It is, however, a fast, busy, and unattractive highway; you'll want to turn off it to explore Piedmont's rustic backwaters among hazelnut groves and vineyards.

One such enchanting drive heads south from Alba to a string of wine villages in the **Langhe hills** (follow signs out of town for Barolo on the SP3). After 8km (5 miles), take the right turn for **Grinzane Cavour,** a

Piedmont's signature wines.

hilltop village built around a castle harboring the **Enoteca Regionale Piemontese Cavour** (www.castellogrinzane.com; ✆ **0173-262-159**), which is open daily from 9am to 7pm (until 6pm Nov–Mar). Here you can enjoy a sampling of local wines from over 300 labels; the fine restaurant is perfect for lunch.

Retrace your route to the main road, turn left, and after another 4km (2½ miles) south, take the right fork to **La Morra,** another settlement perched among vineyards with panoramic views over the rolling, vineyard-clad countryside. There are several cafes and restaurants here in which to taste the local vintages. The **Cantina Comunale di La Morra** at Via Alberto 2 (www.cantinalamorra.com; ✆ **0173-509-204**) doubles as the tourist office and as a representative for local growers, selling Barolo, Nebbiolo, Barbera, and Dolcetto. It's open daily (except Tuesdays, when it's closed) 10am to 12:30pm and 2:30 to 6:30pm.

Barolo is a handsome little village dominated by two ancient castles; it's 5km (3 miles) along the SP58 from La Morra. Here, too, you'll find a choice of restaurants and shops selling the world-renowned red wines from local vineyards. Among these outlets is the **Castello Falletti** (www.enotecadelbarolo.it; ✆ **0173-56-277**), revamped and reopened in May 2014 with a wine bar and an *enoteca* offering tastings in its cavernous cellars. A tasting includes three Barolo wines from different vineyards; costs are 5€ for three wines, 3€ for one. It's open Thursday to Tuesday 10am to 6pm.

Where to Eat & Stay

As well as a smattering of decent urban hotels, the Barolo region is the land of the *agriturismo*, with options to stay on wine estates in the hills of Langhe. Restaurants don't come much classier than the best-found in Piedmont.

Ristorante al Castello di Marc Lanteri ★★★ GOURMET Housed in the fairytale castle at Grinzane Cavour along with an *enoteca* selling the best of the region's wines, this renowned restaurant showcases the food of Michelin-starred chef Marc Lanteri, who took over the kitchen in February 2015. Lanteri, a French chef born on the Italian border, considers his cuisine to be representative of Franco-Piedmont style. He makes everything from old standbys like *foie gras,* French onion

Piedmont's Regional Wines

The wines of Piedmont are of exceptional quality and distinctive taste. They're usually made with grapes unique to the region, and grown on tiny family plots—making the countryside a lovely patchwork of vineyards and small farms.

Often called "the king of reds," **Barolo** is considered one of Italy's top wines, on par with Tuscany's Brunello and the Veneto region's Amarone. It is the richest and heartiest of the Piedmont wines, and the one most likely to accompany game or meat. **Barbaresco,** like Barolo, is made exclusively from the red Nebbiolo grape, although it is less tannic. **Barbera d'Alba** is a smooth, rich red wine, the product of the delightful villages south of Alba (see p. 494). **Dolcetto** is dry, fruity, mellow, and not sweet, as its name leads many to assume. **Nebbiolo d'Alba** is rich, full, and dry.

As far as white wines go, **Spumanti** DOCGs are the sparkling wines that put Asti on the map. **Moscato d'Asti** is a delicious floral dessert wine, and the fiery local **Piedmont** *grappas* are none too shabby either.

---

soup, and traditional Piedmontese *bagna cauda*, to more modern and creative dishes like chestnut flour *pappardelle* or veal tartare with a Nebbiolo wine reduction. Try the "gusto & charme" menu (59€) for a series of small tastes of the chef's cuisine. The chef's American wife Amy serves as the restaurant's sommelier.

Via Castello 5, Grinzane Cavour. www.castellogrinzane.com. ✆ **338-700-1914.** Main courses 15€–20€. Mon 12:15–2pm, Wed–Sun noon–2pm, 7:30–10pm. Closed Jan.

Hotel Castello d'Asti ★★   Don't be put off by the slightly workaday street; this hotel is a find. Tucked into a lush courtyard garden near the *centro storico*, the Castello is in a historic townhouse with an elegantly updated interior. The beautifully appointed rooms are decorated in soft shades of black and cream with luscious marble bathrooms. The suites are more than spacious and all have their own balconies overlooking the gardens; there are also two luxurious self-catering apartments. Downstairs there's a lively bar and a sleek restaurant serving reliably good Piedmontese cuisine and offering more than 300 local wines.

Via G Testa 47, Asti. www.hotelcastelloasti.com. ✆ **0141-351-094.** 11 units. 125€–155€ double; 175€–235€ suite. Rates include breakfast. Free parking. Closed Jan. **Amenities:** Restaurant; bar; room service; Wi-Fi (free).

La Cascina del Monastero ★★★   Perfectly situated for exploring the Barolo wine region, this beautiful 16th-century family-run estate is part laid-back B&B and part winery, all just minutes away from La Morra (see p. 495). Converted from an outbuilding of soft stone and arcading, the suites and apartments are beautifully furnished with exposed timbers, heavy Italian antiques, and brass bedframes. Exposed walls, beams, and wooden floors add to the traditional ambience of the place, while the bathrooms have every modern convenience. Guest facilities include an unusual spa, which has a sauna in what appears to be a massive wine barrel; a sun terrace; and, best of all, the chance to taste the wines produced on the estate. There's no restaurant (there are plenty of choices nearby), but the breakfast buffet kicks off the day in fine style. A camping area is available amid lovely scenery near the main house.

Cascina Luciani 112A, Frazione Annunziata, La Morra. www.cascinadelmonastero.it. ✆ **0173-509-245.** 10 units. 115€–125€ double; 125€–135€ apt. Rates include breakfast. Free parking. Closed Jan and sometimes Feb. **Amenities:** Children's playground; spa; outdoor pool; room service; sauna; Wi-Fi (free).

Palazzo Finati ★★   Hidden away behind a fine *palazzo* facade within easy reach of Alba's gourmet restaurants, the Finati offers a choice of individually designed rooms, some with frescoed ceilings and terraces overlooking the inner courtyard, and all offering a taste of old-fashioned luxury. Rooms can be connected for family stays. The breakfast buffet includes fresh pastries, fruit, local cheeses, and cured hams, all served in a brick-ceilinged, barrel-vaulted dining room.

Via Vernazza 8, Alba. www.palazzofinati.it. ✆ **0173-366-324.** 9 units. 150€–180€ double, 179€–240€ suite. Rates include breakfast. Parking 10€–15€ per day (request in advance). **Amenities:** Wi-Fi (free).

AOSTA ★★ & VALLE D'AOSTA ★★★

Aosta: 113km (70 miles) N of Turin, 184km (114 miles) NW of Milan; Courmayeur-Entrèves: 35km (22 miles) W of Aosta, 148km (92 miles) NW of Turin

Tucked up against the French and Swiss borders in northwest Italy, the Aosta Valley is a land of harsh, snow-capped peaks, lush pastures, thick forests, waterfalls cascading into mountain streams, and romantic castles clinging to wooded hillsides. A year-round stream of skiers, hikers, cyclists, and nature lovers flock to this tiny Alpine region north of Turin for the scenery, outdoor adventure, and rustic gastronomy.

Aosta
ESSENTIALS

GETTING THERE   Aosta is served by 20 **trains** a day to and from **Turin** (2 hr., change in Ivrea or Chivasso; tickets 9.45€) aboard **Trenitalia** (www.trenitalia.com; ✆ **89-20-21**). Bus service to Aosta is much less handy: There are only a couple of direct buses from Turin Porta Nuova per day (most change in Ivrea), and even the direct trip takes 2 hours, the indirect route more than 3. However, a SAVDA bus conveniently connects Aosta hourly to **Courmayeur** (1 hr., 3.50€) and other popular spots in the valley.

Autostrada A5 from Turin shoots up the length of Valle d'Aosta en route to France and Switzerland via the Mont Blanc tunnel; there are numerous exits in the valley. The trip from Turin to Aosta normally takes about 90 minutes, but traffic can be heavy on weekends in the ski season.

VISITOR INFORMATION   The **tourist office** in Aosta (Piazza Porta Praetoria 3; www.lovevda.it; ✆ **0165-236-627**) dispenses a wealth of information on hiking trails, ski lifts and passes, bike rentals, and rafting trips. It's open daily 9am to 7pm.

EXPLORING AOSTA

An appealing mountain town with an ancient heart, Aosta—nick-named "the Rome of the Alps"—is surrounded by snowcapped peaks and steeped in a history that goes back to Roman times. Although you're not going to find much pristine Alpine quaintness here in the Valle d'Aosta's busy tourist center, you will find Roman ruins, medieval bell towers, and chic shops. Aosta's **weekly market** day is Tuesday, when stalls selling food, clothes, and crafts fill the Piazza Cavalieri di Vittorio Veneto.

The new Funivia skyway up Monte Bianco (Mont Blanc).

Well-preserved city walls date from the days when Aosta was one of Rome's most important trading and military outposts. A **Roman bridge** spans the River Buthier and two Roman gates arch gracefully across the Via San Anselmo. The **Porta Pretoria** forms the western entrance to the Roman town and the **Arco di Augusto** the eastern entrance. The **Teatro Romano** and the ruins of the **amphitheater** are north of the Porta Pretoria; the ruins of the **forum** are in an adjacent park. The theater and forum are open generally from 9am–6pm, typically closed for a few hours in the afternoon in the winter, and admission is free. Architectural fragments from these monuments that were found during excavations are displayed in Aosta's **Archaeological Museum** at Piazza Roncas 12 (✆ **0165-275-902**; free admission; Tues-Sun 10am–1pm, 2pm–6pm).

The Valle d'Aosta

Most visitors to the Valle d'Aosta come here for the outdoor activities rather than to sightsee; the region has some of Italy's best hiking trails. In summer climbers, cyclists, and ramblers head for the untamed **Parco Nazionale del Gran Paradiso** (see "Italian Wilderness," p. 499). In winter, the meadows and alpine forests around **Cogne** boast some of the region's best cross-country skiing. There's an **ice rink** in Aosta called Art on Ice at Corso Lancieri di Aosta 47 (✆ **0165-185-7281**), and if you're after something a bit different, consider **dog sledding** (www.dogsledman.com/index.php) near Courmayeur.

However, most visitors come for the **downhill skiing** and snowboarding destinations of **Courmayeur, Breuil-Cervinia**, and the **Monte Rose** ski area around the resort towns of Champoluc and Gressoney. There are trails for all levels, from gentle nursery slopes to black runs and mogul fields. Expert skiers are best off at high-altitude **La Thuile** for excellent off-trail powder and heli-skiing. The ski season kicks off in early December and, weather permitting, runs through April. Altogether there are 800km (500 miles) of ski runs available under the **Valle d'Aosta ski pass**; multi-day passes cost from 133€ for 3 days up to 485€ for 2 weeks. One child under age 8 skis free with each adult that buys the pass. More details are available at www.skivallee.it.

Where to Eat & Stay

In the ski season, many hotels in Valle d'Aosta expect guests to eat on the premises and stay 3 nights or more, but outside busy tourist times, they are more flexible.

The Valle d'Aosta is the land of mountain food—hams and salamis, creamy polenta—and buttery Fontina is the cheese of choice.

Osteria da Nando ★★ FONDUE   This cheery terracotta-colored *osteria* is a true family affair, run under the beady eye of Germana Scarpa, who has been the boss here since 1957. Since then it has become one of Aosta's most popular restaurants for its fondues in many guises, from bourguignonne served with tender beef fillet to *raclette* served with creamy Fontina cheese and chunks of chewy bread, along-side the archetypal Piedmontese dish of *bagna cauda* (anchovy fondue). Desserts are a little basic, French-style crèpes and gateaux, but the wine selection is impressively local.

Via Sant'Anselmo 99. www.osterianando.com. ✆ **0165-44-455.** Main courses 12€–25€. Daily (except closed Tues) noon–2pm, 7:30–10pm. Closed 2 weeks late June to early July.

Ristorante La Palud ★★ PIZZA/SEAFOOD   There are Monte Bianco and glacier views from this buzzing pizzeria, and due to its position near the tunnel into France, it is nearly always packed. With the opening of the new cable-car service, reservations are recommended. It's popular for its deliciously crispy pizzas, creamy polenta dishes, and fresh fish brought up from the Ligurian coast. In summer sit outside on the

---

Italian Wilderness

The little town of Cogne is the gateway to one of Europe's finest parcels of unspoiled wilderness, **Parco Nazionale del Gran Paradiso.** Once the hunting grounds of King Vittorio Emanuele II, this vast and lovely national park—Italy's oldest—encompasses the jagged peaks of **Gran Paradiso** (4,061 m/13,323-ft. high), five valleys, and a total of 703 sq. km (271 sq. miles) of forests and pasture-land. Many Alpine beasts roam wild here, including the ibex (curly-horned goat) and the elusive chamois (small antelope), both of which are nearly extinct in Europe. Humans can roam these wilds via a vast network of well-marked **hiking trails.** As well as being a hikers' paradise, Cogne is also well respected for its 80km (50 miles) of challenging cross-country (Nordic) skiing trails; check www.funivie granparadiso.it for more. The park's main **visitor center** is at Via Alpetta, Ronco Canavese (www.pngp.it/en; ✆ **011-860-6233**). Admission is free.

UP AND over MONT BLANC

Riding high over Mont Blanc—Europe's highest mountain at 4,811m (15,784 ft.)—has to be one of the most awe-inspiring experiences in the Italian Alps. It's an enchanted journey passing over glaciers and steep ravines, mountain lakes, and snowy peaks on the Italian side of the Vallée Blanche.

For years, this epic trek has involved three changes of cable car, starting from the little ski village of **La Palud** (3km/1.75 miles above Courmayeur), and ascending through **Le Pavillon** and **Rifugio Torino** to the viewing terrace at **Punta Helbronner** (3,462 m/11,358 ft.), in the heart of the Mont Blanc Massif. From here it was possible to take the cable car down to **Aiguille de Midi** on the French side of Mont Blanc, and then the Panoramic Mont-Blanc Gondola on into the party-loving resort of **Chamonix**.

However, a new and vastly improved cable-car service run by Funivie del Monte Biano, called **Skyway Monte Bianco**, was being launched in June 2015. The system sees sleek rotating gondolas departing from a swish new station at **Pontal d'Entrèves** (near the entrance to the Mont Blanc tunnel) on a high-speed connection up to Punta Helbronner for a bird's-eye view of Monte Bianco and the surrounding peaks of Gran Paradiso and Monte Cervinia (Matterhorn). Costs and opening hours were not established at the time of writing, but visit www.montebianco.com for an up-to-date report.

Rifugio Torino will continue as a mountain refuge and will connect to Point Helbronner by a 154m (505-ft.) horizontal tunnel and a vertical lift of 70m (230 ft.) blasted out of the mountain. If you venture all the way to Chamonix, the best way back to Courmayeur is to take the SAVDA/SAT bus service through Mont Blanc tunnel. Six buses run each way and the journey takes 45 minutes (www.sat-montblanc.com or www.savda. it; tickets 15€, discounts available for children under age 12).

flower-filled terrace; in winter huddle around the open fire and admire the drifts of snow piled up outside.

Strada la Palud 17, Courmayeur. www.lapalud.it. ℭ **0165-89-169.** Main courses 10€–25€. Mon-Sun noon–3:30pm, 7:30–10:30pm.

Hostellerie du Cheval Blanc ★★   Traditional wooden chalet this is not, but if you're after family comforts and town-center convenience plus Alpine views and a garden, the modern design of the Cheval Blanc (white cow) fits the bill. The hotel is designed around a massive atrium with stylish leather sofas and has two restaurants; Le Petit is fairly expensive, but the Brasserie lends itself to early suppers with kids. The rooms are conventionally decorated in muted shades, and the bathrooms come in highly ornate marble, most with baths as well as showers. For skiers, a winter shuttle runs to the cable car up to Pila, while the pool and sauna provide perfect après-ski relaxation before a night of R&R in the bars of Aosta.

Rue Clavalité 20, Aosta. www.chevalblanc.it. ℭ **0165-239-140.** 55 units. 120€ doubles; 160€–180€ suite. Rates include breakfast. Free parking. **Amenities:** 2 restaurants; bar; children's playroom; indoor pool; gym; sauna; spa; room service; Wi-Fi (free).

GENOA & THE CINQUE TERRE

Hugging the Mediterranean coastline from the French border to the tip of Tuscany lies a crescent-shaped strip of land that makes up the region of Liguria. The pleasures of this region are no secret. Ever since the 19th century, world-weary travelers have been heading for Liguria's resorts, such as San Remo and Portofino, to enjoy balmy weather and sapphire-blue sea. Beyond the beach, the stones and tile of fishing villages, small resort towns, and proud old port cities bake in the sun, and hillsides are fragrant with the scent of bougainvillea and pines.

Liguria is really two coasts. First, the "white sand" stretch west of Genoa known as the **Riviera di Ponente (Setting Sun),** is studded with fashionable resorts, many of which, like San Remo, have seen their heydays fade but continue to entice visitors with palm-fringed promenades and a gentle way of life. The rockier, more rugged, but also more colorful fishing-village-filled stretch to the southeast of Genoa, known as the **Riviera di Levante (Rising Sun),** extends past the posh harbor of Portofino to the ever popular villages of the Cinque Terre.

The province's capital, Genoa, is Italy's busiest port, an ancient center of commerce, and one of history's great maritime powers. Despite its rough exterior, it is an underrated gem filled with architectural delights, Italy's largest historic center, and a sense of "real Italy" that has become hard to come by in many of the country's more popular cities.

GENOA (GENOVA) ★★

142km (88 miles) S of Milan, 501km (311 miles) NW of Rome, 194km (120 miles) E of Nice

With its dizzying mix of the old and the new, **Genoa** is as multilayered as the hills it clings to. It was and is, first and foremost, a port city: an important maritime center for the Roman Empire, boyhood home of Christopher Columbus (whose much-restored house still stands near a section of the medieval walls), and, fueled by seafaring commerce that stretched to the Middle East, one of the largest and wealthiest cities of Renaissance Europe.

Genoa began as a port of the ancient Ligurian people at least by the 6th century B.C. and by the early Middle Ages had become a formidable maritime power, conquering the surrounding coast and the mighty

Previous Page: **Genoa Aquarium.**

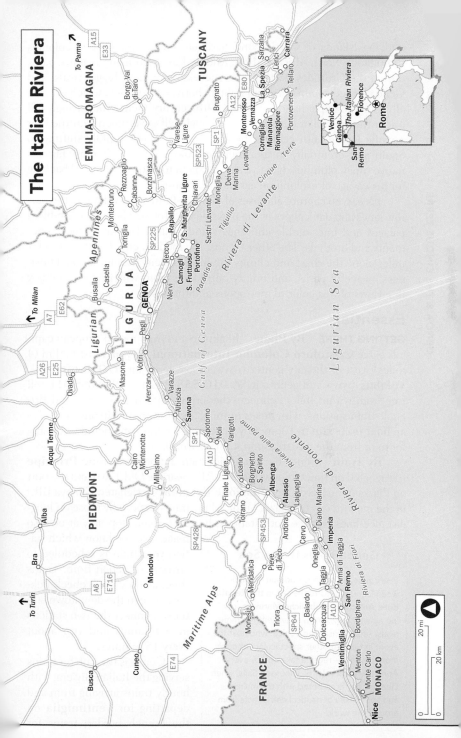

The Italian Riviera

outlying islands of Corsica and Sardinia. Genoa established colonies throughout North Africa and the Middle East, and made massive gains during the Crusades. With bigger success came new, bigger rivals, and Genoa locked commercial and military horns with Venice, which eventually took the upper hand in the late 14th century. Genoa increasingly fell under the control of outsiders, and though self-government returned for a while in the 16th century, by then sea trade was rapidly shifting to Spain and eventually to its American colonies. Genoa's most famous native son, Columbus, had to travel to Spain to find the financial backing for his voyage of exploration across the Atlantic.

It's easy to capture glimpses of Genoa's former glory days on the narrow lanes and dank alleys of the portside Old Town, where treasure-filled palaces and fine marble churches stand next to laundry-draped tenements and brothels. The other Genoa, the modern city that stretches for miles along the coast and climbs the hills, is a city of international business, peaceful parks, and breezy belvederes from which you can enjoy fine views of this colorful metropolis and the sea.

Essentials

GETTING THERE   By Plane Flights to and from most European capitals serve **Cristoforo Colombo International Airport,** just 6.5km (4 miles) west of the city center (www.airport.genova.it; ✆ 010-60-151). **Volabus** (www.amt.genova.it; ✆ 010-558-2414 or 800-085-311 toll free from within Italy) connects the airport with the Principe and Brignole train stations, with buses running the 30-minute trip once or twice an hour from 5am to 10pm; buy tickets on the bus (6€, includes a transfer to or from the city transportation network).

By Train Genoa has two major train stations, **Stazione Principe** (designated on timetables as Genova P.P.) near the Old Town and the port on Piazza Acquaverde, and **Stazione Brignole** (designated Genova BR.) in the modern city on Piazza Verdi. Many trains, especially those on long-distance lines, service both stations; however, some stop only at one, so make sure you know which station your train is scheduled to arrive at or depart from. Trains (free, as they don't check tickets between the downtown stations) connect the two stations in 5 minutes and run about every 15 minutes.

Genoa is the hub for trains serving the Italian Riviera, with hourly trains arriving from and departing for **Ventimiglia** on the French border; trains for

Genoa Takes to the Sea

Every June, an ancient tradition continues when Genoa takes to the sea in the **Regata delle Antiche Repubbliche Marinare,** rowing against crews from its ancient maritime rivals, Amalfi, Pisa, and Venice, who host the event in turn. Another spectacular—though more modern—regatta takes place every April: the **Millevele,** or Thousand Sails, when Genoa's bay is carpeted with the mainsails and spinnakers of nautical enthusiasts from around the world.

Geno

ATTRACTIONS

Acquario di Genova
  (Aquarium) **3**
Cattedrale di San Lorenzo **13**
Galata Museo del Mare **2**
Galleria di Palazzo Bianco **6**
Galleria Nazionale
  di Palazzo Spinola **5**
Piazza Dante **14**

HOTELS

Agnello d'Oro **1**
Best Western City Hotel **10**
Best Western Hotel Metropoli **8**
Hotel Bristol Palace **15**

RESTAURANTS

I Tre Merli **4**
I Tre Merli Antica Cantina **7**
La Berlocca **12**
Maxelâ **11**
Trattoria da Maria **9**

La Spezia, at the eastern edge of Liguria, run even more frequently, as often as three trains an hour during peak times. Check timetables: regional trains make l stop at almost all the coastal resorts, while faster trains stop at only a few of them (for towns covered in this chapter, see individual listings for connections with Genoa). Lots of trains connect Genoa with major Italian cities: **Milan** (one to two per hour; 1½–2 hrs.), **Rome** (hourly; 5–6 hr.), **Turin** (one per hour; regional: 1¾–2 hrs.), **Florence** (hourly but always with a change, usually at Pisa; 3 hr.), **Pisa** (hourly; 1½–3 hrs.).

    By Bus An extensive bus network connects Genoa with other parts of Liguria, and with other Italian and European cities, from the main bus station next to Stazione Principe. It's easiest to reach seaside resorts by the trains that run along the coast, but buses link to many small towns in the region's hilly hinterlands. Contact **PESCI,** Piazza della Vittoria 94r (✆ **010-564-936**), for tickets and information.

By Car   Genoa is linked to other parts of Italy and to France by a convenient network of highways. Genoa has lots of parking around the port and the edges of the Old Town, so you can usually find a spot easily. It can be pricey (1.60€–2.50€ an hour), though in some lots you don't pay for the overnight hours.

By Ferry   Genoa connects to several other major Mediterranean ports, including Barcelona, as well as Sardinia and Sicily by ferry service (www.traghettitalia.it). Most boats leave and depart from the Stazione Marittima (✆ **010-089-8300**), which is on a waterfront roadway, Via Marina D'Italia, about a 5-minute walk south of Stazione Principe. For service to and from the **Riviera Levante,** check with **Tigullio** (www.traghettiportofino.it; ✆ **0185-284-670**) or Golfo Paradiso (www.golfo paradiso.it; ✆**0185-772091**); there's almost hourly service from 9am to 5pm daily in July and August.

VISITOR INFORMATION   The **main tourist office** is on **Via Garib- aldi 12r** across from the beautiful city hall (www.visitgenoa.it; ✆ **010- 557-2903**), open daily 9am to 6:30pm. There are branches also in **Piazza Caricamento** near the aquarium (✆ **010-557-4200**), open daily 9:30am to 6:30pm; and **Cristoforo Colombo airport** (✆ **010- 601-5247**), open daily 9am to 1pm and 1:30 to 5:30pm.

Genoa's twisting alleyways.

GETTING AROUND   Given Genoa's labyrinth of small streets (many of which cannot be negoti- ated by car or bus), the only way to traverse much of the city is on foot—and you'll need a good map. The tourist office gives out terrific maps, but you can also buy an audioguide with map that really helps you navigate the small *vicoli* or backstreets. Genovese are usu- ally happy to direct visitors, but given the geography with which they are dealing, their instructions can be complicated.

BY BUS   Bus tickets (1.60€) are available at newsstands and at ticket booths, *tabacchi* (tobacco- nists, marked by a brown and white T sign), and at the train stations;

A Market Cornucopia

The sprawling **Mercato Orientale,** Genoa's boisterous indoor food market, evokes the days when ships brought back spices and other commodities from the ends of the earth. An excellent place to stock up on olives, herbs, fresh fruit, and other Ligurian products, it is held Monday through Saturday 7:30am to 1pm and 3:30 to 7:30pm, with entrances on Via XX Settembre and Via Galata (about halfway between Piazza de Ferrari at the edge of the Old Town and Stazione Brignole). The district just north of the market (especially Via San Vincenzo and Via Colombo) is a gourmand's dream, with many bakeries, *pasticcerie* (pastry shops), and stores selling pasta and cheese, wine, olive oil, and other foodstuffs.

look for the symbol **AMT** (www.amt.genova.it; ✆ **010-558-2414**). Otherwise, tickets cost 2.60€ on board. You must stamp your ticket when you board. Bus tickets can also be used on the funiculars and public elevators that climb the city's steep hills surrounding the ancient core of the town. Tickets good for 24 hours cost 4.50€, or 9€ for four people (two people travel for free). You can also buy a discounted pack of 10 single tickets for 14€.

BY TAXI   Metered taxis, which you can find at cabstands, are a convenient and safe way to get around Genoa at night. For instance, you may well want to consider taking a taxi from a restaurant in the Old Town to your hotel or to one of the train stations (especially Stazione Brignole, which is a bit farther out). Cabstands at Piazza della Nunziata, Piazza Fontane Marose, and Piazza de Ferrari are especially convenient to the Old Town, or call a **radio taxi** at ✆ **010-5966.**

BY SUBWAY   The city's nascent subway system is a work in progress, as there are still only seven stops on a single line between Piazza De Ferrari and a suburb to the northwest called Certosa (there are convenient stops in between at Stazione Principe and at Dinegro close to the ferry port). The tickets are the same as those used for the bus.

CITY LAYOUT   Genoa extends for miles along the coast, with neighborhoods and suburbs tucked into valleys and climbing the city's many hills. Most sights of interest are in the **Old Town,** a fascinating jumble of old *palazzi,* shabby tenements, cramped squares, and tiny lanes and alleyways clustered on the eastern side of the old port. The city's two train stations are located on either side of the Old Town. As confusing as Genoa's topography is, wherever you are in the Old Town, you are only a short walk or bus or taxi ride from one of these two stations.

Stazione Principe is the closest, just to the west; from **Piazza Acquaverde,** in front of the station, follow **Via Balbi** through **Piazza della Nunziata** and **Via Bensa** to **Via Cairoli,** which runs into Via Garibaldi (the walk will take about 15 min.). **Via Garibaldi,** lined with a succession of majestic *palazzi,* forms the northern flank of the Old Town and is the best place to begin your explorations. Many of the city's most important museums and other major monuments are on and around this street, and from here you can descend into the warren of little lanes, known as ***caruggi,*** that lead through the cluttered heart of the city and down to the port.

From **Stazione Brignole,** walk straight across the broad, open space to Piazza della Vittoria/Via Luigi Cadorna and turn right to follow broad **Via XX Settembre,** one of the city's major shopping avenues, due west for about 15 or 20 minutes to **Piazza de Ferrari,** which is on the eastern edge of the Old Town. From here, **Via San Lorenzo,** accessed by exiting the southwest corner of the square, will lead you past Genoa's cathedral and to the port. To reach Via Garibaldi, go north from Piazza de Ferrari on **Via XXV Aprile** to **Piazza delle Fontane Marose.** This busy square marks the eastern end of Via Garibaldi.

[Fast FACTS] GENOA

Bookstores Genoa's best source for English-language books and other media is **Feltrinelli,** Via Ceccardi 16, near Piazza De Ferrari, just off of Via XX Settembre (www.lafeltrinelli. it; ✆ **010-583-296**).

Crime Genoa is a relatively safe city, but some of the very small alleyways of the Old Town near the port can be sketchy at night, and even during the day they can sometimes make you feel unsafe. Wait for other people, preferably locals, before entering little-trafficked alleyways and avoid any streets that make you feel uneasy. In an **emergency,** call ✆ **113;** this is a free call. There is a **police station** on the cusp of the Old Town and the port at Via Balbi 38/B (✆ **010-254-871**).

Drugstores Pharmacies keep extended hours on a rotating basis; dial ✆ **192** to learn which ones are open late in a particular week. Usually open overnight are **Pescetto,** Via Balbi 185r (✆ **010-246-2697**), across from Stazione Principe; and **Europa,** Corso Europa 676 (✆ **010-397-615**).

Emergencies The general emergency number is ✆ **113;** for an ambulance, dial ✆ **118.** Both are free calls.

Holidays Genoa's patron saint, San Giovanni Battista (Saint John the Baptist), is the same as Turin's and is honored on June 24. For a list of official state holidays, see p. 34.

Hospitals The **Ospedale San Martino,** Largo Rosanna Benzi 10

(✆ **010-5551**), offers a variety of medical services.

Laundry There is a self-service laundromat, **Lavanderia Self-Service,** at Via Gramsci 181R (✆ **340-235-1492;** Mon–Sat 9am–6pm).

Luggage Storage The luggage storage office in Stazione Principe is along track 11 and is open daily 7am to 11pm; the fee is 4€ per piece of baggage for the first 5 hours. It is an additional .60€ per hour for the next 7 hours and then an additional .20€ per hour after that. In Stazione Brignole the storage office is on the ground floor (same hours and rates as Principe), but was closed at press time while the station is under construction.

Post Office Genoa's main post office is at **Piazza**

Dante 4 (☎ **010-591-762**). This office is open Monday through Saturday 8:10am to 7:40pm, while the other offices around town—including those at the two train stations and the airport—have shorter hours.

Telephone The area code for Genoa is ☎ **010.**

Travel Services CTS, Via Colombo 21R (☎ **010-564-366**), specializes in budget travel. It's open Monday to Friday 9:30am to 6:30pm.

Exploring Genoa

Acquario di Genova (Aquarium of Genoa) ★★★ AQUARIUM

Europe's largest aquarium is Genoa's biggest draw and a must-see for travelers with children. The structure alone is remarkable, resembling a ship and built alongside a pier in the old harbor; it's about a 15-minute walk from Stazione Principe and 10 minutes from Via Garibaldi. Inside, more than 50 aquatic displays re-create Red Sea coral reefs, pools in the tropical rainforests of the Amazon River basin, and other marine ecosystems that provide a home for sharks, seals, dolphins, penguins, piranhas, and just about every other kind of water creature. Look out for the tiny orange frogs from Madagascar the size of a thumbnail. During the day, playful seals and dolphins blow trick bubbles. Descriptions are posted in English, and there's a 3-D film on ocean life (ask for printed English narration).
Ponte Spinola (at the port). www.acquariodigenova.it. ☎ **010-23451.** Admission 24€ adults, 16€ seniors 65 and over, 15€ children 4–12. Mon–Fri 9:30am–7:30pm; Sat–Sun 9:30am–8:30pm (July–Aug daily until 10:30pm). Bus: 1, 2, 3, 4, 5, 6, 7, 8, 12, 13, 14, or 15. Metro: Darsena.

Cattedrale di San Lorenzo ★ CATHEDRAL

The austerity of this church's black-and-white-striped 12th-century facade is enlivened ever so slightly by fanciful French Gothic carvings around the portal and the presence of two stone lions. A later addition is the bell tower, completed in the 16th century. In the frescoed interior, chapels house two of Genoa's most notable curiosities: Beyond the first pilaster on the right is a still-unexploded shell fired through the roof from a British ship offshore during World War II; and in the Cappella di San Giovanni (left aisle), a 13th-century crypt contains what crusaders returning from the Holy Land claimed to be relics of John the Baptist. The adjoining treasury appears to specialize in fabled tableware of doubtful provenance: the plate upon which Saint John's head was supposedly served to Salome, a bowl allegedly used at the Last Supper, and a bowl

> ### A Cumulative Ticket
>
> Admission to Genoa's major **palaces and art galleries** is grouped together on the **Card Musei** (12€ for 1 day, 16€ for 2; 13,50€ and 20€ respectively also gets you unlimited use of the city's public transport), which includes entrance to the principal palaces, the Museo Sant'Agostino, San Lorenzo, the Galleria Nazionale di Palazzo Spinola, the Museo di Palazzo Reale, and a handful of other museums around town, plus a discount on admission to the aquarium and movie theaters. Pick it up at any city museum, the airport tourist office, or in one of several bookstores downtown (www.visitgenoa.it).

The black-and-white marble façade of Cattedrale di San Lorenzo.

thought at one time to be the Holy Grail. Less storied but nonetheless magnificent gold and bejeweled objects here reflect Genoa's medieval prominence as a maritime power. Entrance to the treasury is only by guided tour in Italian, but it's still worth seeing what is inside, even if the extent of your Italian is *gelato* and *pizza*.

Piazza San Lorenzo. ✆ **010-254-1250.** Cathedral admission free; treasury 5.50€ adults, 4.50€ seniors and students. Cathedral: Mon–Sat 9am–noon and 3–6pm. Treasury: By half-hour guided tour only (ask when you get there) Mon–Sat 9am–noon and 3–6pm. Bus: 1, 7, 8, 17, 18, 19, or 20.

Galata Museo del Mare (Museum of the Seas) ★★ MUSEUM Genoa's livelihood has always been linked to the sea. While you can wander the port to see boats of every size and type, to truly learn about and appreciate the maritime history of Genoa, a visit to the Galata is a must. The building itself is the oldest surviving construction of the dockyard from the old Republic, where Genovese galleys were built during the 17th century. You enter into the gallery dedicated to the old port with paintings and artifacts of the period, and then it's on to the fantastic, full-scale reproduction of a Genovese "attack ship" (otherwise known as a galley), with fun artifacts and props, and good English translation that will engage all ages.

Ponte Parodi (at the port). www.galatamuseodelmare.it. ✆ **010-234-5655.** Admission 12€ adults, 9€ seniors 65 and over, 7€ children 4–12. Mar–Oct daily 10am–7:30pm; Nov–Feb Tues–Fri 10am–6pm, Sat–Sun 10am–7:30pm (last entry 1 hr. before closing). Bus: 1, 2, 3, 4, 5, 6, 7, 8, 12, 13, 14, or 15. Metro: Darsena (a 10-min. walk to the aquarium or hop on the 1€ shuttle).

Galleria di Palazzo Bianco (White Palace) ★★ MUSEUM Palazzo Bianco (the White Palace) can be considered the oldest and, at the same time, the most recent of the magnificent *palazzi* along ritzy Via Garibaldi, also known as the Strada Nuova. Although it was built during the mid-16th century by Luca Grimaldi, a scion of one of the most important Genovese families, the gorgeoous white facade one sees today was reconstructed in the 18th century. Maria Durazzo Brignole-Sale de Ferrari donated the palace and her art collection to the city in 1884, and its rooms now display an impressive collection of art. Her preference for painters of Spanish and Flemish schools is obvious—Van Dyck, Rubens, Filippino Lippi, Veronese, and Caravaggio all are represented here—but the museum's most notable holding is "Portrait of a Lady," by Lucas Cranach the Elder. A small rooftop terrace offers (for a fee of 3€) panoramic views of the city.

Via Garibaldi 11. www.palazzobianco.museidigenova.it. ℭ **010-557-2193.** Admission 12€ adults, free for EU citizens 18 and under; includes entrance to Palazzo Rosso and Palazzo Tursi. Tues–Fri 9am–7pm; Sat–Sun 10am–7pm. Bus: 18, 19, 20, 30, 35, 37, 39, 40, 41, or 42.

Galleria Nazionale di Palazzo Spinola ★ MUSEUM Another prominent Genovese family, the Spinolas, donated their palace and magnificent art collection to the city only recently, in 1958. One of the pleasures of viewing these works is seeing them amid the frescoed splendor in which the city's merchant/banking families once lived. As in Genoa's other art collections, you will find masterworks that range from native artists like Strozzi, da Messina, Reni, Giordano, and De Ferrari, to van Dyck and other painters of the Dutch and Flemish schools, whom Genoa's wealthy were fond of importing to paint their portraits.

Humble house off Piazza Dante, once owned by Christopher Columbus' father.

Piazza Pellicceria 1. ℭ **010-270-5300.** Admission 4€ adults, 2€ for ages 18–25, free for those under 18 or 65 and over, or pay 12€ for a Card Musei cumulative ticket (see box below). Tues–Sat 8:30am–7:30pm; Sun 1:30–7:30pm. Bus: 1, 3, 7, 8, 18, 20, or 34.

Piazza Dante Though most of this square just south of Piazza de Ferrari is made of 1930s office buildings, one end is bounded by the twin round towers of the reconstructed **Porta Soprana ★★**, a town gate built in 1155. The main draw, though, is the small **house** (rebuilt in the 18th c.), still standing a bit incongruously in a tidy little park below the gate, said to have belonged to **Christopher Columbus's father,** who was a weaver and gatekeeper (whether young Christopher lived here is open to debate).

Bus: 14, 35, 42, 44, or 46.

Via Garibaldi ★★ Many of Genoa's museums and other sights are clustered on and around this street, also known as Strada Nuova, one of the most beautiful in Italy, where Genoa's wealthy families built palaces in the 16th and 17th centuries. Aside from the art collections housed in the **Galleria di Palazzo Bianco** and **Galleria di Palazzo Rosso** (see above), the street contains a wealth of other treasures. The **Palazzo Podesta,** at no. 7, hides one of the city's most beautiful fountains in its courtyard, and the **Palazzo Tursi,** at no. 9, now housing municipal offices, proudly displays artifacts of famous locals: letters written by Christopher Columbus and the violin of Nicolo Paganini (which is still played on special occasions).

Admission free when the offices are open: Mon–Fri 8:30am–noon and 1–4pm. Bus: 19, 20, 30, 32, 33, 35, 36, 41, or 42.

Where to Stay

Despite the draw of the aquarium and its intriguing Old Town, Genoa is still geared more to business travelers. There has been a pleasant boom of new quality accommodations sprouting up, however, as the city starts to turn toward becoming more tourist-friendly. It is best to avoid hotels in the heart of the Old Town, especially around the harbor, as many are a little sketchy. Keep in mind, Genoa books up solid during its annual boat show, the world's largest, in October. The upper end of the price range listed below in most cases applies only the week of the boat show; the maximum the rest of the year is considerably lower, sometimes as much as 25%.

EXPENSIVE

Hotel Bristol Palace ★ This 19th-century *palazzo* is one of Genoa's most regal and popular hotels with its opulent oval staircase and beautiful stained-glass dome. Located in the middle of the city's shopping district, it is surprisingly quiet (with soundproof windows) and perfectly located for exploring the sights and doing a little damage to the wallet. The rooms and bathrooms have all been renovated in classic taste, and an outdoor dining terrace adds even more appeal to this oasis-like lodging in the city center. Although the rack rates are high, you can almost always find a deal online and for weekends.

Via XX Settembre 35. www.hotelbristolpalace.com. ℰ **010-592-541.** 33 units. 119€–470€ double; 249€–699€ junior suite. Rates include buffet breakfast. Parking in garage 25€. **Amenities:** Restaurant; bar; babysitting; bikes; concierge; room service; smoke-free rooms, Wi-Fi (free).

MODERATE

Best Western City Hotel ★★ This nondescript building just off the city's main shopping street is actually a very nice, modern, and well-equipped 4-star hotel. Guest rooms have neutral-toned contemporary decor, flatscreen TVs, and sleek built-ins; family rooms include bunkbeds. Rooms on the upper floors have fantastic views of the city and port. Breakfasts (included) are particularly robust.

Via San Sebastiano 6. www.bwcityhotel-ge.it. ✆ **010-584-707.** 64 units. 109€–275€ double. Rates include breakfast. Parking 22€ in nearby garage. **Amenities:** Bar; room service; smoke-free rooms, Wi-Fi (free).

Best Western Hotel Metropoli ★★ Located on the corner of a lovely square and a pedestrian-only street in the historic center, Hotel Metropoli offers very good lodging with modern amenities, a robust breakfast, and good service. Straightforward guest rooms can be a bit business-like but they are soundproof, clean, and comfortable, with refurbished bathrooms. The staff can help you plan a day of exploring.

Piazza delle Fontane Marose. www.hotelmetropoli.it. ✆ **010-246-8888.** 48 units. 93€–246€ double; 99€–260€ triple. Rates include buffet breakfast. Parking 22€ in nearby garage. **Amenities:** Bar; room service; smoke-free rooms, Wi-Fi (free).

INEXPENSIVE

Agnello d'Oro ★ It's all about location at this converted convent turned low-cost *locanda*. It is just a few blocks away from Stazione Principe and on the edge of the Old Town, which can be viewed from the hotel terrace. Most of the rooms are very basic (think modular, modern furniture without much personality), but some still retain the building's original 16th-century character, with high ceilings (rooms numbered in teens) or vaulted ones (rooms numbered under 10). Some top-floor rooms come with the added charm of balconies and views over the Old Town and harbor (best from no. 56). There's an apartment (3 bedrooms, 2 bathrooms) that sleeps six, perfect for those traveling with a few kids. The owner is friendly, helpful with sightseeing tips, and offers the occasional free *aperitivo* for guests.

Via Monachette 6, off Via Balbi. www.hotelagnellodoro.it. ✆ **010-246-2084.** 17 units. 70€–100€ double; 160€ for 4 people in 3-bedroom apt., 2 more people can be added for 20€ each. Rates include breakfast. Private parking 15€–25€. **Amenities:** Bar; concierge; room service; smoke-free rooms, Wi-Fi (free).

Where to Eat

I Tre Merli ★★ New Yorkers will recognize the name and chic ambience of this restaurant from its now-closed Manhattan outposts. Here in Genoa, their stylish flagship restaurant overlooks the old port, in a high-ceilinged room that's all black-and-white columns and exposed stone walls. Local seafood stars in dishes such as *fritua* (fried fish, squid, and shrimp with crisp vegetables and fried sage); cheese *foccacia* come with artichokes or arugula and Parma ham. I Tre Merli also operates a couple of *enoteche* (wine bars) around the city and an enoteca and "affittacamere" (rooms for rent) in Camogli (see p. 519).

Calata Cattaneo 17. www.itremerli.it. ✆ **010-246-4416**. Main courses 18€–20€. Daily noon–3pm and 7:30–11pm.

Fast . . . and, Oh, So Good

All over Genoa you'll find shops selling **focaccia,** Liguria's answer to pizza, a sort of thick flatbread often stuffed or topped with cheese, herbs, olives, onions, vegetables, or prosciutto. Many of these *focaccerie* also sell *farinata,* a chickpea pancake that usually emerges from the oven in the shape of a big round pizza. Just point and make a hand gesture to show how much you want. Prices are by weight and in most cases a piece of either will cost about 1.50€ to 3€. Most focaccia (especially the ones with cheese) and all *farinata* are better warm, so if the piece you are getting looks like it has been there a while, ask for it to be warmed up.

A favorite spot for both snacks, and right near Stazione Principe, is **La**

Focacceria di Teobaldo ★, Via Balbi 115r (daily 8am–8pm). **Focacceria di Via Lomellini** ★, on Via Lomellini 57/59 in the heart of the Old Town (Mon–Sat 8am–7:30pm), has great *focaccia di Recco* (also called *focaccia al formaggio*), a super-thin focaccia filled with cheese that is the specialty of the nearby town of Recco. **Focaccia & Co.,** Piazza Macelli di Soziglia 91r (Mon–Sat 7am–7:30pm), is right across from Fratelli Klainguti (Piazza Macelli di Soziglia 98; ✆ 010-860-2628), so you can follow up your focaccia with something sweet. Down at Porto Antico, get your focaccia fix (you *will* be addicted after your first taste) at **Il Localino,** Via Turati 8r (Mon–Sat 9am–7pm).

La Berlocca ★ GENOVESE   Once a simple *farinata* (chickpea pancake) shop is now a cozy trattoria serving good food and wine at decent prices, and located in the historic center just a few steps from the port. Dishes are typically Ligurian and include choices from both the sea and garden, all thoughtfully prepared. Try the signature *buridda,* a traditional dish of salted cod, tomatoes, and herbs. There's also a variety of homemade pasta dishes.

Via dei Macelli di Soziglia 47r. ✆ **010-796-3333.** Main courses 9€–20€. Tues–Sat noon–3pm and 7–11pm and until midnight on Fri and Sat; Sun lunch only, with reservation. Closed last week of July to 3rd week of Aug.

Maxelâ ★ MEAT/LIGURIAN   This butcher shop/restaurant is located in the historic center in what is called Soziglia, the "old *via* of butcher shops"; the locale itself oozes with old-world charm. Enter through the butcher shop where diners are invited to choose their cut; you have the choice of having your meat served raw (tartar), grilled, or pan-fried. Next door, the dining room features stone and brick arches, light green tiles irregularly arranged on the walls, and dark wood tables topped with slabs of white marble. Price-fixed meals (ranging from 12€–30€) are available at lunch and dinner, and there's a decent wine list to complement your meal.

Vico inferiore del ferro 9. ✆ **010-247-4209.** Main courses 15€–20€. Mon–Sat noon–2:30pm and 7:30–10:30pm.

Trattoria da Maria ★★ LIGURIAN   One of the simplest trattorias also happens to be one of Genoa's most famous eateries. Sit side by side with lawyers, construction workers, students, and tourists, ignore the unattractive decor, and concentrate on the great mix of dishes this Genovese institution has to offer, on a menu that changes daily. Enjoy flavorful, no-nonsense dishes such as the near-perfect pesto, stuffed anchovies, and even simple fish sautéed in white wine. *Note:* Maria has finally retired and the kitchen is in new hands. Although still a good choice, those who ate there under the former cook may be slightly disappointed.

Vico Testadoro 14r (just off Via XXV Aprile). ☎ **010-581-080.** *Primi* and main courses 5€–9€. Sun and Tues–Fri 11:45am–2:15pm and 7–9:15pm; Mon 11:45am–2:45pm.

Entertainment & Nightlife

The Old Town, some parts of which are sketchy in broad daylight, is especially unseemly at night. Confine late-hour prowls in this area to the well-trafficked streets such as Via San Lorenzo and Via Garibaldi. On the edges of the Old Town, good places to walk at night are around the waterfront, Piazza Fontane Marose, Piazza de Ferrari, and Piazza delle Erbe, where many bars and clubs are located.

PERFORMING ARTS   Genoa has two major venues for culture: the restored **Teatro Carlo Felice,** Piazza de Ferrari (www.carlofelice.it; ☎ **010-589-329**), which is home to Genoa's opera company, and the modern **Teatro Stabile di Genova** (www.teatrostabilegenova.it; ☎ **010-53-421**), on Piazza Borgo Pila near Stazione Brignole, which hosts concerts, dance, and other cultural programs.

THE RIVIERA DI PONENTE: SAN REMO

140km (87 miles) W of Genoa, 56km (35 miles) E of Nice

Gone are the days when Tchaikovsky and the Russian empress Maria Alexandrovna joined a well-heeled mix of *nobils* strolling along San Remo's palm-lined avenues. They left behind an onion-domed Orthodox church, a few grand hotels, and a casino, but **San Remo** is a different sort of town these days. It's still the most cosmopolitan stop on the Riviera di Ponente, as the stretch of coast west of Genoa is called, and caters mostly to sun-seeking Italian families in the summer and, in winter, Milanese who come down to get away from the fog and chilly temperatures of their city.

If you've got a few extra days, base yourself in San Remo and explore further along the coast, all the way to the French border. Train connections are good, and the coastal SS1 road links several charming towns. Highlights include the quiet resort town of **Bordighera** (12km/7.5 miles west of San Remo); one of Europe's finest gardens, **Giardini Hanbury** (28km/20 miles west of San Remo, just past Ventimiglia); and the inland village of **Dolceacqua** (23km/14 miles northwest of San Remo), with its well-preserved medieval core and abandoned castle.

Essentials

GETTING THERE   There are **trains** hourly in both directions between San Remo and Genoa (2–3 hr.). If you're arriving by train, note that San Remo's sleek new underground railway station is a bit of a hike from the center of town and the old port. Trains from Genoa continue west for another 20 minutes to Ventimiglia on the French border. Some trains continue on into France, otherwise, at Ventimiglia you can change onto one of the twice-hourly trains across the border to **Nice,** which is 50 minutes west.

The fastest **driving route** in and out of San Remo is Autostrada A10, which follows the coast from the French border (20 min. away) to Genoa (about 45 min. away). The slower coast road, SS1, cuts right through the center of town.

VISITOR INFORMATION   San Remo's **IAT tourist board** is at Largo Nuvoloni 1 (www.turismoinliguria.it; ✆ **0184-59059;** Mon–Sat 8am–7pm, Sun 9am–1pm), at the corner of Corso Imperatrice/Corso Matteotti.

FESTIVALS   Since the 1950s, the **Sanremo Festival** (mid- to late February; www.sanremo.rai.it) has been Italy's premier music fest, sort of an Italian Grammy Awards, only spread out over several days with far more live performances—by Italian pop stars, international headliners, and plenty of up-and-coming performers. Hotels book up and down the coast (and into France) months in advance. Call the tourist office if you want to try to score tickets.

Exploring San Remo

San Remo's two main thoroughfares are **Via Roma** and **Corso Matteotti.** Corso Matteotti runs between **Piazza Colombo,** with its flower market, and the **casino** (see p. 517), passing through the heart of the bustling, pedestrian-only business district. Here you can shop, sit in cafes, and do a bit of true-Italy people-watching. About midway along Corso Matteotti, turn north on **Via Feraldi** to reach the charming older precincts of town. From **Piazza Mercato,** Via Montà leads into the medieval quarter, **La Pigna,** set on a hill shaped like a pine cone (*la*

A Day at the Beach

The pebbly beach below the Passeggiata dell'Imperatrice is lined with beach stations, where many visitors choose to spend their days: easy to do, because most provide showers, snack bars, beach chairs, lounges, and umbrellas. Expect to spend up to 15€ for a basic lounge, but more like 20€ for a more elaborate sunbed arrangement with umbrella. *Note:* As is standard at most European resort towns without "public" sections of beach (which are usually not very nice anyway), you cannot go onto the beach without paying for at least a lounge chair.

The resort town of San Remo.

pigna is Italian for pine cone). Aside from a few restaurants, La Pigna is a residential quarter, with tall old houses overshadowing narrow lanes that twist and turn up the hillside, with the park-enclosed ruins of a **castle** at the top.

VISITING THE CASINO

San Remo's white palace of a **casino** (www.casinosanremo.it; ℗ **0184-5951**), set intimidatingly atop a long flight of steps across from the old train station and enclosed on three sides by Corso degli Inglesi, is the hub of the local nightlife scene. You can't step foot inside without being properly attired (jacket for gents Oct–June) and showing your passport. You must be 18 or older to enter. Poker tables start at 2€ games, but there are more serious tables that attract high rollers from the length of the Riviera. Gaming rooms are open daily 2:30pm to 2:30am. Things are more relaxed in the rooms set aside for slot machines, where there is no dress code. They are open Sunday to Friday 10am to 2:30am.

Where to Eat & Stay

Ristorante L'Airone ★ LIGURIAN/PIZZA   This cute and always happening restaurant/pizzeria on a pedestrian-only street in the town center serves consistently good food at decent prices. The extensive menu features mostly traditional Ligurian dishes, such as *spaghetti alla vongole* (with clams) and *trofiette al pesto,* but the thin-crust pizza is also excellent. While the decor is cozy and inviting inside, you can also dine in their small garden or in the piazza that fronts the restaurant. Note that pizza is served only in the evening, except for Tuesday and Saturday, when it's also served at lunchtime. The place fills up fast, so reservations are recommended for dinner.

Piazza Eroi Sanremesi 12. www.ristorantelairone.it. ℗ **0184-541-055.** Main courses 7€–17€. Sat–Wed noon–2:30pm; Fri-Wed 7:30–11:30pm.

Hotel Villa Maria ★★ Located on the hillside just above the casino and a quick stroll to the beach, Villa Maria offers comfort and quality in a lovely setting. The hotel's atttributes and reasonable rates make the somewhat outdated style of the guest rooms forgivable. Originally three separate villas, the hotel is spacious and almost regal with its many salons decorated in tasteful fashion from the heydays of the 1920s, 30s, and 40s. Many of these public rooms open to a nicely planted terrace. Pleasant gardens are filled with beautiful roses that flourish all year in the mild winter of the Italian Riviera. Several rooms have balconies facing the sea. Room sizes vary considerably, so ask specifically about what's available when booking or ask to see a few upon arrival. Corso Nuvoloni 30. www.villamariahotel.it. ℂ **0184-531-422.** 38 units, 36 with private bathroom. 77€–140€ double. For half-board (required Easter, Christmas, and Aug 1–15), add 30€ per person. Rates include continental breakfast. Free parking. **Amenities:** Restaurant; concierge; room service; smoke-free rooms.

Royal Hotel ★★★ Thanks to a much-needed restoration, old-world charm and luxury can still be found at this sprawling seafront resort within walking distance of the old town. The majority of rooms have sea views and are tastefully decorated. The gardens and seawater pool are spectacular and allow some reprieve from the sun and heat during the summer months. The buffet breakfast is particularly abundant. Of course, with any 5-star luxury property come jaw-dropping prices—even in the off season. Corso Imperatrice 80. www.royalhotelsanremo.com. ℂ **0184-5391.** 126 units. 279€–665€ double. Rates include buffet breakfast. Free parking. **Amenities:** 3 restaurants; bar; 24-hour room service; babysitting; kid's club; concierge; room service; Wi-Fi (free).

THE RIVIERA DI LEVANTE: CAMOGLI, SANTA MARGHERITA LIGURE & PORTOFINO ★★

Camogli: 26km (16 miles) E of Genoa; Santa Margherita Ligure: 31km (19 miles) E of Genoa; Portofino: 38km (24 miles) E of Genoa; Rapallo: 37km (23 miles) E of Genoa

The coast east of Genoa, the **Riviera di Levante (Shore of the Rising Sun),** is more ruggedly beautiful than the Riviera Ponente, less developed, and hugged by mountains that plunge into the sapphire-colored sea. Three of the coast's most appealing towns are within a few kilometers of one another, clinging to the shores of the Monte Portofino Promontory just east of Genoa: **Camogli, Santa Margherita Ligure,** and little **Portofino.**

Essentials

GETTING THERE One to three **trains** per hour ply the coastline, connecting Genoa with Santa Margherita (25–30 min.) and Camogli (30–45 min.); the trip between Camogli and Santa Margherita takes 5 minutes by train. To get to **Portofino,** take the train to Santa Margherita and then the **Tiguillio** bus (www.tigulliotrasporti.it; ☏ **0185-373-239**), a 25-minute ride via a beautiful coastal road (service every 20 minutes). Tiguillio buses also connect Camogli and Santa Margherita, but because they have to circle the promontory, they take about 30 minutes, a lot longer than the train ride.

In summer, **boats** operated by Golfo Paradiso (www.golfoparadiso. it; ☏ **0185-772-091**) run from Camogli to Portofino and Genoa. **Tiguillio ferries** (www.traghettiportofino.it; ☏ **0185-284-670**) make hourly trips from Santa Margherita to Portofino (15 min.) and Rapallo (15 min.). In summer, there is a boat several days a week to the Cinque Terre. Hours of service vary considerably with the season; schedules are posted on the docks at Piazza Martiri della Libertà.

The fastest car route into the region is Autostrada A12 from Genoa (exit at Recco for Camogli), which takes about 35 to 40 minutes to either Camogli or Santa Margherita. Route SS1 along the coast from Genoa is much slower but more scenic. **Note:** Parking is a challenge in Camogli and Portofino in the summer, and traffic quickly gets clogged on the tiny road between Santa Margherita and Portofino. If you're arriving by car, you would do well to park it in Santa Margherita and take the bus or boat to Portofino.

VISITOR INFORMATION Camogli's tourist office is across from the train station at Via XX Settembre 33 (www. camogliturismo.i; ☏ **0185-771-066**). In **Santa Margherita**, the tourist office is near the harbor at Via XXV Aprile 2B (www.turismoinliguria.it; ☏ **0185-287-485**). The **Portofino** tourist office is at Via Roma 35 (www.turismoinliguria.it; ☏ **0185-269-024**). All are open daily in summer, except Portofino's office is closed on Mondays; expect shorter hours in winter, and a lunchtime closure between noon and 3.

Camogli

Camogli remains delightfully unspoiled, an authentic Ligurian fishing port with tall houses in pastel colors facing the harbor and a nice swath of beach. Given also its excellent accommodations and eateries, Camogli is a lovely place to base yourself while exploring the Riviera Levante. It's also a restful retreat from which you can explore Genoa, which is only about 30 minutes away. One interpretation of Camogli's name is that it derived from *"Ca de Mogge,"* or "House of the Wives" in the local dialect, so named for the women who held down the fort while their husbands went to sea. Another possibility is that it comes from *"Ca a Muggi,"* or "clustered houses," which will seem apt when you are out swimming in the sea and turn to look up at the town's wonderful agglomeration of colorful buildings.

EXPLORING CAMOGLI

Camogli is clustered around its delightful waterfront, from which the town ascends via steep, staircased lanes to Via XX Settembre, one of the few streets in the town proper to accommodate cars (this is where

Getting Festive in Camogli

Camogli throws a well-attended annual party, the **Sagra del Pesce ★★**, on the second Sunday of May, where the town fries up thousands of sardines in a 3.6m-diameter (12-ft.) pan and passes them around for free—a practice that is accompanied by an annual outcry in the press about health concerns and even accusations that frozen fish is used.

The first Sunday of August, Camogli stages the lovely **Festa della Stella**

Maris, during which a procession of boats sails to Punta Chiappa, a spot of land about 1.5km (1 mile) down the coast, and releases 10,000 burning candles. Meanwhile, the same number of candles is set afloat from the Camogli beach. If currents are favorable, the burning candles will come together at sea, signifying a year of unity for couples who watch the spectacle.

the train station, tourist office, and many shops and other businesses are located). Adding to the charm of this setting is the fact that the oldest part of Camogli juts into the harbor on a picturesque little point (once an island). Here ancient houses cling to the little **Castello Dragone** (now closed to the public) and the **Basilica di Santa Maria Assunta** (© **0185-770-130**), originally built in the 12th century but much altered through the ages; its overwhelming baroque interior is open daily 7:30am to noon and 3:30 to 7pm.

Most visitors, though, are drawn to the pleasant **seaside promenade ★** that runs the length of the town. You can swim from the pebbly beach below, and should you feel your towel doesn't provide enough comfort, rent a lounge chair from one of the few beach stations for about 15€—highly recommended in the summer months, when finding even a small piece of pebbly sand is nearly impossible.

WHERE TO EAT & STAY

Bar Primula ★ CAFE/LIGHT FARE   This is considered the "main bar" of Camogli with a prime position along the *lungomare* (promenade). A limited menu of pasta and main courses is served at either lunch or dinner, but Primula is mostly a good spot for simple foods like panini, salads, and the early-evening *aperitivo*.
Via Garibaldi 140. © **0185-770-351.** Pizzas/main courses 9€–15€. Daily 9am–1am.

Vento Ariel ★★ SEAFOOD   We love the old port setting of this popular restaurant almost as much we love its food. Make your way through the medieval archway connecting the *lungomare* to the old port and you'll find the restaurant nestled in the corner facing the *gozzi* (fishing boats of the old harbor). Seafood is done right, with such succulent dishes as *patè di seppie* (cuttlefish mousse), *acchiuge ripiene* (stuffed anchovies) and oven-baked (under a blanket of salt) fresh fish from the gulf (the salt is removed before serving). The wine list is extensive and contains some local, hard-to-find bottles of Vermentino and Pigato, plus the wonderful whites of Liguria. If you can, grab a table outside to drink in the local ambience as well. Reservations are highly recommended.

Calata Porto. ✆ **0185-771-080.** Main courses 15€–28€. Thurs–Tues noon–11:30pm.

Hotel Cenobio dei Dogi ★★

The spectacular position of this resort, combined with the beautifully manicured grounds and old-world charm of the main building, make this Camogli's most popular (and most expensive) hotel. The rooms come in various shapes and sizes, and for the most part are tastefully decorated with a mix of tradition and island flair. (*Note:* There is a *big* difference in size and style between the standard and classic rooms.) The large pool area and private beach—one part terraced stone, one part pebbles—are gorgeous and inviting, making up for the somewhat aloof attitude of the staff.

Via Cuneo 34. www.cenobio.it. ✆ **0185-7241.** 108 units. 200€–250€ standard double with garden view; 240€–360€ standard double with sea view; 240€–320€ classic double with garden view; 370€–480€ classic double with sea view. Rates include buffet breakfast and beach facilities. Free parking. **Amenities:** 2 restaurants, 2 bars; babysitting; concierge; nearby golf course; outdoor saltwater pool; outdoor lighted tennis courts; watersports equipment/rentals; Wi-Fi (free).

La Camogliese ★★

This hotel is super basic, but it's affordable and perfectly located at the entrance of the old village. The large, bright rooms have simple modular furniture and comfortable beds; a few have balconies that require a slight twist of the head to take in the sea view (best from rooms 3 and 16B). Bathrooms are small even by Italian standards, but adequate. Don't stay here to lounge in your room or the hotel's communal areas; but do come for the price and location (which make the hotel fill up fast, especially on weekends and in the summer—book early).

Via Garibaldi 55. www.lacamogliese.it. ✆ **0185-771-402.** 21 units. 80€–115€ double. 2- to 4-night required minimum stay. Rates include breakfast. Parking 15€ (reserve in advance). **Amenities:** Babysitting; concierge; exercise room; outdoor pool; room service; Internet; Wi-Fi (free).

Locanda I Tre Merli ★

This delightful little *locanda* is right on Camogli's charming harbor and each of the five cozy guest rooms has a lovely view of the harbor. Warm, fresh focaccia is served in the morning with a sublime cappuccino. When the weather is decent, breakfast is served outside—a real treat and a slice of true Italian seaside life, with boats arriving and departing, fishermen unloading the catch of the day, and families and small children playing football along the walkway. Be patient with the small staff, who speak barely passable English, and focus on what brought you here—the beautiful setting and ambience.

Via Scalo 5. www.locandaitremerli.com. ✆ **0185-770-592.** 5 units. 170€–250€ double; 210€–250€ triple. **Amenities:** Bar; Wi-Fi (free).

Santa Margherita Ligure

Santa Margherita had one brief moment in the spotlight at the beginning of the 20th century when it was an internationally renowned resort. Fortunately, the seaside town didn't let fame spoil its charm, and now that it's no longer as well-known as its glitzy neighbor Portofino, it could be the Mediterranean retreat of your dreams. A palm-lined harbor, a decent beach, and a friendly ambience make Santa Margherita a fine place to settle down for a few days of sun and relaxation.

EXPLORING SANTA MARGHERITA

Life in Santa Margherita centers on its palm-fringed **waterfront,** a pleasant string of marinas, docks for pleasure and fishing boats, and pebbly beaches, in some spots with imported sand of passable quality. Landlubbers congregate in the cafes that spill out into the town's two seaside squares, Piazza Martiri della Libertà and Piazza Vittorio Veneto.

The train station is on a hill above the waterfront, and a staircase in front of the entrance will lead you down into the heart of town. Santa Margherita's one landmark of note is its namesake **Basilica di Santa Margherita** (open daily 7:30am–noon and 2:30–7pm), just off the seafront on Piazza Caprera and well worth a visit to view the extravagant, gilded, chandeliered interior.

One of the more interesting daily spectacles in town is the **fish market** on Lungomare Marconi from 8am to 12:30pm. On Friday, Corso Matteotti, Santa Margherita's major street for food shopping, becomes an open-air **food market.**

WHERE TO EAT & STAY

La Paranza ★★ GENOVESE/LIGURIAN   Locals say this is one of the best restaurants in town, and one sitting at this family-run trattoria will show you why. While the ambience is nothing special, the menu is

---

Focaccia by the Seaside

It might be the perfect seaside setting, or perhaps there is something in the water, but no matter the reason, Camogli has some of the best focaccia in all of Liguria. Along Via Garibaldi, the promenade above the beach, there are many *focaccerie* to choose from, and though it's hard to go wrong with any of them, **Revello,** at no. 183 (closest to the church; (℃ **0185-770-777**), stands out. There, Tino carries on the tradition passed down by his uncle, who first began pulling focaccia out of the oven here in 1964. Revello is open daily except Tuesday, from 10am to 6pm (summer until 7pm). There are a few benches outside where you can enjoy your loot while watching the kids play soccer in the little square overlooking the beach. **O'Becco** next door also makes some mean focaccia—special mention goes to the one with fresh anchovies, parsley, garlic, and olive oil—and **U Caruggiu** at the other end of Via Garibaldi has kamut (a type of wheat) focaccia on the weekends.

filled with delicious, innovative dishes, from the *bianchetti fritti* (fried baby sardines) to simply grilled-to-perfection fresh fish.

Via Jacopo Ruffini 46. © **0185-283-686.** Main courses 12€–30€. Sun–Sat 12:30–2:20pm and 7:30–10:30pm. Closed Nov.

Grand Hotel Miramare ★★★ "Pure Riviera Elegance" can best describe this once private villa turned top-of-its-class hotel. Just a 10-minute walk from the town center along the road to Portofino, this hotel oozes class and money with carefully restored antique furniture and crystal chandeliers. The rooms are of a good size, mostly with parquet floors and charming stucco decorations on the walls and ceilings. The fifth-floor suites are a bit more modern, larger, and have balconies overlooking the Bay of Tigullio. A lovely (but steep) park rises behind the hotel, from which one can take a pleasant hiking trail to Portofino and enjoy fantastic views of the land and sea. You can also relax at their small, private pebble beach/beach terrace across the busy road.

Via Milite Ignoto 30. www.grandhotelmiramare.it. © **0185-287-013.** 84 units. 215€–253€ double with park view; 317€–531€ double with sea view. Parking 25€. **Amenities:** 2 restaurants, 2 bars; babysitting; concierge; outdoor heated saltwater pool; room service; nearby sauna; nearby golf, tennis, and exercise room; watersports equipment/rentals, Wi-Fi (free).

Hotel Metropole ★★ This popular hotel is just above the port and a 5-minute stroll from the town center. Accommodations are split between the main, modern building and the far-preferable Villa Porticciolo, a dusty red villa right on the beach; the rooms are smaller in the latter, but they're graced with 19th-century stuccoes, and the sea laps practically up against the building. Six rooms on the far end of the garden have large terraces. All other guest rooms have large balconies. The fourth floor is made up of junior suites and one double with sloped ceilings. Two suites on the lower floor of the main building open onto small private gardens. Several rooms can be joined to make family suites, and there's day care at the beach, with a separate area of sand just for the kiddies. The small private beach includes a curved sunbathing terrace and a private boat launch.

Via Pagana 2, Santa Margherita Ligure (GE). www.metropole.it.© **0185-286-134.** 58 units. 192€–290€ double; 154€–334€ double with half board; 178€–358€ double with full board. Rates include buffet breakfast. Parking 15€ outside or 18€ in private garage. **Amenities:** 2 restaurants; bar; babysitting; children's center (in summer); nearby golf course; small exercise room; swimming pool; sauna; watersports equipment/rentals, Wi-Fi (free).

Portofino ★★★

Portofino is almost too beautiful for its own good—in almost any season, you'll be rubbing elbows on Portofino's harborside quays with day-tripping mobs, as well as Italian industrialists, international celebrities, and a lot of rich-but-not-so-famous folks who consider this little town to be the epicenter of the good life. If you make an appearance in the late afternoon

Much of the **Monte Portofino Promontory** can be approached only on foot or by boat (see below), making it a prime destination for hikers. If you want to combine some excellent exercise with magnificent glimpses of the sea through a lush forest, arm yourself with a map from the tourist offices in Camogli, Santa Margherita Ligure, Portofino, or Rapallo, and set out. You can explore the upper reaches of the promontory or aim for the **Abbazia di San Fruttuoso** ((C) 0185-772-703), a medieval abbey that is surrounded by a tiny six-house hamlet and two pebbly beaches. It is 2½ hours away from Camogli and Portofino by a not-too-strenuous inland hike, or 3½ hours away by a cliff-hugging, up-and-down trail. En route, you can clamber down well-posted paths to visit San Rocco, San Niccolò, and Punta Chiappa, a string of fishing hamlets on the shore of the promontory.

Once you reach San Fruttuoso, you may well want to relax on the pebbly beach and enjoy a beverage or meal at one of the seaside bars. You can tour the stark interior of the abbey for 6€ (open June to mid-Sept daily 10am–5:45pm; May Tues–Sun 10am–5:45pm; Mar–Apr and Oct Tues–Sun 10am–3:30pm; and Nov–Feb Sat–Sun 10am–3:30pm). Note,

though, that despite these official hours, the abbey tends to close whenever the last boat leaves. Should you have your scuba or snorkeling gear along, you can take the plunge to visit **Christ of the Depths**, a statue of Jesus erected 15m (49 ft.) beneath the surface to honor sailors lost at sea.

You can also visit San Fruttuoso with one of the **boats** that run almost every hour during the summer months from Camogli. A round-trip costs 12€ (9€ one-way if you then plan to head southward from the abbey) and takes about 30 minutes. For more information, contact Golfo Paradiso (www.golfoparadiso.it; (C) **0185-772-091**). *Note:* Hourly (in summer) Tigullio boats (www.traghettiportofino.it; (C) **0185-284-670**) run to San Fruttuoso from Portofino (20 min.; 8€-12€ round-trip), Santa Margherita (35 min.; 10€–16€ round-trip), and Rapallo (50 min.; 10.50€–17€ round-trip). Bear in mind that the seas are often too choppy to take passengers to San Fruttuoso, because docking there can be tricky. In that case, there are private boats you can take—smaller, rubber crafts capable of bad-weather landings—though they are expensive: From Portofino, you will likely be charged 100€ for up to 12 people.

when the crowds have thinned out a bit, you are sure to experience what remains so appealing about this enchanting place—its indelible beauty.

EXPLORING PORTOFINO

The one thing that won't break the bank in Portofino is the spectacular scenery. Begin with a stroll around the stunning **harbor,** lined with expensive boutiques, eateries, and colorful houses set along the quay and steep green hills rising behind them. One of the most scenic walks takes you uphill for about 10 minutes along a well-signposted path from the west side of town just behind the harbor to the **Chiesa di San Giorgio** ((C) **0185-269-337**), built on the site of a sanctuary Roman soldiers dedicated to the Persian god Mithras. It's open daily 9am to 7pm.

Portofino's harbor at night.

From there, continue uphill for a few minutes more to Portofino's 15th-century **Castello Brown** (www.castellobrown.it; ✆ **0185-267-101**), which has a lush garden and offers great views of the town and harbor below. It costs 5€ (includes access to special exhibitions when they are going on) and is open daily 10am to 7pm from March to October, and the rest of the year on Saturday and Sunday from 10am to 5pm.

For more lovely views on this stretch of coast and plenty of open sea, go even higher up through lovely pine forests to the *faro* (lighthouse).

From Portofino, you can also set out for a longer hike on the paths that cross the **Monte Portofino Promontory** to the Abbazia di San Fruttuoso (see "An Excursion to San Fruttuoso," p. 524), a walk of about 2½ hours from Portofino. The tourist office provides maps.

WHERE TO EAT & STAY

Portofino's charms come at a price. Its few hotels are expensive enough to put them in the "trip of a lifetime" category, and the harborside restaurants can take a serious chunk out of a vacation budget as well. An alternative is to enjoy a light snack at a bar or one of the many shops selling focaccia, and wait to dine in Santa Margherita or one of the other nearby towns.

Ristorante Puny ★★ LIGURIAN   Right on the *piazzetta* in front of the harbor, this colorful restaurant is smack in the middle of it all, so book well in advance. The lengthy menu offers tasty Ligurian dishes including *pappardelle al portofino* (large flat noodles with a mix of tomato and pesto sauce), which may be topped with shrimp, or the heavenly *pesce al forno* baked in bay leaves, or the famed *risotto al curry e gamberi* (curried rice embedded with tiny shrimp). Just be prepared to pay a small fortune for the location, view, food, and being part of the scene.
Piazza Martiri dell'Olivetta 5. ✆ **0185-269-037.** Main courses 16€–30€. Mon–Wed and Fri–Sun 12:30–3:30pm and 7:30–11pm. Closed Jan–Feb.

Hotel Nazionale ★★   Two reasons to choose this hotel for your stay in Portofino: location and price. Rooms are fairly basic with minimal decoration, but you are right on the harbor and paying about a third of what you would at any other hotel in the village or nearby. Several of the rooms are lofted suites with bedrooms upstairs. We highly recommend splurging for one of the five junior suites which enjoy views of the harbor.
Via Roma 8. www.nazionaleportofino.com. ✆ **0185-269-575.** 12 units. 220€–275€ double without sea view; 330€–375€ junior suite with sea view. Rates include breakfast. Parking 25€ in nearby lot. Closed mid-Dec to Mar. **Amenities:** Restaurant; bar; concierge; room service, Wi-Fi (free).

Hotel Splendido ★★★ Splendido has been the Italian Riviera's #1 resort for over 100 years, hosting the likes of Bogart and Bacall, Taylor and Burton, and many more members of the rich and famous club. The former monastery turned 5-star luxury hotel is located on a lush hill of verdant gardens; the structure and grounds are spectacular with 64 guest rooms, including 35 suites, nearly all of which have balconies with spectacular views across and beyond the picturesque harbor. The prices may make your heart stop momentarily.

Salita Baratta 16. www.hotelsplendido.com. ✆ **0185-267-801.** 64 units. 425€–1,000€ double without sea view; 510€–2,000€ double with sea view. Rates include breakfast. Free parking. Closed mid-Dec to Mar. **Amenities:** 3 restaurants; bar; concierge; room service; wellness center; saltwater infinity pool; tennis court; access to hotel's motor boat; Wi-Fi (free).

THE CINQUE TERRE ★★★

Monterosso, the northernmost town of the Cinque Terre: 93km (58 miles) E of Genoa

Rocky coves, dramatic cliffs, and Apennine ridges are the spectacular backdrop to the Cinque Terre (Five Lands), a region which consists of five fishing and wine-making villages dramatically perched along a 11-mile stretch of Italy's Ligurian coast. Terraced vineyards and olive groves climb slopes that are largely inaccessible by road, but have become a hiker's haven stretching southeast from Monterosso al Mare to Vernazza, Corniglia, Manarola, and Riomaggiore.

Not too surprisingly, these charms have not gone unnoticed, and American tourists especially have been coming here in increasing numbers. From May to October (weekends are worst), you are likely to find yourself in a long procession of like-minded, English-speaking trekkers making their way down the coast or elbow to elbow with day-trippers from cruise ships. Even so, the Cinque Terre manages to escape the hubbub that afflicts so many coastlines, and even a short stay here is likely to reward you with one of the most memorable seaside visits of a lifetime.

Essentials

GETTING THERE Cinque Terre towns are served only by local **train** runs. Coming from Florence or Rome, you will likely have to change trains in nearby La Spezia, which has 1 or 2 local trains per hour (6–8 min. to the smaller towns). From Pisa, there are about 6 daily trains to La Spezia (1¼ hr.); from Genoa, there are 1 or 2 direct trains per hour to La Spezia, stopping in Monterosso (1 hr., 40 min. from Genoa) and sometimes Riomaggiore (15 min. further south).

The fastest **driving** route is via Autostrada A12 from Genoa; get off at the Corrodano exit for Monterosso. The drive from Genoa to Corrodano takes less than an hour, while the much shorter 15km (9¼-mile) trip from Corrodano to Monterosso (via Levanto) follows a narrow road and can take half an hour. Coming from the south or Florence, get off Autostrada A12 at La Spezia and follow cinque terre signs.

While Portofino and the Cinque Terre get their just accolades, it would be a shame to overlook some other lovely seaside destinations that also make a great base for exploring the area. When the Cinque Terre is drowning in tourists (a common occurrence May–Sept), these alternatives offer as much beauty, a bit more breathing room, and more options in terms of accommodations—some better in fact!

Set on opposites sides of the stunning Gulf of Poets lie the picturesque seaside medieval villages of **Portovenere** (tourist info: www.portovenere.it; ✆ **0187-790-691**) and **Lerici** (tourist office: ✆ **0187-967-164**). Once arch rivals—Portovenere belonged to Genoa and Lerici to Pisa—both built imposing fortresses to protect themselves from the enemy (and pirates!). These incredible edifices still remain along with charming colorful homes backing up to olive tree–covered hills. Their beautiful harbors hold local fishing boats and yachts alike. One can easily take the spectacular ferry ride up to the Cinque Terre in less than an hour.

To the north of of the Cinque Terre and only a 5-minute train ride from Monterosso is the sunny seaside town of **Levanto** (tourist info: www.levanto.com; ✆ **0187-808-125**) with its large sand beach, lovely historic center, and lodging options ranging from campsites to 4-star hotels.

A few train stops more, you arrive at **Bonassola** (tourist office: ✆ **0187-813-500**), **Moneglia** (tourist office: ✆ **0185-490-576**), and **Sestri Levanto** (tourist info: www.sestri-levante.net; ✆ **0185-459-575**) with its breathtaking "Bay of Silence"; any of these towns offer nice beaches and colorful town centers.

Navigazione Golfo dei Poeti (www.navigazionegolfodeipoeti.it; ✆ **0187-732-987**) runs **ferry service** from the Riviera Levante towns, April to November, though these tend to be day cruises stopping for anywhere from 1 to 3 hours in Vernazza (see description below) before returning.

GETTING AROUND   The best way to see the Cinque Terre is to devote a whole day and hoof it along the trails. See "Exploring the Cinque Terre," below, for details.

Local **trains** make frequent runs (2–3 per hr.) between the five towns; some stop only in Monterosso and Riomaggiore, so check the posted *partenze* schedule at the station first to be sure you're catching a local. One-way tickets between any two towns are available, including one version that is good for 6 hours of travel in one direction, meaning you can use it to town-hop—or you can buy a day ticket good for unlimited trips.

A narrow, one-lane coast road hugs the mountainside above the towns, but all the centers are closed to cars. Parking is difficult and, where available, expensive.

Riomaggiore and Manarola both have small **public parking facilities** just above their towns and minibuses to carry you and your luggage down. The cheapest option is the big open dirt lot right on the seafront in Monterosso. The priciest is the garage in Riomaggiore.

From the port in Monterosso, **Navigazione Golfo dei Poeti** (www.navigazionegolfodeipoeti.it; ☏ **0187-732-987**) makes 8 to 10 trips a day between Monterosso and Riomaggiore (25-min. trip), all stopping in Vernazza and half of them stopping in Manarola as well.

VISITOR INFORMATION The **tourist office** for the Cinque Terre is underneath the train station of Monterosso, Via Fegina 38 (www.turismo inliguria.it; ☏ **0187-817-506**). It's open Easter through September daily 9am to 5pm; hours are reduced the rest of the year. Even when it's closed, you will usually find posted outside the office a display of phone numbers and other useful information, from hotels to ferries.

Additional useful websites for the region include www.cinqueterre.it and www.parconazionale5terre.it.

Exploring the Cinque Terre

Aside from swimming and soaking in the atmosphere of unspoiled fishing villages, the most popular activity in the Cinque Terre is **hiking from one village to the next ★★★** along centuries-old goat paths. Trails plunge through vineyards and groves of olive and lemon trees, hugging seaside cliffs and affording heart-stopping views of the coast and romantic little villages in the distance. The well-signposted walks from village to village range in difficulty and length, but as a loose rule, they get longer and steeper—and more rewarding—the farther north you go.

Depending on your pace, and not including eventual stops for focaccia and *sciacchetrà*, the local sweet wine, you can make the trip between **Monterosso,** at the northern end of the Cinque Terre, and **Riomaggiore,** at the southern end, in about 4½ hours. You should decide whether you want to walk north to south or south to north. Walking south means tackling the hardest trail first, which you may prefer, because you'll get it out of the way and things will get easier as the day goes on and you start to tire. Heading north, the trail gets progressively harder between towns, so you might like this if you want to walk just until you tire and then hop on the train.

The walk from **Monterosso to Vernazza** is the most arduous and takes 1½ hours, on a trail that makes several steep ascents and descents (on the portion outside Monterosso, you'll pass beneath funicular-like cars that transport grapes down the steep hillsides). The leg from **Vernazza to Corniglia** is also demanding and takes another 1½ hours, plunging into some dense forests and involving some lengthy ascents, but is probably the prettiest and most rewarding stretch. Part of the path between **Corniglia and Manarola,** about 45 minutes apart, follows a level grade above a long stretch of beach, tempting you to break stride and take a dip. From **Manarola to Riomaggiore,** it's easy going for about half an hour along a partially paved path known as the Via dell'Amore, so named for its romantic vistas (great to do at sunset).

Walking path above Manarola in the Cinque Terre.

Because all the villages are linked by rail, you can hike as many portions of the itinerary as you wish and take the train to your next destination. Trails also cut through the forested, hilly terrain inland from the coast, much of which is protected as a nature preserve. The tourist office in Monterosso can provide maps. *Note:* At press time, the section between Corniglia and Manarola, and Via dell'Amore were closed indefinitely due to landslides. For updates, visit the Cinque Terre National Park website, www.parconazionale5terre.it.

MONTEROSSO

The Cinque Terre's largest village seems incredibly busy compared to its sleepier neighbors, but it's not without its charms. Monterosso is actually two towns—a bustling, character-filled Old Town built behind the harbor, and a relaxed resort that stretches along the Cinque Terre's **only sand beach.** This is where you'll find the train station and the tiny regional tourist office (upon exiting the station, turn left and head through the tunnel for the Old Town; turn right for the newer town).

The region's most famous art treasure is here: Housed in the **Convento dei Cappuccini,** perched on a hillock in the center of the Old Town, is a "Crucifixion" by Anthony van Dyck, the Flemish master who worked for a time in nearby Genoa (you can visit the convent daily 9am–noon and 4–7pm). While you will find the most conveniences in Monterosso, you'll have a more "rustic" experience if you stay in one of the other four villages.

VERNAZZA

Vernazza may just be the quintessential, postcard-perfect seaside village. Tall, colorful houses (known as *terratetti*) cluster around a natural harbor, where you can swim among the fishing boats; above them a **castle** stands high atop a rocky promontory that juts into the sea (the castle, which is nothing special, is open Mar–Oct daily 10am–6:30pm; admission 2€). The center of town is waterside **Piazza Marconi,** itself a sea of cafe tables. The only Vernazza drawback is that too much good press has turned it into the Cinque Terre's mecca for American tourists.

CORNIGLIA

The quietest village in the Cinque Terre is isolated by its position midway down the coast, its hilltop location high above the open sea, and its hard-to-access harbor. Whether you arrive by boat, train, or the trail from the south, you'll have to climb more than 300 steps to reach the village proper (arriving by trail from the north is the only way to avoid these stairs), which is an enticing maze of little walkways overshadowed by tall houses.

Once there, though, the views over the surrounding vineyards and up and down the coastline are stupendous—for the best outlook, walk to the end of the narrow main street to a belvedere that is perched between the sea and sky. Corniglia is the village most likely to offer a glimpse into life in the Cinque Terre the way it was decades ago.

MANAROLA

Manarola is a near-vertical cluster of tall houses that seems to rise piggyback up the hills on either side of the harbor. In fact, in a region with no shortage of heart-stopping views, one of the most amazing sights is the descent into the town of Manarola on the path from Corniglia: From this perspective, the hill-climbing houses seem to merge into one another to form a row of skyscrapers. Despite these urban associations, Manarola is a delightfully rural village where fishing and winemaking are big business. The region's major **wine cooperative,** Cooperativa Agricoltura di Riomaggiore, Manarola, Corniglia, Vernazza e Monterosso, made up of 300 local producers, is here; call © **0187-920-435** for information about tours of its modern (established 1982) facilities.

RIOMAGGIORE

Riomaggiore clings to the rustic ways of the Cinque Terre while making some (unfortunate) concessions to the modern world. The old fishing quarter has expanded in recent years, and Riomaggiore now has some sections of new houses and apartment blocks. This blend of the old and new is a bit of a shame. The village center still looks like something of 50 years ago, bustling and prosperous in a charming setting, while the "new side" of town seems like a half-effort at maintaining the old mostly in color. A credit to both sides is that many of the lanes end in seaside belvederes.

From the parking garage, follow the main drag down; from the train station, exit and turn right to head through the tunnel for the main part of town (or, from the station, take off left up the brick stairs to walk the Via dell'Amore to Manarola). At press time, this walk was closed indefinitely due to landslides.

That tunnel and the main drag meet at the base of an elevated terrace that holds the train tracks. From here, a staircase leads down to a tiny fishing harbor, off the left of which heads a rambling path that, after a few hundred meters, leads to a pleasant little **beach** of large pebbles.

Where to Stay

Gianni Franzi ★★   The owner of a local trattoria in Vernazza has 23 rooms spread across two buildings; some come with a bathroom, some with excellent views up the coast, all with a steep climb up the streets of the town and then up the stairs within the building. Call ✆ **0187-821-003** to book, or when you arrive in town, stop by the trattoria's harborside bar (if you arrive on a Wed when the trattoria is closed, there is usually somebody there in the afternoon to take care of new arrivals, or else call ✆ **393-900-8155**).

Restaurant address: Piazza G. Marconi 5, Vernazza (SP). www.giannifranzi.it. ✆ **0187-821-003** or 393-900-8155. 23 units. 85€ double with shared bathroom, 100€ double with a shared bathroom and sea view, 120€–140€ double (170€ triple) private bathroom and sea view. Rates include continental breakfast. Closed Jan 10–Mar 10. **Amenities:** Communal sea-view garden/terrace.

Hotel Porto Roca ★★★   Considered the Cinque Terre's only resort, this 4-star hotel in Monterosso is spectacularly positioned upon the cliffside overlooking the village, cemetery, and blue sea below. The addition of a pool and spa have helped make it the most expensive accommodations in the area, too. Most of the rooms are small and in need of a revamp, but once you step out onto your private balcony suspended above the Mediterranean, you can easily forgive the hotel's shortcomings. The pleasant restaurant serves typical Ligurian dishes, and in the warm weather you can have the best seat in town on their cliffside patio. Prices are high even for a "back, small non-seaview" room; we suggest splurging if you can to enjoy the full experience.

Via Corone 1, Monterosso al Mare (SP). www.portoroca.it. ✆ **0187-817-502.** 42 units. 160€–680€ double; 325€–750€ triple, 435€–520€ for a four person family room. Rates include breakfast. Parking 14€ in nearby public lot. Closed Nov–Mar. **Amenities:** Restaurant; bar; concierge; spa/beauty center; pool, room service; Wi-Fi (free).

Il Giardino Incanto ★★   This charming and comfortable family-run B&B is in a converted 16th-century villa just off Via Roma in Monterosso's old village. There are just three rooms and a junior suite, all of which are lovingly decorated with terracotta tiles, vaulted wood-beamed ceilings, and wrought-iron beds. Next to the villa is a lovely garden with lemon trees, lavender, and colorful flowers where breakfast is served, weather permitting. It is a tranquil and relaxing refuge in a town that can be quite busy in high season.

Via Mazzini 18, Monterosso al Mare (SP). www.ilgiardinoincantato.net. ✆ **0187-818-315.** 4 units. 150€–200€ double. Rates include buffet breakfast. Parking 14€ in nearby public lot. Closed early Nov to Apr.

La Mala ★★★   A bit of "beach chic" has come to Vernazza with the stylish four-room *locanda*. The rooms are not large but they are well-designed and -equipped, sunny, and come with great views (sea, village, and/or harbor view). Bathrooms are clean and modern. Room 26 has a small living area and is ideal for families traveling with a child as it can comfortably accommodate a third bed. Guests can enjoy the communal seaside terrace, the perfect spot for a sunset *aperitivo*. There is no reception area so you will be expected to call (or find) the owner, Gian Battista, upon your arrival in the village (specific instructions are given when your reservation is confirmed). There's no breakfast room; instead you are provided with a relatively basic *cornetto* and cappuccino at a local bar.

Via San Giovanni Battista, Vernazza. www.lamala.it. ✆ **334-287-5718.** 4 units. 140€–220€ double with private bathroom. Rates include basic breakfast. Closed Jan 10 to Mar. **Amenities:** Wi-Fi (free).

La Torretta ★★★   Besides La Mala in Vernazza (see above), this charming establishment in Manarola is perhaps the only other "chic retreat" in the Cinque Terre. La Torretta offers lovely rooms and suites in varied sizes, several with sea views and balconies, and all with nice in-room amenities (like choice toiletries). Our favorite rooms are the Junior Design Suite in the main building and the Junior Panoramic Suite in the annex, just a short walk from the main building. The communal solarium is a great place for guests to enjoy an *aperitivo*, paired with beautiful views. Despite its fairly steep price (and position on the hill up from the train station as well!), rooms go quickly here during the season, so best to book way ahead of time.

Vico Volto 20, Manarola. www.torrettas.com. ✆ **0187-920-327.** 11 units. 220€–350€ double. 400€–700€ suites. Rates include breakfast. Closed Nov. **Amenities:** Solarium; Wi-Fi (free).

Ostello Cinque Terre ★   Don't expect luxury here, but a good clean bed and bath at more than reasonable prices make this hostel sell out weeks before the high season. Located in the center of Manarola near the church, it's a pleasant welcome in an area that has few budget accommodations.

Via Riccobaldi 21, Manarola. www.hostel5terre.com. ✆ **0187-920-039.** 21€–25€ for beds in six-bed dorm rooms, 55€–70€ for a room with 2 single beds and private bathroom, or 132€–162€ for 6-bed family room with private bathroom. 2-night minimum stay. Closed mid-Nov to mid-Mar. **Amenities:** Kayak, bike, and snorkel rental; pay laundry; Wi-Fi (free).

Where to Eat

La Lanterna ★ LIGURIAN/SEAFOOD   Arguably, this small trattoria just above the charming harbor in Riomaggiore is the best restaurant in the Cinque Terre (along with Miky, below). Chef Massimo is famous for his impeccable seafood dishes, and from a table on the terrace, you can hear the waves lap against the rocks and watch the local fishermen mend their nets. Seafood is king here, with many Ligurian dishes such as *spaghetti allo scoglio* (spaghetti with mussels and shrimp in a white-wine sauce) or *spaghetti ai ricci di mare* (with sea urchins). Try choosing something from the chalkboard menu, which features the day's fresh delicacies.

Riomaggiore. © **0187-920-589.** *Primi* 9€–12€; *secondi* 10€–22€. Daily 11am–midnight. Closed Nov.

Osteria a Cantina de Mananan ★★ LIGURIAN
This tiny eatery in an old wine cellar carved into the stone of an ancient house in Corniglia is always packed with both locals and tourists—so call ahead (and bring cash; they don't accept credit cards). The menu (written on a blackboard) focuses on fresh and local ingredients, like vegetables from the nearby terraced gardens and seafood from local fishermen. Preparations are simple but packed with flavor; consider grilled and rolled vegetables stuffed with mozzarella, fresh anchovies stuffed with herbs, or the house speciality, *coniglio* (rabbit) roasted in a white sauce. Simply delicious!

Via Fieschi 117, Corniglia. © **0187-821-166.** Main courses 9€–15€. Wed–Mon 12:30–2:30pm and 7:30–9:30pm. Closed Nov, Mon–Fri in Dec, and part of Jan–Feb.

Ristorante Belforte ★★★ LIGURIAN
Being perched on a medieval watch tower overlooking the Mediterranean makes for some pretty fantastic ambience. Eating well on traditional Ligurian dishes makes the experience at the upscale restaurant in Vernazza worth the wait (even if you reserve ahead of time) and the steep price. Notable dishes include the *antipasto di mare,* a selection of six to eight small bites of seafood (we love the *cozze ripiene*, stuffed mussels, when they are in season) and the mixed grilled fish platter. If you are able to nab the single table on a small balcony at sunset, you are in for a romantic treat!

Via Guidoni 42, Vernazza. www.ristorantebelforte.it. © **0187-812-222.** Main courses 16€–27€. Wed–Mon noon–3pm and 7–10:30pm. Closed Nov–Apr.

Ristorante Miky ★ SEAFOOD
This family-run restaurant in Monterosso is considered one of the best in the Cinque Terre. In addition to the friendly service and the tasty, beautifully presented dishes, you can dine in a lovely garden with the smell of lemon and rosemary in the air. Most notable dishes include the grilled calamari, the monkfish ravioli, and *pesce al sale,* which is your choice of fresh fish covered in coarse salt and slowly cooked in a wood-burning oven (the salt is removed before the fish is served). Many dishes are served in large scalloplike dishes made of dough, and in fact all dishes are presented in some artful, creative manner, adding to the already charming ambience. It's not cheap, but the food and setting make it worthwhile. The da Fina family has also opened a *cantina/enoteca* just a few doors down (at Via Fegina 90, © **0187-802-525**) that offers dining alfresco and seaside as well as a bit of nightlife.

Via Fegina 104, Monterosso al Mare. www.ristorantemiky.it. © **0187-817-608.** Main courses 12€–25€. Daily noon–3pm and 7:30pm–late. Closed Nov–Mar.

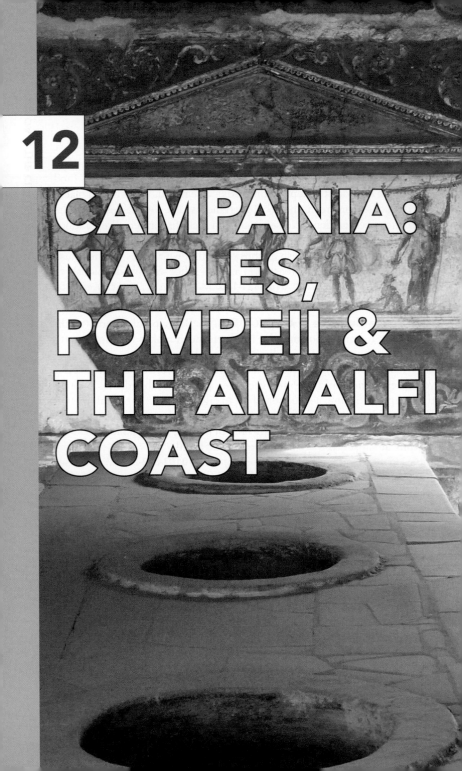

12

CAMPANIA: NAPLES, POMPEII & THE AMALFI COAST

B ienvenuti al sud—welcome to the south. Your first encounter with southern Italy, for better or worse, will probably be Naples. If you've enjoyed the grandeur of Venice, the elegance of Florence, and the awesomeness of monumental Rome, be prepared for a bit of a shock. Naples lives up to its reputation for dirt and grime, delights with its energy and good cheer, and surprises with the sophistication of its monuments and museums. It can be overwhelming, but that's part of the city's allure. And Naples is just the beginning.

There's so much more right around Naples—some of the most extensive remains of the ancient world in Herculaneum and Pompeii; the favorite playgrounds of the rich on Capri and along the Amalfi coast; the natural, ominous wonders of Mt. Vesuvius and the Campo Flegrei; plus miles of coastline and hillsides carpeted with olive groves and orange and lemon orchards. You might want to think of Naples and Campania as Italy on overdrive. Hang on and enjoy the ride.

NAPLES ★★

219km (136 miles) SE of Rome

In Naples, Mt. Vesuvius looms to the east, the fumaroles of the Campo Flegrei hiss and steam to the west, and the isle of Capri floats phantom-like across the gleaming waters of the bay. For all the splendor and drama of this natural setting, one of Italy's most intense urban concoctions is the real show. Naples shoots out so many sensations that it takes a while for visitors to know what's hit them.

Everything seems a bit more intense in Italy's third-largest city, the capital of the south. Dark brooding lanes open to palm-fringed piazzas. Laundry-strewn tenements stand cheek by jowl with grand palaces. Medieval churches and castles rise above the grid of streets laid out by ancient Greeks. No denying it, parts of the city are squalid, yet its museums are packed with riches.

It seems that most of life here transpires on the streets, so you'll witness a lot. The pace can be leisurely in that southern way, and amazingly hectic. When you partake—in a meal, in a *passegiata*, or just in a simple transaction—you'll notice the warmth, general good nature, and a sense of fun. You get the idea—but you won't really, until you experience this fascinating, perplexing, and beguiling city for yourself.

FACING PAGE: **Thermopolia, a bar in Pompeii with frescoes and ancient water jug holders.**

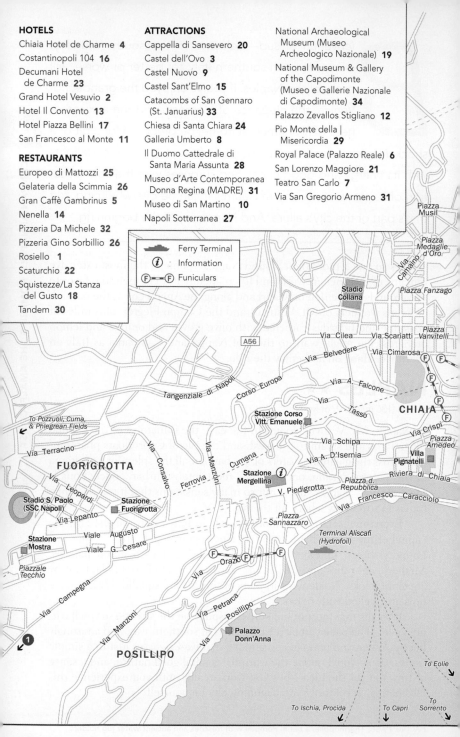

HOTELS

Chiaia Hotel de Charme **4**
Costantinopoli 104 **16**
Decumani Hotel de Charme **23**
Grand Hotel Vesuvio **2**
Hotel Il Convento **13**
Hotel Piazza Bellini **17**
San Francesco al Monte **11**

RESTAURANTS

Europeo di Mattozzi **25**
Gelateria della Scimmia **26**
Gran Caffè Gambrinus **5**
Nenella **14**
Pizzeria Da Michele **32**
Pizzeria Gino Sorbillio **26**
Rosiello **1**
Scaturchio **22**
Squistezze/La Stanza del Gusto **18**
Tandem **30**

ATTRACTIONS

Cappella di Sansevero **20**
Castel dell'Ovo **3**
Castel Nuovo **9**
Castel Sant'Elmo **15**
Catacombs of San Gennaro (St. Januarius) **33**
Chiesa di Santa Chiara **24**
Galleria Umberto **8**
Il Duomo Cattedrale di Santa Maria Assunta **28**
Museo d'Arte Contemporanea Donna Regina (MADRE) **31**
Museo di San Martino **10**
Napoli Sotterranea **27**

National Archaeological Museum (Museo Archeologico Nazionale) **19**
National Museum & Gallery of the Capodimonte (Museo e Gallerie Nazionale di Capodimonte) **34**
Palazzo Zevallos Stigliano **12**
Pio Monte della Misericordia **29**
Royal Palace (Palazzo Reale) **6**
San Lorenzo Maggiore **21**
Teatro San Carlo **7**
Via San Gregorio Armeno **31**

Ferry Terminal
(i) : Information
(F) ▬▬ (F) Funiculars

Piazza Musil
Piazza Medaglie d'Oro
Piazza Fanzago
Stadio Collana
Via Cilea
Via Belvedere
Via Scariatti
Via Cimarosa
Piazza Vanvitelli
A56
Corso Europa
Via A. Falcone
Via Tasso
CHIAIA
Tangenziale di Napoli
Stazione Corso Vitt. Emanuele
Via Schipa
Via Crispi
Piazza Amedeo
To Pozzuoli, Cuma, & Phlegrean Fields
Via Terracino
Via Consalvo
Via Manzoni
Cumana
Via A. D'Isernia
Villa Pignatelli
Riviera di Chiaia
FUORIGROTTA
Ferrovia
Via Leopardi
Stazione Mergellina
Piazza d. Repubblica
Via Francesco Caracciolo
V. Piedigrotta
Stadio S. Paolo (SSC Napoli)
Stazione Fuorigrotta
Piazza Sannazzaro
Terminal Aliscafi (Hydrofoil)
Via Lepanto
Viale Augusto
Stazione Mostra
Viale G. Cesare
Orazio (F) ▬▬ (F)
Piazzale Tecchio
Via Campegna
Via Manzoni
Via Petrarca
Via Posillipo
Palazzo Donn'Anna
POSILLIPO
To Eolie
To Ischia, Procida
To Capri
To Sorrento

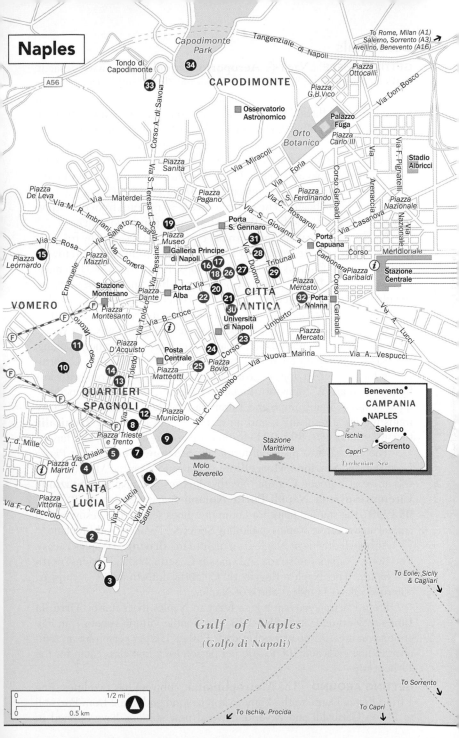

Naples

Capodimonte Park

To Rome, Milan (A1)
Salerno, Sorrento (A3) ↗
Avellino, Benevento (A16)

Tangenziale di Napoli

A56

Tondo di
Capodimonte

34

33

CAPODIMONTE

Piazza
Ottocalli

Via Don Bosco

Piazza
G.B.Vico

Osservatorio
Astronomico

Palazzo
Fuga

Orto
Botanico

Piazza
Carlo III

Via F. Pignatelli

Stadio
Albricci

Via S. Teresa d. Scalzi

Piazza
Sanita

Via Miracoli

Via Foria

Corso A.-di-Savoia

Corso Garibaldi

Arenaccia

Piazza
De Leva

Via M. R. Imbriani

Via Materdei

Piazza
Pagano

Via S. Ferdinando

Piazza
S. Ferdinando

Via C. Rossaroli

Via Casanova

Piazza
Nazionale

Via Nazionale

Via S. Rosa

Via Salvator Rosa

Piazza
Mazzini

Via Conera

Via S. Giovanni a

Porta
S. Gennaro

Porta
Capuana

Corso   Meridionale

Piazza
Leonardo

15

19

Piazza
Museo

Galleria Principe
di Napoli

31

28

Tribunali

Carbonara

Porta
Capuana

Stazione
Centrale

i

Emanuele

Vittorio

Stazione
Montesano

Piazza
Dante

Porta Via

Alba

16 **17**

18 **26**

27

Via Duomo

CITTÀ

ANTICA

29

Piazza
Mercato

Piazza
Garibaldi

Corso Garibaldi

VOMERO

F

F

F

Piazza
Montesanto

Via Toledo

Via B. Croce

22

20

21

30

Università
di Napoli

Umberto

Piazza
Mercato

32

Porta
Nolana

Via A. Lucci

11

Piazza
D'Acquisto

i

23

10

14

13

Corso

Posta
Centrale

24

Corso

25

Piazza
Bovio

Via Nuova Marina

Via A. Vespucci

Piazza
Matteotti

QUARTIERI
SPAGNOLI

12

Piazza
Municipio

9

Via C. Colombo

Stazione
Marittima

V. d. Mille

F

8

Piazza Trieste
e Trento

Via Chiala

5

7

Piazza d.
Martiri

i

4

6

Molo
Beverello

SANTA
LUCIA

Piazza
Vittoria

Via S. Lucia

Via N. Sauro

Via F. Caracciolo

2

i

3

Gulf of Naples
(Golfo di Napoli)

To Eolie; Sicily
& Cagliari
↓

To Sorrento
↓

To Ischia, Procida ↙

To Capri
↓

CAMPANIA

Benevento •

NAPLES

Ischia

Salerno •

Capri

Sorrento •

Tyrrhenian Sea

0 ———— 1/2 mi
0 ———— 0.5 km

Essentials

GETTING THERE   Naples's **Aeroporto Capodichino** (www.gesac.it; ✆ **081-7896259** and 081-7896255), is only 7km (4 miles) from the city center. It receives flights from Italian and European cities, plus a few intercontinental flights. From the airport, you can take a taxi into town (make sure it is an official white taxi with the Naples municipal logo); the flat rate for the 15-minute trip to the train station is 16€, and to Molo Beverello (for ferries to the islands) 19€. There is a convenient bus service to Piazza Municipio and Piazza Garibaldi, called the Alibus, run by the **ANM bus company** (www.anm.it; ✆ **800-639-525;** 3€ one-way from ticket desk, 4€ on board). The bus runs every 30 minutes from the airport (6:30am–11:50pm) and from Piazza Municipio (6am–midnight).

Naples is on the main southern rail corridor and is served by frequent and fast **train service** from most Italian and European cities and towns. EuroStar trains (ES) make very limited stops, InterCity trains (IC) make limited stops, and AltaVelocità (AV) trains are high-speed express trains. Regular trains take between 2 and 2½ hours between Rome and Naples, while the AV train takes only 87 minutes, making it by far the best method of transport between the two cities. The fare is 44€ one-way, but varies, and specials are often available, as are lower rates for advance booking. The same journey on an InterCity train will cost about 22€. Unfortunately for travelers trying to save money, InterCity trains run with less frequency than AV trains do, making cheaper transport quite inconvenient at times. Rail Europe and Eurail pass holders should note that AV trains require a reservation and an extra fee (10€). Contact **Trenitalia** (www.trenitalia.it; ✆ **892-021**) for information, reservations, and fares.

The city has two main rail terminals: **Stazione Centrale,** at Piazza Garibaldi, and **Stazione Mergellina,** at Piazza Piedigrotta. Most travelers will arrive at Stazione Central. Nearby, on Corso Garibaldi, is **Stazione Circumvesuviana Napoli-Porta Nolana** (www.vesuviana.it; ✆ **800-053939**), the starting point for commuter lines serving the Vesuvian and coastal area south of Naples, including Sorrento, Pompeii, and Ercolano.

Although driving *in* Naples is a nightmare, **driving** *to* Naples is easy. The Rome-Naples autostrada (A2) passes Caserta 29km (18 miles) north of Naples. The Naples–Reggio di Calabria autostrada (A3) runs by Salerno, 53km (33 miles) north of Naples.

From Palermo you can take a **ferry** to Naples that's run by **Tirrenia Lines** (www.tirrenia.it; ✆ **892-123**), Via Pontile Vittorio Veneto 1, in Palermo's port area. A one-way ticket costs 35€ to 55€ per person for an armchair in first class and 50€ to 70€ per person for a first-class cabin for the 11-hour trip.

GETTING AROUND   The **Metropolitana** (subway) has two lines: line 1 from Piazza Dante to the Vomero and beyond and line 2 from Pozzuoli to Piazza Garibaldi and beyond. Several new stations have opened in recent years, with more under way. You can also use the urban section of the **Cumana** railroad from Montesanto, which is convenient to Mergellina and other coastal locations north of the city center. Handy **bus** routes include the R lines (R1, R2, R3, R4), with frequent stops at major tourist attractions, and the electric minibuses (marked e) that serve the historic district. **Funiculars** take passengers up and down the steep hills of Naples. The Funicolare Centrale (www.metro.na.it; © **800-568-866**) connects the lower part of the city to Vomero. Daily departures (6:30am–12:30am) are from Piazzetta Duca d'Aosta just off Via Roma. Be careful not to get stranded by missing the last car back. One-way fare for the subway, buses, and funiculars is 1.50€, daily tickets (Biglietto Giornaliero) are 4.50€, valid until midnight the day they are validated, and weekly tickets (Biglietto Settimanale) are 15.80€. You may purchase tickets at newsstands, tobacco shops, and from machines in most metro and funicular stations and at some bus stops; you must validate tickets in the electronic ticket machines in stations or on the bus.

Taxis are an excellent, relatively inexpensive way to get around the city, and are very reliable and strictly regulated. Official taxis are painted white and marked by the comune di napoli. Inside, you'll find a sign listing official flat rates to the seaports, central hotels, and major attractions; don't fret if your driver doesn't use the meter—*not* using the meter is legal for all rides that have established flat rates. Taxis do not cruise but are found at the many taxi stands around town, or, for an extra 1€ surcharge, can be called by phone (© **081-444-444** or 081-555-5555).

As for **driving** around Naples, we have one word: *Don't.* If you're tempted, take a look at the cars on the street. In the rest of Italy, even the simplest models are kept in pristine condition; here, cars look like they've been used in demolition derbies. Car theft is so common that some rental agencies will not extend coverage to drivers planning to go to Naples.

Walking is an excellent way to get around the city center, where sights are fairly close together, but remember: For Neapolitan drivers, red lights are mere suggestions; cross busy streets carefully, and stick with a crowd if possible. Always look both ways when crossing a street, because a lot of drivers scoff at the notion of a one-way street. The zebra stripes (white lines) in the street, indicating where pedestrians have the right of way, mean absolutely nothing here.

VISITOR INFORMATION The **Ente Provinciale per il Turismo,** Piazza dei Martiri 58 (© **081-4107211;** bus: 152), is open Monday to Friday 9am to 2pm, with another office at Stazione Centrale (© **081-268779;** Metro: Garibaldi; Mon–Sat 9am–7pm). The AASCT (www.inaples.it) maintains two excellent tourist information points: Via San Carlo 9 (© **081-402394**) and Piazza del Gesù (© **081-5512701**), both are open daily (Mon–Sat 9:30am–6:30pm; Sun 9:30am–2pm). Any of these offices can give you a free map, an essential piece of equipment when navigating Naples.

The Neighborhoods in Brief

CHIAIA Naples cleans itself up a bit in this seaside and hillside enclave that stretches from Piazza del Plebiscito west along the bay, skirting the seaside park, Villa Communale. By day, strollers follow the bay along the Lungomare di Chiaia all the way to similarly genteel Mergelina. Come evening, crowds head inland for a *passegiata* along Via Chiaia. To join them, just move along with the flow west from Piazza Plebiscito. Before you leave this lovely expanse, find the two bronze equestrian statues, turn your back to the Palazzo Reale, close your eyes, and try to walk between them (it's a local thing—hard to do, but success brings good fortune, along with some stares).

CITTA ANTICA (HISTORICAL CENTER) This warren of many tight lanes, a few avenues, and some boisterous piazzas is also known as the Decumani, and just as often as **Spaccanapoli** (that's the name of the street that runs straight through the center of the neighborhood, as it has ever since the Greeks established a colony here). Roughly, the heart of Naples extends north from seaside Castel Nuovo to the Museo Archeologico Nazionale, and east from Via Toledo and Quartieri Spagnoli to the Porta Nolona Fish Market. Anchoring the southwest corner of this neighborhood, two of Naples' grandest landmarks stand opposite each just off the Piazza Trieste e Trento. The stately **Teatro San Carlo** is one of the world's finest opera houses, resplendent with gilded stucco and plush red velvet. **Galleria Umberto** is one of the world's first shopping malls, a beautiful late-19th-century concoction of domes and steel girding, where commerce transpires in style on beautifully tiled promenades beneath glass arcades.

PIAZZA GARIBALDI No need to linger in this decidedly unsavory quarter of grungy streets and some decidedly unsavory denizens. The train station is here, as is a station of the Circumvesuviana line for Pompeii and Sorrento. Descend into the flashy subway station for the metro and Circumflegrea line. The perpetually torn-up piazza is also a stop on many bus and tram lines, but you'll need to summon the ancient oracle of Cumae to find the right stop—short of her, check with the friendly folks in the tourist office in the train station if they're on duty.

SANTA LUCIA It's been a while since anyone but yachters set sail from this old fisherman's quarter made famous by the song. Neapolitans come here to stroll along seaside Via Mazzuro Sauro and Via Partenope (both closed to traffic) and gaze across the bay toward Capri. The nautical atmosphere cranks up a notch or two once you cross the bridge to Borgo Marinari, the little island where old houses huddle alongside **Castel dell'Ovo** (p. 547).

QUARTIERI SPAGNOLI This is the real Naples, where age-old rituals of city life hang on—just like the laundry that perpetually hangs across the narrow streets. It's not street life you're witnessing but just plain Neapolitan life, because everything seems to transpire in narrow, gridlike streets wedged between Via Toledo on the east and the San Martino hill on the west. Residents talk to one another from balconies, guys in T-shirts lower baskets from windows and haul up cigarettes, and kids play amid street stalls selling everything from fish to votive candles. If it all gets to be a bit much, just keep heading south (toward the bay) and you'll emerge in airy, semicircular Piazza del Plebiscito, where the huge Chiesa di San Francesco di Paola, copied on the Pantheon in Rome, faces the **Palazzo Reale** (p. 548).

VOMERO   Life in Naples never really becomes *too* gentrified, but it calms down quite a bit in the hilltop enclave of the Napoli *bene* (the city's middle and upper classes). Aside from fresh air and spectacular views, this quarter of elegant 19th- and early-20th-century villas (plus one too many banal apartment houses) has two big draws: **Castel Sant'Elmo** (p. 548) and **Certosa San Martino,** a huge monastery that was founded in the 14th century and expanded in the early 17th century into the hilltop landmark that's visible from throughout the city. The trip up here from the center is on the Centrale and Montesanto funiculars.

[FastFACTS] NAPLES

Consulates   The **U.S. Consulate** is on Piazza della Repubblica 1 (http://naples.usconsulate.gov; ℰ **081-5838111**; Metro: Mergellina, tram: 1). Consular services are open Monday to Friday 8am to noon. The **U.K. Consulate,** Via Dei Mille 40 (ℰ **081-4238911;** Metro: Amedeo), is open Monday to Friday (9:30am–12:30pm and 2–4pm). The **Canadian Consulate,** at Via Carducci 29 (www.canada.it; ℰ **081-401338;** Metro: Amedeo), is open Monday to Friday (9am–1:30pm). Citizens of Australia and New Zealand need to go to the embassies or consulates in Rome (see chapter 4).

Drugstores   There are several pharmacies open weekday nights and taking turns on weekend nights. A good one is located in the Stazione Centrale (Piazza

Garibaldi 11; ℰ **081-440211;** Metro: Piazza Garibaldi).

Emergencies   If you have an emergency, dial ℰ **113** to reach the police. For medical care, dial ℰ **118,** but only in an emergency. To find the local Guardia Medica Permanente, ask for directions at your hotel.

Safety   The Camorra-related crime for which Naples is infamous will have little bearing on your visit. Street crime is another story and it's best to err on the side of caution in this city with catastrophically high unemployment, a big drug problem, and lots of dark, empty streets. If you have a money belt, by all means use it. Also use common sense. *Do not* carry a lot of cash, wear expensive jewelry, walk around with a fancy camera

hanging from your neck, place your smartphone on cafe tables, or plunge down dark, deserted lanes at night. *Do* leave your valuables in a safe at your hotel (most rooms are equipped with them). When going out for a meal or excursion, carry only as much cash as you are going to need and only the credit card you will be using, and leave the others behind (including your debit/cash cards unless you need to make a withdrawal). Beware of pickpockets in crowds and on the subways and commuter trains—they're crafty. Do not carry a wallet in your back pocket, of course, or even in your inside jacket pocket, where someone brushing against you can easily get to it. When walking, carry any bags on the side away from the street to thwart thieves whizzing past on motorbikes.

Naples' atmospheric alleyways.

Exploring Naples

Large as Naples is, it's easy to get to the sights you want to see on foot, allowing you to experience one of the city's greatest allures—its street life. From Piazza Trento e Trieste, with the magnificent **Teatro San Carlo** and **Galleria Umberto I**, Via Toledo/Via Roma leads north. To the left is the Quartieri Spagnoli, a neighborhood of tightly packed narrow lanes, while to the right, just beyond Piazza Dante, is the atmospheric historical center of the city, where many of the churches you want to see face airy piazzas. At the northern end of Via Toledo, about a 10-minute walk beyond Piazza Dante, is the celebrated Archaeological Museum.

THE TOP MUSEUMS

Museo d'Arte Contemporanea Donna Regina (MADRE) ★

ART MUSEUM It's not New York's Guggenheim or London's Tate Modern, but the sprawling **Palazzo Regina** in the middle of medieval and baroque Naples provides a dramatic counterpoint for works by such contemporary artists as Anish Kapoor, Richard Serra, and Jeff Koons. Painter Francesco Clemente, who was born in Naples but made his reputation on the international art scene, creates an illusionary experience in two rooms he's decorated with colorful tile floors and frescoes replicating ancient symbols of the city. Conceptual sculptor Anish Kapoor has transformed a room into a white cube with rich blue pigments on the floor that seem to draw you into the bowels of the earth; he also designed the entrance to the Monte S. Angelo subway station just outside the city center to resemble his version of Dante's entrance to the underworld (and perhaps sympathizing with riders that commuting can indeed be hell). Across town, the **Palazzo delle Arti Napoli,** or PAN (Via dei

Mille 60; palazzoartinapoli.net; ℂ **081-7958604**) houses rotating exhibitions of contemporary art.

Via Settembrini 79 (btw. Via Duomo and Via Carbonara). www.madrenapoli.it. ℂ **081-19313016.** Admission 7€ Wed–Sun, free Mon. Mon & Wed–Sat 10:30am–7:30pm, Sun 10:30am–11pm. Bus: E1. Metro: Cavour.

National Archaeological Museum (Museo Archeologico Nazionale) ★★★ MUSEUM   The echoey, dusty, gloomy galleries of the rundown Palazzo degli Studi provide one of the world's great time-travel experiences, from grimy modern Naples back to the ancient world. Two treasure troves in particular should not be missed. The superb **Farnese Collection** of Roman sculpture shows off the pieces snapped up by the enormously wealthy Roman Cardinal Alessandro Farnese, who became Pope Paul III (1543–1549) and was at the top of the Renaissance game of antiquity hunting. His remarkable collection was inherited by Elisabetta Farnese, duchess of Parma, who married Philip V of Spain and whose son and grandson became kings of Naples and brought the collection here in the 18th century. Among Cardinal Farnese's great prizes was the magnificent **Ercole Farnese,** a huge statue of Hercules unearthed at the Baths of Caracalla in Rome. The superhero, son of Zeus, is tuckered out, leaning on his club after completing his 11th Labor. He looks a bit troubled, and who can blame him? After slaying monsters and subduing beasts, he's just learned he has to go into the fray again, descend into Hell, and bring back Cerberus, the three-headed canine guardian. It's a magnificent piece, powerful and wonderfully human at the same time. The colossal **"Toro Farnese,"** 4m (13-ft.) high, is the world's largest-known sculpture from antiquity and is carved out of a single piece of marble. This prize was also unearthed at the Baths of Caracalla, and Cardinal Farnese hired a team of Renaissance masters, Michelangelo among them, to restore it, piecing together bits and pieces here and there. The intricate and delicate work depicts one of mythology's greatest acts of satisfying revenge, when the twin brothers Amphion and Zethus tied Dirce—who had imprisoned and mistreated their mother, Antiope—to the horns of a bull that will drag her to her death.

On the mezzanine and upper floors are mosaics, frescoes, and bronzes excavated from Pompeii and Herculaneum. Seeing these everyday objects from villas and shops hauntingly brings the ruined cities to life, as they show off the residents' tastes and preoccupations. Some, such as baking equipment and signage, are quite mundane, touchingly so; many, such as the bronze statues of the "Dancing Faun" (on the mezzanine), the "Drunken Faun" (top floor), and five life-size female bronzes known as "Dancers" (top floor) show off sophisticated artistry. Most of the mosaics, on the mezzanine, are from the House of Faun, one of the largest residences in Pompeii. The million-plus-piece floor mosaic, "Alexander Fighting the Persians," depicts the handsome, wavy-haired king of Macedonia astride Bucephalos, the most famous steed in antiquity, sweeping into battle with King Darius III of Persia, who's looking a bit concerned in his chariot. The **Gabinetto Segretto** (Secret Room; also on the mezzanine) displays some of the erotica that was commonplace in Pompeii. Some works are from brothels, among them frescoes that show acts lively yet predictable and some bestial (literally, as in Pan copulating with a goat) and others include phallus-shaped oil lamps and huge phalluses placed at doorways to suggest fertility and good fortune. We might titter at the bulges under togas and a fresco from Herculaneum's House of Papyri showing a gent weighing his huge member, but they weren't necessarily intended to be pornography and rather suggest the libertine attitudes of the time.

Piazza Museo 19. http://cir.campania.beniculturali.it/museoarcheologiconazionale. ℭ **081-4422149.** Admission 10€. Daily 9am–7:30pm. Metro: Museo or Cavour.

National Museum & Gallery of the Capodimonte (Museo e Gallerie Nazionale di Capodimonte) ★ MUSEUM

Italy has many better art collections, and the trip here inevitably involves a change of buses or a taxi ride. That said, there's plenty to lure you out to the former hunting preserve of the Bourbon kings. For one, the *bosco reale* (royal woods) are one of the few parks in Naples, and sharing the greenery with picnicking families can be a refreshing change of scenery. The core of the collection is from Elisabetta Farnese, the duchess of Parma who handed down the family's paintings to her children and grandchildren after she became Queen of Spain, and they in turn brought them back to Italy when they became kings of Naples. By the time the works got here, many of the best had found their way into other collections; what remains includes a roster of the greatest Italian and Northern masters, but often secondary works. In fact, the two standout pieces here have nothing to do with the Farneses. Caravaggio executed his dramatic "Flagellation of Christ" for Naples' Church of San Domenico Maggiore (for more on Caravaggio in Naples, see "Bad Boy With a Bruch," p. 546), and it was brought here in the 1970s, not long after another Caravaggio was stolen from a church in Palermo. In the contemporary galleries hangs Andy Warhol's "Mount Vesuvius," an almost-corny comic-book depiction of an eruption that renders the mountain as an age-old icon of volatility. If you've found other royal palaces around town fairly empty, it's because many of the furnishings are upstairs here, in the Royal Apartments. There's enough Sèvres and Meissen to put together a royal feast of epic proportions. Some of the pieces, the Capodimonte ceramics, were fired right here on the grounds throughout the 18th century.

Palazzo Capodimonte, Via Miano 1; also through the park from Via Capodimonte. http://cir.campania.beniculturali.it/museodicapodimonte. ℭ **081-7499111.** Admission 7.50€; 6.50€ after 2pm. Thurs–Tues 8:30am–7:30pm. Bus: R4 (from the Archaeological Museum).

TOP CHURCHES

Cappella di Sansevero ★★ MUSEUM   Only in Naples would a room as colorful, fanciful, mysterious, beautiful, and macabre as this exist. Prince Raimondo di Sangro of Sansevero remodeled his family's funerary chapel in the 18th century, combining the baroque style then in fashion with his own love of complex symbolism and intellectual quests. Neapolitan sculptor Giuseppe Sanmartino crafted "Christ Veiled Under A Shroud," in which a thin transparent covering seems to make Christ's flesh look even more tormented and his suffering greater. (Antonio Canova, the Venetian sculptor, came to Naples to see the work a century later and said he would give 10 years of his life to have created something so beautiful.) The prince's father lies beneath a statue of "Despair on Disillusion," in which a man disentangling himself from a marble net suggests a troubled soul and mind seeking relief—provided by the winged boy who represents intellect. Prince Raimondo's mother, who died at age 20, lies beneath a statue of "Veiled Truth," in which a woman holds a broken tablet, symbol of an interrupted life, with her veil in this case suggesting the unfulfilled promise she took to the grave with her. Raimondo himself is surrounded by colorful floor tiles arranged in a complex maze, symbol of the quest to unravel the secrets of life. Downstairs are two skeletal bodies in which the circulatory systems are perfectly preserved and brightly colored, allegedly with the injection of a substance the prince devised (and the subjects are probably not, as legend has it, the prince's unwilling servants, whom he supposedly scarified in the interest of science).

Via Francesco De Sanctis 19 (near Piazza San Domenico Maggiore). www.museosansevero.it. ✆ **081-5518470.** Admission 7€. Mon and Wed–Sat 10am–6:30pm; Sun 10am–2pm. Closed May 1 and Easter Monday. Metro: Dante.

Chiesa di Santa Chiara ★ CHURCH   Despite its vast, light-filled interior and unabashedly cheerful cloisters, the church of Naples' 13th- to 15th-century French rulers, the House of Anjou, is steeped in a stormy past. It's not a sign of a good marriage when a wife's only desire is to be a nun, but that's what Queen Sancha, second wife of Robert the Wise, wanted, so the king founded Santa Chiara in 1343 as a place for her to retreat from the world. Robert's tomb is in the nave; the poet Boccaccio eulogized him as "unique among kings of our day, friend of knowledge and virtue." His granddaughter Joan was crowned queen here in 1343, launching an enlightened reign nonetheless marred with plotting, intrigue, the murder of a husband, and her own demise at 56, when she was smothered with pillows. Her body was thrown into a deep well on the grounds of Santa Chiara and, once retrieved, she was denied Christian burial because of her heretical anti-papal views; instead she was laid to rest in an unmarked grave under the church floor. During World War II, Allied bombers laid waste to most of the church's colorful frescoes,

BAD BOY WITH A brush

The painter Caravaggio arrived in Naples in 1606, fleeing authorities in Rome after he killed a man in a fight over a debt. With his taste for gambling, prostitutes, young boys, rowdiness, and drunkenness, the tempestuous artist must have felt right at home in colorful Naples. The city was then the second largest in Europe after Paris, with 350,000 inhabitants, more than a few of whom shared Caravaggio's predisposition for recklessness. His sumptuous canvases, with their realistic portrayals of saints and martyrs and dramatic use of light, have become emblematic of the city's emotion-filled baroque style. Three Caravaggio works are in Naples.

The dark, moody, and chaotic "Seven Acts of Mercy" altarpiece is in the chapel of the **Pio Monte della Misericordia,** Via Tribunali 253 (🕿 **081-446944;** Metro: Dante), a fraternity founded by nobles in 1601 to loan money to the poor. As you pick out the merciful acts—St. Martin in the foreground giving his cloak to the beggar is easy (clothing the naked)— you'll probably only detect six. But look again at the scene of the old man sucking at the breast of the young woman: That counts as two, visiting prisoners and feeding the hungry. Classicists might recognize the pair as the Roman Cimon, who was sentenced to death by starvation; his daughter, Pero, secretly suckled him, and this act of family honor won him his release. It's open Thursday to Tuesday 9am to 2pm; admission 5€.

Located in the **Capodimonte gallery** (p. 544), the "Flagellation of Christ" depicts two brutish tormentors whipping a nearly naked Christ with almost rote determination ("another day, another flagellation"); a third is in the foreground, preparing his scourge to join in the action. Lighting emphasizes the arms in action and Christ's twisted, suffering body, providing an almost-hard-to-witness depiction of cruelty in action. This is one of two flagellation scenes Caravaggio painted while he was in Naples (he did this one originally for a family chapel in the Church of San Domenico).

The "Martyrdom of St. Ursula" hangs in the **Palazzo Zevallos Stigliano** (Via Toledo 185; 🕿 **081-425011;** Metro: Montesanto), the lavish headquarters of the Banco Intesa Sanpaolo. Ursula appears relatively unfazed as the king of the Huns, from whom she has just refused an offer of marriage, shoots an arrow into her breast at point-blank range (given that, as legend has it, the 11,000 virginal handmaidens accompanying Ursula on a pilgrimage had just been beheaded, she could not have been terribly surprised at the cruel reaction of her jilted suitor). Caravaggio himself looks on from the background. This was his last painting and the last image we have of him, for he died of fever while returning to Rome a couple of months later. The *palazzo* is open Tuesday to Sunday 10am to 6pm (Sat until 8); admission is 4€.

though a few fragments remain in the reconstructed nave. Other frescoes line the walls of the delightful **cloisters**, where columns are decorated with colorful Mallorca tiles. This is one of the most refreshing corners of Naples, and well worth the 5€ admission fee if you've been walking around the old city and need some peace and quiet.

Church: Via Santa Chiara 49. 🕿 **081-7971235.** Free admission. Mon and Wed–Sat 7:30am–1pm and 4:30–8pm. Cloisters and museum: Admission 5€. Mon and Wed–Sat 9:30am–5:30pm; Sun 10am–2:30pm. Metro: Dante.

Il Duomo Cattedrale di Santa Maria Assunta ★★ CATHEDRAL

Three times a year—the first Saturday in May, September 19, and December 16—all of Naples squeezes into the great cathedral that King Carlo I d'Angio dedicated to San Gennaro in the 13th century. On these dates the dried blood of the city's patron saint liquefies, or sometimes doesn't. Not doing so foretells terrible events for Naples, such as an outbreak of the plague in 1528 or the earthquake in 1980 that killed 2,000 residents. The rest of the year the blood is kept in a vault inside an altar in the **Canella di San Gunnar**, where a reliquary houses the head that soldiers of the Emperor Diocletian severed from the rest of the bishop's body around 305.

Within the cathedral are Naples' two oldest remaining places of worship. The **Capella di Santa Restituta** served as the city's 4th-century basilica and is supported by a forest of columns from a Greek temple, and the **Capella di San Giovanni in Fonte** was a 5th-century baptistery; if you crane your neck and squint (binoculars or a telescopic lens come in handy) you can make out some endearingly rendered frescoes in the dome, including one showing Christ's miracle of the loaves and fishes.

Via del Duomo 147. ⓒ **081-449097.** Free admission to the cathedral, but the archaeological zone is 3€. Mon–Sat 8am–12:30pm and 4:30–7pm; Sun 8am–1:30pm and 5–7:30pm. Metro: Piazza Cavour.

ROYAL NAPLES

Castel dell'Ovo ★★ CASTLE   As every Neapolitan knows, the poet Virgil placed an egg under the foundations of the city's outrageously picturesque seafront fortress (Castle of the Egg) and when it breaks, a great disaster will befall the city. Considering earthquakes, eruptions of nearby Mt. Vesuvius, plague outbreaks, and World II bombings, it's probably safe to assume the egg is no longer intact. The castle is enchanting even without such legends, squeezed onto a tiny island the Greeks first settled almost 3 millennia ago. Built over the foundations of the villa of the Roman emperor Lucullus, it was a royal residence from the 13th through 20th centuries. The little lanes beneath the thick walls are lined with the houses of Borgo Marinaro, a former fisherman's haunt where the ground floors of the quaint house are now occupied by pleasant bars and pizzerias. For

The Castell dell'Ovo.

Neapolitans, a walk across the stout bridge onto the island is a favorite Sunday afternoon outing.

Borgo Marinari (off Via Partenope). ℂ **081-7954593.** Free admission. Mon–Sat 8am–6pm; Sun 8am–2pm. Bus: 152, C25, 140, or E5 to Via Santa Lucia.

Castel Nuovo ★ CASTLE/MUSEUM   Now that the Giotto frescoes that once decorated this palace's chapel have faded away, you can forgo a visit to the fairly uninspired staterooms and art collection and settle for admiring this medieval sea-girt beauty from the outside. As you do so, consider the plight of prisoners who once shared their dungeons with crocodiles imported from Egypt for the express purpose of snacking on the doomed souls. The best view is from the Piazza Municipo, where you can take in the castle's towers, crenellations, and the white-marble Triumphal Arch of Alfonso I of Aragona squeezed between two turrets, a splendid example of early Renaissance architecture.

Piazza Municipio. ℂ **081-795-2003.** Admission 5€. Mon–Sat 9am–7pm. Bus: R1, R2.

Castel Sant'Elmo ★ CASTLE   The Spanish gave this star-shaped fortress atop Vomero Hill its present appearance in the 16th century, taking advantage of a strategic position high above the city. That's the main reason to come up here: the castle still offers the best 360-degree views in town.

Via Tito Angelini. ℂ **081-5784120.** Admission 5€. Wed–Mon 8:30am–9:30pm. Metro: Vanvitelli and then bus V1 to Piazzale San Martino.

Royal Palace (Palazzo Reale) ★ MUSEUM   If your decorating tastes lean toward royal pomp, you'll love following a designated route (accompanied by a dry audio commentary) through some 30 grandiose yet strangely vacuous rooms where Neapolitan royalty ruled and entertained in the 18th and 19th centuries. You won't miss too much if you give this pompous old pile a miss, though it's hard not be impressed by the sweep of the marble double staircase, the opulent Teatrino di Corte (the private theater), and the ridiculously large, tapestry-hung Hall of Hercules (the ballroom). Most seductive of all are the manicured private gardens, tucked away above the city and the Bay of Naples; those, you can enter for free.

Piazza del Plebiscito 1. www.palazzorealenapoli.it. ℂ **081-5808111.** Admission 4€; courtyard and gardens free. Thurs–Tues 9am–7pm. Bus: R2 or R3.

UNDERGROUND NAPLES

Catacombs of San Gennaro (St. Januarius) ★ RELIGIOUS SITE San Gennaro's head is in the duomo, but the rest of him is in his namesake two-story underground cemetery, used from the 2nd through 11th centuries. Some of the city's earliest frescoes (those from Pompeii aside) are here, including one depicting a haloed San Gennaro with Mt. Vesuvius on his shoulders. Even earlier are a charming 2nd-century scene with Adam and Eve and a portrait of a family, with figures of each of the three members added over the years when their times came. Guides (most speaking English) will lead you down the wide aisles past

EVERY DAY IS christmas IN NAPLES

Among the many delights of Naples are the *presepi*, nativity scenes that pop up everywhere, any time of the year and, not surprisingly, come out in force at Christmas time. Figures are carved in wood or fired in ceramic. Mainstays are Mary, Joseph, the infant Jesus, the donkey, the Wise Men, and angels, though the Neapolitan repertoire often expands to soccer stars and other celebrities. The settings are often a lot more elaborate than a humble manger: medieval town squares, rusticated villages with thatched cottages and spinning water-wheels, elaborate caves that look like some troglodyte fantasy.

The **Museo di San Martino** (Largo San Martino 8; *℄* **081-5781769;** admission 6€; open Thurs–Tues 8:30am–7:30pm) shows off the world's largest *presepe*, an 18th-century concoction with hundreds of figures and objects; it's the

museum's most popular display, and it's thronged at Christmastime.

You can piece together your own scene with a walk down **Via San Gregorio Armeno,** where year round, dozens of shops sell figures beginning at about 15€. You can also buy a complete scene for anywhere from 100€ well into five digits, or have one specially made with figures of your family and favorite celebrities (as many Neapolitans do).

As you peruse these holy scenes, be aware that pickpockets flock to the street like sheep to a Bethlehem hillside with the unholy intent of preying on distracted gawkers glued to shop windows. Among the most reputable shops are **Gambardella Pastori,** Via San Gregorio Armeno 40 (*℄* **081-5517107**); **Giuseppe Ferrigno,** Via San Gregorio Armeno 10 (*℄* **081-5523148**); and **Amendola,** Via San Gregorio Armeno 51 (*℄* **081-5514899**).

the frescoed burial niches and early basilicas carved from the *tufa* rock, providing fascinating insights into the city's long past—with a special nod to Sant'Agrippino, a 3rd-century bishop once interred here, who is almost as popular among Neapolitans as San Gennaro.

Via Capodimonte 13. www.catacombedinapoli.it. *℄* **081-7443714.** Admission 8€. Tours Mon–Sat on the hour 10am–5pm; Sun 10am–1pm. Bus: 24 or R4.

Napoli Sotterranea ★ With so much happening above ground, it's hard to see the appeal of "Naples Underground," but guided tours of the city's ancient water works are wildly popular and a surefire hit with kids. Some 2,000 years ago, Romans dug huge cisterns beneath the city and connected them with a system of tunnels. Neapolitans used the ancient water supply well into the 19th century, when some cholera outbreaks necessitated purer sources. The emptied cisterns came in handy as quarries, then as bomb shelters during World War II (some of the wartime furnishings and graffiti remain in place). Adding to the mix is a Greek theater that's been unearthed amid the subterranean network. Tours last about 90 minutes, include some broken-English commentary, and usually meet at Piazza San Gaetano 68, on Via dei Tribunali near the church of San Lorenzo (Metro: Dante); sometimes they meet in front of Café Grumbus in Piazza Trento e Trieste. Exit points vary a bit, too, but

Bags of dried pasta hang in the doorway of a Naples shop.

usually you'll climb out of the dark up a long staircase and emerge into the courtyard of an ordinary-looking apartment house (a good illustration of this city's many age-spanning layers). Aside from climbing stairs, you'll also be asked to squeeze through a very tight passage (not recommended for the claustrophobic or the overweight).

Vico S. Anna di Palazzo, 52. www.lanapolisotterranea.it. ℭ **081-296944.** Admission 9.30€, 6€ for children under 10. Tours in English are scheduled daily, year-round, at 10am, noon, 2pm, and 4pm.

San Lorenzo Maggiore ★ CHURCH The most beautiful of Naples's medieval churches seems to inspire great literature. Petrarch, the medieval master of Italian verse, lived in the adjoining convent in 1345, and it was here on Holy Saturday 1338 that Boccaccio (author of *The Decameron*) supposedly first laid eyes on his muse, Maria d'Aquino. The daughter of a count and countess but rumored to have been the illegitimate daughter of Robert of Anjou, king of Naples, Maria was married but preferred refuge in a convent to life with her debauched husband. For Boccaccio, it was love at first sight; he nicknamed her La Fiametta (Little Flame), wooed her with his romantic epic "Filocoppo," and eventually won her over and convinced her to become his mistress (she jilted him for another man a few years later). You can ponder 14th-century romance as you stroll through the delightful cloisters, then descend a staircase to witness more of the city's multilayered history: Ongoing excavations have unearthed streets from the Greco-Roman city lined with bakeries and shops, porticoes, an entire covered market, and an early Christian basilica.

Piazza San Gaetano, Via Tribunali 316. ℭ **081-290580.** Free admission to church. Mon–Sat 8am–noon and 5–7pm. Excavations: Admission 4€. Mon–Sat 9:30am–5:30pm; Sun 9:30am–1:30pm. Metro: Piazza Cavour.

Where to Stay

Where you stay in Naples makes a difference—as in, enjoyable stay versus "I never want to set foot in this hellhole again." You want a safe neighborhood close to the sights, and our suggestions below meet that criterion. Some good business-oriented hotels have opened near the train station, but this area is not very convenient or, for that matter, particularly savory after dark. Naples hotels often post special Internet rates on their website, especially in summer, which is low season in the city.

EXPENSIVE

Grand Hotel Vesuvio ★★   Old world glamour holds sway in this famed waterfront hostelry that pampers the rich and famous and provides a Grand Tour–worthy experience (with all the 21st-century amenities, including a spiffy spa and small indoor pool). Expanses of shiny parquet, handsome old prints, fine linens on the firm beds, and classic furnishings give the large, bright, and very comfortable guest rooms sophisticated-yet-understated polish. The big perk, though, is the view of the bay, the Castel dell'Ovo, and Mt. Vesuvius outside big glass doors that open to balconies off many rooms and suites. You'll get the same eyeful from the bright salon where a lavish breakfast buffet is served, and from the rooftop restaurant. High-season prices are geared to the pocketbooks of celebrities and dignitaries, though off-season rates and the occasional special offer brings the memorable experience of a stay here within reach of the rest of us.

Via Partenope 45 (off Via Santa Lucia by Castel dell'Ovo). www.vesuvio.it. ✆ **081-7640044.** 160 units. 180€–460€ double. Most rates include buffet breakfast. Parking 25€. Bus: 152, 140, or C25. **Amenities:** 2 restaurants; bar; fitness center and spa; pool (for a fee); room service; smoke-free rooms; Wi-Fi (fee).

MODERATE

Chiaia Hotel de Charme ★   With its bright shops and bars, spiffy, pedestrian-only Via Chiaia may be the city's friendliest address, and this warmly decorated inn that ranges across two floors of an old nobleman's residence does the location justice. Some smaller rooms face interior courtyards and have snug, shower-only bathrooms, while many of the larger ones on the street side (with double panes to keep the noise down) have large bathrooms with Jacuzzi tubs. Decor throughout is sufficiently traditional and regal to suggest the *palazzo's* aristocratic provenance, and services are more wholesome than they were when the place was an upscale brothel. Pastries and snacks are laid out in the sitting room in the afternoon and evening, the buffet breakfast is generous, and the staff is good at recommending restaurants and providing directions.

Via Chiaia 216. www.hotelchiaia.it. ✆ **081-415555.** 33 units. 145€–185€ double. Rates include buffet breakfast. Parking 18€ in nearby garage. Bus: R2. **Amenities:** Bar; concierge; free Wi-Fi in lobby and some rooms.

Costantinopoli 104 ★ A 19th-century Art Nouveau palace that once belonged to a marquis is set in a palm-shaded courtyard that's mere steps from the archeological museum but a world removed from the noisy city—there's even a small swimming pool for a refreshing dip. Contemporary art and some stunning stained glass grace a series of salons; some rooms are traditionally done with rich fabrics and dark wood furnishings, others are more breezily contemporary, and some spread over two levels. The choicest rooms are on the top floor and open directly off a sprawling roof terrace—a magical retreat above the surrounding rooftops and definitely what you should ask for when booking.

Via Santa Maria di Costantinopoli 104 (off Piazza Bellini). www.costantinopoli104. com. ℂ **081-5571035.** 19 units. From 140€ double. Rates include buffet breakfast. Parking 25€. Metro: Museo. **Amenities:** Pool; room service; Wi-Fi (free).

Decumani Hotel de Charme ★★ The heart-of-Naples neighborhood outside the huge portals can be gritty, but these are sprucely regal lodgings, on the piano nobile of the *palazzo* of the last bishop of the Bourbon kingdom, Cardinal Sisto Riario Sforza. Guest rooms surround a vast, fresco-smothered ballroom-cum-breakfast room; all have plush draperies and fabrics and a few antique pieces complementing shiny hardwood floors and timbered ceilings. Larger rooms include small sitting areas and face the quiet courtyard, while many of the smaller, street-facing doubles share small terraces with the adjoining rooms.

Via San Giovanni Maggiore Pignatelli 15 (off Via Benedetto Croce, btw. Via Santa Chiara and Via Mezzocannone). www.decumani.it. ℂ **081-5518188.** 22 units. 135€– 150€ double. Rates includes breakfast. Parking 25€ in nearby garage. Metro: Piazza Dante. **Amenities:** Wi-Fi (free).

San Francesco al Monte ★★ This ex-Franciscan convent just above the Spanish quarter and halfway up the San Martino hill makes the monastic life seem pretty appealing. The hillside location is a handy refuge above the fray but an easy walk or funicular ride away from the sights, and views from all the rooms and several airy glassed-in and outdoor lounges sweep across the city to the bay. The monastic tenants left behind a chapel, a refectory, secret stairways, and all sorts of atmospheric nooks and crannies (one houses an elaborate nativity scene), and their cells have been combined into large, tile-floored guest rooms, all with sitting areas, and some sprawling suites. In the contemplative, sky-high monk's garden, shaded walkways are carved out of the cliffside and a swimming pool and outdoor bar are delightful un-monastic perks.

Corso Vittorio Emanuele 328. www.sanfrancescoalmonte.it. ℂ **081-4239111.** 45 units. 165€–225€ double. Rates include buffet breakfast. Parking 25€. Metro: Piazza Amedeo; Montesanto or Centrale funiculars to Corso Vittorio Emanuele. **Amenities:** Restaurant; bar; pool; room service; Wi-Fi (free).

INEXPENSIVE

Hotel Il Convento ★ If you want to experience a slice of Neapolitan life—as in laundry flapping outside your window—this is the place for you. While the narrow Spagnoli streets outside teem with neighborhood color and busyness, a 17th-century former convent provides all sorts of cozy ambience, with lots of wood beams, brick arches, and terracotta floors. Two rooms are real retreats, with their own planted rooftop terraces, and two others spread over two levels. Main artery Via Toledo is just 2 short blocks away, taking the edge off comings and goings at night. An eager staff will steer you to neighborhood restaurants and shops.

Via Speranzella 137/a. www.hotelilconvento.com. © **081-403977.** 14 units. 85€–110€. Rates include buffet breakfast. Parking 15€ in nearby garage. Bus: R2 to Piazza Municipio. Small pets allowed. **Amenities:** Bar; fitness room and sauna; room service; Wi-Fi (free).

Hotel Piazza Bellini ★★ The archaeological museum and lively Piazza Bellini are just outside the door of this centuries-old palace, but a cool contemporary redo softens the edges of city life. An outdoor living room fills the cobbled courtyard, and the rooms that range across several floors are minimalist chic with warm hardwood floors, neutral tones with warm-hued accents, sleek surfaces that make plenty of space for storage, and Philippe Starck chairs and crisp white linens. Some of the rooms have terraces and balconies, a few are bi-level, and some with limited views are set aside in an "economy" category—but rates for any room in the house are reasonable and make this mellow haven an especially good value.

Via Costantinioli 101. www.hotelpiazzabellini.com. © **081-451732.** 18 units. 100€–160€ double. Metro: Piazza Dante or Piazza Cavour. **Amenities:** Bar; concierge; Wi-Fi (free).

Where to Eat

Neapolitans love to eat, and you'll love dining here, too. What's not to like about a cuisine in which pizza is a staple? Other dishes to look out for include *mozzarella in carrozza* (fried mozzarella in a "carriage"), in which mozzarella is fried between two pieces of bread and topped with a sauce of the chef's design, often with tomatoes and capers; *gnocchi alla sorrentina,* little pockets of potato pasta filled with mozzarella and topped with tomato sauce; *ragu,* a sauce of several meats cooked for hours and served atop pasta, of course, or in a bowl with thick slices of bread; *parmigiana di melanzane* (eggplant parmigiano), yes, the now-ubiquitous dish of fried eggplant, tomato sauce, mozzarella, parmigiano, and basil originated here; *crocchè di patate* (fried potatoes, pronounced "croquet"), mashed with herbs, cheese, sometimes salami, lightly coated in breadcrumbs and fried; and *pasta e fagioli,* beans and pasta, nothing could be more Neapolitan. Think, too, of seafood—any kind, especially *cozze,* mussels, often served *alla marinara* (simmered in tomato sauce)—and *polpette,* succulent little meatballs.

For a sampling of street food—especially the above mentioned *crocchè di patate* and *arancini,* fried rice balls—stop by the stand on the ground floor of **Matteo,** a venerable pizzeria at Via Tribunali 94 (© **081-455262**), open Monday to Saturday 9am to midnight.

Europeo di Mattozzi ★★ NEAPOLITAN/PIZZA/SEAFOOD Just about all Neapolitans rank this attractive center-of-town eatery as a favorite, and the walls covered with copper pots, framed photos, and oil paintings provide welcoming surroundings that suggest that dining here is serious business. Even connoisseurs claim the pizzas are some of the best in town, and if one of the large pies doesn't suffice as a starter, choose from *zuppa di cannellini e cozze* (bean and mussel soup) or *pasta e patate con provola* (pasta and potatoes with melted local cheese). Seafood *secondi* are the house specialties and include *ricciola all' acquapazza* (a local species in a light tomato and herb broth) and *stoccafisso alla pizzaiola* (dried codfish in a tomato, garlic, and oregano sauce). Reservations are a must on weekends.
Via Marchese Campodisola 4. ☎ **081-5521323.** Main courses 12€–18€. Mon–Wed noon–3:30pm; Thurs–Sat noon–3:30pm and 8pm–midnight. Closed 2 weeks in Aug. Bus: R2 or R3 to Piazza Trieste e Trento.

Nenella ★ NEAPOLITAN No one here is going to stand on formality, but the guys at this Spagnoli favorite will make you feel like one of the neighborhood regulars who crowd into the tent-covered terrace or plain white room for the satisfying home cooking. Stick to the specials, listed on a board and recited by one of the busy waiters—*pasta e patate* (pasta and potatoes), maybe some fried fish or roasted pork, and salads of fresh greens. Even when accompanied by wine a meal here won't cost more than 12€ or 15€ a head.
Vico Lungo Teatro 103–105. ☎ **081-414338.** Main courses 6€–8€. Mon–Sat noon–3pm and 7–11pm. Metro: Montesanto.

Pizzeria Da Michele ★★ PIZZA According to about half the residents of Naples, this no-frills, zero-ambience place serves the best pizza in town—the other half would vote for Sorbillo (see below). Take a number at the door and prepare to wait for a table, as the place is always packed. But you won't have to wait long for one of the enormous and simply delicious pizzas that come in just two varieties, *margherita* or *marinara* (toppings are for snobs, say the guys behind the counter): they emerge from the oven in a mere 20 seconds, an act of wizardry that keeps the tables turning quickly. No credit cards accepted.
Via Sersale 1. www.damichele.net. ☎ **081-5539204.** Pizza 4€–5€. Mon–Sat 11am–11pm. Metro: Garibaldi.

Pizzeria Gino Sorbillo ★★ PIZZA Don't let the crowds out front put you off, and don't let one of the other pizza places on Via Tribunali lure you in (a couple of others, also confusingly called Sorbillo, have been set up by other family members). Just make your way through the crowd, give your name to the friendly, bemused woman with the clipboard, and enjoy the partylike atmosphere on the street out front as you wait for a table. The wait is never as long as you think it might be, and once inside you'll probably be ushered to the vast, upstairs dining room where a long menu of pizzas is accompanied by a palatable house wine. This attractive place is the Ritz compared to serious contender Michele (see above). The

Campania is famous for its pizza.

Quattro Stagione (Four Seasons) pizza defies Michele's no-topping policy with its quadrants of mushrooms, salami, prosciutto, and cheese.
Via Tribunali 32. www.sorbillo.it. *©* **081-0331009.** Pizza 4€–5€. Daily noon–3:30 and 7–midnight. Metro: Dante.

Rosiello ★★★ NEAPOLITAN/SEAFOOD   It's a cab ride or long bus trip out to this retreat, on a hilltop above the sea in swanky and leafy Posilipo, but the trip is worth it. Ask your hotel to make reservations and help arrange transport, because a meal on the terrace here is one of the city's great treats. Everything comes from the waters at your feet or the restaurant's extensive vegetable plots on the hillside; even the cheese is local. These ingredients find their way into seafood feasts that might include risotto *alla pescatora* (with seafood) and *pezzogna all'acquapazza* (fish in a light tomato broth), but even a simple pasta here, such as *scialatielli con melanzane e provola* (fresh pasta with local cheese and eggplant), is elegant and simply delicious.
Via Santo Strato 10. www.ristoranterosiello.it. *©* **081-7691288.** Main courses 10€–25€. Thurs–Tues 12:30–4pm and 7:30pm–midnight (May–Sept open daily). Closed 2 weeks each Jan and Aug. Bus: C3 to Mergellina (end of line), and then 140.

Squistezze/La Stanza del Gusto ★★ CREATIVE NEAPOLITAN
Chef Mario Avallone prepares some of the most innovative food in town, and he offers it two ways: In a casual, ground-floor cheese bar/*osteria* (Squistezze) and in a simple-but-stylish upstairs restaurant. Downstairs, daily offerings are written on blackboards and include the best lunch deal in town—a main course of the day, dessert, wine, water, and coffee for 13€. Or, you can pair cheese and *salumi* (cured meats) with carefully chosen wines or what is probably the city's largest selection of craft beers (the staff makes suggestions) or tuck into hearty salads and several unusual specialties, such as *arancino di mare*, a fresh take on classic fried rice balls, in this case concealing a core of fresh seafood. Upstairs, locally

Sweet-Tooth Heaven

On top of their many other sterling qualities, Neapolitans make delicious sweets and desserts. Clam-shaped *sfogliatelle,* filled with ricotta cream and topped with powdered sugar, is the city's unofficial pastry, delicious and available at bars and in pastry shops all over the city. *Il baba* are little cakes soaked in a rum or limoncello syrup and often filled with cream; *delizia al limone* (delicious lemon) consists of sponge-caked soaked with lemon or limoncello syrup, filled with lemon pastry cream, and iced with lemon-flavored whipped cream; and dark, flourless *torta* Caprese, topped with powdered sugar, is the chocolate cake of choice.

Scaturchio, Piazza San Domenico Maggiore 19 (www.scaturchio.it; ✆ **081-5517031**), makes some of the best *sfogliatelle* in town and also serves excellent coffee. Naples's ice cream parlors dispense some of the best gelato in the country; try **Gelateria della Scimmia,** Piazza della Carità 4 (✆ **081-5520272**).

sourced ingredients find their way into dishes that you'll probably want to enjoy on one of several tasting menus that start at 35€; choose one that includes the *variazione di baccalà,* an amazing presentation of salt cod prepared in several different ways.

Via Santa Maria di Costantinopoli 100. www.lastanzadelgusto.com. ✆ **081-401578.** Main courses (upstairs restaurant) 14€–20€. Tues–Sat noon–11:30pm; Sun noon–3pm. Upstairs restaurant Tues–Sat 7–11pm. Closed 3 weeks in Aug. Metro: Piazza Dante or Museo.

Tandem ★ NEAPOLITAN   Take a seat in the simple room or the pleasant little terrace on the lane outside and linger over the house specialty, *ragu.* A lot of locals come here for their fix of this city staple, which comes in two varieties, meat (three or four kinds, slow-cooked) or vegetarian, which is a bit of a desecration. It's served over spaghetti or a choice of other pasta, or by itself with thick slices of bread for dunking, along with carafes of the house wine.

Via Paladino 51. www.ristorantetandemragu.it. ✆ **081-4074833.** Reservations recommended Fri–Sat. *Secondi* 10€–18€. AE, DC, MC, V. Mon–Fri noon–3:30 and 7–11:30 and Sat–Sun noon–4 and 7–midnight. Metro: Piazza Dante.

Entertainment & Nightlife

Neapolitans make the best of balmy evenings by passing the time on cafe terraces. Top choice is the oldest cafe in Naples, with a Liberty-style interior from the 1860s, the elegant **Gran Caffè Gambrinus,** Via Chiaia 1, in Piazza Trento e Trieste (✆ **081-417582**). Another very popular spot is **La Caffetteria,** Piazza dei Martiri 25 (✆ **081-7644243**), top choice for evening *aperitivi.*

OPERA & CLASSICAL MUSIC   The venerable **Teatro San Carlo,** Via San Carlo 98 (www.teatrosancarlo.it; ✆ **081-7972412** or 081-7972331), stages world-class opera, along with dance and orchestral works, Tuesday through Sunday, December through June. Tickets cost between 30€ and 100€.

Associazione Alessandro Scarlatti, Piazza dei Martiri 58 (www.associazionescarlatti.it; *C* 081-406011), organizes a concert series at Castel Sant'Elmo; ticket prices range from 15€ to 25€.

BARS & CLUBS   This is a port, a cosmopolitan city, and a university town all rolled into one, so the Neapolitan nighttime scene is eclectic and lively. **Piazza Bellini,** near the university at the edge of the historical center, is an especially lively destination. *Enoteche,* or wine bars, provide a good choice of wines by the glass and by the bottle, along with a bit of food and usually a relaxed atmosphere. Some top choices are quiet **Berevino,** Via Sebastiano 62 (*C* 081-0605688; closed Mon); **Enoteca Belledonne,** Vico Belledonne a Chiaia 18 (www.enotecabelledonne.com; *C* 081-403162; closed Sun), with a local Chiaia vibe; chic, stark **Barril** (Via Giuseppe Fiorelli 11); and **Trip** (Via Giuseppe Martucci 64; www.tripnapoli.com; *C* 081-19568994), with welcoming overstuffed couches.

Side Trip to Campo Flegrei (The Phlegrean Fields) ★★

On this seaside peninsula just west of Naples, volcanic vents steam and hiss (the name is from the Greek, "Burning Fields"), ruined villas testify to ancient hedonism, and mythic characters and oracles seem to spring to life. Moonlike landscapes are interspersed with lush hillsides carpeted with olive groves and orange and lemon orchards. Rich in history, the area has long evoked colorful storytelling. Our alphabet was invented here, when the Latin language officially adopted the characters used for written communication in Cuma. Nero murdered his mother, the ambitious and villainous Agrippina, outside Baia, the Palm Beach of the ancient world, where Caesar relaxed and Hadrian breathed his last.

GETTING THERE

A day exploring this strange, mythic landscape begins in seaside Pozzuoli, reached from Naples by Line 2 of the Metropolitana (subway) or via the Cumana Railroad (*C* 800-053939), starting from Piazza Montesanto. From Pozzuoli, SEPSA buses run to various nearby sights: Baia, Cumae, Solfatara, and Lago d'Averno (www.sepsa.it; *C* 081-7354965).

POZZUOLI   Screen legend Sophia Loren was born in this seaside town in 1934, contributing a bit of local color, although the main attraction dates much farther back: The **Anfiteatro Flavio,** built in the last part of the 1st century. More than 40,000 spectators could squeeze into its seats, making it the third largest arena in the Roman world. Much of the seating remains intact, as do the subterranean staging areas with "mechanics" that hoisted wild beasts up to the field of slaughter and pumped water to flood the arena for mock naval battles (Via Nicola Terracciano 75; *C* 081-5266007); admission 4€; Wed–Mon 9am–1 hour before sunset).

SOLFATARA   The ancients called this dormant volcano just 2km (1¼ miles) above Pozzuoli "Forum Vulcani" and believed it to be the residence of the god Vulcan and an entrance to Hades. It's easy to see why: lunar landscapes hiss, steam, bubble, and spew sulfurous clouds that reach a temperature of 160°C (320°F). Despite all the bubbling and steaming, the volcano has not erupted since 1198. (Via Solfatara 161, Pouzzoli; ℂ 081-5262341; 6€; daily 8:30am to 1 hr. before sunset.)

BAIA Although most of the villas and thermal baths of this ancient spa town are now underwater, enough remains on terra firma to suggest the grandeur of **Baia,** where Julius Caesar, Nero, and other Roman elite once relaxed and debauched. Seneca the Younger called the place a "vortex of luxury" and a "harbor of vice." It was here that Caligula supposedly had a bridge fashioned from a string of boats and rode across it on his horse, defying the oracle's prediction that he had "no more chance of becoming emperor than of riding a horse across the Gulf of Baiae" (ℂ 081-8687592; admission 4€; Tues–Sun 9am to 1 hr. before sunset). The evocative 16th-century **Castello di Baia** shows off statuary and other artifacts from the ancient city (ℂ 081-5233797; admission 4€; Tues–Sun 9am–2:30pm).

LAGO D'AVERNO This placid lake just north of Baia fills an extinct volcanic crater—and if legends have any truth to them, was once so vaporously lethal that the name derives from a Greek word meaning "without birds," because winged creatures flying over the waters would plunge to their deaths. The Cumaean Sibyl (see below) is said to have ferried Aeneas, son of Aphrodite, across the lake, where he discovered the River Styx, the Gateway to Hades. In the 1st century B.C., Agrippa

The Cave of the Cumaean Sibyl, just outside of Naples.

had a canal dug to connect the lake with the sea, providing safe harbor for Roman ships. A couple of centuries later the Romans built the lakeside **Temple of Apollo**, a huge thermal complex covered with a dome almost as large, but not as long lasting, as the one on the Pantheon in Rome. A large section of well-weathered façade still stands, attesting to its former grandeur.

CUMAE When the Greeks founded nearby Cumae, their first colony on mainland Italy, in the 8th century B.C., they discovered they had a helpful neighbor: the Cumaean Sibyl, who, according to legend, passed on messages from Apollo. A little less poetically, the sibyl's long, narrow trapezoidal tunnel was probably gouged from the rock as part of the colony's defense system. The cave is in an **archaeological park** that also includes temples dedicated to Jupiter and Apollo, later converted into Christian churches (📞 **081-8543060;** admission 2.50€; daily 9am to 1 hr. before sunset). On Via Domitiana, to the east of Cumae, you'll pass the **Arco Felice**, an arch about 20m (64 ft.) high, built by Emperor Domitian in the 1st century A.D.

Side Trip to Pompeii & Herculaneum

24km (15 miles) S of Naples, 237km (147 miles) SE of Rome

On that fateful day, August 24, A.D. 79, the people of Pompeii, a prosperous fishing town, and Herculaneum, a resort just down the coast, watched Mount Vesuvius hurl a churning column of gas and ash 10 miles high into the sky. It was only a matter of time before ash and pumice buried Pompeii and flows of superheated molten rock coursed through the streets of Herculaneum. Volcanic debris quickly hardened into a layer of mud that fossilized everything—furniture, wooden beams, clothing, skeletons, graffiti, mosaics. Terrifying indeed for the ill-fated townsfolk, but lucky for us, the layer of ooze preserved Pompeii and Herculaneum as time capsules. Pompeii is much more extensive than Herculaneum, with more to see, while Herculaneum provides an easier-to-manage, less crowded experience. You could easily do both in one day, though that might be "excavation overload." If you have to choose, Pompeii provides the more sensational experience.

ESSENTIALS

GETTING THERE The **Circumvesuviana Railway** (www.vesuviana.it; 📞 **800-053939**) runs between Naples and Sorrento every half-hour from Piazza Garibaldi. For Herculaneum, get off at Ercolano/Scavi (*scavi* means "archaeological excavation"). Herculaneum is about 20 minutes from Naples and 50 minutes from Sorrento; the entrance is about 10 blocks from the station. Pompeii is about 40 minutes from Naples and 30 minutes from Sorrento; exit the train at Pompeii/Scavi. The entrance is about 45m (150 ft.) from the station at the Villa dei Mister.

To reach either by **car** from Naples, follow the autostrada toward Salerno. If you're coming from Sorrento, head east on SS. 145, where you can connect with A3 (marked napoli). Then take the signposted turnoffs for Pompeii and Herculaneum.

LOGISTICS Hours for both excavation sites are the same: April to October, they are open daily 8:30am to 7:30pm and November to March daily 8:30am to 5pm (last admission 90 min. before close); Admission to each site is 11€, but a cumulative ticket (20€) will grant you access to both as well as other nearby archaeological sites and is good for three consecutive days. You can purchase it at the Circumvesuviana Railway Station, Piazza Garibaldi, in Naples, or at the sites.

TREAD LIGHTLY ON mount vesuvius

Towering, pitch-black Mount Vesuvius looms menacingly over the Bay of Naples. The volcano has erupted periodically since the day of doom, August 24, A.D. 79, when it buried Pompeii and Herculaneum: eruptions occurred in 1631, in 1906, and most recently on March 31, 1944.

It might sound like a dubious invitation, but it's possible to visit the rim of the crater's mouth. As you look down into its smoldering core, you might recall that, a century before the eruption that buried Pompeii, the escaped slave Spartacus, who boldly led an uprising against his Roman captors, hid in the hollow of this crater, which was then covered with vines.

The **Parco Nazionale del Vesuvio** (www.parconazionaledelvesuvio.it;

℗ 081-8653911; admission 8€) contains an observatory at 608m (1,994 ft.) that is the oldest in the world, dating from 1841. The park is open daily from 9am to sunset.

To reach Vesuvius from Naples, take the Circumvesuviana Railway and get off the train at Ercolano station, the 10th stop. From here, you can catch the shuttle bus to the entrance of the park (summer daily 9am–6pm; winter daily 9am–3pm). The cost is 10€. Once at the top, you must be accompanied to the crater by a guide, and the final accompanied ascent will cost another 6.50€. Assorted willing tour guides are found in the bus parking lot; they are available from 9am to about 4pm. For more information, call ℗ **081-7393666** or visit www.vesuvioexpress.it.

The ticket offices at both provide a free map and booklet that will guide you through the site. Inside the entrance at Pompeii, you'll find a **bookstore,** where you can purchase additional guidebooks to the ruins (available in English, complete with detailed photos). Pompeii also has a cafeteria inside the archaeological zone, which is handy for sandwiches and beverages.

If you're visiting the sites on a sunny day, wear sunscreen and bring along a bottle of water. At both sites you can leave bags in checkrooms near the entrances for free.

HERCULANEUM

Excavations began at Herculaneum in the 18th century and continue to this day, with the fairly recent discovery of a beached boat full of desperate souls trying to make an escape by sea. The archaeological remains of Herculaneum, the **Scavi di Ercolano** (Corso Resina; www.pompeii sites.org; ℗ **081-7324311**), give the unsettling impression not of a ruin but of a ghost town from which residents have only recently walked away.

The excavated area stretches from the **Decumanus Maximus** (the town's main street) to what was once the shoreline (now a kilometer to the west); the rest of the Roman town remains inaccessible beneath the buildings of modern Ercolano.

Elegant mosaics of fish, dolphins, and other sea creatures decorate the **Thermal Baths,** with several entrances. The men's section, the Terme

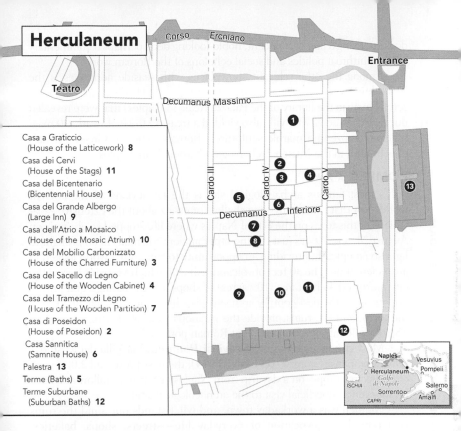

Herculaneum

Corso Ercolano

Entrance

Teatro

Decumanus Massimo

Cardo III Cardo IV Cardo V

Decumanus Inferiore

Naples
Vesuvius
Herculaneum Pompeii
Golfo
di Napoli
ISCHIA Salerno
Sorrento Amalfi
CAPRI

Maschili, has an abundance of practical facilities include a latrine, benches, and shelves for stashing sandals and personal effects. In the Terme Feminili, a mosaic of a naked Triton decorates the floor of the changing rooms.

The **Casa del Tramezzo di Legno (House of the Wooden Partition),** with its perfect facade, is named for a well-preserved wooden screen that separated the atrium from the tablium, a little room that served as an office.

The **Casa a Graticcio (House of the Latticework)** is one of the very few examples of working-class housing that has survived from antiquity; the name-giving lattices, though cheaply made of interwoven cane and plaster, are remarkably well preserved.

The **Casa del Mosaico di Nettuno e Anfitrite (House of the Neptune and Anfitritis Mosaic)** is so called for its bright blue mosaic of the sea god and his nymph. Goods still line the shelves of the adjoining shop.

The **Casa dei Cervi (House of the Stags)** was one of the most elegant houses in town, with terraces and porticos overlooking the sea. Decorations say much about its fun-loving inhabitants: Frescoes depict cheerful and playful cherubs, while courtyards were filled with statues of drunken satyrs and a drunken, peering Hercules. The house is named for a statue of dogs attacking a pair of innocent, noble-looking deer, perhaps a commentary on the cutthroat politics and social echelons of the Roman world.

Among the other elegant showplaces with seaside addresses is the **Villa dei Papiri,** so called because of the 1,000-odd badly charred papyrus scrolls (now in the library of the Palazzo Reale in Naples) that were revealed during excavations. The villa also yielded a treasure trove of nearly 90 magnificent bronze and marble sculptures, Roman copies of Greek originals now housed in the Museo Archeologico Nazionale in Naples.

POMPEII ★★★

Italy's most famous archaeological site is the Disneyland of the ancient world. Not that there's anything shallow or ersatz about the extensive excavations of this town on the Bay of Naples where life stopped so abruptly on August 24, A.D. 79. It's just that no other ancient town has been brought to light so completely, providing an opportunity to step into a world locked in an ancient time. The 30 feet of volcanic ash with which Vesuvius buried the city preserved 44 hectares (109 acres) of shops, civic buildings, and private houses. Over the past century archaeologists have painstakingly uncovered the town, and the ruins provide the vicarious thrill of sharing space with 35,000 residents of a lively, ancient Roman port.

Most visitors come to the **Scavi di Pompeii,** Via Villa dei Misteri 1 (www.pompeiisites.org; ✆ **081-8610744**), the best-preserved 2,000-year-old ruins in Europe, on a day trip from Naples or Sorrento (allow at least 4 hr. for even a superficial visit to the archaeological site).

Pompeii was a workaday town, and what stands out amid the ruins is a remarkable evocation of everyday life—streets, shops, bakeries, brothels, baths. The first thing you'll notice is the typical Roman plan of

The House of the Mysteries in Pompeii.

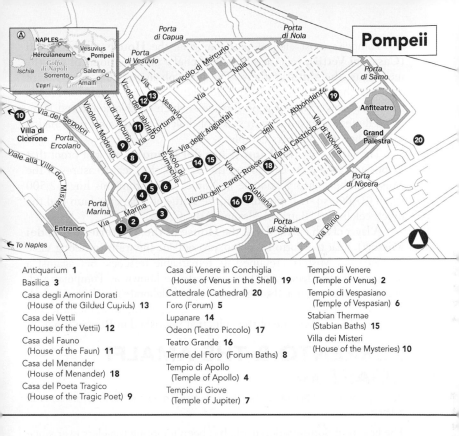

Pompeii

gridlike streets, on which stepping stones appear at every intersection. These were laid down to allow residents to cross the pavement even when the streets were being flushed with water, as they were at least once a day. Raised sidewalks conceal water and sewage pipes. In the center of town is the **Forum (Foro),** the small marketplace that had been severely damaged in an earthquake 16 years before the eruption of Vesuvius and hadn't been repaired when the final destruction came. Surrounding the Forum are the **Basilica** (the city's largest single structure), a law court with a floor plan later adopted by Christian churches, along with the name; the **Temple of Apollo** (Tempio di Apollo), and the **Temple of Jupiter** (Tempio di Giove). The city's bathhouses are among the finest to survive from antiquity. Vividly colored frescoes depicting graphic sex acts in one of them are the subject of ongoing controversy: Were they meant to advertise sexual services available on the upper floors or were they simply amusing decorations?

Unlike Herculaneum, with its seafront district of lavish villas, Pompeii was a proletariat town, and the wealthy lived among the working classes. Their houses are interspersed with shops (which were often combined with dwellings) all over town.

Pompeii's most elegant patrician villa, the **House of the Vettii (Casa dei Vettii),** was the ultimate bachelor pad, the home of wealthy merchants, the Vettii brothers. The huge phallus resting on a pair of scales at the entrance was not intended as a come-hither for female guests but was a sign of good fortune—which the black-and-red Pompeian dining room with its frescoes of delicate cupids and colonnaded garden show the brothers had plenty of.

The **House of the Faun (Casa del Fauno)** is ancient proof that money and good taste can go together. Two of the great treasures of the Museo Archeologico Nazionale in Naples come from this huge, 2,500 sq. m (27,000 sq.-ft.) spread: a bronze statue of a dancing faun and the much-celebrated "Battle of Alexander the Great."

A layer of ash ensured that the **House of the Mysteries (Villa dei Misteri),** near the Porto Ercolano, just outside the walls (go along Viale alla Villa dei Misteri), retained its remarkable frescoes. Set against a background of a deep hue that's come to be known as Pompeian red, figures are shown going through some sort of elaborate rituals that, scholars argue, might be preparations for a wedding or initiation into a sect of Dionysus (Bacchus), one of the cults that flourished in Roman times.

SORRENTO & THE AMALFI COAST ★★

50km (31 miles) S of Naples, 256km (159 miles) SE of Rome, 50km (31 miles) W of Salerno

The beautiful Sorrento peninsula has been tempting travelers ever since Ulysses was forced to fill the ears of his sailors with wax and to tie himself to the mast of his ship to avoid the alluring call of the Sirens. Today, the pull of the sea and imposing rock-bound coast remain as compelling as they were in Homer's day. Even though it's besieged by tourists, graceful old Sorrento is a lovely place, perched high atop a cliff gazing across the sea toward the isle of Capri. The spectacular but nerve-racking Amalfi Drive heads vertiginously east, clinging to cliffs and rounding one bend after another until it comes to Positano, a tile-domed village hugging a near-vertical rock, then to Amalfi, a little seaside town that was once the center of a powerful maritime republic.

As transporting as the green hillsides and azure seas are, as much as the scent of lemon and frangipani entices, the charms of Sorrento and the Amalfi Coast are no secret. You'll do yourself a favor to save the pleasure of a visit for the early spring or fall, before and after the summer crowds, and even then accept the fact that you will not have this slice of paradise to yourself.

Some of the world's most legendary hotels are tucked into the cliffsides around Sorrento and along the Amalfi Coast. The price of one of their attractive and comfortable rooms often comes with sea views, a

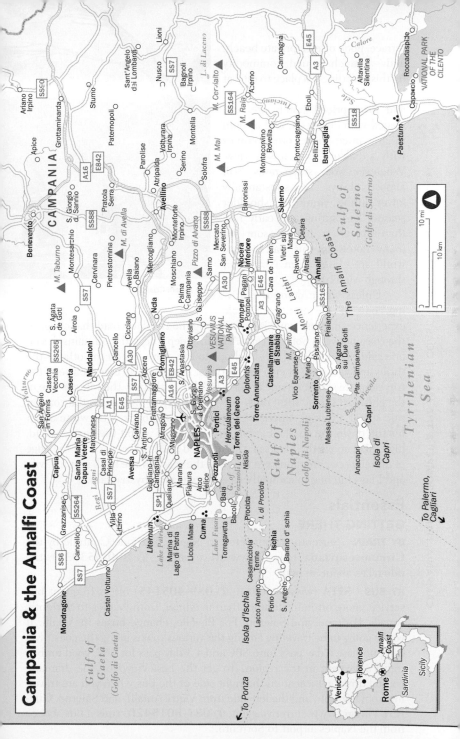

Campania & the Amalfi Coast

CAMPANIA

terrace, pool, often a private beach, and—a much valued commodity on this coastline—a place to retreat from the crowds. Many moderate and lower-priced hotels are also loaded with character, and a room in any price range often comes with a balcony and a sea view. Wherever you stay, rates will almost always be substantially lower during winter and shoulder season, late spring and early fall, than they are in high season (but many hotels in this part of the world are closed from November through March).

The Amalfi Coast.

Unless you're doing the driving, one of the most enjoyable experiences in these parts is riding along the two-lane road that clings to the coast between Sorrento and Amalfi. Steep forested mountainsides on one side, sheer, 150m (500-ft) drops to the azure sea on the other—the thrills and views are of epic proportions. Provided you can get a seat, the trip along this coast on one of the SITA buses that ply the route is one of the cheapest scenic thrill rides anywhere. As you plod down the coast at safe speed, think of American writer John Steinbeck, who wrote about his trip down the coast, "Flaming like a meteor we hit the coast, a road, high, high above the blue sea, that hooked and corkscrewed on the edge of nothing . . . . We didn't see much of the road. In the back seat my wife and I lay clutched in each other's arms, weeping hysterically."

Essentials
GETTING THERE

BY TRAIN Sorrento is connected to Naples' Stazione Centrale by the **Circumvesuviana** railway (www.vesuviana.it; © 800-053939); the ride takes about an hour.

BY BUS **SITA** (www.sitabus.it; © 089-405145) offers frequent bus service, more often in summer than in winter, from Naples to Sorrento, Amalfi, Positano, and Salerno. For Ravello, change buses in Amalfi. If you're going to be traveling among the various towns along the coast, you can purchase a day pass for 6.80€ and a 3-day pass for 16€, good for bus travel anywhere in the region. To get the best views on the dramatic coastal drive, get a seat on the right side of the bus when you are traveling from Sorrento and the left side from Vietri, Amalfi, and Salerno. **Curreri Viaggi** (www.curreriviaggi.it; © 081-8015420) runs a bus service from the Naples airport to Sorrento.

BY BOAT   In summer, ferries and hydrofoils operated by **LMP-Linee Marittime Partenope** (www.consorziolmp.it; ✆ 081-5513236), **NLG-Navigazione Libera del Golfo** (www.navlib.it; ✆ 081-8071812), and **Linee Lauro** (www.alilauro.it; ✆ 081-4972222) make daily runs to and from Sorrento, Naples, Ischia, and Capri. **Volaviamare** (www.volaviamare.it; ✆ 081-4972291) makes trips between Sorrento and Amalfi and Positano. **Metrò del Mare**, at the Marina Piccola in Sorrento (www.metrodelmare.net; ✆ 199-600700), is a summer-only commuter ferry serving the whole coast between Salerno and Bacoli.

BY CAR   Taxis offer a flat rate of 100€ to Sorrento from Naples; or 130€ to Amalfi from the Naples Capodichino Airport. By **car** from Naples, take the A3, exit at Castellammare di Stabia for the SS145 to Sorrento. The SS163 branches off the SS145 before you get to Sorrento and heads over the peninsula to Positano and Amalfi. To get to Ravello, take the SP1 inland from Amalfi. From Naples, allow about 1 hour and 10 minutes for the drive to Sorrento; 1 hour and 25 minutes to Positano or Amalfi; and 1 hour to Ravello.

Sorrento ★★

50km (31 miles) S of Naples

How does that old song, "Come Back to Sorrento," go? *"Vir 'o mare quant'è bello"* . . . or, "See the sea how beautiful it is." You'll be humming a few bars, because the sea, the scented gardens, and sun-drenched vistas that have been luring visitors to this cliff top town for millennia really are beautiful. Monuments are few and far between, but views from the town center Piazza Tasso or a trek down to Marina Grande, a fisherman's port, show off the town's irrepressible appeal. Sorrento provides easy access to Naples as well as such fabled places as Capri, Positano, Amalfi, and the ruins at Pompeii and is usually thronged with happy holidaymakers who, at their best, provide pleasant company.

Choosing a Town

Just about everyone who visits Sorrento and the Amalfi Coast comes away with a favorite town to which they yearn to return. When choosing the place to put down your bags, it's hard to go wrong in this beautiful part of the world, but you may want to take some practical considerations into account. **Sorrento** is the best situated for an exploring base, given its excellent train, bus, and boat connections to Capri, Naples, Pompeii, and Herculaneum, and other towns along the coast. **Positano** is the most picturesque and resortlike, with the best (and most easily accessible) beaches, though getting in and out of town in high season on the traffic-choked coast road can be a nightmare (boats are a pleasant alternative). **Amalfi** provides small-town charm and gives you a two-fer—its beautiful and easy-to-reach neighbor **Ravello**; you can also avoid the worst of the coast traffic by approaching and leaving Amalfi from and to the east through Salerno, with its excellent train connections to Naples.

VISITOR INFORMATION   The **tourist office** in Sorrento is at Via de Maio 35, off Piazza Tasso (www.sorrentotourism.com; ℂ **081-8074033**); it's open Monday to Friday 9am to 4:15pm; in summer it's also open on Saturday mornings. You'll also find an information office in the green caboose just outside the train station; it's open daily 10am to 1pm and 3 to 7pm.

EXPLORING SORRENTO

Sorrento is long and narrow, strung out along the top of seaside cliffs. Just about everything you want to see in town is an easy walk from the train station, with the exception of the town's two ports, which many residents opt to reach by bus. Marina Piccola, directly below Piazza Tasso (bus C or C, 1.20€), is the commercial port where ferries and hydrofoils dock; Marina Grande, below the western edge of town (bus D, 2.20€), is the old fishing port.

The center of town is sunny **Piazza Tasso.** Amid the piazza's cafes, glossy shops, and crowds of promenaders stands a statue of the namesake poet, Tarquato Tasso, who was born in Sorrento into a noble family in 1544. Despite being a darling of royalty and authoring one of Europe's most popular poems, *Jerusalem Delivered*, he spent much of his adult life in a madhouse and died at the age of 51, just before being crowned poet laureate. The piazza dramatically spans a deep gorge; the north end overhangs a steep hillside that descends to Marina Piccola, while to the south you can follow a walkway and look far down into a verdant valley where a settlement flourished alongside a stream as early as the 5th century B.C.

The old town spreads out to the west, bisected by busy **Corso Italia** (closed to car traffic evenings in summer and weekend evenings in winter). Along the corso a few blocks west of the square, at Via Santa Maria della Pieta, is Sorrento's **cathedral** (www.cattedralesorrento.it; ℂ **081/8782248;** admission free; open daily 7:30am–noon and 3–7pm). Frequent rebuilding has rendered the façade rather bland, except for an intriguing arcaded three-story campanile with embedded Roman columns; inside are doors inlaid with scenes of Sorrento life, a map of the town, and an enormous *presepe* (nativity scene), with Mt. Vesuvius looming behind the manger. North of here are the quieter precincts around the gardens of the **Villa Communale.** From there you can take an elevator down to Marina Piccola (1€) or follow a well-marked lane and stairway to the quainter Marina Grande (see p. 569).

Chiesa di San Francisco★ CHURCH   Top choice for the most charming spot in Sorrento goes to the 14th-century Moorish cloisters of this church and convent, where an old pepper tree shades tufa-rock arches interspersed with elaborately capped columns. Just across the street, a statue of St. Francis stands amid the cliffside gardens of **Villa Communale**. Views from one side of this delightful, palm-studded patch of greenery take in the port far below and a broad sweep of the bay of Naples.

Piazza San Francesco. Free admission. Daily 8am–1:30pm and 3:30–8pm.

Sorrento.

Marina Grande ★ CHURCH
Walking past a row of narrow houses squeezed between the steep hillside and the sea, you'll get a sense of Sorrento as an old-time fishing port, though you'll have to contend with shills trying to lure you into restaurants with multi-language menus (a few restaurants down here are excellent, see below). It's a nice walk from Sorrento down to the port (and remember, this is Marina Grande, as opposed to Marina Piccola, the commercial port where ferries disembark). Just follow the well-marked road from the gardens of the Villa Communale; it eventually becomes a staircase and passes beneath a Greek gate—a reminder that Marina Grande was once a separate town that was vulnerable to pirate raids, a much riskier place to live than fortified Sorrento. You can take a dip here, but the small, pebbly beach is less than inviting (for better options, see p. 572). The scene is quite romantic in the evening, with moonlight illuminating the harbor full of bobbing boats. Should you have one limoncello too many while taking in the spectacle, hop on the D bus to get back up the hill.
Marina Grande.

Museo Correale di Terranova ★ CHURCH A walk through these rather plain galleries carved out of an 18th-century villa introduces you to the good life as it's been enjoyed over the past few centuries in this part of the world. Counts Alfredo and Pompeo Correale donated to this museum the collectibles their family had amassed since 1500; the randomness of the assortment is its charm. Neapolitan paintings from the 17th through 19th centuries capture the scenic Sorrento views that have been inspiring travelers since the days of the Grand Tour. Inlaid intarsia furniture is from studios right here in Sorrento, and much of the porcelain was fired in kilns on the grounds of the Capodimonte palace in Naples (some especially delicate-looking pieces are from China and Japan, reflecting the 19th-century aristocratic craze for arts of the Far East). A lovely palm-shaded garden affords stunning views up and down the coast, a welcome spot in which to linger in relative solitude for a spell.
Piazza San Francesco. Free admission. Daily 8am–1:30pm and 3:30–8pm.

WHERE TO STAY
Hotel Antiche Mura ★★ An elegant Art Nouveau–style palazzo built on top of the town's former defensive walls reveals many surprises, including a huge, lovely garden filled with lemon trees surrounding a

pool, while many rooms enjoy precipitous views into the deep gorge that runs through Sorrento. Gracious public lounges flow over a couple of floors and include a conservatory-like breakfast room. Guest quarters are bright and cheerful, with colorful Vietri-tile floors; many have balconies facing the gorge or town, while some are tucked into the garden. Service is as gracious and welcoming as the surroundings.

Via Fuorimura 7 (entrance on Piazza Tasso. www.hotelantichemura.com. ✆ **081-8073523.** 46 units. 80€–250€ double. Rates include buffet breakfast. Parking 10€. **Amenities:** Bar; concierge; pool; Wi-Fi (free).

Grand Hotel Cocumella ★★★

Of all Sorrento's grand hotels, this magically converted monastery is the most beautiful of all, set amid lush gardens above the sea in elegant Sant'Agnello, a residential enclave at the eastern end of town. Rooms created from combined monk's cells are chic and sophisticated, mixing antiques with nice contemporary touches, offset with gleaming white tile floors. Some have seaview terraces while others hang over the orange-scented gardens, where a pool is tucked into the greenery. An elevator descends to the sea and a swimming platform.

Via Cocumella 7, Sant'Agnello. www.hotelantichemura.com. ✆ **081-8782933.** 48 units. 240€–380€ double; Rates include buffet breakfast. **Amenities:** Restaurant; bar; concierge; pool; beach; Wi-Fi (free).

Hotel Rivoli ★

Convenience comes with high style at this strikingly revamped convent right in the center of town. A dramatic glass staircase floats up to the large, airy, and smartly decorated guest rooms and a rooftop breakfast room and terrace, while cozy, antiques-filled reading nooks open off the landings (there's also an elevator). You'll trade a pool and sea views for a center-of-town location—the pedestrian-only old town lanes are just outside the sound-proofed windows, and the train station, port, and bus stops are nearby, making this an especially handy base if you plan on exploring the coast.

Via Santa Maria delle Grazie 16. www.sorrentorivoli.com. ✆ **081-365-4089.** 8 units. 120€–140€ double. Rates include buffet breakfast. Substantial discounts for longer stays. **Amenities:** Wi-Fi (free).

WHERE TO EAT

Sorrento has some good fast-food options geared to its international visitors. For a quick meal and a meat fix, try the veal or chicken kebabs at **Kebab Ciampa,** Via Pieta 23 (www.kebabsorrento.com; ✆ **081-8074595**); they also serve falafel and meatballs. **Star Pub,** Via Luigi de Maio 17 (www.starpub.it; ✆ **081-8773618**) satisfies a craving for a hamburger, and also makes excellent meals-in-themselves salads, washed down with a thoughtful selection of wines and beers.

The best gelato parlor in the whole area is at **Davide,** Via Padre Reginaldo Giuliani 39 (✆ **081-8072092;** closed Wed in winter), where the 60 flavors include deliciously creamy *noci di Sorrento* (Sorrento walnuts), rich *cioccolato con canditi* (dark chocolate cream studded with candied oranges), and *delizia al limone* (a delectable lemon cream).

Il Delfino ★ SORRENTINE   A meal here comes with a perk—the chance to swim off the adjoining pier. That's a good incentive to eat lightly from the snack food menu, though the fresh fish and heaping platters of fresh seafood are tempting—and a popular Sunday afternoon lunch choice, when locals come down to take in the sun and indulge in excellent cooking and friendly service.

Western end of port off Via Marina Grande. ℂ **081-878-2038.** Main courses 12€–24€. Daily 12:30–3:30pm and 6:30–11pm. Closed Nov–Mar.

Inn Bufalito ★ SORRENTINE   The approach is to use only local products, especially buffalo meats and cheeses (buffalo-milk mozzarella is one of the region's most prized specialties). The brown-toned room is meant to give off a rustic vibe, even though the menu and service is decidedly polished. You can enjoy buffalo steaks or pasta with a heavy sauce of buffalo *ragu*, while a platter of cheeses and salamis provides a nice light meal and a taste of the house specialties.

Vico I Foro 21. www.innbufalito.com. ℂ **081-365-6975.** Main courses 12€–24€. Wed–Mon noon–3:30pm and 6:30–11pm. Closed Nov–Feb.

Ristorante Tasso ★★ SORRENTINE   Amalfi prides itself on fresh seafood, and the catch comes to the fore in this casually elegant room that resembles a garden pavilion (and there's also a large garden for al fresco dining). The choices change every day, with two reasonably priced set menus, though you can also dine lightly and a la carte. A little unexpectedly, given the classy surroundings, pizza is a specialty and claimed by many regulars to be the best this side of Naples.

Via Correale 11d. www.ristorantetasso.com. ℂ **081-878-5809.** Main courses 12€–24€. Daily noon–4pm and 7–11:30pm.

Sant'Anna da Emilia ★ SORRENTINE   The simple pleasures of this old boat shed in Marina Grande are well known, so getting a table during the summer rush usually requires a long wait. Patience pays off with some old-time classics, such as *gnocchi alla Sorrentina* (Sorrento-style potato dumplings with cheese and tomato sauce), and *fritto misto* (deep-fried calamari and little fish). The best tables, of course, are on the pier outside. No credit cards are accepted.

Via Marina Grande 62. ℂ **081-807-2720.** Main courses 8.50€–14€. Daily noon–3:30pm and 7:30–11:30pm (closed Tues in winter). Closed Nov–Feb.

An Acquired Taste?

Lunch and dinner in Sorrento and on the Amalfi Coast will often end with a *limoncello*, often complimentary and more often than not homemade. Almost everyone in the region has a time-honored recipe for this potent lemon liqueur.

Many diners are tempted to buy a few bottles to re-create an Amalfitana evening back home; others would rather swallow mouthwash. You'll certainly have the chance to decide for yourself.

SHOPPING

On a walk along palazzo-lined **Via San Cesareo**, Sorrento's main shopping street, you can easily stock up on all sorts of things you don't need, mostly emblazoned with the town's signature lemons. If you decide to succumb to a purchase of the town's ubiquitous *limoncello* liqueur, head out to the charming **Giardini di Cataldo,** just off Corso Italia near the train station (www.igiardinidicataldo.it; **081-878-1888**); in a fragrant lemon and orange grove you can taste and buy *limoncello*, marmalade, and other products made on the premises.

Sorrento craftspeople are known for producing the beautiful inlaid wood designs known as intarsia, as they have for centuries. You can see fine examples at the **Museobottega della Tarisalignea,** Via San Nicola 28 (www.alessandrofiorentinocollection.it), and can even order a beautiful custom-made piece of furniture if you're tempted (admission 8€; Apr–Oct daily 9:30am–1pm and 4–8pm, Nov–Mar daily 9:30am–1pm and 3–7pm). **Gargiulo & Jannuzzi**, Piazza Tasso 1 (✆ **081-8781041**), sells fine pieces with wood intarsia, and you can visit the workshops for a demonstration.

NIGHTLIFE

Epicenter of nightlife in Sorrento seems to be the lively terrace of the **Fauno Bar,** Piazza Tasso 13 (www.faunobar.it; ✆ **081-8781135**), popular for an *aperitivo* (aperitif) and people-watching throughout the day till late into the evening. The adjoining nightclub caters to a mature crowd willing to fork over the 25€ cover charge. Some popular casual bars, usually packed with an international crowd, are **Chantecler,** Via Santa Maria della Pietà 38 (www.chanteclers.com; ✆ **081-8075868**) and the **English Inn,** Corso Italia 55 (✆ **081-8074357**).

The **cloister of San Francesco,** Piazza Francesco Saverio Gargiulo, is the evocative setting for summertime concerts. Contact the tourist office (p. 567) for a schedule of events, including others staged at many restaurants and taverns in town. *Sorrento Musical* is a perennially popular revue of Neapolitan songs hosted by **Teatro Tasso,** Piazza Sant'Antonino (www.teatrotasso.com; ✆ **081-8075525**; tickets cost about 25€ depending on show; 50€ including dinner).

BEACHES

You can swim from a pebbly patch at Marina Grande or rent a beach chair at one of the beach clubs there, but for real sand, take the A bus from Piazza Tasso east to **Meta,** where the beach is often jammed with Neapolitans out for a day in the sun. A more appealing option is west of town, also reachable on the A bus from Piazza Tasso, **Bagno della Regina Giovanna** (Queen Giovanna's Bath) at Punta del Capo, the tip of the Sorrento Peninsula. Here a small rock-sheltered pool of clear water, reached on a path through citrus and olive groves, was once the private harbor of the ancient Roman Villa of Pollio Felice, the ruins of which you can visit at the top of the cliff. Just beyond, also reached by the A bus, is **Marina di Puolo,** a little fishing port where you can swim in a sheltered cove.

Positano ★★

16km (10 miles) E of Sorrento

Hugging a semi-vertical rock formation, Positano is the very essence of picturesque, an enticing collection of pastel-colored houses and majolica domes that spill down a ravine to the sea. Novelist John Steinbeck, who was much taken with Positano during a visit in 1953, described it in words that still ring true: "It is a dream place that isn't quite real when you are there and becomes beckoningly real after you have gone . . . ."

It's not surprising that in the 1960s and 70s Positano was the retreat for *la dolce vita* set. In mid-summer, its throngs of admirers can seem like an invading horde, much like those that attacked the little seaside kingdom back in the 9th to 11th centuries, when it was part of the powerful Republic of the Amalfis, rival to Venice as a sea power.

VISITOR INFORMATION The **tourist office** at Via del Saracino 4 (www. aziendaturismopositano.it; ✆ **089-875067**) is open Monday to Saturday 8:30am to 2pm, with additional hours (3:30–8pm) in July and August.

EXPLORING POSITANO

Whether you arrive by boat or bus, you're in for an uphill or downhill climb along narrow lanes and steep lanes (wear comfortable walking shoes). At some point you'll want to stay put, probably along the sea at **Marina Grande,** where the town's few fishermen still haul up their boats and ferries arrive and depart. Most of the pebbly shoreline is taken up with a beach, backed by restaurants and bars in what were once shipyards and storehouses when Positano was a naval power. From Marina Grande, **Via Positanesi d'America**, a cliffside pedestrian promenade, stretches along the shore past the cape of **Torre Trasita** and a 13th-century lookout to the smaller and slightly more relaxing beach of **Fornillo.**

If you wander up the steps from Marina Grande you'll soon find yourself amid a souk-like sprawl of shops shaded by bougainvillea-laced trellises. The majolica-domed **Collegiata di Santa Maria Assunta ★★**, Piazza Flavio Gioia (✆ **089-875480;** daily 8am–noon and 4–7pm), is Positano's main church, founded as a Benedictine monastery in the 13th century. The "Madonna Nera" (Black Madonna), a Byzantine-style icon above the altar, allegedly gave the town its name when a 12th--century pirate ship carrying the icon sailed into a violent storm. Sailors heard the Madonna on the icon saying "Posa, Posa" ("Put me down") and they took their ship to safety in what would become the harbor of Positano. A relief on the campanile outside curiously shows a wolf nursing seven fish, a clue to how the town once made its living. If you're waiting for a bus at the western bus stop (on the Sorrento side of town) step into the small **Chiesa di Nuova,** Via Chiesa Nuova, for a look at the beautiful majolica tile floor.

WHERE TO STAY

Small, guesthouse-style rooms offer a way to beat Positano's sky-high lodging prices. The tourist office has a full list of bed-and-breakfasts, home stays, and other moderately priced accommodations.

Positano.

Hotel Savoia ★★ You won't find a lot of luxurious amenities, but this hotel's great location right in the heart of Positano, steps from the beach, couples with pleasant decor—bright tile floors, comfortable beds, and attractive traditional furnishings. Some rooms have sea views, and others take in the sweep of the old town climbing the hillside. The old-fashioned ambience comes with a provenance: The D'Aiello family has been running this place since 1936, when Positano was a getaway for a select few, and that's still how they treat their guests. Via Cristoforo Colombo 73, Positano. www.savoiapositano.it. ⓒ **089-875003.** 42 units. 120€–190€ double. Rates include buffet breakfast. Parking 25€ nearby. **Amenities:** Bar; babysitting; concierge; room service; Wi-Fi (free).

La Rosa die Venti ★★ Each of the homey furnished, tile-floored rooms in this house high on a hillside in the quieter part of Positano comes with a big perk—a large planted terrace with a sea view. It's tempting to settle in and stay put here, but moving around town and the coast is easy to do: the beach at Fornillo is at the bottom of the hill, shops and restaurants are nearby, and it's an easy climb up to the bus stop on the coast road or down to the harbor. Via Fornillo 40, Positano. www.larosadeiventi.net. ⓒ **089-875252.** From 130€ double. Rates include breakfast. **Amenities:** Wi-Fi (free).

Photo Op

If you're traveling by car or taxi, just west of Positano on SS 163 keep an eye out for the renowned **Belvedere dello Schiaccone**. This is the best lookout point on the Amalfi Drive, 200m (656 ft.) above sea level. The view extends across palm and citrus groves to the archipelago of Li Galli and Capo Sottile, with the splendid Monte Sant'Angelo a Tre Pizzi in the background.

Palazzo Murat ★★ Gioacchino Murat, Napoleon's brother-in-law and king of Naples, built this enticing and vaguely exotic 18th-century baroque palace near Positano's small port as a summer getaway. It's still a retreat of royal magnitude, set amid a vast garden and orchard dripping with flowering vines and scented with lemons and jasmine. Five especially large rooms, filled with handsome antiques, are in the original palace, and others are in a new yet extremely tasteful addition, where tile floors and traditional furnishings adhere to the historical ambience. Most rooms have balconies, some with sea views, others overlooking the surrounding greenery, tile-domed church of Santa Maria Assunta, and delightful views of the town. Buffet breakfast is served in the garden in good weather.

Via dei Mulini 23, Positano. www.palazzomurat.it. ℂ **089-875177.** 31 units. 200€–450€ double. Rates include buffet breakfast. Parking 25€ nearby. Closed Jan to week before Easter. **Amenities:** Restaurant; concierge; pool; room service; Wi-Fi (free).

WHERE TO EAT

Da Adolfo ★ AMALFITAN/SEAFOOD   One of Positano's old-time favorites makes the most of its beachside location with a laidback ambience and an emphasis on fresh seafood and water views. You can venture into some local specialties here, including mozzarella *alla brace* (grilled on fresh lemon leaves) followed by a beautifully seasoned *zuppa di cozze* (mussel stew). Come for lunch and spend the afternoon, making use of the adjacent changing rooms, showers, and chair-and-umbrella rentals. Sooner or later, though, you'll have to face the 450 rugged steps that climb the hillside up to the road—better yet, take the free water-shuttle service to Marina Grande.

Via Spiaggia di Laurito 40. www.daadolfo.com. ℂ **089-875022.** Main courses 10€–18€. Daily 1–4pm. Closed mid-Oct to early May.

Il Grottino Azzurro ★ AMALFITAN/WINERY   A modest little wine cellar opening onto the street near the top of the town is a favorite with locals, who count on the kitchen for delicious renditions of simple recipes. *Manicaretti* (large ravioli) and cannelloni are filled with meat and baked with cheese and homemade tomato sauce, with extra sauce served on the side, while *spaghetti alla vongole* is piled high with sweet, tender clams from local waters. A good choice of regional wines is on hand.

Via Guglielmo Marconi 158 (SS 163). ℂ **089-875466.** Main courses 10€–16€. Thurs–Tues 12:30–3pm and 7:30–11pm (also Wed in summer).

SHOPPING

Though Positano appears to have sold its soul to the devils of commerce, the endless rows of shops are curiously unenticing. If you must spend money, consider some loungewear, a throwback to the 1970s when Moda Positano was all the rage. A holdover from those days is the excellent **Sartoria Maria Lampo,** Viale Pasitea 12 (www.marialampo. it; ℂ **089-875021**). The town is also famous for handcrafted sandals, often made while you wait. Among the best shoe makers are **D'Antonio,** Via Trara Genoino 13 (ℂ **089-811824**); **Dattilo,** Via Rampa Teglia 19 (ℂ **089-811440**); and **Safari,** Via della Taratana 2 (www.safariposi tano.com; ℂ **089-811440**).

NIGHTLIFE

You can still get a whiff of Positano's jet-set days at **Music on the Rocks,** Via Grotto dell'Incanto 51 (© **089-875874;** www.musicon therocks.it), a two-level dance club carved into the rocks above Spiaggia Grande; the upstairs terrace provides nice views and mellow piano music, while dancing is in the cavelike disco beneath. Right on the beach, **La Buca di Bacco,** Via del Brigantino 35 (© **089-811461;** www.bucapositano.it), has been Positano's prime stop for an after-dinner drink for half a century.

BEACHES

Positano has two in-town beaches, **Spiaggia Grande** and the quieter **Fornillo.** You can swim for free at both, or rent a lounger and umbrella for about 10€. To reach slightly more idyllic settings, step aboard any of the tour boats that set off from Spiaggia Grande for stops at coves along the coast, or rent a rowboat and poke along the rocky shoreline at your own pace. Should you wish to explore the coast on foot, you can follow the *Via degli Incanti* (**Trail of Charms**), a 25km (15-mile) long path between Positano and Amalfi. You'll wend your way through cultivated terraces and citrus groves, enjoying some spectacular views along the way. If you don't want to do the entire trail on one haul, you can catch the coast-road bus at any of the towns and settlements along the way.

Amalfi ★★

19km (12 miles) E of Positano

From the 9th to the 11th century, the seafaring Republic of Amalfi rivaled the great maritime powers of Genoa and Venice, and its capital, Amalfi, still enjoys some prominence today as a major resort on the Amalfi Drive. Set among terraces of lemon groves and olive trees on the slopes of the steep Lattari mountains and the Bay of Salerno, where narrow public beaches flank the harbor, Amalfi is a lovely town that, despite its popularity, doesn't seem crushed by tourism as Positano does—at least not in the early morning and evening hours after the tour buses and boats depart. With its porticos, little squares, stepped medieval streets, and green mountainsides on one side and blue sea on the other, it's a pleasant place to spend some time.

VISITOR INFORMATION The **tourist office** (www.amalfitouristoffice. it; © **089-871107**) is in Palazzo di Città, Corso delle Repubbliche Marinare 19. It's open Monday to Friday 9am to 1pm and 2 to 6pm, Saturday 9am to noon. In winter, it is only open in the morning.

EXPLORING AMALFI

Just outside the old town walls, **Piazza Flavio Gioia** opens onto the harbor: It commemorates the local navigator who some say invented the compass around 1300 (a dubious claim, since sailors were using rudimentary compasses long before then). Let's just say he might have perfected the compass for marine use, and it is bonafide fact that sailors returning to Amalfi provided material for some of the first nautical charts of the Middle Ages. They also came up with a maritime code, the Tavole Amalfitane, that was followed in the Mediterranean for centuries. This document is on view in the **Civic Museum (Museo Civico),** in Town Hall on Piazza Municipio (✆ **089-8736211;** free admission; open Mon–Fri 8am–1pm).

The medieval heart of Amalfi, characterized by covered porticos and narrow streets, stretches from

Bottles of limoncello for sale in Amalfi.

Piazza Duomo, a lovely cathedral square near the sea, into an increasingly narrow ravine. You can easily walk the length of town in ten minutes or so, following Via Amalfi from Piazza Duomo up to the **Paper Museum** (see below).

Arsenale Marinaro ★ HISTORIC SITE   In this medieval shipyard, beneath pointed arches and cross vaults resting on stone pillars, the Republic of Amalfi built galleys up to 40m (131 ft.) that enabled sailors to maintain power over the Mediterranean. Storms have erased much of the complex, but nearby a tile panel created by the artist Renato Rossi in the 1950s depicts Amalfi's commercial empire in the Middle Ages.
Via Matteo Camera (off Piazza Flavio Gioia). Free admission. Easter–Sept 9am–8pm.

Duomo ★★ CHURCH   This monument to Amalfi's rich past, covered in black-and-white facade and mosaics, sits atop a monumental staircase just inland from the sea. The **Cloister of Paradise** (Chiostro del Paradiso), to the left of the entrance, is decidedly Moorish, with a whitewashed quadrangle of interlaced arches and brightly colored geometric mosaics. Amalfi's medieval nobles are entombed in the sarcophagi littered around this exotic enclosure. The **Crypt** houses the remains of St. Andrew, Amalfi's protector saint, one of the Apostles who forsook fishing to join Christ. It was important for Amalfi to have a famous patron, just as Venice had St. Mark, so soldiers brought the remains of Andrew back from Constantinople at the end of the 4th Crusade, in 1206. A painting in the cathedral depicts his crucifixion on an X-shaped cross, and you'll also encounter him on the square below the cathedral, standing amidst a gurgling fountain.
Piazza del Duomo. Duomo: ✆ **089-871059.** Free admission. Nov–Feb daily 10am–5pm; Mar–Oct 9am–9pm. Museum and cloister: ✆ **089-871324.** Free admission.

Museo della Carta (Museum of Paper) ★ MUSEUM Among the many goods Amalfi's sailors and merchants brought back from their voyages was paper, a popular commodity throughout the Middle East that Arab traders had come across in China. From the 13th through the mid-19th century, Amalfi was one of Europe's largest exporters of paper, produced in factories whose ruins now litter the Valle dei Mulini at the inland end of town, where water wheels powered machines that beat linen, cotton, and hemp into paper. In the remains of a once-thriving enterprise, a guide shows off vintage machinery and the product that is still sold in Amalfi shops. Neighboring factories are evocative ruins that you can view from a path through the Valle dei Mulini.

Palazzo Pagliara, Via delle Cartiere 24. ℂ **089-8304561.** www.museodellacarta.it. Admission 4€. Nov–Mar Tues–Sun 10am–3pm; Apr–Nov daily 10am–6:30pm.

WHERE TO STAY

Hotel Lidomare ★ One of Amalfi's few bargains is set on a small square just beyond the main street fray, and provides a lot of pleasant, old-fashioned ambience in a 13th-century palazzo. Some of the enormous, high-ceilinged, tile-floored guest rooms have sea views, and all are furnished with a scattering of antiques and comfy old furnishings. Amalfi's beach is just steps away.

Largo Piccolomini 9. ℂ **089-871332.** 15 units. 103€–145€ double. Rates include continental breakfast. Parking 18€. **Amenities:** Wi-Fi (free).

Hotel Santa Caterina ★★★ One of the world's great getaways provides a stay of a lifetime while making guests feel right at home. Its comfortable yet unpretentious rooms and suites are tucked into gardens and citrus groves hovering above the water. Colorful Vietri tiles and handsome antiques add notes of elegance, while balconies and terraces make the most of the cliffside location. Glassed-in elevators and a winding garden path descend to a private beach and saltwater swimming pool, and memorable meals are served in a vine-covered, glassed-in dining room and on a seaside terrace in good weather. Several private bungalows with private pools tucked into citrus groves provide the ultimate getaway.

Via Nazionale 9. www.hotelsantacaterina.it. ℂ **089-871012.** 49 units. 420€–790€ double. Rates include lavish buffet breakfast. Parking 15€. Closed Nov–Mar. **Amenities:** 2 restaurants; bar; beach; concierge; gym; pool; room service; spa; Wi-Fi (free).

Residenza Luce ★★★ These lovely rooms near the town center are at the top of the list for an affordable stay in Amalfi. Half of the beautifully decorated, tile-floored units are bi-level, with sleeping lofts tucked above living areas; many have balconies and all have large windows overlooking medieval lanes and squares. A sunny rooftop breakfast room overlooks the surrounding hills, while the beach and port are just steps away.

Via Fra Gerardo Sasso. www.residenzaluce.it. ℂ **089-871537.** 8 units. 90€–140€ double. Rates include buffet breakfast. **Amenities:** Wi-Fi (free).

The Eerie Emerald Grotto

The millennia-old Emerald Grotto (Grotta di Smeraldo) gives Capri's Blue Grotto (p. 585) a run for its money. This chamber of stalactites and stalagmites, some underwater, produces transcendent light effects. The ceramic nativity scene is artificial, added in the 1950s and making a trip through the grotto a popular Christmastime pilgrimage. The only way to get into the grotto is by boat from Amalfi's docks (10€ roundtrip); you'll transfer to a small rowboat for a leisurely glide through the grotto. You can visit daily 9am to 4pm, provided that the seas are calm enough not to bash boats to bits.

WHERE TO EAT

Da Gemma ★ SEAFOOD/AMALFITAN   Amalfi's old-time classic, in warm-hued rooms tucked behind the cathedral and in the hands of the Grimaldi family for several generations, holds high standards for the seafood it serves to a loyal and discerning clientele. The house *zuppa di pesce* is a meal in itself, prepared only for two, and equally memorable is a special pasta, *paccheri all'acquapazza,* made with shrimp and monkfish. The dessert of choice is *crostata* (pie with jam), made with pine nuts and homemade marmalades of lemon, orange, and tangerine. Reservations, especially on weekends, are a must.

Via Frà Gerardo Sasso 11. www.trattoriadagemma.com. ⓒ **089-871345.** Main courses 16€–26€. Daily 12:30–2:45pm and 7:30–11pm (closed Wed Nov to mid-Apr). Closed 6 weeks Jan to early Mar.

L'Abside ★★ SEAFOOD/AMALFITAN   If this charming small place were more formal you could call it a temple of gastronomy, as it occupies part of a former church. As is, the delightful, white-washed and arched room adds even more charm to a delicious meal (also served on a terrace out front in good weather). Seafood and vegetables are so fresh that even a simple bruschetta with anchovies is memorable, and a bounty of sea creatures also make a showing atop several homemade pastas and in garden fresh salads.

Piazza dei Dogi. www.ristorantelabside.it. ⓒ **089-873586.** Main courses 9€–20€. Daily 12:30–2:45pm and 7:30–11pm.

Ristorante Al Mare ★ PIZZA/AMALFITAN   The bamboo-roofed, al fresco dining terrace at the Santa Caterina Hotel (see above) is an alluring spot for a seaside lunch. The menu offers a nice choice of pizzas, grilled fish, and pastas that include the hotel specialty, *tagilolini limone,* homemade noodles with a lemon cream sauce. All dishes come with a big dash of informal glamor.

Via Nazionale 9. www.hotelsantacaterina.it. ⓒ **089-871012.** Main courses 20€–35€, pizzas from 20€. May–Oct daily 12:30–3:30pm.

BEACHES

Amalfi's beaches are two pebbly strips on either side of the harbor. For a large stretch of sand, take the footpath to **Atrani**, a pretty village that's an easy 15-minute stroll eastward. Leaving town, follow the sidewalk along the main road until you come to a staircase (signposted for Atrani) up to a path that is really a series of alleyways between hillside houses; it soon drops down to the sea again.

Ravello ★★★

7km (4 miles) N of Amalfi

Clinging to a mountainside overlooking the sea, Ravello can seem like a world removed from the clamor down on the coast. This sense of escape, along with views and some of the world's most splendid gardens, has long made this aerie 1,000 feet above the coast a refuge for the rich and famous. Its eclectic group of admirers includes Richard Wagner, D.H. Lawrence, Greta Garbo, and Gore Vidal. Like they did, you'll come up here not to do too much but stroll in the gardens, gaze up and down the coastline, and maybe relax for a few days in one of many villas converted into luxury hotels.

VISITOR INFORMATION   Ravello's **tourist office,** Via Roma 18 (www.ravellotime.it), is open daily from 9am to 7pm; November to May it closes at 6pm.

EXPLORING RAVELLO

The heart of town is **Piazza del Vescovado,** a terrace overlooking the valley of the Dragone, and the adjacent **Piazza del Duomo**. Climb up steep, stepped Via Richard Wagner (behind the tourist office) to reach **Via San Giovanni del Toro**, which is lined with some of Ravello's grandest medieval palaces, built as hilltop retreats for wealthy merchant families of the Amalfi Republic and now housing some of Italy's most distinguished hotels.

Villa Cimbrone ★ The eccentric Englishman Lord Grimthorpe (who also designed London's Big Ben) redid this grand 14th-century villa in 1904. The lavish salons and gardens soon became associated with the 20th-century elite, few more elusive than Greta Garbo, who hid out here in 1937 with her lover, the conductor Leopold Stokowski. The high point of the lavish gardens, quite

Wine Tasting

The wines produced in the harsh, hot landscapes of Campania seem stronger, rougher, and, in many cases, more powerful than those grown in gentler climes. You'll encounter them in shops and restaurant tables. Ones to try are Lacryma Christi (Tears of Christ), a white that grows in the volcanic soil near Naples, Herculaneum, and Pompeii; Taurasi, a potent red; and Greco di Tufo, a pungent white laden with the odors of apricots and apples.

literally, is the **Belvedere Cimbrone,** where you'll have the dizzying sensation of being suspended between sea and sky.

Via Santa Chiara 26. www.villacimbrone.it. ℰ **089-857459,** for hotel reservations. Admission 6€ adults, 4€ children. Daily 9am–sunset. Last admission 30 min before close.

Villa Rufolo ★★ The 14th-century poet Boccaccio was so moved by this onetime residence of kings and popes that he included it as background in one of his tales. The most famous visitor to the Moorish-influenced palace was Richard Wagner, who composed an act of *Parsifal* here and used the surroundings for his *Garden of Klingsor*. Paths wind through flower gardens to lookout points high above the coastline.

Piazza Duomo. www.villarufolo.it. ℰ **089-857621.** Admission 5€. Summer daily 9am–8pm; winter daily 9am–sunset. Last admission 15 min earlier.

WHERE TO STAY & EAT

Cumpa' Cosimo ★ AMALFITAN Netta Bottone runs the restaurant her family started back in 1929, serving generous portions of pastas (including an extravaganza with seven pastas topped with seven different sauces) and big platters of *frittura di pesce* (fish fry) and some very well done lamb and veal dishes. Artichokes and other vegetables are right out of the nearby garden plots. Whatever you order, Netta herself may well serve it with a flourish and a kiss on the cheek.

Via Roma 44. ℰ **089-857156.** Main courses 11€–18€; pizza 6€–10€. Daily 12:30–3pm and 7:30–11pm. Closed Mon Nov–Feb.

Palazzo Avino ★★★ A 12th-century patrician palace strikes just the right balance between comfort and opulence, with enough antiques, Vietri ceramic floors, and fine linens to satisfy the most discerning guests. Especially winning are the views that, making the most of Ravello's aerielike position, extend for miles up and down the coast. They're enjoyed through the huge windows in just about every room, on the rooftop terrace with two Jacuzzis, and from the sumptuous gardens and pool that cascade partway down the cliff, and from the hotel's formal restaurant, the double-Michelin-starred **Rossellinis.** Open for dinner only, Rossellinis serves such sublime creations as ravioli stuffed with squid, and cod in an olive crust, which pair with local wines for a memorable, if not inexpensive, evening. A free shuttle takes guests down to the **Clubhouse by the Sea** (open May–Sept), the hotel's beach club where there is a small outdoor pool, a waterside terrace with lounge chairs and umbrellas, and a **casual restaurant.**

Via San Giovanni del Toro 28, Ravello. www.palazzoavino.com. ℰ **089-818181.** 44 units. 350€–710€ double. Rates include lavish buffet breakfast. Parking 34€. Closed mid-Oct to Mar. **Amenities:** Restaurant, bar; concierge; gym; Jacuzzi; pool; room service; spa; Wi-Fi (free).

CAPRI ★★★

5km (3 miles) off the tip of the Sorrentine peninsula

Rugged, mountainous Capri (pronounced *Cap*-ry, not Ca-*pree*), lying just off the tip of the Sorrentine Peninsula, has beguiled the ancient Greeks, Roman emperors, and legions of modern visitors. VIPs, millionaires, and just plain folks delight in the spectacular scenery and impossibly azure seas that surround the rugged coasts. Most visitors come on day trips from Naples and Sorrento, but the longer you stay, the more charms this enchanting beauty reveals. Ah, but be forewarned—you might well find the island to be a charmless tourist trap. If you're visiting on a summertime daytrip and disembark any time between 10am and 5pm your impressions will probably only be of crowds and long lines—you might wait hours to get on the bus or funicular up to Capri town from the port, hours to get on the chair lift from Anacapri up Monte Solaro, hours to board a boat to be rowed through the Grotto Azzurra. To avoid the greatest crush, arrive as early as you can or plan on staying late or staying over. Actually, to enjoy the island at its best, you might want to forgo a summertime visit altogether and visit in the spring or early fall.

Essentials

GETTING THERE   You can easily reach Capri from either Naples or Sorrento, and in summer there's also service from Amalfi and Positano. From Naples's Molo Beverello dock (take a taxi from the train station), the **hydrofoil** (*aliscafo*) takes just 45 minutes and departs several times daily (some stop at Sorrento); a one-way trip costs 19€. Regularly scheduled **ferry** (*traghetto*) service, departing from Porta di Massa, is cheaper but takes longer (about 1½ hr.; 17€ each way). Contact **Caremar** (www. caremar.it; ℭ **199-116655**) for ferry schedule; for hydrofoils, try **SNAV** (www.snav.it; ℭ **081-4285555**).

From Sorrento, go to the dock at Marina Piccola (just below Piazza Tasso), where you can board one of the **fast ferries** (*nave veloce*) run by Caremar or a hydrofoil run by **Gescab** (www.gescab.it; ℭ **081-8781430**). The hydrofoils are slightly faster (trip time is 20 min., compared to 25 min.) and cost 15€ one-way; a one-way ticket for the fast ferry is 13€. Departures are 11 times per day from 7:15am to 7:15pm (the last boat back leaves Capri at 6:30pm).

Gescab (ℭ **081-811986**) also runs a service between Amalfi and Positano and Capri from April through October. Hydrofoils cost 18€ oneway, and a ferry ticket goes for 16€ one-way.

GETTING AROUND   The island is serviced by funiculars, taxis, and buses. From the ferry dock in Marina Grande, take the funicular or a bus to **Capri Town** (1.80€ for either, buy tickets at the office near the funicular terminal, from newsstands or tobacco shops, or from the driver). Buses also run **between Capri and Anacapri** about every 15 minutes

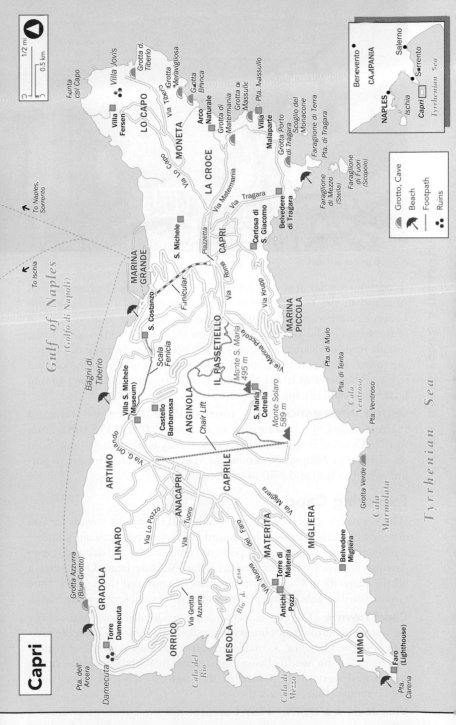

Capri

Gulf of Naples
(Golfo di Napoli)

To Ischia

To Naples, Sorrento

To Naples, Sorrento

Bagni di Tiberio

MARINA GRANDE

S. Costanzo

Scala Fenicia

Villa S. Michele (Museum)

Castello Barbarossa

ANGINOLA

Chair Lift

IL PASSETIELLO

Monte S. Maria 495 m

S. Maria Cetrella

Monte Solaro 589 m

ARTIMO

LINARO

GRADOLA

Grotta Azzurra (Blue Grotto)

Damecuta

Torre Damecuta

Pta. dell' Arcera

Via G. Orlandi

Via Lo Pozzo

Via Tuoro

ANACAPRI

CAPRILE

Via Grotta Azzurra

ORRICO

MESOLA

Rio d. Cessa

Via Nuova

MATERITA

Torre di Materita

Antichi Pozzi

MIGLIERA

Belvedere Migliera

Via Migliera

Grotta Verde

Cala Marmolata

Cala del Rio

Cala di Mezzo

LIMMO

Faro (Lighthouse)

Pta. Carena

S. Michele

Piazzetta

Funicular

CAPRI

Certosa di S. Giacomo

Via Roma

Via Tragara

Via Krupp

Via Matermania

LA CROCE

MONETA

LO CAPO

Punta del Capo

Villa Jovis

Grotta d. Tiberio

Villa Fersen

Via Lo Capo

Grotta Meravigliosa

Grotta Bianca

Arco Naturale

Grotta di Matermania

Grotta di Massullo

Pta. Massullo

Villa Malaparte

Grotta Porto di Tragara

Scoglio del Monacone

Faraglione di Terra

Pta. di Tragara

Belvedere di Tragara

Faraglione di Mezzo (Stella)

Faraglione di Fuori (Scopolo)

Via Marina Piccola

MARINA PICCOLA

Pta. di Mulo

Pta. di Terita

Cala Ventroso

Pta. Ventroso

Tyrrhenian Sea

Tyrrhenian Sea

Legend

🐚 Grotto, Cave

☂ Beach

••••• Footpath

•• Ruins

Inset map

NAPLES

CAMPANIA

Berevento

Salerno

Sorrento

Ischia

Capri

Tyrrhenian Sea

1/2 mi

0.5 km

A hilltop garden on Capri.

throughout the day. If you wish to explore farther, there's a chair lift from Anacapri to the top of **Monte Solaro** (see below), and buses run between Anacapri and the **Faro** (lighthouse) at the far southwestern tip of the island or the **Grotto Azzurra**, on the northwestern coast. Taxis, usually readily available and eager at the port and at taxi stands outside the towns) are expensive (about 15€ for the short ride from the port up to Capri) but are a welcome alternative when you encounter long lines to board buses and the funicular.

VISITOR INFORMATION   The **tourist office** is in Capri town on Piazzetta Italo Cerio (www.capritourism.com; ℰ **081-8375308**). From April to October, it's open Monday to Saturday 8:30am to 8:30pm, Sunday 8:30am to 2:30pm; November to March, hours are Monday to Saturday 9am to 1pm and 3:30 to 6:30pm.

Exploring Capri

Whether or not Capri's beauty will transcend the tourist crowds for you depends on your tolerance levels and when you come. Avoid summer weekends especially, when Neopolitans come over for the day and Italian daytrippers come from as far away as Rome. And take heart: Once you get off the Piazzetta in Capri Town and have been rowed through the Blue Grotto, you'll be able to find plenty of almost-tranquil spots on the island.

Capri Town ★ TOWN   Capri's mountainside main town is an enticing warren of narrow lanes lined with walled villa gardens. Town life radiates from the Piazzetta, a small square that at times is so full of visitors that it's called the "world's living room." From there the old town's narrow streets lead west to the **Giardini di Augusto,** terraced pine-shaded public gardens that overlook the sea.

Villa Jovis ★★ RUIN   From Capri Town, a stroll of about 2.4km (1½ miles) ends with a steep climb to the northeastern tip of the island and the most sumptuous and best-preserved of the 12 villas built by Roman emperors. Tiberius spent the final years of his reign here and installed elaborate baths, forcing his architects to devise an ingenious system of canals and cisterns to collect rainwater. The covered Loggia Imperiale follows the cliff edge to the Salto di Tiberio, a 330m-high (1,083-ft.) precipice from which Tiberius allegedly used to hurl those who did not please him. The views are stunning. Admission is 2€ and it is open daily 9am until sunset (the ticket booth closes 1 hr. before sunset).

Marina Piccola ★ BEACH   The island's largest beach, on the southern shore, provides views of the **Faraglioni,** three rock stacks that jut out of the sea. The outermost rock is home to a particular type of bright blue lizard that is found nowhere else on the planet. The beach is nothing much, just a pebbly strip, but the water is clean and crystal clear.

Blue Grotto (Grotta Azzurra) ★★ NATURAL WONDER   Italy's tourist trap extraordinaire can be beguiling, despite all the hassle it entails—the frenzy of climbing off a motorboat into a small rowboat, lying back, squeezing through a narrow opening, and being rowed out again just as you beginning to enjoy the experience. The magical colors of the water and walls of this huge grotto are extraordinary, even more so than they appear in countless photographs. Little wonder postcard writers have rhapsodized about it since it became part of the tourist circuit in the 19th century. (Actually, a small, ancient Roman dock suggests this outlet of a vast system of shoreline caverns was known long before then.) It's open daily 9am to 1 hour before sunset. In summer, boats leave frequently from the harbor at Marina Grande, transporting passengers to the grotto's entrance for 17€ roundtrip (and that includes the fee for the rowboat that takes you inside). If you get to the entrance to the Blue Grotto under your own steam (via bus from Anacapri), you'll still pay 13.50€ to be rowed in. The boat trip out from Marina Grande is well worth the few extra euros, as it delivers sea-level views of the island's spectacular cliffs.

Anacapri ★★ TOWN   Capri's second town, perched on heights surrounded by vineyards, is a pleasant place where, once away from the main square, island life transpires somewhat independently of visitors. The **Church of San Michele** is delightfully colorful, made so by a **majolica floor** picturing Adam and Eve's expulsion from the Garden of Eden, accompanied by a unicorn, a goat, and other unlikely creatures (admission 2€; Apr–Oct daily 9am–7pm, Nov–Mar 10am–2pm; closed the first 2 weeks of Dec). **Villa San Michele** was the home of Swedish doctor and writer Axel Munthe, who built this house in the 19th century on the ruins of one of Tiberius's villas. The gardens are lovely, with peaceful, flower-lined paths that lead to a terrace with panoramic views (www.sanmichele.eu; ✆ **081-8371401;** admission 6€; Nov–Feb 9am–3:30pm, Mar 9am–4:30pm, Apr and Oct 9am–5pm, May–Sept 9am–6pm). The chairlift **Seggiovia Monte Solaro** (✆ **081-8371428**) departs from Via Caposcuro and whisks you to the top of **Monte Solaro,** Capri's highest peak, in 12

Take a Hike

Following the trails along Capri's cliffs allows you to soak in the island's beauty and get away from the crowds. The *Scala Fenicia* (Phoenician Staircase) descends—or climbs, depending on which way you go—from **Anacapri to Capri**. The steep path (with no authenticated connection to the ancient peoples of its name) is basically a long staircase with 881 steps—and many superb views. Another good hike is the descent from **Monte Solaro** (p. 585), on a clearly marked dirt path, after you've taken the chairlift ride to the top. Stop by the tourist office (p. 584) to pick up a map of the paths.

minutes. Tickets cost 7€ one-way, 9€ round-trip, free for children 8 and under; lifts run March through October 9:30am to 4:30pm.

Where to Eat & Stay

Grottelle ★ CAPRESE   On the panoramic terrace, a simple meal of *zuppa di fagioli* (bean soup) and *spaghetti con pomodoro e basilica* (with fresh tomatoes and basil) comes with a view of the Arco Naturale, a wonder, wave-buffeted formation in the surf far below. To find this delightful spot, wander through the little lanes east of the Piazzetta.

Via Arco Naturale 13, Capri. ✆ **081-8375719.** Main courses 15€–30€. Fri–Wed noon–3pm and 7–11pm. Closed Nov–Mar.

Pulalli Wine Bar ★★ CAMPANIAN   To find a hideaway in the jam-packed Piazzetta just look up, to this little terrace next to the clock tower. A bird's-eye view comes with wine, a selection of cheeses, or a meal—the *risotto al limone* (lemon-flavored risotto) is specially transporting in this magical setting.

Piazza Umberto I 4, Capri. ✆ **081-8374108.** Main courses 10€–25€. Wed–Mon noon–3pm and 7pm–midnight. Closed Nov to just before Easter.

Capri Palace ★★★   If you find it hard to leave the island, a perfect place to give into temptation is this delightful getaway in Anacapri on the slopes of Monte Solaro. Everything here seems geared to soothing relaxation: An expanse of green lawn surrounds the swimming pool, lounges are quiet oases with contemporary flair, and guest rooms are done in restful creams with rose-colored tile floors and white linens and upholstery. Some suites have private pools, and some rooms look across the sea all the way to Vesuvius, but even the quiet outlooks over the green flanks of Monte Solaro are relaxing. A shuttle bus runs to the port, Capri Town, and a delightful beach club where platforms make it easy to dip into the Mediterranean.

Via Capodimonte 2, Anacapri. www.capri-palace.com. ✆ **081-9780111.** 79 units. 340€–1,250€ double. Rates include buffet breakfast. Closed Oct 17–Mar 31. No children under 10 accepted June–Aug. **Amenities:** 2 restaurants; bar; beach club; heated pool; room service; spa; Wi-Fi (free).

SICILY

13

S icily has been conquered, settled, and abandoned by dozens of civilizations, from the Phoenicians, Greeks, and Carthaginians in antiquity, to the Arabs, Berbers, Moors, and Normans in the Middle Ages, to the Spanish and Bourbons in the Renaissance, and finally, finally the (at least nominally) Italian modern era. It's an intricate and violent story that nonetheless left a fascinating legacy. Touring the relics of Sicily's tumultuous past can sometimes make you feel that you're visiting several different countries at once.

At 25,708 sq. km (9,926 sq. miles), Sicily is not only the largest island in the Mediterranean but also the largest region in Italy. This triangle-shaped land is home to the first known parliament in the western world (Palermo), the oldest continental tree (Sant'Alfio, near Catania), the highest and most active volcano in Europe (Mount Etna), and the most extensive archaeological park (Selinunte).

Though it's only separated from the mainland by the 4km-wide (2½ miles) Stretto di Messina, Sicily has a palpable, captivating sense of otherness. Some Sicilians will refer to a trip to the mainland as "going to Italy." The island offers the full package of Italian travel experiences: evocative towns, compelling art, impressive architecture, and ruins older than anything in Rome. Alongside the jewels of Sicily's glorious Classical past (Agrigento, Siracusa, Segesta, Tindari, Morgantina, Piazza Armerina) you'll see unique baroque cities rebuilt after devastating earthquakes (Catania, Noto, Scicli, Ragusa, and Modica)—and, sadly, also hideous postwar concrete monsters (Palermo, Catania, Messina, Agrigento).

The island's geographic palette goes from the sere, chalky southeast to the brooding slopes of Mt. Etna to the brawny headlands of Palermo and the gentle, agricultural landscapes of the east—all surrounded by cobalt seas and beaches where you can swim from May to October. The colors and natural contrasts are shaped by the elements like nowhere else on Earth; African and Alpine fauna live spectacularly on the same island.

Then, of course, too, there are the Sicilians themselves: The descendants of Greek, Carthaginian, Roman Vandal, Arab, Norman, and Spanish conquerors. They can be welcoming yet suspicious, taciturn and at the same time garrulous, deeply tied to traditions yet always yearning to break away from distasteful precedents. True to stereotypes, Sicilians are a passionate people, and their warmth can make even everyday transactions memorable.

PREVIOUS PAGE: Il Agrigento at sunset.

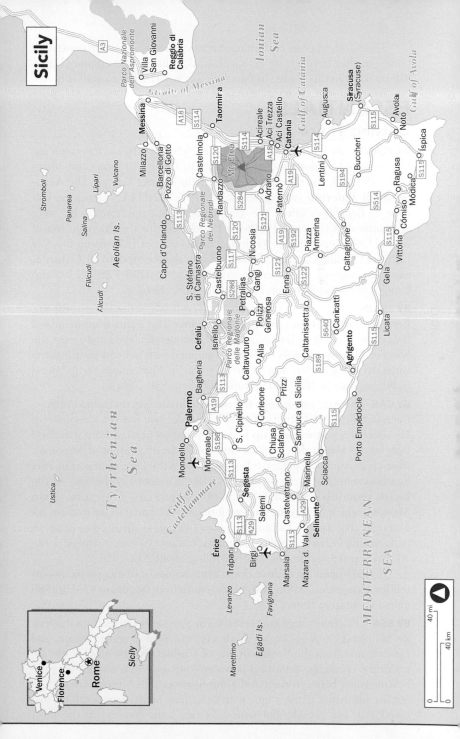

Thousands of years of domination may have created stark contradictions, but they have left an archaeological, cultural, and culinary legacy like no other in this world. In Goethe's words, "The key to it all is here."

ESSENTIALS
Getting There

BY PLANE   By far the easiest way to reach Sicily is by air. Palermo's airport is served by dozens of daily flights to Rome (50 min.) and Milan (1 hr., 15 min.), and nonstops to airports throughout Europe. The **Aeroporto di Palermo** (www.gesap.it; © **091-7020111**), known as Falcone e Borsellino (after the two anti-Mafia magistrates who were assassinated in the early 1990s) or Punta Raisi for the dramatic spit of coastal land it occupies, is 31km (19 miles) west of Palermo on the A29 highway. Outside Catania in eastern Sicily, the **Aeroporto di Catania,** aka Fontanarossa (www.aeroporto.catania.it; © **095-7239111**), also handles domestic flights and European connections.

BY TRAIN   Trains to Sicily are operated by Italy's national rail company, **Ferrovie dello Stato** (www.trenitalia.com). The trains from mainland Italy come down from Rome and Naples through Calabria and across the Strait of Messina to Sicily on ferries equipped with railroad tracks on the cargo deck. It's a novel way to arrive in Sicily. Many more Sicily-bound trains originate in Naples (trip time to Palermo: 9–10 hr.).

BY CAR   Yes, you can drive to the island of Sicily. No, there's no bridge—the much-discussed Straits of Messina bridge has not yet materialized. However, the northeastern tip of Sicily is only separated from mainland Italy by the 5km-wide (3-miles) Stretto di Messina (Strait of Messina), which is crossed by regular car ferries between the Calabrian port of Villa San Giovanni (just north of Reggio Calabria, essentially the "toe" of the Italian peninsula's boot shape) and the Sicilian city of Messina. From Messina, which lies on the well-maintained A20 and A18 autostrade, it's a straight shot west to Palermo (233km/145 miles; about 2 hr.) or south to Taormina (52km/32 miles; 45 min.), Catania (97km/60 miles; 1 hr., 15 min.), and Siracusa (162km/100 miles; about 2 hr.).

If you're planning to drive down from Naples or Rome, prepare yourself for a long ride: 721km (448 miles) south from Naples or 934km (580 miles) south from Rome.

BY SEA   Palermo's large port is served by passenger ferries from the Italian mainland cities of Naples, Civitavecchia (near Rome), Livorno, and Genova, and from the Sardinian city of Cagliari. Nearly all of these are nighttime crossings, departing between 7pm and 9pm and arriving the next morning between 6am and 8am. Some of these ferries are tricked out like miniature cruise ships, with swimming pools, beauty salons, discos, gyms, and presidential suites. Ferries from Naples are the most numerous, operating daily year-round. The Naples-Palermo route is run by **SNAV** (www.snav.it; ✆ **081-4285555**) and **Tirrenia Lines** (www.tirrenia.it; ✆ **892123** or 02-26302803). With either company, the ferry trip takes 11 hours, although there is also a faster, more expensive daytime hydrofoil service that takes 6 hours (summer only). From Civitavecchia, which is the port that cruise ships use when visiting Rome, **Grandi Navi Veloci** (www.gnv.it; ✆ **010-2094591**) has ferries to Palermo that depart at 8pm, arriving in Palermo the next morning at 8am. Schedules vary depending on weather conditions, so always call on the day of departure even if you've already confirmed your reservation the day before.

Getting Around

Sicilian roads, as in the rest of Italy, are generally signposted well. Before taking the wheel acquire a good road map *(carta stradale),* such as that published by Touring Editore, available at newsstands and bookshops.

Bus travel in Sicily is excellent, with good connections between most cities. Buses are clean and modern, with comfortable upholstered seats, air-conditioning, and smooth suspensions. The main bus companies in Sicily are **Interbus** (www.interbus.it; ✆ **091-6167919;** also goes by the names **Etna Trasporti, Segesta,** and **Sicilbus,** depending on which part of Sicily you're in), and **Cuffaro** (www.cuffaro.info; ✆ **091-6161510**), which operates buses between Palermo and Agrigento.

Passenger rail service on the island is generally spotty and slow, with limited routes and antiquated, dirty coaches. The bus is almost always a better option everywhere except along the north coast between Palermo and Messina.

TAORMINA ★★★

53km (33 miles) N of Catania, 53km (33 miles) S of Messina, 250km (155 miles) E of Palermo

Guy de Maupassant, the 19th-century French short-story writer, played the tourist shill and wrote, "Should you only have one day to spend in Sicily and you ask me 'what is there to see?' I would reply 'Taormina' without any hesitation. It is only a landscape but one in which you can find everything that seems to have been created to seduce the eyes, the mind and the imagination." Lots of visitors have felt the same way. The Roman poet Ovid loved Taormina, and 18th-century German man of letters Wolfgang Goethe put the town on the Grand Tour circuit when he extolled its virtues in his widely published diaries. Oscar Wilde was one of the gentlemen who made Taormina, as writer and dilettante Harold Acton put it, "a polite synonym for Sodom," and Greta Garbo is one of many film legends who have sought a bit of privacy here.

It could be said that with its beauty and sophistication Taormina has a surfeit of star quality itself. The town often seems more international than Sicilian and has so many admirers that visitors often outnumber locals. Then again, perched precariously on a steep cliff halfway between the sinister slopes of Mount Etna and the glittering Ionian Sea, its captivating alleyways lined with churches and *palazzi,* Taormina is almost over-the-top beautiful, and what could be more Sicilian than that?

Essentials

GETTING THERE Taormina is well served by buses, most of which connect through Catania. From Catania's Fontanarossa airport, there are nine Taormina-bound buses per day, stopping in downtown Catania before heading up the coast to Taormina. Travel time by bus from Catania to Taormina is about 1½ hours; tickets are about 5€ one-way. Full schedules are available from **Interbus** (www.etnatrasporti.it). Taormina's bus station is on Via Pirandello, near Porta Messina, on the north end of town.

If you're arriving by **car** from Messina, head south along A18, following signs for Catania. From Catania, take the A18 north, toward Messina. Exit the autostrada at the Taormina exit, which lies just north of a series of highway tunnels. Find out if your hotel has parking and if there's a fee, and get very clear instructions about how to arrive—Taormina is a mind-boggling maze of tiny one-way streets and hairpin turns. Otherwise, take advantage of the large public **parking garages** just outside the old town, both clearly signposted with blue "P"s on all roads that approach Taormina. On the north side of town, **Parking Lumbi** (ⓒ 0942-24345) charges 14€ per day (16€ per day in Aug) and has a free shuttle from the garage to the Porta Messina gate of Taormina proper. On the south end of town, **Parking Porta Catania** (ⓒ 0942-620196) is another multilevel garage with slightly higher rates than Lumbi (15€ per day, 17€ per day in Aug) but with the advantage of being practically in town (it's just 100m/328 ft. from the Porta Catania city gate). Down by the beach at Mazzarò, in the vicinity of the lower cablecar station, is **Parking Mazzarò** (14€ per day, 16€ in Aug).

It's also possible to take the **train** to Taormina, on a line between Messina and Catania, each between 40 minutes and 1½ hours away, depending on the speed of your train. See www.trenitalia.com for complete schedules. Keep in mind that Taormina's train station, which is shared with the seaside town of Giardini-Naxos, lies down the hill from town, 1.6km (1 mile) away. From the station, you have to take a bus up the hill to Taormina proper (9am–9pm, every 15–45 min.; 2€ one-way), or a taxi (about 15€).

VISITOR INFORMATION The **tourist office** is in Palazzo Corvaja, Piazza Santa Caterina (ⓒ **0942-23243** or 0942-24941; Mon–Thurs 8:30am–2pm and 4–7pm, and Fri 8:30am–2pm). Here you can get a free map, hotel listings, bus and rail timetables, and a schedule of summer cultural events staged at the **Teatro Greco** (Greek Theater; see p. 604).

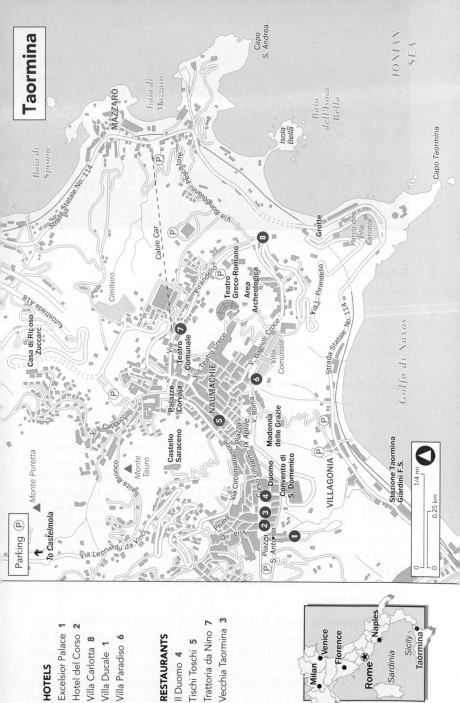

Taormina

HOTELS

Excelsior Palace **1**
Hotel del Corso **2**
Villa Carlotta **8**
Villa Ducale **1**
Villa Paradiso **6**

RESTAURANTS

Il Duomo **4**
Tischi Toschi **5**
Trattoria da Nino **7**
Vecchia Taormina **3**

Parking ⓟ

← To Castelmola

▲ Monte Puretta

Baia di Spisone

MAZZARO

Isola di Mazzaro

Strada Statale No. 114

Autostrada A18

Casa di Riposo Zuccaro

Cimitero

Cable Car

Via Bonifacini Pescaia

Capo S. Andrea

IONIAN SEA

Baia dell'Isola Bella

Isola Bella

Capo Taormina

Pirandello

Via Teatro Greco
Via Teatro Comunale
Palazzo Corvaja
NAUMACHIE

Teatro Greco-Romano
Area Archeologica

V. Bagnoli Croce
Villa Comunale

⑦ ⑥ ⑤

Castello Saraceno

Monte Tauro

Salita Branco

Via Cappuccini

Via Circonvallaz.

Corso Umberto IX Aprile

Piazza IX Aprile

Madonna delle Grazie

Convento di S. Domenico

V. Roma

Duomo ④ ③ ②

Piazza S. Antonio ⓟ

Via D. Primo

Via Leonardo da Vinci

Via L. Pirandello

Grotte

Parco di Villa Caronia

VILLAGONIA

Strada Statale No. 114

Golfo di Naxos

Stazione Taormina
Giardini F.S.

① ⑧

0   1/4 mi
0   0.25 km

Milan
Venice
Florence
Rome ✴
Naples
Sardinia
Sicily
Taormina

593

The resort town of Taormina.

Exploring Taormina

Just about everything to see in Taormina unfolds from the main pedestrian drag, **Corso Umberto I**, which slices through town from Porta Messina, in the north, to Porta Catania, in the south. It only takes about 10 minutes to walk the length of the Corso. Taormina is also a handy base for day trips to Mount Etna—the high-altitude visitor areas are only about 1 hour away by car.

Teatro Greco (Teatro Antico) ★★★ RUINS   With their penchant for building in beautiful settings, the Greeks perched the second-largest ancient theater in Sicily, after the one in Siracusa, on the rocky flanks of Mount Tauro. The backdrop of smoldering Mount Etna and the sea crashing far below certainly provided as much drama as any theatrical production. Romans rebuilt much of the theater, adding the finishing touches on what we see today in the 2nd century A.D., and put the arena to use for gladiatorial events. In ruin, but with much of the hillside *cavea*, or curved seating area, intact, the theater is still the setting for performances and film screenings, greatly enhanced by columns and arches framing the sea and volcano in the background. Check with TaorminaArte's headquarters, Corso Umberto 19 (www.taoarte.it; ✆ **0942-21142**), or at the tourist office for exact dates and show times.

Via del Teatro Greco. ✆ **0942-21142.** Admission 8€. Apr–Sept daily 9am–7pm; Oct–Mar daily 9am–4pm.

Villa Comunale ★★★ PARK/GARDEN   Of all the colorful characters who have spent time in Taormina, the one leaving the biggest mark may have been Lady Florence Trevelyan, who in the late 19th century created these beautiful gardens, now the city park also known as Parco Duca di Cesarò. Lady Trevelyan allegedly was asked to leave Britain after an entanglement with Edward, Prince of Wales, son of Queen Victoria. She settled in Taormina, married, and lived quite happily in the lovely, adjacent villa that is now the hotel Villa Paradiso (see below). Her liaison with a farmer, much of it conducted amid these groves and terraces, supposedly inspired D.H. Lawrence's "Lady Chatterley's Lover." Lady Trevelyan built the stone and brick pavilions in the park for bird watching and entertaining—it's too bad the gates are swung shut at sunset, because these fanciful follies would be perfect for whiling away a hot summer night. During the day, the 3 hectares (7½ acres) of beautifully groomed terraces provide a nice respite from the busy town, filled as they are with luxuriant Mediterranean vegetation, cobblestone walkways, picturesque stone stairways, and a sinuous path lining the park's eastern rim with superb views over the sea.

Via Bagnoli Croce. No phone. Free admission. Daily 8:30am–7pm (6pm in winter).

Where to Stay

The hotels in Taormina are the best in Sicily. All price ranges are available, with accommodations ranging from army cots to sumptuous suites.

If you're driving to a hotel at the top of Taormina, call ahead to see what arrangements can be made for your car. Ask for exact driving directions as well as instructions on where to park—the narrow, winding, one-way streets can be bewildering once you get here.

Excelsior Palace ★ Not a palace, really, but a sprawling pink grand hotel from the early 20th century that is conveniently tucked into one end of town just off Corso Umberto. Rooms here have not been upgraded since, well, since a time when burnt-orange bathroom tiles and floral carpets were all the rage. They're well maintained, though, and every one has a view—many of Mt. Etna and the coastline—and many have little balconies with just enough room for two chairs. Though the place is often filled with groups, service is personal, attentive, and old-world, with waiters in ties and jackets serving cocktails in frumpy lounges full of overstuffed, slipcovered couches and armchairs. In the magnificent garden, many verdant acres are draped over a promontory high above the town and sea, the setting for a magnificently perched swimming pool—which in itself makes this a good summertime choice.

Via Toselli 8. www.excelsiorpalacetaormina.it. ✆ **0942-23975.** 85 units. From 65€–125€ double. Rates include buffet breakfast. **Amenities:** Restaurant; bar; concierge; pool; Wi-Fi in public areas (free).

Hotel del Corso ★ You'll forgo spas, pools, and other chic luxuries in these fairly basic lodgings right in the heart of town, on Corso Umberto near the Duomo, but you won't give up views of the sea and Mt. Etna. They fill the windows of many of the rooms and spread out below the top floor lounge, breakfast room, and sun terrace; some rooms have less dramatic but pleasing views of the town. Black-and-white terrazzo floors, iron bedsteads, and soothing neutral colors add a lot of spark to the comfortable guest rooms, a choice few of which have small balconies. Book well in advance, especially on weekends, when this good-value property fills up fast.

Corso Umberto 328. www.hoteldelcorsotaormina.com. ✆ **0942-628698.** 15 units. 70€–110€ double. Rates include buffet breakfast. **Amenities:** Wi-Fi (free).

MEET mighty MOUNT ETNA

Warning: Always get the latest report from the tourist office before setting out for a trip to Mount Etna. Adventurers have been killed by a surprise "belch" (volcanic explosion). Mount Etna remains one of the world's most active volcanoes, with sporadic gas, steam, lava, and ash emissions from its summit.

Looming menacingly over the coast of eastern Sicily, Mount Etna is the highest and largest active volcano in Europe. The peak changes in size over the years but it currently soars 3,324m (10,906 ft.). Etna has been active in modern times: In 1928, the little village of Mascali was buried under lava, and powerful eruptions in 1971, 1992, 2001, and 2003 caused extensive damage to facilities nearby. Throughout the year, episodes of spectacular but usually harmless lava fountains, some hundreds of meters high, are not uncommon, providing a dramatic show for viewers in Taormina.

Etna has figured in history and in Greek mythology. Empedocles, the 5th-century B.C. Greek philosopher, is said to have jumped into its crater in the belief that he would be delivered directly to Mount Olympus to take his seat among the gods. It was under Etna that Zeus crushed the multiheaded, viper-riddled dragon Typhoeus, thereby securing domination over Olympus. Hephaestus, the god of fire and blacksmiths, made his headquarters in Etna, aided by the single-eyed Cyclops. The Greeks warned that when Typhoeus tried to break out of his prison, lava erupted and earthquakes cracked the land. That must mean that the monster nearly escaped on March 11, 1669, one of the most violent eruptions ever—it destroyed Catania, about 27km (17 miles) away.

Etna is easy to reach by car from Taormina. The fastest way is to take the E45 autostrada south to the Acireale exit. From here, follow the brown Etna signs west to Nicolosi, passing through several smaller towns along the way. From Nicolosi, keep following the Etna signs up the hill toward **Rifugio Sapienza** (1,923m/6,307 ft.), the starting point for all expeditions to the crater. Here, there's a faux–Alpine hamlet with tourist shops and services, cheap and ample parking, as well as the base station of the **Funivia del Etna** cable car (www.funiviaetna.com; ✆ **095-914141;** daily 9am–4:30pm), which takes you to the Torre del Filosofo (Philosopher's Tower) station at 2,900m (9,514 ft.). You can also hike up to the station, but it's a strenuous hike that takes about 5 hours. From there, to reach the authorized crater areas at about 3,000m (9,843 ft., as close to the summit as visitors are allowed), you'll climb into white, *Star Wars*-ish off-road vehicles that make the final ascent over a scrabbly terrain of ash and dead ladybugs (dead ladybugs are everywhere on Mount Etna). Conditions at the crater zone are thrilling, but the high winds, exposure, and potential sense of vertigo are not for the faint of heart.

The round-trip cost of going to the top of Etna, including the cable car ride, the off-road vans, and the requisite authorized guide at the crater zone, is about 55€. Etna is not a complicated excursion to do on your own, but if you'd prefer to go with a tour, Taormina is chock-full of agencies that organize Etna day trips.

Villa Carlotta ★★★   This 1920s stone villa vaguely resembling a castle is an enchanting getaway at the edge of town—another creation of Andrea and Rosaria Quartucci, who work such magic at Villa Ducale (below). A wall of Byzantine catacombs adds an air of mystery, but what wins you over is the classic-yet-contemporary style and wonderful sense of privacy and comfort. Most of the warm-hued, stylish rooms have terraces and sea views, and many overlook the luxuriant rear gardens where a swimming pool is tucked into the greenery. As at Villa Ducale, service is personalized and attentive, and a shuttle bus makes a run down to the beach. Villa Carlotta also operates the sumptuous Taormina Luxury Apartments (www.taorminaluxuryapartments.com), just up the street.

Via Pirandello 81. www.hotelvillacarlottataormina.com. © **0942-626058.** 23 units. 200€–350€ double. Closed Jan–early Mar. **Amenities:** Restaurant; concierge; health club; pool; Wi-Fi (free).

Villa Ducale ★★★   Andrea and Rosaria Quartucci have fashioned a family villa perched high on a hillside above the town into a warm and stylish getaway with flower-planted terraces, Mediterranenan gardens, and extraordinary eagle's-nest views that extend as far as Calabria. Distinctive rooms and suites, in the villa and a house across the road, are done in Sicilian chic, with stylish and extremely comfortable furnishings set against warm hues that play off terracotta floors; they are enlivened with beams, arches, and other architectural details, equipped with luxurious baths, and fitted out with fine linens and works by local artists. Service is exceedingly warm and personal, and a lavish buffet breakfast and complimentary sunset cocktails, accompanied by a spread of Sicilian appetizers, are served on a living room–like terrace; lunch and dinner are available on request. The hotel has no pool, but there's a Jacuzzi, and a shuttle makes a run to a private beach, and also to town.

Via Leonardo da Vinci 60. www.villaducale.com. © **0942-28153.** 15 units. 240€–400€ double. Rates include buffet breakfast. Parking 10€. Closed Jan–early Mar. **Amenities:** Jacuzzi; room service; Wi-Fi (free).

Villa Paradiso ★   Lady Florence Trevelyan, who created the beautiful gardens that are now the Villa Communale, lived in this villa until her death in 1907, and it passed to the Martorana family, three generations of whom have proven to be charming hoteliers. Family antiques, comfy armchairs and couches, and paintings (many presented by guests over the years) fill lounges and bright, handsomely decorated guest rooms, where balconies and sun-drenched sitting alcoves face the sea. Breakfast and dinners are served in a top-floor, glassed-in restaurant, Settimo Cielo (Seventh Heaven), which it really seemes to be. Between June and October, the hotel offers free shuttle service and free entrance to the Paradise Beach Club, about 6km (4 miles) to the east, in the seaside resort of Letojanni.

Via Roma 2. www.hotelvillaparadisotaormina.com. © **0942-23921.** 37 units. 130€–210€ double. **Amenities:** Restaurant; bar; room service; Wi-Fi (fee).

Where to Eat

The ultimate Sicilian summer refreshment, the sorbetlike *granita,* is perfect at **Bam Bar,** not far from the Grand Hotel Timeo at Via di Giovanni 45 (© **0942-24355**). Specialties are the almond (*mandorla*) or white fig (*fico bianco*), but there are usually more than a dozen flavors to choose from.

Il Duomo ★★ SICILIAN   The decor leaves something to be desired, with harsh lighting and a green-and-orange color scheme—to avoid it, choose a table near the large window overlooking the Duomo, or better yet in good weather, on the side terrace. Fortunately, the food doesn't take any such liberties in taste and sticks to traditional Sicilian recipes, with some well-conceived modern twists. This is the best place in town to try pasta con sarde (with sardines and breadcrumbs); the fish is commendably fresh and nicely enlivened with capers, tomatoes, and olives.
Vico Ebrei. www.ristorantealduomo.it. © **0942-625656.** Main courses 10€–16€. Tues–Sun 12:30–3pm and 7:30–10:30pm.

Tischi Toschi ★★★ SICILIAN/SEAFOOD   A warm-hued yellow room facing a delightful little piazza and decorated with old ceramics is the setting for creative takes on old Sicilian classics. Even *pasta alla Norma* (with eggplant and ricotta) seems like a work of art here, and is thoughtfully topped with a grilled eggplant. Venture further, though, into some dishes you might not encounter in many other places—some top choices, if they're being served, are *insalata di pesce stocco*, a salad made from dried cod, raw fennel, and tomato dressed with olive oil and parsley, and *sarde a beccafico*, sardines stuffed with pine nuts and fennel and served with lemon and orange. Accompany anything with the delicious fried artichokes, and end a meal with the heavenly, refreshing lemon jelly.
Via F. Paladini 3. © **339-3642088.** Main courses 8€–18€. Daily noon–3pm and 6:30–11pm.

Trattoria da Nino ★ SICILIAN   Good, no-nonsense Sicilian *cucina casalinga* (home cooking) is the recipe for success in this unpretentious, brightly lit room (with an airy terrace in warm weather) across from the upper station of the cable car. Pastas are house-made (deliciously delicate gnocchi, little potato dumplings, are served *alla Norma,* with eggplant and ricotta), and the fish is fresh and served simply grilled. Nino's is a local institution, a 50-year veteran of the Taormina dining scene, and it's always packed; they don't take reservations for groups of fewer than six.
Via Pirandello 37. www.trattoriadanino.com. © **0942-21265.** Main courses 8€–18€. Daily noon–3pm and 6:30–11pm.

Vecchia Taormina ★★ SICILIAN   One of Taormina's longtime favorites keeps a steady stream of regulars happy with what are reputed to be the best pizzas around. The *pizza alla Norma,* the ingredients of the classic Sicilian pasta on a flaky crust, makes good on the claim. The kitchen also does nice versions of spaghetti con vongole (with clams), or topped with fresh sardines and breadcrumbs, as well as other classics, and serves them in two cozy rooms and a delightful multilevel terrace in an alleyway outside.
Vico Ebre 3. © **0942-625589.** Main courses 10€–15€. Thurs–Tues 7:30–10:30pm.

Outdoor Pursuits

To reach the best and most popular beach, **Lido Mazzarò,** you have to go south of town via a cable car (✆ **0942-23605**) that leaves from Via Pirandello every 15 minutes (3€ round-trip). This soft, finely pebbled beach is one of the best equipped in Sicily, with bars, restaurants, and hotels. You can rent beach chairs, umbrellas, and watersports equipment at kiosks from April to October. To the right of Lido Mazzarò, past the Capo Sant'Andrea headland, is the region's prettiest cove, where twin crescents of beach sweep from a sand spit out to the minuscule **Isola Bella** islet.

North of Mazzarò are the long, wide beaches of **Spisone** and **Letojanni,** more developed but less crowded than **Giardini,** the large, built-up resort beach south of Isola Bella. A local bus leaves Taormina for Mazzarò, Spisone, and Letojanni, and another heads down the coast to Giardini.

Shopping

Shopping is all too easy in Taormina—just walk along **Corso Umberto I**. Ceramics are one of Sicily's most notable handicrafts, and Taormina's shops are among the best places to buy them on the island, as the selection is excellent. **Giuseppa di Blasi,** Corso Umberto I 103 (✆ **0942-24671**), has a nice range of designs and specializes in the highly valued "white pottery" from Caltagirone. Mixing the new and the old, **Carlo Panarello Antichità,** Corso Umberto I 122 (✆ **0942-23910**), offers Sicilian ceramics (from pots to tables) and also deals in eclectic antique furnishings, paintings, and engravings.

Side Trips from Taormina

CASTELMOLA

Taormina gets high praise for its gorgeous views, but for connoisseurs of scenic outlooks, the real show takes place in the village of Castelmola, an eagle's nest 3km (2 miles) northwest of Taormina, and about 300m (1,000 ft.) feet higher. The Ionian Sea seems to stretch to the ends of the earth from up here, and you'll be staring right into the northern flanks of Mt. Etna. For the full experience, make the trip up on foot, following routes that begin at Porta Catania and Porta Messina (the tourist office or any hotel desk can give you directions); the Porta Messina trail passes a section of the Roman aqueduct and the Convento dei Cappuccini, where you can pause for views and a breather. Either route involves an hour or so of fairly strenuous walking, but once at the top, stop at Castelmola's **Bar Turrisi** (Piazza Duomo 19; ✆ **0942-28181;** 10am–1am, and until 3am weekends and holidays) for a glass of *vino alla mandorla* (almond wine) and a look at its peculiar art collection. If that's more walking than you care to do, you can also drive up to Castelmola (park below the village and walk in) or take an orange local bus that runs more or less hourly from Porta Messina (2.20€ round-trip).

GOLE DELL'ALCANTARA

In a series of narrow gorges on the Alcantara (Al-*cahn*-ta-rah) river, rushing ice-cold water fed by snow melt on Mt. Etna darts and dashes over fantastically twisted volcanic rock, creating a scenic spectacle that's especially refreshing on a hot day. The basalt rock formations were sculpted into these wild shapes thousands of years ago by cool water flowing over molten debris during eruptions on Mount Etna. The gorge is now protected as **Parco Fluviale dell'Alcanta** (www.parcoalcantara. it; © 0942-985010), though ticket booths, turnstiles, and elevators into the gorge lend an amusement-park aura. You can get away from the crowds with a hike along the riverbed, stopping now and then to lounge on flat riverside rocks and wade and even swim in the chill water. From October to April, only the upper area of the park, with an overlook trail above the gorge, is open. It costs 8€ to enter the park (open daily 7am–7:30pm). Amenities include a gift shop, cafeteria, picnic areas, and toilets. You can reach the Gole dell'Alcantara by car from Taormina (a 35-min. drive) or you can take **Interbus** (www.interbus.it; © 0942-625301) for the 1-hour trip, with several daily departures from Taormina. The round-trip fare is 6€. Organized excursions (from 25€) to the gorges are also offered by many bus tour operators in Taormina, often in conjunction with a visit to Mount Etna.

SIRACUSA ★★

This small, out-of-the-way southern city packs a one-two punch. Siracusa was one of the most important cities of Magna Graecia (Greater Greece), rivaling even Athens in power and influence, and the still-functioning Teatro Greco, where Aeschylus premiered his plays, is one of many landmarks of the ancient metropolis. The charming historical center, on miniscule Ortigia Island, belongs to a much later time, the 18th century, when palaces and churches were built in an ebullient baroque style following the earthquake of 1693.

Siracusa might seem far removed, but in making the trip to the southeast coast you'll be following in the illustrious footsteps of the scientist Archimedes, statesman Cicero, evangelist St. Paul, martyr St. Lucy, painter Caravaggio, and naval hero Admiral Lord Horatio Nelson, all of whom left a mark on this rather remarkable place.

Essentials

GETTING THERE   Siracusa is 1½ hours south of Taormina on the A18. It's 3 hours southeast of Palermo on the A19 and A18, and 3 hours east of Agrigento on the SS540, A19, and A18. Siracusa is also well connected with the rest of Sicily by bus and train, though buses are generally more efficient and frequent than trains. **Interbus buses** (www.etnatra sporti.it) run almost hourly between Siracusa and Catania and several times a day between Siracusa and Palermo. Train travel usually requires a change in Cantania; for information, contact www.trenitalia.com © **892021.** Both trains and buses arrive in Siracusa at the station on Via Francesco Crispi, centrally located between the Parco Archeologico (Archaeological Park) and Ortygia.

GETTING AROUND   You won't need a car, just your own two feet and perhaps a few bus or cab rides to see the best of Siracusa proper. However, if you're using Siracusa as a base for exploring southeastern Sicily, you may arrive here by car—in which case, inquire about parking with your hotel or rental agency before arriving.

VISITOR INFORMATION   The **tourist office,** at Via San Sebastiano 43 (© **0931-481232**), is open Monday to Friday 8:30am to 1:30pm and 3 to 6pm, Saturday 8:30am to 1:30pm. There's another office in the historic center at Via della Maestranza 33 (© **0931-65201**); it's open Monday to Friday 8:15am to 2pm and 2:30 to 5:30pm, Saturday 8:15am to 2pm.

Exploring Siracusa

Ortigia Island is Siracusa's *centro storico,* a mostly pedestrian zone where narrow alleys lined with romantic 18th-century *palazzi* spill onto Piazza del Duomo, the most beautiful square in Sicily. The ancient ruins lie a good half-hour walk north of Ortigia along Corso Gelone.

ORTIGIA ISLAND ★★★

The historic center of Siracusa is an island only about 1 sq. km (¾ sq. mile), with breezy, palm-shaded seaside promenades fringing its shores. Most of the island is baroque, with grandiose palaces and churches lining narrow lanes and flamboyant piazzas, though Ortigia was settled in ancient times—as ancients believed, when Leto stopped by to give birth to Artemis, one of the twins she conceived with Zeus (she continued on her way and delivered Apollo on the Greek island of Delos).

The first landmark you'll come to after you cross Ponte Umbertino from the mainland is the **Temple of Apollo,** the oldest Doric temple in Sicily. The Apollion would have measured 58m × 24m (190 ft. × 79 ft.) when it was built in the 6th century B.C. It later served as a Byzantine church, then a mosque, then a church again under the Normans and is now an evocative ruin, with the temple platform, a fragmentary colonnade, and an inner wall rising in the middle of Piazza Pancali.

The **Piazza del Duomo,** one of the most beautiful squares in Sicily, is all about theatrics—a sea of white marble softened by pink oleander and surrounded by flamboyant palaces enlivened with elaborate stone filigree work and wrought-iron balconies. The Duomo itself (open daily 8am–noon and 4–7pm) is frothily baroque, almost too playful to be religious. The two tiers of tall Doric columns that define its remarkable facade were originally part of Siracusa's 5th-century B.C. Temple of Athena, one of the best-known sights of the ancient world, built

Siracusa's Ortigia Island.

to celebrate a Greek victory over the Carthaginians. Cicero, the Roman orator and traveler, reported that the temple was filled with gold, the doors were made of gold and ivory, and a statue of Athena atop the pediment was visible for miles out to sea. Romans made off with the gold, but a statue of the Virgin stands atop the pediment like Athena once did. Other ancient columns are a looming presence in the apse of the church, which was first fashioned from the temple around the 7th century.

On the south side of the square is the pretty church of **Santa Lucia alla Badia,** with a tall, marble baroque facade embellished with twisted columns, pediments, and a wrought-iron balcony. Lucia, a plucky 4th-century Siracusan virgin, is the city's patron; born of wealth, from an early age she adapted Christian principles and was determined to give her worldly goods to the poor. Her piousness and generosity annoyed the young man to whom she had once been betrothed, and out of spite for seeing Lucia's sizable dowry squandered in such a way, the youth denounced her to Roman authorities. Lucia was condemned to prostitution, but refused to be dragged off to a brothel. Authorities then tied her to a pillar and lit a fire beneath her, but she proved to be flame resistant. Finally, a soldier plunged a sword into her throat. You'll see depictions of this gruesome act throughout Siracusa and the rest of Sicily, where the saint is very popular (tamer versions show the saint holding the sword that killed her).

Also on Piazza del Duomo is an entrance to the **Hypogeum** (no phone; admission 3€; Tues–Sun 9am–1pm and 4–8pm), a network of underground chambers and corridors dug as air-raid shelters in World War II.

Historians spout some mumbo-jumbo about the water that feeds **Fonte Aretusa,** a lovely shoreline spot where papyrus grows in a shallow pool fed by a spring that supplied Siracusa with fresh water for millennia. Classical myth, however, tells a different story: The nymph Aretusa was bathing in a river in Greece when the river god Alpheus took a liking to her. She asked for help in avoiding his advances, and Artemis, goddess of the wilderness and protectress of young women, turned her into a river that emerged here. Not to be thwarted, Alpheus followed suit, and the two of them bubble forth for eternity.

The elegant 13th-century palace **Galleria Regionale Palazzo Bellomo** (Via Capodieci 16; ℂ **0931-69511;** admission 8€; Tues–Sat 9am–7pm, Sun 9am–1pm), houses Sicilian works from the Middle Ages through the 20th century, including two great masterpieces. Antonello da Messina's **"Annunciation"** (1474) shows the artist's remarkable attention to detail: Tall windows, beams, columns, the Virgin's bed, and a blue-and-white vase compose an intricately rendered interior, with bright light infusing the spaces. The scene is typical of the Flemish paintings that were popular in Naples, where Messina studied when he left his native Sicily while still a teenager. Caravaggio's **"Burial of St. Lucia"** was commissioned in the late fall of 1608, when the artist had just escaped from a prison in Malta and come to Siracusa. Note how, with his characteristic lighting, the artist highlights the muscular grave-diggers, showing their brute strength, while the mourners seem small and meek in the background. A shaft of light falls on Lucia's face and neck, showing the stab wound that killed her; she is a study in serenity, having entered the heavenly kingdom.

THE ANCIENT RUINS ★★★

Of all the Greek cities of antiquity that flourished in Sicily, Siracusa was the most important, a formidable competitor of Athens. In its heyday, it dared take on Carthage and even Rome. Sprawling Greek and Roman ruins are these days surrounded by an unremarkable section of the modern city. To reach the ruins, walk north along Corso Gelone (or better yet, take bus no. 1, 3, or 12, or a cab from Ortigia's Piazza Pancali) or take buses 11, 25, or 26 from the front of Siracusa's central train station.

Castello Eurialo ★ RUINS Part of a massive, 27km (16-mi) long defense system, this 4th-century B.C. fortress is surrounded by three trenches, connected by underground tunnels. These supposedly impregnable defenses were never put to the test: Siracusa fell to the Romans in 212 B.C. without a fight, because the entire garrison was celebrating the feast of Aphrodite. Legend has it that it was here that the Greek mathematician Archimedes famously cried "Eureka!" having discovered the law of water displacement while taking a bath. The evocative ruin overlooking the Siracusan plain is the best-preserved Greek castle in the Mediterranean. The defenses are at the far end of the archaeological zone, about 5km (3 miles) outside the city center near a village called Belvedere; buses 25 and 26 along Corso Gelone pass the entrance.

Piazza Eurialo 1, off Viale Epipoli in the Belvedere district. ℂ **0931-481111.** Admission 4€; 10€ when combined with Parco Archeologico and Museo Archeologico. Daily 9am–5:30pm.

Catacombe di San Giovanni ★★ RUINS Spooky subterranean chambers, installed in underground aqueducts that had been abandoned by the Greeks, contain some 20,000 ancient Christian tombs. They are entered through the Church of San Giovanni, now in ruin but holy ground for centuries; it was the city's cathedral until it was more or less leveled by an earthquake in 1693. St. Paul allegedly preached here when he stopped in Siracusa around A.D. 59, and a church was erected to commemorate the event in the 6th century. The Cripta di San Marciano (Crypt of St. Marcian) honors a popular Siracusan martyr, a 1st-century A.D. bishop who was tied to a pillar and flogged to death on this spot.

Piazza San Giovanni, at end of Viale San Giovanni. No phone. Admission 5€. Tues–Sun 9:30am–12:30pm and 2:30–4:30pm. Closed Feb.

Museo Archeologico Regionale Paolo Orsi (Paolo Orsi Regional Archaeological Museum) ★★★ MUSEUM One of Italy's finest archaeological collections shows off artifacts from southern Sicily's prehistoric inhabitants through the Romans, showcasing pieces in stunning modern surroundings. Amid prehistoric tools and sculptures are the skeletons of a pair of dwarf elephants, as intriguing to us as they were to the ancients: It's believed that the large central orifice (nasal passage) of these skeletal beasts inspired the myth of the one-eyed Cyclops. Early Greeks left behind a (much-reproduced) grinning terracotta Gorgon that once adorned the frieze of the temple of Athena (see **Duomo**, above) to ward off evil. You'll also see scores of votive cult statuettes devoted to Demeter and Persephone—mother and daughter goddesses linked to fertility and the harvest. Legend had it that Hades, god of the underworld, abducted Persephone in Sicily and carried her down to his realm; with a bit of negotiating between angry Demeter and the other gods, it was agreed that Persephone could return to Earth but must descend to resume her duties as queen of the underworld for part of the year, when in her absence winter descends upon the lands above. The museum's most celebrated piece is the **Landolina Venus**, a Roman copy of an original by the great classical Greek sculptor Praxiteles. The graceful and modest goddess, now headless, rises out of marble waves; French writer Guy de Maupassant, visiting in 1885, called her "the perfect expression of exuberant beauty."

In the gardens of the Villa Landolina in Akradina, Viale Teocrito 66. ℭ **0931-464022.** Admission 8€ or 14€ with combo ticket that includes Parco Archeologico della Neapolis. Tues–Sat 9am–6pm; Sun 9am–1pm.

Parco Archeologico della Neapolis ★★★ RUINS Many of Siracusa's ancient ruins are clustered in this archaeological park at the western edge of town, immediately north of Stazione Centrale.

The **Teatro Greco** ★★★ (Greek Theater) was hewn out of bedrock in the 5th century B.C., with 67 rows that could seat 16,000 spectators. It was reconstructed in the 3rd century B.C., appears now much as it did

A Gigantic Teardrop Runs Through It

The tallest building in Siracusa is the bizarre **Santuario della Madonna delle Lacrime** (Our Lady of Tears Sanctuary, Via Santuario 33; ✆ **0931-21446;** free admission; daily 8am–noon and 4–7pm), a monstrous cone of contemporary architecture (built in 1993) halfway between Ortigia and the archaeological zone. Meant to evoke a sort of angular teardrop and rising 74m (243 ft.) with a diameter of 80m (262 ft.), it houses a statue of the Madonna that supposedly wept for 5 days in 1953. Alleged chemical tests showed that the liquid was similar to that of human tears. Pilgrims flock here, and you'll see postcards of the weepy Virgin around Siracusa. In the interior, vertical windows stretch skyward to the apex of the roof. A charlatan TV evangelist and his rapt congregation would not look out of place here.

then, and is still the setting for ancient drama in the spring and early summer. Tickets cost 30€ to 70€. For information, contact **INDA,** Corso Matteotti 29, Siracusa (www.indafondazione.org; ✆ **0931-487200**).

Only the ancient theaters in Rome and Verona are larger than the **Anfiteatro Romano,** created during the rein of Augustus, around 20 B.C. Gladiators sparred here, and a square hole in the center of the arena suggests that machinery was used to lift wild beasts from below. Some historical evidence suggests that the arena could be flooded for mock sea battles called *naumachiae;* pumps could also have flooded and drained a reservoir in which crocodiles are said to have fed on the corpses of victims killed in the games. The Spanish carted off much of the stonework to rebuild the city fortifications when they conquered Siracusa in the 16th century, but some of the seats remain—the first rows would have been reserved for Roman citizens, those right above for wealthy Siracusans, and the last rows for the hoi polloi.

What is now a lush grove of lemon and orange trees, the **Latomia del Paradiso** (Quarry of Paradise) was at one time a fearsome place, vast, dark, and subterranean—until the cavern's roof collapsed in the great earthquake of 1693. Originally prisoners were worked to death here to quarry the stones used in the construction of ancient Siracusa. Certainly the most storied attraction in the park is the **Orecchio di Dionisio** (Ear of Dionysius). The Greeks created this tall and vaguely ear-shaped cave by digging into the cliff, simply to expand the limestone quarry for water storage—but something about this huge cavern has always inspired more dramatic accounts. When the flamboyant painter Caravaggio lived in Siracusa in the early 17th century, he playfully dubbed the cavern the Ear of Dionysus, after the 5th- to 4th-century B.C. ruler of Greek Siracusa, and backed that up with a wild story: that Dionysus had imprisoned political opponents in the cave because of its unique acoustic effect—he could sit near the opening and hear every word they said. Other legends, completely unfounded, say the cave's occupants were Athenians captured by Dionysus' mercenaries during the Peloponnesian Wars; this version claims that he liked the way the cave's acoustics amplified their screams as they were tortured. Almost as fascinating is the well-documented purpose of the **Ara di Ierone** (or, Altar of Heron): Fifth-century B.C. Greeks built the altar, 196m (636 ft.) long and 23m (75 ft.) wide and approached by enormous ramps, for the sacrifice of 450 bulls at one time.

Via Del Teatro (off the intersection of Corso Gelone and Viale Teocrito), Viale Paradiso. © **0931-66206.** Admission 10€ or 14€ with combo ticket that includes archaeological museum. Daily 9am–6pm (until 4:30pm on certain summer evenings when performances are held in the theater).

Where to Stay

The best place to stay in Siracusa is Ortigia, with enough character, charm, and comfortable choices to keep the most discerning traveler happy. A good agency for apartments in Ortigia is **Case Sicilia** (www.casesicilia.com; © **339-2983507**). For villas, **Think Sicily** (www.thinksicily.com) has a carefully edited list of well-equipped properties in and around Siracusa.

Algilà Ortigia Charme Hotel ★   A slightly exotic air pervades this old stone palace at the edge of the sea. Built around a peaceful inner courtyard with a splashing fountain, it's accented throughout with carefully restored stone work and wooden beams, offset by beautiful multicolor tiles and other rich details. Rooms combine conventional luxury, with all the modern amenities, and a surfeit of four-poster beds, antiques, and tribal kilims; many have sea views. The in-house restaurant serves Sicilian classics and seafood beneath a beautiful wooden ceiling.

Via Vittorio Veneto 93. www.algila.it. © **0931-465186.** 30 units. 174€–400€ double. Rates include buffet breakfast. **Amenities:** Restaurant; room service; Wi-Fi (free, in lobby).

Approdo delle Sirene ★★   This natty little inn occupies two floors of a seaside apartment house, beautifully refashioned as light-filled quarters with a slightly nautical flair, as becomes the sparking blue water just beyond the tall windows. In the contemporary-styled guest rooms, polished wood floors offset handsome blond furnishings, striped fabrics, and bold colors. Several rooms have French doors opening to small balconies, though some rooms are sky-lit only—flooded with light but without outlooks. The sunny breakfast room/lounge and terrace provide plenty of views, however. The hosts, a mother-and-son team, Fiora and Friedrich, are a hospitable on-the-scene presence and can arrange all kinds of tours and excursions. They even have bikes available for guests' use (no charge).

Riva Garibaldi 15. www.apprododellesirene.com. © **0931-24857.** 8 units. 80€–130€ double. 2-night minimum stay June–Aug. Rates include buffet breakfast. **Amenities:** Bikes, Wi-Fi (free).

Domus Mariae Benessere Guest House ★   The Ursiline sisters who still occupy a wing of this seaside convent have found their calling as innkeepers. They provide large, bright rooms that are functional bordering on vaguely luxurious, with plush headboards on extremely comfortable beds, attractive rugs on tile floors, and lots of counter and storage space in the large bathrooms. Some rooms have sea views, while others face an atrium-like courtyard. Some surprising indulgences given the surroundings are a lovely roof terrace and a lower level spa, with a small pool and Jacuzzi available to all guests. An in-house restaurant serves a rather monastic breakfast (included in room rates, though coffee is extra) as well as a well-prepared dinner featuring healthful Mediterranean fare.
Via Veneto 89. www.domusmariaebenessere.com. © **0931-24854.** 21 units. From 60€ double. Rates include buffet breakfast. **Amenities:** Bikes (free), pool, Wi-Fi (free).

Hotel Gutkowski ★★   Two old houses facing the sea at the edge of Ortigia are warm, hospitable, and capture the essence of southern Italy—Sicilian hues on the walls, colorful floor tiles, and views of the blue water or sun baked roofs of the old city. Each room is different, some with balconies, some with terraces, and furnishings throughout are functional but chosen with care to provide restful simplicity—old Sicilian and vintage mid-century pieces offset contemporary tables and bedsteads. A rooftop terrace serves as an outdoor living room for much of the year, and the bar serves not only regional wines but also one or two well-prepared dishes in the evenings for guests only.
Lungomare Vittorini 26. www.guthotel.it. © **0931-465861.** 25 units. From 90€ double. Rates include buffet breakfast. **Amenities:** Bar; Wi-Fi (free).

Where to Eat

Caseificio Borderi, tucked in among piles of fresh fish in Ortigia's colorful morning market at 6 Via die Benedictis (© **329-9852500**), is a mandatory stop on the food circuit for its huge selection of house-made cheeses, cured meats, olives, and wine; the staff hands out samples and makes delicious sandwiches (about 3€).

Archimede ★★ SEAFOOD   This Siracusa institution has been serving meals in white-washed, vaulted dining rooms since 1938; it's remained a favorite for a night out, even through those long post-war years when the surrounding neighborhood moldered in neglect. Specialties veer toward such Sicilian classics as spaghetti with *ricci* (sea urchin), tagliolini al *nero di seppie* (pasta with cuttlefish ink), and *pesce all'acqua pazza* (fish cooked with garlic, tomatoes, capers, and olives); many fans claim that no one in Sicily makes them better. The kitchen is also equipped with a wood-fired oven that turns out what many Siracusans consider to be the best pizza in town, available in different sizes, including one that's perfect as a starter.
Via Gemmallaro 8. www.trattoriaarchimede.it. © **0931-69701.** Main courses 12€–24€. Mon–Sat 12:30–3:30pm and 7:30–11:30pm.

Bienvenuti al Sud ★ SICILIAN/CREATIVE   Sicilian towns are full of casual eateries like this—barebones storefronts with open kitchens and plastic tables. Locals know the ones that serve the best food, and this simple, four-table room operated by an enthusiastic young husband-and-wife team is one of Ortigia's hidden gems (it's on a back street behind the Duomo). Chef Christian serves the specialties you'd encounter in a Sicilian home and he enhances the homey ambience as he chats from the kitchen while he prepares linguine al neonate (baby fish), fresh from the market fish baked with capers and olives, and a simple but delicious gnocchi alla Palermitiana, with eggplant, mozzarella, and tomatoes. Dinner is often followed by a complimentary glass of almond wine.

Via della Concillazione 22. ✆ 0931-64046. Main courses 9€–12€. Daily 7pm–midnight, lunch some days.

Don Camillo ★★ SIRACUSAN/SEAFOOD   The top contender with Archimede (see above) for old-time Siracusa favorite is slightly more formal, with lots of polished antiques offsetting the handsomely tiled floors and rows of vintage wines. House specialties, like spaghetti *delle Sirene* (with sea urchin and shrimp in butter) and *tagliata al tonno* (with sliced tuna), have been drawing loyal regulars here for years. On weekends especially, join the many Siracusan families who fill the vaulted rooms decorated with vintage photos of Ortigia.

Via Maestranza 96. www.ristorantedoncamillosiracusa.it. ✆ **0931-67133.** Main courses 14€–24€. Mon–Sat 12:30–3pm and 7:30–10:30pm.

Side Trips from Siracusa
BEACHES NEAR SIRACUSA

Some of the best, unspoiled shoreline in all of Italy is on Sicily's southeastern coast. **Fontane Bianche** is the closest beach to Siracusa, 15 minutes away. It's an almost-square bay with laid-back beach clubs and luxurious deep sand. **Lido di Noto,** 15 minutes from the baroque hill town of Noto, is a lively beach with great waterfront restaurants. Half the beach is private beach clubs (where you pay around 10€ for day use of a lounge chair, umbrella, and shower facilities), and half is free public access. Between Noto and Pachino is the **Vendicari Nature Reserve,** where beaches are small and hard to find but the scenery is beautiful. Thousands of migratory birds nest here every year. A few miles south of the autostrada on SP19, park at the Agriturismo Calamosche to reach **Calamosche**. It's a 15-minute walk down a nature path to reach the intimate cove, framed by rock cliffs and sea caves. The water is a calm, perfectly dappled teal. **Isola delle Correnti ★★**, a little over an hour south of Siracusa at the southeastern tip of the island, is one of the best beaches on Sicily. It's a bit more windswept and wavy than the other spots. On a clear day, you can see Malta, which is just 100km (60 miles) to the south.

NOTO ★★★

31km (19 miles) SW of Siracusa

Dubbed the "Stone Garden" because of its sheer beauty, this little town has a main street, Corso Vittorio Emanuele, lined with rich-looking buildings of golden stone, some of the most captivating on the island. What's more, Noto is set amid olive groves and almond trees on a plateau overlooking the Asinaro Valley, providing lovely outlooks.

GETTING THERE   Take the A18 autostrada south for 27km (17 miles), then exit and head north up a hill, following blue signs toward Noto. Near town, be sure to follow the yellow signs toward Noto's *"centro storico"* (brown "Noto Antica" signs lead to the ruins of the old city, quite some distance from town.) The drive from Siracusa takes about 35 minutes. It's also easy to reach Noto by bus (55 min. each way; 6€ round-trip), with either **AST** (www.aziendasicilianatrasporti.it) or **Interbus** (www.interbus.it), which offer about a dozen buses per day from Ortigia or Siracusa train station. Buses arrive at Noto's Piazzale Marconi, a 5-minute walk from the *centro storico.*

VISITOR INFORMATION   The **tourist office** at Via Gioberti 13 (© **0931-836503**) is open May to September daily from 9am to 1pm and 3:30 to 6:30pm; from October to April it's open Monday through Friday, 8am to 2pm and 3:30 to 6:30pm.

Exploring Noto

Noto, a hill town on the flanks of Mount Alviria, was a flourishing place in the late 17th century, having outgrown its medieval core and expanded into

The hill town of Noto.

new streets lined with palaces and convents. Then, on January 11, 1693, it all came tumbling down, as the strongest earthquake in Italian history leveled Noto and much of the rest of southeastern Sicily. The ruins of that old city can be seen at the "Noto Antica" archaeological site outside of town.

The good to come out of such a devastating tragedy, however, is that Noto was rebuilt—not on the same site but on the banks of the River Asinaro, and not haphazardly, but in splendid, unified baroque style. Noto is a stage-set of honey-colored limestone, with curvaceous facades, curling staircases, and potbellied wrought-iron balconies. You will be surrounded by all this theatricality on a walk down **Corso Vittorio Emanuele III,** though things hit a high note on a side street, **Via Nicolaci.** Be sure not to miss the beautiful elliptical facade of the **Chiesa di Montevirgine** church, and the playful **Palazzo Villadorata** (or Palazzo Nicolaci), where expressive maidens, dwarves, lions, and horses support the balconies.

Work on the 18th-century landmarks is ongoing (the **Duomo** was just rebuilt after a 1997 collapse), while much of the rest of the town seems to languish in disrepair—suggesting that in Noto the attitude is, "If it ain't baroque, don't fix it."

PIAZZA ARMERINA ★★★

134km (83) miles NW of Siracusa, 158km (98 miles) SE of Palermo

Why do travelers make such an effort to get to this dusty, sun-baked hilltown in the center of Sicily? There's one very simple reason: To see the richest collection of Roman mosaics in the world, at the **Villa del Casale,** in the countryside 5km (3 miles) outside of town. Here, from elevated walkways you'll gaze down upon wild beasts, bikini-clad exercisers, superheroes, and the monsters of myth, depicted in glorious and colorful mosaic tableaux. The masterful ancient craftsmanship is in a near-miraculous state of preservation, and provides a fascinating window into 4th-century A.D. preoccupations—but even more than that, looking at these brilliant mosaic scenes is as entertaining as watching a good film, one in glorious Technicolor.

Essentials

GETTING THERE From Taormina, Siracusa, or anywhere in the east, take the A19 west from Catania, exit at Dittaino, and head south following blue signs for Piazza Armerina. From Palermo, take the A19 east and south, exit at Caltanissetta, then immediately look for signs for Piazza Armerina. (The route is SS626 south to SS122 east to SS117bis.) You can reach the nearby town of Piazza Armerina by **SAIS bus** (www.sais autolinee.it; ✆ **800-211020**); from Palermo (a 2-hr trip) there are 5 buses a day, 3 on weekends; coming from Siracusa or other east coast towns, take a bus from Enna (40 min; 4 buses a day). Once in Piazza Armerina, take local bus B to the site (15 min; runs daily 9-noon and 3-6pm). Taxis also eagerly await visitors.

Exploring Villa Romana del Casale

Built between 310 and 340, this enormous villa of a rich and powerful landowner was the center of a vast agricultural estate. It was almost completely covered by a landslide in the 12th century, but this natural disaster turned out to be a blessing, as the mud preserved almost 38,000 square feet of mosaic flooring. Rediscovered in the 19th century, the glorious villa was excavated and restored beginning in the early 20th century.

The place must have been magnificent, more a palace than a mere villa, with 40 rooms, many of them clad in marble, frescoed, and equipped with fountains and pools. Terme, or steam baths (Rooms 1–7) heated the villa with steam circulating through cavities (now exposed) in the floors and walls. The villa was obviously built to impress, and the ostentation reached its height in the mosaics of mythology, hunting, flora and fauna, and domestic scenes that carpeted most of the floors. Given the style and craftsmanship, they were probably the work of master artists from North Africa.

The villa's 40 rooms are arranged around a garden courtyard, or peristyle. Take time as you wander through the rooms simply to enjoy the mosaics, noticing the expressions, colors, and playfulness of many of these scenes. Remember, the mosaics were intended to delight visitors.

Corridors of the **peristyle** (Room 13) contain the splendid Peristyle mosaic, a bestiary of birds, plants, wild animals, and more

Villa Romana del Casale.

13

SICILY

Piazza Armerina

611

domesticated creatures such as horses. Adjoining it to the baths is the **Palestra** (exercise area, Room 15) where mosaics depict a chariot race at Rome's Circus Maximus.

Along the north side of the peristyle is the **Sala degli Eroti Pescatori** ★ (Room of the Fishing Cupids, Room 24), probably a bedroom. The occupant would have drifted off to a busy scene of four boatloads of winged cupids harpooning, netting, and trapping various fish and sea creatures.

Just past those rooms is the **Sala della Piccola Caccia** (*Piccola caccia* meaning "small hunt," Room 25) where hunters in togas and leggings go after deer, wild boar, birds, and other small game as Diana, goddess of the hunt, looks on. In one scene the hunters roast their kill under a canopy.

The long hall to the east is the **Corridoio della Grande Caccia ★★★,** or Corridor of the Great Hunt (Room 28), measuring 65m (197 ft.) in length. The mosaics depict men capturing panthers, leopards, and other exotic animals, loading them onto wagons for transport, and finally onto a ship in an eastern-looking port. They're obviously bound for Rome, where they will be part of the games in the Colosseum.

A cluster of three rooms east of the north (right-hand side) end of the Grande Caccia corridor includes the **Vestibolo di Ulisse e Polifemo** (Vestibule of Ulysses and Polyphemus, Room 47), where the Homeric hero proffers a *krater* of wine to the Cyclops (here with three eyes instead of one, and a disemboweled ram draped casually over his lap) in hopes of getting him drunk. Adjacent is the **Cubicolo con Scena Erotica** (Bedroom with Erotic Scene, Room 46), where a seductress, with a side gaze and a nicely contoured rear end, embraces a young man.

Off the southwest side of the Grande Caccia corridor is one of the most amusing rooms of all, the **Sala delle Palestrite,** Room of the Gym Girls (Room 30). Their skimpy strapless bikinis would be appropriate for a beach in the 21st century, but ancient literary sources tell us that this was actually standard workout apparel 1,700 years ago—the bandeau top was called the *strophium,* and the bikini bottom the *subligar.* The girls are engaged in various exercises—curling dumbbells, tossing a ball, and running.

South of the central block of the villa and peristyle is the **Triclinium** (Room 33), a large dining room with a magnificent rendition of the Labors of Hercules. In the central apse, the mosaics depict the Gigantomachy (Battle of the Giants), in which five mammoth creatures are in their death throes after being pierced by Hercules's poisoned arrows.

PALERMO ★★★

233km (145 miles) W of Messina, 721km (447 miles) S of Naples, 934km (579 miles) S of Rome

In Palermo, street markets evoke Middle Eastern souks, and famous monuments bear the exotic artistic signature of the Arab-Norman 12th century, when Palermo was one of Europe's greatest cultural and intellectual centers. The city is Sicily's largest port, its capital, and a jumble of contradiction. Parts of some neighborhoods remain bombed out and not yet rebuilt from World War II; unemployment, poverty, traffic, crime, and crowding are rampant. Yet Palermo boasts some of the greatest sights and museums in Italy, and looming over it all is crown-shaped Monte Pellegrino, what Goethe called "the most beautiful headland on earth."

Essentials

GETTING THERE Many travelers arrive via Palermo's dramatically situated **Falcone-Borsellino airport** (aka Punta Raisi; www.gesap.it; ✆ 091-7020273), on the sea among tall headlands 25km (16 miles) northwest of the city center. Palermo is well served by flights from all over Italy and many European cities. In summer, a few weekly nonstop flights also arrive from North America. All the major rental car companies have operations here, although if you drive into Palermo with a rental car, get clear directions and parking information from your hotel. An easier way to reach the center from the airport is with the shuttle bus run by **Prestia e Comandè** (✆ 091-580457). The buses depart every half-hour from 5am to 11pm; the trip takes 45 minutes and costs 7€ one-way. In central Palermo, the bus stops at the main train station, at Via Emerico Amari (port), and at Teatro Politeama. There's also a direct train called the **Trinacria Express** (www.trenitalia.com; ✆ 091-7044007; 1 hr.; 6€) from Palermo airport to Palermo central station. Taxis are plentiful but expensive; expect to pay about 50€ from the airport to town.

If you're arriving in Palermo from another place in Sicily by **rail,** all trains come into Palermo Stazione Centrale, just south of the historic center. **Buses** from elsewhere in Sicily arrive at a depot adjacent to the train station.

GETTING AROUND Walking is the best way to get around Palermo, because distances are never great within the historic center. To reach greater Palermo destinations (like the catacombs) or farther-flung locales (such as Mondello and Monreale), buses run by **AMAT** (✆ 091-350111) cost 1.30€ per ride.

VISITOR INFORMATION Official **tourist information offices** are located at Falcone-Borsellino (Punta Raisi) airport (✆ 091-591698; Mon–Sat 8:30am–7:30pm), and in the city center at Piazza Castelnuovo 35 (✆ 091-6058351; Mon–Fri 8:30am–2pm and 2:30–6:30pm). The website of Palermo's tourism board is www.palermotourism.com.

SAFETY Palermo is home to some of the most skilled pickpockets on the continent. Don't flaunt expensive jewelry, cameras, or wads of bills. Women who carry handbags are especially vulnerable to purse snatchers on Vespas. Police squads operate mobile centers throughout the town to help combat street crime.

Neighborhoods in Brief

Palermo is divided into four historical districts, or *mandamenti,* that spread out from **Quattro Canti,** or Four Corners. The actual name of the square is Piazza Vigliena, after the viceroy who commissioned it, and it marks the intersection of **Via Maqueda** (which runs north–south) and **Corso Vittorio Emanuele** (which runs east–west, east toward the seafront from here). The square is also known as Theater of the Sun, because at any given time of day, the sun will shine on one of the four corners.

ALBERGHERIA Located southwest of the Quattro Canti, this is the oldest of the four *mandamenti;* it is also known as the mandamento Palazzo Reale because the Phoenicians first laid the foundations of what would become the royal place on the highest part of the city. These were the streets roamed by the 18th-century soothsayer and charlatan Giuseppe Balsamo (aka Count Cagliostro), an adventurer, traveler, swindler, forger, and thief who spent time in the Bastille after allegedly stealing a diamond necklace from Marie Antoinette; he was finally tried by the Inquisition and died in a Roman prison. The Albergheria is filled with tiny, dimly lit alleyways barely wide enough for a person to walk along, and decaying buildings in dire need of repair; it is unsavory in some patches, despite the ever-growing presence of cafes and eateries. Still, there are some very exquisite corners—especially the splendid Piazza Bologni, with is noble palaces and a statue of Charles V, and the historic market **Il Ballarò** extending from Piazza Bologni to Corso Tukory (see p. 616).

IL CAPO The northwestern neighborhood, enclosed within Via Maqueda, Corso Vittorio Emanuele, Via Papireto and Via Volturno, has a warren of tiny, winding streets and alleyways spread out behind the Teatro Massimo. At its heart is the largest and the most bazaarlike of Palermo's markets, also called **Il Capo** (see p. 616). The Capo was once the headquarters of the secret society of the Beati Paoli, the legendary sect that robbed from the rich and gave to the poor; pickpockets still adhere to this age-old principle, so watch your wallet.

CASTELLAMMARE Owing its name to the castle that once overlooked the sea, this northeastern quadrant is bordered by Corso Vittorio Emanuele, Via Cavour, Via Roma, and Via Crispi. Though heavily bombed by the Allies during 1943, the neighborhood houses some spectacular palazzi and churches, such as the **Oratorio del Rosario di Santa Cita** and the **Oratorio di San Lorenzo** (p. 614). The centuries-old market **La Vucciria,** once the beating heart of Palermo, is located here (see p. 616). Though only a smattering of its vibrancy remains, you'll still see butcher shops called *carnizzerie,* fishmongers scaring shoppers with large heads of swordfish, precarious houses that look as though they might crumble any time (some have in recent years), and tiny, hole-in-the-wall eateries that may seem shady and improvised, but are often excellent.

Palermo

Villa Trabia

Giardino Inglese

Milan
Venice
Florence
Rome ★
Naploc
Sardinia
Palermo
Sicily

Villa Malfitana

Via Melaspina
Via Giacomo Cusmano
Via Sammartiro
Via Principe di Villafranca
Via XX Settembre
Via della Libertà
Via Archimede

Piazza Lolli

Borgo Vecchio

Corso Scina

Via Dante

Via Antonio Veneziano
Via Villa Florio
Via Houel
Via Fllppo Juvara
Via Goethe

Teatro Politeama

Piazza Sturzo

Piazza Castelnuovo

Via Emerico Amari

Via del Mare

C. Finocchiaro
Via Polara

Piazza S. Oliva

Via Principe di Belmonte
Pza. Florio

Via Francesco Crispi

Via Marco Polo
Via Pietro Ranzano
Amedeo

Via P. Aragona

Via Mariano Stabile **1**

NEW CITY

Via Sammuzzo

Via Gaetano Mosca

Piazza di Giustizia

Via Volturno
Teatro Massimo

Piazza Verdi **2**

Via Cavour

Via Flippo Patti

Capo Market

Via Sant' Agostino

Via S. Basilio
Via Bandiera

Via Scquarcialupo **3**

4

Chiesa di S. Domenico

Piazza S. Domenico

La Cala

Duomo **17**

Via del Celso

Vucciria Market

OLD CENTER

Corso

Via

Vittorio

Quattro Canti **16**

Emanuele

Piazza Marina

18 ←

Pal. dei Normanni

Villa Bonanno

Via della Vittoria

San Francesco d'Assisi **9**

8
7

Piazza Magione **10**

Foro Italico

Piazza Indipendenza

Cappella Palatina **19**

Via Porta di Castro

15

5

Via Roma

11

Corso Pisani

Ballarò Market

Via Alloro

13 **12**

Corso Re Ruggero
Via del Bene dettini

20

Via Antonio Mongitore
Via Alberghieria

Via del Bosco

Via Divisi

Piazza Rivoluzione

Santa Teresa

Corso Tukory

Via Garibaldi

LA KALSA

14

Via Lincoln

0 ——— 1/4 mi
0 ——— 250 m

Piazza G. Cesare

Stazione Centrale

ATTRACTIONS

Catacombs of the Capuchins
(Catacombe dei Cappuccini) **18**

Chiesa della Martorana/
San Cataldo **15**

Duomo **17**

Galleria Regionale della Sicilia
(Regional Gallery)/Palazzo **13**

Museo Archeologico Regionale
"Antonino Salinas" (Regional
Archaeological Museum) **2**

Oratorio del Rosario
di San Domenico **4**

Oratorio di San Lorenzo **8**

Oratorio di Santa Cita **3**

Palazzo dei Normanni
and Cappella Palatina **19**

San Giovanni degli Eremiti **20**

Stanza al Genio **14**

HOTELS

Butera 28 **11**

Central Palace **16**

Grand Hotel Piazza Borsa **9**

Hotel Ariston **1**

Hotel Porta Felice **10**

RESTAURANTS

Antica Focacceria
San Francesco **7**

Casa del Brodo **5**

Ferro di Cavallo **6**

Ottava Nota **12**

Do Some Market Research

You can't do justice to Palermo without swinging through one of its street markets. Nowhere is Palermo's multicultural pedigree more evident than at the stalls of the sadly declining **La Vucciria** (on Via Argenteria, north of Via Vittorio Emanuele and east of Via Roma), **Ballarò** (in Piazza Ballarò), and **Capo** (from Via Porta Carini south toward the cathedral). These open-air markets go on for blocks and blocks, hawking everything from spices to seafood to sides of beef to toilet paper to handicrafts to electronics. Ballarò and Capo, west and north of the train station, are where more real Palermitans shop. Delve even deeper into Palermo's market culture at the neighborhood **Borgo Vecchio** market (along Via Ettore Ximenes to Via Principe di Scordia) in the newer part of the city, northwest of Piazza Politeama. Antiques vendors with many unusual buys lie along the Piazza Peranni, off Corso Vittorio Emanuele.

LA KALSA   A thousand years ago, Arabs settled the southeast quadrant, La Kalsa, which is bounded by Via Lincoln, Via Roma, Corso Vittorio Emanuele, and the Foro Italico. The neighborhood still has an exotic feel to it. Time was, even 10 years ago, when the quarter was so insalubrious that walking down the narrow lanes was risky business. It's still wise to avoid some emptier areas after dark, though these are rather rare these days, as restaurants and bars have opened in old *palazzi*.

NEW CITY   As you head north along Via Maqueda, the streets grow broader but also more nondescript. The monumental **Teatro Massimo**, at Piazza Verdi, roughly marks the division between the Old City and the New City. Via Maqueda becomes Via Ruggero Séttimo as it heads north through the modern town, emptying into the massive double squares at Piazza Politeama, site of the **Teatro Politeama Garibaldi.** North of the square is Palermo's swankiest street, **Viale della Libertà,** running up toward Giardino Inglese (the English Gardens). This is the area where the Art Nouveau movement triumphed in the city, as is still visible in the kiosks at Piazza Castelnuovo and in Piazza Verdi, but many of these priceless edifices were torn down by unscrupulous builders to make way for ugly cement behemoths that mar the elegance of the neighborhood.

Exploring Palermo

Most of everything you want to see is within walking distance of the Quattro Canti, where Via Maqueda meets Via Vittorio Emanuele.

Catacombs of the Capuchins (Catacombe dei Cappuccini) ★
CEMETERY   In 1599, the occupants of the adjoining Capuchin monastery discovered that the bodies of the brothers they placed in their catacombs soon became naturally mummified, and Sicilians began demanding to be buried along with them. In these chambers, the corpses of some 8,000 people in various stages of preservation now hang from walls and recline in open caskets. It would be easy to write the spectacle off as eerie

(which it certainly is) or even a bit vampy, but for the deceased and the loved ones they left behind, a spot here provided a bit of comforting immortality. Wearing their Sunday best, the dead are grouped according to sex and rank—men, women, virgins, priests, nobles, professors (possibly including the painter Velasquez, though his presence here is questionable), and children. This last grouping includes the most recent resident, 2-year-old Rosalia Lombardo, who died in 1920 and whom locals have dubbed "Sleeping Beauty." Giuseppe Tommasi, prince of Lampedusa and author of one of the best-known works of Sicilian literature, *The Leopard*, was buried in the cemetery next to the catacombs in 1957. His great-grandmother, the model for the princess in the novel, is in the catacombs.

Capuchins Monastery, Piazza Cappuccini 1. (℘ **091-212117.** Admission 3€. Daily 9am–noon and 3–5pm (until 7pm in summer). Closed holidays. Bus: 327.

Chiesa della Martorana/San Cataldo ★★ CHURCH These two Norman churches stand side by side, separated by a little tropical garden. George of Antioch, Roger II's Greek admiral, founded Santa Maria dell'Ammiraglio in 1141; the church was later renamed **Chiesa della Martorana** for Eloisa Martorana, who founded a nearby Benedictine convent. The nuns gained the everlasting appreciation of Palermitans when they invented marzipan, and *frutta di Martorana*—sweets in which marzipan is fashioned into the shape of little fruits—has outlived the order. George of Antioch, for his part, had a love of Byzantine mosaics and hired the North African craftsmen who had just completed their work on the **Cappella Palatina** (see p. 620) to also cover this church's walls, pillars, and floors with stunning mosaics in deep hues of ivory,

Shopping at a local market in Palermo.

green, azure, red, and gold. Christ crowns Roger II, George appears in a Byzantine robe, and Christ appears again in the dome, surrounded by angels. The Arab geographer/traveler Ibn Jubayr visited Palermo in 1166 and called the church "the most beautiful monument in the world." In 1266 Sicilian nobles met here and agreed to offer the crown to Peter of Aragon, ending a bloody uprising against French rule known as the Sicilian Vespers. A baroque redo has rendered the interior a little less transporting than it was then, but it's still beautiful.

Maio of Bari, chancellor to William I, began the tiny **Chiesa di San Cataldo** next door in 1154, but he died before it was completed in 1160, so the church was left unfinished. The red domes and the lacy crenellation around the tops of the walls are decidedly Moorish, while the stone interior, with three little cupolas over the nave, evoke the Middle Ages—all the more so since traces were removed of the church's use over the years as a hospital and post office.

Piazza Bellini 2, adjacent to Piazza Pretoria. (℃ **091-6161692.** La Martorana: Free admission. Mon–Sat 9:30am–1pm and 3:30–6:30pm; Sun 8:30am–1pm. San Cataldo: 2€. Tues–Fri 9am–5pm; Sat–Sun 9am–1pm. Bus: 101 or 102.

Duomo ★ CATHEDRAL   All those who came, saw, and conquered in Palermo left their mark on this cathedral, an architectural pastiche that lies somewhere between exquisite and eyesore. It is, however, noble enough as befits the final resting place of Roger II, the first king of Sicily, who died in 1154, and other Norman–Swabian royalty. Neapolitan architect Ferdinando Fuga began a restoration in 1771 that gave the exterior and the interior an all-encompassing neoclassical style, adding a cupola that sticks out like a sore thumb on the original Norman design. With a little attention you can pick out some of the original elements: four impressive campaniles (bell towers) from the 14th century; the middle portal from the 15th century; and the south and north porticos from the 15th and 16th centuries. Take note of the column on the left of the south portico: It was recycled from a mosque and is inscribed with a verse from the Koran.

Piazza Cattedrale. (℃ **091-334373.** Duomo: free admission; crypt and treasury: 1€ each. Mon–Sat 9:30am–1:30pm and 2:30–5:30pm. Bus: 101, 104, 105, 107, or 139.

Galleria Regionale della Sicilia (Regional Gallery)/Palazzo Abatellis ★★★ MUSEUM   Center stage at this fine collection is the late–15th century *palazzo* that houses it, built around two courtyards and beautifully restored in the 1950s. On display is an array of the arts in Sicily from the 13th to the 18th centuries, though it's hard to get beyond the gallery's most celebrated work, the **"Trionfo della Morte" ("Triumph of Death").** Dating from 1449 and of uncertain attribution, this huge study in black and gray is prominently displayed in a two-story ground-floor gallery (once you've looked at it up close, climb the stairs to the balcony for an overview). Death has never looked worse—a fearsome skeletal demon astride an undernourished steed, brandishing a scythe as he leaps over his victims (allegedly members of Palermo aristocracy, who

THE oratories OF GIACOMO SERPOTTA

Some of Palermo's most delightful places of worship are oratories, private chapels funded by private societies and guilds and usually connected to a larger church. Giacomo Serpotta, a native master of sculpting in stucco, decorated several oratorios in the early 18th century. Most are open Monday through Friday 10am to 1pm and 3 to 6pm, Saturday 10am to 1pm, though hours vary. You'll be charged 2€ admission, but your ticket is good at at least one other oratory.

Serpotta was a member of the Society of the Holy Rosary, and he decorated the society's **Oratorio del Rosario di San Domenico** (Via dei Bambinai; ℂ 091-332779) with his delightfully expressive *putti* (cherubs), who are locked forever in a playground of happy antics. His 3-D reliefs depict everything from the Allegories of the Virtues to the Apocalypse of St. John to a writhing "Devil Falling from Heaven." Anthony van Dyck, the Dutch master who spent time in Palermo in the 1620s, did the "Madonna of the Rosary" over the high altar.

Serpotta also worked on the **Oratorio di San Lorenzo** (Via dell'Immacolatella;

ℂ **091-332779**) between 1698 and 1710, creating panels relating the details of the lives of St. Francis and St. Lawrence to create what critics have admiringly called "a cave of white coral." Some of the most expressive of the stuccoes depict the martyrdom of Lawrence, who was roasted to death and nonchalantly informed his tormentors, "I'm well done. Turn me over." Among the reliefs are serene-looking statues of the Virtues, amid them naked *putti* romping gaily. Caravaggio's last large painting, a "Nativity," once hung over the altar, but it was stolen in 1969 and never recovered.

The all-white **Oratorio del Rosario di Santa Cita** (Via Valverde 3; ℂ **091-332779**) houses Serpotta's crowning achievement, a detailed relief of the Battle of Lepanto, in which a coalition of European states defeated the Turks, more or less preventing the expansion of the Ottoman Empire into Western Europe. Serpotta's cherubs, oblivious to international affairs, romp up and down the walls and climb onto window frames.

were none too pleased with the portrayal). The painter is believed to have depicted himself in the fresco, seen with an apprentice praying in vain for release from the horrors of Death, the poor and hungry, looking on from the side, have escaped such a gruesome fate for the time being. The precision of this astonishing work, including details of the horse's nostrils and the men and women in the full flush of their youth, juxtaposed against such darkness, suggests the Surrealism movement that came to the fore 400 years later.

The second masterpiece of the gallery, in room 4, is a refreshing antidote, and also quite modern-looking: the white-marble, slanted-eyed bust of **"Eleonora di Aragona,"** by Francesco Laurana. The Dalmatian-born sculptor was in Sicily from 1466 to 1471, and he captured this likeness of Eleanor, daughter of King Ferdinand I of Naples, shortly before she married Ercole d'Este and became the duchess of Ferrara. Of the Sicilian artists on display, Antonello da Messina stands out, with an "Annunciation" in room 11. (It is one of the two Annunciations he painted; the other is at the Bellomo museum in Siracusa, see p. 603). This one is probably the artist's most famous work, completed in 1476 in Venice. He depicts the Virgin as an adolescent girl, sitting at a desk with a devotional book in front of her, clasping her cloak modestly to her chest. She raises her hand, seemingly to us viewers but probably to Gabriel, who has just delivered the news that she is to be the mother of the son of God. Considering that news, her expression is remarkably serene. This is one of the most lovely and calming works anywhere.

Via Alloro 4, Palazzo Abatellis. ℂ **091-6230011.** Admission 8€ adults, 4€ children. Tues–Sun 9am–1:30pm and 2:30–6:30pm. Bus: 103, 105, or 139.

Museo Archeologico Regionale "Antonino Salinas" (Regional Archaeological Museum) ★★★

The first thing to know about this stunning collection of antiquities is that you may not see it, as the museum was closed indefinitely in 2011 for a much-needed renovation. When it is open, the former convent of the Filippini, built around a lovely cloister, displays a head-spinning repository of artifacts from the island's many inhabitants and invaders: Phoenicians, Greeks, Saracens, and Romans. The museum's most important treasures are metopes (temple friezes) from once-great Selinunte on the southern coast. Sumptuous, detailed marbles depict Perseus slaying Medusa, the Rape of Europa by Zeus, Actaeon being transformed into a stag, and other scenes that bring these myths vividly to life. Among the other artifacts—anchors from Punic warships, mirrors used by the Etruscans, and a joyful Roman statue of "Satyr Filling a Drinking Cup"—is a rare Egyptian find: The **Pietra di Palermo** (Palermo Stone), a black stone slab dating from 2700 B.C. that is known as the Rosetta stone of Sicily. Discovered in Egypt in the 19th century, it was in transit for the British Museum in London when it was shuffled off to the corners of a Palermo dock. The hieroglyphics reveal the inscriber's attention to detail: a list of pharaohs, details of the delivery of 40 shiploads of cedarwood to Snefru, and flood levels of the Nile.

Piazza Olivella 24. ℂ **091-6116805.** Closed temporarily. Admission 4€ adults, 2€ children 18 and under. Tues–Fri 8:30am–1:30pm and 2:30–6:30pm; Sat–Sun and holidays 8:30am–1:30pm. Bus: 101, 102, 103, 104, 107, or Linea Rossa.

Palazzo dei Normanni ★★ and Cappella Palatina ★★★

PALACE The cultural influences of Sicily collide in this palace, which dates back to the 8th century B.C., when Punic administrators set up an outpost in the highest part of the city. In the 9th century A.D. the Arabs built a palace on the spot for their emirs and their harems, and in the 12th century the Normans turned what was essentially a fortress into a sumptuous royal residence. Here Frederick II presided over the early 13th-century court of minstrels and literati that founded the Schola Poetica Siciliana, which marked the birth of Italian literature. Spanish viceroys took up residence in the palace in 1555, and today most of the vast maze of rooms and grand halls houses the seat of Sicily's semiautonomous regional government.

Arab–Norman cultural influences intersect most spectacularly in the **Cappella Palatina**, a chapel covered in glittering Byzantine mosaics from 1130 to 1140. It was finished in time for the coronation of Roger II, who proved to be not only the most powerful of European kings but also the most enlightened. High in the cupola at the end of the apse is Christ Pantocrator (as usual in this iconic image, he holds the New Testament in his left hand and makes the gesture of blessing with his right hand). He is surrounded by saints and biblical characters, some interpreted a little less piously than usual—Adam and Eve happily munch on the forbidden fruit, and rather than showing any remorse for their act of defiance, they greedily reach for a second piece. Shame prevails in the next scene, when God steps in reproachfully and the naked couple covers themselves with leaves. The mosaics are vibrant in the soft light, and the effect is especially powerful in scenes depicting waters, as in the flood and the Baptism of Christ—in these, water appears actually to be shimmering.

More scenes appear on the wooden ceiling, done in a three-dimensional technique using small sections of carved wood, known in Arabic as *muqarnas*. A team of carpenters and painters was brought in from Egypt to create the playfully secular scenarios of dancers, musicians, hunters on horseback, drinkers, even banqueters in a harem. You'll see them best with binoculars or a telephoto lens.

Visits to the **Royal Apartments** are escorted, as this is a seat of government. Tours are almost always conducted in Italian; ask if there is

Mosaics in the Cappella Palatina.

an usher on duty who can speak English. The apartments are not open to the public when the Sicilian parliament is in session—meeting in the **Salone d'Ercole**, named for the mammoth 19th-century frescoes depicting the "Twelve Labours of Hercules" (pundits like to say this is apt decoration for legislators wading through government bureaucracy). The fairly pompous staterooms from the years of Spanish rule give way to earlier remnants, among them the **Sala dei Presidenti**; this stark chamber was hidden in the bowels of the palace for several centuries, completely unknown until 2002, when an earthquake knocked down one of the walls and unveiled an untouched, medieval relic. The **Torre Gioaria** (tower of the wind) is a harbinger of modern air-conditioning systems: A fountain in the middle of the tower (since removed) spouted water that cooled the breezes coming from the four hallways. In the Torre Gioaria is the Sala di Ruggero II, decorated with mosaics of nature and hunting scenes. Much less hospitable are the **Segrete**, or dungeons, where the cold stone walls are etched with primitive scenes of Norman warships. The otherwise enlightened Frederick II is said to have taken his interest in science to perverse lengths in these chambers, where he shut prisoners in casks to see whether or not their souls could be observed escaping through a small hole at the moment of death. He also imprisoned children, forbidding any interaction beyond sucking and bathing, to see if they would develop a natural language that would provide clues to the speech God gave Adam and Eve.

Frederick was fascinated by the stars and brought many astronomers and astrologers to his court. His Bourbon successors shared the interest and in 1790 added an astronomical observatory, still functioning, at the top of the **Torre Pisana**. From these heights in 1801 the priest Fra Giuseppe Piazza discovered Ceres, the first asteroid known to mankind.

Piazza del Parlamento. www.ars.sicilia.it. ℮ **091-626833.** Admission 8.50€, free for children 17 and under. Admission 7€ Tues–Thurs, when the Royal Apartments are closed due to Parliamentary meetings. Mon–Sat 8:15am–5pm; Sun 8:15am–12:15pm. Bus: 104, 105, 108, 109, 110, 118, 304, or 309.

San Giovanni degli Eremiti ★ CHURCH   Palermo's most romantic landmark is a simple affair, part Arab, part Norman, with five red domes atop a portico, a single nave, two small apses, and a squat tower. As befits the humble Spanish recluse it honors, St. John of the Hermits, the church is almost devoid of decoration, though the surrounding citrus blossoms and flowers imbue the modest structure with an other-worldy aura. Adding to the charms of the spot is a Norman cloister, with a Moorish cistern in the center, part of a Benedictine monastery that once stood here.

Via dei Benedettini 3. ℮ **091-6515019.** Admission 6€ adults; 3€ students, seniors, and children. Tues–Sat 9am–1pm and 3–7pm; Sun 9am–6:30pm. Bus: 109 or 318.

Where to Stay

Palermo has some excellent hotels, with rates much lower than they are in Rome or Florence. For convenience and atmosphere, don't stay too far beyond the neighborhoods in the old center (see above).

Ariston Hotel ★★   The sixth floor of an apartment building near Teatro Massimo is a welcoming retreat, with bright, airy rooms spread along a corridor off a comfortable lounge. Luxuries don't extend much beyond free coffee and tea, but the premises are spotless, owner/manager Giuseppe is a welcoming host, and the plain but pleasing furnishings and a smattering of modern art hit just the right tasteful notes—all making this place an excellent value.

Via Mariano Stabile 139. www.aristonpalermo.it. ℮ **091-3322434.** 8 units. 59€–75€ double. **Amenities:** Wi-fi (free). Bus: 101.

Butera 28 ★★★ The 17th-century Lanza Tomasi Palace, facing the seafront, is the home of Duke Gioacchino Lanza Tomasi, the adoptive son of Prince Giuseppe Tomasi di Lampedusa, author of one of the greatest works of modern Italian literature, *The Leopard*. The gracious duke and his charming wife, Nicoletta, have converted 12 apartments of their *palazzo* to short-stay apartments, filling them with family pieces and all the modern conveniences, including full kitchens and, every traveler's dream come true, washing machines. Apartments have one or two bedrooms; some have sea views and terraces, some are multilevel, and all have beautiful hardwood or tile floors and other detailing. The duchess also offers cooking classes, and she and the duke are on hand to provide a wealth of advice to help you get the most out of their beloved Palermo.

Via Butera 28. www.butera28.it. ✆ **333-316-5432.** 12 units. From 70€ double. **Amenities:** Kitchens, Wi–Fi (free). Bus: 103, 104, 105, 118, or 225.

Centrale Palace ★★ A wonderful location just steps off the Quattro Canti puts this much-redone yet still grand *palazzo* within easy reach of most sights. Public rooms, including a vast frescoed salon where breakfast is served, evoke the 1890s Belle Époque age when the 17th-century *palazzo* was first converted to a hotel. The good-sized guest rooms above are comfortably functional, with some luxe touches like rich fabrics and mosaic-tiled bathrooms; double-pane windows in the front rooms keep the street noise at bay. A rooftop sun terrace offers a retreat from the city below, with views that extend across the rooftops to Monte Pellegrino. There's an airy dining room up here, and you may want to linger well into a warm summer night.

Via Vittorio Emanuele 327 (at Via Maqueda). www.centralepalacehotel.it. ✆ **091-336666.** 104 units. 140€–271€ double. Some rates include buffet breakfast. Parking 18€. **Amenities:** 2 restaurants; bar; exercise room; sauna; room service; babysitting; Wi–Fi (free). Bus: 103, 104, or 105.

Grand Hotel Piazza Borsa ★★ A conglomeration of three historic buildings seems to take in a bit of every part of Palermo's past—the banking floor and grand offices of the old stock exchange, a monastery, and a centuries-old *palazzo*. These elements come together atmospherically in surroundings that include a cloister, open-roofed atrium, paneled dining rooms, and frescoed salons. Guest rooms are a bit more businesslike, though large and plushly comfortable, with hardwood floors and furnishings that cross traditional with some contemporary flair; the best have balconies overlooking the surrounding churches and palaces. A spa and exercise area includes a sauna and steam room.

Via dei Cartari 18. www.piazzaborsa.com. ✆ **091-320075**. 103 units. 120€–200€ double. Rates include buffet breakfast. **Amenities:** Restaurant; bar; babysitting; concierge; Wi–Fi (free). Bus: 103, 104, 105, 118, or 225.

Hotel Porta Felice ★ It's a sign that the old Kalsa district is on the upswing that this elegant and subdued retreat has risen amid a once derelict block of buildings just off the seafront. Marble-floored public areas are coolly soothing, while guest rooms are sleekly contemporary, with just

MEN OF dishonor

Members of the Sicilian Mafia (or "Men of Honor," as they like to be called) traditionally operated as a network of regional bosses who controlled individual towns by setting up puppet regimes of thoroughly corrupt officials. It was a sort of devil's bargain with the national Christian Democrat Party, which controlled Italy's government from World War II until 1993 and, despite its law-and-order rhetoric, tacitly left Cosa Nostra alone as long as the bosses got out the party vote.

The Cosa Nostra trafficked in illegal goods, of course, but until the 1960s and 1970s, its income was derived mainly from low-level protection rackets, funneling state money into its own pockets, and ensuring that public contracts were granted to fellow mafiosi (all reasons why Sicily has experienced unchecked industrialization and modern growth at the expense of its heritage and the welfare of its communities). But in the 1970s the younger generation of Mafia underbosses got into the highly lucrative heroin and cocaine trades, transforming the Sicilian Mafia into a world player on the international drug-trafficking circuit—and raking in the dough. This ignited a clandestine Mafia war that, throughout the late 1970s and 1980s, generated headlines of bloody Mafia hits. The new generation was wiping out the old and

turning the balance of power in their favor.

This situation gave rise to the first Mafia turncoats, disgruntled ex-bosses and rank-and-file stoolies who told their stories, first to police prefect Gen. Carlo Alberto Dalla Chiesa (assassinated 1982) and later to crusading magistrates Giovanni Falcone (killed May 23, 1992) and Paolo Borsellino (murdered July 19, 1992), who staged the "maxitrials" of mafiosi that sent hundreds to jail. The magistrates' 1992 murders, especially, drew public attention to the dishonorable methods of the new Mafia and, perhaps for the first time, began to stir true shame.

On a broad and culturally important scale, it is these young mafiosi, without a moral center or check on their powers, who have driven many Sicilians to at least secretly break the unwritten code of omertà, which translates as "homage" but means "silence," when faced with harboring or even tolerating a man of honor. The Mafia still exists in Palermo, the small towns south of it, and the provincial capitals of Catania, Trapani, and Agrigento. Throughout the rest of Sicily, its power has been slipping. The heroin trade is a far cry from construction schemes and protection money, and the Mafia is swiftly outliving its usefulness and its welcome.

enough antique pieces and expanses of hardwood to suggest traditional comforts. A rooftop bar and terrace is a welcome refuge, while the downstairs health spa is geared to ultimate relaxation.

Via Butera 35. www.hotelportafelice.it. © **091-617-5678.** 33 units. 130€–240€ double. Rates include buffet breakfast. **Amenities:** Bar; spa; Wi-Fi (free). Bus: 103, 104, 105, 118, or 225.

Where to Eat

Palermitans dine well on the fresh seafood and other bounty of the city markets, and they have a laudable appreciation for sweets. Legendary pastry shops like **Mazzara** (Via Generale Magliocco 19; © **091-321443**) will fill you up with cassata, cannoli, *frutta martorana* (marzipan sweets), and gelato, while the opulent **Antico Caffè Spinnato** (Via Principe di Belmonte 115; www.spinnato.it; ✆ **091-583231**), established in 1860, is the place to linger over a pastry and coffee. While exploring the Kalsa quarter, you can satisfy a sweet tooth at **Ciccolateria Lorenzo,** near the Palazzo Abatellis at Via Quattro Aprile 7 (✆ **091-840846;** closed Mon.), with a wonderful selection of cakes and the best hot chocolate in Palermo, and at **Antica Gelateria Patricola,** on the waterfront at Foro Umberto 1—try the Riso di Paradise, a concoction of chocolate, rice, and whipped cream, and you'll come back daily (closed in winter).

Antica Focacceria San Francesco ★ SICILIAN/SNACKS Palermo street fare is good anywhere you have it, but it's especially savory in the atmospheric, marble-floored surroundings of this institution founded in 1834. If you've shied away from buying a *panino con la milza* (a bread roll stuffed with slices of boiled spleen and melted cheese) from a street vendor, you might want to jump in and try this delicious specialty here. You can also snack or lunch on *panelle* (deep-fried chickpea fritters), *ararancini di riso* (rice balls stuffed with tomatoes and peas or mozzarella), *focaccia farcita* (flat pizza baked with various fillings), or a number of other sandwiches, curtly dispensed from a busy counter.
Via A. Paternostro 58. www.afsf.it. ✆ **091-320264.** Sandwiches 3€–5€. Daily 11am–11pm (closed Tues Oct–Mar). Bus: 103, 105, or 225.

Casa del Brodo ★ SICILIAN With a setting in two plain rooms on the edge of the now sadly diminished Vucciria market, this century-old institution serves old Sicilian specialties that you might not encounter outside of home kitchens. *Fritelle di fava* (fava beans) are fried with vegetables and cheese; *carni bollite* (boiled meats) is a tantalizing assortment of tender, herb-flavored meats; and the *macco di fave* (meatballs and tripe) is a carnivore's delight. The namesake *brodo* (broth) is served several different ways, best as tortellini in brodo, with house-made pasta. If in doubt, order one of the fixed-price menus.
Corso Vittorio Emanuele 175. www.casadelbrodo.it. ✆ **091-321655.** Main courses 8€–16€; fixed-price menus from 20€. Wed–Mon 12:30–3pm and 7:30–11pm (closed Sun June–Sept). Bus: 103, 104, 105, 118, or 225.

Ferro di Cavallo ★ SICILIAN Bright red walls seem to rev up the energy to high levels in this ever-busy favorite, but the buzz is really about the good, plain food served at very reasonable prices. There's a menu, and a decent *antipasti* platter offers a nice sampling of *panelle* (fried chickpea fritters) and other street food, but go with the daily specials to get the full flavor of the kitchen. The preference is for beans and celery, broad beans and vegetables, meatballs in tomato sauce, boiled veal, and other classics. Service hovers between nonchalant and brusque, but the jovial atmosphere compensates, and you'll pay very little for your homey meal.
Via Venezia 20. www.ferrodicavallopalermo.it. ✆ **091-331835.** Main courses 7€. Mon–Sat 10am–3:30pm and 7:45–11:30pm. Bus: 103, 104, 105, 118, or 225.

Ottava Nota ★★ SICILIAN   "New Sicilian" is in full force at the most exciting of the restaurants that have opened in the once derelict Kalsa district in recent years, where the sleek surroundings are the setting for creative takes on Sicilian classics. Tuna tartare is served with avocado, risotto is laced with leeks and tuna caviar, and eggplant meatballs are topped with tomato cream. Duck, beef, and fish are market fresh and beautifully prepared, but you may not want to go beyond the pastas with fresh seafood—linguine with scallops, risotto with shrimp, tagliatelle with sea urchins. Service is strictly old-school—friendly and attentive—and a meal usually begins with a complimentary glass of prosecco.

Via Butera 55. ⓒ **091-6168601.** Main courses 10€–20€. Mon 8–11pm, Tues–Sun 12:30–3:30pm and 8–11pm. Bus: 103, 104, 105, 118, or 225.

Entertainment & Nightlife

Palermo is a cultural center of some note, with an opera and ballet season running from November to July. The principal venue for cultural presentations is the restored **Teatro Massimo** ★★, Piazza G. Verdi (www.teatromassimo.it; ⓒ **091-6053111**), which boasts the third largest indoor stage in Europe. Francis Ford Coppola shot the climactic opera scene here for *The Godfather: Part III.* Built between 1875 and 1897 in a neoclassical style, the theater was restored in 1997 to celebrate its 100th birthday. Ticket prices range from 10€ to 125€. The box office is open Tuesday to Sunday 10am to 3pm. **Note:** The Teatro Massimo can be visited Tuesday through Sunday from 10am to 3pm. Visits cost 5€. Guided tours in English are given Tuesday through Saturday from 10am to 3pm (bus: 101, 102, 103, 104, 107, 122, or 225).

Side Trips from Palermo

For Palermitans, a warm summer day means one thing—a trip to **Mondello Lido,** 12km (7½ miles) west of Palermo, where Belle Epoque Europeans once came to winter. Their Art Nouveau villas face a sandy beach that stretches for about 2km (1¼ miles), though there's little or no elbow room in July and August. Bus no. 806 makes the 15-minute trip to Mondello from Piazza Sturzo behind the Teatro Politeama.

Should you wish to do more than lie on a beach, many other sights are within easy reach of Palermo. The tour below are our best picks.

MONREALE ★★★
10km (6 miles) S of Palermo

On the Mons Regalis overlooking the Conca d'Oro (the Golden Valley), this hilltop village would be just another of the many that dot this fertile area south of Palermo if it weren't for its majestic Duomo, one of Italy's greatest medieval treasures, carpeted in shimmering mosaics. The locals even have a saying, "To come to Palermo without having seen Monreale is like coming in like a donkey and leaving like an ass."

GETTING THERE The **AST bus** (www.aziendasicilianatrasporti.it; © 840-000323) leaves about every hour or so throughout the day from Palermo's Piazza Giulio Cesare (Central Train station) and Piazza Indipendenza (2.10€ one-way). If you are **driving** (it's about a 30 minute drive), leave your vehicle at the municipal car park at Via Ignazio Florio. From there you can take a cab or walk up the 99 steps that lead to the cathedral.

Exploring the Duomo

Duomo ★★ CATHEDRAL   Legend has it that William II had the idea of this cathedral in a dream when, during a hunting expedition, he fell asleep under a carob tree. While slumbering, the Virgin Mary appeared to him, indicating where a treasure chest was located—and with this loot he was to build a church in her honor. Legends aside, William's ambition to leave his mark was the force behind the last—and the greatest—of Sicily's Arab-Norman cathedrals with Byzantine interiors. Best of all, the cathedral in Monreale never underwent any of the "improvements" that were applied to the cathedral of Palermo, and therefore its original beauty was preserved.

For the most part, the exterior of the building is nothing remarkable. But inside, mosaics comprise some 130 individual scenes, depicting biblical and religious events, covering some 6,400 sq. m (68,889 sq. ft.), and utilizing some 2,200 kg (4,850 lb.) of gold. The shop in the arcade

The cathedral of Monreale.

outside the entrance sells a detailed plan of the mosaics with a legend detailing what's what, a mandatory aid to enjoying the spectacle; binoculars are also handy.

Episodes from the Old Testament are depicted in the central nave (a particularly charming scene shows Noah's Ark riding the waves) while the side aisles illustrate scenes from the New Testament. Christ Pantocrator, the Great Ruler, looks over it all from the central apse; actually, he gazes off to one side, toward scenes from his life. Just below is a mosaic of the Teokotos (Mother of God) with the Christ child on her lap, bathed in light from the small window above the main entrance. Among the angels and saints flanking Teokotos is Thomas à Becket, the Archbishop of Canterbury who was murdered on the orders of William's father-in-law, Henry II (this is one of the earliest portraits of the saint; he is the second from the right).

William II is buried here, and also honored with a mosaic showing him being crowned by Christ. The heart of St. Louis, or Louis IX, a 13th-century king of France, rests in the urn in which it was placed when the king died during a crusade in Tunisia; the urn was transported to Sicily, then ruled by Louis's younger brother, Charles of Anjou.

The lovely cloisters adjacent to the cathedral are an Arabesque fantasy, surrounded by 228 columns topped with capitals carved with scenes from Sicily's Norman history. A splendid fountain in the shape of a palm tree adds to the romance of the place.

Piazza Guglielmo il Buono. ✆ **091-6404413.** Free admission to the cathedral; 2€ north transept and treasury; 2€ roof; 8€ cloisters, 4€ ages 18–25, free for children 17 and under and EU citizens 65 and over. Mon–Sat 8am–1pm and 2:30–6:30pm, Sun 8am–1pm; Cloisters: daily 9am–7pm.

CEFALÙ ★★

81km (50 miles) E of Palermo

The former fishing village of Cefalù, anchored between the sea and a craggy limestone promontory, has grown into a popular resort, though it will never be a rival to Taormina. If you saw the Oscar-winning film *Cinema Paradiso,* you've already been charmed by the town, though the filmmakers wisely left out the hordes of white-fleshed northern Europeans who roast themselves on the crescent-shaped **beach**, one of the best along the northern coast. Towering 278m (912 ft.) above the beach and town is **La Rocca,** a massive and much-photographed crag. The Greeks thought it evoked a head, so they named the village Kephalos, which in time became Cefalù. It's a long, hot, sweaty climb up to the top, but once there, the view is panoramic, extending all the way to the skyline of Palermo in the west or to Capo d'Orlando in the east.

GETTING THERE From Palermo, some three dozen **trains** (www.trenitalia.com; ✆ **892021**) head east to Cefalù (trip time: 1 hr.). Trains pull into the Stazione Termini, Piazza Stazione (✆ **892021**). **SAIS buses** (✆ **091-6171141**) run between Palermo and Cefalù.

By **car,** follow Route 113 east from Palermo to Cefalù; count on at least 1½ hours of driving time (longer if traffic is bad). Once in Cefalù, park along either side of Via Roma for free, or pay 1€ per hour for a spot within one of the two lots signposted from the main street; both are within an easy walk of the town's medieval core.

VISITOR INFORMATION The **Cefalù Tourist Office,** Corso Ruggero 77 (✆ **0921-421050**), is open Monday to Saturday 8am to 7:30pm, Sunday 9am to 1pm. Closed on Sunday in winter.

Exploring Cefalù

Getting around Cefalù on foot is easy—no cars are allowed in the historic core. The city's main street is **Corso Ruggero,** which starts at Piazza Garibaldi, site of one of a quartet of gateways to the town.

Duomo ★★★ CHURCH Anchored on a wide square at the foot of towering La Rocca, the twin-towered facade of the duomo forms a landmark visible for miles around. Legend has it that Roger II ordered this mighty church to be constructed in the 12th century after his life was spared in a violent storm off the coast. In reality, he probably built it to flex his muscle with the papacy and show the extent of his power in Sicily. Inside are more mosaics, and even if you've become inured to the charms of these shimmering scenes in Palermo and Monreale, you're in for a bit of a surprise: This being a Norman church, Christ is depicted as a blond, not a brunette. In his hand is a Bible, a standard accessory in these images of Christ the Pantocrator (the Ruler), with the verse, "I am the light of the world; he who follows me shall not walk in darkness." Columns in the nave are said to be from the much-ruined Temple of Diana halfway up La Rocca (you'll stop to inspect the rest of the stony remains if you make the climb to the top).
Piazza del Duomo. ✆ **0921-922021.** Free admission. Summer daily 8am–noon and 3:30–7pm; off season daily 8am–noon and 3:30–5pm.

Museo Mandralisca MUSEUM There is only one reason to step into this small museum, and it's a compelling one: "Ritratto di un Uomo Ignoto" ("Portrait of an Unknown Man"), a 1470 work by the Sicilian painter Antonello da Messina. Seeing this young man with a sly smile and twinkling eyes—some scholars say he was a pirate from the island of Lipari—is an experience akin to seeing the "Mona Lisa," and you won't have to fight your way through camera-wielding crowds to do so.
Via Mandralisca 13. ✆ **0921-421547.** Admission 5€. Daily 9am–1pm and 3–7pm.

Where to Eat

For cakes and cookies, stop by **Pasticceria Serio Pietro,** V. G. Giglio 29 (✆ **0921-422293**), which also sells more than a dozen flavors of the most delicious gelato in town.

Osteria del Duomo ★★ SICILIAN/SEAFOOD A prime spot across from the duomo with great views of the Rocca alone would make this a worthy stop, and the fresh seafood does justice to the locale.

The Old Town of Cefalù.

Seafood salads are a perfect choice for lunch on a summer's day, and piscivores will love the *carpaccio de pesce* (raw, thinly sliced fish). Carnivores can tuck into the similarly excellent carpaccio of beef. Try to reserve ahead on weekends.

Via Seminario 3. © **0921-421838.** Main courses 8€–16€. Tues–Sun noon–midnight. Closed mid-Nov to mid-Dec.

SEGESTA ★★★

75km (47 miles) SW of Palermo

The **Tempio di Segesta**, one of the best-preserved ancient Doric temples in all of Italy, proves yet again that the Greeks had a remarkable eye for where to build. Part of the ruined ancient city of Segesta, for millennia this beautiful structure in a lonely field overlooking the sea has been delighting those lucky enough to set eyes upon it. The temple was especially popular with 18th-century artists traveling in Sicily, whose paintings usually included herds of sheep and cattle in or surrounding the temple.

GETTING THERE From Palermo, three trains a day make the 1¾- to 2-hour journey. The station is about a 1km (½-mile) walk to the park entrance. It's more convenient to reach Segesta **by bus; Tarantola** (© **0924-31020**) operates four buses from Piazza Giulio Cesare (Central Train Station) in Palermo (journey time: 1¾ hour).

By **car,** take the autostrada (A29) running between Palermo and Trapani. The exit at Segesta is clearly marked. The journey takes a little under an hour from Palermo.

Exploring the Parco Archaeologico (The Archaeological Park)

The archaeological site, which is outside the modern town of Calatafimi, is still the subject of study by archaeologists from around the world. There's a small, canopied eating area opposite the only cafe, where visitors can unwind or rest during their visit.

Parco Archaeologico Segesta ★★★ RUINS   The **Tempio di Segesta (Temple of Segesta)** stands on a 304m (997-ft.) hill, on the edge of a deep ravine carved by the Pispisa River. Built in the 5th century B.C., it was never finished; the columns were never fluted and the roof was never placed on top. This, of course, does not affect the temple's greatest assets: the view down the hillside to the sea and the views of the temple from afar. Segesta's other great sight is the perfectly preserved **Teatro (Theater),** hewn out of rock at the top of 431m (1,414 ft.) Mount Barbaro (it's accessible by a hike of 4km [2½ miles] or by buses that run every half hour, cost 1.50€). The *cavea* of 20 semicircular rows could seat 4,000 spectators, who enjoyed views across the surrounding farmland to the Gulf of Castellamare. Those stunning views surely competed with any performance—and still do, during summertime stagings of operas, concerts, and plays.

Parco Archaelogico Segesta. ✆ **0924-952356**. Combined ticket with Parco Archeologico in Selinunte (p. 632), valid for 3 days: 9€ adults, 4.50€ ages 18–25, free children 17 and under. Mar daily 9am–6pm, Apr–Sept daily 8:30am–7pm, Oct–Feb daily 9am–5pm. Ticket office closes 1 hr before park closes.

SELINUNTE ★★★
122km (76 miles) SW of Palermo

This westernmost Greek colony was one of the most powerful cities in the world, home to 100,000 inhabitants, when the great Carthiginian general Hannibal virtually destroyed it in 409 B.C. He spared only the temples—not out of respect for the deities, but to preserve the loot they housed. Today the vast archaeological park comprises 270 hectares (670 acres), making it Europe's largest archaeological site. Selinunte is not just large, but also beautiful, a bucolic spot where you can walk amid the ruins, gaze out to sea, and ponder what life might have been like millennia ago. As you walk amid the wildflowers and smell the wild herbs, remember that the name of the town name comes from the Greek word *selinon,* meaning parsley.

GETTING THERE   Selinunte is on the southern coast of Sicily and is most easily reached by **car.** From Palermo, take the A29 autostrada and get off at Castelvetrano, following the signs thereafter. Allow about 2 hours for the trip.

If you prefer to take the **train** (www.trenitalia.it; ✆ **892021**) from Palermo, you can get off at Castelvetrano, 23km (14 miles) from the ruins. The trip from Palermo to Castelvetrano takes a little over 2 hours (you need to change trains); once at Castelvetrano, board a **bus** for the final lap of the journey to Selinunte. **Autoservizi Salemi** (www.autoservizisalemi.it; ✆ **0923-981120**), which also operates a service from Palermo to Castelvetrano, will take you to the archaeological park in 20 minutes.

VISITOR INFORMATION   The tourist office at Via Giovanni Caboto (✆ **0924-46251**), near the archaeological park, is open Monday to Saturday 8am to 2pm and 3 to 8pm, Sunday 9am to noon and 3 to 6pm.

The Temple of Segesta.

Exploring the Archaeological Park

Given the enormity of the area, allow yourself at least 3 hours to visit, preferably in the early morning. Bring or buy drinks before starting your visit, as you can get rather thirsty under the sun. Ecotour Selinunte runs a hop-on-hop-off service to all the sites within the park on a train of golf carts. For more info, visit www.selinunteservice.com or call ✆ **347-1645862.**

Parco Archeologico Selinunte ★★★ RUINS   The archaeological grounds are designated into three distinct zones: The East Hill and temples, the Acropolis and ancient city, and the Sanctuary of Demeter Malophorus. You will most likely start your visit from the East Hill, adjacent to the main entrance. (Note that archeologists are still trying to determine which deity each of the Doric temples was dedicated to—for now, they are simply denoted by letters of the alphabet.) The **East Hill** was the sacred district of the city, with three temples surrounded by an enclosure. Temple E, which was in all probability dedicated to Hera (Juno), was built between 490 and 480 B.C. and has a staggering 68 columns. The Metopes, the reliefs that are the pride and joy of the archaeological museum in Palermo, are from this temple. Temple F is the oldest of the trio, built between 560 and 540 B.C.; in its original state, it had a double row of 6 columns at the eastern entrance and 14 columns on either side. Temple G, now an impressive heap of rubble except for a lone standing column, was destined to be of colossal proportions if it had been completed in 480 B.C.; even so, it is the second largest temple in Sicily.

Atop a plateau, the **Acropolis,** a district of gridlike streets surrounded by defensive walls, was the center of social and political life. Here stood most of Selinunte's important public and religious buildings, as well as the residences of the town's aristocrats. Temple C, the earliest surviving temple of ancient Selinus, was built here in the 6th century B.C.; it stands surrounded by 14 of its resurrected 17 columns. From the

Acropolis, you cross the now-dry Modione River to the **Sanctuary of Demeter Malophorus,** the ruins of several shrines to Demeter, goddess of fertility. The custom was for worshipers to place stone figurines in the shrines to honor Demeter; as many as 12,000 such figurines have been unearthed.

Parco Archeologico Selinunte. ℂ **0924-46540** Combined ticket with Parco Archeologico in Segesta (p. 631), valid for 3 days: 9€ adults, 4.50€ ages 18–25, free children 17 and under. Daily 9am to 1 hour before sunset.

AGRIGENTO & THE VALLEY OF THE TEMPLES ★★★

129km (80 miles) SE of Palermo

Colonists from Crete or Rhodes established Akragas in the 7th century B.C., and by the 5th century B.C. the city was one of the great Mediterranean powers, with close to 200,000 residents. The Greek poet Pindar described Akragas as the most beautiful city "inhabited by mortals" but commented that its citizens "feasted as if there were no tomorrow." The city poured part of its enormous wealth into temples erected along a ridge overlooking the sea, their bright pediments becoming well-known landmarks along southern sea routes. Carthage and Rome fought over the city for several centuries until Akragas became part of the Roman Empire in 210 B.C. Tumbled by earthquakes, plundered for marble, and overgrown from neglect, today the temples are merely proud remnants of ancient grandeur.

Essentials

GETTING THERE   Agrigento is about 2½ hours by **car** from either Palermo or Siracusa. From Palermo, cut southeast on the SS121, which becomes SS189 before it finally reaches Agrigento. From Siracusa, take the A18 autostrada north to Catania and the A19 west toward Enna; just past Enna, exit the A19 and follow signs south through Caltanissetta and down to Agrigento. The "coastal route" from Siracusa—taking the SS115 all the way—may look more direct on the map but is much more time-consuming, up to 5 hours on an often very curvy, two-lane road.

   Bus connections between Palermo and Agrigento are fairly convenient: **Cuffaro** (www.cuffaro.info; ℂ **0922-403150**) runs nine buses per day each way and drops you right in front of the entrance to the archaeological site; the trip takes 2 hours and costs 8.30€ one-way or 13€ round-trip. Bus service from Siracusa takes at least 4 hours.

   Taking the **train** to Agrigento is a hassle. The main rail station, **Stazione Centrale,** is at Piazza Marconi (ℂ **892021**); from there you then have to take a cab or local bus (lines 1, 2, or 3) to the temples, 10 minutes away. The train trip from Palermo takes 2 hours and costs 8€; there are 12 trains daily. From Siracusa, you must change in Catania; the full 6-hour trip costs 20€ one-way.

The Tempio della Concordia, Valley of the Temples, at Agrigento.

VISITOR INFORMATION The **tourist office,** in the modern town at Piazzale Aldo Moro 7 (✆ 0922-20454), is open Sunday through Friday 8am to 1pm and 3 to 8pm, Saturday 8am to 1pm. Another tourist office is at Via Empedocle 73 (✆ **0922-20391**), open Monday to Friday 8am to 2:30pm and Wednesday also from 3:30 to 7pm.

Exploring the Ruins

The park is divided into eastern and western zones, with entrances at each.

Parco Valle dei Templei ★★★ RUINS   In the eastern zone are Agrigento's three best-preserved temples. **The Temple of Hercules (Tempio di Ercole)** is the oldest, dating from the 6th century B.C. At one time the temple sheltered a celebrated statue of Hercules, though it has long since been plundered. Gaius Verres, the notoriously corrupt 1st-century B.C. governor of Sicily, had his eyes on the statue as he looted temples across the island, though there is no record of Verres (who was exiled for his misdeeds) getting this prize. Eight of 36 columns have been resurrected, while the others lie rather romantically scattered in the tall grass and wildflowers; they still bear black sears from fires set by Carthaginian invaders.

The **Tempio della Concordia (Temple of Concord),** surrounded by 34 columns, has survived almost intact since its completion in 430 B.C. It was never plundered because it was shored up as a Christian basilica in the 6th century, and its foundations rest on soft soil, absorbing the shock of earthquakes. The **Temple of Juno** had no such structural resiliency and was partly destroyed in an earthquake, though 30 columns and sections of the colonnade have been restored. A long altar was used for wedding ceremonies and sacrificial offerings.

The western zone would have been the setting of the largest temple in the Greek world, if the **Temple of Jove/Zeus (Tempio di Giove)** had ever been completed—and if what was built had not been toppled in earthquakes. A copy of an 8m-tall telamon (a sculpted figure of a man with arms raised) lies on its back amid the rubble; the original is the pride of the Museo Archeologico. The **Temple of Castor and Pollux (Tempio di Dioscuri** or **Tempio di Castore e Polluce),** with four Doric columns intact, honors Castor and Pollux, the twins who were patrons of seafarers; Demeter, the goddess of marriage and of the fertile earth; and Persephone, the daughter of Zeus and the symbol of spring.

Parco Valle dei Templei. www.lavalledeitempli.eu. ✆ **0922-621611**. Admission 8€. Daily 8:30am–7pm. Separate admission 8€ for evening hours, July–Aug Mon–Fri until 9:30pm, Sat–Sun until 11pm; Sat until 11:30 rest of year.

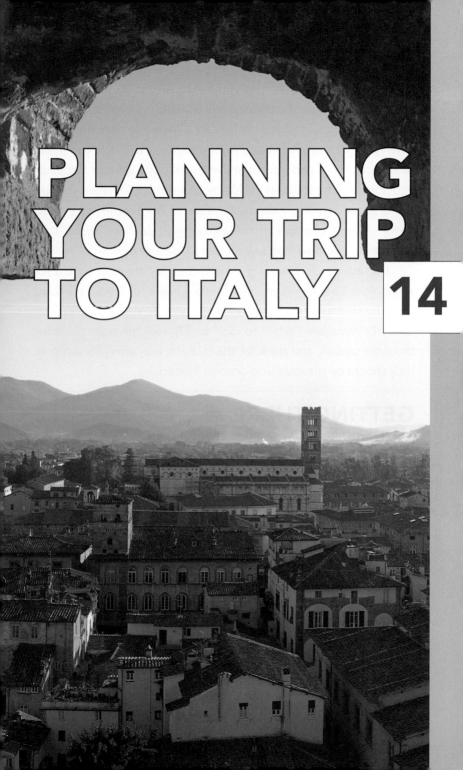

PLANNING YOUR TRIP TO ITALY

14

taly is loaded with "must see" cities and sights, and most of us have limited vacation time. You want to get there efficiently, get around by road or rail without hassle, and spend as much time soaking up the atmosphere of *Bella Italia* as you can. This chapter shows you how. It may be a long way from home, but when you get there Italy need not be expensive: Below you'll find advice on where and how to shave travel costs without trimming your fun. (And for the best budget accommodations when you get there, see this guide's individual chapters.) Want some more good news? Recent changes in the exchange rate have made Italy cheaper to visit now than any time in at least a decade.

For advice on planning time-limited or themed itineraries around the country—if you only have a week, or if you're a food lover, for example—turn to chapter 3. If you do your homework on special events (see "When to Go," p. 33), pick the right place for the right season, and pack for the climate, preparing for a trip to Italy should be pleasant and uncomplicated.

GETTING THERE
By Plane

If you're flying across an ocean, you'll most likely land at Rome's **Leonardo da Vinci–Fiumicino Airport** (FCO; www.adr.it/fiumicino), 40km (25 miles) from the center, or **Milan Malpensa** (MXP; www.milanomalpensa-airport.com), 45km (28 miles) northwest of central Milan. Rome's much smaller **Ciampino Airport** (CIA; www.adr.it/ciampino) serves low-cost airlines connecting to European cities and other destinations in Italy. It's the same story with Milan's **Linate Airport** (LIN; www.milanolinate-airport.com). For information on getting to central Rome from its airports, see p. 60; for Milan, see p. 427.

FLYING DIRECTLY TO VENICE, BERGAMO, BOLOGNA, PISA, OR PALERMO

Carriers within Europe fly direct to several smaller Italian cities. Among the most convenient for Italy's highlights are Venice's **Marco Polo Airport** (VCE; www.veniceairport.it), Bergamo's **Orio al Serio Airport** (BGY; www.sacbo.it), Bologna's **Marconi Airport** (BLQ; www.bologna-airport.it), Pisa's **Galileo Galilei Airport** (PSA; www.pisa-airport.com), and **Palermo Airport** (PMO; www.gesap.it), Sicily.

For information on getting into central Venice from the airport, see p. 361. For reaching Florence from Pisa Airport, see p. 164. Florence is also connected with Bologna Airport, by the **Appennino Shuttle** (www. appenninoshuttle.it; ✆ **055-585-271**). The direct bus runs 10 times each day and the journey takes between 80 and 90 minutes. Tickets cost 25€, 10€ ages 5 to 10, free ages 4 and under; book online ahead of time for a 5€ per passenger discount. Buses arrive at and depart from Piazzale Montelungo, close to Florence's Santa Maria Novella rail station.

Several services connect Bergamo's airport with Milan's Stazione Centrale, including **Orioshuttle** (www.orioshuttle.com; ✆ **035-330-706**). The service runs approximately half-hourly all day, a little less frequently on weekends. Journey time is 50 minutes. Tickets cost from 4€ if you book online ahead of time.

For information on arriving in Sicily via Palermo's airport, see p. 590.

Begin thinking about flying plans at least 6 months ahead of time. Consider exchange rate movements: Fares may be calculated in US dollars or euros, depending on the airline. The key window for finding a **deal** is usually between 5 and 6 months ahead of your departure according to a massive study of some 21 million fare transactions by the Airline Reporting Corporation (a middleman between travel agencies and the airlines). They also found that those who booked on a Sunday statistically found the best rates (on average they paid 19% less than those who booked midweek). Run searches through the regular online agents such as Expedia, as well as metasearch engines like **DoHop.com, Kayak. com, Skyscanner.net,** and **Momondo.com**. For complex journeys, with multiple departures, doing multiple searches (so affordable intra-European airlines such as Germanwings, EasyJet and Ryanair show up on the search) is a good way to find deals; a specialist flight agent such as **RoundtheWorldFlights.com** or **AirTreks.com** will also likely save you money.

By Train

Italy's major cities are well connected to Europe's rail hubs. You can arrive in Milan on direct trains from France (Nice, Paris, Lyon) by TGV, or from Switzerland, and connect from there to Venice or Florence or Rome (see "Getting Around," below). Direct trains from central and Eastern Europe arrive at Verona and Venice. TGV services connect France with Turin.

Thello (www.thello.com) also operates an overnight service connecting Paris with Milan and Venice. After crossing the Alps in the dead of night, the train calls at Milan, Brescia, Verona, Vicenza, and Padua, before arriving in Venice around 9:30am. For Florence, Rome, and points south, alight at Milan (around 6am) and switch to Italy's national high-speed rail lines; see below. Accommodation on the Thello train is in sleeping cars, as well as in six- and four-berth couchettes. Prices range from 35€ per person for the cheapest fare in a six-berth couchette to 290€ for sole occupancy of a sleeping car. It's worth paying the extra for private accommodations if you can.

Book in advance online or with **Rail Europe** (www.raileurope.com; ✆ **800-622-8600**) or **International Rail** (www.internationalrail.com; ✆ **+44-871-231-0790**).

GETTING AROUND
By Car

Much of Italy is accessible by public transportation, but to explore vineyards, countryside, and smaller towns, a car will save you time. You'll get the **best rental rate** if you book your car far ahead of arrival. Try such websites as **Kayak.com, CarRentals.co.uk, Skyscanner.net,** and **Momondo.com** to compare prices across multiple rental companies and agents. Car rental search companies usually report the lowest rates being available between 6 and 8 weeks ahead of arrival. Rent the smallest car possible and request a **diesel** rather than a petrol engine, to minimize fuel costs.

You must be 25 or older to rent from many agencies (although some accept ages 21 and up, at a premium price).

The legalities and contractual obligations of renting a car in Italy (where accident rates are high) are more complicated than those in almost any other country in Europe. You also must have nerves of steel, a sense of humor, and a valid driver's license or **International Driver's Permit.** Insurance on all vehicles is compulsory.

Note: If you're planning to rent a car in Italy during high season, you should **book well in advance.** It's not unusual to arrive at the airport in Rome in June or July to find that every agent is all out of cars, perhaps for the whole week.

It can sometimes be tricky to get to the *autostrada* (fast highway) from the city center or airport, so consider renting or bringing a GPS-enabled device, or installing an offline sat-nav app on your phone. In bigger cities you will first have to get to the *tangenziale,* or beltway, which will eventually lead to your highway of choice. The beltway in Rome is known as the Grande Raccordo Anulare, or "Big Ring Road."

The going can be slow almost anywhere, especially on Friday afternoons leaving the cities and Sunday nights on the way back into town, and rush hour around the cities any day of the week can be epic. Driving for a day or so either side of the busy *ferragosto* (August 15) holiday is to be avoided *at all costs.* See **www.autostrade.it** for live traffic updates and a road-toll calculator.

Autostrada tolls can get expensive, costing approximately 1€ for every 15km (10 miles), which means that it costs about 18€ for a trip from Rome to Florence. Add in the high price of fuel (averaging over

1.50€ *per liter* at time of writing) and car rental, and it's often cheaper to take the train, even for two people.

Before leaving home, you can apply for an **International Driving Permit** from the American Automobile Association (www.aaa.com; ✆ **800/622-7070** or 650/294-7400). In Canada, the permit's available from the Canadian Automobile Association (www.caa.ca; ✆ **416/221-4300**). Technically, you need this permit and your actual driver's license to drive in Italy, though in practice your license itself often suffices. Visitors from within the EU need only take their domestic driver's license.

Italy's equivalent of AAA is the **Automobile Club d'Italia (ACI**; www.aci.it). They're the people who respond when you place an emergency call to ✆ **803-116** (✆ 800-116-800 from a non-Italian cellphone) for road breakdowns, though they do charge for this service if you're not a member.

DRIVING RULES   Italian drivers aren't maniacs; they only appear to be. Spend any time on a highway and you will have the experience of somebody driving up insanely close from behind, headlights flashing. Take a deep breath and don't panic: This is the aggressive signal for you to move to the right so he (invariably, it's a "he") can pass, and until you do he will stay mind-bogglingly close. On a two-lane road, the idiot passing someone in the opposing traffic who has swerved into your lane expects you to veer obligingly over toward the shoulder so three lanes of traffic can fit—he would do the same for you. Probably. Many Italians seem to think that blinkers are optional, so be aware that the car in front could be getting ready to turn at any moment.

Autostrade are toll highways, denoted by green signs and a number prefaced with an *A,* like the A1 from Milan to Florence, Rome, and Naples. A few fast highways aren't numbered and are simply called a *raccordo,* a connecting road between two cities (such as Florence–Siena and Florence–Pisa).

Strade statali (singular is *strada statale*) are state roads, sometimes without a center divider and two lanes wide (although sometimes they can be a divided four-way highway), indicated by blue signs. Their route numbers are prefaced with an SS, as in the SS11 from Milan to Venice. On signs, however, these official route numbers are used infrequently. Usually, you'll just see blue signs listing destinations by name with arrows pointing off in the appropriate directions. The *strade statali* can be frustratingly slow due to traffic, traffic lights, and the fact that they bisect countless towns: When available, pay for the autostrada.

The **speed limit** on roads in built-up areas around towns and cities is 50 kmph (31 mph). On two-lane roads it's 90 kmph (56 mph) and on the highway its 130 kmph (81 mph). Italians have an astounding disregard for these limits. However, police can ticket you and collect the fine on the spot. The blood-alcohol limit in Italy is .05%, often achieved with just two small drinks; driving above the limit can result in a fine of up to

6,000€, a driving ban, or imprisonment. The blood-alcohol limit is set at zero for anyone who has held a driver's license for under 3 years.

Safety belts are obligatory in both the front and the back seats; ditto child seats or special restraints for minors under 1.5 meters (5 ft.) in height, though this latter regulation is often ignored. Drivers may not use a handheld cellphone while driving—yet another law that locals seem to consider optional.

PARKING On streets, **white lines** indicate free public spaces, **blue lines** are pay public spaces, and **yellow lines** mean only residents are allowed to park. Meters don't line the sidewalk; rather, there's one machine on the block where you punch in coins corresponding to how long you want to park. The machine spits out a ticket that you leave on your dashboard.

If you park in an area marked *parcheggio disco orario,* root around in your rental car's glove compartment for a cardboard parking disc (or buy one at a gas station). With this device, you dial up the hour of your arrival and display it on your dashboard. You're allowed *un'ora* (1 hr.) or *due ore* (2 hr.), according to the sign. If you do not have a disk, write your arrival time clearly on a sheet of paper and leave it on the dash.

Parking lots have ticket dispensers, but exit booths are not usually manned. When you return to the lot to depart, first visit the office or automated payment machine to exchange your ticket for a paid receipt or token, which you will then use to get through the exit gate.

ROAD SIGNS A **speed limit** sign is a black number inside a red circle on a white background. The **end of a speed zone** is just black and white, with a black slash through the number. A red circle with a white background, a black arrow pointing down, and a red arrow pointing up means **yield to oncoming traffic,** while a point-down red-and-white triangle means **yield ahead.**

Many city centers are closed to traffic and a simple white circle with a red border, or the words *zona pedonale* or *zona traffico limitato,* denotes a **pedestrian zone** (you can sometimes drive through to drop off baggage at your hotel); a white arrow on a blue background is used for Italy's many **one-way streets;** a mostly red circle with a horizontal white slash means **do not enter.** Any image in black on a white background surrounded by a red circle means that image is **not allowed** (for instance, if the image is two cars next to each other, it means no passing; a motorcycle means no Harleys permitted; and so on). A circular sign in blue with a red circle-slash means **no parking.**

Gasoline (gas or petrol), *benzina,* can be found in pull-in gas stations along major roads and on the outskirts of town, as well as in 24-hour stations along the autostrada. Almost all stations are closed for the *riposo* and on Sundays (except for those on the autostrade), but the majority of them have a machine that accepts cash. Unleaded gas is *senza piombo.* Diesel is *gasolio.*

By Train

Italy, especially the northern half, has one of the best train systems in Europe with most destinations connected. The train is an excellent option if you're looking to visit the major sites without the hassle of driving. The vast majority of lines are run by the state-owned **Ferrovie dello Stato,** or FS (www.trenitalia.com; ✆ **89-20-21**). A private operator, **Italo** (www.italotreno.it; ✆ **06-07-08**) operates on the Turin–Milan–Florence–Rome–Naples–Salerno high-speed line, and the branch from Bologna northward to Padua and Venice.

Travel durations and the prices of the tickets vary considerably depending on what type of train you are traveling on. The country's principal north–south high-speed line links Turin and Milan to Bologna, Florence, Rome, Naples, and Salerno. Milan to Rome, for example, takes under 3 hours on the quick train, and costs 86€ if you want to travel on the spot, though you can find tickets as low as 20€ if you buy ahead and travel in off-peak hours. Rome to Naples takes 70 minutes and costs 43€ (walk-up fare) on the fast train, or you can spend 12€ for a trip on a slower train that takes just over twice as long. If you want to bag the cheapest fares on high-speed trains, aim to **book around 100 to 120 days before your travel dates.** You can do everything online. Both Italo and the state railway operate a ticketless system: Just show your confirmation email (which has a unique PNR code).

Types of Trains   The speed, cleanliness, and overall quality of Italian trains vary. **High-speed trains** usually have four classes: Standard, Premium, Business, and Executive on the state railway; Smart, eXtra Large, First, and Club Executive on Italo. The cheapest of these, on both operators, is perfectly comfortable, even on long legs of a journey. These are Italy's premium rail services. The **Frecciarossa** and **Italo** trains are the nicest of the nice and the fastest of the fast (Italy's bullet train). They operate on the Turin–Milan–Florence–Rome–Naples line, and run up to 300 kmph (186 mph). The **Frecciargento** uses similar hardware, but goes a bit slower; it links Naples, Rome, Florence, Verona, and Venice at speeds of up to 250 kmph (155 mph). With a maximum speed of 200 kmph (124 mph), the **Frecciabianca** links Milan and Turin with Venice and cities down the Adriatic coastline as far as Italy's heel. It also connects Rome and Genoa in just over 3½ hours. They are all generically called *Le Frecce*. Speed and cleanliness come at a price, with tickets for the high-speed trains usually costing around three times as much as a slower "regional" train. On high-speed services you **must make a seat reservation** when you buy a ticket. If you are traveling with a rail pass (see below), you must pay a 10€ supplementary fee to ride them and reserve a seat. Passes are not valid (yet) on Italo.

Intercity (IC) trains are one step down, both in speed and in comfort, but are a valid option that also requires a seat reservation. The slower **Regionale** (**R**) and **Regionale Veloce** (**RV**) make many stops. Old *Regionale* rolling stock is slowly being replaced, but they can still sometimes be on the grimy side of things. They are also ridiculously cheap: A Venice–Verona second-class R or RV (there's no difference in practice) ticket will put you back only 8.60€ compared with 23€ on the Frecciabianca. You can't prebook seats on R or RV services, nor is there any price advantage to booking tickets ahead of travel.

Overcrowding is often a problem on standard services (that is, not the high-speed trains) Friday evenings, weekends, and holidays, especially in or out of big cities, or just after a strike. In summer, the crowding escalates, and any train going toward a beach in August bulges like an overstuffed sausage.

Train Travel Tips When buying a regular ticket, ask for either *andata* (one-way) or *andata e ritorno* (round-trip). The best way to avoid presenting yourself on the train with the wrong ticket is to tell the person at the ticket window exactly what train you are going to take, for example, "the 11:30am train for Venice." Regular R or RV tickets are not valid on high-speed trains.

If you don't have a ticket with a reservation for a particular seat on a specific train, then you must **validate you ticket by stamping it in the little yellow box** on the platform before boarding the train. If you board a train without a ticket, or without having validated your ticket, you'll have to pay a hefty fine on top of the ticket or supplement, which the conductor will sell you. If you knowingly board a train without a ticket or realize once onboard that you have the wrong type of ticket, your best bet is to search out the conductor, who is likely to be more forgiving because you found him and made it clear you weren't trying to ride for free.

Schedules for all trains leaving a given station are printed on yellow posters tacked up on the station wall (a similar white poster lists all the arrivals). These are good for getting general guidance, but keep your eye on the electronic boards and television screens that are updated with delays and track *(binario)* changes. You can also get official schedules (plus more train information, also in English) and buy tickets at both www.trenitalia.com and **www.italotreno.it**.

In the big cities (especially Milan and Rome) and major tourist destinations (above all Venice and Florence), ticketing lines can be dreadfully long. Don't be scared of the **automatic ticket machines.** They are easy to navigate, allow you to follow instructions in English, accept cash and credit cards, and can considerably cut down the stress of waiting in an interminably slow line. *Note:* You can't buy international tickets at automatic machines.

Stations tend to be well run, with luggage storage facilities at all but the smallest and usually a good bar attached that serves surprisingly palatable food. If you pull into a dinky town with a shed-size station, find the nearest bar or *tabacchi,* and the man behind the counter will most likely sell tickets.

Travel Times Between the Major Cities

CITIES	DISTANCE	(FASTEST) TRAIN TRAVEL TIME	DRIVING TIME
Florence to Venice	281km/174 miles	1 hr., 50 min.	3 hr.
Florence to Milan	298km/185 miles	1 hr., 40 min.	3½ hr.
Milan to Venice	267km/166 miles	2¼ hr.	3¼ hr.
Milan to Rome	572km/355 miles	2 hr., 55 min.	5½ hr.
Rome to Florence	277km/172 miles	1½ hr.	3 hr.
Rome to Naples	219km/136 miles	1 hr., 10 min.	2½ hr.
Rome to Turin	669km/415 miles	4 hr.	6½ hr.
Rome to Venice	528km/327 miles	3hr., 20 min.	5½ hr.

SPECIAL PASSES & DISCOUNTS   To buy the **Eurail Italy Pass,** available only outside Europe and priced in U.S. dollars, contact **Rail Europe** (www.raileurope.com). You have 1 month in which to use the train a set number of days; the base number of days is 3, and you can add up to 5 more. For adults, the first-class pass costs $222, second class is $179. Additional days cost $30 to $35 more for first class, roughly $25 for second class. For youth tickets (25 and under), a 3-day pass is $179/$146 and additional days about $20 each. Saver passes are available for groups of two to five people traveling together **at all times,** and amount to a saving of about 15% on individual tickets.

When it comes to regular tickets, if you're **25 and under,** you can buy a 40€ **Carta Verde (Green Card)** at any Italian train station. This gets you a 10% break on domestic trips (walk-up fares only) and 25% off international connections for 1 year. Present it each time you buy a ticket. An even better deal is available for anyone **61 and over** with the **Carta d'Argento (Silver Card):** 15% off domestic walk-up fares and 25% off international, for 30€ (the Carta d'Argento is free for those 76 and over). Children 11 and under ride half-price while kids under 4 don't pay, although they also do not have the right to their own seat. On state railways, there are sometimes free tickets for children 14 and under traveling with a paying adult; ask about "Bimbi gratis" when buying your ticket.

By Bus

Although trains are quicker and easier, you can get just about anywhere on a network of local, provincial, and regional bus lines. Keep in mind that in smaller towns, buses exist mainly to shuttle workers and schoolchildren, so the most runs are on weekdays, early in the morning, and usually again in midafternoon.

In a big city, the **bus station** for trips between cities is usually near the main train station. A small town's **bus stop** is usually either in the main square, on the edge of town, or the bend in the road just outside the main town gate. You should always try to find the local ticket vendor—if there's no office, it's invariably the nearest newsstand or *tabacchi* (signaled by a sign with a white t), or occasionally a bar—but you can usually also buy tickets on the bus. You can sometimes flag down a bus as it passes on a country road, but try to find an official stop (a small sign tacked onto a telephone pole). Tell the driver where you're going and ask him courteously if he'll let you know when you need to get off. When he says, *"È la prossima fermata,"* that means yours is the next stop. *"Posso scendere a…?"* (*Poh-*so *shen-*dair-ay ah…?) is "Can I get off at…?"

By Plane

These days, the only internal air connection you will likely want to make is to the island of **Sicily.** There's choice to fit round pretty much any itinerary. From Milan, **easyJet** (www.easyjet.com) and **Alitalia** (www.alitalia.com) connect Milan's Malpensa Airport with both Palermo and Catania in Sicily. **Meridiana** (www.meridiana.it) flies Milan Linate to Catania. **Ryanair** (www.ryanair.com) connects Bergamo with Palermo, Trapani, and Catania. Direct **Rome** to Sicily routes are operated by Alitalia, Meridiana, and Ryanair. Alitalia, **Volotea** (www.volotea.com), and **Air One** (www.flyairone.com) operate direct flights between **Venice** and Palermo. Volotea and Air One also fly from Venice or Verona to Catania, and from Verona or Turin to Palermo. Air One flies to Catania from Pisa. Volotea also connects Catania with Genoa, as well as Palermo with Genoa, Bari, and Naples. EasyJet links Naples and Catania.

[FastFACTS] ITALY

Area Codes The **country code** for Italy is **39.** Former **city codes** (for example, Florence 055, Venice 041, Milan 02, Rome 06) are incorporated into the numbers themselves. Therefore, you must dial the entire number, *including the initial zero,* when calling from *anywhere* outside or inside Italy and even within the same town. For example, to call Milan from the United States, you must dial **011-39-02,** then the local phone number. Phone numbers in Italy can range anywhere from 6 to 12 digits in length.

ATMs The easiest and best way to get cash away from home is from an ATM (automated teller machine), referred to in Italy as a *bancomat.* ATMs are prevalent in Italian cities and while every town usually has one, it's good practice to fuel up on cash in urban centers before traveling to villages or rural areas.

Be sure to confirm with your bank that your card is valid for international withdrawal and that you have a four-digit PIN. (Some ATMs in Italy will not accept any other number of digits.) Also, be sure you know your daily withdrawal limit before you depart. *Note:* Many banks impose a fee every time you use a card at another bank's ATM, and that fee can be higher for international transactions (up to $5 or more) than for domestic ones. In addition, the bank from which you withdraw cash may charge its own fee, although this is not common practice in Italy.

Business Hours

General open hours for **stores, offices,** and **churches** are from 9:30am to noon or 1pm and again from 3 or 3:30pm to 7:30 or 8pm. The early afternoon shutdown is the *riposo*, the Italian siesta (in the downtown area of large cities, stores don't close for the *riposo*). Most stores close all day Sunday and many also on Monday (morning only or all day). Some services and business offices are open to the public only in the morning. **Banks** tend to be open Monday through Friday 8:30am to 1:30pm and 2:45 to 4:15pm. Traditionally, **state museums** are closed Mondays. Most of the large museums stay open all day long otherwise, although some close for *riposo* or are only open in the morning (9am–2pm is popular). Some churches open earlier in the morning, and the largest often stay open all day, though the last hour or so of opening is usually taken up with an evening service, during which tourist visits are frowned upon.

Customs

Foreign visitors can bring along most items for personal use duty-free, including merchandise valued up to $800.

Disabled Travelers

A few of the top museums and churches have installed ramps at their entrances, and several hotels have converted first-floor rooms into accessible units. Other than that, you may not find parts of Italy easy to tackle. Builders in the Middle Ages and the Renaissance didn't have wheelchairs or mobility impairments in mind when they built narrow doorways and spiral staircases, and preservation laws prevent Italians from doing much about this in some areas.

Some buses and trains can cause problems as well, with high, narrow doors and steep steps at entrances—though the situation on public transportation, especially the railways, is improving. For those with disabilities who can make it onto buses and trains, there are usually seats reserved for them, and Italians are quick to give up their space for somebody who looks like they need it more than them.

Accessible Italy (www.accessibleitaly.com; ✆ **378-0549-941-111**) provides travelers with info about accessible tourist sites and places to rent wheelchairs, and also sells organized "Accessible Tours" around Italy. Disabled travelers should call **Trenitalia** (✆ **199-303060**) for assistance on the state rail network. Italo has a couple of dedicated wheelchair spaces on every service: Call ✆ **06-07-08.**

Doctors & Hospitals

See individual chapters for details of emergency rooms and walk-in medical services.

Drinking Laws

People of any age can legally consume alcohol in Italy, but a person must be 16 years old in order to be served alcohol in a restaurant or a bar. Noise is the primary concern to city officials, and so bars generally close around 2am, though alcohol is commonly served in clubs after that. Supermarkets carry beer, wine, and spirits.

Electricity

Italy operates on a 220-volt AC (50 cycles) system, as opposed to the U.S. 110-volt AC (60 cycles) system. You'll need a simple adapter plug to make the American flat pegs fit the Italian round holes and, unless your appliance is dual-voltage (as some hair dryers, travel irons, and almost all laptops are), an electrical currency converter. You can pick up the hardware at electronics stores, luggage shops, and airports.

Embassies & Consulates

The **U.K. Embassy** (www.gov.uk/government/world/italy.it; ✆ **06-4220-0001**) is in Rome at Via XX Settembre 80a. The **British Consulate-General** is in Milan at Via San Paolo 7 (✆ **02-7230-0237**).

The **U.S. Embassy** is in Rome at Via Vittorio Veneto 121 (http://italy.usembassy.gov; ✆ **06-46-741**). There are also **U.S. Consulates General** in **Florence,** at Lungarno Vespucci 38 (http://florence.usconsulate.gov; ✆ **055-266-951**); in **Milan,** at Via Principe Amedeo 2/10 (http://milan.usconsulate.gov; ✆ **02-290-351**); and in **Naples,** in Piazza della Repubblica (http://naples.usconsulate.gov; ✆ **081-583-8111**).

Emergencies

The best number to call in Italy (and the rest of Europe) with a **general emergency** is ℭ **112,** which connects you to the *carabinieri* who will transfer your call as needed. For the **police,** dial ℭ **113;** for a **medical emergency** and to call an **ambulance,** the number is ℭ **118;** for the **fire department,** call ℭ **115.** If your car breaks down, dial ℭ **116** for **roadside aid** courtesy of the Automotive Club of Italy. All are free calls, but roadside assistance is a paid-for service for nonmembers.

Family Travel

Italy is a family-oriented society. A crying baby at a dinner table is greeted with a knowing smile rather than with a stern look. Children almost always receive discounts, and maybe a special treat from the waiter, but the availability of such accoutrements as child seats for cars and dinner tables is more the exception than the norm. (The former, however, is a legal requirement: Be sure to ask a rental car company to provide one.) There are plenty of parks, offbeat museums, markets, ice-cream parlors, and vibrant street-life scenes to amuse even the youngest children. Child discounts apply on public transportation, and at public and private museums. **Prénatal** (www.prenatal.com) is the premier toddler and baby chain store in Italy.

Health

You won't encounter any special health risks by visiting Italy. The country's public health care system is generally well regarded. The richer north tends to have better **hospitals** than the south.

Italy offers universal health care to its citizens and those of other European Union countries (U.K. nationals should remember to carry an EHIC: See **www.nhs.uk/ehic**). Others should be prepared to pay medical bills upfront. Before leaving home, find out what medical services your **health insurance** covers. *Note:* Even if you don't have insurance, you will always be treated in an emergency room.

Pharmacies offer essentially the same range of generic drugs available in the United States and internationally. Pharmacies are ubiquitous (look for the green cross) and serve almost like miniclinics, where pharmacists diagnose and treat minor ailments, like flu symptoms and general aches and pains, with over-the-counter drugs. Carry the generic name of any prescription medicines you take, in case a local pharmacist is unfamiliar with the brand name. Pharmacies in cities take turns doing the night shift; normally there is a list posted at the entrance of each pharmacy informing customers which pharmacy is open each night of the week.

Insurance

Italy may be one of the safer places you can travel in the world, but accidents and setbacks can and do happen, from lost luggage to car crashes. For information on traveler's insurance, trip cancellation insurance, and medical insurance while traveling, please visit **www.frommers.com/tips**.

Internet Access

Internet cafes are in healthy supply in most Italian cities, though don't expect to find them in every small town. If you're traveling with your own computer or smartphone, you'll find wireless access in almost every hotel, but if this is essential for your stay make sure you ask before booking and certainly don't always expect to find a connection in a rural *agriturismo* (disconnecting from the 21st century is part of their appeal). In a pinch, hostels, local libraries, and some bars will have some sort of terminal for access. Several spots around Venice, Florence, Rome, and other big cities are covered with free Wi-Fi access provided by the local administration, but at these and any other Wi-Fi spots around Italy, antiterrorism laws make it obligatory to register for an access code before you can log on. Take your passport or other photo ID when you go looking for an Internet point. Rome's Leonardo da Vinci–Fiumicino Airport offers free Wi-Fi. Florence's discount **Firenze Card** (p. 171) comes with 72 hours of free city Wi-Fi included.

Internet Train (www.internettrain.it) is a national franchise chain with Internet points in Rome, Florence, Verona, Pisa, and elsewhere in Italy.

LGBT Travelers

Italy as a whole, and northern Italy in particular, is gay-friendly. Homosexuality is legal, and the age of consent is 16. Italians are generally more affectionate and physical than North Americans in all their friendships, and even straight men occasionally walk down the street with their arms around each other—however, kissing anywhere other than on the cheeks at greetings and goodbyes will draw attention. As you might expect, smaller towns tend to be less permissive than cities.

Italy's national associations and support networks for gays and lesbians are **ARCI-Gay and ArciLesbica.** The national websites are **www.arcigay.it** and **www.arcilesbica.it**, and most sizable cities have a local office (although not Venice). In **Verona,** the office is at Via Nichesola 9 (www.arcigayverona.org; ☏ **346-979-0553**); in **Milan,** Via Bezzecca 3 (www.arcigaymilano.org; ☏ **02-5412-2225**); and in **Rome,** Via Zabaglia 14 (www.arcigayroma.it; ☏ **06-6450-1102**). See **www.arcigay.it/comitati** for a searchable directory.

Mail & Postage

Sending a postcard or letter up to 20 grams, or a little less than an ounce, costs .95€ to other European countries, 2.30€ to North America, and a whopping 3€ to Australia and New Zealand. Full details on Italy's postal services are available at **www.poste.it** (some in English).

Mobile Phones

GSM (Global System for Mobile Communications) is a cellphone technology used by most of the world's countries that makes it possible to turn on a phone with a contract based in Australia, Ireland, the U.K., Pakistan, or almost every other corner of the world and have it work in Italy without missing a beat. (In the U.S., service providers like Sprint and Verizon use a different technology—CDMA—and phones on those networks won't work in Italy unless they also have GSM compatibility.)

Also, if you are coming from the U.S. or Canada, you may need a multiband phone. All travelers should activate "international roaming" on their account, so check with your home service provider before leaving.

But—and it's a *big* but—using roaming can be very expensive, especially if you access the Internet on your phone. It is usually much cheaper, once you arrive, to buy an Italian SIM card (the removable plastic card found in all GSM phones that is encoded with your phone number). This is not difficult, and is an especially good idea if you will be in Italy for more than a week. You can **buy a SIM card** at one of the many cellphone shops you will pass in every city. The main service providers are TIM, Vodafone, Wind, and 3 *(Tre)*. If you have an Italian SIM card in your phone, local calls may be as low as .10€ per minute, and incoming calls are free. Value prepaid data packages are available for each, as are micro- and nano-SIMs, as well as prepaid deals for iPads and other tablets. If you need 4G data speeds, you will pay a little more. Not every network allows **tethering**—be sure to ask if you need it. Deals on each network change regularly; for the latest see the website of one of this guide's authors: **www.donaldstrachan.com/dataroamingitaly**. *Note:* Contract cellphones are often "locked" and will only work with a SIM card provided by the service provider back home, so check to see that you have an unlocked phone.

Buying a phone is another option, and you shouldn't have too much trouble finding one for about 30€. Use it, then recycle it or eBay it when you get home. It will save you a fortune versus alternatives such as roaming or using hotel room telephones.

Money & Costs

Frommer's lists exact prices in the local currency. The currency conversions quoted below were correct at press time. However, rates fluctuate, so before departing, consult a currency exchange website, such as **www.oanda.com/convert/classic**, to check up-to-the-minute rates.

Like many European countries, Italy uses the euro as its currency. Euro coins are issued in denominations of .01€, .02€, .05€, .10€, .20€, and .50€, as well as 1€ and 2€; bills come in denominations of 5€, 10€, 20€, 50€, 100€, 200€, and 500€.

Bus ticket (from/to anywhere in the city)	1.50€
Double room at Capo d'Africa (very expensive)	380€–430.00€
Double room at Lancelot (moderate)	130€–196.00€
Double room at Beehive (inexpensive)	70€—80€
Dinner for one, with wine, at Glass (very expensive)	95.00€
Dinner for one, with wine, at La Barrique (moderate)	30.00€
Dinner for one, with wine, at Li Rioni (inexpensive)	15.00€
Glass of wine at a bar	4.00€–8.00€
Coca-Cola (standing/sitting in a bar)	2.50€/4.50€
Cup of espresso (standing/sitting in a bar)	.90€/2.50€

The evolution of international computerized banking and consolidated ATM networks has led to the triumph of plastic throughout the Italian peninsula—even if cold cash is still the most trusted currency in mom-and-pop joints. However, it is always a good idea to carry some cash, as small businesses may accept only cash or may claim that their credit card machine is broken to avoid paying fees to the card companies. Traveler's checks have gone the way of the Stegosaurus.

You'll get the best rate if you **exchange money** at a bank or one of its ATMs. The rates at "cambio/change/wechsel" exchange booths are invariably less favorable but still better than what you'd get exchanging money at a hotel or shop (a last-resort tactic only).

Visa and **MasterCard** are almost universally accepted. Some businesses also take **American Express,** especially at the higher end, but few take **Diners Club.**

Finally, be sure to let your bank know that you will be traveling abroad to avoid having your card blocked after a few days of big purchases far from home. ***Note:*** Many banks assess a 1% to 3% "transaction fee" on **all** charges you incur abroad (whether you're using the local currency or your native currency).

Police
For emergencies, call 📞 **112** or 📞 **113.** Italy has several different police forces, but there are only two you'll most likely ever need to deal with. The first is the *carabinieri* (📞 **112**), who normally only concern themselves with serious crimes, but point you in the right direction. The *polizia* (📞 **113**), whose city headquarters is called the *questura*, is the place to go for help with lost and stolen property or petty crimes.

Safety
Italy is a remarkably safe country. The worst threats you'll likely face are the pick-pockets who sometimes frequent touristy areas and public buses; keep your hands on your camera at all times and your valuables in an under-the-clothes money belt or inside zip-pocket. Don't leave anything valuable in a rental car overnight, and leave nothing visible in it at any time. If you are robbed, you can fill out paperwork at the nearest police station *(questura),* but this is mostly for insurance purposes or to get a new passport issued—don't expect them to spend any resources hunting down the perpetrator. In general, avoid public parks at night. The areas around city rail stations are often unsavory, but rarely worse than that. Otherwise, there's a real sense of personal security for travelers in Italy.

Senior Travel
Seniors and older people are treated with a great deal of respect and deference, but there are few specific programs, associations, or concessions made for

them. The one exception is on admission prices for museums and sights, where those ages 60 or 65 and older will often get in at a reduced rate or even free. There are also special train passes and reductions on bus tickets and the like in many towns (see "Getting Around," p. 638). As a senior in Italy, you're *un anziano* or if you're a woman, *un'anziana*, "elderly"—it's a term of respect, and you should let people know you're one if you think a discount may be in order.

Smoking
Smoking has been eradicated from inside restaurants, bars, and most hotels, so smokers tend to take outside tables at bars and restaurants. If you're keen for an alfresco table, you are essentially choosing a seat in the smoking section; requesting that your neighbor not smoke may not be politely received.

Student Travelers
An **International Student Identity Card (ISIC)** qualifies students for savings on rail passes, plane tickets, entrance fees, and more. The card is valid for 1 year. You can apply for the card online at **www.myisic.com** or in person at **STA Travel** (www.statravel.com; ✆ **800/781-4040** in North America). If you're no longer a student but are still 26 and under, you can get an **International Youth Travel Card (IYTC)** and an **International Teacher Identity Card (ITIC)** from the same agency, either of which entitles you to some discounts. Students will also find that many university cities offer ample student discounts and inexpensive youth hostels.

Taxes
There's no sales tax added onto the price tag of purchases in Italy, but there is a 22% value-added tax (in Italy: IVA) automatically included in just about everything except basic foodstuffs like milk and bread. Entertainment, transport, hotels, and dining are among a group of goods taxed at a lower rate of 10%. For major purchases, you can get IVA refunded.

Tipping
In **hotels,** service is usually included in your bill. In family-run operations, additional tips are unnecessary and sometimes considered rude. In fancier places with a hired staff, however, you may want to leave a .50€ daily tip for the maid and pay the bellhop or porter 1€ per bag. In **restaurants,** a 1€ to 3€ per person "cover charge" is automatically added to the bill and in some tourist areas, especially Venice, another 10 to 15% is tacked on (except in the most unscrupulous of places, this will be noted on the menu somewhere; if unsure you should ask, è incluso il servizio?). It is not necessary to leave any extra money on the table, though it is not uncommon to leave up to 5€, especially for good service. Locals generally leave nothing. At **bars and cafes,** you can leave something very small on the counter for the barman (maybe 1€ if you have had several drinks), though it is not expected; there is no need to leave anything extra if you sit at a table, as they are likely already charging you double or triple the price you'd have paid standing at the bar. It is not necessary to tip **taxi** drivers, though it is common to round up the bill to the nearest euro or two.

Toilets
Aside from train stations, where they cost about .50€ to use, and gas/petrol stations, where they are free (with perhaps a basket seeking donations), public toilets are few and far between. Standard procedure is to enter a cafe, make sure the bathroom is not *fuori servizio* (out of order), and then order a cup of coffee before bolting to the facilities.

Websites
Following are some of our favorite sites to help you plan your trip: **www.italia.it/en** is the official English-language tourism portal for visiting Italy; **www.arttrav.com** is good for cultural travel, exhibitions, and openings, especially in Florence and Tuscany; and, naturally, **www.frommers.com/destinations/Italy**, for more of our expert advice on the country.

Index

PHOTO CREDITS

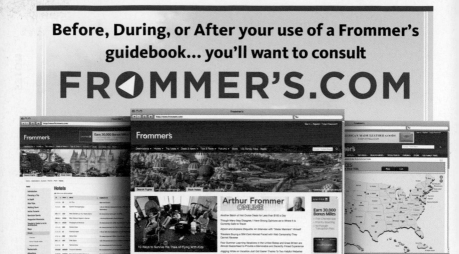